REVISED EDITION

GRADUATE MANAGEMENT ADMISSION TEST

BY

Gary R. Gruber, Ph.D.

AND

Edward C. Gruber, Ph.D.

MONARCH
PRESS

MONARCH PRESS
New York

1985 PRINTING

Copyright © 1971, 1973, 1975, 1976, 1978, 1979, 1980 by Edward C. Gruber

Published by Monarch Press
A Division of Simon & Schuster, Inc.
Simon & Schuster Building
1230 Avenue of the Americas
New York, N.Y. 10020

MONARCH PRESS and colophon are registered trademarks of Simon & Schuster, Inc.

Manufactured in the United States of America

ISBN: 0-671-18995-6

10 9 8 7 6 5 4 3

Contents

Important Tips about the GMAT

GENERAL TIPS

Tip 1. *See the GMAT Format.* Refer to "The Format of The Recently Revised GMAT" (page 5). Note the various sections which you will have on the exam.

Tip 2. *Read the directions carefully.* Familiarize yourself (*before* you take test) with the directions for each type of question — Reading Recall, Math Ability, Business Judgment (Data Evaluation and Data Application), Data Sufficiency, Verbal Ability (Antonyms, Analogies, Sentence Completions), Grammar and Usage, Reading Comprehension. Not understanding the instructions for a question-type may cause you to lose considerable credit.

Tip 3. *Take the first Practice Test.* After you have attended to Tips 1 and 2 (above), take the first Practice Test, beginning on page 11. Put yourself under strict examination conditions while you are taking the Practice Test. Allow no interruptions and *observe the time limits strictly.* Do the same for Practice Tests 2, 3, 4, and 5 — and do the same on your actual GMAT.

Tip 4. *When you are sure about the answer.* If you recognize one of the choices immediately as the correct choice, don't spend any time looking at the other choices. Mark your answer paper with the choice that "hit" you. There is no need, in this case, to waste your time considering the other choices that are necessarily incorrect.

Tip 5. *What about guessing?* Take "educated guesses." If, in a question, you know that one of the five choices is incorrect, you are at a guessing advantage. One-quarter of a correct answer is deducted for each incorrect answer as a correction for haphazard guessing.

Tip 6. *When you meet a tough question.* Don't spend too much time on a hard question. Return to it later — you will probably have the time to do so. Each question counts as much as any other. Therefore, try to "pile up" as many correct answers as you can, as fast as you can.

Tip 7. *When you skip a question.* If you skip any question, be sure to skip that number on your answer sheet. Be sure that each answer you mark is in the space numbered the same as the question you are answering in your test.

Tip 8. *Toward the end of the test.* If you still have some time before the proctor announces the end of the test, spend the few remaining minutes as follows:

1. *Check unanswered questions* — Be sure that you have answered every question that you can.

2. *Check double answers* — Make sure that your answer sheet has only one answer for each question. It two choices are marked, you will receive no credit even though one of them is right.

1

SPECIFIC TIPS *

READING COMPREHENSION

(A) "Reading Comprehension" is different in form from "Reading Recall." (See below.)

(B) You will have "Reading Comprehension" and/or "Reading Recall" on your GMAT.

(C) The "Reading Comprehension" section is likely to have four passages.

(D) As you answer the questions based on these passages, you are permitted to look back at the passages.

(E) Each reading passage is between 500 to 1000 words in length.

(F) The reading passages vary in theme. The passages are usually selected from the areas of History, Sociology, Economics, Psychology, Science, Literature, Art, and Music.

(G) Some of the passages are quite difficult to comprehend — others are relatively easy.

(H) *Underline* important words and phrases as you read each passage. When you start answering the questions for this passage, quick reference to the underlinings will aid you in answering the questions.

(I) Read as widely as possible — everything in sight that is worthwhile reading. Newspaper reading (various sections) is especially helpful in preparing for the "Reading Comprehension" part of the GMAT.

READING RECALL

(not permitted to look back)

(A) The "Reading Recall" part is likely to have three passages.

(B) Each reading passage is between 500 and 1000 words in length.

(C) The "Reading Recall" passages are, for the most part, economy-oriented or business-oriented.

(D) "Reading Recall" in the GMAT consists of two distinct sections — the Reading Part (three passages) and the Recall Part (the questions to be answered).

(E) You are allowed 15 minutes to read all three passages — then 15 minutes to answer the questions which are based on these three passages. While you are reading the passages, you are not permitted to look ahead at the questions for these passages. While you are answering the questions, you are not permitted to look back at the passages.

* Subject to revision since one form of the GMAT may vary somewhat from another form in regard to test format.

(F) There are usually 30 questions in the Recall Part — 10 questions in each of the three passages.

(G) Underline important words and phrases as you read each passage. Then, when you finish reading the passage, go over what you have underlined. This will help you to remember vital things about the passage when the time comes to answer the questions based on this passage.

(H) Read as widely as possible in preparing for the "Reading Recall" question-type. Read everything in sight that is worthwhile reading. Newspaper reading (various sections) is especially helpful in preparing for GMAT "Reading Recall."

BUSINESS JUDGMENT

(A) There are two separate question divisions. About two-thirds of the Business Judgment questions are the "data evaluation" type. The remaining one-third consists of the "data application" type.

(B) Read the passage in an analytical manner. Underline important words and phrases as you read the passage. When you start answering the questions for the passage, quick reference to the underlinings will aid you in answering the questions.

(C) To answer the "data evaluation" questions:
 1. Have a clear understanding of each of the elements which make up the problem situation:

    (a) **Major Objective**
    (b) **Major Factor**
    (c) **Minor Factor**
    (d) **Major Assumption**
    (e) **Unimportant Issue**

(D) To answer the "data application" questions:

 1. Be on the lookout for specific and relevant information appearing in the passage. Sometimes a chart or list is included — sometimes it is not.

 2. In making your calculations, be sure that you include all of the required calculation steps.

(E) Study "Tips for Answering Business Judgment Questions," beginning on page 495.

MATH ABILITY

(A) The "Math Ability" section requires background in the basics of Arithmetic, Algebra, Plane Geometry, and Graphs and Charts. Use the "Math Refresher" section (beginning on page 411) to good advantage.

(B) Compose your own questions and answers by using the graphs and charts which appear in newspapers, magazines, and textbooks. This will provide you with excellent practice.

DATA SUFFICIENCY

(A) Study "Tips for Solving Data Sufficiency Problems," beginning on page 473.

(B) Solve the "55 Practice Problems in Data Sufficiency," beginning on page 476.

GRAMMAR AND USAGE

(A) This question-type consists of single-sentence questions. Four words or phrases are underlined in each sentence. You are to select the underlined part (A *or* B *or* C *or* D) which is *incorrect* in accordance with the rules of standard written English for grammar, correct usage, and choice of words. If there is no error in the sentence, you are to fill in answer space E.

(B) Study "Grammar and Usage Refresher," beginning on page 503.

VERBAL ABILITY

(A) You may get this question-type on your GMAT.

(B) The "Verbal Ability" section consists of three separate parts: Antonyms (Opposites), Analogies, and Sentence Completions.

(C) The number of questions is about equally divided among these three different types of "Verbal Ability."

The Format of the Recently Revised GMAT*
[Beginning with the June 1982 Administration]

8 SECTIONS OF THE GMAT	NUMBER OF MINUTES
SECTION 1: ** READING COMPREHENSION (Reading of 3 or 4 passages with questions)	30 min.

or

READING RECALL (Answering questions about 3 passages without looking back at the passages)	30 min.
SECTION 2: MATH ABILITY	30 min.

5-MINUTE BREAK

SECTION 3: BUSINESS JUDGMENT	30 min.
SECTION 4: DATA SUFFICIENCY	30 min.
SECTION 5: ** GRAMMAR AND USAGE, SENTENCE CORRECTION, or VERBAL ABILITY	30 min.
SECTION 6: BUSINESS JUDGMENT	30 min.
SECTION 7***	30 min.
SECTION 8***	30 min.

240 = TOTAL MINUTES [4 HOURS]

*Subject to modifications since the GMAT has several different forms.

**Refer to "A Note from the Authors" on the inside front cover.

***Two of the eight sections in your GMAT will have experimental questions that do not count. These experimental sections are not known to the test-taker. In the above format, we have considered Sections 7 and 8 as the sections that are experimental. These experimental sections may be a REPEAT of other sections in the GMAT—or they may be new question-types measuring analytical ability.

5 GMAT Practice Tests ⟶

Part One

5 GMAT Practice Tests
Patterned after the Actual Test

The best way to prepare for the GMAT is to work with questions similar to those which appear on the actual test. On the following pages, you will find five Practice Tests— each very much like the actual GMAT. The "real" test and each "practice" test have the

    (a) same types of questions
    (b) same time limit*
    (c) same level of difficulty

These Practice Tests are not copies of the actual test. The actual test is copyrighted and may not be duplicated. The primary purpose of your taking each Practice Test is to help you diagnose your weaknesses so that you can proceed, without delay, to eliminate those weaknesses.

As you take these Practice Tests in the book, you will find many of the questions very hard to answer. Bear in mind that the *level of difficulty of the Practice Tests is the same as that of the actual tests*. We could have made the Practice Tests in the book much easier — but that would have given you a false impression of what the actual exam is really like. This would have been misleading and harmful to you. Remember, too, that no candidate is expected to get a perfect score.

*30 minutes for each section beginning with the June 1982 GMAT.

7

Practice Test 1 ⟶

USE THIS SHEET FOR YOUR ANSWERS
PRACTICE TEST 1

Section 1: Reading Comprehension

1 Ⓐ Ⓑ Ⓒ Ⓓ Ⓔ	6 Ⓐ Ⓑ Ⓒ Ⓓ Ⓔ	11 Ⓐ Ⓑ Ⓒ Ⓓ Ⓔ	16 Ⓐ Ⓑ Ⓒ Ⓓ Ⓔ	21 Ⓐ Ⓑ Ⓒ Ⓓ Ⓔ
2 Ⓐ Ⓑ Ⓒ Ⓓ Ⓔ	7 Ⓐ Ⓑ Ⓒ Ⓓ Ⓔ	12 Ⓐ Ⓑ Ⓒ Ⓓ Ⓔ	17 Ⓐ Ⓑ Ⓒ Ⓓ Ⓔ	22 Ⓐ Ⓑ Ⓒ Ⓓ Ⓔ
3 Ⓐ Ⓑ Ⓒ Ⓓ Ⓔ	8 Ⓐ Ⓑ Ⓒ Ⓓ Ⓔ	13 Ⓐ Ⓑ Ⓒ Ⓓ Ⓔ	18 Ⓐ Ⓑ Ⓒ Ⓓ Ⓔ	23 Ⓐ Ⓑ Ⓒ Ⓓ Ⓔ
4 Ⓐ Ⓑ Ⓒ Ⓓ Ⓔ	9 Ⓐ Ⓑ Ⓒ Ⓓ Ⓔ	14 Ⓐ Ⓑ Ⓒ Ⓓ Ⓔ	19 Ⓐ Ⓑ Ⓒ Ⓓ Ⓔ	24 Ⓐ Ⓑ Ⓒ Ⓓ Ⓔ
5 Ⓐ Ⓑ Ⓒ Ⓓ Ⓔ	10 Ⓐ Ⓑ Ⓒ Ⓓ Ⓔ	15 Ⓐ Ⓑ Ⓒ Ⓓ Ⓔ	20 Ⓐ Ⓑ Ⓒ Ⓓ Ⓔ	25 Ⓐ Ⓑ Ⓒ Ⓓ Ⓔ

Section 2: Math Ability

26 Ⓐ Ⓑ Ⓒ Ⓓ Ⓔ	32 Ⓐ Ⓑ Ⓒ Ⓓ Ⓔ	38 Ⓐ Ⓑ Ⓒ Ⓓ Ⓔ	44 Ⓐ Ⓑ Ⓒ Ⓓ Ⓔ	50 Ⓐ Ⓑ Ⓒ Ⓓ Ⓔ
27 Ⓐ Ⓑ Ⓒ Ⓓ Ⓔ	33 Ⓐ Ⓑ Ⓒ Ⓓ Ⓔ	39 Ⓐ Ⓑ Ⓒ Ⓓ Ⓔ	45 Ⓐ Ⓑ Ⓒ Ⓓ Ⓔ	51 Ⓐ Ⓑ Ⓒ Ⓓ Ⓔ
28 Ⓐ Ⓑ Ⓒ Ⓓ Ⓔ	34 Ⓐ Ⓑ Ⓒ Ⓓ Ⓔ	40 Ⓐ Ⓑ Ⓒ Ⓓ Ⓔ	46 Ⓐ Ⓑ Ⓒ Ⓓ Ⓔ	52 Ⓐ Ⓑ Ⓒ Ⓓ Ⓔ
29 Ⓐ Ⓑ Ⓒ Ⓓ Ⓔ	35 Ⓐ Ⓑ Ⓒ Ⓓ Ⓔ	41 Ⓐ Ⓑ Ⓒ Ⓓ Ⓔ	47 Ⓐ Ⓑ Ⓒ Ⓓ Ⓔ	53 Ⓐ Ⓑ Ⓒ Ⓓ Ⓔ
30 Ⓐ Ⓑ Ⓒ Ⓓ Ⓔ	36 Ⓐ Ⓑ Ⓒ Ⓓ Ⓔ	42 Ⓐ Ⓑ Ⓒ Ⓓ Ⓔ	48 Ⓐ Ⓑ Ⓒ Ⓓ Ⓔ	54 Ⓐ Ⓑ Ⓒ Ⓓ Ⓔ
31 Ⓐ Ⓑ Ⓒ Ⓓ Ⓔ	37 Ⓐ Ⓑ Ⓒ Ⓓ Ⓔ	43 Ⓐ Ⓑ Ⓒ Ⓓ Ⓔ	49 Ⓐ Ⓑ Ⓒ Ⓓ Ⓔ	55 Ⓐ Ⓑ Ⓒ Ⓓ Ⓔ

Section 3: Business Judgment

56 Ⓐ Ⓑ Ⓒ Ⓓ Ⓔ	61 Ⓐ Ⓑ Ⓒ Ⓓ Ⓔ	66 Ⓐ Ⓑ Ⓒ Ⓓ Ⓔ	71 Ⓐ Ⓑ Ⓒ Ⓓ Ⓔ	76 Ⓐ Ⓑ Ⓒ Ⓓ Ⓔ
57 Ⓐ Ⓑ Ⓒ Ⓓ Ⓔ	62 Ⓐ Ⓑ Ⓒ Ⓓ Ⓔ	67 Ⓐ Ⓑ Ⓒ Ⓓ Ⓔ	72 Ⓐ Ⓑ Ⓒ Ⓓ Ⓔ	77 Ⓐ Ⓑ Ⓒ Ⓓ Ⓔ
58 Ⓐ Ⓑ Ⓒ Ⓓ Ⓔ	63 Ⓐ Ⓑ Ⓒ Ⓓ Ⓔ	68 Ⓐ Ⓑ Ⓒ Ⓓ Ⓔ	73 Ⓐ Ⓑ Ⓒ Ⓓ Ⓔ	78 Ⓐ Ⓑ Ⓒ Ⓓ Ⓔ
59 Ⓐ Ⓑ Ⓒ Ⓓ Ⓔ	64 Ⓐ Ⓑ Ⓒ Ⓓ Ⓔ	69 Ⓐ Ⓑ Ⓒ Ⓓ Ⓔ	74 Ⓐ Ⓑ Ⓒ Ⓓ Ⓔ	79 Ⓐ Ⓑ Ⓒ Ⓓ Ⓔ
60 Ⓐ Ⓑ Ⓒ Ⓓ Ⓔ	65 Ⓐ Ⓑ Ⓒ Ⓓ Ⓔ	70 Ⓐ Ⓑ Ⓒ Ⓓ Ⓔ	75 Ⓐ Ⓑ Ⓒ Ⓓ Ⓔ	80 Ⓐ Ⓑ Ⓒ Ⓓ Ⓔ

Section 4: Data Sufficiency

81 Ⓐ Ⓑ Ⓒ Ⓓ Ⓔ	87 Ⓐ Ⓑ Ⓒ Ⓓ Ⓔ	93 Ⓐ Ⓑ Ⓒ Ⓓ Ⓔ	99 Ⓐ Ⓑ Ⓒ Ⓓ Ⓔ	105 Ⓐ Ⓑ Ⓒ Ⓓ Ⓔ
82 Ⓐ Ⓑ Ⓒ Ⓓ Ⓔ	88 Ⓐ Ⓑ Ⓒ Ⓓ Ⓔ	94 Ⓐ Ⓑ Ⓒ Ⓓ Ⓔ	100 Ⓐ Ⓑ Ⓒ Ⓓ Ⓔ	106 Ⓐ Ⓑ Ⓒ Ⓓ Ⓔ
83 Ⓐ Ⓑ Ⓒ Ⓓ Ⓔ	89 Ⓐ Ⓑ Ⓒ Ⓓ Ⓔ	95 Ⓐ Ⓑ Ⓒ Ⓓ Ⓔ	101 Ⓐ Ⓑ Ⓒ Ⓓ Ⓔ	107 Ⓐ Ⓑ Ⓒ Ⓓ Ⓔ
84 Ⓐ Ⓑ Ⓒ Ⓓ Ⓔ	90 Ⓐ Ⓑ Ⓒ Ⓓ Ⓔ	96 Ⓐ Ⓑ Ⓒ Ⓓ Ⓔ	102 Ⓐ Ⓑ Ⓒ Ⓓ Ⓔ	108 Ⓐ Ⓑ Ⓒ Ⓓ Ⓔ
85 Ⓐ Ⓑ Ⓒ Ⓓ Ⓔ	91 Ⓐ Ⓑ Ⓒ Ⓓ Ⓔ	97 Ⓐ Ⓑ Ⓒ Ⓓ Ⓔ	103 Ⓐ Ⓑ Ⓒ Ⓓ Ⓔ	109 Ⓐ Ⓑ Ⓒ Ⓓ Ⓔ
86 Ⓐ Ⓑ Ⓒ Ⓓ Ⓔ	92 Ⓐ Ⓑ Ⓒ Ⓓ Ⓔ	98 Ⓐ Ⓑ Ⓒ Ⓓ Ⓔ	104 Ⓐ Ⓑ Ⓒ Ⓓ Ⓔ	110 Ⓐ Ⓑ Ⓒ Ⓓ Ⓔ

(continued on next page)

Section 5: Grammar and Usage

111 Ⓐ Ⓑ Ⓒ Ⓓ Ⓔ	116 Ⓐ Ⓑ Ⓒ Ⓓ Ⓔ	121 Ⓐ Ⓑ Ⓒ Ⓓ Ⓔ	126 Ⓐ Ⓑ Ⓒ Ⓓ Ⓔ	131 Ⓐ Ⓑ Ⓒ Ⓓ Ⓔ
112 Ⓐ Ⓑ Ⓒ Ⓓ Ⓔ	117 Ⓐ Ⓑ Ⓒ Ⓓ Ⓔ	122 Ⓐ Ⓑ Ⓒ Ⓓ Ⓔ	127 Ⓐ Ⓑ Ⓒ Ⓓ Ⓔ	132 Ⓐ Ⓑ Ⓒ Ⓓ Ⓔ
113 Ⓐ Ⓑ Ⓒ Ⓓ Ⓔ	118 Ⓐ Ⓑ Ⓒ Ⓓ Ⓔ	123 Ⓐ Ⓑ Ⓒ Ⓓ Ⓔ	128 Ⓐ Ⓑ Ⓒ Ⓓ Ⓔ	133 Ⓐ Ⓑ Ⓒ Ⓓ Ⓔ
114 Ⓐ Ⓑ Ⓒ Ⓓ Ⓔ	119 Ⓐ Ⓑ Ⓒ Ⓓ Ⓔ	124 Ⓐ Ⓑ Ⓒ Ⓓ Ⓔ	129 Ⓐ Ⓑ Ⓒ Ⓓ Ⓔ	134 Ⓐ Ⓑ Ⓒ Ⓓ Ⓔ
115 Ⓐ Ⓑ Ⓒ Ⓓ Ⓔ	120 Ⓐ Ⓑ Ⓒ Ⓓ Ⓔ	125 Ⓐ Ⓑ Ⓒ Ⓓ Ⓔ	130 Ⓐ Ⓑ Ⓒ Ⓓ Ⓔ	135 Ⓐ Ⓑ Ⓒ Ⓓ Ⓔ

Section 6: Business Judgment

136 Ⓐ Ⓑ Ⓒ Ⓓ Ⓔ	141 Ⓐ Ⓑ Ⓒ Ⓓ Ⓔ	146 Ⓐ Ⓑ Ⓒ Ⓓ Ⓔ	151 Ⓐ Ⓑ Ⓒ Ⓓ Ⓔ	156 Ⓐ Ⓑ Ⓒ Ⓓ Ⓔ
137 Ⓐ Ⓑ Ⓒ Ⓓ Ⓔ	142 Ⓐ Ⓑ Ⓒ Ⓓ Ⓔ	147 Ⓐ Ⓑ Ⓒ Ⓓ Ⓔ	152 Ⓐ Ⓑ Ⓒ Ⓓ Ⓔ	157 Ⓐ Ⓑ Ⓒ Ⓓ Ⓔ
138 Ⓐ Ⓑ Ⓒ Ⓓ Ⓔ	143 Ⓐ Ⓑ Ⓒ Ⓓ Ⓔ	148 Ⓐ Ⓑ Ⓒ Ⓓ Ⓔ	153 Ⓐ Ⓑ Ⓒ Ⓓ Ⓔ	158 Ⓐ Ⓑ Ⓒ Ⓓ Ⓔ
139 Ⓐ Ⓑ Ⓒ Ⓓ Ⓔ	144 Ⓐ Ⓑ Ⓒ Ⓓ Ⓔ	149 Ⓐ Ⓑ Ⓒ Ⓓ Ⓔ	154 Ⓐ Ⓑ Ⓒ Ⓓ Ⓔ	159 Ⓐ Ⓑ Ⓒ Ⓓ Ⓔ
140 Ⓐ Ⓑ Ⓒ Ⓓ Ⓔ	145 Ⓐ Ⓑ Ⓒ Ⓓ Ⓔ	150 Ⓐ Ⓑ Ⓒ Ⓓ Ⓔ	155 Ⓐ Ⓑ Ⓒ Ⓓ Ⓔ	160 Ⓐ Ⓑ Ⓒ Ⓓ Ⓔ

Section 7: Verbal Ability

161 Ⓐ Ⓑ Ⓒ Ⓓ Ⓔ	166 Ⓐ Ⓑ Ⓒ Ⓓ Ⓔ	171 Ⓐ Ⓑ Ⓒ Ⓓ Ⓔ	176 Ⓐ Ⓑ Ⓒ Ⓓ Ⓔ	181 Ⓐ Ⓑ Ⓒ Ⓓ Ⓔ
162 Ⓐ Ⓑ Ⓒ Ⓓ Ⓔ	167 Ⓐ Ⓑ Ⓒ Ⓓ Ⓔ	172 Ⓐ Ⓑ Ⓒ Ⓓ Ⓔ	177 Ⓐ Ⓑ Ⓒ Ⓓ Ⓔ	182 Ⓐ Ⓑ Ⓒ Ⓓ Ⓔ
163 Ⓐ Ⓑ Ⓒ Ⓓ Ⓔ	168 Ⓐ Ⓑ Ⓒ Ⓓ Ⓔ	173 Ⓐ Ⓑ Ⓒ Ⓓ Ⓔ	178 Ⓐ Ⓑ Ⓒ Ⓓ Ⓔ	183 Ⓐ Ⓑ Ⓒ Ⓓ Ⓔ
164 Ⓐ Ⓑ Ⓒ Ⓓ Ⓔ	169 Ⓐ Ⓑ Ⓒ Ⓓ Ⓔ	174 Ⓐ Ⓑ Ⓒ Ⓓ Ⓔ	179 Ⓐ Ⓑ Ⓒ Ⓓ Ⓔ	184 Ⓐ Ⓑ Ⓒ Ⓓ Ⓔ
165 Ⓐ Ⓑ Ⓒ Ⓓ Ⓔ	170 Ⓐ Ⓑ Ⓒ Ⓓ Ⓔ	175 Ⓐ Ⓑ Ⓒ Ⓓ Ⓔ	180 Ⓐ Ⓑ Ⓒ Ⓓ Ⓔ	185 Ⓐ Ⓑ Ⓒ Ⓓ Ⓔ

Section 8: Sentence Correction

186 Ⓐ Ⓑ Ⓒ Ⓓ Ⓔ	194 Ⓐ Ⓑ Ⓒ Ⓓ Ⓔ	202 Ⓐ Ⓑ Ⓒ Ⓓ Ⓔ	210 Ⓐ Ⓑ Ⓒ Ⓓ Ⓔ	218 Ⓐ Ⓑ Ⓒ Ⓓ Ⓔ
187 Ⓐ Ⓑ Ⓒ Ⓓ Ⓔ	195 Ⓐ Ⓑ Ⓒ Ⓓ Ⓔ	203 Ⓐ Ⓑ Ⓒ Ⓓ Ⓔ	211 Ⓐ Ⓑ Ⓒ Ⓓ Ⓔ	219 Ⓐ Ⓑ Ⓒ Ⓓ Ⓔ
188 Ⓐ Ⓑ Ⓒ Ⓓ Ⓔ	196 Ⓐ Ⓑ Ⓒ Ⓓ Ⓔ	204 Ⓐ Ⓑ Ⓒ Ⓓ Ⓔ	212 Ⓐ Ⓑ Ⓒ Ⓓ Ⓔ	220 Ⓐ Ⓑ Ⓒ Ⓓ Ⓔ
189 Ⓐ Ⓑ Ⓒ Ⓓ Ⓔ	197 Ⓐ Ⓑ Ⓒ Ⓓ Ⓔ	205 Ⓐ Ⓑ Ⓒ Ⓓ Ⓔ	213 Ⓐ Ⓑ Ⓒ Ⓓ Ⓔ	221 Ⓐ Ⓑ Ⓒ Ⓓ Ⓔ
190 Ⓐ Ⓑ Ⓒ Ⓓ Ⓔ	198 Ⓐ Ⓑ Ⓒ Ⓓ Ⓔ	206 Ⓐ Ⓑ Ⓒ Ⓓ Ⓔ	214 Ⓐ Ⓑ Ⓒ Ⓓ Ⓔ	222 Ⓐ Ⓑ Ⓒ Ⓓ Ⓔ
191 Ⓐ Ⓑ Ⓒ Ⓓ Ⓔ	199 Ⓐ Ⓑ Ⓒ Ⓓ Ⓔ	207 Ⓐ Ⓑ Ⓒ Ⓓ Ⓔ	215 Ⓐ Ⓑ Ⓒ Ⓓ Ⓔ	223 Ⓐ Ⓑ Ⓒ Ⓓ Ⓔ
192 Ⓐ Ⓑ Ⓒ Ⓓ Ⓔ	200 Ⓐ Ⓑ Ⓒ Ⓓ Ⓔ	208 Ⓐ Ⓑ Ⓒ Ⓓ Ⓔ	216 Ⓐ Ⓑ Ⓒ Ⓓ Ⓔ	224 Ⓐ Ⓑ Ⓒ Ⓓ Ⓔ
193 Ⓐ Ⓑ Ⓒ Ⓓ Ⓔ	201 Ⓐ Ⓑ Ⓒ Ⓓ Ⓔ	209 Ⓐ Ⓑ Ⓒ Ⓓ Ⓔ	217 Ⓐ Ⓑ Ⓒ Ⓓ Ⓔ	225 Ⓐ Ⓑ Ⓒ Ⓓ Ⓔ

Practice Test 1

SECTION 1: READING COMPREHENSION

Time: 30 minutes

> *Directions:* Each of the reading passages in this section is followed by questions based on its content. After reading the passage, choose the best answer to each question. The questions are to be answered on the basis of what is stated or implied in the passage.

Our knowledge of man's first appreciation of the great values of freedom of speech and press comes to us from what we refer to as the classical period of Greece, some five centuries more or less before the Christian era. It reaches us largely through fragments of the writings of ancient philosophers and poets, such as Diogenes, Plato, Aristotle, Homer, Aeschylus, Aristophanes, and others. We learn from their writings the high value they placed on being left free from governmental censorship of what they said and wrote. And the writings of these ancient poets and philosophers must have echoed the ideas of preceding generations, that citizens need a right to communicate their ideas to the public in order to protect themselves against arbitrary or tyrannical governments. So we know that by the golden age of Greece, men, striving to enjoy good government, had reached that stage in their thinking in which they *knew* that freedom of speech and press was an essential means of obtaining it.

The Greek states, Athens in particular, long boasted that within their domains word and speech were free. Socrates, in responding to a young sophist's complaints, said, "Strange it were, my good fellow, if having come to Athens, where there is the greatest freedom of speech in all Greece, you alone should be denied that here" (Plato, *Gorgias*). And in Euripides' play the *Phoenissae* we find Jocasta saying, "License to say what one thinks is the mark by which the free are distinguished from slaves." Yet the words of these writers were not always matched by the deeds of their governments, which occasionally lapsed into periods of censorship and repression of views during which people with unpopular opinions were frequently tried, convicted, and punished for daring to express their refusal to conform to the prevailing beliefs and customs.

The lessons against governmental supervision of thought, speech, and press taught by the life and death of Socrates were passed on to Rome. While that bold and warlike country was never able to allow complete freedom of speech and press to criticize governmental affairs, it did pay lip service to the doctrine, and in certain fields and on certain occasions permitted such freedoms to prevail. These concepts were transmitted to England both by the Roman occupation and control of England, and through the Norman conquest of that country. As the years rolled on, and successive British rulers oppressed their subjects more severely, complaints against government were more and more heard. Scattered protests of the people came to be voiced by organized groups or committees, sometimes with open revolutionary overtones. Magna Carta resulted from one of the best known and most successful of these movements. In A.D. 1215 King John was compelled to grant *in writing* numerous privileges, immunities, and benefits to his insurgent barons and many benefits to other groups as well.

1. Which Greek philosopher was sentenced to death for " . . . daring to express (his) refusal to conform to prevailing beliefs and customs?"

    (A) Socrates
    (B) Plato
    (C) Aristotle
    (D) Aristophanes
    (E) Euclid

2. Which event in 20th century Greece has contradicted the ancient Greek values?

    (A) the feud with Turkey about Cyprus
    (B) the growth of the Communist Party
    (C) the censorship of the press under the military regime of the late 1960's
    (D) the admission of Greece into NATO
    (E) the expulsion of the German troops

3. From which countries has America gained its democratic heritage?

        I. Greece
       II. Rome
      III. England
      IV. China

    (A) I, II, and IV only
    (B) I, II, and III only
    (C) II, III, and IV only
    (D) I, III, and IV only
    (E) I, II, III and IV

4. What prompted the demand for a Magna Carta in England?

    (A) dreadful actions by the peasants against the upper classes
    (B) barbarian attacks
    (C) the crowning of Charlemagne as the Holy Roman Emperor
    (D) the complaints of a small group of revolutionaries
    (E) the rising of the barons against the king

5. The "golden age" of a nation is

    (A) the period in which materialism replaces intellectualism
    (B) a time when the nation is on the gold standard
    (C) the age that follows the "silver age"
    (D) its most flourishing period
    (E) the period just before the nation falls

Queen Victoria ruled the British Empire for more than 63 years—the longest reign in England's history. During her lifetime, England was more prosperous than it had ever been before.

But if England prospered under her rule, Queen Victoria's own family did not. For in her *genes*—the coded chemical units that pass on characteristics from one generation to another—she carried an often fatal *genetic defect.* She was a carrier of *hemophilia* (heem-oh-FEEL-ee-uh), a disease in which the blood clots, or *coagulates,* very slowly.

Strangely, only Victoria's *male* descendants became "bleeders." All of her daughters and granddaughters were apparently healthy. Yet many later gave birth to hemophiliac sons.

The genes—including defective ones—are strung like beads on objects known as *chromosomes.* These are found within every human cell. Each normal human cell carries 46 chromosomes—two sets of 23. One set of 23 chromosomes originally comes from the mother's ovum—the egg cell. The other set of 23 comes from one of the father's sperm cells. Each set carries a complete "blueprint" for the "design" of a human being.

When the egg is fertilized by the sperm, both sets of chromosomes come together within the egg. But they do not necessarily produce a "blend" of characteristics. Why? Because some genes can *control* their "matching" gene (say, eye-color gene) from the other parent. These "controller" genes are called *dominants.* The genes that can be controlled are called *recessives.* Whenever a dominant gene and a recessive gene are paired, the individual *always* develops the characteristic of the dominant gene.

The gene that causes hemophilia is recessive. If it is paired with a "healthy" gene, the individual does not develop the symptoms of hemophilia. But even so, the gene is still present. It can be passed along to the *next* generation.

This explains why not all of Victoria's children actually suffered from hemophilia. But why should Victoria's daughters *never* get the disease?

One particular set of chromosomes that we inherit are known as X and Y chromosomes.

Egg cells contain only X chromosomes. A female thus always passes along X chromosomes. But sperm cells contain either an X or Y chromosome. A male can pass along one or the other.

The gene that causes hemophilia is *always* linked to the X chromosome. Thus it is a *sex-linked gene.*

As you recall, each normal cell contains 46 chromosomes—23 donated by the mother and 23 donated by the father. In a female—such as Queen Victoria—such cells hold two X chromosomes. And, in Victoria, only one of these chromosomes held the defective gene. Since a female's egg cells hold only *one* X chromosome, there was a 50 per cent chance of any of Victoria's children inheriting the defective gene.

What's more, since the gene is also recessive, a female will not show the symptoms of the disease if she has one *non*-hemophilic X in her cells. (Victoria's daughters *had* one non-hemophilic X in their cells.)

But the male has only *one* X that he inherits from his mother. Without an "opposite" X, the defective X becomes dominant. Thus, Victoria's sons would become hemophiliacs if they inherited her defective X chromosome.

Queen Victoria probably never knew that she carried the defective hemophilia gene. Her doctors could not explain the disease or even treat it.

But today, medical scientists not only know the genetic basis of the disease, but how to control it as well. Hemophilia is caused by the lack of a *protein*—one of the building blocks of tissue—in the blood. This protein is called Factor VIII or AHF—*antihemophilic factor*. Without this protein, the blood of hemophiliacs clots extremely slowly.

One important method of treating hemophiliacs is to concentrate AHF extracted from the *plasma* of donated blood. Plasma is the thin, watery part of the blood that contains many blood proteins. When the AHF is injected into a hemophiliac, his blood begins to clot normally.

6. A female descendant of Queen Victoria could never be the victim of hemophilia due to the fact that

   (A) she contains both X and Y chromosomes
   (B) both of her genes are always recessive and so she will never contract the disease
   (C) she has two X chromosomes, and one counteracts the other
   (D) she contains only Y chromosomes, which never carry the gene for hemophilia
   (E) she has neither an X nor a Y chromosome

7. A characteristic very similar to hemophilia is

   (A) hair color
   (B) Rh blood factor
   (C) skin pigmentation
   (D) color-blindness
   (E) tallness

8. The determining factors of the hereditary characteristics of an individual are know as

   (A) genes
   (B) chromosomes
   (C) amino acids
   (D) blood cells
   (E) blueprints

9. The human sperm cell contains

   (A) 44 chromosomes and 2 X chromosomes
   (B) 46 chromosomes
   (C) 23 chromosomes
   (D) 23 chomosomes, and 1 X and 1 Y chromosome
   (E) a varying number of chromosomes

10. If $\overset{*}{X}$ stands for a chromosome with the gene for hemophilia, and X stands for a chromosome with a normal gene, a boy with hemophilia will result from parents whose chromosomes are

   (A) XX × XY
   (B) $\overset{*}{X}$X × XY
   (C) XX × X$\overset{*}{Y}$
   (D) XX × $\overset{*}{X}$Y
   (E) XX × YY

11. The protein needed by a hemophiliac can be found in and obtained from

   (A) tissues of the body
   (B) human gametes
   (C) egg cells
   (D) water
   (E) blood plasma

12. The child of brown-eyed parents, where brown is dominant over blue and and the mother is pure brown while the father is hybrid, will

   (A) always have either pure or hybrid brown eyes
   (B) always have pure brown eyes
   (C) have a 50-50 chance of having brown or blue eyes
   (D) have a 25% chance of having blue eyes and a 75% chance of brown eyes
   (E) always have pure blue eyes

When we use a word in speech and writing, its most obvious purpose is to point to some thing or relation or property. This is the word's "meaning." We see a small four-footed animal on the road and call it a "dog," indicating that it is a member of the class of four-footed animals we call dogs. The word "dog" as we have used it there has a plain, straight-forward, "objective" meaning. We have in no way gone beyond the requirements of exact scientific description.

Let us suppose also that one grandparent of the dog was a collie, another was an Irish terrier, another a fox terrier, and the fourth a bulldog. We can express these facts equally scientifically and objectively by saying that he is a dog of mixed breed. Still we have in no way gone beyond the requirements of exact scientific description.

Suppose, however, that we had called that same animal a "mongrel." The matter is more complicated. We have used a word which objectively means the same as "dog of mixed breed," but which also arouses in our hearers an emotional attitude of disapproval toward that particular dog. A word, therefore, can not only indicate an object, but can also suggest an emotional attitude toward it. Such suggestion of an emotional attitude does go beyond exact and scientific discussion because our approvals and disapprovals are individual — they belong to ourselves and not to the objects we approve or disapprove of. An animal which to the mind of its master is a faithful and noble dog of mixed ancestry may be a "mongrel" to his neighbor whose chickens are chased by it.

Once we are on the lookout for this difference between "objective" and "emotional" meanings, we shall notice that words which carry more or less strong suggestions of emotional attitudes are very common and are ordinarily used in the discussion of such controversial questions as those of politics, morals, and religion. This is one reason why such controversies cannot yet be settled.

There is a well-known saying that the word "firm" can be declined as follows: I am *firm,* thou are *obstinate,* he is *pigheaded.* That is a simple illustration of what is meant. "Firm," "obstinate," and "pigheaded" all have the same objective meaning — that is, following one's own course of action and refusing to be influenced by other people's opinions. They have, however, different emotional meanings: "firm" has an emotional meaning of strong approval, "obstinate" of mild disapproval, "pigheaded" of strong disapproval.

In much the same way when, during the World War, thoughts were dominated by emotions, the newspapers contrasted the *spirit* of our heroic boys with *ruthlessness* of the *Huns*, and the *heroism* of our troops with the enemy's *savagery*. Now, with the more objective attitude that has been brought by the lapse of time, we can look back and see that *spirit* and *ruthlessness* are objectively the same thing, only the one word has an emotional meaning of approval, the other of disapproval. We can see, too, that a soldier going forward under shellfire to probable death is doing the same thing whether he is a German or one of our own countrymen, and that to distinguish between them by applying the word *savagery* to the action of the one and *heroism* to that of the other is to distort reality by using words to make an emotional distinction between two actions which are objectively identical.

13. The author's point in the first three paragraphs is that

   (A) there is no real difference between calling a dog a mongrel or calling it a dog of mixed breed
   (B) "a dog of mixed breed" in an emotional term
   (C) "mongrel" is an objective term
   (D) words may suggest emotional attitudes as well as objective meanings
   (E) "sticks and stones can break my bones but names will never hurt me"

14. The author maintains that

   (A) in discussing scientific subjects, emotional words are often used to make meanings clearer
   (B) in discussing controversial questions, objective terms are generally used to help clarify meanings
   (C) in discussing scientific subjects, objective terms are generally used, in order to avoid controversy
   (D) in discussing controversial questions, emotional terms are used very often
   (E) the use of emotional terms has little or no influence in political or religious discussions

15. The author believes that people have disagreements on many subjects partially because

   (A) people have not learned how to get along with each other without conflict and argument
   (B) words used in discussing those subjects carry emotional overtones which tend to antagonize people
   (C) words with objective meanings mean different things to different persons, and must be used carefully
   (D) politics, morals, and religion cause controversies that cannot yet be settled
   (E) of racial, religious, and political differences

16. Regarding war, the author believes that in World War I

   (A) our men showed spirit and heroism, while the Germans displayed ruthlessness and savagery
   (B) although our men acted heroically, there were occasions when they were almost as ruthless as the Germans
   (C) there was no difference at all between the actions of the Americans and of the Germans
   (D) at the time of the war, most people thought that both sides had fought equally bravely, but with the passage of time they began to realize how savage the Germans had really been
   (E) American newspapers unfairly used emotional words to describe the military action

17. In the best scientific position to appraise the worthwhileness of this selection would be a scholar in the field of

   (A) history
   (B) biology
   (C) politics
   (D) military tactics
   (E) linguistics

18. Which of these synonym pairs includes a term which would most likely result in an emotional reaction?

   (A) teacher – instructor
   (B) god – deity
   (C) congressman – representative
   (D) hardhat – laborer
   (E) dictionary – lexicon

   Why have the schools failed? Why boycotts and strikes, why the high school SDS, why the battles over long hair, underground newspapers, and expressions of independent student opinion? Why are there cops in the corridors and marijuana in the gym lockers? Why is it that most students panic when they're invited to work on their own, to study independently? Why is it that most students are more interested in what the teacher wants or what's going to be on the test than they are in understanding the subject that's ostensibly under study? Why bells, monitors, grades, credits, and requirements? Why do most students learn to cheat long before they learn how to learn? Yes, there are exceptions – there are teachers who ask real questions and schools that honor real intellectual distinction and practice real democracy. But a system that requires all children (except the very rich who can buy their way out) to attend a particular school for a specified period – that, in other words, sentences everyone to twelve years of schooling – such a system can and must be judged by its failures.

Everything that we could not, or would not, do somewhere else we expected to be done in the schools. And in the process we thought we saw what in fact does not exist. The greatest failure of American educational journalism in the last decade is that its practitioners refused to believe what they saw, and reported instead what they were supposed to see. Thus we have been inundated with millions of words about the new math, the new physics, the compensatory this and advanced that, about BSCS and PSSC, about IPI and SMSG, about individual progress and head start, upward bound, and forward march. And thus also we have read, with increasing incomprehension, about student uprisings, protests and boycotts and strikes. But few of us ever described the boredom, the emptiness, the brutality, the stupidity, the sheer waste of the average classroom.

What choices does a fifteen-year-old have in the average high school? Choices as to courses, teacher, or physical presence? What does he do most of the day? He sits—and maybe listens. Follow him, not for a few minutes, but for six hours a day, 180 days a year. What goes on in the class? What is it about, what questions are asked? Is it about the real world? Is it about an intellectually honest discipline? Is it about the feelings, passions, interests, hopes, and fears of those who are present? No. It is a world all of its own. It is mostly about nothing.

It worked as long as the promise of schooling itself appeared credible – that is, as long as the proffered reward looked more like a rainbow and less like a mirage, before the end of the road was crowded with people reporting back that the trip wasn't worth it. It is not necessary again to describe the travesties of the average classroom or the average school. But it is important to point out the nothingness of schooling because nothingness (or conformity and repression and boredom) is necessary to the system. Which is not to suggest an Establishment conspiracy to keep children docile so they will become satisfactory candidates for the military-industrial complex. No one planned schools this way, nor have teachers and principals betrayed them: The schools do what they do out of a structural necessity, because we don't know enough about learning, and because social mythology permits very little else.

Any single, universal public institution—and especially one as sensitive as the public school—is the product of a social quotient verdict. It elevates the lowest common denominator of desires, pressures, and demands into the highest public virtue. It cannot afford to offend any sizable community group, be it the American Legion, the B'nai B'rith, or the NAACP. Nor can it become a subversive enterprise that is designed to encourage children to ask real questions about race or sex or social justice or the emptiness and joys of life. Occasionally, of course, it does do these things, but rarely in a significant and consistent manner. Students who ask real questions tend to be threatening to teachers, parents, and the system. They destroy the orderliness of the management procedure, upset routines, and question prejudices. The textbook, the syllabus, the lesson plan are required not only because most teachers are lost without them, but because they represent an inventory for the community, can be inspected to ascertain the purity of the goods delivered. Open-ended programs, responsive to the choices and interests of students, are dangerous not only because all real questions are dangerous, but because they cannot be preinspected or certified for safety. The schools are not unresponsive to the immediate demands of the society. They are doing precisely what most Americans expect.

19. The author is critical of

    (A) permitting the students to choose courses and teachers
    (B) teachers who ask real questions and practice real democracy
    (C) the use of textbooks in the classroom
    (D) having a principal as the head of a school
    (E) curricular innovations such as new math and new physics

20. The selection illustrates a cause and effect relationship between campus unrest and

    (A) classroom boredom
    (B) underground newspapers
    (C) drug use
    (D) the American Legion
    (E) the six-hour school day

21. It is the author's contention that organizations such as the American Legion, the B'nai B'rith, and the NAACP

    (A) encourage children to ask good questions
    (B) are politically wholesome
    (C) destroy the orderliness of classroom management procedures
    (D) prepare the way for adequate instruction concerning race, sex, and social justice
    (E) stand in the way of programs that are responsive to student interest

22. "Why is it that most students panic when they're invited to work on their own, to study independently?" (paragraph 1)

    (A) They are afraid of their teachers.
    (B) Schools do not teach them to be self-sufficient.
    (C) Their parents spoil them at home.
    (D) They are not old enough to work on their own.
    (E) They do not know enough about the "hard knocks" of life.

23. The passage indicates that students fail because

    (A) they are stupid and shiftless
    (B) they are exposed to studies that are too difficult for them
    (C) teachers do not have the required teaching background
    (D) external problems such as the war and racial antagonisms interfere with study
    (E) schools and society have failed them

24. Which statement, according to the passage, is *not* true?

(A) Schools do not relate to student interest.
(B) The average student in a classroom sits most of the day.
(C) School administrators generally do what the adult society wants them to do.
(D) It is not the high schools, but the colleges, which have failed.
(E) Teachers and parents do not, as a rule, favor searching questions on the part of students.

25. Which of the following does the author seem to favor?

  I. American educational journalism
 II. Open-ended school programs
III. The new math and the new physics

(A) I only
(B) II only
(C) III only
(D) I and II only
(E) I, II and III

IF YOU FINISH BEFORE THE TIME IS UP, GO OVER YOUR WORK FOR THIS SECTION ONLY. DO NOT TURN TO ANY OTHER SECTION OF THE TEST. WHEN THE TIME IS UP, GO ON TO THE NEXT SECTION.

SECTION 2: MATH ABILITY

Time: 30 minutes

Directions: Each of the problems in this section is followed by five alternatives lettered A through E. Solve each problem and then choose the correct answer. Note that diagrams are not necessarily drawn to scale. Scratchwork may be done on available space on the pages of this section.

26. Successive discounts of 30% and 10% on an item are equivalent to a single discount of what percent?

    (A) 40%   (D) 33⅓%
    (B) 35%   (E) 25%
    (C) 37%

27. It takes Bill 4 hours to do a job. It takes Joe 2 hours to do the same job. How many such jobs could they do together in 4 hours?

    (A) 1   (D) 7
    (B) 3   (E) 9
    (C) 5

28. John eats ⅛ of a pie. The next day his sister Jean and her friends eat ⅘ of the remaining pie. What percent of the original pie is left?

    (A) 7½%   (D) 70%
    (B) 17½%   (E) 82½%
    (C) 30%

29. A stenographer does typing work at the following rate: 5¢ per sheet of typing paper used and $3.00 per hour of typing. He can type 60 words a minute, and types on paper which holds 30 lines per page, and 10 words per line. How much will he charge to type an 1800-word paper, with two carbon copies?

    (A) $2.40   (D) $9.15
    (B) $4.10   (E) $10.50
    (C) $6.50

30. Mr. Puresilver makes a down payment of $300 on an $1100 purchase. He must pay 8% interest on the balance. How many months will it take Mr. Puresilver to pay the balance if he pays $30 a month?

(A) 28   (D) 37
(B) 29   (E) 40
(C) 30

31. A car cost a dealer $2500. The dealer raised the price by $200, and then deducted $1/9$ of the new price. What percent of the original cost was the car sold for?

(A) 25%   (D) 96%
(B) 100%   (E) none of the above
(C) 108%

Question 32 refers to the following chart:

SURVEY OF INCOMES
(IN THOUSANDS OF DOLLARS)

		Number interviewed	Average 1965 income	Average 1969 income
Business	Men	30	25	35
	Women	5	15	20
Teaching	Men	15	11	12
	Women	15	9	11
Sports	Men	10	15	18

32. What group's wages increased by the greatest percentage between 1965 and 1969?

(A) businessmen   (D) women teachers
(B) businesswomen   (E) sportsmen
(C) men teachers

33. An item which originally sold for $140 was discounted by 40%, and then by 20%. What was the final selling price?

(A) $67.20   (D) $80.00
(B) $72.00   (E) $84.00
(C) $76.80

34. An art collector is given a 60-piece collection of geometric figures. 15% of the figures are spheres. How many spheres must be added to the collection so that 25% will be spheres?

(A) 6 (D) 9
(B) 7 (E) 10
(C) 8

35. A man wishes to cover his 9-foot by 9-foot room with square tiles, all the same size. He wants to use white and black squares, in checkerboard fashion, so that there is a black square at each corner. All these conditions can be met if

(A) the tiles measure 4 inches on each side
(B) the tiles measure 6 inches on each side
(C) the tiles measure 8 inches on each side
(D) the tiles measure 4 inches, 6 inches, *or* 8 inches on each side
(E) all of the above are true

36. Cashew nuts cost 20¢ more per pound than peanuts. If 15 pounds of peanuts cost just as much as 10 pounds of cashews, how much do cashews cost per pound?

(A) 60¢ (D) 25¢
(B) 50¢ (E) 15¢
(C) 40¢

37. In order to obtain admission into a special school program, all applicants must take a special exam, which is passed by three out of every five applicants. Of those who pass the exam, one-fourth are finally accepted. What is the percentage of all applicants who *fail* to gain admission into the program?

(A) 55 (D) 85
(B) 60 (E) 90
(C) 75

38. Of the following, which one will yield the greatest amount of simple interest?

(A) $ 20 at 2% per year for 6 years
(B) $ 25 at 2% per year for 3 years
(C) $ 50 at 4% per year for 1¾ years
(D) $100 at 4% per year for 9 months
(E) $150 at 8% per year for 3 months

39. A car was initially priced at $3000. The price was reduced 20% and then raised 10%. What was the total reduction in price?

   (A) $125   (D) $540
   (B) $270   (E) $840
   (C) $360

40. The Stock Market rose 35¢, 40¢, 25¢, and 50¢ on 4 successive days. What rise is necessary on a fifth day for the average gain to be 30¢?

   (A) 30¢   (D) 0¢
   (B) 10¢   (E) 25¢
   (C) 25¢

41. Estimate L if $L = \dfrac{.1003}{\sqrt[3]{\dfrac{31.97}{2.03} \times \dfrac{11.912}{2.98}}}$

   (A) $\frac{1}{3}$ (D) $\frac{1}{40}$
   (B) $\frac{1}{30}$ (E) 40
   (C) $\frac{1}{4}$

42. The sum of five whole numbers is 146. If m is the largest of the five numbers, what is the smallest value that m can have?

   (A) 30   (D) 27
   (B) 35   (E) 41
   (C) 28

43. If all the children in a class pay 35¢, they can buy enough food for a party. If another twenty children chip in, each child need only pay 21¢ for the same total amount of food. How many children are there in the class?

   (A) 25   (D) 35
   (B) 30   (E) 38
   (C) 33

Question 44

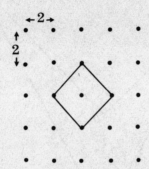

44. If the horizontal distance between two consecutive dots is 2 and the vertical distance between two consecutive dots is also 2 as shown in the diagram above, what is the area of the square region above?

(A) $2\sqrt{2}$ (D) 16
(B) 4   (E) 32
(C) 8

45. $^2\!/_9$ of $^3\!/_5$ is equal to x times $^5\!/_6$. What is the value of x?

(A) $^1\!/_9$ (D) $^{81}\!/_{25}$
(B) $^4\!/_9$ (E) $^1\!/_{75}$
(C) $^4\!/_{25}$

46. A car can travel 30 miles per hour going uphill and 60 miles per hour going downhill. What is its average speed, in miles per hour, if it goes 100 miles uphill and then 50 miles downhill?

(A) 40   (D) 45
(B) 36   (E) $48\,^1\!/_2$
(C) $33\,^1\!/_3$

47. Which of the following must be positive?

     I. the product of 2 positive numbers
     II. the product of 2 negative numbers
     III. the sum of 2 negative numbers

(A) I only   (D) I and II only
(B) II only   (E) I, II, and III
(C) I and III only

48.

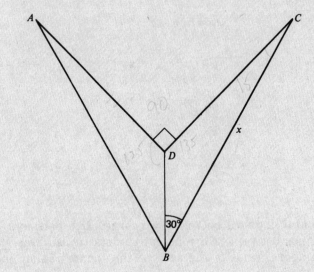

In the diagram, if triangle *ABD* and triangle *BCD* are congruent, what is the length of *DC*?

(A) $\dfrac{x\sqrt{3}}{4}$

(B) $\dfrac{2x}{5}$

(C) $\dfrac{x}{3}$

(D) $\dfrac{2x\sqrt{2}}{3}$

(E) $\dfrac{x\sqrt{2}}{2}$

49. A cow is tied to a pole in the middle of a field, with a 14-foot rope. If the cow eats 100 square feet of grass a day, for how many days will the cow have enough to eat?

(A) 2
(B) 18
(C) 24
(D) 7
(E) 6

50. During the first month, the population of an ant colony was 500 ants. It was discovered that for the *n*th month, the population was given by the formula $500(n^2 - n + 1)$. Find the increase in population from the fourth month to the fifth month.

(A) 4000
(B) 2000
(C) 3600
(D) 3218
(E) 2400

51. Jay types *m* words in *n* minutes; John types *p* words in *q* minutes. The ratio of Jay's typing rate to John's rate is

(A) $\dfrac{m}{p}$

(B) $mnpq$

(C) $\dfrac{mq}{pn}$

(D) $m + q - p - n$

(E) $\dfrac{mn}{pq}$

52. The price of a $100 suit was reduced 20%. Later the price was reduced another 10%. These two reductions had the same effect as a single reduction of

   (A) 32%
   (B) 24%
   (C) 30%

   (D) 28%
   (E) 37½%

53. A Mid-Western railway company charges $3.75 per pound for each item 10 lbs or less, shipped one mile, and $3.25 per pound for each item over 10 lbs, shipped one mile. The fee the company will charge per one mile shipment of 20 forty pound items sent in 5 equal one-mile shipments is

   (A) $520
   (B) $640
   (C) $580

   (D) $720
   (E) $840

54. In an electronics firm, 5 Type-A parts are permanently attached to 2 Type-B parts. In June, 1974, 1000 Type-B parts were shipped abroad. The stock of parts was contained in drawers and each drawer contained 500 Type-A parts. How many drawers were emptied of the Type-A and Type-B parts for the shipment abroad in June, 1974?

   (A) 2
   (B) 3
   (C) 4

   (D) 5
   (E) 6

55. A teacher requests that his annual salary be paid in twelve equal payments instead of ten. If each of the ten payments is m dollars, how many dollars will each of the twelve payments be?

   (A) $m - 3$

   (B) $\dfrac{6m}{5}$

   (C) $\dfrac{5m}{6}$

   (D) $10m - 12$

   (E) $12m - 10$

IF YOU FINISH BEFORE THE TIME IS UP, GO OVER YOUR WORK FOR THIS SECTION ONLY. DO NOT TURN TO ANY OTHER SECTION OF THE TEST. WHEN THE TIME IS UP, GO ON TO THE NEXT SECTION.

SECTION 3: BUSINESS JUDGMENT

Time: 30 minutes for all of Section 3

QUESTIONS ON DATA EVALUATION

Directions: Read the passage. After the passage are Data Evaluation questions (in phrase form) that relate to the passage. Answer each question by choosing the appropriate letter for your answer.

(A) **Major Objective.** The phrase indicates a Major Objective of the business executive in the situation described in the passage.

(B) **Major Factor.** The phrase indicates a Major Factor in the business executive's arriving at a decision. The passage specifically mentions a circumstance or consideration that is fundamental in his coming to the decision.

(C) **Minor Factor.** The phrase indicates a Minor Factor in the business executive's arriving at a decision. The passage specifically states a circumstance or consideration that is secondary in his coming to a decision.

(D) **Major Assumption.** The phrase indicates a Major Assumption in the business executive's arriving at a decision. He is taking for granted certain circumstances or occurrences in his decision-making.

(E) **Unimportant Issue.** The phrase indicates an Unimportant Issue in the business executive's arriving at a decision. The issue is of no importance or of no relevance in his decision-making.

Bill Stevens had been operating a steel foundry in Fargo, North Dakota for over twenty years. The plant was small, and was thus unable to accommodate large contract offers from the automobile and aircraft industries. However, the foundry was able to remain economically solvent by successfully bidding on small contracts, particularly on those offered by companies which manufactured heavy machinery.

In the spring of 1977, Fargo, North Dakota was hit by a devastating earthquake. Fortunately, there were few injuries, although much personal property, including the Stevens' foundry, was completely demolished.

Stevens was not a man who sulked over the events of the past. Immediately following this unfortunate catastrophe, he began to consider various methods of reconstructing his business. However, he soon realized that he possessed neither the time nor the resources nor the overall business judgment necessary to arrive at a satisfactory decision on his own. Upon the advice of an associate, he therefore sought the assistance of the consulting firm, Karmen and Baylor. He wrote them the following letter:

Gentlemen:

Prior to the spring of 1977, I was the operator of a small steel foundry in Fargo, N.D. Because of the earthquake that has hit this area, my business has been destroyed. My insurance company has promised that I will be completely reimbursed for the loss. I am therefore anxious to quickly rebuild the foundry with these payments.

I have considered reconstructing the plant in Fargo. I already own the land, and have established a good reputation in the area. This would keep soliciting and advertising costs to a minimum. However, as the earthquake has proven, the terrain is extremely unstable. In addition, because of the lack of adequate space, the new plant would not be any larger than the old one. Since I am rebuilding, I would like to have the opportunity to expand my operation.

I am therefore determined to relocate, and it is in this respect that I seek your assistance. Primarily, I am looking for a site with room for expansion, so as to be able to accept larger contracts. Furthermore, I insist that the terrain be certified as stable, since I would hate to experience another quake. In addition, I am seeking a location that is relatively free from competition and legal problems. I would like this land to cost less than $100,000, although I am prepared to pay as much as $120,000. I would greatly appreciate your help in this matter.

Sincerely,

Bill Stevens

After three months, Stevens received this report:

Dear Mr. Stevens:

The search for alternative sites which you commissioned is now complete. Four members of our staff have come up with possible locations. While none of these sites is perfect, they should all be considered.

In addition, I have assessed the market value of the land that you now own at $10,000. However, it is my feeling that the value will double in the next three years, and therefore suggest that you do not rush to sell it. In any case, here are the findings of our staff.

Mr. Drucker explored a land site in Briarcliff, North Dakota. He found the land to be moderately priced at $30,000 although building costs on this site would run an additional $60,000. Furthermore, Drucker projects the costs of soliciting and advertising at this site to be $22,000. The land is quite stable, and there is much room for expansion. However, this area has had a history of union problems, and only last year there was a general strike.

Mr. Haney found a potential location in Fairlane, South Dakota. The land is extremely cheap at $18,000, and the cost of building is moderate at $48,000. However, the stability of the land could not be verified. Furthermore, the site is located in an area of strong competition, and soliciting and advertising costs for it are thus projected to be approximately $35,000.

Mr. Douglas found a site in Bayville, Montana. The land is expensive — $46,000. However, it has been certified by geologists to be one hundred percent stable. There are no labor problems, and the demand for a foundry in this area seems to be high. The building costs would be quite reasonable at $37,000, and soliciting and advertising should not exceed $15,000. The only drawback is that this location is rather far away from most of the large contractors, and shipping costs would thus be higher than in any of the other locations.

Finally, Mr. Bodine visited Crispwater, Idaho, and found there a possible site. At $24,000, the land is quite reasonable, and, like all the other locations, it is quite spacious. The cost of building would be $42,000, and additional soliciting and advertising costs would run $20,000. Although the land cannot be certified to be one hundred per cent stable, the chance of an earthquake in this location is very slight. A major problem here is that the cost of complying with the Idaho Pollution Statutes would be exceedingly high, and would tend to restrict production. In addition, these laws are likely to get harsher in the coming years.

We have prepared a chart to simplify the comparison of the various costs of relocation. We hope you arrive at satisfactory choice.

Sincerely,

Martin Baylor

Karmen & Baylor Consultants

LOCATION	LAND COST	BUILDING COST	SOLICITING AND ADVERTISING COSTS	TOTAL COST
Fargo, N. D. (original location)	0	$68,000	$5,000	$73,000
Briarcliff, N.D.	$30,000	$60,000	$22,000	$112,000
Fairlane, S.D.	$18,000	$48,000	$35,000	$101,000
Bayville, Montana	$46,000	$37,000	$15,000	$98,000
Crispwater, Idaho	$24,000	$42,000	$20,000	$86,000

*Choose the appropriate letter (A or B or C or D or E)
for these phrases in accordance with the given directions.*

56. Desirability of rebuilding business
57. Emotional effects of moving on Stevens' children
58. Relocating on acceptable site
59. Ability of geologists to accurately gauge the stability of terrain
60. Effects of pollution legislation on a foundry
61. Remaining in Fargo, North Dakota
62. Increasing size of foundry
63. Distance of the Bayville location from large contractors
64. Ability of Karmen & Baylor to adequately advise Stevens of his alternatives
65. Total cost of each location
66. Amount of consultation fee charged by firm
67. Undesirable effects of union problems on the foundry
68. Advisability of relocation over reconstruction in Fargo
69. Accommodating large contracts from big businesses
70. Desirability of having room for expansion
71. The number of people injured in the earthquake
72. Avoiding the experience of another earthquake
73. Effects of competition on soliciting and advertising costs
74. Reimbursement of losses by Stevens' insurance company
75. Stability of each site's terrain

QUESTIONS ON DATA APPLICATION

Directions: The questions below are to be answered with reference to the same passage (above). For each question, select the correct answer from each of the five choices given.

76. All of the following are given as reasons for Stevens' desire to relocate *except*

    I. Legal restrictions of original location
    II. Unstable terrain of original location
    III. Size of original location
    IV. Competition from other foundries

    (A) I, III only
    (B) I, III, IV only
    (C) IV only
    (D) I, IV only
    (E) II, III only

77. Three years from now, how would one expect the value of the Fargo land to compare with the present values of the other landsites?

    (A) It would be the cheapest.
    (B) It would be more expensive than one of the other sites.
    (C) It would be more expensive than two of the other sites.
    (D) It would be more expensive than three of the other sites.
    (E) It would be more expensive than all of the other sites.

78. Stevens' insurance policy allowed for the payment of all damages in excess of $24,000. If the damages incurred from the earthquake totaled $125,000, how many of the relocation alternatives would Stevens be able to afford if he relied solely on the insurance payments to finance his move? (Do not consider consultation fees.)

    (A) none
    (B) one
    (C) two
    (D) three
    (E) four

79. Stevens is obligated to pay the consultation fee of $10,000 to Karmen and Baylor only if he selects one of their alternatives. Therefore, he would save *at least* how much more by reconstructing the foundry in Fargo than by relocating in one of the four landsites?

    (A) $35,000
    (B) $13,000
    (C) $49,000
    (D) $38,000
    (E) $23,000

80. On the basis of the evidence given and the objectives sought, which alternative would be Stevens' best choice?

    (A) Fargo
    (B) Briarcliff
    (C) Fairlane
    (D) Bayville
    (E) Crispwater

IF YOU FINISH BEFORE THE TIME IS UP, GO OVER YOUR WORK FOR THIS SECTION ONLY. DO NOT TURN TO ANY OTHER SECTION OF THE TEST. WHEN THE TIME IS UP, GO ON TO THE NEXT SECTION.

SECTION 4: DATA SUFFICIENCY

Time: 30 minutes

Directions: Each of the questions below is followed by two statements, labeled (1) and (2), in which certain data are given. In these questions you do not actually have to compute an answer, but rather you have to decide whether the data given in the statements are *sufficient* for answering the question. Using the data given in the statements *plus* your knowledge of mathematics and everyday facts (such as the number of days in July), you are to blacken the box on the answer sheet under

(A) if statement (1) ALONE is sufficient but statement (2) alone is not sufficient to answer the question asked.

(B) if statement (2) ALONE is sufficient but statement (1) alone is not sufficient to answer the question asked,

(C) if BOTH statements (1) and (2) TOGETHER are sufficient to answer the question asked, but NEITHER statement ALONE is sufficient,

(D) if EACH statement is sufficient by itself to answer the question asked,

(E) if statements (1) and (2) TOGETHER are NOT sufficient to answer the question asked and additional data specific to the problem are needed.

81. The average salary of the employees of Company XYZ is $100 per week. How many employees earn more than the average?

    (1) There are 10 employees in Company XYZ.
    (2) Exactly eight employees earn $100 per week.

82. Which is the longest side of triangle ABC?

    (1) Angle A is 100°.
    (2) Angle B is 20°.

83. What is the value of x?

    (1) x is an integer greater than 5 and less than 13.
    (2) x is divisible by both 2 and 3.

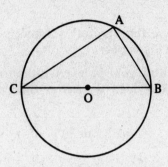

84. In the figure above, what is the length of AC, provided BC is a straight line and O is the center of the circle?

    (1) AB = 6 inches.
    (2) The radius of circle O is 5 inches.

85. Who is the shortest: Jim, George, or Andy?

    (1) George is shorter than Andy.
    (2) Andy is 10% taller than Jim.

86.

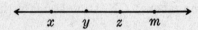

Is $zm > 0$ on the number line above?

    (1) $y = 0$
    (2) $x = -2$

87. How much does Ann weigh?

    (1) If she were twice as heavy, she would be 10 pounds lighter than her mother.
    (2) If she were to lose 30 pounds, she would be 75% of her present weight.

88. What is the value of x?

    (1) $\dfrac{2}{x} = \dfrac{27}{2}$
    (2) $x + 0.76 = 0.3$

89. How many people in Littletown have both blond hair and blue eyes?

    (1) 150 people have blond hair, 840 people have blue eyes.
    (2) Littletown has a population of 2000.

90. How much do 10 oranges cost?

    (1) A dozen oranges cost 60¢.
    (2) If the cost of the 10 oranges was decreased by 10%, they would cost 63¢.

91. Which would have the greatest volume: a gram of gold, a gram of lead, or a gram of copper?

    (1) A cubic inch of gold is heavier than a cubic inch of lead.
    (2) A cubic foot of lead is heavier than a cubic foot of copper.

92. Which is greater: $z\%$ of $2x$ or $m\%$ of 5 $(m > 0)$?

    (1) $x > \dfrac{5}{2}$

    (2) $z > m$

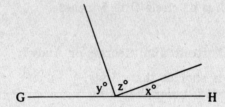

93. In the diagram above, GH is a straight line. What is the value of z?

    (1) $y = 70$
    (2) $x + y = 100$

94. What is the average age of the students in Henry's class?

    (1) There are 30 students in the class.
    (2) 29 students in the class are exactly 16 years old.

95. R varies directly as S. What is R when S is 5?

    (1) R is 10 when S is 6.
    (2) R increases when S increases.

96. How many miles per gallon can Mr. Hart get on his car?

    (1) He used two tankfuls of gasoline on an 800 mile trip.
    (2) The tank of Mr. Hart's car holds 20 gallons.

97. Is triangle JHG an acute triangle?

    (1) The lengths of the sides of the triangle are 5, 12, and 13.
    (2) Triangle JHG has a 5° angle.

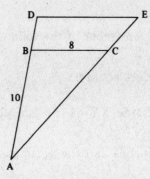

98. In the diagram above, triangle ABC is similar to triangle ADE. AB is 10 and BC is 8. What is the length of DE?

    (1) BD = 5
    (2) AB + AC = 25

99. What is the area of a certain rectangle?

    (1) The length is 5 more than twice the width.
    (2) The perimeter of the rectangle is 20.

100. Angles A and B are supplementary. What is the measure of angle A?

    (1) Angle A is greater than twice angle B.
    (2) Twice angle A plus angle B equals 310°.

101. Is y, an integer, divisible by 30.

    (1) y is divisible by 30.
    (2) y is divisible by 5.

102. Who can run faster, George or Simon?

    (1) George can run around a track 5 times in 320 seconds.
    (2) Simon can run 100 yards in 12.4 seconds.

103. Which is the shortest of 3 worms?

    (1) The sum of the lengths of the worms is 3 inches.
    (2) Worm A is 1 inch long and Worm C is $\frac{1}{2}$ inch long.

104. How many bushels of corn can a farmer grow on his farm?

    (1) The farmer owns 530 acres.
    (2) Each corn stalk can yield 5 pounds of corn.

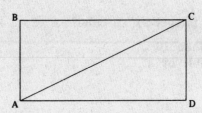

105. What is the area of the rectangle shown above?

    (1) AD is 10 feet long, AC is 14 feet long.
    (2) The perimeter is 30 feet.

106. Is a certain number X a member of the following set? {4, 5, 8, 18, 20}

    (1) X is divisible by 7.
    (2) X is an odd perfect square.

107. What is the length of side XY of the isosceles triangle XYZ?

    (1) Angle Z equals 51°.
    (2) ZX = ZY = 15 inches and the perimeter is 40 inches.

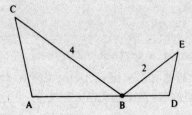

108. In the diagram above, triangle ABC is similar to triangle BDE. BC is 4 units long and BE is 2 units long. What is the length of AD? (Angle CBA = Angle EBD and Angle A = Angle D.).

    (1) BD is 1.6 units long.
    (2) AC is 3 units long.

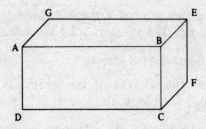

109. What is the volume of the rectangular prism shown above?

    (1) BC = 2 inches, BE = 1½ inches.
    (2) The area of face ADCB is 10 square inches.

110. Is the positive integer "x" a cube?

    (1) x is less than 16.
    (2) x is divisible by 8.

IF YOU FINISH BEFORE THE TIME IS UP, GO OVER YOUR WORK FOR THIS SECTION ONLY. DO NOT TURN TO ANY OTHER SECTION OF THE TEST. WHEN THE TIME IS UP, GO ON TO THE NEXT SECTION.

SECTION 5: GRAMMAR AND USAGE

Time: 30 minutes

Directions: In each question, you will find a sentence with four words (or phrases) underlined. In some sentences one of the underlined words (or phrases) is incorrect in the light of the rules of standard written English for grammar, correct usage, and choice of words. No sentence has more than one error. You are to assume that the rest of the sentence (whatever is not underlined) is correct. If you find an error, choose the letter (A *or* B *or* C *or* D) of that underlined word (or phrase) which is incorrect. If you find no error, fill in answer space E.

111. The union delegates who are going to the convention in Miami Beach
         A   B   C
     are Thompson, Steinmetz, and me. No error.
                                 D   E

112. After being wheeled into the infirmary, the nurse at the desk asked
                           A   B   C
     me several questions. No error.
            D   E

113. Us boys insist on your giving them what is theirs and us what is
       A   B   C
     ours. No error.
      D   E

114. We hear dissent from a young man who, we firmly believe, is not
             A   B
     about to pay compliments to our political leaders or to the local
           C   D
     draft board. No error.
             E

115. She wore a dress to the party that was far more attractive than
         A   B   C
     the other girls. No error.
         D   E

116. Controversial matters involving the two groups were discussed; never-
                           A   B
     theless, most of the representatives remained calm. No error.
           C   D   E

117. If he had laid quietly under the tree as he had been instructed to do,
     $\overline{}_{A}$ $\overline{}_{B}$ $\overline{}_{C}$
we would have found him. No error.
$\overline{}_{D}$ $\overline{}_{E}$

118. If one reads a great many articles in *Elementary English,* you will
                     $\overline{}_{A}$ $\overline{}_{B}$
become familiar with the problems of the beginning teacher of read-
       $\overline{}_{C}$ $\overline{}_{D}$
ing. No error.
    $\overline{}_{E}$

119. Down the field came the students of South High School: members of
     $\overline{}_{A}$
the newly organized, somewhat incompetent band; drum majorettes
                     $\overline{}_{B}$
in white, spangled skirts; and the team, muddy and wretched.
          $\overline{}_{C}$ $\overline{}_{D}$
No error.
$\overline{}_{E}$

120. If I would have been there, I certainly would have taken care of the
     $\overline{}_{A}$ $\overline{}_{B}$ $\overline{}_{C}$
problem in a hurry. No error.
        $\overline{}_{D}$ $\overline{}_{E}$

121. Between you and I, I am convinced that this painting by Dali shows
                    $\overline{}_{A}$ $\overline{}_{B}$
greater artistry than that of Picasso. No error.
        $\overline{}_{C}$ $\overline{}_{D}$ $\overline{}_{E}$

122. He believes in witchcraft, but he doubts that they ride on broom-
        $\overline{}_{A}$ $\overline{}_{B}$ $\overline{}_{C}$ $\overline{}_{D}$
sticks. No error.
       $\overline{}_{E}$

123. Being that you are interested in the outcome of the election, let us
     $\overline{}_{A}$ $\overline{}_{B}$ $\overline{}_{C}$
wait until the final tally has been made. No error.
                        $\overline{}_{D}$ $\overline{}_{E}$

124. The retreat of the enemy soldiers into caves and tunnels are deceiving
        $\overline{}_{A}$ $\overline{}_{B}$
the oncoming infantrymen. No error.
     $\overline{}_{C}$ $\overline{}_{D}$ $\overline{}_{E}$

125. The <u>millennium</u> <u>will have arrived</u> when parents give <u>appropriate</u>
           A   B   C

     responsibilities to <u>we</u> teenagers. <u>No error.</u>
                   D   E

126. In <u>contrast to</u> <u>Arnold's</u> intellectual prowess <u>was</u> his <u>slovenly</u> appear-
            A   B   C   D

     ance and his nervous demeanor. <u>No error.</u>
                                     E

127. The crisis <u>in</u> the <u>Middle East</u> is one of the topics that
               A   B

     <u>has been discussed</u> at our <u>weekly</u> forums. <u>No error.</u>
              C   D   E

128. I <u>wouldn't</u> be interested in buying this <u>here</u> farm <u>even</u> if you <u>were</u>
       A   B   C   D

     to offer it to me for a hundred dollars. <u>No error.</u>
                                         E

129. The trouble <u>with</u> a good many people in our country is that they
                  A

     have <u>vested</u> interests – <u>that is,</u> they are concerned with <u>theirselves</u>
           B   C   D

     first and foremost. <u>No error.</u>
                       E

130. There is no sense in <u>getting</u> angry with <u>them</u> radicals <u>just</u> because
                        A   B   C

     they disagree <u>with</u> you. <u>No error.</u>
                  D   E

131. There <u>seem</u> <u>nowadays</u> to be little of the optimism that <u>imbued</u> our
            A   B   C

     ancestors <u>with</u> courage and hope. <u>No error.</u>
                D

132. The high school graduate, if <u>he</u> is eighteen or nineteen, <u>has</u> these
                             A   B

     <u>alternatives:</u> attending college, finding a job, or <u>the army.</u> <u>No error.</u>
         C   D   E

133. Since it was an <u>unusually</u> warm day, the dog <u>laid</u> under the tree
A   B

<u>all afternoon</u> without barking at <u>passersby</u> — something he
C   D

usually does. <u>No error.</u>
E

134. There <u>was</u> only an apple and three pears <u>in the refrigerator</u> when
A   B

we <u>came home</u> after a <u>weekend</u> in the country. <u>No error.</u>
C   D   E

135. The Chairman <u>of the Board</u> of Directors made it <u>clear</u> at the meeting
A   B

that he <u>will not</u> step down from his position <u>as chairman</u>. <u>No error.</u>
C   D   E

IF YOU FINISH BEFORE THE TIME IS UP, GO OVER YOUR WORK FOR THIS
SECTION ONLY. DO NOT TURN TO ANY OTHER SECTION OF THE TEST.
WHEN THE TIME IS UP, GO ON TO THE NEXT SECTION.

SECTION 6: BUSINESS JUDGMENT

Time: 30 minutes for all of Section 6

QUESTIONS ON DATA EVALUATION

Directions: Read the passage. After the passage are Data Evaluation questions (in phrase form) that relate to the passage. Answer each question by choosing the appropriate letter for your answer.

(A) **Major Objective.** The phrase indicates a Major Objective of the business executive in the situation described in the passage.

(B) **Major Factor.** The phrase indicates a Major Factor in the business executive's arriving at a decision. The passage specifically mentions a circumstance or consideration that is fundamental in his coming to the decision.

(C) **Minor Factor.** The phrase indicates a Minor Factor in the business executive's arriving at a decision. The passage specifically states a circumstance or consideration that is secondary in his coming to a decision.

(D) **Major Assumption.** The phrase indicates a Major Assumption in the business executive's arriving at a decision. He is taking for granted certain circumstances or occurrences in his decision-making.

(E) **Unimportant Issue.** The phrase indicates an Unimportant Issue in the business executive's arriving at a decision. The issue is of no importance or of no relevance in his decision-making.

Bromley's Fantasyland had long been a landmark of Southern Wyoming. For years, the famous amusement park, with its multitude of rides, games, and other attractions, had provided entertainment for both children and adults alike. The park was owned and operated by Mr. Bromley and his son George. The staff consisted of approximately two hundred employees.

While generating a sizable profit for the greater part of its existence, Fantasyland was now running at a loss. To account for this dilemma, Mr Bromley blamed several factors. Inclement weather, he claimed, had forced the closing of the amusement park for a number of days during the peak summer vacation period. In addition, rising fuel costs had sharply reduced the profit margin obtained through the operation of various rides. Finally, "Spacetown," a newly developed amusement center, had begun to win over a segment of his clientele. In an effort to improve the situation, the owner called in his son George, in addition to Mr. Ken Jefferson, the senior staff member, to discuss the matter.

Mr. Bromley: On the one hand, there is no cause for immediate action. We may view the problems incurred through bad weather and fuel prices simply as freak ocurrences and hope that they do not recur. However, I feel it is foolish to run a business based on chance. Furthermore, if things keep up at their present rate, I will be forced to lay off as many as twenty-five per cent of the staff. I have always enjoyed a very cordial relationship with my employees and would hate to lay any of them off. I therefore feel it absolutely necessary to devise a plan which will guarantee that never again will Fantasyland finish a year in the red. To this end, we should address ourselves to our competition. Let us expand our facilities to meet those of "Spacetown." As I see it, all that we lack is a comparable roller coaster. The construction of a new one would cost $20,000, and would require an initial investment of fifty per cent. I would expect the job to be completed within two years.

Jefferson: It seems to me that there is no need to compete with "Spacetown" on their level. We have been in existence for many years and have developed a strong reputation for service to the community. Surely we do not have to match them "ride for ride." However, I suggest that we harness the inclement weather that we have been having, and use it to our advantage. During the months of November through March, our area has averaged fifteen inches of snow per month. With this much natural powder, we have the potential for an excellent ski slope. In speaking to a number of landscapers, I have found that the task would require an initial investment of $15,000, and would run $48,000 overall. The construction should take no longer than a year and a half, but I have known similar jobs to take two years.

Mr. Bromley: Your suggestion is interesting but it ignores several problems. The ski slope would make use only of the winter snow, when, in actuality, it has been the excessive rainfall of the past summer which has hurt our business. In addition, most of our staff know nothing about the management of a ski slope. I think we should stick to something we know.

George: I have studied the prospect of putting Fantasyland under a giant enclosure, and have determined that the project would run $52,000 with an initial deposit of seventy-five per cent required.

Jefferson: Could we possibly raise that much capital on such short notice?

Mr. Bromley: Yes. The First National Bank has offered me a credit line of $120,000 at an annual interest rate of 22% per year. However, this applies only to the first eighteen months of the loan, following which the interest rate doubles. It is, therefore, to our advantage to complete the construction as early as possible so as to quickly pay back the loan with the newly generated income.

George: The advantages gained by enclosing Fantasyland in a domed structure are significant. First of all, we would forever rid ourselves of the dependence on good weather. Secondly, in an indoor environment, our rides would operate more efficiently and would waste less fuel. Finally, we would be offering our clientele a feature that "Spacetown" could not match.

In addition, we could continue to operate Fantasyland even while the enclosure is under construction. The reason for this is that the dome will be produced at the manufacturer's plant, and will be shipped to Fantasyland ready to be quickly assembled. The construction of a new roller coaster, however, will necessitate the closing of Fantasyland for at least six months due to safety regulations, resulting in the loss of an expected $80,000 in income.

Mr. Bromley: What must be realized is that all of the previous projects must be accompanied by an aggressive advertising campaign. My experience tells me that this will probably cost in the area of $40,000. We should therefore consider the possibility of building a new electric generator which would drastically reduce our fuel costs. The generator would require an initial investment of $10,000, and would cost $95,000. It would require no advertising. However, I have been told that such machines take five years to build.

George: I think that we have discussed a number of viable alternatives. We should select a project that will best guarantee that the crises of the past year will not repeat, and yet we must arrive at a decision that is economically sound, and that will perpetuate Fantasyland's fine record of service to the community.

OPTION	INITIAL COST	CONSTRUC-TION COST	ANTICIPATED TIME TO COMPLETE	CONSTRUC-TION COST + ADVERTISING
Roller Coaster	$10,000	$20,000	2 years	$60,000
Ski Slope	$15,000	$48,000	1½ years	$88,000
Enclosure	$39,000	$52,000	1 year	$92,000
Generator	$10,000	$95,000	5 years	$95,000

Choose the appropriate letter (A or B or C or D or E) *for these phrases in accordance with the given directions.*

136. Maintaining Fantasyland's staff of 200 employees
137. Time required to build an electric generator
138. Maintaining community service of Fantasyland
139. Material from which the dome-like enclosure was made
140. Ability to obtain a loan from the First National Bank
141. Length of time required for each project to be completed
142. The staff's lack of expertise in running a ski slope
143. Shielding Fantasyland from natural and economic hardships
144. Continued competition from Spacetown
145. Salary of each employee
146. Profitability of Spacetown
147. Proximity of Spacetown to Fantasyland
148. Devising a mechanism to insure the solvency of Fantasyland
149. Total cost of each project
150. Possibility of delays in construction of ski slope
151. Withstanding competition from Spacetown
152. The inadvisability of running a chancy business
153. Cost of operating roller coaster
154. Method by which the enclosure is built and assembled
155. Original number of employees at Fantasyland

QUESTIONS ON DATA APPLICATION

Directions: The questions below are to be answered with reference to the same passage (above). For each question, select the correct answer from each of the five choices given.

156. All of the following are given as motivations for Mr. Bromley to improve or to expand Fantasyland *except*

    I. Competition from another amusement park
    II. Poor relations with his staff
    III. Sharply reduced income
    IV. Insufficient advertising

    (A) I only
    (B) II and IV only
    (C) I, II, and III only
    (D) I and III only
    (E) I, II, III, and IV

157. If Bromley were to receive a 50% discount on advertising costs by electing to build a roller coaster, how would the total cost of this project compare with that of the enclosure (excluding interest payments)?

    (A) lesser by $32,000
    (B) greater by $48,000
    (C) lesser by $52,000
    (D) greater by $28,000
    (E) lesser by $20,000

158. Which of the following is the most serious disadvantage of the ski slope project?

    (A) The time required to build it
    (B) The uncertainty of its ability to generate a sizable income
    (C) Its inability to function in the summer months
    (D) The unfamiliarity of the staff with running a ski slope
    (E) The cost of building such a project

159. Assuming that Bromley had planned to pay back his loan in a lump sum exactly six months after the completion of Fantasyland's refurbishment, approximately how much more would he owe the bank if he chose to build the generator than if he chose to construct a roller coaster? (Consider only construction costs.)

    (A) $75,000
    (B) $183,000
    (C) $225,000
    (D) $154,000
    (E) $258,000

160. On the basis of the evidence given and the objectives sought, which alternative would be Bromley's best choice?

    (A) Roller Coaster
    (B) Ski-slope
    (C) Enclosure
    (D) Generator
    (E) Postponement of any action

IF YOU FINISH BEFORE THE TIME IS UP, GO OVER YOUR WORK FOR THIS SECTION ONLY. DO NOT TURN TO ANY OTHER SECTION OF THE TEST. WHEN THE TIME IS UP, GO ON TO THE NEXT SECTION.

SECTION 7: VERBAL ABILITY

Time: 30 minutes

Part A — Antonyms

Directions: In each question, you will find a capitalized word which is followed by five choices. Select from these choices that word whose meaning is *opposite* to the meaning of the capitalized word.

161. ENDEMIC

 (A) bright
 (B) satanic
 (C) academic
 (D) tyrannical
 (E) foreign

162. OBESE

 (A) willing
 (B) remarkable
 (C) convex
 (D) underweight
 (E) bland

163. ABERRANT

 (A) average
 (B) dull
 (C) capable
 (D) flippant
 (E) apparent

164. GELID

 (A) hard
 (B) warm
 (C) soft
 (D) cold
 (E) medium

165. HOI POLLOI

 (A) cannibalism
 (B) tyranny
 (C) the past
 (D) bottoms up
 (E) aristocracy

166. PRECURSORY

 (A) slandering
 (B) satisfactory
 (C) succeeding
 (D) unpretentious
 (E) glassy

167. INCREDULOUS

 (A) tolerable
 (B) gullible
 (C) vicious
 (D) creditable
 (E) not injurious

168. ASKEW

 (A) straight
 (B) silent
 (C) curious
 (D) aching
 (E) acceptable

Part B — Analogies

Directions: In each question, you will first see two capitalized words. Try to establish a relationship between these two words. Then select from the five lettered word-pairs that word pair which bears a relationship which is the same as that of the two capitalized words.

169. WEALTH : LUXURIES ::

(A) enemies : friends
(B) sandwich : bread
(C) ticket : admission
(D) crying : sympathy
(E) story : moral

170. PEAK : SUMMIT ::

(A) mutation : change
(B) gun : soldier
(C) elementary : advanced
(D) switch : current
(E) foreign : native

171. ANGLE : DEGREE ::

(A) letter : alphabet
(B) milk : quart
(C) area : square inch
(D) time : minutes
(E) society : classes

172. SHIP : HARBOR ::

(A) flower : garden
(B) village : people
(C) nest : bird
(D) editor : newspaper
(E) car : garage

173. NOSE : NASAL ::

(A) ear : aural
(B) apparent : evident
(C) fragrant : perfume
(D) wise : wisdom
(E) tree : branches

174. GLOVE : HAND ::

(A) teeth : chewing
(B) neck : collar
(C) coat : pocket
(D) stocking : leg
(E) shoe : lace

175. LEND : BORROW ::

(A) abridge : lengthen
(B) award : deserve
(C) begin : start
(D) dictate : govern
(E) seed : plant

176. MUSIC : GUITAR ::

(A) stamping : noise
(B) water : ocean
(C) windows : house
(D) words : typewriter
(E) tears : sorrow

Part C — Sentence Completions

Directions: In each of the following sentences, one or two words are missing. From the five choices, select that choice which fits in best with the rest of the sentence.

177. A child should not be _____ as being either very shy or over-aggressive.

   (A) instructed
   (B) refrained
   (C) intoned
   (D) categorized
   (E) distracted

178. The fact is that surface fleets are becoming increasingly _____ _____ in the nuclear age, but the Navy, understandably, is reluctant to _____ this.

   (A) powerful .... redress
   (B) obsolete .... concede
   (C) diverse .... resist
   (D) mechanized .... disrupt
   (E) complex .... enhance

179. Some people respond to a threat of rejection by becoming very _____, while others _____ and become again like little dependent children.

   (A) concise .... objectify
   (B) militant .... regress
   (C) impulsive .... diminish
   (D) indignant .... revive
   (E) amiable .... procrastinate

180. Not only did he display _____ manners, but his whole attitude betrayed his _____ for these people whom he considered his inferiors.

   (A) elegant .... frustration
   (B) peculiar .... anxiety
   (C) revolting .... adoration
   (D) abominable .... contempt
   (E) benign .... attrition

181. His choice for the new judge won the immediate _____ of city officials, even though some of them had _____ about him.

   (A) acclaim .... reservations
   (B) disdain .... information
   (C) apprehension .... dilemmas
   (D) vituperation .... repercussions
   (E) enmity .... preconceptions

182. While the _____ goal is to meet the specific learning needs of each child, the long-range aim is to develop his ability to assume the _____ for his own learning.

    (A) real .... initiative
    (B) supposed .... requirements
    (C) immediate .... responsibility
    (D) apparent .... desire
    (E) innate .... preparation

183. The fact that the _____ of confrontation is no longer as popular as it once was _____ progress in race relations.

    (A) practice .... inculcates
    (B) reticence .... indicates
    (C) glimmer .... foreshadows
    (D) insidiousness .... reiterates
    (E) technique .... presages

184. The purpose of this approach is to initiate _____ correctional steps whenever the need for them arises.

    (A) invidious
    (B) appropriate
    (C) residual
    (D) perceptible
    (E) irreversible

185. Without the _____ to think imaginatively, man could never have developed _____.

    (A) premonition .... civilization
    (B) inhibition .... aesthetics
    (C) apparatus .... presumption
    (D) capacity .... architecture
    (E) animosity .... creation

IF YOU FINISH BEFORE THE TIME IS UP, GO OVER YOUR WORK FOR THIS SECTION ONLY. DO NOT TURN TO ANY OTHER SECTION OF THE TEST. WHEN THE TIME IS UP, GO ON TO THE NEXT SECTION.

SECTION 8: SENTENCE CORRECTION

Time: 30 minutes

Directions: Each sentence is partly or wholly under-lined. In some cases, what is underlined is correct — in other cases, it is incorrect. The five choices that follow each sentence represent various ways of writing the underlined part. Choice A is the same as the original underlining but Choices B, C, D, and E are different. If, in your judgment, the original sentence is better than any of the changed sentences, select Choice A. If another choice produces the only correct sentence, select that other choice (B or C or D or E).

In making your choice, you should observe the rules of standard written English. Your choice must fulfill the requirements of correct grammar, diction (word choice), sentence structure, and punctuation.

If a choice changes the meaning of the original sentence, do not make that choice.

186. Driving a racing car on a speedway is in some ways like when you are riding a horse on a bridle path.

   (A) is in some ways like when you are riding
   (B) in some ways is in the same class as riding
   (C) is in some ways similar to when you are riding
   (D) is in some ways similar to riding
   (E) is like a ride in some ways of

187. Seeing their father, the cigarettes were immediately concealed by the children.

   (A) Seeing their father, the cigarettes were immediately concealed by the children.
   (B) Their father being seen by them, the children immediately concealed the cigarettes.
   (C) The children having seen their father, the cigarettes were concealed immediately.
   (D) When the children saw their father, they immediately concealed the cigarettes.
   (E) When their father was seen, the children immediately concealed the cigarettes.

188. Barrymore had many wives, Garrick one, but each is remembered not for his women but for his talent.

   (A) Barrymore had many wives, Garrick one
   (B) Barrymore had many wives, Garrick having one
   (C) Barrymore having many wives, Garrick just one
   (D) Barrymore has had many wives, but Garrick only one
   (E) Barrymore had many wives, Garrick had only one wife

189. Biologists often say that <u>it is not chemists or physicists but that they have</u> the answer to the improvement of life on earth.

   (A) it is not chemists or physicists but that they have
   (B) it is not chemists or physicists but they have
   (C) they, and not chemists or physicists have
   (D) it is not chemists or physicists but it is they who have
   (E) it is they, not chemists or physicists, who have

190. The underprivileged student is getting a better <u>education, there are better teachers for them</u> and better facilities.

   (A) education, there are better teachers for them
   (B) education; he has better teachers
   (C) education; they have better teachers
   (D) education, he has better teachers
   (E) education; because he has better teachers

191. <u>When the university administration changed its role from that of a judge and prosecutor to that of an adviser and friend,</u> not only did the students stop their demonstrations but they also sided with the administration against the outsiders.

   (A) When the university administration changed its role from that of a judge and prosecutor to that of an adviser and friend
   (B) When the university administration changed its role from that of a judge and prosecutor to an adviser and friend
   (C) When the university administration changed its role from that of a judge and prosecutor to one of an adviser and friend
   (D) As a result of the administration's changing its role from judge and prosecutor to that of adviser and friend
   (E) As to the university administration, in changing its role from that of a judge and prosecutor to that of an adviser and friend

192. The Soviet Union has reorganized and modernized its intelligence network in the Western Hemisphere toward the goal of diminshing and <u>to possibly replace</u> United States influence.

   (A) to possibly replace
   (B) possibly to replace
   (C) possibly replacing
   (D) to replace possibly
   (E) for replacement of

193. In the next booklet, <u>the sales manager and personnel director will tell you something about his work.</u>

    (A) the sales manager and personnel director will tell you something about his work

    (B) the sales manager who is also director of personnel will tell you something about their work

    (C) the sales manager who is also personnel director will tell you something

    (D) the sales manager and personnel director will tell you something as it applies to his work

    (E) the sales manager and the personnel director will tell you something about what his work is

194. I have enjoyed the study of the Spanish language not only because of its beauty but also <u>to make use of it in business.</u>

    (A) to make use of it in business

    (B) because of its use in business

    (C) on account it is useful in business

    (D) one needs it in business

    (E) since all business people use it

195. Known to every man, woman, and child in the town, <u>friends were never lacking to my grandfather.</u>

    (A) friends were never lacking to my grandfather

    (B) my grandfather was not lacking to his friends

    (C) friends never lacked my grandfather

    (D) my grandfather never lacked no friends

    (E) my grandfather never lacked friends

196. No sooner had he entered the room <u>when the lights went out</u> and everybody began to scream.

    (A) when the lights went out

    (B) than the lights went out

    (C) and the lights went out

    (D) but the lights went out

    (E) the lights went out

197. John, whose mother is a teacher, <u>is not so good a student as many other friends</u> I have with no academic background in their families.

    (A) is not so good a student as many other friends

    (B) is not as good a student like many other friends

    (C) is not quite the student as are other friends

    (D) as a student is not a good as many other friends

    (E) does not have the studious qualities of many other friends

198. After our waiting in line for three hours, <u>much to our disgust, the tickets had been sold out</u> when we reached the window.

  (A) much to our disgust, the tickets had been sold out
  (B) the tickets had been, much to our disgust, sold out
  (C) the tickets had been sold out, much to our disgust,
  (D) the sold-out tickets had, much to our disgust, been disposed of
  (E) and much to our disgust, the tickets had been sold out

199. When the members of the committee are at odds, <u>and when also, in addition, they are in the process</u> of offering their resignations, problems become indissoluble.

  (A) and when also, in addition, they are in the process
  (B) and also when they are in the process
  (C) and when, in addition, they are in the process
  (D) they are in the process
  (E) and when the members of the committee are in the process

200. <u>There is no objection to him joining the party</u> if he is willing to fit in with the plans of the group.

  (A) There is no objection to him joining the party
  (B) There is no objection on him joining the party
  (C) There is no objection to his joining the party
  (D) No objection will be raised upon him joining the party
  (E) If he decides to join the party, there will be no objection

201. Further acquaintance with the memoirs of Elizabeth Barrett Browning and Robert Browing enable us to appreciate the depth of influence that two people <u>of talent can have on one another.</u>

  (A) of talent can have on one another
  (B) of talent can exert on one another
  (C) with talent can have one for the other
  (D) of talent can have on each other
  (E) who are talented can have

202. <u>If you saw the amount of pancakes he consumed</u> at breakfast this morning, you would understand why he is so overweight.

  (A) If you saw the amount of pancakes he consumed
  (B) If you would see the amount of pancakes he consumed
  (C) When you see the amount of pancakes he consumed
  (D) If you saw the number of pancakes he consumed
  (E) If you had seen the number of pancakes he consumed

203. The debutante went to the concert with her fiancé wearing a sheer blouse.

    (A) The debutante went to the concert with her fiancé wearing a sheer blouse.
    (B) The debutante went to the concert, wearing a sheer blouse, with her fiancé.
    (C) The debutante, wearing a sheer blouse, went to the concert with her fiancé.
    (D) With her fiancé, wearing a sheer blouse, the debutante went to the concert.
    (E) To the concert, wearing a sheer blouse, went the debutante with her fiancé.

204. Briefly the functions of a military staff are to advise the commander, transmit his instructions, and the supervision of the execution of his decisions.

    (A) and the supervision of the execution of his decisions
    (B) also the supervision of the execution of his decisions
    (C) and supervising the execution of his decisions
    (D) and supervise the execution of his decisions
    (E) and have supervision of the execution of his decisions

205. The 15-round decision that Frazier was given over Ali was not popular with all of the boxing fans.

    (A) The 15-round decision that Frazier was given over Ali
    (B) Frazier's 15-round decision over Ali
    (C) The Frazier 15-round decision over Ali
    (D) The decision of 15 rounds that Frazier was given over Ali
    (E) Ali's 15-round decision that Frazier was given over him

206. Tricia Nixon was just engaged and was born on St. Patrick's Day.

    (A) Tricia Nixon was just engaged and was born on St. Patrick's Day.
    (B) Tricia Nixon was just engaged, she was born on St. Patrick's Day.
    (C) On St. Patrick's Day Tricia Nixon was born, she was just engaged.
    (D) Tricia Nixon, born on St. Patrick's Day, was just engaged.
    (E) Tricia Nixon was engaged and she was born on St. Patrick's Day.

207. As no one knows the truth as fully as him, no one but him can provide the testimony needed to clear the accused of the very serious charges.

    (A) as fully as him, no one but him
    (B) as fully as he, no one but him
    (C) as fully as he, no one but he
    (D) as fully as he does, no one but he
    (E) as fully as he does, no one but he alone

208. After the defendant charged him with being prejudiced, the judge withdrew from the case.

    (A) After the defendant charged him with being prejudiced
    (B) On account of the defendant charged him with being prejudiced
    (C) Charging the defendant with being prejudiced
    (D) Upon the defendant charging him with being prejudiced
    (E) The defendant charged him with being prejudiced

209. Although the mourners differed in color and in dress, they all sat silently together for an hour to honor Whitney M. Young Jr.

    (A) Although the mourners differed in color and in dress
    (B) Because the mourners differed in color and in dress
    (C) The mourners having differed in color and in dress
    (D) When the mourners differed in color and in dress
    (E) The mourners differed in color and in dress

210. To avoid the hot sun, our plans were that we would travel at night.

    (A) To avoid the hot sun, our plans were that we would travel at night.
    (B) To try to avoid the hot sun, our plans were for travel at night.
    (C) Our plans were night travel so that we could avoid the hot sun.
    (D) We planned to travel at night, that's how we would avoid the hot sun.
    (E) To avoid the hot sun, we made plans to travel at night.

211. Whatever she had any thoughts about, they were interrupted as the hotel lobby door opened.

    (A) Whatever she had any thoughts about
    (B) Whatever her thoughts
    (C) Whatever be her thoughts
    (D) What her thoughts were
    (D) What thoughts

212. The use of radar, as well as the two-way radio, make it possible for state troopers to intercept most speeders.

    (A) make it possible
    (B) makes it possible
    (C) allows the possibility
    (D) makes possible
    (E) make it a possibility

213. Irregardless what reasons or excuses are offered, there is only one word for his behavior: cowardice.

    (A) Irregardless what reasons or excuses are offered
    (B) Regardless about what reasons or excuses he may offer
    (C) Since he offered reasons and excuses
    (D) Nevertheless he offered reasons and excuses
    (E) No matter what reasons and excuses are offered

214. What a man cannot state, he does not perfectly know.

    (A) What a man cannot state, he does not perfectly know.
    (B) A man cannot state if he does not perfectly know.
    (C) A man cannot perfectly know if he does not state.
    (D) That which a man cannot state is that which he cannot perfectly know.
    (E) What a man cannot state is the reason he does not perfectly know.

215. Professional writers realize that they cannot hope to effect the reader precisely as they wish without care and practice in the use of words.

    (A) they cannot hope to effect
    (B) they cannot hope to have an effect on
    (C) they cannot hope to affect
    (D) they cannot hope effecting
    (E) they cannot try to affect

216. I've met two men whom, I believe, were policemen.

    (A) whom, I believe,
    (B) who, I believe
    (C) each, I believe,
    (D) and I believe they
    (E) who

217. Such people never have and never will be trusted.

    (A) never have and never will be trusted
    (B) never have and will be trusted
    (C) never have trusted and never will trust
    (D) never have been trusted and never will be trusted
    (E) never have had anyone trust them and never will have anyone trust them

218. Your employer would have been inclined to favor your request if you would have waited for an occasion when he was less busy.

    (A) if you would have waited for an occasion
    (B) if you would only have waited for an occasion
    (C) if you were to have waited for an occasion
    (D) if you waited for an occasion
    (E) if you had waited for an occasion

219. I find Henry James' prose style more difficult to read than James Joyce.

(A) I find Henry James' prose style more difficult to read than James Joyce.
(B) I find Henry Jame's prose style more difficult to read than James Joyce'.
(C) I find Henry James's prose style more difficult to read than James Joyce's.
(D) I find the prose style of Henry James more difficult to read than James Joyce.
(E) Henry James' prose style I find more difficult to read than I find James Joyce.

220. Neither Dr. Conant nor his followers knows what to do about the problem.

(A) Neither Dr. Conant nor his followers knows what to do about the problem.
(B) Neither Dr. Conant or his followers knows what to do about the problem.
(C) Neither Dr. Conant nor his followers know what to do about the problem.
(D) Neither Dr. Conant nor his followers knows what to do as far as the problem goes.
(E) As to the problem, neither Dr. Conant nor his followers knows what to do.

221. Although I know this house and this neighborhood as well as I know myself, and although my friend here seems not hardly to know them at all, nevertheless he has lived here longer than I.

(A) and although my friend here here seems not hardly to know them at all.
(B) and even though my friend here seems hardly to know them at all
(C) and in spite of the fact that my friend doesn't hardly seem to know them at all
(D) and because my friend here hardly seems to know them at all
(E) my friend here seems hardly to know them at all

222. So I leave it with all of you: Which came out of the open door — the lady or the tiger.

(A) the lady or the tiger.
(B) the lady or the Tiger!
(C) the Tiger or the lady.
(D) the Lady or the tiger.
(E) the lady or the tiger?

223. The machine is not easy to fool, <u>it isn't altogether foolproof either.</u>

    (A) it isn't altogether foolproof either
    (B) or is it foolproof
    (C) and it isn't completely fooled by anyone
    (D) nor is it entirely foolproof
    (E) so it isn't altogether foolproof

224. The police and agents of the F.B.I. <u>arrested the owner of a Madison Avenue art gallery yesterday</u> and charged him with receiving paintings stolen last November.

    (A) arrested the owner of a Madison Avenue art gallery yesterday
    (B) yesterday arrested the owner of a Madison Avenue art gallery
    (C) arrested the owner yesterday of a Madison Avenue art gallery
    (D) had the owner of a Madison Avenue art gallery yesterday arrested
    (E) arranged the arrest yesterday of a Madison Avenue art gallery owner

225. At the end of the play about women's liberation, the leading lady cautioned the audience not to judge womanhood by the way <u>she dresses.</u>

    (A) she dresses
    (B) she dressed
    (C) they dress
    (D) they dressed
    (E) it dresses

IF YOU FINISH BEFORE THE TIME IS UP, GO OVER YOUR WORK FOR THIS SECTION ONLY. DO NOT TURN TO ANY OTHER SECTION OF THE TEST. WHEN THE TIME IS UP, THE TEST IS OVER

NOW THAT YOU HAVE COMPLETED PRACTICE TEST 1

1. Turn to the Answer Key on pages 62-64. Do not consider Sections 7 and 8.

2. Count your **correct answers.**

3. Count your **incorrect answers.**

4. Deduct ¼ of the number of incorrect answers from the number of correct answers to get a **"raw score"** of _____.

5. Your **"scaled score"** for this test, according to the Raw Score/Scaled Score Table on page 88, is _____.

ANSWER KEY FOR PRACTICE TEST 1

Section 1: Reading Comprehension

1. A	6. C	11. E	16. C	21. E
2. C	7. D	12. A	17. E	22. B
3. B	8. A	13. D	18. D	23. E
4. E	9. C	14. D	19. E	24. D
5. D	10. B	15. B	20. A	25. B

Section 2: Math Ability

After each answer, there is a hyphenated number (or numbers) in parentheses. This hyphenated number is keyed to Math Refresher (beginning on page 411). The number *before* the hyphen indicates the Math area of the problem:

1 = ARITHMETIC
2 = ALGEBRA
3 = PLANE GEOMETRY
5 = GRAPHS AND CHARTS

The number *after* the hyphen gives you the section (within the Math area) that explains the rule or principle involved in solving the problem.

26. C (1-25)	36. A (2-11, 2-22)	46. B (2-31, 2-34)
27. B (2-32)	37. D (1-25)	47. D (2-2, 2-3)
28. B (1-4, 1-25)	38. C (1-24)	48. E (3-4, 3-7)
29. A (1-17, 1-15)	39. C (1-25)	49. E (3-6)
30. B (1-25)	40. D (2-34)	50. A (2-12)
31. D (1-5, 1-25)	41. D (1-27)	51. C (2-26)
32. A (5-2, 2-25)	42. A (2-34)	52. D (1-25)
33. A (1-24)	43. B (2-11, 2-22)	53. A (Basic Arith.)
34. C (1-25)	44. C (3-4)	54. D (2-28)
35. A (1-28)	45. C (2-22)	55. C (2-13)

ANSWER KEY FOR PRACTICE TEST 1 (continued)

Section 3: Business Judgment

56. D	65. B	74. D
57. E	66. E	75. B
58. A	67. C	76. D
59. D	68. D	77. B
60. C	69. A	78. D
61. E	70. D	79. E
62. A	71. E	80. D
63. C	72. A	
64. D	73. C	

Section 4: Data Sufficiency

81. C	91. C	101. A
82. A	92. C	102. E
83. E	93. B	103. C
84. C	94. E	104. E
85. E	95. A	105. A
86. A	96. C	106. D
87. B	97. A	107. B
88. D	98. A	108. A
89. E	99. C	109. C
90. D	100. B	110. C

Section 5: Grammar and Usage

111. D	120. B	129. D
112. C	121. A	130. B
113. A	122. C	131. A
114. E	123. A	132. D
115. D	124. B	133. B
116. E	125. D	134. A
117. A	126. C	135. C
118. B	127. E	
119. E	128. B	

Section 6: Business Judgment

136. A	145. E	154. C
137. C	146. E	155. E
138. A	147. E	156. B
139. E	148. A	157. D
140. D	149. B	158. D
141. B	150. C	159. E
142. C	151. A	160. C
143. A	152. D	
144. C	153. C	

ANSWER KEY FOR PRACTICE TEST 1 (continued)

Section 7: Verbal Ability

161. E	170. A	179. B
162. D	171. C	180. D
163. A	172. E	181. A
164. B	173. A	182. C
165. E	174. D	183. E
166. C	175. A	184. B
167. B	176. D	185. D
168. A	177. D	
169. C	178. B	

Section 8: Sentence Correction

186. D	200. C	214. A
187. D	201. D	215. C
188. A	202. E	216. B
189. E	203. C	217. D
190. B	204. D	218. E
191. A	205. A	219. C
192. C	206. D	220. C
193. A	207. B	221. B
194. B	208. A	222. E
195. E	209. A	223. D
196. B	210. E	224. B
197. A	211. B	225. E
198. C	212. B	
199. C	213. E	

EXPLANATORY ANSWERS FOR PRACTICE TEST 1

Section 1: Reading Comprehension

1. **(A)** Socrates (469-399 B. C.), accused of impiety and innovation, was forced to commit suicide by drinking hemlock. In addition, the first sentence of the third paragraph hints at the answer.

2. **(C)** After reading the first paragraph, one should realize that Ancient Greece's values included freedom of speech and press. The censorship of the press in Greece in the late 1960's contradicts these beliefs.

3. **(B)** The first paragraph states that first Greece was a cradle for democratic thought. The third paragraph adds that this thought was passed on to the Romans and then on to the English.

4. **(E)** The last sentence of the third paragraph states: "In A.D. 1215 King John was compelled to grant *in writing* numerous privileges, immunities, and benefits to his insurgent barons and many benefits to other groups as well."

5. **(D)** See paragraph 1 (last sentence): "So we know.. means of obtaining it."

6. **(C)** Paragraph 9 states that egg cells contain only X chromosomes, never Y. Paragraph 13 says that a male lacks the "opposite" X chromosome, and the hemophilia gene becomes dominant in him. In the female this never happens.

7. **(D)** Both hemophilia and color-blindness are known to be sex-linked characteristics, being carried along the sex chromosomes and identifiable with one sex.

8. **(A)** Paragraph 2 states this to be the function of genes.

9. **(C)** Paragraph 4 tells us that a human cell has 46 chromosomes, with two sets of 23 each contributed by the two human gametes.

10. **(B)** Of all the choices given, only choice B is possible, as only females can be carriers of hemophilia. The female is signified with a double X.

11. **(E)** The last paragraph tells us that blood plasma contains AHF, the protein which causes blood to clot.

12. **(A)** Because brown is dominant over blue and both parents have brown eyes, it is impossible for a blue-eyed child to come about. The child's eyes would be either hybrid brown or pure brown, as seen in the following chart:

    B = brown
    b = blue
    BB = pure brown
    Bb = hybrid brown

    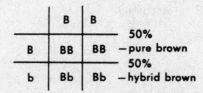

13. **(D)** See middle of third paragraph—"A word.. toward it". Each of the other choices is the opposite of the fact.

14. **(D)** See beginning of fourth paragraph. Choice A is obviously wrong. Choice B is wrong since the author believes that this is just what is not being done; choice C is true in itself but is not mentioned in the passage. Choice E is wrong as indicated in the last sentence of the fourth paragraph.

15. **(B)** See beginning of fourth paragraph. Note that choice D, while using selected words from the selection, does not give the author's reason for the disagreements, as asked for, but merely states that they exist.

16. **(C)** See last paragraph. The author is of course emphasizing that in war, savagery and heroism are almost identical, as we can generally see if we are not involved in the situation.

17. **(E)** This article is essentially one of linguistics, the scientific study of language.

18. **(D)** The expression "hardhat" has emotional significance for many. We won't elaborate here lest we bring to the fore emotional reactions on the part of the reader.

19. **(E)** See paragraph 2: "Thus we have been inundated with millions of words . . . and forward march"

20. **(A)** See paragraph 2, last two sentences: "And thus also . . . waste of the average classroom."

21. **(E)** See paragraph 5 in which the influence of such organizations as the American Legion, the B'nai B'rith, and the NAACP is discussed.

22. **(B)** See paragraph 3: "What does he do most of the day? . . It is mostly about nothing."

23. **(E)** Throughout the selection, the failure of the schools and society is brought out.

24. **(D)** Criticism in this article is leveled primarily at the secondary school system. For example, see paragraph 3: "What choices does a fifteen-year-old have in the average high school?"

25. **(B)** The author does not favor "I" —see paragraph 2: "The greatest failure of American educational journalism . . . reported instead what they were supposed to see." He does not favor "III"— again, see paragraph 2: "Thus we have been inundated with millions of words about the new math, the new physics . . ." The author implies that he favors "II" —see the last paragraph: "Open-ended programs, responsive to the choices and interests of students, are dangerous . . . certified for safety."

EXPLANATORY ANSWERS FOR PRACTICE TEST 1 (continued)

Section 2: Math Ability

26. **(C)** Let P = original price
    P' = price after the first discount
    and P'' = price after the second discount.
    Since $30\% = {}^3/_{10}$ and $10\% = {}^1/_{10}$,

$$P' = P - {}^3/_{10}P = {}^7/_{10}P$$
$$P'' = P' - {}^1/_{10}P' = {}^9/_{10}P'$$
$$P'' = ({}^9/_{10})({}^7/_{10})P = {}^{63}/_{100}P$$

Since P'' is 63% of P, the two discounts are equivalent to a single discount of 37%.

27. **(B)** In 4 hours Bill does 1 job and Joe does $^4/_2$ or 2 jobs. Together they do 3 jobs.

28. **(B)** First John eats $^1/_8$ or $12^1/_2\%$ of the pie. Then his sister and her friends eat $^4/_5$ of the remaining pie. ($^7/_8$ of the pie remains since John ate $^1/_8$ of the pie.) $^4/_5$ or $^7/_8$ of the pie equals $\dfrac{4}{5} \times \dfrac{7}{8} = \dfrac{7}{10}$ which is equivalent to 70% of the remaining pie. Since John has already eaten $12^1/_2\%$ of the whole pie, $70\% + 12^1/_2\%$ or $82^1/_2\%$ of the original pie has been eaten. The amount of pie remaining is found by subtracting $82^1/_2\%$ from 100%. $17^1/_2\%$ of the original pie remains.

29. **(A)** There are two charges here: a paper charge and a time charge. The paper charge equals 5¢ times the number of sheets used. Since each page holds 30 lines of 10 words each (300 words per page), the length of the paper will be $1800 \div 300$, or 6 pages; but since two additional copies of each page must be made, the total number will be $6 + (2)(6) = 18$. At 5¢ a page, 18 pages will cost $0.90. At a rate of 60 words per minute, 1800 words can be typed in $(1800 \div 60)$, or 30 minutes (which equals $^1/_2$ hour). Thus, the time charge will equal $^1/_2 \times \$3.00$, or $1.50. Therefore, adding the paper charge to the time charge, we get: $\$0.90 + \$1.50 = \$2.40$.

30. **(B)** Since he paid $300, he must pay a balance of $800 on the $1100 purchase. On this $800, an 8% interest must be paid. $800 \times .08 = \$64$. Mr. Puresilver must pay another $864. Each month he pays $30. To find how many months he needs to pay, we divide $864 by $30. $\dfrac{28}{\$30)\$864}$ months plus a remainder of $24. He will pay this $24 in this next month. Therefore 29 months is the correct answer.

31. **(D)** $2500 + \$200 = \$2700$. Then, $\$2700 - \dfrac{1}{9}(\$2700) = \$2400$. Now, $2400 is $\dfrac{2400}{2500} \times 100$ or 96% of $2500.

32. **(A)** The businessmen's income went up from 25 to 35 thousand dollars, an increase of $^{10}/_{25}$ or 40%.

33. **(A)** A 40% discount from $140 reduces the price by $(.4)(\$140) = \$56$, to $84. A further discount of 20% reduces this amount by $(.2)(\$84) = \$16.80$, to $67.20.

34. **(C)** 15% of 60 figures are spheres. 9 figures are spheres. In order to find how many spheres must be added so that 25% of the figures are spheres, set up the following algebraic expression:

    Let x be the number of additional spheres.

$$\frac{9 + x}{60 + x} = .25$$

$$9 + x = 15 + .25x$$
$$.75\,x = 6$$
$$x = 8$$

35. **(A)** Since the colors of the squares along the edge of the room will alternate, there will have to be an *odd* number of tiles on each edge if both corners can be black. If the tiles are 4 inches each, then there will

be (108 ÷ 4), or 27 tiles per side, so the conditions can be satisfied. (Note: 108 inches = 9 feet) If we use 6-inch tiles, we will have (108 ÷ 6), or 18 tiles, an even number, per side. If we used 8-inch tiles, we would have (108 ÷ 8), or 13½ tiles per side; this is not possible, since we specified squares of equal size. Thus, the only possible choice of the ones given is the 4-inch tile.

36. **(A)** Let x equal the cost per pound of peanuts.

$x + 20$ is the cost per pound of cashews

From the information given in the problem we know that

$$15x = 10(20 + x)$$
$$15x = 200 + 10x$$
$$5x = 200$$
$$x = 40$$

Cashews cost $x + 20 = 40 + 20 = 60¢$.

37. **(D)** Two-fifths, or 40% of the applicants fail on the examination. Of the 60% remaining, three-fourths fail to get into the program (this represents 45% of the total number of applicants). Thus, the total number of failures is equal to 40% + 45%, or 85%.

38. **(C)** Interest = Principal × Rate × Time Using this formula find the interest of each one. Choice C yields the greatest interest:

$$\text{Interest} = (\$50)(.04)(1\tfrac{3}{4})$$
$$= \$3.50$$

Remember: Convert months to years if the interest rate is given in years.

39. **(C)** When the $3000 car was reduced by 20% its new price was

$$\$3000 - 20\% \text{ of } \$3000 =$$
$$\$3000 - \$600 =$$
$$\$2400$$

The raise of 10% changed it to

$$\$2400 + 10\% \text{ of } \$2400 =$$
$$\$2400 + \$240 =$$
$$\$2640$$

The total reduction was

$$\$3000 - \$2640 = \$360.$$

40. **(D)** The average of the five gains is the sum of the gains divided by 5. Let the unknown fifth gain be G. Then the average gain is

$$\frac{35¢ + 40¢ + 25¢ + 50¢ + G}{5} = 30¢.$$

which we are told in the average. Adding and dividing by 5 we find $30¢ + \dfrac{G}{5} = 30¢$.

Therefore G = 0¢.

41. **(D)** In our estimate for L, we will approximate L as

$$\frac{.1003}{\sqrt[3]{\dfrac{31.97}{2.03}} \times \dfrac{11.912}{2.98}}$$

$$\cong \frac{.1}{\sqrt[3]{\dfrac{32}{2}} \times \dfrac{12}{3}}$$

This is equal to $\dfrac{\dfrac{1}{10}}{\sqrt[3]{64}} = \dfrac{\dfrac{1}{10}}{4} = \dfrac{1}{40}$

42. **(A)** m is smallest when the sum of the four other numbers is a maximum, while none of the four numbers is greater than m. This is possible when all five numbers are very close to their average. Since the average of 146 is about 29, let the four numbers be each equal to 29. Since 29 + 29 + 29 + 29 = 116, m must be 146 − 116 or 30 which is greater than 29. Since m can no longer be the largest number if $m = 29$, the smallest value that m can be is 30.

43. **(B)** Let x equal the number of children in the class.
$35x = 21(x + 20)$
Thus, $35x = 21x + 420$; $14x = 420$
Accordingly, $x = 30$

44. **(C)** The length of one side of the square is given as

$$\sqrt{2^2 + 2^2} = \sqrt{8}$$

The area of the square is

$$\sqrt{8} \times \sqrt{8} = 8.$$

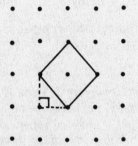

45. **(C)** We are given the equation:

$$\frac{2}{9} \cdot \frac{3}{5} = x \cdot \frac{5}{6}.$$

Multiplying both sides by $^6/_5$, we obtain:

$$\frac{2}{9} \cdot \frac{3}{5} \cdot \frac{6}{5} = x.$$

Performing the indicated multiplication on the left (after appropriate cancellation), we obtain:

$$\frac{2 \cdot 1 \cdot 2}{1 \cdot 5 \cdot 5} = \frac{4}{25} = x.$$

46. **(B)** It travels for 100 miles going at 30 miles per hour. This would take $3\frac{1}{3}$ hours, since

$$\text{Distance} = \text{Rate} \times \text{Time}$$

$$100 = 30x$$
$$x = 3\frac{1}{3}$$

To go the final 50 miles at 60 miles per hour takes

$$\frac{50}{60} = \frac{5}{6} \text{ hour.}$$

The total time required was $3\frac{1}{3} + \frac{5}{6} = 4\frac{1}{6}$ hours.
The total distance traveled was 150 miles.

The average rate is

$$\frac{150 \text{ miles}}{4\frac{1}{6} \text{ hours}} = \frac{150}{\left(\frac{25}{6}\right)} = \frac{6(150)}{25}$$

$$= 36 \text{ miles per hour}$$

47. **(D)** If a and b are two positive numbers, then their product, ab, is also positive. $-a$ and $-b$ are negative but their product, $(-a)(-b) = ab$, is positive. Also, the sum of $-a$ and $-b$ is $-a + (-b) = -(a + b)$ which is negative. Therefore, statements I and II are true.

48. **(E)** Draw AC. Since triangles ABD and BCD are congruent, $AB = BC$, $AD = CD$, and $\angle ABD = \angle CBD = 30°$.
$\angle ABC = \angle ABD + \angle CBD = 60°$
Since $AB = BC$, $\angle BAC$ and $\angle ACB$ must also be 60°, and triangle ABC is equilateral.

$$AC = x$$

In right triangle ADC,

$$(AD)^2 + (DC)^2 = x^2$$
$$2(DC)^2 = x^2$$
$$(DC)^2 = \frac{1}{2}x^2$$
$$DC = \frac{x}{\sqrt{2}} = \frac{x\sqrt{2}}{2}$$

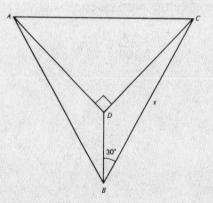

49. **(E)** The cow can eat grass inside a circle with radius 14 feet. The area of this is

$$\pi r^2 = \frac{22}{7}(14^2) = \frac{22}{7}(196) = 616 \text{ sq. ft.}$$

Dividing this by 100 square feet, we get 6 full days of food.

50. **(A)** The population during the fifth month was

$$500(5^2 - 5 + 1) = 500(21)$$
$$= 10500$$

The population during the fourth month was

$$500(4^2 - 4 + 1) = 500(13)$$
$$= 6500$$

The increase was $10500 - 6500 = 4000$.

51. **(C)** Jay's rate is $\frac{m}{n}$. John's rate is $\frac{p}{q}$. The ratio is $\frac{m/n}{p/q}$ or $\frac{mq}{pn}$.

52. **(D)** After the first reduction of 20% the $100 suit cost

$$100 - 20\% \text{ of } 100$$
$$100 - 20 \text{ or } \$80$$

Then this $80 suit is reduced another 10%.

$$80 - 10\% \text{ of } 80$$
$$80 - 8 \text{ or } \$72$$

Thus, the total reduction was $100 - 72$ or $28.
Therefore the net reduction was

$$\frac{28}{100} = 28\%.$$

53. **(A)** Since 20 forty pound items are sent in 5 equal shipments, $\frac{20}{5}$ forty pound items are shipped in one shipment. Since each 40 pound item is over 10 pounds, the company will charge $3.25 \times 40 = $130 for each item per shipment. There are $\frac{20}{5} = 4$ items each shipment so for each shipment the company will charge $130 \times 4 = $520.

54. **(D)** Since for every 5 Type-A parts there are 2 Type-B parts, there must have been 2500 Type-A parts shipped abroad. This is because we must have the ratio:

$$5 : 2 = 2500 : 1000$$

or

$$\frac{5}{2} = \frac{2500}{1000}$$

Since each drawer contained 500 Type-A parts, and 2500 Type-A parts were shipped abroad, $2500 \div 500 = 5$, and 5 drawers were emptied of Type-A and Type-B parts.

55. **(C)** If he received 10 payments of m dollars each, his annual salary was $10m$ dollars.

He now receives a monthly payment of

$$\frac{10m}{12} = \frac{5m}{6} \text{ dollars}$$

EXPLANATORY ANSWERS FOR PRACTICE TEST 1 (continued)

Section 3: Business Judgment

56. **(D)** This is a major assumption which the decision maker has considered from the very outset.

57. **(E)** This statement is clearly an unimportant issue. At no point in Stevens' letter does he even mention that he has any children. The correct answer is thus Choice E.

58. **(A)** Here we are presented with a major objective. Stevens sought to consult Karmen and Baylor precisely to find a suitable place for relocation. The correct answer is thus Choice A.

59. **(D)** This statement is a major assumption and the correct answer is Choice D. Stevens insisted that he relocate on a guaranteed stable terrain. He therefore must be operating under the assumption that the stability of terrains can be measured, and that the measurement can be done accurately.

60. **(C)** The effects of pollution legislation on production is a factor that applies only to one of the alternatives — the Crispwater site. Moreover, the factor does not greatly affect the merits of that alternative. This statement must therefore be a minor factor, and the correct answer is Choice C.

61. **(E)** This statement represents a false objective. At no point in his letter does Stevens indicate a particular desire to remain in Fargo. This statement is thus an unimportant issue, and the correct answer is Choice E.

62. **(A)** In his letter, Stevens expresses the desire to expand the foundry so as to be able to accept larger contracts. Expanding the foundry is thus one of Stevens' major objectives and the correct answer is Choice A.

63. **(C)** This statement applies only to one of the alternatives — the Bayville location. It is therefore a minor factor in the decision-making process and the correct answer is Choice C.

64. **(D)** This statement is a major assumption on the part of Stevens, and the correct answer must therefore be Choice D. Stevens is relying on the firm to present him with viable alternatives. He must therefore assume that they are able to adequately advise him on this matter.

65. **(B)** Here we are presented with a major factor in the decision-making process. We are evaluating the total cost as it applies to each of the land-sites. The correct answer is thus Choice B.

66. **(E)** This statement is clearly an unimportant issue. Nowhere in the passage is there any mention of the fact that Karmen and Baylor are even charging a fee. The correct answer must therefore be Choice E.

67. **(C)** The effects of union problems applies to only one of the alternatives — the Briarcliff site. This statement must thus be a minor factor, and the correct answer is Choice C.

68. **(D)** In his letter, Stevens claims to have examined the prospect of reconstruction and appears to be convinced that relocation would be a better alternative. Acting on this assumption, he approaches the consulting firm. Our statement is thus a major assumption, and the correct answer is Choice D.

69. **(A)** Stevens would like to expand his foundry so as to be able to accept larger contracts from big industries. This is

one of his primary objectives. Therefore, the correct answer is Choice A.

70. **(D)** This is a major assumption since Stevens supposes that it is important to have room for expansion. It is not a factor because it does not affect the decision.

71. **(E)** The passage does mention that few people were injured in the earthquake, but this is of no consequence to the business problem at hand. This statement is therefore an unimportant issue, and the correct answer is Choice E.

72. **(A)** Recall that Stevens insists that the terrain be stable, as he would "hate to experience another quake." This statement thus represents a major objective on the part of Stevens, and the correct answer is Choice A.

73. **(C)** Only one of the alternatives, the Fairlane site, encounters the problem of competition. This statement therefore applies to only one of the locations and is thus a minor factor. The correct answer is Choice C.

74. **(D)** Stevens is anxious to rebuild the foundry with his insurance payments. He is therefore acting under the assumption that he will be reimbursed by the insurance company. The correct answer is thus Choice D.

75. **(B)** The stability of the terrain is one of Stevens' primary concerns. Furthermore, this statement applies to all of the alternatives.We are thus presented with a major factor, and the correct answer must be Choice B.

76. **(D)** Recall that Stevens complains that his present location is both unstable (as was proven by the earthquake), and too small. At no point does he make any reference to legal restrictions or competition in the original site. He merely expresses the preference that future locations be free of these problems. The correct answer is thus Choice D.

77. **(B)** Three years from now, the value of the Fargo site will be double its present value, or $20,000. This figure is greater than that of only one of the locations, the Fairlane site, which costs $18,000. The correct answer is thus Choice B.

78. **(D)** If the damages incurred total $125,000, and the insurance company will deduct $24,000 from this amount, then Stevens will receive $101,000 in insurance payments. He will then be able to afford all but one of the four relocation alternatives, namely the Briarcliff site. The correct answer is thus Choice D.

79. **(E)** Recall that reconstructing the foundry in Fargo was not one of the firm's suggestions. Stevens came up with that idea on his own. Therefore, if he chooses that alternative, he pays no consultation fee. Now, the cheapest of the firm's alternatives would be the Crispwater site at $86,000. Adding to this figure the consultation fee, we arrive at a sum of $96,000. This represents a savings of $23,000 over the cost of rebuilding in Fargo, and is thus the minimum amount that Stevens would save by choosing this alternative. The correct answer is thus Choice E.

80. **(D)** To solve this problem, we must turn to Stevens' original objectives and see which of the alternatives best meets them. Firstly, he is looking for a location that will offer him the opportunity to expand. This effectively eliminates the Fargo site as it is too small. Next, he is looking for a site with a stable terrain. This eliminates the Fairlane site, as the stability could not be verified. Legal restrictions force the Crispwater site to drop out of contention, and a prohibitive cost ($112,000) in addition to union problems eliminates the Briarcliff site. We are left with the Bayville location which, although not perfect, best satisfies Stevens' requirements. The correct answer is thus Choice D.

EXPLANATORY ANSWERS FOR PRACTICE TEST 1 (continued)

Section 4: Data Sufficiency

81. **(C)** The statements alone are insufficient to answer the question but taken together we can see the answer would be "one employee earns more than $100 per week." We know that 8 of the 10 employees earn exactly the average, $100 per week. This leaves 2 employees with unknown salaries. For the average to remain at $100 per week, one employee must earn more than $100 and one must earn less than $100.

82. **(A)** Statement (1) alone is needed to answer the question. Angle A is 100° and must be the largest angle in the triangle (a triangle can have only one obtuse angle). The largest side of a triangle is opposite the largest angle. Statement (2) alone does not provide an answer.

83. **(E)** Both statements taken together do not provide enough data to solve the problem. There are two possible answers if we use both statements: x could be either 6 or 12.

84. **(C)** Both statements are needed to solve the problem. Triangle ABC is a right triangle since it is inscribed in a semi-circle. To find the length of AC we must know the lengths of the other two sides. Statement (1) gives us the length of AB and (2) gives us the length of BC, just double the radius. You can now use the Pythagorean Theorem to obtain the length of AC.

85. **(E)** The second statement tells us that Jim is shorter than Andy, and the first statement says George is shorter than Andy. We still don't know who is shorter, George or Jim.

86. **(A)** If $y = 0$, then $z > 0$ and $m > z > 0$, since points z and m are on the right side of point y. Thus z and m are both greater than 0 so

    $$zm > 0$$

    Therefore statement (1) is sufficient to answer the question.

    If we apply statement (2) we have $x = -2$.

    If z is negative and m is positive, then $zm < 0$.

    If z is positive and m is positive then $zm > 0$.

    Thus statement (2) alone is not sufficient to answer the original question.

87. **(B)** Statement (1) is of little use since we do not know how much Ann's mother weighs. Statement (2) can be used to solve the problem. Let x equal Ann's present weight. 75% is the same as $\frac{3}{4}$.

    We can set up the following equation:

    $$x - 30 = \tfrac{3}{4} x$$

    This equation can be solved for x.

88. **(D)** Cross-multiplying in Equation (1) we obtain

    $$27x = (2)(2)$$

    Thus

    $$x = \frac{(2)(2)}{27}$$

    Therefore by applying statement (1), the value of x can be determined.

    Subtracting 0.76 from both sides of Equation (2), we obtain

    $$x = 0.3 - 0.76$$

and so the value of x can be determined. Therefore Choice D is correct.

89. **(E)** We do not have enough data to solve the problem. It is possible that anywhere from 0 to 150 people in Littletown have both blond hair and blue eyes.

90. **(D)** We can answer the question with the use of statement (1) alone by setting up the following proportion:

$$\frac{10}{x} = \frac{12}{60\cancel{c}}$$

x can be found by cross-multiplying and solving the equation.

We can answer the question with the use of statement (2) alone by using the following equation:

$$y - \frac{1}{10}y = 63\cancel{c}$$

This equation can be solved for y.

91. **(C)** Statement (1) shows us that if we take equal volumes of gold and lead, the lead is lighter. Statement (2) says if we take equal volumes of lead and copper, the copper is lighter. Thus, copper is the lightest per volume. From this we conclude that one gram of copper would be the greatest volume.

92. **(C)** $z\%$ of $2x$ can be rewritten as

$$\frac{z}{100}(2x);$$

$m\%$ of 5 can be rewritten as

$$\frac{m}{100}(5).$$

Thus we want to determine which is greater: $\frac{z}{100}(2x)$ or $\frac{m}{100}(5)$?

Applying statement (1) only, does not tell us anything about the relative values of z and m, so statement (1) is not sufficient to answer the original question.

Applying statement (2) only, does not tell us the value of x, so, here again, we cannot answer the original question.

However, applying both statements (1) and (2) we have

(1) $x > \dfrac{5}{2}$

(2) $z > m$.

Therefore,

$$(x)(z) > \left(\frac{5}{2}\right)m.$$

Multiplying both sides of the above inequality by 2 we obtain

$$2xz > 5m.$$

Dividing both sides of this last inequality by 100 we obtain

$$\frac{2xz}{100} > \frac{5m}{100}$$

which answers our original question. Thus Choice C is correct.

93. **(B)** GH is a straight line, so we know

$$x + y + z = 180.$$

Statement (2) alone tells us that

$$x + y = 100.$$

Combining these two facts we get

$$z = 80.$$

Statement (1) alone does not provide enough information to solve the problem.

94. **(E)** 29 students are 16 years old, but since we don't know the age of the remaining student, we cannot find the average age.

95. **(A)** We are given that R varies directly as S. Thus, $R = kS$ where k is a constant of proportionality. By substituting the values given in statement (1) we can write

$$10 = k(6)$$

and we can easily solve for k.

$$k = 5/3$$

To find R when S equals 5 merely write

$$R = (5/3)(5).$$

Statement (2) is of no help in solving the problem.

96. **(C)** If we use both statements (1) and (2) we can solve the problem. Mr. Hart went 800 miles on two tanks, or 40 gallons of gasoline. We can get miles per gallon by dividing 800 by 40.

97. **(A)** If the sides of a triangle satisfy the relationship

$$a^2 + b^2 = c^2$$

then it is a right triangle. The lengths of the sides stated in (1) satisfy this relationship so the triangle must be right and we can answer the question. Statement (2) however does not provide useful information since any kind of triangle can have a 5° angle.

98. **(A)** Using the fact that BD is 5, we can see that AD is 15 and we can set up the proportion:

$$\frac{10}{15} = \frac{8}{DE}$$

By cross-multiplying, we can obtain an equation which can be solved for DE. Statement (2) does not help us solve the problem.

99. **(C)** Statement (1) and statement (2) can both be written as equations in two variables:

Let l represent the length of the rectangle.

Let w represent the width of the rectangle.

Statement (1) says
$$l = 2w + 5.$$
Statement (2) says
$$2l + 2w = 20.$$

We can solve these two equations in two unknowns simultaneously and obtain values for the length and width of the rectangle. Their product is the area.

100. **(B)** Statement (1) does not aid in solving the problem. Statement (2) tells us
$$2A + B = 310°$$
Since the angles are supplementary, we know
$$A + B = 180°$$
Subtracting the second equation from the first, we get
$$A = 130°$$

101. **(A)** If y is divisible by 30, it must also be divisible by all the factors of 30. 15 is a factor of 30. Statement (2) does not provide enough information to answer the question.

102. **(E)** Using both pieces of data we still cannot solve the problem since we do not know how long the track is.

103. **(C)** From statement (1) we know that Worm A + Worm B + Worm C = 3 inches.
From statement (2) we know that Worm A = 1 inch   Worm B = ½ inch. Substituting these values into the first equation, we have
$$1 + \text{Worm B} + \tfrac{1}{2} = 3 \text{ inches}$$
or simply
$$\text{Worm B} = 1\tfrac{1}{2} \text{ inches.}$$
Thus, we can see that Worm C is the shortest.

104. **(E)** In order to answer the question, we would have to know yet another bit of information. We would need to know how many corn stalks can be grown on an acre. The two statements alone do not provide enough data.

105. **(A)** By using the Pythagorean Theorem on the right triangle ACD, and the data provided in statement (1), it is possible to find out the length of CD. The area of the rectangle is the length of AD times the length of CD. The perimeter alone, as provided in statement (2), is insufficient to solve the problem.

106. **(D)** From statement (1) alone we see that the answer would be "no" since none of the members of the set is divisible by 7. From statement (2) alone we see that the answer would be "no" since none of the members of the set is an odd square.

107. **(B)** Statement (1) is of little value. Statement (2) however, enables us to solve the problem. The perimeter is 40. Thus,

XY + ZX + ZY = 40 inches

Substitute the lengths of ZX and ZY and solve for XY.

ZX = ZY = 15

XY + 15 + 15 = 40 inches

XY = 10 inches.

108. **(A)** Using the length of BD as provided in statement (1) we can set up the following proportion:

$$\frac{4}{2} = \frac{AB}{1.6}$$

By cross-multiplying, we can obtain an equation which can be solved for AB. The length of AD can be found by adding the lengths of AB and BD. Statement (2) is not particularly useful in solving this problem.

109. **(C)** The volume of the rectangular prism can be found by multiplying the area of face ADCB by the length of edge BE.

110. **(C)** Statement (1) tells us that x is one of the integers 1, 2 . . . , 15. Statement (2) narrows down the choice to just one possiblility, 8, and thus allows us to answer the question.

EXPLANATORY ANSWERS FOR PRACTICE TEST 1 (continued)

Section 5: Grammar and Usage

111. **(D)** "... are Thompson, Steinmetz, and *I*."
The predicate nominative form is *I* (not *me*).

112. **(C)** "... into the infirmary, *I* was asked several questions by the nurse at the desk."
It is *I* who was being wheeled—not the *nurse*. The participial construction should modify the subject. In the original sentence, the subject is *nurse*.

113. **(A)** "*We* boys insist ..."
The pronoun-adjective which modifies a subject (*boys* in this case) must take the subject form *we* (not *us*).

114. **(E)** All underlined parts are correct.

115. **(D)** "... than *those* of the other girls."
We have an improper ellipsis here. The dress that the girl wore was more attractive than the dresses of the other girls—not more attractive than the other girls.

116. **(E)** All underlined parts are correct.

117. **(A)** "If he *had lain* ..."
The past perfect tense form of *to lie* is *had lain* (not *had laid*). The past perfect tense form of *to lay*—meaning to place or to put—is *had laid*.

118. **(B)** "... *one* will become ..."
Do not shift the number or person of a noun if the noun represents another noun which precedes in the sentence. In the original sentence, *one* and *you* refer to the same person. Since *one* is third person and *you* is second person, we have a shift error.

119. **(E)** All underlined parts are correct.

120. **(B)** "If I *had been* there ..."
In a contrary-to-fact conditional construction in past time, sequence of tenses requires the past perfect subjunctive form (*had been*) in the "if" clause instead of the future perfect subjunctive form (*would have been*).

121. **(A)** "Between you and *me* ..."
The object of the preposition *between* must be an objective case form (*me*—not *I*).

122. **(C)** "... that *witches* ride on broomsticks."
The pronoun *they* must have an antecedent, which is obviously *witchcraft*. But since witchcraft is a singular abstract noun, the plural personal pronoun *they* cannot be used here. Accordingly, we must substitute a noun, such as *witches*, for the pronoun. The word *witches*, of course, has no antecedent because it is a noun. Only pronouns have antecedents.

123. **(A)** "*Since* you are interested ..."
Being that is unacceptable for *since* or *because*.

124. **(B)** "... into caves and tunnels *is deceiving* ..."
Since the subject (*retreat*) is singular, the verb must be singular (*is* deceiving—not *are* deceiving).

125. **(D)** "... to *us* teenagers."
The pronoun-adjective modifying the object of the preposition must be objective in form. *Teenagers* is the object of the preposition *to*. The pronoun-adjective modifying teenagers must, therefore, be the object form (*us*—not *we*).

126. **(C)** "... *were* his slovenly appearance and his nervous demeanor."
The two subjects (*appearance* and *demeanor*) constitute plurality. We must, accordingly, have a plural verb (*were*—not *was*).

127. **(E)** All underlined parts are correct.

128. **(B)** "... in buying *this farm* ..."
The expression *this here* is unacceptable for *this*.

129. **(D)** "... are concerned with *themselves* ..."
The correct form of the reflexive pronoun is *themselves*—not *theirselves*.

130. **(B)** ". . . angry with *those* radicals . . ."
The adjective-pronoun *those* must be used to modify the noun *radicals*. The pronoun *them* cannot be used to modify a noun.

131. **(A)** "There *seems* nowadays little of the optimism . . ."
The subject of the sentence (*little*) is singular and it therefore takes a singular verb (*seems* – not *seem*).

132. **(D)** ". . . attending college, finding a job, or *joining the army*."
The need for parallelism requires *joining the army*, in order to have a balanced construction with the preceding gerund phrases (*attending college* and *finding a job*).

133. **(B)** ". . . the dog *lay* under the tree . . ."
The past tense of the verb *lie* is *lay* — not *laid*.

134. **(A)** "There *were* only an apple and three pears . . ." The subject of the sentence is plural (*an apple and three pears*). Therefore the verb must be plural (*were* — not *was*). Incidentally, the word *there* is not the subject — it is an expletive.

135. **(C)** ". . . that he *would* not step down . . ." Since the verb of the main clause (*made*) is in the past tense, the verb of the subordinate clause must also be in the past tense (*would speak*). Incidentally, *would speak* is a past subjunctive.

EXPLANATORY ANSWERS FOR PRACTICE TEST 1 (continued)

Section 6: Business Judgment

136. **(A)** This item represents a major objective of Mr. Bromley, the owner of Fantasyland. Early in the passage he expresses his desire to continue the cordial relationship he shares with his employees, and not to lay anyone off. The correct answer is thus Choice A.

137. **(C)** This item applies specifically to one alternative — namely, the generator. Much of the discussion in the passage involves a number of general considerations applied to various options. Therefore, this item represents a minor factor to the decision-making process, and the answer is Choice C.

138. **(A)** This is a major objective as can be seen from the last statement in the passage.

139. **(E)** This item is irrelevant to the decision process. The material is of little concern to Bromley, and the correct answer is clearly Choice E.

140. **(D)** Bromley is relying on the bank to provide him with the necessary funding for new construction. His ability to obtain this funding is a major assumption on his part, and the correct answer is Choice D.

141. **(B)** This item represents a general consideration which can be applied to all of the alternatives. It is a major factor in making the decision, and the correct answer is Choice B.

142. **(C)** This is a factor which applies only to a specific concern — the ski slope. The correct answer is Choice C, since the item is a minor factor in the decision process.

143. **(A)** This is clearly a major objective of the owners of Fantasyland. Recall Bromley's desire to guarantee that never

again will Fantasyland finish a year in the red. The correct answer is thus Choice. A

144. **(C)** Bromley was worried about the competition from Spacetown but he did not have a major concern about Spacetown. Note that Bromley does not *assume* continued competition from Spacetown. It is obvious that Spacetown will continue to compete.

145. **(E)** We are not concerned with the salary of each employee, but only with the fact that, if economic difficulties continue, the employees are in danger of being laid off. The item is irrelevant, and the answer is Choice E.

146. **(E)** The profitability of Spacetown is irrelevant to the decision maker.

147. **(E)** The proximity of Spacetown to Fantasyland is irrelevant. All that matters is that Spacetown is a competitor. Clearly, the correct answer is Choice E.

148. **(A)** This item is a direct paraphrase of the passage. Bromley calls for a means to guarantee that Fantasyland never closes a year in the red. The correct answer is thus Choice A, as the item is a major objective.

149. **(B)** Here we have a general consideration which is applied to each alternative. It is, of course, a major factor in the decision process, and the answer is Choice B.

150. **(C)** This is a factor that influences the decision-making, but it is not a major factor. Note also that the construction will take up to about two years if delays do occur.

151. **(A)** Mr. Bromley makes clear his desire to withstand competition from Spacetown. It is, therefore, a major objective

in the decision making process and the correct answer is Choice A.

152. **(D)** Bromley maintains that it is foolish to run a business based on chance. This is a major assumption in his decision. Thus, the correct answer is Choice D.

153. **(C)** The cost of operating a roller coaster was not seriously considered but the cost is still, of course, a factor. Thus it is a minor factor.

154. **(C)** The method by which the enclosure is built and assembled allows the park to remain open. It is a minor factor in the decision process as it applies only to one specific alternative, and the correct answer is Choice C.

155. **(E)** We are not concerned with any specific fact about the employees at Fantasyland (neither their salary nor their number). Such points are irrelevant to the decision process. The correct answer is Choice E.

156. **(B)** It is clear from the passage that both reduced income and competition from Spacetown are motivations for Mr. Bromley to refurbish Fantasyland. However, nowhere does he complain of insufficient advertising, nor does he refer to poor relations with his staff. Thus Choice B, which contains items II and IV only, is the correct answer.

157. **(D)** Including advertising, the cost of the enclosure is $92,000, while the cost of the roller coaster, with the accompanying loss of $80,000 expected income, is $140,000. Taking into account the 50% advertising discount, the price of the roller coaster becomes $120,000, or

$28,000 greater than the cost of the enclosure. The correct answer is thus Choice D.

158. **(D)** Neither the time required to build the ski slope nor its cost are particularly prohibitive. Furthermore, nowhere in the passage does anyone express doubts over its ability to make money. True, it will not function in the summer months, but this is not the most serious disadvantage. Recall that Bromley concluded his criticism of the ski slope with the statement, "I maintain that we stick to something we know." The correct answer is thus Choice D.

159. **(E)** This problem is a difficult mathematical one. The loan for the generator would be paid back after five and a half years, while the loan for the roller coaster would be returned after two and a half years. Examining the interest arrangement, we observe that after 5½ years, the borrower must pay 209% interest on the principal. This would amount to $198,550 in the case of the generator. Added to the principal, we arrive at a figure of $293,550. Now, for 2½ years, the total interest rate amounts to 77%. In the case of the roller coaster, a total of $35,400 would have to be returned. The margin in cost would thus be $258,150, or approximately $258,000. The correct answer is thus Choice E.

160. **(C)** Only Choice C, the enclosure, addresses all the problems originally cited by Bromley. It offers a feature that Spacetown cannot match, it will aid in reducing fuel costs, and it shields against inclement weather hazards. Furthermore, it is readily financible. The correct answer is thus Choice C.

EXPLANATORY ANSWERS FOR PRACTICE TEST 1 (continued)

Section 7: Verbal Ability

PART A — ANTONYMS

161. **(E)** ENDEMIC: native; peculiar to a country or people.
Antonym: *foreign.*

162. **(D)** OBESE: excessively fat; corpulent; overweight.
Antonym: *underweight.*

163. **(A)** ABERRANT: straying; abnormal; exceptional.
Antonym: *average.*

164. **(B)** GELID: chilly; frigid.
Antonym: *warm.*

165. **(E)** HOI POLLOI: the common people; the masses.
Antonym: *aristocracy.*

166. **(C)** PRECURSORY: preliminary; introductory.
Antonym: *succeeding.*

167. **(B)** INCREDULOUS: not believing.
Antonym: *gullible.*

168. **(A)** ASKEW: awry; crooked.
Antonym: *straight.*

PART B — ANALOGIES

169. **(C)** Wealth enables one to obtain luxuries just as a ticket enables one to obtain admission. Choice D might be correct if sympathy were replaced by something material, as luxuries and admission are both material things.

170. **(A)** Summit is simply another word for a peak, just as change is another word for a mutation. None of the other choices are synonymous.

171. **(C)** The smallest measuring unit of an angle is usually a degree and the smallest measuring unit of an area is usually a square inch. Time can also be measured in seconds. Milk can also be measured in pints.

172. **(E)** Just as a ship is always entering or leaving a harbor, where it is naturally suited, a car is always entering or leaving a garage, where it too is suited. None of the other choices are analogous in this way.

173. **(A)** The adjective directly relating to the nose is nasal, as the adjective directly relating to the ear is aural. In Choice C, not only is the adjective placed first, which does not match the original analogy, but many adjectives exist which can describe perfume; fragrant is only one of them.

174. **(D)** Just as a glove is made to fit and cover the hand, a stocking is made to fit and cover the leg. None of the other choices express this type of relationship.

175. **(A)** The opposite of lending something is to borrow it; the opposite of abridging or shortening something is to lengthen it. This analogy of opposites exists in none of the other choices.

176. **(D)** Music will be produced from a guitar only if a skilled person is handling the instrument. In the same way, words will be produced from a typewriter only if a skilled person is handling it. Choice A could possibly be correct if the words were reversed.

PART C — SENTENCE COMPLETIONS

177. **(D)** A child should not be *classified or put into the category* of being either very shy or over-aggressive.

178. **(B)** Although the first word of each choice might fit the sentence, none of the pairs together make sense except Choice B.

179. **(B)** Words of opposite meaning are called for here. The key word is "while." Also, the second word, whose meaning is somewhat explained by "and become again like little dependent children," must mean to go back or retreat to an earlier state — to regress.

180. **(D)** This sentence calls for a pair of words that support or intensify each other. Key: "Not only . . . but also."

181. **(A)** This sentence calls for two words of contrasting nature, as shown by the words "even though." The only pair that has this contrast in meaning is Choice A.

182. **(C)** Since the first-mentioned goal contrasts with the second one, it must be the opposite of "long-range"; that is, immediate.

183. **(E)** The only other choice that would fit the first word is Choice A, but its second word would not make sense in this context.

184. **(B)** Appropriate steps are the steps necessary or advisable in a given situation.

185. **(D)** Another choice for the first blank might be Choice C, but its second word could not be used in this context.

EXPLANATORY ANSWERS FOR PRACTICE TEST 1 (continued)

Section 8: Sentence Correction

186. **(D)** Choice A is incorrect because "like when" is ungrammatical. Choice B is incorrect because it is too indirect. Choice C is incorrect because "similar to when" is ungrammatical. Choice D is correct. Choice E is incorrect because it is awkwardly expressed.

187. **(D)** Choice A is incorrect because the present participle "Seeing" is incorrectly modifying "the cigarettes." Choices B, C, and E are too roundabout. Choice D is correct.

188. **(A)** Choice A is correct. Choice B is incorrect because the nominative absolute construction "Garrick having one" throws the sentence out of balance. Choice C is incorrect because we need a finite verb ("had"), not the participle "having". Choice D is incorrect because the present perfect tense ("has had") should be replaced by the past tense ("had"). Choice E is too wordy.

189. **(E)** Choice A is incorrect because it is awkward and because the pronoun "they" has an indefinite antecedent. Choice B is incorrect for the same reason. Choice C is incorrect — it would be correct if changed to "they, not chemists and physicists, have." Choice D is too wordy. Choice E is correct.

190. **(B)** Choice A is incorrect because we have a run-on sentence. The comma should be replaced by a semicolon or a period. Choice A is incorrect for another reason: the singular pronoun "him" (not "them") should be used because the antecedent ("student") of the pronoun is singular. Choice B is correct. Choice C is incorrect because the pronoun "they" should be singular. Choice D is incorrect because it creates a run-on sentence. Choice E is incorrect — the semicolon should be eliminated.

191. **(A)** Choice A is correct. Choice B is incorrect because of the improper ellipsis of the words "that of" which should precede "an adviser and friend." Choice C is incorrect, because the word "one" should be replaced by the words "that of." Choices D and E are incorrect because they are too indirect. Moreover, in Choice D, right after the words "its role" we should place the words "that of."

192. **(C)** Choice A is incorrect because we should have a gerund ("replacing") to balance with the previous gerund "diminishing." Moreover, there is no need to split the infinitive ("to . . . replace"). Choice B is incorrect also because of lack of gerund balance. Choice C is correct. Choice D is incorrect because of lack of gerund balance and because of awkwardness. Choice E is incorrect because of awkwardness.

193. **(A)** Choice A is correct. If you are questioning the singularity of the possessive pronoun-adjective "his," it is correct. The subject of the sentence consists of a singular compound subject, "the sales manager and personnel director." If we wanted to indicate plurality here, we would have to insert the article "the" before the second member ("personnel director") of the compound subject. Choice B is incorrect because "their" must refer to a plural antecedent. Choice C is incorrect because it changes the meaning of the original sentence. Choice D is awkward. Choice E is too wordy.

194. **(B)** Choice A is incorrect because it does not parallel the structure of "not only because of its beauty." Choice B is correct. Choices C, D, and E are incorrect for the same reason that Choice A is incorrect — the lack of parallel structure. Moreover, Choice C is incorrect because "on account" cannot be used as a subordinate conjunction.

195. **(E)** The past participle "known" must modify the subject of the sentence. Choices A and C are, therefore, incorrect because the subject must be "grandfather" — he is the one (not "friends") that is "known to every man, woman, and child in the town." Choice B changes the meaning of the original sentence. Choice D has a double negative ("never ... no..."). Choice E is correct.

196. **(B)** Choice A is incorrect since the correct expression is "no sooner ... than ..." Choice B is correct. Choices C, D, and E are incorrect because we must have the "no sooner ... than" construction.

197. **(A)** Choice A is correct. Choice B is incorrect for two reasons: (1) We use the adverb "so" instead of "as" in a negative comparison; (2) "like" may not be used instead of "as" in this type of comparison. Choice C is awkward. Choice D is roundabout. Choice E changes the meaning of the original sentence.

198. **(C)** The problem in this question is the correct placement of the modifier. The prepositional phrase "much to our disgust" is an adverbial phrase showing result. The phrase, therefore modifies the verb "had been sold out." Accordingly, the phrase should, in this sentence, follow right after the verb it modifies. Choice C, therefore, is correct and the other choices are incorrect. Choice D, incidentally, is incorrect for another reason — it is illogical: the sold-out tickets are obviously disposed of when they are sold out.

199. **(C)** Choice A is incorrect because in this sentence "also" means the same as "in addition." Choice B is awkward. Choice C is correct as a subordinate clause which parallels the preceding subordinate clause. Choice D creates a run-on sentence. Choice E is too wordy.

200. **(C)** Choices A, B, and D are incorrect because of the use of "him joining." The word "joining" is a gerund in this sentence. Its possessive pronoun-adjective must be "his" — not "him." Choice B, moreover, has the unidiomatic expression "objection on." Choice C is correct. Choice E changes the meaning of the original sentence.

201. **(D)** The expression "one another" refers to three or more; "each other" refers to two only. Therefore, Choices A and B are incorrect and Choice D is correct. Choice C is awkward. Choice E changes the meaning of the original sentence.

202. **(E)** The past contrary-to-fact conditional form is "had seen." Therefore, Choices A, B, C, and D are all incorrect. Choice E is correct. Moreover, Choice C has the wrong tense and the wrong tense sequence. Note also that "amount" refers to mass whereas "number" refers to countable units.

203. **(C)** A misplaced modifier may create a very embarrassing situation — so we can observe in the original sentence. We certainly don't want the fiancé wearing a sheer blouse. Such a blouse clearly belongs on the female. Choices A and D are, therefore, incorrect. Choice B is incorrect because it may appear that the concert is wearing the sheer blouse. Choice C is, of course, correct. Choice E is not acceptable because (1) the phrase "wearing a sheer blouse" is a "squinting" modifier, and (2) the sentence would be inappropriately poetic.

204. **(D)** We are looking for *balanced construction* in this question. Note that the correct Choice D gives us a balanced infinitive construction: "to advise," "(to) transmit", and "(to) supervise." None of the other choices offers this balanced construction.

205. **(A)** Choice A is correct. Choices B and C are incorrect because Frazier did not "own" the decision — it was rendered by the judges and the referee. Choice D is too roundabout. Choice E changes the meaning of the original sentence — and it is too roundabout.

206. **(D)** The important thing is that Tricia Nixon had (finally) become engaged. Choice D, alone, brings out the primary importance of the engagement and the secondary importance of her being born on St. Patrick's Day. Moreover, Choices B and C are run-on sentences.

207. **(B)** Choice A is incorrect because the nominative form ("he") is required: "as fully as him" is wrong. Choice B is correct. Choices C, D, and E are incorrect because the object of the preposition must have an objective case form — the preposition "but" must be followed by the object case form "him."

208. **(A)** Choice A is correct. Choice B is incorrect because "on account" may not be used as a subordinate conjunction. Choice C is incorrect because it gives the meaning that the judge is doing the charging. Choice D is incorrect because the possessive noun ("defendant") modifying the gerund ("charging") must take the form "defendant's." Choice E creates a run-on sentence.

209. **(A)** Choice A is correct. Choices B, C, and D are incorrect because they change the meaning of the original sentence. Choice E creates a run-on sentence.

210. **(E)** Choices A and B are incorrect because they give the idea that the plans are trying to avoid the hot sun. Choice C is awkward. Choice D is a run-on sentence. Choice E is correct.

211. **(B)** Choice A is too wordy. Choice B is correct. Choice C is incorrect because it changes the tense of the original sentence — "Whatever (may) be her thoughts" is in the present tense. Choice D does not retain the meaning of the original sentence. Choice E makes no sense.

212. **(B)** Choices A and E are incorrect because the subject word "use" requires a singular verb ("makes"). Choice B is correct. Choices C and D are awkward.

213. **(E)** "Irregardless" (Choice A) is incorrect. "Regardless about" (Choice B) is unidiomatic. Choices C and D change the meaning of the original sentence. Moreover, Choice D makes the sentence ungrammatical. Choice E is correct.

214. **(A)** Choice A is correct. Choices B, C, and E change the meaning of the original sentence. Choice D is too wordy.

215. **(C)** The infinitive "to effect" means "to bring about" — this is not the meaning intended in the original sentence. Therefore. Choices A, B, and D are incorrect. Choice C is correct. Choice E changes the meaning of the original sentence.

216. **(B)** In the original sentence, "who" should replace "whom" as the subject of the subordinate clause ("who were policemen"). "I believe" is simply a parenthetical expression. Therefore, Choice A is incorrect and Choice B is correct. Choice C creates a run-on sentence. Choice D improperly changes the sentence from a complex type to a compound type. Choice E does not retain the meaning of the original sentence.

217. **(D)** Choices A and B suffer from improper ellipsis. Choice C changes the meaning of the original sentence. Choice D is correct. Choice E is too wordy.

218. **(E)** Sequence of tenses in a past contrary-to-fact condition requires the "had waited" form in the "if" clause. Therefore Choices A, B, C, and D are incorrect and Choice E is correct.

219. **(C)** We are concerned here with the apostrophe use with a singular name ending in "s." We are also concerned with improper ellipsis. In Choice A, "James' " is correct but we must either say "to read than *the prose style* of James Joyce" or "to read than James Joyce's." In Choice B, "Jame's" is incorrect — his name is not "Jame." Choice C is correct. Choices D and E are incorrect for the same reason that Choice A is incorrect — improper ellipsis.

220. **(C)** Choice A is incorrect because in a "neither .. nor" construction, the number of the verb is determined by the "nor" subject noun ("followers"). Since "followers" is plural, the verb must be plural ("know"). Choices B, D, and E are incorrect for the same reason. Moreover, Choice B is incorrect for another reason: the correlative form is "neither . . . nor" — not "neither . . . or". Choice C is correct.

221. **(B)** Avoid the double negative. Choices A and C suffer from the double negative fault. Choice B is correct. Choice D changes the meaning of the original sentence. Choice E creates a run-on sentence.

222. **(E)** The original sentence is interrogative. Accordingly, the sentence must end with a question mark. Choice E is correct.

223. **(D)** Choice A is incorrect because it creates a run-on sentence. Choice B fails to include the all-inclusive ("altogether," "completely," "entirely") idea of the original sentence. Choice C changes the meaning of the original sentence. Choice D is correct. Choice E changes the meaning of the original sentence.

224. **(B)** The adverb "yesterday" should, in this sentence, be placed before the modified verb ("arrested"). Therefore, Choices A and C are incorrect and Choice B is correct. Choices D and E are too roundabout.

225. **(E)** The singular historical present tense should be used here. Reasons: (1) a general truth is being expressed — this requires the present tense; (2) "womanhood" is singular. Also, the personal pronoun "it" must be used since its antecedent is "womanhood" — an abstract noun. Therefore Choice E is correct and all the other choices are incorrect.

What to Do Now
to Improve Your GMAT Score

1. Determine your Scaled Score by referring to the Raw Score/Scaled Score Table on the next page.

2. On the basis of your analysis of your incorrect answers on the Practice Test you have just taken, indicate your strengths and weaknesses in the Self-Appraisal Charts on page 89-90.

3. Then proceed to Practice Test 2.

4. Repeat the foregoing procedure for Practice Test 3, 4, and 5.

RAW SCORE/SCALED SCORE TABLE FOR CONVERTING YOUR
PRACTICE TEST RAW SCORE TO YOUR SCALED SCORE

When you get your GMAT score, you will find that it consists of 3 digits. This is your so-called Scaled Score which is usually the basis that graduate schools use to determine your acceptability.

The GMAT has a range from 200 to 800. There is no passing or failing score on the test. 500 is the average score and about two-thirds of the test-takers receive scores between 400 and 600. Very few examinees score above 750 or below 250.

This Scaled Score is derived by a statistical process from the Raw Score. The Raw Score is the number of items you answered correctly minus $\frac{1}{4}$ of the number of items you answered incorrectly. A Scaled Score of 500 is equivalent to a 50th percentile ranking – that is, about half of those taking the test scored better than you and half scored below you.

The following unofficial Raw Score/Scaled Score Table will give you a rough idea of what your Scaled Score should be for each GMAT Practice Test that you take. The final two sections in each of the five Practice Tests in the book — Section 7 and Section 8 — are not included in the following table because these two sections in the actual GMAT are likely experimental and will vary from form to form in question-type and in number of questions.

Note that the GMAT Scaled Scores are rounded so that the third digit will always be zero — for example 580, 590, 600.

RAW SCORE/SCALED SCORE TABLE

RAW SCORE*		SCALED SCORE	RAW SCORE*		SCALED SCORE	RAW SCORE*		SCALED SCORE
160-165**	......	800	143	......	630	101-103	......	460
159	......	790	142	......	620	98-100	......	450
158	......	780	141	......	610	95-97	......	440
157	......	770	140	......	600	92-94	......	430
156	......	760	138-139	......	590	89-91	......	420
155	......	750	136-137	......	580	86-88	......	410
154	......	740	134-135	......	570	83-85	......	400
153	......	730	132-133	......	560	80-82	......	390
152	......	720	130-131	......	550	77-79	......	380
151	......	710	128-129	......	540	74-76	......	370
150	......	700	126-127	......	530	71-73	......	360
149	......	690	122-125	......	520	68-70	......	350
148	......	680	118-121	......	510	65-67	......	340
147	......	670	114-117	......	500	62-64	......	330
146	......	660	110-113	......	490	59-61	......	320
145	......	650	106-112	......	480	56-58	......	310
144	......	640	104-105	......	470	53-55	......	300

52 and below ... 290 and below

* After ¼ of the number of incorrect answers has been deducted from the number of correct answers.

** Do not include Sections 7 and 8 in your calculation.

SELF-APPRAISAL CHARTS

The charts below offer a convenient method to determine where your GMAT strengths and weaknesses lie. Circle the appropriate box in accordance with the number of *correct answers* which you counted for each section of the Practice Test that you have administered to yourself.

Self-Appraisal Chart

for Practice Tests 1, 3, and 5*

	Reading Comprehension Section 1 (25 Questions)	Math Ability Section 2 (30 Questions)	Business Judgment Section 3 and Section 6 (50 Questions)	Data Sufficiency Section 4 (30 Questions)	Grammar & Usage Section 5 (25 Questions)
EXCEL-LENT	23 to 25	27 to 30	46 to 50	27 to 30	23 to 25
GOOD	18 to 22	23 to 26	38 to 45	23 to 26	18 to 22
FAIR	14 to 17	18 to 22	28 to 37	18 to 22	14 to 17
POOR	10 to 13	11 to 17	20 to 27	11 to 17	10 to 13
VERY POOR	0 to 9	0 to 10	0 to 19	0 to 10	0 to 9

* Do not consider Sections 7 and 8 since they vary from test to test.

Self-Appraisal Chart

for Practice Tests 2 and 4*

	Reading Recall Section 1 (30 Questions)	Math Ability Section 2 (30 Questions)	Business Judgment Section 3 and Section 6 (50 Questions)	Data Sufficiency Section 4 (30 Questions)	Grammar & Usage *or* Verbal Ability Section 5 (25 Questions)
EXCEL-LENT	27 to 30	27 to 30	46 to 50	27 to 30	23 to 25
GOOD	23 to 26	23 to 26	38 to 45	23 to 26	18 to 22
FAIR	18 to 22	18 to 22	28 to 37	18 to 22	14 to 17
POOR	11 to 17	11 to 17	20 to 27	11 to 17	10 to 13
VERY POOR	0 to 10	0 to 10	0 to 19	0 to 10	0 to 9

* Do not consider Sections 7 and 8 since they very from test to test.

Practice Test 2 ⟶

USE THIS SHEET FOR YOUR ANSWERS
PRACTICE TEST 2

Section 1: Reading Recall

1 Ⓐ Ⓑ Ⓒ Ⓓ Ⓔ   7 Ⓐ Ⓑ Ⓒ Ⓓ Ⓔ   13 Ⓐ Ⓑ Ⓒ Ⓓ Ⓔ   19 Ⓐ Ⓑ Ⓒ Ⓓ Ⓔ   25 Ⓐ Ⓑ Ⓒ Ⓓ Ⓔ
2 Ⓐ Ⓑ Ⓒ Ⓓ Ⓔ   8 Ⓐ Ⓑ Ⓒ Ⓓ Ⓔ   14 Ⓐ Ⓑ Ⓒ Ⓓ Ⓔ   20 Ⓐ Ⓑ Ⓒ Ⓓ Ⓔ   26 Ⓐ Ⓑ Ⓒ Ⓓ Ⓔ
3 Ⓐ Ⓑ Ⓒ Ⓓ Ⓔ   9 Ⓐ Ⓑ Ⓒ Ⓓ Ⓔ   15 Ⓐ Ⓑ Ⓒ Ⓓ Ⓔ   21 Ⓐ Ⓑ Ⓒ Ⓓ Ⓔ   27 Ⓐ Ⓑ Ⓒ Ⓓ Ⓔ
4 Ⓐ Ⓑ Ⓒ Ⓓ Ⓔ   10 Ⓐ Ⓑ Ⓒ Ⓓ Ⓔ   16 Ⓐ Ⓑ Ⓒ Ⓓ Ⓔ   22 Ⓐ Ⓑ Ⓒ Ⓓ Ⓔ   28 Ⓐ Ⓑ Ⓒ Ⓓ Ⓔ
5 Ⓐ Ⓑ Ⓒ Ⓓ Ⓔ   11 Ⓐ Ⓑ Ⓒ Ⓓ Ⓔ   17 Ⓐ Ⓑ Ⓒ Ⓓ Ⓔ   23 Ⓐ Ⓑ Ⓒ Ⓓ Ⓔ   29 Ⓐ Ⓑ Ⓒ Ⓓ Ⓔ
6 Ⓐ Ⓑ Ⓒ Ⓓ Ⓔ   12 Ⓐ Ⓑ Ⓒ Ⓓ Ⓔ   18 Ⓐ Ⓑ Ⓒ Ⓓ Ⓔ   24 Ⓐ Ⓑ Ⓒ Ⓓ Ⓔ   30 Ⓐ Ⓑ Ⓒ Ⓓ Ⓔ

Section 2: Math Ability

31 Ⓐ Ⓑ Ⓒ Ⓓ Ⓔ   37 Ⓐ Ⓑ Ⓒ Ⓓ Ⓔ   43 Ⓐ Ⓑ Ⓒ Ⓓ Ⓔ   49 Ⓐ Ⓑ Ⓒ Ⓓ Ⓔ   55 Ⓐ Ⓑ Ⓒ Ⓓ Ⓔ
32 Ⓐ Ⓑ Ⓒ Ⓓ Ⓔ   38 Ⓐ Ⓑ Ⓒ Ⓓ Ⓔ   44 Ⓐ Ⓑ Ⓒ Ⓓ Ⓔ   50 Ⓐ Ⓑ Ⓒ Ⓓ Ⓔ   56 Ⓐ Ⓑ Ⓒ Ⓓ Ⓔ
33 Ⓐ Ⓑ Ⓒ Ⓓ Ⓔ   39 Ⓐ Ⓑ Ⓒ Ⓓ Ⓔ   45 Ⓐ Ⓑ Ⓒ Ⓓ Ⓔ   51 Ⓐ Ⓑ Ⓒ Ⓓ Ⓔ   57 Ⓐ Ⓑ Ⓒ Ⓓ Ⓔ
34 Ⓐ Ⓑ Ⓒ Ⓓ Ⓔ   40 Ⓐ Ⓑ Ⓒ Ⓓ Ⓔ   46 Ⓐ Ⓑ Ⓒ Ⓓ Ⓔ   52 Ⓐ Ⓑ Ⓒ Ⓓ Ⓔ   58 Ⓐ Ⓑ Ⓒ Ⓓ Ⓔ
35 Ⓐ Ⓑ Ⓒ Ⓓ Ⓔ   41 Ⓐ Ⓑ Ⓒ Ⓓ Ⓔ   47 Ⓐ Ⓑ Ⓒ Ⓓ Ⓔ   53 Ⓐ Ⓑ Ⓒ Ⓓ Ⓔ   59 Ⓐ Ⓑ Ⓒ Ⓓ Ⓔ
36 Ⓐ Ⓑ Ⓒ Ⓓ Ⓔ   42 Ⓐ Ⓑ Ⓒ Ⓓ Ⓔ   48 Ⓐ Ⓑ Ⓒ Ⓓ Ⓔ   54 Ⓐ Ⓑ Ⓒ Ⓓ Ⓔ   60 Ⓐ Ⓑ Ⓒ Ⓓ Ⓔ

Section 3: Business Judgment

61 Ⓐ Ⓑ Ⓒ Ⓓ Ⓔ   66 Ⓐ Ⓑ Ⓒ Ⓓ Ⓔ   71 Ⓐ Ⓑ Ⓒ Ⓓ Ⓔ   76 Ⓐ Ⓑ Ⓒ Ⓓ Ⓔ   81 Ⓐ Ⓑ Ⓒ Ⓓ Ⓔ
62 Ⓐ Ⓑ Ⓒ Ⓓ Ⓔ   67 Ⓐ Ⓑ Ⓒ Ⓓ Ⓔ   72 Ⓐ Ⓑ Ⓒ Ⓓ Ⓔ   77 Ⓐ Ⓑ Ⓒ Ⓓ Ⓔ   82 Ⓐ Ⓑ Ⓒ Ⓓ Ⓔ
63 Ⓐ Ⓑ Ⓒ Ⓓ Ⓔ   68 Ⓐ Ⓑ Ⓒ Ⓓ Ⓔ   73 Ⓐ Ⓑ Ⓒ Ⓓ Ⓔ   78 Ⓐ Ⓑ Ⓒ Ⓓ Ⓔ   83 Ⓐ Ⓑ Ⓒ Ⓓ Ⓔ
64 Ⓐ Ⓑ Ⓒ Ⓓ Ⓔ   69 Ⓐ Ⓑ Ⓒ Ⓓ Ⓔ   74 Ⓐ Ⓑ Ⓒ Ⓓ Ⓔ   79 Ⓐ Ⓑ Ⓒ Ⓓ Ⓔ   84 Ⓐ Ⓑ Ⓒ Ⓓ Ⓔ
65 Ⓐ Ⓑ Ⓒ Ⓓ Ⓔ   70 Ⓐ Ⓑ Ⓒ Ⓓ Ⓔ   75 Ⓐ Ⓑ Ⓒ Ⓓ Ⓔ   80 Ⓐ Ⓑ Ⓒ Ⓓ Ⓔ   85 Ⓐ Ⓑ Ⓒ Ⓓ Ⓔ

Section 4: Data Sufficiency

86 Ⓐ Ⓑ Ⓒ Ⓓ Ⓔ   92 Ⓐ Ⓑ Ⓒ Ⓓ Ⓔ   98 Ⓐ Ⓑ Ⓒ Ⓓ Ⓔ   104 Ⓐ Ⓑ Ⓒ Ⓓ Ⓔ   110 Ⓐ Ⓑ Ⓒ Ⓓ Ⓔ
87 Ⓐ Ⓑ Ⓒ Ⓓ Ⓔ   93 Ⓐ Ⓑ Ⓒ Ⓓ Ⓔ   99 Ⓐ Ⓑ Ⓒ Ⓓ Ⓔ   105 Ⓐ Ⓑ Ⓒ Ⓓ Ⓔ   111 Ⓐ Ⓑ Ⓒ Ⓓ Ⓔ
88 Ⓐ Ⓑ Ⓒ Ⓓ Ⓔ   94 Ⓐ Ⓑ Ⓒ Ⓓ Ⓔ   100 Ⓐ Ⓑ Ⓒ Ⓓ Ⓔ   106 Ⓐ Ⓑ Ⓒ Ⓓ Ⓔ   112 Ⓐ Ⓑ Ⓒ Ⓓ Ⓔ
89 Ⓐ Ⓑ Ⓒ Ⓓ Ⓔ   95 Ⓐ Ⓑ Ⓒ Ⓓ Ⓔ   101 Ⓐ Ⓑ Ⓒ Ⓓ Ⓔ   107 Ⓐ Ⓑ Ⓒ Ⓓ Ⓔ   113 Ⓐ Ⓑ Ⓒ Ⓓ Ⓔ
90 Ⓐ Ⓑ Ⓒ Ⓓ Ⓔ   96 Ⓐ Ⓑ Ⓒ Ⓓ Ⓔ   102 Ⓐ Ⓑ Ⓒ Ⓓ Ⓔ   108 Ⓐ Ⓑ Ⓒ Ⓓ Ⓔ   114 Ⓐ Ⓑ Ⓒ Ⓓ Ⓔ
91 Ⓐ Ⓑ Ⓒ Ⓓ Ⓔ   97 Ⓐ Ⓑ Ⓒ Ⓓ Ⓔ   103 Ⓐ Ⓑ Ⓒ Ⓓ Ⓔ   109 Ⓐ Ⓑ Ⓒ Ⓓ Ⓔ   115 Ⓐ Ⓑ Ⓒ Ⓓ Ⓔ

(continued on next page)

Section 5: Grammar and Usage

116 Ⓐ Ⓑ Ⓒ Ⓓ Ⓔ   121 Ⓐ Ⓑ Ⓒ Ⓓ Ⓔ   126 Ⓐ Ⓑ Ⓒ Ⓓ Ⓔ   131 Ⓐ Ⓑ Ⓒ Ⓓ Ⓔ   136 Ⓐ Ⓑ Ⓒ Ⓓ Ⓔ
117 Ⓐ Ⓑ Ⓒ Ⓓ Ⓔ   122 Ⓐ Ⓑ Ⓒ Ⓓ Ⓔ   127 Ⓐ Ⓑ Ⓒ Ⓓ Ⓔ   132 Ⓐ Ⓑ Ⓒ Ⓓ Ⓔ   137 Ⓐ Ⓑ Ⓒ Ⓓ Ⓔ
118 Ⓐ Ⓑ Ⓒ Ⓓ Ⓔ   123 Ⓐ Ⓑ Ⓒ Ⓓ Ⓔ   128 Ⓐ Ⓑ Ⓒ Ⓓ Ⓔ   133 Ⓐ Ⓑ Ⓒ Ⓓ Ⓔ   138 Ⓐ Ⓑ Ⓒ Ⓓ Ⓔ
119 Ⓐ Ⓑ Ⓒ Ⓓ Ⓔ   124 Ⓐ Ⓑ Ⓒ Ⓓ Ⓔ   129 Ⓐ Ⓑ Ⓒ Ⓓ Ⓔ   134 Ⓐ Ⓑ Ⓒ Ⓓ Ⓔ   139 Ⓐ Ⓑ Ⓒ Ⓓ Ⓔ
120 Ⓐ Ⓑ Ⓒ Ⓓ Ⓔ   125 Ⓐ Ⓑ Ⓒ Ⓓ Ⓔ   130 Ⓐ Ⓑ Ⓒ Ⓓ Ⓔ   135 Ⓐ Ⓑ Ⓒ Ⓓ Ⓔ   140 Ⓐ Ⓑ Ⓒ Ⓓ Ⓔ

Section 6: Business Judgment

141 Ⓐ Ⓑ Ⓒ Ⓓ Ⓔ   146 Ⓐ Ⓑ Ⓒ Ⓓ Ⓔ   151 Ⓐ Ⓑ Ⓒ Ⓓ Ⓔ   156 Ⓐ Ⓑ Ⓒ Ⓓ Ⓔ   161 Ⓐ Ⓑ Ⓒ Ⓓ Ⓔ
142 Ⓐ Ⓑ Ⓒ Ⓓ Ⓔ   147 Ⓐ Ⓑ Ⓒ Ⓓ Ⓔ   152 Ⓐ Ⓑ Ⓒ Ⓓ Ⓔ   157 Ⓐ Ⓑ Ⓒ Ⓓ Ⓔ   162 Ⓐ Ⓑ Ⓒ Ⓓ Ⓔ
143 Ⓐ Ⓑ Ⓒ Ⓓ Ⓔ   148 Ⓐ Ⓑ Ⓒ Ⓓ Ⓔ   153 Ⓐ Ⓑ Ⓒ Ⓓ Ⓔ   158 Ⓐ Ⓑ Ⓒ Ⓓ Ⓔ   163 Ⓐ Ⓑ Ⓒ Ⓓ Ⓔ
144 Ⓐ Ⓑ Ⓒ Ⓓ Ⓔ   149 Ⓐ Ⓑ Ⓒ Ⓓ Ⓔ   154 Ⓐ Ⓑ Ⓒ Ⓓ Ⓔ   159 Ⓐ Ⓑ Ⓒ Ⓓ Ⓔ   164 Ⓐ Ⓑ Ⓒ Ⓓ Ⓔ
145 Ⓐ Ⓑ Ⓒ Ⓓ Ⓔ   150 Ⓐ Ⓑ Ⓒ Ⓓ Ⓔ   155 Ⓐ Ⓑ Ⓒ Ⓓ Ⓔ   160 Ⓐ Ⓑ Ⓒ Ⓓ Ⓔ   165 Ⓐ Ⓑ Ⓒ Ⓓ Ⓔ

Section 7: Reading Comprehension

166 Ⓐ Ⓑ Ⓒ Ⓓ Ⓔ   171 Ⓐ Ⓑ Ⓒ Ⓓ Ⓔ   176 Ⓐ Ⓑ Ⓒ Ⓓ Ⓔ   181 Ⓐ Ⓑ Ⓒ Ⓓ Ⓔ   186 Ⓐ Ⓑ Ⓒ Ⓓ Ⓔ
167 Ⓐ Ⓑ Ⓒ Ⓓ Ⓔ   172 Ⓐ Ⓑ Ⓒ Ⓓ Ⓔ   177 Ⓐ Ⓑ Ⓒ Ⓓ Ⓔ   182 Ⓐ Ⓑ Ⓒ Ⓓ Ⓔ   187 Ⓐ Ⓑ Ⓒ Ⓓ Ⓔ
168 Ⓐ Ⓑ Ⓒ Ⓓ Ⓔ   173 Ⓐ Ⓑ Ⓒ Ⓓ Ⓔ   178 Ⓐ Ⓑ Ⓒ Ⓓ Ⓔ   183 Ⓐ Ⓑ Ⓒ Ⓓ Ⓔ   188 Ⓐ Ⓑ Ⓒ Ⓓ Ⓔ
169 Ⓐ Ⓑ Ⓒ Ⓓ Ⓔ   174 Ⓐ Ⓑ Ⓒ Ⓓ Ⓔ   179 Ⓐ Ⓑ Ⓒ Ⓓ Ⓔ   184 Ⓐ Ⓑ Ⓒ Ⓓ Ⓔ   189 Ⓐ Ⓑ Ⓒ Ⓓ Ⓔ
170 Ⓐ Ⓑ Ⓒ Ⓓ Ⓔ   175 Ⓐ Ⓑ Ⓒ Ⓓ Ⓔ   180 Ⓐ Ⓑ Ⓒ Ⓓ Ⓔ   185 Ⓐ Ⓑ Ⓒ Ⓓ Ⓔ   190 Ⓐ Ⓑ Ⓒ Ⓓ Ⓔ

Section 8: Error Recognition

191 Ⓓ Ⓥ Ⓖ Ⓞ   198 Ⓓ Ⓥ Ⓖ Ⓞ   205 Ⓓ Ⓥ Ⓖ Ⓞ   212 Ⓓ Ⓥ Ⓖ Ⓞ   219 Ⓓ Ⓥ Ⓖ Ⓞ
192 Ⓓ Ⓥ Ⓖ Ⓞ   199 Ⓓ Ⓥ Ⓖ Ⓞ   206 Ⓓ Ⓥ Ⓖ Ⓞ   213 Ⓓ Ⓥ Ⓖ Ⓞ   220 Ⓓ Ⓥ Ⓖ Ⓞ
193 Ⓓ Ⓥ Ⓖ Ⓞ   200 Ⓓ Ⓥ Ⓖ Ⓞ   207 Ⓓ Ⓥ Ⓖ Ⓞ   214 Ⓓ Ⓥ Ⓖ Ⓞ   221 Ⓓ Ⓥ Ⓖ Ⓞ
194 Ⓓ Ⓥ Ⓖ Ⓞ   201 Ⓓ Ⓥ Ⓖ Ⓞ   208 Ⓓ Ⓥ Ⓖ Ⓞ   215 Ⓓ Ⓥ Ⓖ Ⓞ   222 Ⓓ Ⓥ Ⓖ Ⓞ
195 Ⓓ Ⓥ Ⓖ Ⓞ   202 Ⓓ Ⓥ Ⓖ Ⓞ   209 Ⓓ Ⓥ Ⓖ Ⓞ   216 Ⓓ Ⓥ Ⓖ Ⓞ   223 Ⓓ Ⓥ Ⓖ Ⓞ
196 Ⓓ Ⓥ Ⓖ Ⓞ   203 Ⓓ Ⓥ Ⓖ Ⓞ   210 Ⓓ Ⓥ Ⓖ Ⓞ   217 Ⓓ Ⓥ Ⓖ Ⓞ   224 Ⓓ Ⓥ Ⓖ Ⓞ
197 Ⓓ Ⓥ Ⓖ Ⓞ   204 Ⓓ Ⓥ Ⓖ Ⓞ   211 Ⓓ Ⓥ Ⓖ Ⓞ   218 Ⓓ Ⓥ Ⓖ Ⓞ   225 Ⓓ Ⓥ Ⓖ Ⓞ

Practice Test 2

SECTION 1A: READING RECALL

Time: 15 minutes

Directions: Read the following three passages. While you are reading these passages, bear in mind you will be asked to recall certain facts and ideas about what you have read here. After the reading time limit of 15 minutes, you will not be permitted to turn back to these passages. The questions based on these passages will be given to you after the proctor announces that time is up for the reading of these three passages.

FIRST PASSAGE

Thus at the extreme left stand the Marxists, whose prediction of the ultimate undoing of our system is little changed from the days of Karl Marx himself. Their prophecy we know; their persuasion is that we should line up on the side of history, as they see it. It is not a blueprint of the future which the Marxists try to sell us, but a sense of historical participation, of joining the winning team, of riding the "wave of the future." If Russia or China were not there as an object lession in applied Marxism, their urgings might be a more formidable competitor for our belief. As things now stand, the rigors which are the price of rapid collectivist growth have an appeal only to the most miserable peoples in the world—those who have never known anything but a beggar's lot. Perhaps our task is to understand with genuine compassion the hard choice that history has enjoined on the poor—and to attempt in every way to facilitate their escape from poverty.

To the right of the Marxists are the socialists. Many of them are Marxian in their prognosis of capitalism's end, but they are not Marxian in their prediction of things to come. The Marxists extol the inevitability of history; the socialists extol the idea of liberty inherent in social change. The Marxists are not so much interested in What Comes Next—but this is the very heart and essence of the socialist persuaders. Whether the society of the future is to be centralized or built on old-fashioned guilds; whether it is to be entirely planned, or only partially so; the extent to which the consumer should have a voice, and the extent to which the producer should be heard—these are the burning questions of socialism—but not of communism. While the Marxists hold out the prospect of blindly and trustingly enlisting oneself with the inexorable process of history, the socialists ask us to join them in *shaping* history as they wish it.

Next on the spectrum of prophecy and persuasion are the advocates of managed capitalism. Unlike the socialists, they do not believe that capitalism must disappear, and unlike the socialists they do not want to displace the institution of private ownership with public ownership. Their central philosophy is something else again: they feel that capitalism can be maintained *if* we intervene sufficiently to make it viable. Left to itself, they say, capitalism may run off the rails—if not its economic rails, then its moral rails. Given a strong policy of guidance, it can continue to prosper. Hence we are asked to ensure our futures with a strong pillar of government investment, with active enforcement of antimonopoly laws, with the encouragement of public activity as well as private. This road to the future lies in *making* capitalism work – rather than in relying on its inner stability.

Not so, say the next group of public counselors, the protagonists of the Right-of-Center. Capitalism can work only in an atmosphere of hands-off. While liberal aims may be commendable, the liberal means are incompatible with the essence of a market economy itself. Leave the system alone and it will fare well; try to patch it up and you will only succeed in hopelessly paralyzing it.

It is some such spectrum of prophecy and persuasion that we face.

As we listen to the debates which now surround us – and which will command our attention as long as our society survives – we can recognize the voices of the past. Adam Smith still speaks to us from the platform to the Right; Karl Marx seeks to enroll us in the legions of the Left. We can distinguish the voice of John Stuart Mill in the words of the socialists, and that of John Maynard Keynes in the arguments of the liberal capitalist reformers. The analytic insight of Ricardo, the gloomy presentiments of Malthus, the vision of the more utopian Utopians, the complacency of the Victorians, the disquietude of the underworld, the shrewd skepticism of Veblen – they are all there.

SECOND PASSAGE

Despite the history-making civil rights struggle of the 1960's and the new movement for women's rights, the economic role of the black woman in America remains more severely limited by discrimination – racial and sexual – than that of any other major group.

In the coming decade, however, fortified by her uncommon experience as co-breadwinner in the family, the black woman can be expected to move with the tide of social change into far wider participation in business and in all higher-paying occupations — quite possibly in advance of white women.

Such optimism should not obscure certain gray realities about the present, however. Today, just as 10 or 50 years ago, the "typical black" woman worker is still to be found among the thousands who line up at ghetto bus stops starting at dawn each morning to get to their jobs as maids, laundresses, and baby nurses in whites' homes.

The nearly four million non-white working women (90 per cent black) earn much less than any other group of workers because of their concentration in low-paid occupations. Their median income in 1970 was $3,050, compared with $5,175 for nonwhite men and $7,300 for white men, according to the Department of Labor.

Among black women across the nation, even the well-paid skilled stenographer is still a rarity, and if the high-ranking black female business executive exists, I have yet to hear of her.

Even so, black women have the advantage of — in the masterful understatement of one government report — "a strong attachment to the labor force." Even among mothers of children aged 6 to 17, 62 per cent of black women work, the Labor Department reports. (An equally revealing figure is that for women in the child-rearing ages of 25 to 34, 57 per cent of black women in this group work, compared with 41 per cent of white women.)

The reason for this unusually heavy participation in the labor market is clear. Throughout the history of black people in the Western Hemisphere, nearly all black women have been obliged to play an economic role central to the survival of their families, alongside their husbands or in their stead.

As a result, black women unwittingly are the co-makers and beneficiaries of a form of sexual egalitarianism brought about by oppressive conditions and economic necessity, and not shared by most white women.

Within the black community, there is already the groundwork for equality between the sexes born of interdependence in a constant fight against deprivation. This has contributed to a strength of purpose and responsbility among black women that makes them disproportionately success-oriented. Black women are *doers*.

The indicators of the black woman's movement upward in the labor market are strong. The number of non-white women in professional and technical occupations about doubled in the 1960's. Average educational attainment of nonwhite women rose spectacularly during the last two decades and is now very close to the white (male or female) average.

Perhaps the most interesting finding of this study was that black coeds were far more likely than whites to choose job-oriented college courses (steering away from humanities) *and twice as likely to major in business fields.*

Drawing upon the talents of black women such as these, who are trained to be executives, should be fairly easy for a business world that is going to find itself pressed hard by government to do just that. A more demanding task will be to find ways to develop the resources represented by the hundreds of thousands of black women who have recently entered American corporations in lower-level positions.

If business treats these women on the same kind of timetable as white women, it will be decades before even a modest movement up the promotional ladder can be achieved.

Black women will be available in large numbers to figure prominently in the advances made toward both racial and sexual integration of American business.

THIRD PASSAGE

Many people who are willing to concede that the railroad must be brought back to life are chiefly thinking of bringing this about on the very terms that have robbed us of a balanced transportation network — that is, by treating speed as the only important factor, forgetting reliability, comfort and safety, and seeking some mechanical dodge for increasing the speed and automation of surface vehicles.

My desk is littered with such technocratic fantasies, hopefully offered as "solutions." They range from old-fashioned monorails and jet-propelled hovercraft (now extinct) to a more scientific mode of propulsion at 2,000 miles an hour, from completely automated highway travel in private cars to automated vehicles a Government department is now toying with for "facilitating" urban traffic.

What is the function of transportation? What place does locomotion occupy in the whole spectrum of human needs? Perhaps the first step in developing an adequate transportation policy would be to clear our minds of technocratic cant. Those who believe that transportation is the chief end of life should be put in orbit at a safe lunar distance from the earth.

The prime purpose of passenger transportation is not to increase the amount of physical movement but to increase the possibilities for human association, cooperation, personal intercourse, and choice.

A balanced transportation system, accordingly, calls for a balance of resources and facilities and opportunities in every other part of the economy. Neither speed nor mass demand offers a criterion of social efficiency. Hence such limited technocratic proposals as that for high-speed trains between already overcrowded and overextended urban centers would only add to the present lack of functional balance and purposeful organization viewed in terms of human need. Variety of choices, facilities and destinations, not speed alone, is the mark of an organic transportation system. And, incidentally, this is an important factor of safety when any part of the system breaks down. Even confirmed air travelers appreciate the railroad in foul weather.

If we took human needs seriously in recasting the whole transportation system, we should begin with the human body and make the fullest use of pedestrian movement, not only for health but for efficiency in moving large crowds over short distances. The current introduction of shopping malls, free from wheeled traffic, is both a far simpler and far better *technical* solution than the many costly proposals for introducing moving sidewalks or other rigidly automated modes of locomotion. At every stage we should provide for the right type of locomotion, at the right speed, within the right radius, to meet human needs. Neither maximum speed nor maximum traffic nor maximum distance has by itself any human significance.

With the over-exploitation of the motor car comes an increased demand for engineering equipment, to roll ever wider carpets of concrete over the bulldozed landscape and to endow the petroleum magnates of Texas, Venezuela and Arabia with fabulous capacities for personal luxury and political corruption. Finally, the purpose of this system, abetted by similar concentration on planes and rockets, is to keep an increasing volume of motorists and tourists in motion, at the highest possible speed, in a sufficiently comatose state not to mind the fact that their distant destination has become the exact counterpart of the very place they have left. The end product everywhere is environmental desolation.

If this is the best our technological civilization can do to satisfy genuine human needs and nurture man's further development, it's plainly time to close up shop. If indeed we go farther and faster along this route, there is plenty of evidence to show that the shop will close up without our help. Behind our power blackouts, our polluted environments, our transportation breakdowns, our nuclear threats, is a failure of mind. Technocratic anesthesia has put us to sleep. Results that were predictable — and predicted! — half a century ago without awakening any response still find us unready to cope with them — or even to admit their existence.

IF YOU FINISH BEFORE THE TIME IS UP, GO OVER THESE PASSAGES. DO NOT TURN TO THE QUESTIONS FOR THESE PASSAGES NOR TO ANY OTHER SECTION OF THE TEST. WHEN THE 15 MINUTES ARE UP, GO ON TO SECTION 1B WHICH CONTAINS THE QUESTIONS FOR THESE PASSAGES.

SECTION 1B: READING RECALL

Time: 15 minutes

Directions: Answer the following questions on the basis of what is stated or implied in the passages which you have just read. You are not permitted at any time to turn back to the passages.

QUESTIONS FOR FIRST PASSAGE

1. Proceeding from Left to Right on the economic spectrum, one would find

   (A) Marx – Smith – Mill – Keynes
   (B) Mill – Keynes – Marx – Smith
   (C) Smith – Mill – Keynes – Marx
   (D) Keynes – Mill – Marx – Smith
   (E) Marx – Mill – Keynes – Smith

2. The founder of Capitalism is

   (A) Adam Smith
   (B) Thomas Malthus
   (C) Friedrich Engels
   (D) John Maynard Keynes
   (E) Thorstein Veblen

3. The "gloomy presentiments of Malthus" refers to Malthus' prediction that

   (A) government would take over the operation of all industry
   (B) the world's food supply would become insufficient for its population
   (C) economics would no longer be a factor in the history of nations
   (D) there would be a great class struggle between the workers and the capitalists
   (E) capitalism would eventually be overthrown by communism

4. Advocates of managed capitalism, differing from socialists, believe that

   (A) private ownership should not be displaced by public ownership
   (B) the government should not get involved at all in industry
   (C) the government should own all industry
   (D) the capitalist economy must disappear
   (E) capitalism should be left to itself

5. The existence of Russia and China has made Marxism

   (A) a more formidable competitor of our system
   (B) a system with appeal to all nations of the world
   (C) the dominant economic philosophy in North America
   (D) a model for many of the Western Hemisphere nations
   (E) a system with appeal only to the poorest peoples of the world

6. Favoring capitalism with the qualification that monopolies should be carefully supervised are the

   (A) Socialists
   (B) Rightists
   (C) managed capitalism advocates
   (D) What Comes Next advocates
   (E) Utopians

7. The Marxists believe in

   (A) the encouragement of public, as well as private, activity
   (B) liberty inherent in social change
   (C) a strong pillar of government investment
   (D) a society built on old-fashioned guilds
   (E) the inevitablity of history

8. According to the author, socialists believe in

   (A) riding the "wave of the future"
   (B) rapid collectivist growth
   (C) shaping history
   (D) the inevitability of history
   (E) suppressing liberty to achieve social change

9. The Right of Center advocates believe

   (A) in patching up the market
   (B) in putting capitalism back on the tracks
   (C) managed capitalism can succeed
   (D) that liberal policies interfere with the proper functioning of the market economy
   (E) in old-fashioned guilds

10. The author classifies John Stuart Mill among the

    (A) socialists
    (B) Marxists
    (C) capitalist reformers
    (D) free market advocates
    (E) liberals

QUESTIONS FOR SECOND PASSAGE

11. According to the article, the group facing greatest job discrimination is

   (A) black men
   (B) black women
   (C) the uneducated or those without college degrees
   (D) mothers of children aged 6-17
   (E) black female business executives

12. From the information presented, one can assume that twenty-seven-year-old black women

   (A) are just as likely as white women to be working
   (B) do not constitute a large segment of the work-force
   (C) are more likely than white women to be working
   (D) generally work as domestics in a white home
   (E) average the same level of educational achievement as white women

13. The article states that black women are "doers" because

   (A) hundreds of thousands of them have highly competitive positions in American corporations
   (B) the number of female professionals doubled in the 60's
   (C) they are making conscious attempts for social change
   (D) their struggle against deprivation makes them success-oriented
   (E) black coeds shun the humanities when choosing college courses

14. The author concludes that the task that lies ahead is

   (A) finding a way to make use of the black women who hold low-level corporate positions
   (B) the assimilation of young black female executives into the business world
   (C) promoting college attendance of business courses among black coeds
   (D) allowing black mothers with school-age children to remain at home
   (E) the achieving of equal business status with whites

15. The author states that black women have obtained a degree of sexual equality not attained by most white women because

   (A) black women are born "doers"
   (B) non-whites of both sexes face equal discrimination
   (C) in recent years, black women have made proportionately greater gains than white women
   (D) they are more inclined than white women to share responsibility with their husbands for assuring their families' survival
   (E) the civil rights struggle brought about exclusive advancements for the non-white population

16. According to the article, indications of the black woman's advancement are

      I. her increased representation in professional and technical corporations
     II. her presence in thousands of lower-level positions in U.S. corporations today
    III. her educational achievements which are almost equal in level to the white average

    (A) I only
    (B) I and II only
    (C) II only
    (D) I and III only
    (E) III only

17. The author implies that the government will

    (A) exercise an attitude of "benign neglect" toward the problem of job discrimination
    (B) continue to supply accurate income level statistics
    (C) continue to understate the role that non-white women will play in the American economy
    (D) pressure corporations to hire black female executives
    (E) rate elimination of job discrimination as a top-priority Labor Department concern

18. The author would most likely attribute the lack of equal employment opportunities to

    (A) the attitude business holds toward white as well as black women in regard to their moving up the promotional ladder
    (B) the limitations of the civil rights movement in the 1960's
    (C) government-financed business training programs for non-white unemployed
    (D) the flooding of the job market by black female professionals
    (E) the expanding growth of new American corporations

19. The author says that the most interesting finding in the study was that

    (A) black men earn more then either black or white women
    (B) black coeds were far more likely to choose job-oriented college courses than fine arts courses
    (C) black women earn much less than white women
    (D) black professionals earn as much as white professionals
    (E) education has little bearing on a black woman's earning power

20. The "typical black" woman worker

    (A) is becoming more militant
    (B) supports her family alone
    (C) works at a low-level secretarial job
    (D) enjoys only sporadic employment
    (E) works as a maid, laundress, or baby nurse

QUESTIONS FOR THIRD PASSAGE

21. The author criticizes most railroad advocates because their emphasis is primarily on

    (A) monetary costs
    (B) speed
    (C) traffic flow
    (D) reliability
    (E) pollution

22. The author states that the purpose(s) of transportation is (are)

    I. to move people from place to place efficiently
    II. to increase social contact
    III. to open up opportunities

    (A) I only
    (B) II only
    (C) III only
    (D) I and II only
    (E) I, II and III

23. A solution advocated by the author for transporting masses of people over short distances involves

    (A) jet-propelled hovercraft
    (B) automated vehicles
    (C) conveyor belts
    (D) moving side walks
    (E) pedestrian malls

24. Excessive reliance on the automobile, according to the author, is associated with

    (A) the enrichment of the oil industry
    (B) monopoly power
    (C) our transportation breakdown
    (D) inefficiency in transportation
    (E) a policy of comfort and convenience at all costs

25. It can be inferred that the author would oppose

    (A) a balanced transportation system
    (B) shopping malls
    (C) an expansion of the interstate highway system
    (D) less emphasis on technological solutions
    (E) sacrificing speed for comfort

26. The author predicts that if we continue our present transportation policy

    (A) we will succumb to a technocratic dictatorship
    (B) our society may die
    (C) we will attain a balanced transportation system
    (D) rockets and planes will predominate
    (E) human needs will be surrendered

27. According to the article, the fulfillment of human needs will require

   (A) far greater use of walking
   (B) more resources devoted to transportation
   (C) abandoning the profit system
   (D) a better legislative policy
   (E) a automated travel

28. The author believes that the nation has placed too great an emphasis on all of the following *except*

   (A) speed
   (B) traffic flow
   (C) diversity
   (D) maximizing distance
   (E) technological needs

29. It may be inferred that the author is a(n)

   (A) highway engineer
   (B) historian
   (C) railroad industry spokesman
   (D) lawyer
   (E) oil baron

30. It is stated in the article that safety in transportation is aided by the existence of

   (A) remote air-to-ground control for airplanes
   (B) technological sophistication
   (C) a variety of transport modes
   (D) fail-safe systems
   (E) a combination of surface and sub-surface systems

IF YOU FINISH BEFORE THE TIME IS UP, GO OVER YOUR WORK FOR THIS RECALL PART ONLY. DO NOT TURN BACK TO THE READING PASSAGES NOR TO ANY OTHER SECTION OF THE TEST. WHEN THE 15 MINUTES ARE UP, GO ON TO THE NEXT SECTION.

SECTION 2: MATH ABILITY

Time: 30 minutes

Directions: Each of the problems in this section is followed by five alternatives lettered A through E. Solve each problem and then choose the correct answer. Note that diagrams are not necessarily drawn to scale. Scratchwork may be done on available space on the pages of this section.

31. The mileage on a car was 3740 when the gas tank was one-half full. When the tank was empty the mileage was 3890. If the car averages 15 miles to the gallon, how much can the gas tank hold?

    (A) 20 gallons
    (B) 15 gallons
    (C) 22½ gallons
    (D) 10 gallons
    (E) 12 gallons

32. If the price of a dress is now $18.00 and it has undergone successive reductions of 20% and 10%, what was its price originally?

    (A) $21.70
    (B) $36.00
    (C) $25.00
    (D) $24.50
    (E) $28.25

Question 33 refers to the following chart:

RAILROAD TIMETABLE			
City	Arrival Time	Departure Time	Cumulative Mileage
A	-------	9:00am	0
B	9:15am	9:20	12
C	10:40	10:55	100
D	11:25	11:30	140
E	12:15pm	12:25pm	185
F	12:40	12:45	190
G	1:45	2:00	250
H	2:30	-------	275

33. What was the train's average speed for the trip from city *B* to city *C* (to the nearest mile per hour)?

    (A) 56 miles per hour
    (B) 59 miles per hour
    (C) 62 miles per hour
    (D) 64 miles per hour
    (E) 66 miles per hour

34. A store loses a tenth of its merchandise due to theft. An insurance company reimburses the store for two-fifths of the lost merchandise. In January, the insurance company paid the store $5150 for stolen merchandise. What was the value of the store's total inventory in January?

    (A) $2,060   (D) $128,750
    (B) $12,875   (E) $160,000
    (C) $51,500

35. A regular working day is 8 hours and a regular week is 5 working days. A man is paid $2.40 per regular hour and $3.20 per hour overtime. If he earns $432 in 4 weeks, what is the total number of hours he works?

    (A) 180   (D) 195
    (B) 175   (E) 200
    (C) 160

36. A company sells pens at a price of $1.00 per dozen, but gives a 15% discount on any order which exceeds twelve dozen. If a merchant wants to get three thousand pens, how much will he have to pay?

    (A) $174.25   (D) $235.00
    (B) $205.00   (E) $250.00
    (C) $212.50

37. If gasoline costs 30¢ per gallon or 40¢ per gallon, how far can a driver who uses equal amounts of the two kinds of gas drive for $3.50? He gets 15 miles to the gallon on the average.

    (A) 100 miles   (D) 35 miles
    (B) 300 miles   (E) 515 miles
    (C) 150 miles

38. Peaches cost 25¢ per pound, and nectarines sell for 35¢ per pound. A grocer wants to make a 15 pound mixture and sell it for 33¢ per pound. How many pounds of nectarines should he use?

    (A) 12   (D) 2
    (B) 5   (E) 3
    (C) 8

Questions 39–40 are based on the graph below.

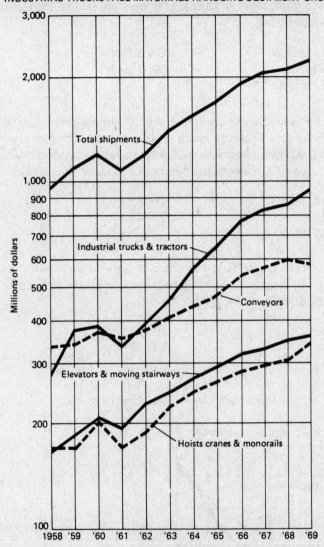

INDUSTRIAL TRUCKS PACE MATERIALS HANDLING EQUIPMENT GROWTH

39. In 1966, what was the difference, in millions of dollars, between the value of conveyors produced and the value of hoists, cranes, and monorails produced?

(A) 130
(B) 250
(C) 300
(D) 375
(E) 540

40. What was the greatest single yearly increase in the value of produced trucks and tractors?

(A) $100 million
(B) $240 million
(C) $130 million
(D) $75 million
(E) $50 million

41. The dimensions of a rectangular room are 12 feet 10 inches by 10 feet 1 inch. If square tiles of the same size are to cover the floor completely without any overlapping and if only whole tiles are used, what is the largest possible length for the side of a square tile?

    (A) 11 inches
    (B) 9 inches
    (C) 8 inches
    (D) 1 foot
    (E) 1 inch

42. X and Y work in the same factory. X can produce 45 articles in 1 hour and Y can produce 40 in 1 hour. During one week, Y worked 5 more hours than X but produced the same number of articles as X. How many hours did X work that week?

    (A) 45
    (B) 40
    (C) 50
    (D) 43
    (E) 44

43. At a certain party, first the ratio of boys to girls was 5 to 3. If, after 10 boys left, the ratio became 1 to 1, how many people were originally at the party?

    (A) 48
    (B) 32
    (C) 64
    (D) 40
    (E) 56

Questions 44-46 refer to the following graphs.

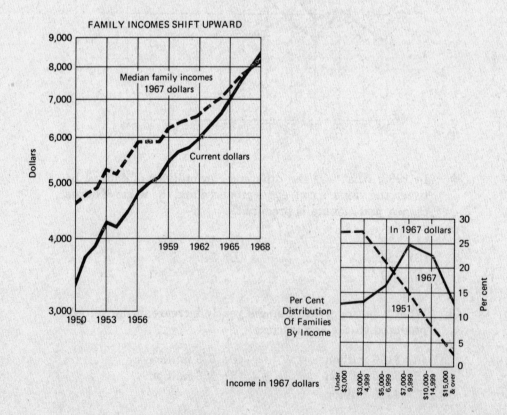

FAMILY INCOMES SHIFT UPWARD

Median family incomes 1967 dollars

Current dollars

Per Cent Distribution Of Families By Income

In 1967 dollars

1967

1951

Income in 1967 dollars

44. Given a random sample of 200 families in 1967, how many could be expected to earn $7,000-$9,999?

    (A) 12   (D) 50

    (B) 25   (E) cannot be determined

    (C) 40

45. In 1953, what was the ratio of the value of 1967 dollars to the value of current dollars?

    (A) 2:1   (D) 31:30

    (B) 15:9   (E) 1:1

    (C) 26:21

46. In 1951, what per cent of families earned $5000 or more?

    (A) 73   (D) 27

    (B) 62   (E) 11

    (C) 46

Base your answers to Questions 47–48 on the following graph.

DISTRIBUTION OF BUSINESS ADMINISTRATION MAJORS IN VARIOUS GRADUATE SCHOOLS

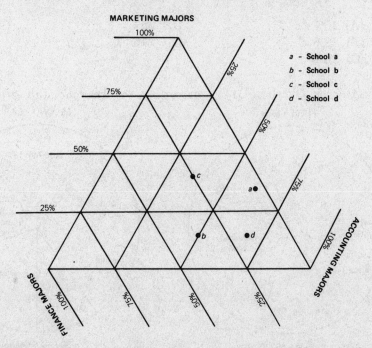

The above graph describes what percentage of students in the business administration department of each of four schools, a, b, c, and d, major in Marketing, Finance, and Accounting. (The business administration department in each of these schools consists of the disciplines Marketing, Finance, and Accounting, only.) The vertices of the large triangle denote 100% and the opposite sides of each of the vertices denote 0%.

47. Approximately what percentage of students in the business administration department of School c major in Marketing?

(A) 20%   (D) 50%
(B) 30%   (E) 5%
(C) 40%

48 Which school has the greatest percentage of Finance majors?

(A) School a   (D) School d
(B) School b   (E) This cannot be determined
(C) School c   from the information given.

49. If 95% of all men work, and ⅖ of them are unskilled laborers, what per cent of male workers are not unskilled laborers?

(A) 60%   (D) 63%
(B) 61%   (E) 64%
(C) 62%

50. A farmer buys 12 cows for $210 apiece. He sells them 2 years later for a total price of $3000. What percent of profit did he make per cow?

(A) 10%   (D) 25%
(B) 19%   (E) 27%
(C) 20%

Answer Question 51–52 according to the following graphs:

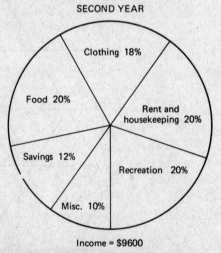

FIRST YEAR

Food 20%
Clothing 15%
Saving 15%
Rent and housekeeping 25%
Misc. 10%
Recreation 15%
Income = $8000

SECOND YEAR

Clothing 18%
Food 20%
Rent and housekeeping 20%
Savings 12%
Recreation 20%
Misc. 10%
Income = $9600

THE TWO GRAPHS SHOW HOW A MAN SPENT HIS INCOME DURING TWO YEARS.

51. What was the man's percent of increase of income?

(A) 10%   (D) 25%
(B) 15%   (E) 12½%
(C) 20%

52. How much more did he spend on clothing during the second year than the first?

   (A) $476
   (B) $528
   (C) $256

   (D) $360
   (E) $300

53. A man with a number of bookshelves, has put 80 books on each shelf. If he adds 3 bookshelves, then each of all of the bookshelves will hold only 50 books. How many books does he have altogether?

   (A) 369
   (B) 200
   (C) 300

   (D) 80
   (E) 400

54. The sum of three consecutive integers is 210. What is the product of the first two integers?

   (A) 4692
   (B) 4830
   (C) 4899

   (D) 4970
   (E) 5112

55. If the ratio a to c is $3/4$ and the ratio of b to c is $5/6$, what is the ratio of a to b?

   (A) $5/8$
   (B) $2/5$
   (C) $3/4$

   (D) $19/12$
   (E) $9/10$

56. A man is driving on a 360-mile-trip. If his average speed is 42 miles per hour for the first 231 miles, what must his average speed be for the rest of the trip in order to finish the entire trip in 8 hours?

   (A) 49 mph
   (B) 51.6 mph
   (C) 50.5 mph

   (D) 45 mph
   (E) none of the above

57. If p is a whole number which is greater than 16, but less than 35, and $x = \dfrac{p+2}{8}$, how many integer values may x have?

   (A) none
   (B) one
   (C) two
   (D) three
   (E) more than three

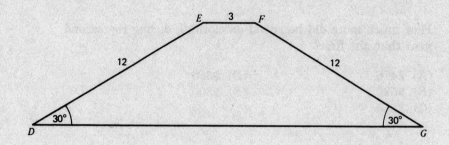

58. What is the area of isosceles trapezoid *DEFG*?

(A) 9

(B) $9 + 36\sqrt{3}$

(C) $18 + 6\sqrt{3}$

(D) $18 + 36\sqrt{3}$

(E) 36

59. A box is made by using rectangles of area 24 as the sides. The bottom of the box is a square of area 9. The volume of the box is

(A) 216

(B) 72

(C) 96

(D) 33

(E) 81

60. For which value of *m* is·it impossible to have a triangle with sides *m*, *m* + 2, *m* + 3?

(A) 1

(B) 1½

(C) 3

(D) π

(E) 9

IF YOU FINISH BEFORE THE TIME IS UP, GO OVER YOUR WORK FOR THIS SECTION ONLY. DO NOT TURN TO ANY OTHER SECTION OF THE TEST. WHEN THE TIME IS UP, GO ON TO THE NEXT SECTION.

SECTION 3: BUSINESS JUDGMENT

Time: 30 minutes for all of Section 3

QUESTIONS ON DATA EVALUATION

Directions: Read the passage. After the passage are Data Evaluation questions (in phrase form) that relate to the passage. Answer each question by choosing the appropriate letter for your answer.

(A) **Major Objective.** The phrase indicates a Major Objective of the business executive in the situation described in the passage.

(B) **Major Factor.** The phrase indicates a Major Factor in the business executive's arriving at a decision. The passage specifically mentions a circumstance or consideration that is fundamental in his coming to the decision.

(C) **Minor Factor.** The phrase indicates a Minor Factor in the business executive's arriving at a decision. The passage specifically states a circumstance or consideration that is secondary in his coming to a decision.

(D) **Major Assumption.** The phrase indicates a Major Assumption in the business executive's arriving at a decision. He is taking for granted certain circumstances or occurrences in his decision-making.

(E) **Unimportant Issue.** The phrase indicates an Unimportant Issue in the business executive's arriving at a decision. The issue is of no importance or of no relevance in his decision-making.

James Callan was a salesman for the Zenith Furniture Store, a high-grade home furnishings store in a large eastern city. Carl Krover, one of his friends, suggested that they form a partnership in a retail furniture store.

Mr. Callan was 30 years old, and had been employed by the Zenith store since his graduation from high school. While in high school he held several jobs in the retail field. Shortly after graduation he married one of his classmates. They had three children, two boys (ages 7 and 6) and a four-year-old daughter. During his 11 years with Zenith, he had progressed satisfactorily, and was considered one of the most promising salesmen in the organization. He was paid a salary of $600 per month and a commission on sales. He earned $15,000 a year.

Mr. Krover received a college degree in chemistry in 1950. He first went to work as a salesman for a large chemical firm, but after three years, because he did not like to be away from home so much, he resigned to accept a position as a salesman with a large real-estate firm. This firm specialized in developing shopping centers. Mr Krover was married and had one son, who was three years old. Upon the death of his father, he had inherited $50,000.

The firm for which Mr. Krover worked constructed all the buildings in a shopping center according to its architectural plans and then leased the stores to selected individuals. A few months before, the company had completed such a center in the suburban section of the city in which the Zenith store was located, and all the stores except one had been leased. This building was a one-story structure 130' deep with a 70' frontage. There were ample parking facilities behind the store, and an important city boulevard, on which city busses passed at regular intervals, served as the main street in the shopping area.

The downtown section of the city was about four miles away. In this section, there were six large furniture stores and five department stores that sold furniture. These firms were old established companies that had been in business from 35 to 90 years.

The real estate company wanted to lease the vacant building to someone who would open a furniture store, and had tried unsuccessfully to get one of the larger downtown stores to open a branch. Mr Krover had worked on the project and was familiar with the terms of the lease, which he believed were very attractive. The lease provided for a minimum guarantee of $200 per month or 5 per cent of sales, whichever was greater.

Mr. Krover had always wanted to go into business for himself and had decided that if he could get somone who knew the furniture business to form a partnership with him, they should do well in this location. He approached the real estate company with his plan, and was given a period of 30 days to decide whether or not he would take the lease. Mr Callan had sold him most of the furniture for his home, and he believed that Callan was the kind of person with whom he would like to become associated. He approached him, therefore, with the partnership offer.

Although Mr. Krover had no experience in the furniture business, he was well-known in the city and believed that he had the ability to learn the business in a relatively short period. Besides the $50,000 his father had left him, he had about $1,500 in government bonds. Mr. Callan owned his home but did not have any capital to invest in the partnership.

No other store in this shopping center sold furniture, appliances, floor coverings, or draperies. The real-estate company was willing to give Callan and Krover exclusive rights to handle these items because its policy was to have only one store of each kind (with the exception of food outlets) in its shopping areas.

Mr. Callan was enthusiastic about the partnership idea and immediately began investigating its possibilities. He told Mr. Krover that he believed they should specialize in high-grade home furnishings and attempt to build a reputation as "interior decorators." He stated that they might anticipate an inventory turnover about three times a year and suggested stock distribution as shown in Schedule I.

Schedule I

Planned Stock Distribution

	Per cent
Major furniture	50
Appliances	15
Draperies	15
Floor coverings	15
Miscellaneous items	5

The manager of the Zenith Furniture Store, in applying a "rule of thumb" principle, had told Mr. Callan that if the partnership was to do a $100,000 volume the first year, they would need about $50,000, two-thirds of which would be tied up in inventory and accounts receivable within a short period of time.

Both Mr. Krover and Mr. Callan believed that it would be easy for the partnership to sell at least $100,000 the first year, and because Mr. Krover was willing to put up the necessary capital at 4 per cent interest, they began to estimate what return they would get.

Mr. Callan went to the manager of the Zenith Furniture Store and secured permission to use the expense control budget which he had introduced successfully eight years before. This budget was set up on a percentage of sales basis.

Schedule II

Expense Control Budget

	Per cent
Sales	100
Cost of goods sold	60
Gross profit	40
Expenses:	
Occupancy (rent, heat, light and power) 7%	
Employees' wages 9	
Advertising 1	
Administration 10	
Bad debt losses 2	
Delivery 3	
Warehousing 4	36
Net profit	4

On the basis of the information in Schedule II, Mr. Callan and Mr. Krover prepared what they considered an adequate budget for the proposed first year of operation. A copy of their budget appears in Schedule III.

Schedule III

Planned budget for first year of operation

	Expenses Percentage of sales	Projected budget on basis of sales of $100,000
Sales	100%	$100,000
Cost of goods sold	60	60,000
	40%	$ 40,000
Expenses:		
Lease	5%	$ 5,000
Heat, light, and power	1	1,000
Employees' wages	4	4,000
Advertising	1	1,000
Bad debt losses	1	1,000
Delivery	3	3,000
Warehousing	4	4,000
Administration	3	3,000
Salaries of partners	10	10,000
Interest on loan	2	2,000
	34%	$ 34,000
Net profit	6%	$ 6,000

Mr. Callan and Mr. Krover were pleased with the planned budget and envisioned a prosperous business. As Mr. Krover stated, "Even if our sales are no greater than $100,000, we will still each earn $5,000 salary and receive $3,000 as our share of profits. There is no reason why, during our first year, we cannot sell $200,000, which will double our profit."

In the meantime, Mr. Callan called on a number of furniture manufacturers and was assured that the partnership could secure a representative list of major brand furniture items. Several of the major appliance manufacturers were also willing to give the partnership limited franchises. There seemed to be no significant problems involved in buying an adequate stock of all the items which the store would need.

Mr. Krover and Mr. Callan decided that the area in which the store was located was a growing one. One thousand homes had been constructed in the past five years, and there was enough room for an additional 300 units. The families were relatively young and, in many instances, both the husband and wife worked.

Without attempting to secure any additional data, Mr. Krover decided to form a partnership with Mr. Callan and shortly thereafter opened their furniture store.

Choose the appropriate letter (A or B or C or D or E)
for these phrases in accordance with the given directions.

61. The background and experience of Mr. Callan
62. Leasing of stores to selected individuals
63. Mr. Krover's inheritance of $50,000
64. Provisions of the lease
65. Decision about whether to take lease before thirty-one days
66. Mr. Krover's ability to learn business in a relatively short period of time
67. Specialization in high-grade home furnishings
68. Stock distribution of major furniture as one-half stock
69. Sales of $200,000 the first year
70. Adequate preparation of budget (Schedule III)
71. Assurance of securing major brand furniture items
72. Location of store
73. Planned profit of 6% of sales
74. Inability of Mr. Callan to invest with capital
75. Mr. Krover's college degree in chemistry
76. Unsuccessful attempt of real estate company to get one of the downtown stores to open up a branch
77. Mr. Krover's desire to go into business for himself or with a partner
78. Formation of partnership in retail store
79. Mr. Krover's inexperience in the furniture business
80. The assurance of the granting of exclusive rights to sell furniture, appliances, floor coverings, and draperies.

QUESTIONS ON DATA APPLICATION

Directions: The questions below are to be answered with reference to the same passage (above). For each question, select the correct answer from each of the five choices given.

81. At the Zenith store Mr. Callan earned a yearly commission of

    (A) $10,000   (D) $7800
    (B) $15,000   (E) $6000
    (C) $9000

82. According to the planned budget for the first year of operation, Mr. Krover expects to earn (excluding interest)

    (A) $4000   (D) $10,000
    (B) $6000   (E) $12,000
    (C) $8000

83. Which of the following would adversely affect the success of the new store?

        I. The parking facilities behind the store
       II. The traffic on the streets near the store
      III. The downtown section of the city

    (A) I only
    (B) II only
    (C) III only
    (D) II and III only
    (E) I and III only

84. One of Mr. Callan's long range goals was to

    (A) go back to school
    (B) become a corporate executive
    (C) own a large department store
    (D) become manager of Zenith Furniture Store
    (E) be known as an interior decorator

85. Mr. Krover's attitude toward business could be deemed

    (A) optimistic but uncritical
    (B) optimistic but very skeptical
    (C) cautious
    (D) unenthusiastic
    (E) critical and insightful

IF YOU FINISH BEFORE THE TIME IS UP, GO OVER YOUR WORK FOR THIS SECTION ONLY. DO NOT TURN TO ANY OTHER SECTION OF THE TEST. WHEN THE TIME IS UP, GO ON TO THE NEXT SECTION.

SECTION 4: DATA SUFFICIENCY

Time: 30 minutes

Directions: Each of the questions below is followed by two statements, labeled (1) and (2), in which certain data are given. In these questions you do not actually have to compute an answer, but rather you have to decide whether the data given in the statements are *sufficient* for answering the question. Using the data given in the statements *plus* your knowledge of mathematics and everyday facts (such as the number of days in July), you are to blacken the box on the answer sheet under

(A) if statement (1) ALONE is sufficient but statement (2) alone is not sufficient to answer the question asked.

(B) if statement (2) ALONE is sufficient but statement (1) alone is not sufficient to answer the question asked.

(C) if BOTH statements (1) and (2) TOGETHER are sufficient to answer the question asked, but NEITHER statement ALONE is sufficient.

(D) if EACH statement is sufficient by itself to answer the question asked.

(E) if statements (1) and (2) TOGETHER are NOT sufficient to answer the question asked and additional data specific to the problem are needed.

86. What is the cost of two pounds of apples?

    (1) Ten apples weight 4.1 pounds, on the average.
    (2) Ten pounds of apples costs $3.00.

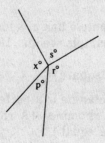

87. What is the value of "r" in the diagram above?

    (1) s = 90.
    (2) t = 130.

88. A chorus is composed of altos, tenors, sopranos, and basses. How many basses are in the chorus?

    (1) There are 10 tenors in the chorus.
    (2) All the altos and sopranos are girls and there are 40 girls in the chorus.

89. Each car of a train is 18 feet long and the cars are separated from each other by a distance of two feet. How many cars are there in a certain train?

    (1) The length of the train is 118 feet.
    (2) It takes the train 5 seconds to pass a post by the side of the tracks.

90. A long distance runner has just completed running 28 miles. How long did it take him to finish the journey?

    (1) He averaged 8 miles per hour.
    (2) Running at the same rate, he could have run 12 miles in $1\frac{1}{2}$ hours.

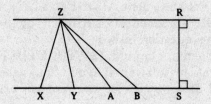

91. In the figure above, what is the ratio of the area of triangle ZXY to the area of triangle ZAB?

    (1) XY = AB
    (2) RS = 5 inches

92. What is the density (weight divided by volume) of the moon rock Lunite?

    (1) The only known sample has a volume of 18 cubic centimeters.
    (2) The only known sample weighs 190 grams.

93. Is rectangle VBNM a square?

    (1) The area of the rectangle is a perfect square (4, 16, 25, 49, etc.).
    (2) The rectangle is a rhombus. (A rhombus is a 4-sided figure, all sides of which are equal.)

94. A television set was originally priced at $250. What percent discount was placed on its original price?

    (1) The store has 5 of these television sets left.
    (2) If the store were to sell all of these remaining television sets, it would receive $1000 for them.

95. Is side GF of triangle GFD 5 inches long?

   (1) GD = FD
   (2) GD = 2 inches

96. Is "z" divisible by 6?

   (1) z is divisible by 4 and 9.
   (2) z is divisible by 12.

97. How many blocks does Joseph live from the train station?

   (1) He can walk to the station in 10 minutes.
   (2) He is 1 mile from the station and the average length of a block is 330 feet.

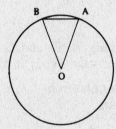

98. In the diagram above, how many degrees are there in angle OAB?

   (1) OA = 4 inches
   (2) Angle AOB = 30°

99. An apple orchard contains 180 apple trees. How many gallons of apple juice can it produce?

   (1) Each tree provides an average of 240 apples.
   (2) Each apple can produce 1 cup of apple juice.

100. What was the average mark on the Math final in Kaye's class?

   (1) The sum of all the marks is 1680.
   (2) Kaye's mark, 84, was above average.

101. Y is a whole number. How many digits does Y have?

   (1) The square of Y has three digits.
   (2) 2Y has two digits.

102. What is the average yearly increase in the cost of a car?

   (1) In 1968 the average cost of a car was $2800.
   (2) In 5 years the cost of a car rose $620.

103. All the secretaries working at a certain office drink either coffee or tea or both. How many drink both?

    (1) There are 60 secretaries at the office.
    (2) 24 secretaries drink tea.

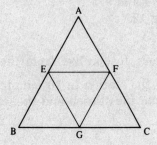

104. In the figure above, points E, F, and G are the midpoints of sides AB, AC, and BC respectively. What is the length of AC?

    (1) Triangle EFG is equilateral.
    (2) EG is 5 inches long.

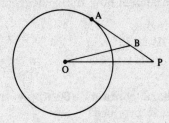

105. In the figure shown above, OP is 10 inches and AP is tangent to the circle. What is the radius of the circle?

    (1) OB is 8 inches long.
    (2) AP is 8 inches long.

106. What is the width of the widest of four rivers?

    (1) The most narrow river is 240 yards across.
    (2) The average width is 570 yards across.

107. Jim, Harry, and Fred have a total of 58 marbles. How many marbles does Fred have?

    (1) Fred has 5 less than twice as many as the number that Jim has and Harry has 3 more than Jim.
    (2) Fred has 7 more than Harry and Jim has 10 less than Fred.

108. A horse ran 100 miles without stopping. What was its average speed in miles per hour?

   (1) The entire journey takes from 8 P.M. one day to 4 A.M. the following day.
   (2) The horse ran 20 miles per hour for the first 50 miles.

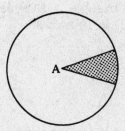

109. The radius of the circle shown above is 18 inches. What is the area of the shaded portion?

   (1) Angle A is 30°.
   (2) The circumference of the circle is 36π.

110. Which is heavier, a cubic inch of liquid A or a cubic inch of liquid B?

   (1) A 20-cubic-inch container filled with liquid B weighs 96 ounces. The container is virtually weightless.
   (2) A cubic foot of liquid A weighs 635 ounces.

111. How many tons of cement will be needed for the foundation of an apartment building?

   (1) The entire building will require 8000 tons of cement.
   (2) The volume of the cement needed for the foundation is 1000 cubic yards.

112. On a certain auto race track, cars average 160 MPH. What is the length of the track?

   (1) On straight sections, cars can go 180 MPH.
   (2) Average lap time (once around the track) is 1 minute, 4 seconds.

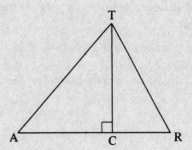

113. What is the length of segment TC in the triangle above?

  (1) The area of the triangle is 80 square inches.
  (2) The length of TR is 10 inches.

114. In triangle WER what is the measure of Angle E?

  (1) Twice Angle E minus the sum of the other two angles is 90°.
  (2) Triangle WER is a right triangle.

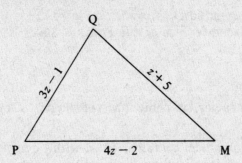

115. In the figure above, what is the value of z?

  (1) The perimeter is 26.
  (2) PQ = QM.

IF YOU FINISH BEFORE THE TIME IS UP, GO OVER YOUR WORK FOR THIS
SECTION ONLY. DO NOT TURN TO ANY OTHER SECTION OF THE TEST.
WHEN THE TIME IS UP, GO ON TO THE NEXT SECTION.

SECTION 5: GRAMMAR AND USAGE

Time: 30 minutes

Directions: In each question, you will find a sentence with four words (or phrases) underlined. In some sentences one of the underlined words (or phrases) is incorrect in the light of the rules of standard written English for grammar, correct usage, and choice of words. No sentence has more than one error. You are to assume that the rest of the sentence (whatever is not underlined) is correct. If you find an error, choose the letter (A *or* B *or* C *or* D) of that underlined word (or phrase) which is incorrect. If you find no error, fill in answer space E.

116. The reason <u>her</u> and her cousin decided <u>to take</u> the train instead of
         A   B
the plane was that <u>there was</u> a forecast over the radio about an
                          C
<u>impending</u> storm. <u>No error.</u>
      D   E

117. <u>Though</u> Seaver pitched <u>real</u> well, the Orioles <u>scored</u> four runs in
       A   B   C
the ninth inning <u>as a result of</u> two Met errors. <u>No error.</u>
                      D   E

118. Jim and <u>him</u>, after spending several hours trying to ascertain the
            A
<u>whereabouts</u> of the missing children, <u>finally</u> discovered them in
      B   C
their <u>aunt's</u> house. <u>No error.</u>
         D   E

119. <u>After</u> the critics see the two plays, they <u>will</u>, as a result of <u>their</u>
       A   B   C
experience and background, be able to judge which is the <u>most</u> ef-
                                                             D
fective and moving. <u>No error.</u>
                        E

120. Each of the <u>hotel's</u> 500 rooms <u>were equipped</u> with <u>high</u> quality
                   A   B   C
<u>air conditioning</u> and television. <u>No error.</u>
      D   E

121. A textbook <u>used</u> in a college class <u>usually always</u> <u>contains</u> an in-
            A   B   C
     troduction, a glossary, and <u>an annotated</u> bibliography. <u>No error.</u>
                                  D   E

122. On any <u>given</u> weekend—especially holiday <u>weekends</u>—the number
       A   B   C
     of highway deaths <u>is</u> predictable. <u>No error.</u>
                   D   E

123. The <u>youth</u> of today are <u>seemingly</u> more sophisticated than were
         A   B
     <u>they're</u> parents <u>at</u> the corresponding age. <u>No error.</u>
      C   D   E

124. The sun <u>hadn't hardly</u> set when the mosquitoes began <u>to sting</u> so
              A   B
     <u>annoyingly</u> that we had to <u>run off</u> from the picnic grounds. <u>No error.</u>
        C   D   E

125. The lilacs in my <u>Uncle Joe's</u> garden smell <u>sweetly</u> <u>at</u> this time
                    A   B C
     <u>of the year.</u> <u>No error.</u>
         D   E

126. A wise <u>and</u> experienced administrator <u>will assign</u> a job to <u>whomever</u>
           A   B   C
     is <u>best qualified.</u> <u>No error.</u>
         D   E

127. <u>Being that</u> the United States has a food surplus, it is <u>hard to see</u>
      A   B
     why <u>anyone</u> in our country <u>should go</u> hungry. <u>No error.</u>
          C   D   E

128. Unless <u>there</u> can be some assurance of increased pay, factory <u>morale,</u>
          A   B
     <u>all ready</u> low, will collapse <u>completely.</u> <u>No error.</u>
       C   D   E

129. A series of debates between the major candidates were scheduled
    $\overline{}_{A}$ $\overline{}_{B}$ $\overline{}_{C}$
    for the Labor Day weekend. No error.
    $\overline{}_{D}$ $\overline{}_{E}$

130. As she was small, her huge eyes and her long black hair were neither
    $\overline{}_{A}$ $\overline{}_{B}$ $\overline{}_{C}$
    outstanding or attractive. No error.
    $\overline{}_{D}$ $\overline{}_{E}$

131. We did the job as good as we could; however, it did not turn out to
    $\overline{}_{A}$ $\overline{}_{B}$ $\overline{}_{C}$ $\overline{}_{D}$
    be satisfactory. No error.
    $\overline{}_{E}$

132. If we are given the opportunity to stage a play, whose to decide
    $\overline{}_{A}$ $\overline{}_{B}$ $\overline{}_{C}$
    which play we shall produce? No error.
    $\overline{}_{D}$ $\overline{}_{E}$

133. If I would have had more time, I would have written a much more
    $\overline{}_{A}$ $\overline{}_{B}$ $\overline{}_{C}$
    interesting and a far more thorough report. No error.
    $\overline{}_{D}$ $\overline{}_{E}$

134. More leisure, as well as an abundance of goods, are attainable through
    $\overline{}_{A}$ $\overline{}_{B}$ $\overline{}_{C}$ $\overline{}_{D}$
    automation. No error.
    $\overline{}_{E}$

135. Morphine and other narcotic drugs are valuable medically; if mis-
    $\overline{}_{A}$ $\overline{}_{B}$
    used, however, it can cause irreparable damage. No error.
    $\overline{}_{C}$ $\overline{}_{D}$ $\overline{}_{E}$

136. An old miser who picked up yellow pieces of gold had something
    $\overline{}_{A}$ $\overline{}_{B}$
    of the simple ardor of a child who picks out yellow flowers. No error.
    $\overline{}_{C}$ $\overline{}_{D}$ $\overline{}_{E}$

137. If we here in America <u>cannot live</u> <u>peaceably</u> and happily <u>together</u>,
                       A   B   C
     we cannot hope that nations which have different living conditions
     — different economic standards, different aspirations, different
     mores, different interests — <u>to live</u> peaceably with us. <u>No error</u>.
                                       D   E

138. Although Marilyn <u>was not invited</u> <u>to the wedding</u>, she would
                          A   B
     <u>very much</u> have liked <u>to have gone</u>. <u>No error</u>.
         C   D   E

139. Every man, woman, and child <u>in this community</u> <u>are</u> now aware of
                                       A   B
     <u>the terrible consequences</u> <u>of the habit</u> of smoking. <u>No error</u>.
              C   D   E

140. The inexperienced teacher had difficulty in controlling the students
     <u>whom</u> she <u>was escorting</u> on a visit to the chemical factory, because
       A   B
     it <u>stunk</u> <u>so</u>. <u>No error</u>.
        C   D   E

IF YOU FINISH BEFORE THE TIME IS UP, GO OVER YOUR WORK FOR THIS
SECTION ONLY. DO NOT TURN TO ANY OTHER SECTION OF THE TEST.
WHEN THE TIME IS UP, GO ON TO THE NEXT SECTION.

SECTION 6: BUSINESS JUDGMENT

Time: 30 minutes for all of Section 6

QUESTIONS ON DATA EVALUATION

Directions: Read the passage. After the passage are Data Evaluation questions (in phrase form) that relate to the passage. Answer each question by choosing the appropriate letter for your answer.

(A) **Major Objective.** The phrase indicates a Major Objective of the business executive in the situation described in the passage.

(B) **Major Factor.** The phrase indicates a Major Factor in the business executive's arriving at a decision. The passage specifically mentions a circumstance or consideration that is fundamental in his coming to the decision.

(C) **Minor Factor.** The phrase indicates a Minor Factor in the business executive's arriving at a decision. The passage specifically states a circumstance or consideration that is secondary in his coming to a decision.

(D) **Major Assumption.** The phrase indicates a Major Assumption in the business executive's arriving at a decision. He is taking for granted certain circumstances or occurrences in his decision-making.

(E) **Unimportant Issue.** The phrase indicates an Unimportant Issue in the business executive's arriving at a decision. The issue is of no importance or of no relevance in his decision-making.

Ten years ago American Laboratories, a manufacturer of cosmetics, brought out a dental cosmetic that when applied to the teeth gave them a pearl-like luster. It would cover dingy, discolored, nicotine stained teeth, even gold fillings. The product had been clinically tested in a prominent dental school and found harmless to teeth and gums. Since the product was marketed purely as a cosmetic, it could not be reviewed by the American Dental Association.

The product was put on the market, and sales were tested in about eight department stores located in big cities, coast to coast. Original sales were good but repeats seemed very poor. The product was put aside for the following reasons:

1. Lack of promotion of the product.

2. The product was originally priced to retail at one dollar. Since then, production costs have increased. American Laboratories also priced the product at a level which fit the general price pattern of the rest of its cosmetic line.

3. Repeat business on the product was not what the company expected. Experience with selling the product showed that a follow-up on each sale was required to develop a profitable percentage of repeat business. This was necessary because practice was required in learning efficient application. At a price of one dollar, there simply was not enough margin available to perform this service.

4. The dental cosmetic was only a small specialty item for American Laboratories. Their primary interest was a line of cosmetics with an annual volume in the millions. When this product didn't go as expected originally, it was neglected.

Two years ago, J. Burton, an advertising man, discovered the sleeping product while looking for new accounts for his firm. American Laboratories told him that they would not invest another dime in promoting the product and that the product was for sale.

The product fired Burton's imagination. It was the only product of its kind on the market. Its nearest competition was a dental recap job on discolored teeth, which cost hundreds of dollars. Therefore, Burton formed a company that became the selling agent for the product. He was given control over promotion and pricing, and for his investment of time and money he was given an option to buy the property outright at a specified figure within a period of six months. Burton felt this would be ample time in which to determine the value of the property.

Features of the product

1. The product is applied with a small brush that comes with the container. A thin coating gets the best results. It is also necessary that the teeth be dry when applying the cosmetic.

2. A bottle will last approximately two months if the applications are made daily.

3. The cosmetic can be applied in about the same time as lipstick.

Burton and Company set up the following marketing policy:

1. The retail price was raised to $2.50. This change was necessary to compensate for increased production costs, to improve the product, to restyle the package, and to allow an adequate promotional budget.

2. Burton set out to learn why so many original purchasers did not become repeaters. In most cases the answer was simple: "They did not follow directions exactly." The company, therefore, developed a beauty consultant service to give a personalized follow-up on every purchase and to pin-point the directions.

3. Distribution was through leading department stores on an exclusive area basis. Direct mail distribution was contemplated for the near future. Advertisements were planned for the pulp magazines soliciting direct mail business. All orders from people in an exclusive area would be forwarded to the store.

4. Price terms with Burton outlets were $2.50 less 40 per cent less 2 per cent ten days E.O.M.

5. Burton also allowed a "20 per-cent-off-invoice" appropriation for local advertising purposes.

6. Burton used P.M.'s to obtain the names and addresses of each customer. Each salesclerk was to be paid $2.00 for every 12 sales of the product if he recorded the required information on the P.M. slip. The company also believed that this arrangement would result in more active cooperation from salesclerks.

As a result of the Burton Company's merchandising plans, the auditor set up a planned profit per unit as given in Schedule I.

Although Burton's unit profit would be low, he believed that when he could get a larger volume of business his product and shipping costs could be reduced to $0.40 per unit.

In the first five months the company was fairly successful in placing its product in a number of the leading department stores in the New England and Middle Atlantic States. However, Burton was just about able to meet costs.

Schedule I

Planned profit per unit

Retail price per unit $2.50

Less allowances and expenses:

40% allowance to outlets	$1.00	
20% allowance for advertising	.30	
P.M. discount	.17	
Beauty consultant service	.10	
Cost of product and shipping	.50	
Sales expense	.20	
Administration expense	.15	2.42
Planned profit per unit		$0.08

He was not sure whether this condition was due to the difficulty of reaching his selective potential market or whether it was just the natural high costs of missionary promotion in an attempt to develop volume business.

If the failure to earn a profit was caused by the high cost of selective distribution, Burton would then refuse his option of buying the product. However, if it was due only to the high missionary costs, he could then hope to realize future profits when his product had wider acceptance.

Choose the appropriate letter (A or B or C or D or E) *for these phrases in accordance with the given directions.*

141. Nature of competitive products on the market
142. Low retail price per unit
143. Ample time to make a decision on purchase of property
144. Locality of manufacturing facilities of product
145. Discovery of why many original buyers did not purchase the product a second time
146. Failure to earn profit due to high missionary costs
147. Failure to earn profit due to high cost of selective distribution
148. Unwillingness of American Laboratories to invest more money in promoting product
149. The geographical location of the dental recap industries
150. The primary interests of American Laboratories
151. The high cost of dental recap jobs
152. Encouragement of original purchasers to buy product again
153. Price of the property
154. Ability to meet costs
155. Inability of American Laboratories to effectively promote product
156. Ability to lower shipping costs
157. Decision on purchase before six months
158. Features of the product
159. Sound marketing policy

QUESTIONS ON DATA APPLICATION

Directions: The questions below are to be answered with reference to the same passage (above). For each question, select the correct answer from each of the five choices given.

160. Which of the following marketing policies did Burton originally institute?

      I. Direct mail distribution
     II. Increase of retail price from American Laboratories retail price
    III. A discount to stores which advertised the product

    (A) I only
    (B) II only
    (C) III only
    (D) II and III only
    (E) I, II, and III

161. When Burton's volume of business increased, Burton felt that he could reduce the cost of product and shipping per unit by

    (A) 10¢
    (B) 20¢
    (C) 30¢ .
    (D) 40¢
    (E) 50¢

162. According to Schedule I, how many units will Burton have to sell in order to make a profit closest to the retail price of the unit?

    (A) 30
    (B) 31
    (C) 32
    (D) 33
    (E) 34

163. If administration expenses amount to $15,000, what can we expect the beauty consultant service to cost during the same time period?

    (A) $5,000
    (B) $10,000
    (C) $15,000
    (D) $20,000
    (E) $40,000

164. The main reason why people who bought the product the first time did not buy the product subsequently, was most likely due to the fact that

    (A) the cost of the product was too high to warrant repeated purchases
    (B) the lifespan of the product could be prolonged depending on how the product was used
    (C) the product was a "novelty" item
    (D) directions for the use of the product were not clear or simple enough
    (E) the American Dental Association did not approve the product

165. The primary reason that Burton became interested in the product was because

    (A) of the uniqueness of the product
    (B) of the low cost of the product
    (C) the product was for sale
    (D) Burton wanted a cosmetic line for his firm
    (E) the cosmetic industry had great potential

IF YOU FINISH BEFORE THE TIME IS UP, GO OVER YOUR WORK FOR THIS SECTION ONLY. DO NOT TURN TO ANY OTHER SECTION OF THE TEST. WHEN THE TIME IS UP, GO ON TO THE NEXT SECTION.

SECTION 7: READING COMPREHENSION

Time: 30 minutes

Directions: Each of the reading passages in this section is followed by questions based on its content. After reading the passage, choose the best answer to each question. The questions are to be answered on the basis of what is stated or implied in the passage.

NMR, a type of spectroscopy that can give a "fingerprint" characteristic of compounds, has recently been used to give a "fingerprint" of proteins and to investigate changes occurring in them as they carry out their functions.

5 Proteins are complex molecules made up chiefly of amino acid residues arranged in a chain, the positions along which are numbered for the convenience of investigators. Proteins that are analogous in different organisms may show great similarity in their sequence of amino acid residues, particularly if they are related by common descent 10 or if they perform the same function in different organisms, or both. For example, in one protein recently investigated from two similar bacteria, it was found that, in one organism, tyrosine (Tyr) was in both positions 2 and 30, while in the other, tyrosine was only in position 2, and phenylalanine (Phe) was in position 30. In addition, the investigators 15 created a modified protein from the former by chemically replacing the first tyrosine with a phenylalanine residue.

Residues 2 and 30 in the protein under discussion are each physically adjacent to an iron-sulfur cluster. Such clusters are the only units (sites) in the protein that are oxidized and reduced. Residue 2 is close to one 20 cluster, and residue 30 is close to the other. When reduction occurs, it is reflected in the NMR spectrum of the protein, particularly in the NMR spectrum of residues 2 and 30.

It was found that when the three proteins were oxidized, the NMR results of the two residues under discussion were very nearly the same. 25 However, upon complete reduction, the NMR results for Tyr^2 and Phe^{30} in one protein were significantly different from each other, the results for Tyr^2 and Tyr^{30} in the other protein were both like the results for Tyr^2 in the first protein, and the results for Phe^2 and Tyr^{30} in the modified protein were also like the results for Tyr^2 in the first protein.

30 Although the NMR results of the residue in position 2 in the two natural proteins were essentially the same, it was found in a separate experiment that there was a 50 mV difference between the two proteins in the redox potential of the oxidation-reduction site neighboring residue 2. Within the second protein, the NMR results of residues 2 and 30 were 35 significantly different, whereas the difference in redox potential between

the two oxidation-reduction sites was insignificant, around 10 mV. From this it was shown that the NMR results of the residues do not correlate with the redox potential of the neighboring oxidation-reduction sites. It was then suggested that the differences in the NMR results of the
40 residues upon reduction may reflect differences in the physical orientation of these residues to the oxidation-reduction sites.

166. The investigators showed that

   (A) proteins can be modified and replaced in the organism, much like surgery in humans
   (B) proteins take on a rigid shape when used for experiments
   (C) the function of proteins is to carry out oxidation-reduction reactions
   (D) redox potential of oxidation-reduction sites cannot be used as a predictor of NMR results
   (E) NMR of amino acid residues can be used to measure the redox potential of neighboring oxidation-reduction sites

167. It can be assumed that the notation Tyr^2 means

   (A) there are two Tyr residues in the protein
   (B) a tyrosine residue occurs in position 2
   (C) Tyr is an abbreviation for tyrosine
   (D) the residue in position 2 has been modified by the experimentor
   (E) the amount of tyrosine in the protein has to be squared for computations about the experiment

168. Which of the following *cannot* be inferred from the passage?

   (A) The experimenters did not substitute phenylalanine for tyrosine in position 30.
   (B) Proteins that are not related by common descent can be similar in amino acid sequence.
   (C) Upon reduction, residue 2 always gives the same NMR results.
   (D) Each of the proteins under discussion has two oxidation-reduction sites.
   (E) None of the above.

169. The passage indicates that in the material under discussion

   (A) the oxidation-reduction sites can function independently of one another
   (B) reduction must have occurred for the NMR method to be applicable
   (C) each amino acid residue has only two iron-sulfur clusters in it
   (D) 50 mV is small enough to be negligible
   (E) none of the above is true

170. The basic experimental role of the residues specifically discussed here was to

(A) reduce the adjacent iron-sulfur cluster

(B) lower the redox potentials of all reduction sites

(C) be a probe in investigating the oxidation-reduction sites

(D) link the experiment to other organisms that might have the same residues in their proteins

(E) show that common descent is not necessary for proteins to have similar compositions of amino acid residues in bacteria

171. The evidence given in the passage indicates that

(A) the residue in position 30 always stays oxidized

(B) phenylalanine causes changes in NMR results of the protein diagnostically different from the results obtained with tyrosine

(C) in the protein when one oxidation-reduction site is reduced the other is oxidized as a consequence

(D) when the protein is incompletely reduced, each oxidation-reduction site must be partly reduced

(E) none of the above is true

In his compact and modestly titled book, "About Behaviorism," Dr. B.F. Skinner, the noted behavioral psychologist, lists the 20 most salient objections to "behaviorism or the science of behavior," and he has gone on to answer them both implicitly and explicitly. He has answers
5 and explanations for everyone.

For instance, to those who object "that behaviorists deny the existence of feelings, sensations, ideas, and other features of mental life," Dr. Skinner concedes that "a good deal of clarification" is in order. What such people are really decrying is "methodological behaviorism," an earlier
10 stage of the science whose goal was precisely to close off mentalistic explanations of behavior, if only to counteract the 2,500-year-old influence of mentalism. But Dr. Skinner is a "radical behaviorist." "Radical behaviorism . . . takes a different line. It does not deny the possibility of self-observation or self-knowledge or its possible usefulness. . . . It re-
15 stores introspection. . . ."

For instance, to those who object that behaviorism "neglects innate endowment and argues that all behavior is acquired during the lifetime of the individual," Dr. Skinner expresses puzzlement. Granted, "A few behaviorists . . . have minimized if not denied a genetic contribution, and
20 in their enthusiasm for what may be done through the environment, others have no doubt acted as if a genetic endowment were unimportant, but few would contend that behavior is 'endlessly malleable.'" And Dr. Skinner himself, sounding as often as not like some latter-day Social Darwinist, gives as much weight to the "contingencies of survival" in
25 the evolution of the human species as to the "contingencies of reinforcement" in the lifetime of the individual.

For instance, to those who claim that behaviorism "cannot explain creative achievements—in art, for example, or in music, literature, science, or mathematics," Dr. Skinner provides an intriguing ellipsis. "Contingencies of reinforcement also resemble contingencies of survival in the production of novelty. . . . In both natural selection and operant conditioning the appearance of 'mutations' is crucial. Until recently, species evolved because of random changes in genes or chromosomes, but the geneticist may arrange conditions under which mutations are particularly likely to occur. We can also discover some of the sources of new forms of behavior which undergo selection by prevailing contingencies or reinforcement, and fortunately the creative artist or thinker has other ways of introducing novelties."

And so go Dr. Skinner's answers to the 20 questions he poses—questions that range all the way from asking if behaviorism fails "to account for cognitive processes" to wondering if behaviorism "is indifferent to the warmth and richness of human life, and . . . is incompatible with the . . . enjoyment of art, music, and literature and with love for one's fellow men."

But will it wash? Will it serve to silence those critics who have characterized B. F. Skinner variously as a mad, manipulative doctor, as a naive 19th-century positivist, as an unscientific technician, and as an arrogant social engineer? There is no gainsaying that "About Behaviorism" is an unusually compact summary of both the history and "the philosophy of the science of human behavior" (as Dr. Skinner insists on defining behaviorism). It is a veritable artwork of organization. And anyone who reads it will never again be able to think of behaviorism as a simplistic philosophy that reduces human beings to black boxes responding robotlike to external stimuli.

Still, there are certain quandaries that "About Behaviorism" does not quite dispel. For one thing, though Dr. Skinner makes countless references to the advances in experiments with human beings that behaviorism has made since it first began running rats through mazes six or seven decades ago, he fails to provide a single illustration of these advances. And though it may be true, as Dr. Skinner argues, that one can extrapolate from pigeons to people, it would be reassuring to be shown precisely how.

More important, he has not satisfactorily rebutted the basic criticism that behaviorism "is scientistic rather than scientific. It merely emulates the sciences." A true science doesn't predict in advance what it will accomplish when it is firmly established as a science, not even when it is posing as "the philosophy of that science." A true science simply advances rules for testing hypotheses.

But Dr. Skinner predicts that behaviorism will produce the means to save human society from impending disaster. Two key concepts that keep accreting to that prediction are "manipulation" and "control." And so, while he reassures us quite persuasively that his science would practice those concepts benignly, one can't shake off the suspicion that he was advancing a science just in order to save society by means of "manipulation" and "control." And that is not so reassuring.

172. According to the passage, Skinner would be most likely to agree that

    (A) studies of animal behavior are applicable to human behavior

    (B) introspection should be used widely to analyze conscious experience

    (C) behaviorism is basically scientific

    (D) behavioristic principles and techniques will be of no use in preventing widespread disaster

    (E) an individual can form an infinite number of sentences which he has never heard spoken

173. The reader may infer that

    (A) Skinner's philosophy is completely democratic in its methodology

    (B) behaviorism, in its early form, and mentalism were essentially the same

    (C) the book "About Behaviorism" is difficult to understand because it is not well structured

    (D) methodological behaviorism preceded both mentalism and radical behaviorism

    (E) the author of the article has found glaring weaknesses in Skinner's defense of behaviorism

174. When Skinner speaks of "contingencies of survival" (line 24) and "contingencies of reinforcement" (lines 25-26), the word "contingency" most accurately means

    (A) frequency of occurrence

    (B) something incidental

    (C) a quota

    (D) dependence on chance

    (E) one of an assemblage

175. The author of the article says that Skinner sounds "like some latter-day Social Darwinist" (lines 23-24) most probably because Skinner

    (A) is a radical behaviorist who has differed from methodological behaviorists

    (B) has predicted that human society faces disaster

    (C) has been characterized as a 19th-century positivist

    (D) has studied animal behavior as applicable to human behavior

    (E) believes that the geneticist may arrange conditions for mutations to occur

176. It can be inferred from the passage that "extrapolate" (line 60) means

    (A) to gather unknown information by extending known information

    (B) to determine how one organism may be used to advantage by another organism

    (C) to insert or introduce between other things or parts

    (D) to change the form or the behavior of one thing to match the form or behavior of another thing

    (E) to transfer an organ of a living thing into another living thing

177. One *cannot* conclude from the passage that

    (A) Skinner is a radical behaviorist but not a methodological behaviorist

    (B) "About Behavior" does not show how behaviorists have improved in experimentation with human beings

    (C) only human beings are used in experiments conducted by behaviorists

    (D) methodological behaviorism rejects the introspective approach

    (E) the book being discussed is to the point and well organized

178. In Skinner's statement that "few would contend that behavior is endlessly malleable," (line 22) he means that

    (A) genetic influences are of primary importance in shaping human behavior

    (B) environmental influences may be frequently supplemented by genetic influences

    (C) self-examination is the most effective way of improving a behavior pattern

    (D) the learning process continues throughout life

    (E) psychologists will never come to a common conclusion about the best procedure for studying and improving human behavior

The idea of androgyny apparently takes a little getting used to. First responses tend either toward bewilderment or hostility. The word itself is easily enough defined for the bewildered: comprising the Greek words anthro (male) and gyne (female), it suggests the unity rather than the necessary separation of what we have come to think of as masculine and feminine qualities.

For the hostile, who in some sense feel threatened by this unfamiliar idea, further assurance is required. Androgyny does not mean the loss of all distinctions; those who are terrified by the word probably envision everyone, man and woman, dressed indistinguishably, like members of the Chinese Army. Those who are terrified further assume that in robbing us of clearly delineated sexual models, androgyny will rob us of all order and sanity. If we are to have more than two accepted role models—in youth, the quarterback and the cheerleader, in later life, the corporation manager and the corporation manager's wife—will we not in fact be diving off the edge of an ordered world into the abyss?

To which one must answer: between the quarterback and the cheerleader, we have lost too much of our humanity; we have come close to losing humanity altogether. What is more, the possibilities for companionship between men and women can only be heightened by androgynous energy. For androgyny implies not only that couples may find or create their own pattern of passion or conversation, but that marriage may become joyful for those who are neither quarterbacks nor cheerleaders and do not now wish to play those roles.

25   The received ideas of masculine and feminine have operated in three destructive ways. First, by insisting on the masculinity of men and the femininity of women, we have locked individuals into prisons of gender, where their response is likely to be either a mindless acquiescence, or violence and rebellion. Second, the overly defined distinction between the
30 received ideas of masculinity and femininity has brought about a sexual polarization in our society that deprives both men and women of their common humanity in relation to one another, and has separated what should have been joined. Third, by placing in power those men at the most "masculine" end of the spectrum of human possibility, we have en-
35 dangered our own survival.

    My hope for the idea of androgyny is that it will not become another fad, briefly puffed up by the media, but soon mentioned only to groans of boredom. That is the danger. But if, as I believe, the androgynous ideal reaches back into the very roots of our literature, religions and
40 ancient wisdom, it will prevail. Present at the birth of every religion, submerged or subverted in most religions thereafter, androgyny hints at a new equilibrium in an unbalanced world. Those who are unmoved by an appeal to humanity's mythic origins might reflect upon the undeniable impact of modern technology, which has freed the sexes from biologically
45 differentiated social and economic roles and from the behavioral patterns traditionally associated with them.

    Is androgyny, then, women's liberation hiding out under an alias? Only to the extent that the shift of political power from men, who have it all, to women, who have almost none, may help to create a situation in
50 which the androgynous ideal is more nearly possible. The record of civilization has been, largely, the record of a move away from androgyny. And yet the androgynous ideal has contrived to reassert itself in the course of civilization, not always named or recognized, but nonetheless there: among the Greeks, in the Jesus of the Gospels, in the great medieval
55 century that produced Dante, in Shakespeare and the Renaissance. Even in the Victorian age, that least androgynous of eras, the ideal was preserved half hidden in the imaginative works of most of the great novelists.

    In an androgynous world, men would be unable to escape their humanity by putting on the aggressive attitudes of maleness; women would
60 be unable to escape theirs by adopting the passive attitudes society has urged on females. This seems a small enough price if we can bring humanity, to its salvation, back toward the center of the masculine-feminine spectrum. We may even discover the gentleness of men, the forcefulness of women, and not be afraid.

179. The author of the article would encourage

    (A) a woman to wear clothes much like the clothes of her husband
    (B) a female to try out for a position on a professional football team
    (C) a male to insist upon being served in a beauty parlor
    (D) a woman to be dominating if such is her inclination
    (E) women to fight side by side with men in an infantry battle against the enemy

180. The passage indicates that

(A) androgyny is a movement that will likely enjoy only brief duration

(B) a male or a female could do equally well as a quarterback or a cheerleader

(C) Greek history and Victorian novels show a clearcut move away from male-female unity

(D) androgyny, to be effective, requires a radical change in current sexual techniques

(E) a married couple will relate better if they are androgynous

181. That "the androgynous ideal has contrived to reassert itself in the course of civilization" (lines 52-53) is well exemplified in the person of

(A) Marie Antoinette

(B) Madame Curie

(C) Marilyn Monroe

(D) the typical "first lady"

(E) the average female typist

182. We may infer that the writer's attitude toward the "fem lib" movement is one that is

(A) favorable

(B) unfavorable

(C) indifferent

(D) cautious

(E) puzzled

183. The phrase "prisons of gender" (line 27) refers to a situation such as

(A) the lonesomeness that many men and women experience

(B) the difficulty of a male's meeting the "right" female and vice versa

(C) a distinction between "the men's room" and "the ladies' room"

(D) jails for men and jails for women

(E) the male confined to the role of "lord and provider"

184. The passage indicates that

(A) the Renaissance was more amenable to androgyny than any previous age

(B) a corporation manager's wife is likely to be androgynous

(C) Jesus was favorable to androgyny

(D) androgynous males are more likely to be gentle than non-androgynous males

(E) religious leaders have tended to favor androgyny

The first problem that confronts the student in his effort to acquire a speaking knowledge of a modern foreign language is its pronunciation. Before he can begin to learn any part of the grammar or to assemble the most elementary vocabulary, he must be able to recognize the sounds

5 of the language as uttered by native speakers, and must be able to produce them himself in a way that natives will understand him. Phonetics is the science of analyzing, describing and classifying such speech sounds and their method of enunciation.

A phonetically trained foreign student of English is likely to observe
10 many differences of which the average speaker of English is unaware. He will differentiate the aspirated "p" (air is released from the mouth during pronunciation) in "pin" and "appear" from the unaspirated "p" (air is not released from the mouth during pronunciation) in "spin" and "upper"; the short "n" in "hence" from the longer "n" in "hens."
15 Knowledge about whether such differences are important cannot be obtained simply by asking the informant. If the latter is sophisticated enough to understand such finespun questions, he is probably literate in his native language and hence likely to be misled by the way in which words are written, by the tradition of the schools, and by other equally
20 fallible guides; and if he is unspoiled by education the chances are that questions about the identity of words will only baffle him.

If the student were to take the approach of learning and listing every sound in the language, he would probably err in listing too much. Instead of giving a clear picture of the language, such a list would com-
25 plicate the vocabulary and obscure the grammar with a profusion of incidental and irrelevant particulars, signifying nothing but the acuteness of the writer's ear. A purely phonetic description makes it impossible to distinguish the really significant features from the accidental and personal features which inevitably form part of every utterance. It is only
30 by discovering the significant features of any utterance, the constants in a mass of irrelevant variables, that we can lay the foundation for linguistic study.

The student must learn which of the many observable phonetic differences in a language are useful. As a linguist, his task must be to
35 classify the facts of speech and to reveal the system of the language by formulating general statements covering a large number of objectively different but socially equivalent events. He will discover that certain sounds occurring in similar positions (e.g., at the beginning of utterances) serve to distinguish meanings, such as the "p" and "b" in "pit" and "bit,"
40 while others in similar positions do not, such as the two varieties of "p" mentioned above. He will be able to divide the phonetic differences observable in the language into distinctive and nondistinctive differences, thereby performing a phonemic analysis, by which he will organize the speech sounds of a language into phonemes.

45 Sounds which are phonetically similar and which do not distinguish meaning can be classed together in one phoneme. If two or more sounds are so distributed in the forms of a language that none of them ever occurs in exactly the same position in words as any of the others, that is, they are in complementary distribution, and if all of the sounds in ques-
50 tion are phonetically similar, then they are classed in the same phoneme and are called allophones. To the rule that allophones of the same phoneme never occur in the same position, there is one exception. There may be, in some particular positions, free variation between two or more allophones.

55 To illustrate the principle of complementary distribution, we shall list here some of the sounds found to occur in utterances of north central United States English. Aspirated "t" occurs at the beginning of words before a vowel ("tin," "tomorrow"); within words between vowels if the following vowel has the louder stress ("attack"); within words after
60 any consonant except "s" and before a stressed vowel ("captivity"); at the end of words after a vowel or any consonant, but here in free variation with unaspirated "t" and with unreleased "t" (the "t" is never really finished), for example, in "at," "apt," "act," "cast," "raft."

Unaspirated "t" occurs at the beginning of words before "ch" and
65 voiceless "r" ("chew," "true"); at the end of words after a vowel or any consonant, but here in free variation with aspirated "t" and unreleased "t," and so forth.

When the list is completed it will be found that there are eight varieties of "t" all in complementary distribution.

185. In the passage, the informant is

   (A) a linguist
   (B) a polyglot able to help the student
   (C) a native speaker
   (D) a student of a foreign language
   (E) a reliable guide if his ear is sufficiently acute

186. The author implies that

   (A) literacy is a useful aid in the maintenance of correct grammar
   (B) education spoils many a promising foreign guide
   (C) knowing how to spell can correct improper pronunciation
   (D) conventional education gives no clear understanding of systematic speech patterns
   (E) in etymology the irrelevant variables must be weeded out

187. The passage indicates

   I.   that knowing the position of sounds in words does not help in carrying out phonemic analysis
   II. that in writing one symbol could be used for a phoneme because its variations are inherent in its definition
   III. that someone who might suggest that languages evolve in a systematic manner has a basis in spoken speech for such a suggestion
   IV. that free variation can be useful in showing subtle shades of meaning within a dialect

   (A) II and III only
   (B) I and II only
   (C) II only
   (D) IV only
   (E) none of the above

188. Different speech sounds are socially equivalent when

    (A) they sound almost the same
    (B) they are useful and complementary to each other
    (C) they do not distinguish meaning
    (D) different phonemes have the same allophone
    (E) native speakers cannot hear them

189. Which is true of phonemic study?

    (A) It looks for allophones that require free variation.
    (B) It describes the enunciation of speech sounds and classifies them.
    (C) It lists all the speech sounds of a language no matter how long the list is.
    (D) It requires simply phonetic similarity in defining a phoneme.
    (E) none of the above

190. Complementary distribution

    (A) occurs when all the sounds in question are phonetically similar
    (B) occurs when phonemes are transcribed by the linguist
    (C) of sounds that are enunciated similarly indicates that they are co-allophones
    (D) of sounds that serve to distinguish meaning would indicate that they are probably unapprehended by the native speaker
    (E) is required for the definition of any phoneme

IF YOU FINISH BEFORE THE TIME IS UP, GO OVER YOUR WORK FOR THIS SECTION ONLY. DO NOT TURN TO ANY OTHER SECTION OF THE TEST. WHEN THE TIME IS UP, GO ON TO THE NEXT SECTION.

SECTION 8: ERROR RECOGNITION

Time: 30 minutes

Directions: Among the sentences in this group are some which cannot be accepted in formal, written English for one or another of the following reasons:

Poor Diction: The use of a word which is improper either because its meaning does not fit the sentence or because it is not acceptable in formal writing.

Examples

The audience was strongly *effected* by the senator's speech.

The dean made an *illusion* to the Boer War in his talk.

Verbosity: Repetitious elements adding nothing to the meaning of the sentence and not justified by any need for special emphasis.

Examples

At that time there was *then* no right of petition.

In the last decade television production has advanced *forward* with great strides.

Faulty Grammar: Word forms and expressions which do not conform to the grammatical and structural usages required by formal written English (errors in case, number, parallelism, and the like).

Examples

Everyone in the delegation had *their* reasons for opposing the measure.

The commission decided to reimburse the property owners, to readjust the rates, and that they would extend the services in the near future.

No sentence has more than one kind of error. Some sentences have no errors. Read each sentence carefully; then on
your answer sheet blacken the box under:

> **D** if the sentence contains an error in diction;
> **V** if the sentence is verbose;
> **G** if the sentence contains faulty grammar;
> **O** if the sentence contains none of these errors.

191. The union delegates who are going to the convention in Miami Beach are Thompson, Steinmetz, and me.

192. This glittering diamond is the most unique gem of all.

193. Our boss becomes enamored about every pretty girl who walks into his office.

194. The poem was full of illusions to mythology.

195. Down the field came the students of South High School: members of the newly organized, somewhat incompetent band; drum majorettes in white, spangled skirts; and the team, muddy and wretched.

196. He believes in witchcraft, but he doubts that they ride on broomsticks.

197. We were eager to purchase two tickets for the evening performance of "Rigoletto" irregardless of what they would cost us.

198. The crowd became so vehement when the politician insulted them that the police had to rescue him.

199. She wore a dress to the party that was far more attractive than the other girls.

200. The children used colored glass to observe the ellipse of the sun.

201. We hear dissent from a young man who, we firmly believe, is not about to pay compliments to our political leaders or to the local draft board.

202. If one reads a great many articles in *Elementary English*, you will become familiar with the problems of the beginning teacher of reading.

203. Usually the instructor of this class generally arrives on time but so far he is already fifteen minutes late.

204. The crisis in the Middle East is one of the topics that have been discussed at our weekly forums.

No sentence has more than one kind of error. Some sentences have no errors. Read each sentence carefully; then on your answer sheet blacken the box under:

D if the sentence contains an error in diction;
V if the sentence is verbose;
G if the sentence contains faulty grammar;
O if the sentence contains none of these errors.

205. There seem nowadays to be little of the optimism that imbued our ancestors with courage and hope.

206. Taking a cold shower is often so enervating that one feels stronger and wideawake afterward.

207. The governor concurred with his adviser and agreed that the project should be started at once.

208. The meat and vegetables were embroiled together over an open fire.

209. Why do you imply from what I have just exclaimed that I think you are old-fashioned in your attire?

210. At the time you speak about there was then no opportunity to bring your case to court.

211. The machinery was dissembled and prepared for storage.

212. John Kennedy held the public's attention by the charisma of his personality.

213. At this point, it is not known or determined whether the midi will replace the mini.

214. If I would have been there, I certainly would have taken care of the problem in a hurry.

215. Between you and I, I am convinced that this painting by Dali shows greater artistry than that of Picasso.

216. The detective suspicioned that some kind of plan was being contrived to abduct the youth.

217. The mainspring is an indispensable component of a watch.

218. The theory was so esoteric and difficult to understand that efforts to popularize it were unsuccessful.

No sentence has more than one kind of error. Some sentences have no errors. Read each sentence carefully; then on your answer sheet blacken the box under:

D If the sentence contains an error in diction;
V If the sentence is verbose;
G If the sentence contains faulty grammar;
O If the sentence contains none of these errors.

219. Being that you are interested in the outcome of the election, let us wait until the final tally has been made.

220. The retreat of the enemy soldiers into caves and tunnels are deceiving the oncoming infantrymen.

221. I am really and truly sorry for what I have done.

222. Narcotics are often used to militate pain.

223. If he had lain quietly under the tree as he had been instructed to do, we would have found him.

224. The high school graduate, if he is eighteen or nineteen, has these alternatives: attending college, finding a job, or the army.

225. In contrast to Arnold's intellectual prowess was his slovenly appearance and his nervous demeanor.

IF YOU FINISH BEFORE THE TIME IS UP, GO OVER YOUR WORK FOR THIS SECTION ONLY. DO NOT TURN TO ANY OTHER SECTION OF THE TEST. WHEN THE TIME IS UP, THE TEST IS OVER

NOW THAT YOU HAVE COMPLETED PRACTICE TEST 2

1. Turn to the Answer Key on pages 148-149. Do not consider Sections 7 and 8.
2. Count your **correct answers**.
3. Count your **incorrect answers**.
4. Deduct ¼ of the number of incorrect answers from the number of correct answers to get a "raw score" of _____.
5. Your "**scaled score**" for this test, according to the Raw Score/Scaled Score Table on page 88, is _____.

ANSWER KEY FOR PRACTICE TEST 2

Sections 1A and 1B: Reading Recall

1. E	7. E	13. D	19. B	25. C
2. A	8. C	14. A	20. E	26. B
3. B	9. D	15. D	21. B	27. A
4. A	10. A	16. D	22. D	28. C
5. E	11. B	17. D	23. E	29. B
6. C	12. C	18. A	24. A	30. C

Section 2: Math Ability

After each answer, there is a hyphenated number (or numbers) in parentheses. This hyphenated number is keyed to Math Refresher (beginning on page 411). The number *before* the hyphen indicates the Math area of the problem:

$$1 = \text{ARITHMETIC}$$
$$2 = \text{ALGEBRA}$$
$$3 = \text{PLANE GEOMETRY}$$
$$5 = \text{GRAPHS AND CHARTS}$$

The number *after* the hyphen gives you the section (within the Math area) that explains the rule or principle involved in solving the problem.

31. A (2-31)	41. A (3-6, 1-28)	51. C (5-3, 1-25)
32. C (1-25, 2-22)	42. B (2-32, 2-22)	52. B (5-3, 1-25)
33. E (5-5)	43. D (2-26, 2-25)	53. E (2-11, 2-22)
34. D (1-10)	44. D (5-4)	54. B (1-28)
35. B (1-18)	45. C (5-4, 2-26)	55. E (2-12, 2-20)
36. C (1-25)	46. C (5-4, 1-25)	56. B (2-31)
37. C (1-18)	47. C (5-4)	57. C (1-29)
38. A (2-11, 2-22)	48. B (5-4)	58. D (3-7, 3-4, 3-6)
39. B (5-4)	49. A (1-22)	59. B (3-7)
40. C (5-4)	50. B (1-25)	60. A (3-4)

Section 3: Business Judgment

61. B	66. D	71. B	76. E	81. D
62. C	67. A	72. B	77. B	82. C
63. B	68. A	73. A	78. A	83. C
64. B	69. D	74. E	79. E	84. E
65. A	70. D	75. E	80. B	85. A

ANSWER KEY FOR PRACTICE TEST 2 (continued)

Section 4: Data Sufficiency

86. B	92. C	98. B	104. B	110. C
87. E	93. B	99. C	105. B	111. E
88. E	94. C	100. E	106. E	112. B
89. A	95. C	101. A	107. D	113. E
90. D	96. D	102. B	108. A	114. A
91. A	97. B	103. E	109. A	115. D

Section 5: Grammar and Usage

116. A	121. B	126. C	131. B	136. E
117. B	122. E	127. A	132. C	137. D
118. A	123. C	128. C	133. A	138. D
119. D	124. A	129. C	134. C	139. B
120. B	125. B	130. D	135. C	140. C

Section 6: Business Judgment

141. B	146. B	151. B	156. D	161. A
142. B	147. B	152. A	157. A	162. B
143. D	148. E	153. B	158. B	163. B
144. E	149. E	154. A	159. A	164. D
145. B	150. E	155. E	160. D	165. A

Section 7: Reading Comprehension

166. D	171. E	176. A	181. B	186. D
167. B	172. A	177. C	182. A	187. A
168. E	173. E	178. B	183. E	188. C
169. E	174. D	179. D	184. C	189. E
170. C	175. D	180. E	185. C	190. C

Section 8: Error Recognition

191. G	198. O	205. G	212. O	219. G
192. V	199. G	206. D	213. V	220. G
193. D	200. D	207. V	214. G	221. V
194. D	201. O	208. D	215. G	222. D
195. O	202. G	209. D	216. D	223. O
196. G	203. V	210. V	217. O	224. G
197. D	204. O	211. D	218. V	225. G

EXPLANATORY ANSWERS FOR PRACTICE TEST 2

Section 1: Reading Recall

1. **(E)** See paragraph 6: "Adam Smith still speaks to us..."

2. **(A)** In 1776, *The Wealth of Nations*, by Adam Smith, was published, in which, for the first time, the principles of capitalism were voiced, Also, see paragraph 6: "Adam Smith still speaks to us from the platform to the Right..."

3. **(B)** Malthus believed that the world's population was increasing in geometric progression (2, 4, 8, 16, 32...), while the world's food supply was increasing in an arithmetic progression (1, 2, 3, 4, 5...). At some time in the future, the food supply will be insufficient for the population, according to Malthus.

4. **(A)** See paragraph 3: "Unlike the socialists..."

5. **(E)** See paragraph 1: "If Russia or China were not there..."

6. **(C)** See paragraph 3: "Hence we are asked to ensure... laws."

7. **(E)** See paragraph 2: "The Marxists extol the inevitability of history..."

8. **(C)** See paragraph 2: "...the socialists ask us to join them in shaping history..."

9. **(D)** See paragraph 4: "...liberal means are incompatible with the essence of a market economy itself."

10. **(A)** See paragraph 6: "We can distinguish the voice of John Stuart Mill in the words of the socialists..."

11. **(B)** See paragraph 1: "...the economic role of the black woman in America remains more severely limited by discrimination... than that of any other major group."

12. **(C)** See paragraph 6: "... for women ... 25 to 34, 57 per cent of black women in this group work, compared with 41 per cent of white women.

13. **(D)** See paragraph 9: "... a constant fight against deprivation. This has contributed to a strength of purpose and responsibility among black women that makes them disproportionately success-oriented. Black women are *doers*."

14. **(A)** See paragraph 12: "A more demanding task will be to find ways to develop the resources represented by hundreds of thousands of black women who have recently entered American corporations in lower-level positions."

15. **(D)** See paragraph 7: "... black women... play an economic role central to the survival of their families, alongside their husbands..." Then see paragraph 8: "... black women ... are the ... beneficiaries of a form of sexual egalitarianism... not shared by most white women."

16. **(D)** See paragraph 10: "The indicators of the black woman's movement upward in the labor market are strong. The number of nonwhite women in professional and technical occupations about doubled in the 1960's. Average educational attainment of nonwhite women rose spectacularly during the last two decades and is now very close to the white... average."

17. **(D)** See paragraph 12: "Drawing upon the talents of black women who are trained to be executives, should be fairly easy for a business world that is going to find itself pressed hard by government to do just that."

18. **(A)** See paragraph 13: "If business treats these women on the same kind of

timetable as white women, it will be decades before even a modest movement up the promotional ladder can be achieved."

19. **(B)** See paragraph 11: "... the most interesting finding... was that black coeds were far more likely than whites to choose job-oriented college courses (steering away from the humanities)..."

20. **(E)** See paragraph 3: "... the "typical black" woman worker is still to be found among the thousands who line up... to get to their jobs as maids, laundresses, and baby nurses in whites' homes."

21. **(B)** See the first paragraph: "Many people who are willing to concede that the railroad must be brought back to life are chiefly thinking of bringing this about... by treating speed as the only important factor..."

22. **(D)** See the fourth paragraph: "The prime purpose of passenger transportation is not to increase the amount of physical movement but to increase the possibilities for human association, coperation, personal intercourse and choice."

23. **(E)** See paragraph 6: "... "The current introduction of shopping malls... is a ...far better *technical* solution than the many costly proposals for introducing moving-sidewalks or other rigidly automated modes of locomotion."

24. **(A)** See the next to last paragraph: "With the over-exploitation of the motor car comes an increased demand... to endow the petroleum magnates... with fabulous capacites for personal luxury..."

25. **(C)** See the next to last paragraph: "With the over-exploitation of the motor car comes an increased demand... to roll ever wider carpets of concrete over the bulldozed landscape..."

26. **(B)** See the last paragraph: "... If indeed we go farther and faster along this route, there is plenty of evidence to show that the shop will close up without our help."

27. **(A)** See paragraph 6: "If we took human needs seriously... we should make the fullest use of pedestrian movement..."

28. **(C)** See paragraph 5: "... Variety of choices, facilities, and destinations, not speed alone, is the mark of an organic transportation system."

29. **(B)** Judging from the time-perspective of the author, and the more general nature of the article, Choice B would be the best answer.

30. **(C)** See paragraph 5: "... And [variety] is an important factor of safety when any part of the system breaks down."

EXPLANATORY ANSWERS FOR PRACTICE TEST 2 (continued)

Section 2: Math Ability

31. **(A)** The car traveled 3890 minus 3740 or 150 miles on half a tank. Since the car goes 15 miles on one gallon, it traveled these 150 miles on about 10 gallons. This is half the tank. The tank can hold 20 gallons.

32. **(C)** Let x represent the price of the dress originally. Then: $x - 20\%x$, or $x - \frac{1}{5}x$, or $\frac{4}{5}x$ represents the price of the dress after the first reduction and $\frac{4}{5}x - 10\%\left(\frac{4}{5}x\right)$, or $\frac{4}{5}x - \left(\frac{1}{10} \cdot \frac{4}{5}\right)x$, or $\frac{18}{25}x$ represents the price now.

$$\frac{18}{25}x = \$18.00$$
$$x = \$25.00$$

33. **(E)** Average speed = distance traveled ÷ time of travel. Distance traveled = $100 - 12 = 88$ miles. Time traveling equals 80 minutes (the difference between the time of departing from B, 9:20, and the time of arrival at C, 10:40). 80 minutes equals $\frac{4}{3}$ hour, so the speed in miles per hour equals $88 \div (\frac{4}{3}) = 66$ miles per hour.

34. **(D)** The insurance company reimburses the store for two-fifths of the stolen merchandise which represents a tenth of the total inventory. Therefore the insurance company reimburses the store for $\frac{1}{10} \times \frac{2}{5}$ or $\frac{1}{25}$ of the total inventory.

$5150 represents $\frac{1}{25}$ of the total inventory. The value of the total inventory is $\dfrac{\$5150}{\frac{1}{25}}$ or $128,750.

35. **(B)** Working 40 regular hours a week for 4 weeks, or 160 hours, he would earn $160 \times$ $2.40 or $384. Since he earns $432, then $432 - $384 or $48 would come from working overtime. Since he is paid $3.20 per hour overtime, he works for $48 ÷ $3.20 or 15 hours of overtime. Therefore, he works a total of $160 + 15$ or 175 hours.

36. **(C)** 3000 pens = $(3000 \div 12)$ dozen = 250 dozen. At a price of $1 per dozen, this comes to $250. But then a 15% discount is allowed, so the final cost is only $250 - (.15)(\$250) = (.85)(\$250) = \$212.50$

37. **(C)** On the average, he pays 35¢ for a gallon of gas. For $3.50 he can buy 10 gallons. Since each gallon takes him 15 miles, he can go a total of $10 \cdot 15$ or 150 miles.

38. **(A)** We let x = number of pounds of nectarines needed. Therefore, $15 - x$ pounds of peaches must also be in the mixture. From the statement of the problem:

$$.25(15 - x) + .35x = .33(15) = 4.95$$

giving:

$$.10x = 1.20 \quad \text{or} \quad x = 12$$

Therefore, 12 pounds of nectarines are needed.

39. **(B)** According to the graph, the value of conveyors produced in 1966 was about 540 million dollars, while hoists were valued at about 290 million dollars. This is a difference of 250 million dollars.

40. **(C)** The value in the *year* 1966 was about $780 million and the value in 1965 was $650 million. The difference is $130 million. At first glance it might appear that 1958–1959 showed the largest increase but the difference there is only about $100 million. The reason the line is steepest there is that the scale is not uniform.

41. **(A)** The floor is 12 feet 10 inches by 10 feet 1 inch or 154 inches by 121 inches. In order to cover the floor with only whole tiles, the length of a side of the square tile must divide into both 154 inches and 121 inches exactly. The largest possible length is 11 inches.

42. **(B)** Let x = number of hours X worked. Then $x + 5$ is the number of hours Y worked.
$$40(x + 5) = 45x$$
$$40x + 200 = 45x$$
$$5x = 200$$
$$x = 40$$

43. **(D)** Let x = original number of boys. Let y = original number of girls.
$$\frac{x}{y} = \frac{5}{3}$$
$$3x = 5y$$
After 10 boys left the ratio is 1 to 1 or the same number of boys and girls,
$$x - 10 = y$$
By substitution, $3x = 5(x - 10) = 5x - 50$
$$2x = 50$$
$$x = 25$$
$$y = 15$$
Therefore, there were originally $25 + 15$ or 40 people at the party.

44. **(D)** The graph at the bottom tells us that in 1967 25% of families were in the $7,000–$9,999 bracket. 25% of 200 is 50.

45. **(C)** In 1953, $5200 1967 dollars were the same as $4200 current dollars. The ratio of the value is 5200:4200 or reduced, 26:21.

46. **(C)** From the lower graph we see that in 1951, 27% earned less than $3000 and 27% earned $3000–$4999. This adds up to 54%. The remaining 46% earned more than $5000.

47. **(C)** We draw a line from point c parallel to the base of the Marketing majors vertex. It intersects the left side of the large triangle at about the 40% mark.

48. **(B)** Point b has the greatest vertical distance from the base of the vertex of the Finance majors.

49. **(A)** If ⅖ of all workers are unskilled laborers, $1 - ⅖$ or ⅗ of all workers are not unskilled laborers. ⅗ = 60%.

50. **(B)** When the farmer sells the cows for $3000, he is receiving $250 per cow. Since he bought each cow for $210, his profit is $40 per cow. Profit divided by original price will give the percentage profit per cow. $\frac{\$40}{\$210} = \frac{4}{21} = .19 = 19\%$

51. **(C)** He earned $8000 the first year and $9600 the second year. He earned $1600 more and the percent of increase was 20%.

52. **(B)** The first year, he spent 15% of $8000 or $1200. The second year, he spent 18% of $9600 or $1728. He spent $1728 − $1200 or $528 more.

53. **(E)** Call the number of bookshelves which the man had originally x. Then his total original number of books was $80x$. After he added new bookshelves there were $x + 3$ bookshelves, but with only $80 - 30$, or 50 books on each one. The number of books, $50(x + 3)$ is still the same and an equation can be set up:
$$80x = 50(x + 3)$$
$$80x = 50x + 150$$
$$30x = 150$$
$$x = 5$$
If there were 5 bookshelves originally, then there were 80×5, or 400 books.

54. **(B)** Let x, $x+1$, and $x+2$ represent the consecutive integers. Their sum,
$3x + 3 = 210$. $x = 69$ and $x + 1 = 70$.
The product of 69 and 70 is 4830.

55. **(E)** $\frac{a}{c} = \frac{3}{4}$ and $\frac{b}{c} = \frac{5}{6}$
Since $\frac{a}{c} \div \frac{b}{c} = \frac{a}{c} \times \frac{c}{b} = \frac{a}{b}$,
$$\frac{a}{b} = \frac{3}{4} \div \frac{5}{6} = \frac{3}{4} \times \frac{6}{5} = \frac{9}{10}.$$

56. **(B)** Since the average speed for the first 231 miles is 42 mph, it takes him $^{231}/_{42}$ or $5\frac{1}{2}$ hours to cover the first 231 miles. In order to finish the trip in 8 hours, he must drive the rest of the trip in $8 - 5\frac{1}{2}$ or $2\frac{1}{2}$ hours.

$$\text{Average speed} = \frac{360 - 231}{2\frac{1}{2}}$$
$$= 129 \times \frac{2}{5}$$
$$= 51.6 \text{ mph}$$

57. **(C)** If $x = \frac{(p+2)}{8}$ is a whole number, then $(p + 2)$ must be divisible by 8. Since p falls between 16 and 35, the only values of p which satisfy the condition are 22 and 30 (in other words, the only values for $p + 2$ are 24 and 32). Since there are only two acceptable values of p, there are correspondingly two possible integral values of x.

58. **(D)** Divide the trapezoid into recognizable figures. The sum of the areas of these figures is equal to the sum of the entire trapezoid.

    First drop perpendiculars from E and F to points on line DG which we will call X and Y. Therefore FYG and EXD are 2 congruent right triangles (They are congruent because 2 corresponding angles and sides are equal.) In a right triangle which has an angle of 30°, the side opposite the 30° angle is equal to half the hypotenuse. Therefore FY is equal to $\frac{1}{2}$ of 12, or 6. The area of rectangle $EFYX$ is base times height; $(3)(6) = 18$.

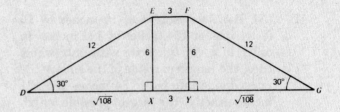

Now let's find the areas of the triangles. Since they are congruent, the area of one will equal the area of the other. Use the Pythagorean Theorem to find YG. $(6)^2 + (YB)^2 = (12)^2$. $36 + s^2 = 144$.
$$s^2 = 108$$
$$s = \sqrt{108}$$
To find the area of a right triangle, multiply the legs and divide by 2. The area of triangle FYG (and DEX) is $\frac{1}{2}(6)(\sqrt{108}) = 3\sqrt{108}$.

The area of the trapezoid is equal to the sum of the areas of rectangle $EFYX$, triangle FYG, and triangle DEX. This equals $18 + 2(3\sqrt{108})$. ($\sqrt{108} = (\sqrt{36})(\sqrt{3}) = 6\sqrt{3}$.)
The total area is $18 + 6\sqrt{108}$ or $18 + 36\sqrt{3}$.

59. **(B)** The sides of the bottom are all 3. Therefore the dimensions of rectangles must be 8 by 3. The volume is then $3 \cdot 3 \cdot 8$ or 72.

60. **(A)** If m equals 1 then the sides of the triangle would be 1, 3, and 4. This is impossible since $1 + 3 = 4$. For any triangle, the sum of the lengths of two sides must be *greater* than the third side.

EXPLANATORY ANSWERS FOR PRACTICE TEST 2 (continued)

Section 3: Business Judgment

61. **(B)** The excellent background and experience of Mr. Callan was a major factor for Callan and Krover in making the decision to open the retail store.

62. **(C)** The firm's policy of leasing the stores to selected individuals enabled Callan and Krover to consider leasing the store. Therefore, the leasing of stores to selected individuals is a minor factor. It is not a major factor because it does not fall into the class of the important considerations for opening the store.

63. **(B)** Mr. Krover's inheritance of $50,000 enabled Callan and Krover to open the store. It was a major factor because $50,000 was the amount of capital needed to do an adequate amount of business the first year.

64. **(B)** Mr. Krover believed that the terms of the lease were very attractive. Therefore, we can assume that this was incentive enough for him to consider pursuing the project.

65. **(A)** Mr Krover was given a period of thirty days to make up his mind about taking the lease. Thus he had to make a decision whether or not to take the lease before thirty-one days.

66. **(D)** This is a major assumption since Mr. Krover had no experience in the furniture business and only believed that he had the ability to learn the business in a relatively short period.

67. **(A)** Mr. Callan believed that they should specialize in high-grade home furnishings. Thus this was a major objective.

68. **(A)** The planned stock distribution in Schedule I shows major furniture comprising of 50% of the total stock.

69. **(D)** Mr. Krover's *assumption* was that he may sell $200,000 worth of merchandise the first year. He does not state this sale as an *objective* especially because the budget is created with $100,000 - not $200,000 - worth of sales in mind.

70. **(D)** Mr. Callan and Mr. Krover prepared what they considered to be an adequate budget. Mr. Callan used a previous budget, from a previous firm, as a model for their own budget. He did not investigate how the needs of his previous firm may have differed from the needs of his potential store, thus possibly warranting two very different budgets.

71. **(B)** Mr. Callan called on a number of furniture manufacturers and was assured that the partnership could secure a representative list of major brand furniture items. This assurance was a major factor in Callan's and Krover's decision to open up the furniture store.

72. **(B)** Mr. Krover and Mr. Callan decided that the area in which the store was located was a growing one. They had obtained the number of homes that had been constructed in the past five years and other information relevant to the location of the store. Thus the location of the store was a major factor in Krover's and Callan's decision to open up the store.

73. **(A)** The planned profit of 6% of sales was a major objective since it was part of the planned budget. *Planned* is a keyword here since *planned profit* is an objective whereas *profit* alone may have been an assumption as in question 69 (see above).

74. **(E)** The inability of Mr. Callan to invest any capital was unimportant since

Mr. Krover had enough capital to open up the store.

75. **(E)** Mr. Krover's college degree in chemistry was an unimportant issue. However, it did give him the opportunity to work as a salesman for a large chemical firm, which led to his acceptance of a position as salesman with a large real estate firm and this subsequently led to his interest in opening up a retail store. But the college degree in chemistry, alone, was an unimportant issue.

76. **(E)** The unsuccessful attempt of the real estate company to get one of the downtown stores to open a branch allowed Krover and Callan to compete for the lease. This was, however, already resolved and not contributory to their decision.

77. **(B)** Mr. Krover's desire to go into business for himself or with a partner was a major factor in his opening the retail store. Note that *desire* to go into business could not be an objective. However, if the statement were worded "owner-operated business," it could be an objective.

78. **(A)** The formation of a partnership in the retail furniture store was a major objective of the decision makers.

79. **(E)** Mr. Krover's inexperience in the furniture business is an irrelevant issue since he was making a decision already knowing that he was inexperienced. As far as the business prospering, his inexperience would be a factor. But we are not concerned with the business prospering — we are concerned with the factors that influenced Mr. Krover in arriving at his decision.

80. **(B)** The assurance of the granting of exclusive rights to sell furniture, appliances, etc., was an important consideration because competition would be minimized as a result.

81. **(D)** Mr. Callan was paid a salary of $600 per month or $7,200 per year. He earned a total of $15,000 per year. $15,000 — $7,200 = $7,800. Thus, Mr. Callan earned $7,800 in commissions for the year.

82. **(C)** According to Schedule III, each partner earns $5,000 in salaries and $3,000 in profits, totaling $8,000.

83. **(C)** The parking facilities behind the store were ample, so I is incorrect. There was an important city boulevard, on which city busses passed at regular intervals, so II is incorrect. The downtown section of the city had six large furniture stores and five department stores which sold furniture. These firms were established. Therefore these stores would be competitive with Krover's and Callan's store. Thus III is correct.

84. **(E)** Mr. Callan told Mr. Krover that he believed that they should specialize in high grade home furnishings and attempt to build a reputation as "interior decorators."

85. **(A)** Mr. Krover's attitude toward business would be deemed as optimistic and uncritical. He was generally optimistic about the store. Specifically, he was optimistic when he said that he did not feel that there was any reason why they couldn't sell $200,000 during the first year. He was uncritical in saying that the $200,000 sales would double their profits. It is not necessarily true that twice the sales doubles the profits since other variables are involved when sales increase by that amount. For example, if they sold $200,000 of merchandise, they might need much more storage space, which could reduce their profit percentage.

EXPLANATORY ANSWERS FOR PRACTICE TEST 2 (continued)

Section 4: Data Sufficiency

86. **(B)** Using the data contained in statement (2) we can write the proportion

$$\frac{x}{2} = \frac{\$3.00}{10}$$

where x represents the cost of two pounds of apples. By cross-multiplying, we can obtain an equation which can be solved for x.
Statement (1) provides no useful information.

87. **(E)** We know, from simple geometry, that

$$s + t + p + r = 360$$

Statements (1) and (2) provide us with the values of s and t. In order to find the value of r, we must still be given the value of p. The given data is insufficient.

88. **(E)** The two statements tell us how many tenors there are and the number of altos plus sopranos. However, in order to calculate now the number of basses in the chorus, we must know how many singers there are in the entire chorus. This information is not provided.

89. **(A)** Let Y be the number of cars in the train. There will be $(Y - 1)$ two-foot separations. The total length of the train will be

$$18\,Y + 2\,(\,Y - 1\,).$$

If we set this equal to 118 feet, using statement (1), we have an equation which can be solved for Y.
  Statement (2) is of little use here since we do not know the speed at which the train was traveling.

90. **(D)** Distance = Rate $\times$ Time. Using statement (1) we can write

$$28 \text{ miles} = 8\,\frac{\text{miles}}{\text{hour}} \times \text{T}$$

Thus

$$\text{T} = \frac{28}{8}\,\text{hour}$$

Statement (2) could also be used since

$$\frac{12 \text{ miles}}{1\frac{1}{2} \text{ hours}} = 8\,\frac{\text{miles}}{\text{hour}}$$

Thus, we see that statement (2) provides the same information as statement (1).

91. **(A)** The two triangles are of equal height. Statement (1) tells us that the triangles have equal bases. Thus, the desired ratio is 1 since the areas (base $\times$ height $\times \frac{1}{2}$) are equal.
Statement (2) does not provide useful information.

92. **(C)** Statement (1) provides us with the volume of a sample and statement (2) provides us with its weight. To find the density we need only divide the weight by the volume.

93. **(B)** Statement (1) is not helpful since non-square rectangles can have square areas: for example, a rectangle 2 by 8. Statement (2) is helpful, since a rhombus is a parallelogram with equal sides. Thus, a rectangle that is a rhombus is a square.

94. **(C)** Using the two statements we can see that 5 television sets are on sale for $1000. This means that each set is now priced at $200. From this information we can calculate the percent discount from the original price of $250.

95. **(C)** The first and second statements tell us that GD = FD = 2 inches. This information is enough to enable us to

answer the question posed. Side GF is not 5 inches long since it is impossible to have a triangle with sides of length 2, 2, and 5. In a triangle, the sum of the lengths of any two sides must be greater than the length of the third side.

96. **(D)** If a number is divisible by 4, it must be divisible by 2. Similarly, if a number is divisible by 9 it must be divisible by 3. Thus, statement (1) tells us that z is divisible by both 2 and 3. If a number is divisible by both 2 and 3, it must be divisible by their product, 6.

Statement (2) also provides us with an answer to the question. A number divisible by 12 is also divisible by the factors of twelve. 6 is a factor of twelve.

97. **(B)** Statement (1) is of little help in solving the problem since we do not know how quickly Joseph walks.

Statement (2) can be used to find the answer. 1 mile is 5280 feet. To find the number of blocks, merely divide 5280 by 330.

98. **(B)** Since OA and OB are radii of the same circle, they are of equal length and the triangle is isosceles. Thus, Angle OAB = Angle OBA. Statement (2) tells us that Angle AOB = 30°

$$\angle OAB + \angle AOB + \angle OBA = 180°$$
Substituting we get

$$\angle OAB + 30° + \angle OAB = 180°$$
which can be solved to give us the measure of $\angle OAB$.

The length of OA as provided by statement (1) is not helpful in solving this problem.

99. **(C)** By using the data from both statements we can calculate the amount of apple juice produced. There are 180 × 240 × 1 cups of juice and 16 cups per gallon.

100. **(E)** Statement (1) provides us with the sum of the marks. In order to find

the average, it is necessary to know the number of people in the class. This information is not provided, and the data given in statement (2) is of no aid.

101. **(A)** The first statement provides enough information. The square of Y must be between 100 and 999 so Y must be between 10 and 31. Y must therefore have two digits.
Statement (2) gives insufficient data. If 2Y is between 10 and 99, Y is between 5 and 49 and can have 1 or 2 digits.

102. **(B)** The average yearly increase can be calculated by using the data of statement (2): divide $620 by 5.

Statement (1) does not help us solve the problem.

103. **(E)** The two statements tell us the total number of secretaries and the number of tea drinkers. We still need to know the number of coffee drinkers to answer the question.

104. **(B)** The information provided in statement (2) is enough to solve the problem. In any triangle, the line joining the midpoints of two sides is one — half the length of the third side. Thus, AC is twice 5 inches.

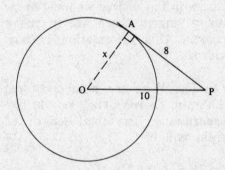

105. **(B)** Ignore segment OB and construct OA, a radius of the circle. Triangle OAP is a right triangle. Since we know the length of OP and AP from statement (2), we can use the Pythagorean Theorem to find the length of OA.

106. **(E)** The two statements do not give enough data. The width of the widest river could be anywhere from 714 to 1560 yards.

107. **(D)** The initial statement can be written algebraically:

Let J represent the number of marbles Jim has.

Let H represent the number of marbles Harry has.

Let F represent the number of marbles Fred has.

Given: $J + H + F = 58$

Statement (1) says
$$F = 2J - 5 , H = J + 3$$

These expressions for F and H can be substituted into the equation $J + H + F = 58$ and we obtain an equation in J:

$$J + (2J - 5) + (J + 3) = 58.$$

This can be solved for J. Once we have the value of J, we can find the value of F from $F = 2J - 5$

Statement (2) says

$$F = H + 7 , J = F - 10.$$

The first expression can be rewritten as
$$H = F - 7$$
Again we can substitute these expressions into the original equation and eventually solve for F.

108. **(A)** From 8 P.M. to 4 A.M. is 8 hours. To get the average speed, merely divide 100 miles by 8 hours. Statement (2) is of no aid.

109. **(A)** From the radius of the circle, we can calculate the total area:
$$\text{Area} = \pi R^2 = \pi (18)^2$$
The area of the shaded

portion is $\dfrac{30}{360}$ of the total area.

Statement (2) provided no new information. It is the same as saying that the radius is 18.

110. **(C)** Statement (1) tells us that each

cubic inch of liquid B weighs $\dfrac{96}{20}$ ounces.

Statement (2) tells us that 144 cubic inches (one cubic foot) of liquid A weighs 635 ounces. Thus, one cubic inch

of liquid A weighs $\dfrac{635}{144}$ ounces. By comparing these two fractions, we can decide which liquid weighs more.

111. **(E)** The two statements provide two unrelated bits of data. With this data, it is not possible to answer the question.

112. **(B)** Distance = Rate × Time. From the information provided in statement (2), we can find the length of the track. We know the average rate is 160 MPH and we know the average time. Their product, after appropriate unit conversions, is the distance.

113. **(E)** The area of a triangle is one-half the product of the base and the height. TC is the height of the triangle but its corresponding base is AR. The data given tells us the length of TR, not AR, so we cannot use this information to find the length of TC.

114. **(A)** From basic geometry we know that
Angle E + angle W + angle R = 180°
Statement (1) says
2(angle E) − (angle W + angle R) = 90°
Adding these two equations together we get
3(angle E) = 270°
Angle E = 90°
Statement (2) does not help us answer the question.

115. **(D)** From statement (1) we have
$(3z - 1) + (z + 5) + (4z - 2) = 26$
This is an equation that can be solved for z.
From statement (2) we have
$$3z - 1 = z + 5$$
This too is an equation that can be solved for z.

EXPLANATORY ANSWERS FOR PRACTICE TEST 2 (continued)

Section 5: Grammar and Usage

116. **(A)** "The reason *she* and her cousin . . ."
The subject form of the personal pronoun is *she*—not *her*.

117. **(B)** "Though Seaver pitched *really* well . . ."
The adverb *well* must be modified by another adverb such as *really*—not by an adjective such as *real*.

118. **(A)** "Jim and *he* . . . finally discovered . . ."
Jim and *he* are the compound subjects of the verb *discovered*. The subject form of the pronoun is *he*—not *him*.

119. **(D)** ". . . the *more* effective and moving."
In a comparison of two things (such as two plays), we use the comparative degree *(more)*—not the superlative degree *(most)*.

120. **(B)** "Each of the hotel's 500 rooms *was* equipped . . ."
The singular subject *(Each)* requires a singular verb *(was equipped*—not *were equipped)*.

121. **(B)** "A textbook . . . usually contains . . ."
One cannot use the two words *usually* and *always* together because one word contradicts the other. *Usually* means almost all the time; *always* means all the time.

122. **(E)** All underlined parts are correct.

123. **(C)** ". . . than were *their* parents . . ."
The possessive adjective *their* modifies the noun *parents*. The contraction *they're* means *they are*.

124. **(A)** "The sun *had hardly* set . . ."
The expression *hadn't hardly* is always incorrect.

125. **(B)** "The lilacs . . . smell *sweet* . . ."
We use the predicate adjective *(sweet)* after the copulative verb *(smell)*. The use of the adverb *sweetly* is incorrect in this case.

126. **(C)** ". . . to *whoever* is best qualified."
Since the underlined word is the subject of the subordinate clause, *whoever* (the nomina-

tive form) must be used. *Whomever* is the objective form.

127. **(A)** "*Since* the United States has a food surplus . . ."
Being that is always incorrect for *since* or *because*.

128. **(C)** ". . . factory morale, *already* low . . ."
All ready means everybody (is) ready. The adverb *already* modifying the adjective *low* is correct here.

129. **(C)** "A series of debates . . . *was* scheduled . . ."
Series is a collective noun with a feeling of singularity. As a singular subject, it takes a singular verb *(was scheduled)*.

130. **(D)** ". . . neither outstanding *nor* attractive."
The correlative conjunctions are *neither . . . nor*—not *neither . . . or*.

131. **(B)** "We did the job as *well* as we could . . ."
The adverb *well* must be used to modify the verb *did*. The adjective *good* is incorrect for such modification.

132. **(C)** ". . . *who's* to decide . . .
The interrogative pronoun-adjective *whose* should not be used here. We mean: *who is (who's)*.

133. **(A)** "If I *had had* more time . . ."
In a contrary to fact condition in the past, the "if clause" must have a past perfect subjunctive form *(had had)*.

134. **(C)** "More leisure . . . *is* attainable . . ."
Since the subject *(leisure)* is singular, the verb must be singular *(is attainable)*.

135. **(C)** ". . . *they* can cause irreparable damage."
We have a plural subject: *Morphine* and *drugs*. Accordingly, the pronoun which occurs later in the sentence must be plural *(they)* since a pronoun must agree with its antecedent in number.

136. **(E)** All underlined parts are correct.

137. **(D)** "... we cannot hope that nations ... *will live* peaceably with us."
The clause beginning with *that nations ...* requires a finite verb *(will live)*—not an infinitive *(to live)*.

138. **(D)** "... she would very much have liked *to go*." A present infinitive *(to go)* — not a past infinitive *(to have gone)* is used after a verb which is in the perfect tense *(would have liked)*.

139. **(B)** "... *is* now aware of ..."
A compound subject *(man, woman, and child)* which is introduced by *every* must have a singular verb *(is now aware* — not *are* now aware).

140. **(C)** "... because it *stank* so."
The past tense of the verb *stink* is *stank* — not *stunk*. The present perfect tense, however, is *has stunk*.

EXPLANATORY ANSWERS FOR PRACTICE TEST 2 (continued)

Section 6: Business Judgment

141. **(B)** The facts that the product was the only product of its kind on the market and the nearest competition was a dental recap job which cost hundreds of dollars, led Burton to consider developing the marketing of the product. Thus the nature of competitive products on the market is a major factor in Burton's arrival at a decision.

142. **(B)** The low retail price per unit is a major factor in the consideration to market the unit since the closest competitor charges hundreds of dollars for a dental recap job.

143. **(D)** This is a major assumption since Burton feels that there would be ample time in which to determine the value of the property.

144. **(E)** This is an unimportant issue since the locality of the manufacturing facilities is not directly relevant to the situation.

145. **(B)** This is a major factor in Burton's making the decision as to whether to take the option to forge ahead or to drop the product.

146. **(B)** Burton believed that if the failure to earn a profit was due only to the high missionary costs, he could hope to realize future profits when his product had wider acceptance. Thus the failure to earn a profit due to the high missionary costs is a major factor affecting Burton's decision.

147. **(B)** This is a major factor because if the failure to earn a profit was due to the high cost of selective distribution, Burton would refuse his option of buying the product.

148. **(E)** The unwillingness of American Laboratories to invest more money in promoting the product was an unimportant issue in *Burton's* decision to market the product.

149. **(E)** This is an unimportant issue since it is of minor importance where the geographical location of the dental recap industries is.

150. **(E)** American Laboratories is "out of the picture" concerning Burton's decision to market the product. Therefore, this item is an unimportant issue.

151. **(B)** The high cost of dental recap jobs was a major factor in Burton's decision to market the product. This is because the low cost of Burton's product would allow Burton to compete favorably with the closest competitor.

152. **(A)** One of the main problems with the product was that many original purchasers did not buy the product a second time. Thus, one of Burton's major objectives was to encourage original purchasers to buy the product again.

153. **(B)** Since Burton was just about able to meet costs, the price of the property was a major factor in Burton's arriving at a decision.

154. **(A)** A major problem was that Burton was just about able to meet costs. Thus Burton's ability to meet costs is a major objective.

155. **(E)** This is an unimportant issue since Burton already decided to consider the product and his present decision is not affected by a previous situation concerning American Laboratories.

156. **(D)** Burton *believed* that when he could get a larger volume of business, both his product costs and his shipping costs could be reduced to 40 cents per unit.

157. **(A)** Burton's decision whether or not to purchase the product before six months was a major objective because he was given the option to buy within a period of six months.

158. **(B)** This is a major factor since the features of the product account for why Burton believes the product is the only product of its kind on the market.

159. **(A)** A sound marketing policy was a major objective of Burton. He wanted to institute a sound policy so that he may determine whether or not it was worthwhile for him to buy the product from American Laboratories.

160. **(D)** Burton increased the retail price from $1 to $2.50. Thus Policy II is correct. Burton allowed a "20 percent-off-invoice" appropriation for local advertising purposes. Thus Policy III is correct. Direct mail distribution was contemplated for the near future. Thus Policy I is incorrect.

161. **(A)** When Burton was able to attain a larger volume of business, he believed that his product and shipping costs could be reduced to 40 cents per unit. According to Schedule I, costs of product and shipping were 50 cents per unit. Thus 50 cents — 40 cents = 10 cents.

162. **(B)** The profit per unit is $0.08. The retail price of the unit is $2.50. Dividing $2.50 by $0.08 will give us the number of units that Burton will have to sell to make a profit equal to the retail price of the unit. This number is $31\frac{1}{4}$ which is closest to 31.

163. **(B)** Since the administration expense per unit is 15 cents and the beauty consultant service cost per unit is 10 cents, administration costs and beauty consultant service costs are in a ratio of 15 to 10. Therefore, if administration expenses are $15,000, beauty consultant services must be $10,000.

164. **(D)** Burton discovered that in most cases the reason why purchasers did not become repeaters was because the purchasers did not follow the directions for use of the product exactly. Therefore the directions for use of the product may have not been clear or simple enough.

165. **(A)** What primarily interested Burton in the product was that it was the only product of its kind on the market. Therefore, Choice A is correct. Although Choices B, C, D, and E may have indeed been reasons for Burton's interest, they were not primary reasons.

EXPLANATORY ANSWERS FOR PRACTICE TEST 2 (continued)

Section 7: Reading Comprehension

166. **(D)** The correct answer is Choice D, which is stated in lines 36-38. Choice A cannot be the answer because, although a protein was modified, no protein was replaced in the organism in this passage. Choices B and C can be eliminated because no such statements were made. Choice E is wrong because it is contradictory to the investigators' findings stated in lines 36-38 (and contradictory to the correct Choice D).

167. **(B)** We are told that a tyrosine (Tyr) residue occurs in two positions, which are 2 and 30 (lines 11-13), and later the article uses the notations Tyr^2 and Tyr^{30} (lines 25-29). Consideration of both these passages allows one to make the proper assumption and to pick the correct answer, Choice B. Choice A contradicts the passage, which states that the protein had sometimes one and sometimes two tyrosine residues, depending on the organism (lines 11-13). Choice C is a bad choice because it gives an incomplete truth, leaving the superscript in the notation unexplained. Choice D is not the answer since the notation system is used regardless of whether the residue has been modified or not (lines 25-29). Choice E is not the answer because the reader is introduced to no computations.

168. **(E)** All the answers can be inferred from the passage; therefore, Choice E is correct. Choice A can be inferred by the reader in lines 14-16. Choice B was indicated to be true in lines 7-10. Choice C was indicated to be the case in lines 25-29. Choice D can be inferred from lines 17-20, especially the phrase "the other" in line 20.

169. **(E)** None of the answers is indicated in the passage; therefore, Choice E is correct. Choice A is true but is not indicated in the passage. All the others are specifically contraindicated. Choice B is contraindicated by the fact that NMR results were obtained when the protein was oxidized (lines 23-24), as well as when it was reduced (lines 25-29). Choice C is wrong because it is the protein, not the amino acid, which contains two iron-sulfur clusters. Choice D is wrong because 50 mV is treated as worthy of mention while a smaller number (10 mV) is described as insignificant (lines 30-36).

170. **(C)** Choice C is correct because it reflects the overall approach of the experimentors. Lines 20-22 in particular indicate that the residues "reflect" what is happening in the protein. If the reader did not realize the above, he could still have arrived at Choice C by elimination of all the others. Choice A is inappropriate because lines 20-22 state that when reduction occurs it is reflected in the residues. No statement is made that residues cause effects. Similarly, Choice B is wrong because there is no mention of a relationship of causality between the residues and the oxidation-reduction sites (iron-sulfur clusters). Choice D is wrong because the experiment was not carried out for purposes of comparison with other organisms. Instead the experiment was carried out to investigate changes occurring during protein function (lines 1-4). Choice E is wrong because it is peripheral to the main point of the experiment and is treated as an aside when it is mentioned (lines 7-10).

171. **(E)** Choice E is correct because all the others are wrong. Choice A is wrong because it is explained in the text that the iron-sulfur clusters, not the amino acid residues, are the sites of oxidation and reduction (lines 17-19). Choice B is wrong because the result for Phe^2 was like the result for Tyr^2 upon reduction (lines 25-29). The result for Phe^{30} was

different from the result for Tyr² (lines 25-29), and hence different from the result for Phe². Therefore, Phe cannot be said to give any diagnostic result. The concepts in Choices C and D are never raised in the passage; therefore, these Choices are inappropriate.

172. **(A)** Choice A is correct. See lines 60-61: "... as Skinner argues, that one can extrapolate from pigeons to people ..." Choice B is incorrect because, though Skinner agrees that introspection may be of some use (lines 12-15), nowhere does the article indicate that he suggests wide use of the introspective method. Choice C is incorrect since Skinner, so the author says (lines 62-63), "has not satisfactorily rebutted ... rather than scientific." Choice D is incorrect because lines 68-69 state that "... Skinner predicts ... impending disaster." Choice E is incorrect because there is nothing in the passage to indicate this statement. Incidentally, this point of view (Choice E) is held by Noam Chomsky of linguistics fame.

173. **(E)** Choice A is incorrect. See lines 69-to end of passage: "Two key concepts ... not so reassuring." Choice B is incorrect. See lines 9-12: "... an earlier stage of ... influence of mentalism." Choice C is incorrect. See lines 51-54: "It is a veritable ... to external stimuli." Choice D is incorrect since mentalism evolved before methodological and radical behaviorism. See lines 8-14: "What such people ... its possible usefulness." Choice E is correct. The passage, from line 54 to the end, brings out weaknesses in Skinner's presentation.

174. **(D)** Choice D is correct. Skinner, in line 22, says "... few would contend that behavior is 'endlessly malleable'." Also, see lines 29-35: "Contingencies of reinforcement ... likely to occur." In effect, Skinner is saying that behavior cannot always, by plan or design, be altered or influenced; behavior must depend, to some extent, on the element of chance.

175. **(D)** Choice D is correct. Skinner is

known for his experiments with pigeons. Also, rats have been used frequently by behaviorists in experimentation. See lines 55-61. In addition, see lines 31-32: "In both natural ... is crucial." The other choices are not relevant to Darwin or his work.

176. **(A)** Choice A is correct. The word "extrapolate" is derived from the Latin "extra" (outside) and "polire" (to polish). The other choices do not define "extrapolate."

177. **(C)** Choice A is incorrect because Choice A is true according to line 12. Choice B is incorrect because Choice B is true according to lines 55-59. Choice C is correct because Choice C is *not* true according to lines 58-61. Choice D is incorrect because Choice D is true according to lines 8-15. Choice E is incorrect because Choice E is true according to lines 48-51.

178. **(B)** Choice A is incorrect. See lines 16-18: "... to those who object ... Skinner expresses puzzlement." Choice B is correct because Skinner, a radical behaviorist, though believing that environmental influences are highly important in shaping human behavior, nevertheless states in lines 29-32: "Contingencies of reinforcement ... is crucial." Operant conditioning is, according to behaviorists, a vital aspect of learning. Choice C is incorrect. Although Skinner accepts introspection (lines 14-15) as part of his system, nowhere does he place primary importance on introspection. Choice D is incorrect. Though Skinner may agree with this choice, nowhere in the passage does he state or imply this opinion. Choice E is incorrect. The word "malleable" means capable of being shaped or formed — from the Latin "malleare" meaning "to hammer." The quote in the stem of the question says, in effect, that few people would say that behavior can always be shaped.

179. **(D)** Choice A is incorrect. See lines 8-11: "Androgyny does not ... of the Chinese Army." Choices B, C, and E are

incorrect because nowhere in the passage does the author encourage or imply encouragement of such actions so contrary to our mores. Choice D is correct. See the last sentence of the passage: "We may even discover the gentleness of men, the forcefulness of women, and not be afraid."

180. **(E)** Choice A is incorrect. See lines 38-40: "But if, as I believe . . . it will prevail." Choice B is incorrect. The author is merely stating (lines 13-16) that we ought not to be confined to "two accepted role models" (line 13). Choice C is incorrect. The statement of Choice C is contradicted by lines 51-57: "And yet the androgynous ideal . . . of the great novelists." Choice D is incorrect. The author suggests no alteration of current sexual practice. Choice E is correct. See lines 21-24: "For androgyny implies . . . to play those roles."

181. **(B)** The androgynous ideal is expressed in lines 4-6: " . . . unity rather than the necessary separation of what we have come to think of as masculine and feminine qualities." Accordingly, Choice B is correct because Madame Curie is revered as one of history's great scientists — a role we long have associated with the male sex. Choices A, C, D, and E are incorrect because these four women represent society's typical females — sex objects and the weaker sex.

182. **(A)** Choice A is correct. See lines 47-50: "Is androgyny . . . more nearly possible." Choices B, C, D, and E are incorrect because nowhere in the passage does the author show or imply such attitudes.

183. **(E)** Choice E is correct. The thrust of this article is that we should fight against "a sexual polarization in our society that deprives both men and women of their common humanity in relation to one another, and has separated what should have been joined." (lines 30-33) Choices A and B are incorrect because they have nothing to do with this sexual polarization. Choices C and D are incorrect be-

cause the author states in lines 8-9: "Androgyny does not mean the loss of all distinctions. . . . "

184. **(C)** Choice A is incorrect. The author cites earlier periods that were marked by some androgynous feeling but he does not indicate relative strengths of such a feeling. See lines 53-55: " . . . among the Greeks . . . and the Renaissance." Choice B is incorrect. The author refers to the corporation manager and his wife as "clearly delineated sexual models" (line 12) and the author states in lines 11-13: "Those who are terrified . . . all order and sanity." Choice C is correct. See lines 51-55: "And yet . . . Jesus of the Gospels. . . . " Choice D is incorrect because the passage does not state or imply this. Choice E is incorrect. See lines 40-41: "Present at the birth of every religion, submerged or subverted in most religions thereafter. . . . "

185. **(C)** This question tests ability to determine the meaning of a word from context. Consideration of related words (*e.g.*, information) could have aided too. The context, lines 9-16, shows that the person who is asked for information is the informant (line 16). Further context (lines 16-21, especially 16-17) and previous context (lines 3-6) indicate that the informant is probably a native speaker. This choice of answer, while it may be only a guess at first, is strengthened by elimination of the other four choices. Choice D can be eliminated when it is realized that the student is doing the asking (lines 9-10). Choice E can be eliminated upon consideration of lines 15-16, which indicate that the informant is not a good source of knowledge. Choices A and B are ruled out because one would not state about these choices what is stated about the informant (lines 16-21); normally one would consider that these choices are less likely than the others to be misled by the factors stated (lines 16-21).

186. **(D)** Lines 16-21 indicate that conventional education is deficient in something

having to do with language. This is identified over the course of the following two paragraphs, especially in lines 24-25, "... a clear picture of the language ..." and in line 35, "... the system of the language ..." Choices A and C are contraindicated by the author's claim that the literate person is likely to be misinformed or misled about language (lines 16-21). Choice B is inappropriate because the article says nothing of talent squelched by education, nor does it speak of guides in the meaning that this word usually has when it is used alone: a person who shows the way to a newcomer. Choice E is inappropriate because the article never mentions etymology.

187. **(A)** Proposition I is contraindicated by lines 46-51 and by the examples (lines 57-67) which show that position is taken into account in defining phonemes. The truth of Proposition II is indicated in lines 45-51, which state that certain kinds of variation are classified in a single class. Common sense tells us that a single thing, in this case a class of sounds, need not be designated by multiple symbols. The truth of Proposition III is attested by the main point of the passage, which is that spoken speech has a system in it it (lines 34-37). Proposition IV is not true since it has been explained that free variation is a property of parts of a phoneme (lines 52-54) and that parts of a phoneme are by definition not capable of distinguishing meaning (lines 37-46, especially 45-46). Moreover, Proposition IV is not upheld by the examples in line 63. Choice A is correct because it includes both true Propositions. Choices B and D are wrong because they include false Propositions. Choices C and E are wrong because they do not include both true Propositions.

188. **(C)** The passage indicates that the student of linguistics separates speech sounds which distinguish (are distinctive of) meaning from those which do not (lines 37-44). If speech sounds do not distinguish meaning, then they must be socially equivalent (lines 34-37). This is

illustrated by the examples of free variation (lines 57-63). Therefore, Choice C is correct. Choice A is wrong because, even though socially equivalent sounds may be similar, the condition of social equivalence is the non-distinction of meaning, as explained just above. Choice B is incorrect because it is nonsensical in relation to the passage. In the passage, useful distinctions are those which distinguish meaning (lines 34-41), and such sounds cannot be socially equivalent. Moreover, the passage spoke of complementary distribution (lines 46-51), not complementary sounds. Choice D is wrong because the passage depicts allophones only as members of the same phoneme (lines 46-52). Choice E is wrong because, although native speakers may not habitually recognize nondistinctive phonetic differences, nothing in the passage suggests that they cannot recognize them should they be pointed out. Indeed, the author probably would not give his English examples if he believed that his English readers were incapable of recognizing them.

189. **(E)** Choice E is correct because all the others are wrong. Choice A is wrong because nothing is said of allophones' requiring free variation, but rather it is said that free variation may exist between allophones (lines 52-54). Choice B is wrong because it applies to phonetic study (lines 6-8), not phonemic study. Choice C is wrong because phonemic study organizes, not lists, speech sounds (lines 41-44). Choice D is wrong because, in addition to phonetic similarity, non-distinction of meaning is required as a criterion of a phoneme (lines 45-46).

190. **(C)** This answer is given explicitly in the passage (lines 46-51); therefore, Choice C is correct. Choice A is wrong because the criteria given for complementary distribution (lines 46-51) pertain to the distribution of sounds, as well as their similarity. Choice B is wrong because complementary distribution is a feature of the language (lines 46-51), not of the transcription. Choice D is

wrong because it is the sounds that do *not* distinguish meaning which are generally unapprehended by the native speaker (lines 9-10). Moreover, this choice makes little sense, since the pronoun "they" has no clear antecedent. Choice E is wrong because the passage does not state that complementary distribution is required; it only indicates that complementary distribution can occur (lines 46-51).

EXPLANATORY ANSWERS FOR PRACTICE TEST 2 (continued)

Section 8: Error Recognition

191. **(G)** " . . . are Thompson, Steinmetz, and *I*." The predicate nominative form is *I* (not *me*).

192. **(V)** "This gem is *unique*."
Something that is unique is the only one of its kind. You cannot, therefore, use the comparative or superlative degree with unique.

193. **(D)** "becomes enamored *of* . . . "
The preposition *of* (not *about*) should follow *enamored*.

194. **(D)** The poem was full of *allusions* to mythology.
An *illusion* is a false idea, a misconception.
An *allusion* is a reference to something.

195. **(O)** The sentence contains no errors.

196. **(G)** " . . . that *witches* ride on broomsticks." The pronoun *they* must have an antecedent, which is obviously *witchcraft*. But since witchcraft is a singular abstract noun, the plural personal pronoun *they* cannot be used here. Accordingly, we must substitute a noun, such as *witches*, for the pronoun. The word *witches*, of course, has no antecedent because it is a noun. Only pronouns have antecedents.

197. **(D)** . . . "*regardless* of what they would cost us." The word *irregardless* is nonstandard.

198. **(O)** The sentence contains no errors.

199. **(G)** " . . . than *those* of the other girls." We have an improper ellipsis here. The dress that the girl wore was more attractive than the dresses of the other girls — not more attractive than the other girls.

200. **(D)** "The children used colored glass to observe the *eclipse* of the sun."
An *ellipse* is a plane curve formed by a conic section.
An *eclipse* is a partial or complete obscuring. It is highly advisable to use something like colored glass when you are watching the sun's eclipse.

201. **(O)** The sentence contains no errors.

202. **(G)** " . . . *one* will become . . . "
The pronoun *(you)* must agree with its antecedent *(one)* in person, number, and gender. Since *one* is third person and *you* is second person, we have a shift error.

203. **(V)** "Usually the instructor of this class *arrives* . . . "
Usually and *generally* are synonyms in this sentence. There is, therefore, no need to use both words.

204. **(O)** The sentence contains no errors.

205. **(G)** "There *seems* nowadays little of the optimism . . . "
The subject of the sentence (*little*) is singular and it therefore takes a singular verb (*seems* — not *seem*).

206. **(D)** "Taking a cold shower is often so *invigorating* that one feels stronger and wideawake afterward."
Enervating means weakening. *Invigorating* means animating.

207. **(V)** "The governor *concurred* with his adviser that . . . "
The verb *concur* means *agree*.

208. **(D)** "The meat and vegetables were *broiled* together over the open fire."
To embroil means to involve in an argument.

209. **(D)** "Why do you *infer* from what I have just exclaimed . . . "
The speaker *implies* — the listener *infers*.

210. **(V)** "At *the time* you speak about, there was no . . . "

At the time and *then* mean the same thing in this sentence.

211. **(D)** "The machinery was *disassembled* and prepared for storage."
Dissemble means to conceal, to disguise, to cover up.
Disassemble means to take apart.

212. **(O)** The sentence contains no errors.

213. **(V)** "At this point, *it is not* known whether . . ."
If something is *not known* it is understood that it is *not determined*.

214. **(G)** "If I *had been* there . . ."
In a contrary-to-fact conditional construction in past time, sequence of tenses requires the past perfect subjunctive form (*had been*) in the "if" clause instead of the future perfect subjunctive form (*would have been*).

215. **(G)** "Between you and *me* . . ."
The object of the preposition *between* must be an objective case form (*me* — not *I*).

216. **(D)** "The detective *suspected* . . ."
The verb is *to suspect* — not to suspicion. Of course, *suspicion* may be used as a noun.

217. **(O)** The sentence contains no errors.

218. **(V)** "The theory was so *esoteric* that efforts . . . "
Something that is *esoteric* is necessarily *difficult to understand*.

219. **(G)** "*Since* you are interested . . ."
Being that is unacceptable for *since* or *because*.

220. **(G)** ". . . into caves and tunnels *is deceiving* . . ."
Since the subject (*retreat*) is singular, the verb must be singular (*is* deceiving — not *are* deceiving).

221. **(V)** "I am really sorry . . ."
The expression *really and truly* is tautological. A tautology is needless repetition.

222. **(D)** "Narcotics are often used to *mitigate* pain."
To *militate* means to have influence or effect — militate is used with *against*. *Mitigate* means to relieve.

223. **(O)** The sentence contains no errors.

224. **(G)** ". . . attending college, finding a job, or *joining the army*."
The need for parallelism requires *joining the army*, in order to have a balanced construction with the preceding gerund phrases (*attending college* and *finding a job*).

225. **(G)** " . . . *were* his slovenly appearance and his nervous demeanor."
The two subjects (*appearance* and *demeanor*) constitute plurality. We must, accordingly, have a plural verb (*were* — not *was*).

Practice Test 3 ⟶

USE THIS SHEET FOR YOUR ANSWERS

PRACTICE TEST 3

Section 1: Reading Comprehension

1 Ⓐ Ⓑ Ⓒ Ⓓ Ⓔ   6 Ⓐ Ⓑ Ⓒ Ⓓ Ⓔ   11 Ⓐ Ⓑ Ⓒ Ⓓ Ⓔ   16 Ⓐ Ⓑ Ⓒ Ⓓ Ⓔ   21 Ⓐ Ⓑ Ⓒ Ⓓ Ⓔ
2 Ⓐ Ⓑ Ⓒ Ⓓ Ⓔ   7 Ⓐ Ⓑ Ⓒ Ⓓ Ⓔ   12 Ⓐ Ⓑ Ⓒ Ⓓ Ⓔ   17 Ⓐ Ⓑ Ⓒ Ⓓ Ⓔ   22 Ⓐ Ⓑ Ⓒ Ⓓ Ⓔ
3 Ⓐ Ⓑ Ⓒ Ⓓ Ⓔ   8 Ⓐ Ⓑ Ⓒ Ⓓ Ⓔ   13 Ⓐ Ⓑ Ⓒ Ⓓ Ⓔ   18 Ⓐ Ⓑ Ⓒ Ⓓ Ⓔ   23 Ⓐ Ⓑ Ⓒ Ⓓ Ⓔ
4 Ⓐ Ⓑ Ⓒ Ⓓ Ⓔ   9 Ⓐ Ⓑ Ⓒ Ⓓ Ⓔ   14 Ⓐ Ⓑ Ⓒ Ⓓ Ⓔ   19 Ⓐ Ⓑ Ⓒ Ⓓ Ⓔ   24 Ⓐ Ⓑ Ⓒ Ⓓ Ⓔ
5 Ⓐ Ⓑ Ⓒ Ⓓ Ⓔ   10 Ⓐ Ⓑ Ⓒ Ⓓ Ⓔ   15 Ⓐ Ⓑ Ⓒ Ⓓ Ⓔ   20 Ⓐ Ⓑ Ⓒ Ⓓ Ⓔ   25 Ⓐ Ⓑ Ⓒ Ⓓ Ⓔ

Section 2: Math Ability

26 Ⓐ Ⓑ Ⓒ Ⓓ Ⓔ   32 Ⓐ Ⓑ Ⓒ Ⓓ Ⓔ   38 Ⓐ Ⓑ Ⓒ Ⓓ Ⓔ   44 Ⓐ Ⓑ Ⓒ Ⓓ Ⓔ   50 Ⓐ Ⓑ Ⓒ Ⓓ Ⓔ
27 Ⓐ Ⓑ Ⓒ Ⓓ Ⓔ   33 Ⓐ Ⓑ Ⓒ Ⓓ Ⓔ   39 Ⓐ Ⓑ Ⓒ Ⓓ Ⓔ   45 Ⓐ Ⓑ Ⓒ Ⓓ Ⓔ   51 Ⓐ Ⓑ Ⓒ Ⓓ Ⓔ
28 Ⓐ Ⓑ Ⓒ Ⓓ Ⓔ   34 Ⓐ Ⓑ Ⓒ Ⓓ Ⓔ   40 Ⓐ Ⓑ Ⓒ Ⓓ Ⓔ   46 Ⓐ Ⓑ Ⓒ Ⓓ Ⓔ   52 Ⓐ Ⓑ Ⓒ Ⓓ Ⓔ
29 Ⓐ Ⓑ Ⓒ Ⓓ Ⓔ   35 Ⓐ Ⓑ Ⓒ Ⓓ Ⓔ   41 Ⓐ Ⓑ Ⓒ Ⓓ Ⓔ   47 Ⓐ Ⓑ Ⓒ Ⓓ Ⓔ   53 Ⓐ Ⓑ Ⓒ Ⓓ Ⓔ
30 Ⓐ Ⓑ Ⓒ Ⓓ Ⓔ   36 Ⓐ Ⓑ Ⓒ Ⓓ Ⓔ   42 Ⓐ Ⓑ Ⓒ Ⓓ Ⓔ   48 Ⓐ Ⓑ Ⓒ Ⓓ Ⓔ   54 Ⓐ Ⓑ Ⓒ Ⓓ Ⓔ
31 Ⓐ Ⓑ Ⓒ Ⓓ Ⓔ   37 Ⓐ Ⓑ Ⓒ Ⓓ Ⓔ   43 Ⓐ Ⓑ Ⓒ Ⓓ Ⓔ   49 Ⓐ Ⓑ Ⓒ Ⓓ Ⓔ   55 Ⓐ Ⓑ Ⓒ Ⓓ Ⓔ

Section 3: Business Judgment

56 Ⓐ Ⓑ Ⓒ Ⓓ Ⓔ   61 Ⓐ Ⓑ Ⓒ Ⓓ Ⓔ   66 Ⓐ Ⓑ Ⓒ Ⓓ Ⓔ   71 Ⓐ Ⓑ Ⓒ Ⓓ Ⓔ   76 Ⓐ Ⓑ Ⓒ Ⓓ Ⓔ
57 Ⓐ Ⓑ Ⓒ Ⓓ Ⓔ   62 Ⓐ Ⓑ Ⓒ Ⓓ Ⓔ   67 Ⓐ Ⓑ Ⓒ Ⓓ Ⓔ   72 Ⓐ Ⓑ Ⓒ Ⓓ Ⓔ   77 Ⓐ Ⓑ Ⓒ Ⓓ Ⓔ
58 Ⓐ Ⓑ Ⓒ Ⓓ Ⓔ   63 Ⓐ Ⓑ Ⓒ Ⓓ Ⓔ   68 Ⓐ Ⓑ Ⓒ Ⓓ Ⓔ   73 Ⓐ Ⓑ Ⓒ Ⓓ Ⓔ   78 Ⓐ Ⓑ Ⓒ Ⓓ Ⓔ
59 Ⓐ Ⓑ Ⓒ Ⓓ Ⓔ   64 Ⓐ Ⓑ Ⓒ Ⓓ Ⓔ   69 Ⓐ Ⓑ Ⓒ Ⓓ Ⓔ   74 Ⓐ Ⓑ Ⓒ Ⓓ Ⓔ   79 Ⓐ Ⓑ Ⓒ Ⓓ Ⓔ
60 Ⓐ Ⓑ Ⓒ Ⓓ Ⓔ   65 Ⓐ Ⓑ Ⓒ Ⓓ Ⓔ   70 Ⓐ Ⓑ Ⓒ Ⓓ Ⓔ   75 Ⓐ Ⓑ Ⓒ Ⓓ Ⓔ   80 Ⓐ Ⓑ Ⓒ Ⓓ Ⓔ

Section 4: Data Sufficiency

81 Ⓐ Ⓑ Ⓒ Ⓓ Ⓔ   87 Ⓐ Ⓑ Ⓒ Ⓓ Ⓔ   93 Ⓐ Ⓑ Ⓒ Ⓓ Ⓔ   99 Ⓐ Ⓑ Ⓒ Ⓓ Ⓔ   105 Ⓐ Ⓑ Ⓒ Ⓓ Ⓔ
82 Ⓐ Ⓑ Ⓒ Ⓓ Ⓔ   88 Ⓐ Ⓑ Ⓒ Ⓓ Ⓔ   94 Ⓐ Ⓑ Ⓒ Ⓓ Ⓔ   100 Ⓐ Ⓑ Ⓒ Ⓓ Ⓔ   106 Ⓐ Ⓑ Ⓒ Ⓓ Ⓔ
83 Ⓐ Ⓑ Ⓒ Ⓓ Ⓔ   89 Ⓐ Ⓑ Ⓒ Ⓓ Ⓔ   95 Ⓐ Ⓑ Ⓒ Ⓓ Ⓔ   101 Ⓐ Ⓑ Ⓒ Ⓓ Ⓔ   107 Ⓐ Ⓑ Ⓒ Ⓓ Ⓔ
84 Ⓐ Ⓑ Ⓒ Ⓓ Ⓔ   90 Ⓐ Ⓑ Ⓒ Ⓓ Ⓔ   96 Ⓐ Ⓑ Ⓒ Ⓓ Ⓔ   102 Ⓐ Ⓑ Ⓒ Ⓓ Ⓔ   108 Ⓐ Ⓑ Ⓒ Ⓓ Ⓔ
85 Ⓐ Ⓑ Ⓒ Ⓓ Ⓔ   91 Ⓐ Ⓑ Ⓒ Ⓓ Ⓔ   97 Ⓐ Ⓑ Ⓒ Ⓓ Ⓔ   103 Ⓐ Ⓑ Ⓒ Ⓓ Ⓔ   109 Ⓐ Ⓑ Ⓒ Ⓓ Ⓔ
86 Ⓐ Ⓑ Ⓒ Ⓓ Ⓔ   92 Ⓐ Ⓑ Ⓒ Ⓓ Ⓔ   98 Ⓐ Ⓑ Ⓒ Ⓓ Ⓔ   104 Ⓐ Ⓑ Ⓒ Ⓓ Ⓔ   110 Ⓐ Ⓑ Ⓒ Ⓓ Ⓔ

(continued on next page)

Section 5: Grammar and Usage

111 Ⓐ Ⓑ Ⓒ Ⓓ Ⓔ   116 Ⓐ Ⓑ Ⓒ Ⓓ Ⓔ   121 Ⓐ Ⓑ Ⓒ Ⓓ Ⓔ   126 Ⓐ Ⓑ Ⓒ Ⓓ Ⓔ   131 Ⓐ Ⓑ Ⓒ Ⓓ Ⓔ
112 Ⓐ Ⓑ Ⓒ Ⓓ Ⓔ   117 Ⓐ Ⓑ Ⓒ Ⓓ Ⓔ   122 Ⓐ Ⓑ Ⓒ Ⓓ Ⓔ   127 Ⓐ Ⓑ Ⓒ Ⓓ Ⓔ   132 Ⓐ Ⓑ Ⓒ Ⓓ Ⓔ
113 Ⓐ Ⓑ Ⓒ Ⓓ Ⓔ   118 Ⓐ Ⓑ Ⓒ Ⓓ Ⓔ   123 Ⓐ Ⓑ Ⓒ Ⓓ Ⓔ   128 Ⓐ Ⓑ Ⓒ Ⓓ Ⓔ   133 Ⓐ Ⓑ Ⓒ Ⓓ Ⓔ
114 Ⓐ Ⓑ Ⓒ Ⓓ Ⓔ   119 Ⓐ Ⓑ Ⓒ Ⓓ Ⓔ   124 Ⓐ Ⓑ Ⓒ Ⓓ Ⓔ   129 Ⓐ Ⓑ Ⓒ Ⓓ Ⓔ   134 Ⓐ Ⓑ Ⓒ Ⓓ Ⓔ
115 Ⓐ Ⓑ Ⓒ Ⓓ Ⓔ   120 Ⓐ Ⓑ Ⓒ Ⓓ Ⓔ   125 Ⓐ Ⓑ Ⓒ Ⓓ Ⓔ   130 Ⓐ Ⓑ Ⓒ Ⓓ Ⓔ   135 Ⓐ Ⓑ Ⓒ Ⓓ Ⓔ

Section 6: Business Judgment

136 Ⓐ Ⓑ Ⓒ Ⓓ Ⓔ   141 Ⓐ Ⓑ Ⓒ Ⓓ Ⓔ   146 Ⓐ Ⓑ Ⓒ Ⓓ Ⓔ   151 Ⓐ Ⓑ Ⓒ Ⓓ Ⓔ   156 Ⓐ Ⓑ Ⓒ Ⓓ Ⓔ
137 Ⓐ Ⓑ Ⓒ Ⓓ Ⓔ   142 Ⓐ Ⓑ Ⓒ Ⓓ Ⓔ   147 Ⓐ Ⓑ Ⓒ Ⓓ Ⓔ   152 Ⓐ Ⓑ Ⓒ Ⓓ Ⓔ   157 Ⓐ Ⓑ Ⓒ Ⓓ Ⓔ
138 Ⓐ Ⓑ Ⓒ Ⓓ Ⓔ   143 Ⓐ Ⓑ Ⓒ Ⓓ Ⓔ   148 Ⓐ Ⓑ Ⓒ Ⓓ Ⓔ   153 Ⓐ Ⓑ Ⓒ Ⓓ Ⓔ   158 Ⓐ Ⓑ Ⓒ Ⓓ Ⓔ
139 Ⓐ Ⓑ Ⓒ Ⓓ Ⓔ   144 Ⓐ Ⓑ Ⓒ Ⓓ Ⓔ   149 Ⓐ Ⓑ Ⓒ Ⓓ Ⓔ   154 Ⓐ Ⓑ Ⓒ Ⓓ Ⓔ   159 Ⓐ Ⓑ Ⓒ Ⓓ Ⓔ
140 Ⓐ Ⓑ Ⓒ Ⓓ Ⓔ   145 Ⓐ Ⓑ Ⓒ Ⓓ Ⓔ   150 Ⓐ Ⓑ Ⓒ Ⓓ Ⓔ   155 Ⓐ Ⓑ Ⓒ Ⓓ Ⓔ   160 Ⓐ Ⓑ Ⓒ Ⓓ Ⓔ

Section 7: Reading Recall

161 Ⓐ Ⓑ Ⓒ Ⓓ Ⓔ   167 Ⓐ Ⓑ Ⓒ Ⓓ Ⓔ   173 Ⓐ Ⓑ Ⓒ Ⓓ Ⓔ   179 Ⓐ Ⓑ Ⓒ Ⓓ Ⓔ   185 Ⓐ Ⓑ Ⓒ Ⓓ Ⓔ
162 Ⓐ Ⓑ Ⓒ Ⓓ Ⓔ   168 Ⓐ Ⓑ Ⓒ Ⓓ Ⓔ   174 Ⓐ Ⓑ Ⓒ Ⓓ Ⓔ   180 Ⓐ Ⓑ Ⓒ Ⓓ Ⓔ   186 Ⓐ Ⓑ Ⓒ Ⓓ Ⓔ
163 Ⓐ Ⓑ Ⓒ Ⓓ Ⓔ   169 Ⓐ Ⓑ Ⓒ Ⓓ Ⓔ   175 Ⓐ Ⓑ Ⓒ Ⓓ Ⓔ   181 Ⓐ Ⓑ Ⓒ Ⓓ Ⓔ   187 Ⓐ Ⓑ Ⓒ Ⓓ Ⓔ
164 Ⓐ Ⓑ Ⓒ Ⓓ Ⓔ   170 Ⓐ Ⓑ Ⓒ Ⓓ Ⓔ   176 Ⓐ Ⓑ Ⓒ Ⓓ Ⓔ   182 Ⓐ Ⓑ Ⓒ Ⓓ Ⓔ   188 Ⓐ Ⓑ Ⓒ Ⓓ Ⓔ
165 Ⓐ Ⓑ Ⓒ Ⓓ Ⓔ   171 Ⓐ Ⓑ Ⓒ Ⓓ Ⓔ   177 Ⓐ Ⓑ Ⓒ Ⓓ Ⓔ   183 Ⓐ Ⓑ Ⓒ Ⓓ Ⓔ   189 Ⓐ Ⓑ Ⓒ Ⓓ Ⓔ
166 Ⓐ Ⓑ Ⓒ Ⓓ Ⓔ   172 Ⓐ Ⓑ Ⓒ Ⓓ Ⓔ   178 Ⓐ Ⓑ Ⓒ Ⓓ Ⓔ   184 Ⓐ Ⓑ Ⓒ Ⓓ Ⓔ   190 Ⓐ Ⓑ Ⓒ Ⓓ Ⓔ

Section 8: Sentence Correction

191 Ⓐ Ⓑ Ⓒ Ⓓ Ⓔ   199 Ⓐ Ⓑ Ⓒ Ⓓ Ⓔ   207 Ⓐ Ⓑ Ⓒ Ⓓ Ⓔ   215 Ⓐ Ⓑ Ⓒ Ⓓ Ⓔ   223 Ⓐ Ⓑ Ⓒ Ⓓ Ⓔ
192 Ⓐ Ⓑ Ⓒ Ⓓ Ⓔ   200 Ⓐ Ⓑ Ⓒ Ⓓ Ⓔ   208 Ⓐ Ⓑ Ⓒ Ⓓ Ⓔ   216 Ⓐ Ⓑ Ⓒ Ⓓ Ⓔ   224 Ⓐ Ⓑ Ⓒ Ⓓ Ⓔ
193 Ⓐ Ⓑ Ⓒ Ⓓ Ⓔ   201 Ⓐ Ⓑ Ⓒ Ⓓ Ⓔ   209 Ⓐ Ⓑ Ⓒ Ⓓ Ⓔ   217 Ⓐ Ⓑ Ⓒ Ⓓ Ⓔ   225 Ⓐ Ⓑ Ⓒ Ⓓ Ⓔ
194 Ⓐ Ⓑ Ⓒ Ⓓ Ⓔ   202 Ⓐ Ⓑ Ⓒ Ⓓ Ⓔ   210 Ⓐ Ⓑ Ⓒ Ⓓ Ⓔ   218 Ⓐ Ⓑ Ⓒ Ⓓ Ⓔ   226 Ⓐ Ⓑ Ⓒ Ⓓ Ⓔ
195 Ⓐ Ⓑ Ⓒ Ⓓ Ⓔ   203 Ⓐ Ⓑ Ⓒ Ⓓ Ⓔ   211 Ⓐ Ⓑ Ⓒ Ⓓ Ⓔ   219 Ⓐ Ⓑ Ⓒ Ⓓ Ⓔ   227 Ⓐ Ⓑ Ⓒ Ⓓ Ⓔ
196 Ⓐ Ⓑ Ⓒ Ⓓ Ⓔ   204 Ⓐ Ⓑ Ⓒ Ⓓ Ⓔ   212 Ⓐ Ⓑ Ⓒ Ⓓ Ⓔ   220 Ⓐ Ⓑ Ⓒ Ⓓ Ⓔ   228 Ⓐ Ⓑ Ⓒ Ⓓ Ⓔ
197 Ⓐ Ⓑ Ⓒ Ⓓ Ⓔ   205 Ⓐ Ⓑ Ⓒ Ⓓ Ⓔ   213 Ⓐ Ⓑ Ⓒ Ⓓ Ⓔ   221 Ⓐ Ⓑ Ⓒ Ⓓ Ⓔ   229 Ⓐ Ⓑ Ⓒ Ⓓ Ⓔ
198 Ⓐ Ⓑ Ⓒ Ⓓ Ⓔ   206 Ⓐ Ⓑ Ⓒ Ⓓ Ⓔ   214 Ⓐ Ⓑ Ⓒ Ⓓ Ⓔ   222 Ⓐ Ⓑ Ⓒ Ⓓ Ⓔ   230 Ⓐ Ⓑ Ⓒ Ⓓ Ⓔ

Practice Test 3

SECTION 1: READING COMPREHENSION

Time: 30 minutes

Directions: Each of the reading passages in this section is followed by questions based on its content. After reading the passage, choose the best answer to each question. The questions are to be answered on the basis of what is stated or implied in the passage.

First of all, modern propaganda is based on scientific analyses of psychology and sociology. Step by step, the propagandist builds his techniques on the basis of his knowledge of man, his tendencies, his desires, his needs, his psychic mechanisms, his conditioning—and as much on social psychology as on depth psychology. He shapes his procedures on the basis of our knowledge of groups and their laws of formation and dissolution, of mass influences, and of environmental limitations. Without the scientific research of modern psychology and sociology there would be no propaganda, or rather we still would be in the primitive stages of propaganda that existed in the time of Pericles or Augustus. Of course, propagandists may be insufficiently versed in these branches of science; they may misunderstand them, go beyond the cautious conclusions of the psychologists, or claim to apply certain psychological discoveries that, in fact, do not apply at all. But all this only shows efforts to find new ways: only for the past fifty years have men sought to apply the psychological and sociological sciences. The important thing is that propaganda has decided to submit itself to science and to make use of it. Of course, psychologists may be scandalized and say that this is a misuse of their science. But this argument carries no weight; the same applies to our physicists and the atomic bomb. The scientist should know that he lives in a world in which his discoveries will be utilized. Propagandists inevitably will have a better understanding of sociology and psychology, use them with increasing precision, and as a result become more effective.

Second, propaganda is scientific in that it tends to establish a set of rules, rigorous, precise, and tested, that are not merely recipes but impose themselves on every propagandist, who is less and less free to follow his own impulses. He must apply, increasingly and exactly, certain precise formulas that can be applied by anybody with the proper training—clearly a characteristic of a technique based on science.

Third, what is needed nowadays is an exact analysis of both the environment and the individual to be subjected to propaganda. No longer does the man of talent determine the method, the approach, or the subject; all that is now being calculated (or must be calculated). Therefore, one type of propaganda will be found suitable in one situation and completely useless in another. To undertake an active propaganda operation, it is necessary to make a scientific, sociological, and psychological analysis first, and then utilize those branches of science, which are becoming increasingly well known. But, here again, proper training is necessary for those who want to use them with their full effectiveness.

Finally, one last trait reveals the scientific character of modern propaganda: the increasing attempt to control its use, measure its results, define its effects. This is very difficult, but the propagandist is no longer content to have obtained, or to believe he has obtained, a certain result; he seeks precise evidence. Even successful political results do not completely satisfy him. He wants to understand the how and why of them and measure their exact effect. He is prompted by a certain spirit of experimentation and a desire to ponder the results. From this point on, one can see the beginning of scientific method. Admittedly, it is not yet very widespread, and those who analyze results are not active propagandists but philosophers. Granted, that reveals a certain division of labor, nothing more. It indicates that propaganda is no longer a self-contained action, covering up for evil deeds. It is an object of serious thought, and proceeds along scientific channels.

1. The usefulness of a propaganda technique is determined by

   (A) the individual and the environment of the individual at whom the propaganda is aimed
   (B) the background of the propagandist
   (C) the media available to the propagandist
   (D) the geographical area in which the propaganda is used
   (E) none of the above since an appraisal must wait till after the propaganda has been used

2. Propaganda has been brought from its primitive stages by

   (A) increased knowledge of physicists
   (B) evolution
   (C) modern sociology and psychology
   (D) the experimental biologist
   (E) all of the above

3. All of the following reveal an increasing use of science and scientific method in the field of propaganda *except*

   (A) the use of modern sociology
   (B) the establishment of a set of rules for propagandists
   (C) the use of propaganda techniques of Pericles
   (D) attempts to control the use of propaganda
   (E) the use of depth psychology

4. The author believes that the argument that science has been misused by the propagandist is false because

   (A) propaganda is not an evil use of sociology
   (B) propaganda methods, if arrived at scientifically, can be helpful
   (C) physicists – not propagandists – created the atom bomb
   (D) the work of the scientist often becomes known because of propaganda
   (E) no one can really define what a science is

5. Of the following, the propagandist would be *least* interested in basing his analyses on

   (A) Freud's theories of repression
   (B) Newton's law of gravitation
   (C) Pavlov's theory of conditioning
   (D) Dewey's theory of teaching
   (E) Thorndike's theories of learning

6. The author's attitude toward propaganda is one of

   (A) suspicion
   (B) humor
   (C) indecision
   (D) distrust
   (E) approval

A history extending over more than two thousand years; a political power that spread all through western Asia and even into Egypt; an intense and rich religious life; a copious literary, artistic, and scientific output: such are the main features of the civilization of the Babylonians and Assyrians, or, to give them their collective name, the Akkadians. But during the past few years a problem of fundamental importance has arisen in regard to the origins and the constituent elements of that civilization: it is questioned whether it was original or derivative, an independent creation or a reworking over of material already in existence.

At the beginning of this century, when the theory of 'pan-Babylonism', which derived all the elements of ancient culture from Babylonia, was in fashion, who would have thought that the tables would be turned so completely? But in fact the rediscovery of the Sumerians is more and more clearly showing that the Babylonian and Assyrian religious conceptions, the content of their literary works, and the themes of their arts and sciences have their precedents in the Sumerian civilization. Inevitably one asks whether even that which still seems original may not sooner or later be attributable to prototypes at present unknown.

The Babylonians and Assyrians are Semitic peoples. They originate in the movements of the nomads who periodically pressed outward from the desert expanses of Arabia and tried to infiltrate into the Mesopotamian valley. This origin deserves closer attention: while providing the link which connects Mesopotamia with other Semitic civilizations, it may again and again afford hints or clues to the identification of distinctive cultural features which, as we have just remarked, is as difficult to achieve as it is necessary for a proper understanding.

Nowhere, perhaps, is the nature of the relationship between the Sumerians and the Semites more clearly exemplified than in their religious beliefs. In the Babylonian and Assyrian pantheon, we meet once more with three great cosmic gods of the Sumerians: Heaven, Air, and Earth. Their names also remain the same: Anu, Enlil, and Ea (Enki). There is also the astral trinity: the Moon, the Sun, and Venus (the morning star); but the names are different: Sin, Shamash, and Ishtar.

The national gods present a different picture, for by their very nature these are not easily transferred from one people to another. Babylonia and Assyria each have their own gods, to whom great honor is accorded. In Babylonia, the Hammurabi dynasty exalts the national god, called Marduk, and henceforth he retains his place at the head of the heavenly hierarchy, being regarded as the creator and orderer of the universe. In Assyria the name of the national god is the same as that of the people and their capital: Ashur; and he possesses the same warlike attributes that are characteristic of his people.

7. The Babylonians and Assyrians belonged to the race of

   (A) Mesopotamians
   (B) Akkadians
   (C) Egyptians
   (D) Sumerians
   (E) Semites

8. The question put forth by the author at the beginning of the article deals with the subject of

   (A) derivation
   (B) religion
   (C) politics
   (D) independence
   (E) economy

9. Babylonia is to Assyria as Marduk is to

   (A) Anu
   (B) Moon
   (C) Ashur
   (D) Sin
   (E) Venus

10. Hammurabi, King of Babylon in the 20th century B.C., is well known for his law code, which states the following:

    (A) "Know thyself"
    (B) "An eye for an eye, a tooth for a tooth"
    (C) "You never cross the same river twice"
    (D) "He who laughs last laughs best"
    (E) "There is always time for courtesy"

11. The article implies a warlike society in

    (A) Sumeria
    (B) Assyria
    (C) Babylon
    (D) countries that were monotheistic
    (E) countries that were polytheistic

Length and time are relative concepts. If two spaceships pass each other with uniform velocity, observers on each ship will find that astronauts on the other ship are thinner and moving about more slowly. If the relative speed is great enough, they will seem to move like actors in a slow-motion picture. All phenomena with periodic movements will seem reduced in speed: tuning forks, balance-wheel watches, heartbeats, vibrating atoms, and so on. A six-foot astronaut, standing erect in a horizontally moving ship, will still appear six feet tall, but his body will seem thinner in the line of travel. When he lies down with his body in line with the ship's motion, his body will be restored to normal width but he will now seem shorter from head to toes.

If two spaceships actually could pass each other with a relative speed great enough to make such changes significant, all sorts of technical difficulties would make it virtually impossible for observers on either ship to *see* such changes. Writers like to explain relativity by using oversimplified dramatic illustrations. These colorful illustrations do not describe changes that actually could be observed, either by the human eye or by any instruments presently known. They should be thought of as changes that could, in principle, be inferred by the astronauts on the basis of measurements, with sufficiently precise instruments and after making necessary corrections for the velocity of light.

In addition to changes in length and time, there also are relativistic changes in mass. Mass, in a rough sense, is a measure of the amount of matter in an object. A lead ball and a cork ball may be the same size, but the lead ball is more massive. It contains a greater concentration of matter.

There are two ways to measure an object's mass. It can be weighed or it can be determined how much force is needed to accelerate the object by a certain amount. The first method is not a very good one, because the results vary with the local strength of gravity. A lead ball, carried to the top of a high mountain, will weigh a trifle less than before, although its mass remains exactly the same. On the moon its weight would be considerably less than on the earth. On Jupiter its weight would be considerably more.

The second method of measuring mass gives the same result regardless of whether one is on the earth, the moon, or Jupiter; but it is subject to a different and odder kind of variation. To determine the mass of a moving object by this method, one must measure the force required to accelerate it by a certain amount. Clearly, a stronger push is needed to start a cannonball rolling than to start a cork ball rolling. Mass measured in this way is called *inertial mass* to distinguish it from *gravitational mass* or weight. Such measurements cannot be made without making measurements of time and distance. The inertial mass of a cannonball, for example, is expressed by the amount of force required to increase its speed (distance per unit time) by so much per unit of time. As we have seen, time and distance measurements vary with the relative speed of object and observer. As a result, measurements of inertial mass also vary.

12. Which one of the following phenomena is not a periodic movement (a movement which repeats itself) ?

    (A) vibrating atoms
    (B) tuning forks
    (C) a freely falling object
    (D) pendulums swinging
    (E) a rocking chair

13. In which direction would the body of an astronaut seem to be distorted in a moving space ship?

    (A) in the line of the ship's motion
    (B) in all directions
    (C) dependent on the astronaut's position
    (D) opposite to the ship's motion
    (E) upside down

14. Mass is the

    (A) number of chemical bonds in a molecule of iron
    (B) amount that an object weighs
    (C) earth's attraction for an object
    (D) amount of matter an object contains
    (E) difference between earth weight and moon weight

15. Why is weighing a poor way to measure an object's mass?

    (A) Any scale will always be slightly inaccurate in weighing.
    (B) The results of weighing vary with the effect of gravity.
    (C) The inertial mass will not remain constant.
    (D) All objects are known to gain weight as they age.
    (E) Mass changes with temperature variation.

16. Why will measurements of inertial mass vary?

    (A) The density of an object affects its inertial mass.
    (B) There are two different scales for measuring inertial mass.
    (C) Time and distance measurements are relative.
    (D) An object's acceleration cannot be kept constant.
    (E) Weather changes may be responsible for variations.

17. Which statement is *not* true?

    (A) To measure inertial mass, we measure the force which is necessary to accelerate that mass by a certain amount.
    (B) The tendency on the part of those who seek to explain relativity is to be dramatic and over-simple.
    (C) The relative speed of an object and the one who watches that object affects the time and distance measurements of that object.
    (D) An object on earth loses weight if it is transferred to the moon.
    (E) A balloon and an iron ball, both of which are perfect circles and of the same size, have the same mass.

"I suppose you Americans have twice our income per capita, but that is just a way of lying with statistics. This is a better country to live in, we all know that: more comfortable, less worried, a satisfactory life. The fact that we show up poorer in the figures does not really matter."

The man speaking was not smug or idle but one of the hardest-working, toughest-thinking figures at the center of the British Establishment. His views would certainly be echoed by many American visitors to contemporary Britain, who find here a humane respite from the tensions of their own country.

Alas, the formula is turning out to be not quite so simple. It seldom is.

The British are becoming increasingly aware that they face a dilemma about their way of life. If they stick to their relatively comfortable, easy-going habits, this country will slip steadily downward in the international economic standings. And as that fact becomes apparent, it is bound to produce a new kind of social unrest here.

Average per capita income in Britain is now somewhat less than half that in the United States: $1,690 in 1970, compared with the U.S. figure of $3,750. But America is really too distant for comparison, geographically and psychologically. More to the point is Britain's standing in Europe.

Ten years ago the British had the third highest gross national product per capita in Europe, trailing only the Swedes and the Swiss. Now Britain is ninth in that league, behind Sweden, Switzerland, Denmark, France, Norway, Germany, Belgium and the Netherlands.

Those are not just figures in the abstract. They mean, in the real world, that British executives now get lower rewards than French, that automobile workers on the Continent are catching up to, and passing, British wage rates. Whether specifically aware of continental comparisons or not, British workers feel their own rising expectations are not being met.

Ford's British plants have been on strike now for more than five weeks. Henry Ford 2nd has been threatening to cut back his investment in Britain because of persistent labor unrest. It is not only this big strike but also endless little ones about this grievance or that; last year they cost Ford $50 million in lost production.

The sensible thing, it seems, would be for the Ford workers to open the way to higher earnings by being more productive — working harder, more steadily, with fewer disputes. But some psychologists here would argue that the squabbles and tea breaks are mechanisms to deal with the dreary pressures of the assembly line. In other words, British workers really do not want to be more efficient; they prefer a less tidy life.

If this were still an island unto itself, that would be fine. But Ford can and does make cars elsewhere. Similarly, the comfortable life worked beautifully at Rolls-Royce — with feeble management and padded payrolls —until the bitter facts of international aeroengine competition told.

The dilemma may be even more painful in the area of personal services than in manufacturing. For it is those labor-intensive services, still so complete and courteous, that make life pleasant for the British and their visitors.

There is the smiling young man who pops into your train compartment to offer coffee and biscuits. Or the nurse who comes into your hospital room instead of answering the patient's buzz over a loudspeaker because she is too busy. Or the postman who slips the mail through the slot in your front door twice a day and occasionally asks how you're keeping.

They have all been possible because they accepted low wages, and now they do not want to. The answer is to mechanize, to eliminate unneeded workers. But then it will no longer be Britain. As Rene Cutforth of the British Broadcasting Corporation said about more efficiency in the postal service:

"The postman is only a viable economic unit if he is serving a machine, not a village. The fact that he prefers the village and the village prefers him cannot for a moment hold up the inevitable march of progress."

And so Britain faces the probable necessity of doing things, to maintain contentment, that in fact will make her less contented. A German correspondent here was asked once whether he did not mind the strikes, the faulty telephones, the bumbling. "Oh no," he said. "If you change it too much, it will be like Germany."

18. In the article, the phrase "labor-intensive" is used to describe

    (A) employee-training programs
    (B) the cause of Britain's labor unrest
    (C) the system of labor employed in most British factories
    (D) the suggested solution to Britain's economic problems
    (E) jobs that render personal services

19. The article quotes a member of the British Establishment who believes that

    (A) Britain's per capita income is not an accurate gauge of living standards
    (B) American visitors do not see the social unrest in Britain
    (C) the niceties of British life more than make up for corporate inefficiency.
    (D) the British economy has been exploited by American interests
    (E) Britain's GNP standing in Europe is steadily declining

20. The author implies that the Ford Motor Company

    (A) has arranged to relocate out of Britain
    (B) has adapted its production policies to suit workers' habits
    (C) cannot tolerate worker inefficiency
    (D) has come out on top in its competition with Rolls Royce
    (E) is able to cope with small-scale strikes

21. The article states that psychologists attribute frequent factory squabbles to

    (A) personal problems
    (B) disillusionment with the failing British system
    (C) worker-employer hostilities
    (D) worker attempts to alleviate assembly-line monotony
    (E) employee dissatisfaction with factory production roles

22. The author implies that Rolls Royce

    (A) was one of the many businesses succumbing to British inflation
    (B) will be bought out by Ford Motor Company
    (C) joined the exodus of big business out of Britain
    (D) overpaid its employees
    (E) had poor management

23. The author concludes that maintaining contentment in Britain

(A) is closely related to improving efficiency
(B) will be made possible only by attracting foreign investors
(C) rests upon citizens' acceptance of low per capita income
(D) is contingent upon maintaining the comfortable, tension-free pace that exemplifies British life
(E) is dependent upon reaching the American level of per capita income

24. It can be inferred from the article that Henry Ford 2nd

(A) agrees that the condition of the British economy is satisfactory
(B) feels his British investments are on the verge of becoming liabilities
(C) will ride out economic instabilities in Britain
(D) will initate the use of labor-saving innovative production methods
(E) will continue to pay higher than average wages

25. According to the article, the British worker

I. is content with his wages
II. is finding that pay expectations are not materializing
III. in general, receives a salary lower than that of other European workers

(A) I only
(B) II only
(C) III only
(D) II and III only
(E) I, II, and III

IF YOU FINISH BEFORE THE TIME IS UP, GO OVER YOUR WORK FOR THIS SECTION ONLY. DO NOT TURN TO ANY OTHER SECTION OF THE TEST. WHEN THE TIME IS UP, GO ON TO THE NEXT SECTION.

SECTION 2: MATH ABILITY

Time: 30 minutes

Directions: Each of the problems in this section is followed by five alternatives lettered A through E. Solve each problem and then choose the correct answer. Note that diagrams are not necessarily drawn to scale. Scratchwork may be done on available space on the pages of this section.

26. If s oranges cost v cents, how many dollars will w dozen oranges cost?

   (A) $\dfrac{sw}{v}(12)$

   (B) $\dfrac{100}{v}\, 12\; sw$

   (C) $\dfrac{12}{100}\,\dfrac{vw}{s}$

   (D) $\dfrac{(v + 100)\; w}{12\; s}$

   (E) $\dfrac{v}{s}(100\; w)$

27. 25% of 1/9 is the same as 33⅓% of what?
   (A) 1/27   (D) 1/6
   (B) 1/36   (E) 1/8
   (C) 1/12

28. What is the net price of a vase costing $125, after successive discounts of 20% and 10%?

   (A) $100.00   (D) $106.25
   (B) $ 90.00   (E) $122.50
   (C) $112.50

29. A student has an average of 75% in four courses one term. What must be his average in five courses the next term to raise his combined average to 80%?

   (A) 87%   (D) 82%
   (B) 85%   (E) 86%
   (C) 84%

30. Anne has 3 blouses, 4 skirts, and 2 pairs of shoes. How many different outfits can she wear, if an outfit consists of any blouse worn with any skirt and either pair of shoes?

    (A) 8
    (B) 12
    (C) 24
    (D) 9
    (E) 48

31. If the tax on a $150 refrigerator is $14, at the same rate what is the tax on a $225 refrigerator?

    (A) $12
    (B) $16
    (C) $18
    (D) $21
    (E) $24

32. A rectangle 20 inches long and 10 inches wide is tiled completely with square tiles $\frac{1}{2}$ inch on each side. How many tiles are needed?

    (A) 60
    (B) 100
    (C) 200
    (D) 400
    (E) 800

Questions 33–34

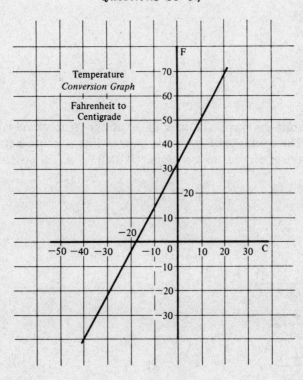

33. From the graph, what is the approximate Fahrenheit temperature corresponding to 10°C?

   (A) 50°
   (B) 55°
   (C) 45°
   (D) 60°
   (E) 40°

34. Which temperature reads the same in degres on both Centigrade and Fahrenheit scales?

   (A) −10
   (B)   10
   (C) −30
   (D) −40
   (E) −20

35. In a certain theater, the price of a ticket for a child is ⅓ that of an adult. The price for 3 children and 3 adults is $21.60. What is the price for an adult ticket?

   (A) $2.10
   (B) $2.40
   (C) $3.60
   (D) $6.00
   (E) $5.40

36. A $400 coat sells for how much after successive discounts of 10% and 5%?

   (A) $325
   (B) $342
   (C) $340
   (D) $357
   (E) $338

37. Two containers have volumes of u and v respectively and are each ⅓ full. The contents of both are poured into a container of volume w. What part of the latter container is full?

   (A) $\dfrac{1}{3}$

   (B) $\dfrac{2}{3}$

   (C) $\dfrac{2(u + v)}{3w}$

   (D) $\dfrac{u + v}{3w}$

   (E) $\dfrac{u + v}{9w}$

38. What percent of 200 is .001% of $2^2 \times 5^3$?

(A) .0025%
(B) .025%
(C) .0145%
(D) .00005%
(E) .2500%

39. The surface area of a cube is 600 square inches. It is cut up into smaller cubes of surface area of 150 square inches each. How many smaller cubes were formed?

(A) 8
(B) 6
(C) 12
(D) 10
(E) 6

40. A catalog advertises successive discounts of 15% and 10% on tape recorders. What is the net price of a $200 tape recorder?

(A) $150
(B) $153
(C) $160
(D) $152.50
(E) $140.25

Questions 41–44

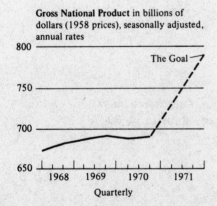

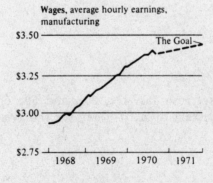

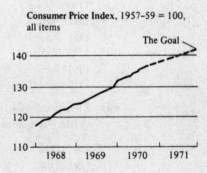

41. What was the approximate percentage increase in Gross National Product (GNP) from the start of 1968 to the end of the third quarter of 1970?

(A) 2.2%
(B) 3%
(C) 4.2%
(D) 5%
(E) 6.2%

42. What was the approximate percentage increase in hourly wages from the start of 1968 to the end of the third quarter of 1970?

    (A) 28%
    (B) 32%
    (C) 10%
    (D) 12%
    (E) 17%

43. Which of the following is *not* a true statement according to the graphs above?

    (A) The GNP has increased slowly from 1968-70.
    (B) The increase in wages has kept pace with the Consumer Price Index from 1968-70.
    (C) The goal is to slow down the rate of growth of the GNP.
    (D) The goal is to increase the rate of growth of the GNP.
    (E) The goal is to slow down the rate of growth of wages.

44. What is the approximate ratio of the expected increase of wages in 1971 to the increase in wages in 1969?

    (A) 1 : 4
    (B) 1 : 2
    (C) 2 : 1
    (D) 3 : 1
    (E) 2 : 5

45. A testee got 45 problems wrong out of 120. If the problems were marked on a basis of 100%, the testee's mark was closest to

    (A) 50%
    (B) 63%
    (C) 72%
    (D) 81%
    (E) 84%

46. The Stock Market rose 35¢, 40¢, 25¢, and 50¢ on 4 successive days. What rise is necessary on a fifth day for the average gain to be 30¢?

    (A) 30¢
    (B) 10¢
    (C) 25¢
    (D) 0¢
    (E) 25¢

47. If $y \sqrt{.09} = 6$, what is the value of y?

    (A) 2
    (B) .2
    (C) 20
    (D) $\dfrac{2}{3}$
    (E) 3

48. If there are exactly four times as many women teachers in a school as men teachers, which of the following *cannot* be the number of teachers in the school?

   (A) 42   (D) 55
   (B) 45   (E) 60
   (C) 50

49. $\frac{1}{3}$ added to $\frac{1}{4}$ is equal to $\frac{1}{5}$ of

   (A) $\frac{12}{35}$ (D) $\frac{12}{5}$

   (B) $\frac{35}{12}$ (E) $\frac{7}{12}$

   (C) $\frac{5}{12}$

50. A man drives a distance of 120 miles at an average speed of 40 miles per hour, and then returns at an average speed of 60 miles per hour. What is his average speed in miles per hour for the entire trip?

   (A) 45   (D) 52
   (B) 48   (E) 54
   (C) 50

51. Under which of the following conditions must $u \times v$ be positive?

   (A) $u > 0$

   (B) $\frac{u}{v} > 0$

   (C) $u > v$
   (D) $v > 0$
   (E) $u - v < 0$

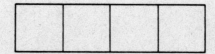

52. In the figure above, four squares have been placed side by side to form a rectangle of perimeter 140. What is the area of each square?

   (A) 400
   (B) 360
   (C) 300
   (D) 256
   (E) 196

53. A poster is cut down by 10% of its width and 30% of its height. What percent of the original area remains?

    (A) 37
    (B) 60
    (C) 63
    (D) 80
    (E) 70

54. If 8 men can paint a fence in 3 hours, how many hours will it take 6 men to do the same job? Assume each man works uniformly at the same rate.

    (A) 4
    (B) $2\frac{1}{4}$
    (C) $2\frac{3}{4}$
    (D) $4\frac{1}{2}$
    (E) 5

55. City A is x miles from New York, city B is y miles from New York, and City C is z miles from New York and lies between city A and city B. All three cities lie to the left of New York. If A, B, C, and New York are all on a straight line, and $x > y$,

    (A) $x < y < z$
    (B) $y > z > x$
    (C) $z < x < y$
    (D) $x > z > y$
    (E) $y < x < z$

IF YOU FINISH BEFORE THE TIME IS UP, GO OVER YOUR WORK FOR THIS SECTION ONLY. DO NOT TURN TO ANY OTHER SECTION OF THE TEST. WHEN THE TIME IS UP, GO ON TO THE NEXT SECTION.

SECTION 3: BUSINESS JUDGMENT

Time: 30 minutes for all of Section 3

QUESTIONS ON DATA EVALUATION

Directions: Read the passage. After the passage are Data Evaluation questions (in phrase form) that relate to the passage. Answer each question by choosing the appropriate letter for your answer.

(A) **Major Objective.** The phrase indicates a Major Objective of the business executive in the situation described in the passage.

(B) **Major Factor.** The phrase indicates a Major Factor in the business executive's arriving at a decision. The passage specifically mentions a circumstance or consideration that is fundamental in his coming to the decision.

(C) **Minor Factor.** The phrase indicates a Minor Factor in the business executive's arriving at a decision. The passage specifically states a circumstance or consideration that is secondary in his coming to a decision.

(D) **Major Assumption.** The phrase indicates a Major Assumption in the business executive's arriving at a decision. He is taking for granted certain circumstances or occurrences in his decision-making.

(E) **Unimportant Issue.** The phrase indicates an Unimportant Issue in the business executive's arriving at a decision. The issue is of no importance or of no relevance in his decision-making.

The Magna Corporation is one of the largest companies in the United States, and apart from being a major defense contractor, is also diversified into a number of important industrial product areas. Mr. Roberts, general manager of the tube department within the Microwave Components Division, has to make a decision as to whether the department should start to manufacture complete microwave ovens or should continue to make only the tube components for microwave oven manufacturers.

The electronics industry is considered to be very competitive and one where high technology is required, together with abundant capital. While the tube department has no experience in manufacturing ovens, Roberts feels that it has a competitive advantage in being skilled in the production of the components, and the corporation has abundant capital. Moreover, Roberts is confident that raw materials will continue to be readily available.

Demand for ovens appears to be growing. One growth area seems to be restaurants where faster food preparation, cheaper labor cost, and easier cleaning of ovens is spurring demand. The restaurant business as a whole appears to be thriving and over the past ten years, while the number of eating and drinking establishments has declined nearly 20% on a per capita basis, the dollar value of sales has increased. Up to four years ago, the $100,000-and-over restaurants accounted for 31.2% of all restaurant sales, and during the past four years, with total restaurant sales growing 16%, the $100,000 restaurants increased their share of the total to 36.1%. In the last four years, the number of $100,000 restaurants has increased to 25,000 — a growth of 25%. An even greater percentage growth in number and share of market has occurred in the sub-group of restaurants with yearly sales of over $300,000.

Roberts also believes that the food-vending industry is showing rapid growth, and possibly through consumer awareness the food-vending machines may encourage consumers to buy their own microwave ovens for their own home use. Moreover, there is greater volume potential in the sale of household ovens than there is in other oven-sale markets.

As a supplier of components, the tube department has no control over the microwave oven manufacturers who can choose tube suppliers at will. Full production of ovens, however, will mean that the tube department will have to consider new sales outlets (restaurants, food-vending companies, and possibly homeowners). The marketing program will differ according to whether emphasis is placed on the restaurant, food-vending, or homeowner business. The tube department has no marketing experience in these areas, nor does it have knowledge of the food industry. This worries Roberts since he is especially concerned with reducing risk. His aim of increasing profit and reducing risk might be better served through joint ventures with food manufacturers and food-vending machine companies rather than through manufacturing and handling the ovens completely within the tube department. He wants to see the prestige of the Magna Corporation (and his own) increase, but there may be other products which the tube department could manufacture — products which might offer more potential for increasing such prestige. Roberts is considering products for household or general industrial use.

Roberts realizes that this whole operation may be beyond the scope of the relatively small tube department but the project could be assigned to some other division of the Magna Corporation, if necessary. Roberts will, of course, keep senior management informed of progress with the project.

Choose the appropriate letter (A or B or C or D or E)
for these phrases in accordance with the given directions.

56. Increase in demand for microwave ovens

57. The attempt to reduce risk

58. Experience in marketing ovens

59. The use of capital more productively elsewhere

60. Labor cost in the restaurant business

61. Possibility of reducing risk through joint venture

62. Prestige of the Magna Corporation

63. Size of the tube department

64. Knowledge of technology

65. Supply of necessary raw materials

66. Easier cleaning of microwave ovens

67. Knowledge of the food industry

68. Current demand for microwave ovens

69. Compatibility with defense work

70. Growth of $300,000 restaurants

71. Approval by senior management

72. Employment for subordinates in the tube department

QUESTIONS ON DATA APPLICATION

Directions: The questions below are to be answered with reference to the same passage (above). For each question, select the correct answer from each of the five choices given.

73. Which of the following reasons is (are) given for Mr. Roberts' investigation into the manufacture of ovens?

    I. Reduction of risk
    II. Quicker delivery of ovens to the consumer
    III. Less need for capital

    (A) I only
    (B) I and II only
    (C) II and III only
    (D) III only
    (E) I, II, and III

74. Which of the following is Roberts considering?

    I. Joint ventures
    II. Manufacture of complete ovens
    III. More defense contracts

    (A) I only
    (B) I and II only
    (C) II and III only
    (D) III only
    (E) I, II, and III

75. Which of the following may influence Roberts' decision to stress marketing to restaurants?

    I. Consumer awareness of microwave ovens for household use
    II. Oven-cleaning problems
    III. Labor costs

    (A) I only
    (B) I and II only
    (C) II and III only
    (D) III only
    (E) I, II, and III

76. What advantages does the tube department have?

    I. Ample size
    II. Oven-marketing experience
    III. Technological skill

    (A) I only
    (B) I and II only
    (C) II and III only
    (D) III only
    (E) I, II, and III

77. Which of the following items is (are) assumed?

      I. Increasing demand for microwave ovens
     II. Availability of sales outlets
    III. Approval by senior management

(A) I only
(B) I and II only
(C) II and III only
(D) III only
(E) I, II, and III

78. Over the past ten years the number of eating and drinking establishments has

(A) declined more than 20%
(B) declined at least 5% on a per capita basis
(C) not affected dollar volume of sales
(D) declined between 6% and 20%
(E) not changed

79. In the past four years the $100,000-and-over restaurants have

(A) increased their share of total restaurant sales for that class of restaurant by less than 6%
(B) increased in number to approximately 300,000
(C) declined in number by 25%
(D) had faster growth than the $300,000 restaurants
(E) been stable in performance

80. Potential sales of ovens to the restaurant business is

(A) at least 10% greater than to the vending machine business
(B) at least 20% less than to the vending machine business
(C) less than the combined potential of sales to the vending machine business and the household market
(D) approximately equal to the combined potential of sales to the vending machine business and the household market
(E) unknown

IF YOU FINISH BEFORE THE TIME IS UP, GO OVER YOUR WORK FOR THIS SECTION ONLY. DO NOT TURN TO ANY OTHER SECTION OF THE TEST. WHEN THE TIME IS UP, GO ON TO THE NEXT SECTION.

SECTION 4: DATA SUFFICIENCY

Time: 30 minutes

Directions: Each of the questions below is followed by two statements, labeled (1) and (2), in which certain data are given. In these questions you do not actually have to compute an answer, but rather you have to decide whether the data given in the statements are *sufficient* for answering the question. Using the data given in the statements *plus* your knowledge of mathematics and everyday facts (such as the number of days in July), you are to blacken the box on the answer sheet under

- (A) if statement (1) ALONE is sufficient but statement (2) alone is not sufficient to answer the question asked.
- (B) if statement (2) ALONE is sufficient but statement (1) alone is not sufficient to answer the question asked.
- (C) if BOTH statements (1) and (2) TOGETHER are sufficient to answer the question asked, but NEITHER statement ALONE is sufficient.
- (D) if EACH statement is sufficient by itself to answer the question asked.
- (E) if statements (1) and (2) TOGETHER are NOT sufficient to answer the question asked and additional data specific to the problem are needed.

81. A gold ring weighs 1 ounce. The ring is not pure gold but is mixed with copper. What is the value of the metal in the ring?

    (1) Gold is worth $35 per ounce.
    (2) 50% of the weight of the ring is due to copper.

82. A certain number, k, is a member of the set [4, 9, 16, 25, 36]. What is k?

    (1) k^2 is divisible by 8.
    (2) k is divisible by a cube other than 1.

83. In triangle LKJ, Angle L is x° and Angle K is y°. Is the triangle obtuse?

    (1) $40 < x < 50$.
    (2) $20 < y < 30$.

84. All the boys at Camp Ola play baseball or soccer or both. 60 boys play baseball. 50 boys play soccer. How many boys are there at the camp?

    (1) 15 boys play both baseball and soccer.
    (2) 35 boys play soccer only.

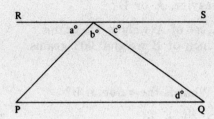

85. In the diagram shown above, line RS is parallel to PQ. What is the value of d?

    (1) a = 60
    (2) b = 90

86. Three cars — car A, car B, and car C — go from Barktown to Dogtown. Car A goes 60 MPH, car B goes 30 MPH, and car C goes 120 MPH. How far is it between the two towns?

    (1) Car A arrives 15 minutes ahead of car B.
    (2) Car C arrives 7½ minutes ahead of car A.

87. How tall is the tallest of three buildings?

    (1) The average height of the buildings is 55 feet.
    (2) The shortest building is 25 feet tall.

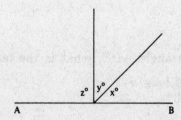

88. In the figure above, AB is a straight line. What is the value of y?

    (1) 2x + 3y + 2z = 420
    (2) y = 2x, z = 3x

89. How many students in Beth's class received over 80 on the math test?

    (1) The sum of all the marks of her class was 2400.
    (2) The class average on the test was 80.

90. Which gas is heavier, A or B?

    (1) One cubic foot of A weighs 1.2 grams.
    (2) One cubic inch of B weighs .003 grams.

91. b is an integer. What is the value of b?

    (1) $5b + 7 \geqslant 3b + 13$
    (2) $b^2 \leqslant 10$

92. Tom, Fred, and Robert earned $160 together. How much did Robert earn?

    (1) Three times Robert's earnings minus twice the sum of the earnings of Fred and Tom is $80.
    (2) Tom earned twice as much as Fred.

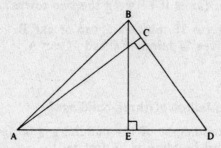

93. In the triangle above, what is the length of altitude BE?

    (1) AD = 10 feet
    (2) BD = 9 feet

94. In the isosceles triangle ADE, what is the length of AD?

    (1) AE is 4 units long.
    (2) Angle E is 90°.

95. Sam's backyard is 100 feet long and 50 feet wide. How much did it cost to plant grass there?

    (1) A bag of grass seed costs 89¢.
    (2) Sam mixed the grass seed with clover seed which costs 49¢ per bag.

96. How much does an egg cost?

    (1) There are 10 boxes in a case of eggs.
    (2) A box of eggs costs 72¢.

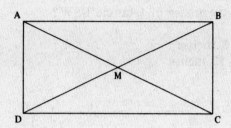

97. In rectangle ABCD, what is the measure of angle BDC?

    (1) Angle AMB measures 134°.
    (2) Angle DBC measures 67°.

98. How old is Sam?

    (1) 14 years from now he will be 2 years older than triple his present age.
    (2) He is 3 years older than his brother.

99. What is the circumference of the circle?

    (1) The radius is 4.
    (2) The area is 16π.

100. How tall is the tallest of 3 boys?

    (1) Their average height is 5 feet 9 inches.
    (2) The sum of the heights of two of the boys is 11 feet 4 inches.

101. When does a train that leaves Debsock at midnight arrive in Larborn?

    (1) The train travels 100 miles per hour.
    (2) Debsock is 636 miles from Larborn.

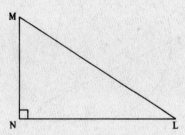

102. What is the length of MN?

    (1) ML = 16 inches.
    (2) NL is twice the length of MN.

103. What is the perimeter of triangle BSW?

    (1) BS = 5 inches
    (2) SW = 12 inches

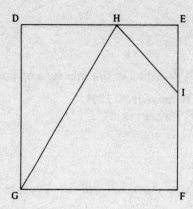

104. In square DEFG, what is the measure of angle HGF?

    (1) Angle HIE measures 43°.
    (2) Angle DHG measures 32°.

105. What is the average profit per cow?

    (1) The farmer had bought 6 cows for $1500.
    (2) The farmer sold the 6 cows for $2400.

106. What is today's date (month and day)?

    (1) In two weeks, it will be the first of a month.
    (2) Two weeks ago, it was the first of a month.

107. Is U greater than V?

    (1) $3U = 2V$.
    (2) $U^2 > V$.

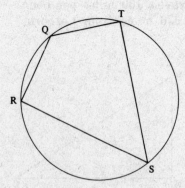

108. What is the measure of angle QRS?

    (1) Arc QTS measures 180°.
    (2) QS is a diameter of the circle.

109. *Y* and *Z* are points on line segment *WX* and *Z* lies between *W* and *Y*. What is the length of *YZ*?

    (1) $WZ = \quad YX$
    (2) $YX = 3$ inches

110. Who earned the least money — Tim, Alan, or Charles?

    (1) Alan earned $1\frac{1}{2}$ times as much as Charles.
    (2) Tim earned 35% of the money.

IF YOU FINISH BEFORE THE TIME IS UP, GO OVER YOUR WORK FOR THIS SECTION ONLY. DO NOT TURN TO ANY OTHER SECTION OF THE TEST. WHEN THE TIME IS UP, GO ON TO THE NEXT SECTION.

SECTION 5: GRAMMAR AND USAGE

Time: 30 minutes

Directions: In each question, you will find a sentence with four words (or phrases) underlined. In some sentences one of the underlined words (or phrases) is incorrect in the light of the rules of standard written English for grammar, correct usage, and choice of words. No sentence has more than one error. You are to assume that the rest of the sentence (whatever is not underlined) is correct. If you find an error, choose the letter (A *or* B *or* C *or* D) of that underlined word (or phrase) which is incorrect. If you find no error, fill in answer space E.

111. We were terrified by sounds: the screaming of the wind; the rest-
            A   B

     less rustle of leaves in the trees; and the sudden, overwhelming ex-
         C   D

     plosions of thunder. No error.
                     E

112. His dog having barked a warning, the watchman who
               A

     had been assigned to guard the valuable truckload of chemicals
           B

     pulled out his gun quick and proceeded to search out a possible
                C   D

     intruder. No error.
             E

113. Your employer would have been inclined to favor your request if
                     A

     you would have waited for an occasion when he was less busy with
         B   C

     other more important matters. No error.
           D   E

114. Popular impressions about slang are often erroneous: their is no
                A   B

     necessary connection, for example, between what is slang and what
                 C   D

     is ungrammatical. No error.
               E

115. After all the performers <u>had finished</u> their performances, I knew
A
the winner to be <u>he</u> <u>whom</u> I had singled out <u>the moment</u> I had
B   C   D
met him. <u>No error.</u>
E

116. <u>Nor</u> has the writer even the satisfaction of calling his reader a fool
A
for misunderstanding him, since he seldom hears <u>of</u> it; it is the
B
reader who calls the writer a fool <u>for</u> not being able to express
C
<u>hisself.</u> <u>No error.</u>
D   E

117. Struggling <u>hard</u> against almost <u>insuperable odds</u>, he was unable,
A   B
<u>to effect</u> even a small change in the <u>course</u> of the vehicle. <u>No error.</u>
C   D   E

118. I appreciate <u>you</u> helping me <u>to do</u> the dishes, but I wish you would
A   B
<u>lay</u> them down on the table more <u>carefully.</u> <u>No error.</u>
C   D   E

119. Looking through the <u>main gate</u> at the southwest corner of the park
A
where the bridle path <u>emerges</u> from the wood, <u>the blooming lilac</u>
B   C
can be seen in <u>great sprays</u> of purple, lavender, and white. <u>No error.</u>
D   E

120. <u>No sooner</u> had be <u>begun</u> to speak <u>when</u> an ominous muttering
A   B   C
<u>arose</u> from the audience. <u>No error.</u>
D   E

121. Separate vacations by husband and wife are <u>much esteemed</u> in cer-
A
tain circles, but if such holidays <u>last</u> more than a year <u>or so</u>, even
B   C
the most liberal raise <u>there</u> eyebrows. <u>No error.</u>
D   E

122. Proud of his skill <u>in serving</u> liquor, he <u>poured</u> some of the wine
                            A   B

into his own glass first so that he <u>would get</u> the cork
                                    C

<u>and not the lady.</u> <u>No error.</u>
      D   E

123. The captain of the squad was a sophomore, one of last <u>year's</u>
                                               A

<u>freshman</u> team, a player of great intelligence, and, <u>above all,</u>
   B   C

<u>endurance.</u> <u>No error.</u>
   D   E

124. Everyone <u>is expected</u> <u>to attend</u> the afternoon session <u>but</u> the field
             A   B   C

supervisor, the sales manager, and <u>I.</u> <u>No error.</u>
                               D   E

125. No one who <u>has seen</u> him work in the laboratory <u>can deny</u> that
               A   B

Williams has an <u>interest and an</u> <u>aptitude</u> for chemical experimenta-
                C   D

tion. <u>No error.</u>
     E

126. Manslaughter is <u>where</u> a person <u>is killed</u> <u>unlawfully</u> <u>but without</u>
                A   B   C   D

premeditation. <u>No error.</u>
          E

127. The reason teenagers <u>tend</u> to follow the trend while <u>openly</u> declaring
                   A   B

<u>themselves</u> nonconformists is <u>because</u> they are really insecure.
   C   D

<u>No error.</u>
   E

128. <u>Its</u> not generally <u>known</u> that the word "buxom" <u>originally</u> came
    A   B   C

from the <u>Old English</u> verb meaning "to bend." <u>No error.</u>
          D   E

129. A <u>great many</u> educators <u>firmly</u> believe that English is one of the
       A   B

<u>poorest</u> taught subjects in high school <u>today.</u> <u>No error.</u>
  C   D   E

130. Developed by the research engineers of Dupont, the government
                         A   B
       considers the new explosive a sure deterrent to war. No error.
                                       C   D   E

131. Baseball, football, and soccer have all been approved as
                                             A
       extracurricular activities. From either of them a coach can earn
            B   C
       several hundreds of dollars each season. No error.
               D   E

132. After I listened to the violinist and cellist, and enjoyed their
              A   B
       interpretations, I hurried home to practice. No error.
                       C   D   E

133. Most of the citizens have no doubt that the Mayor taking a firm
                               A   B
       stand in the matter of clamping down on drug peddlers will bear
                                  C
       immediate results in ridding the city of these vermin. No error.
                         D   E

134. Having sat the bag of dirty clothes on a bench in the apartment
          A   B
       building laundry room, Mrs. Williams chatted with a neighbor
                                      C
       until a washing machine was available. No error.
                             D   E

135. None of the crew members who flew with me over Hanoi is
                                A   B
       happy today about the destruction caused in that bombing mission.
                   C   D
       No error.
        E

IF YOU FINISH BEFORE THE TIME IS UP, GO OVER YOUR WORK FOR THIS SECTION ONLY. DO NOT TURN TO ANY OTHER SECTION OF THE TEST. WHEN THE TIME IS UP, GO ON TO THE NEXT SECTION.

SECTION 6: BUSINESS JUDGMENT

Time: 30 minutes for all Section 6

QUESTIONS ON DATA EVALUATION

Directions: Read the passage. After the passage are Data Evaluation questions (in phrase form) that relate to the passage. Answer each question by choosing the appropriate letter for your answer.

(A) **Major Objective.** The phrase indicates a Major Objective of the business executive in the situation described in the passage.

(B) **Major Factor.** The phrase indicates a Major Factor in the business executive's arriving at a decision. The passage specifically mentions a circumstance or consideration that is fundamental in his coming to the decision.

(C) **Minor Factor.** The phrase indicates a Minor Factor in the business executive's arriving at a decision. The passage specifically states a circumstance or consideration that is secondary in his coming to a decision.

(D) **Major Assumption.** The phrase indicates a Major Assumption in the business executive's arriving at a decision. He is taking for granted certain circumstances or occurrences in his decision-making.

(E) **Unimportant Issue.** The phrase indicates an Unimportant Issue in the business executive's arriving at a decision. The issue is of no importance or of no relevance in his decision-making.

Mr. Storr is considering whether he should resign from his present job and start his own business. Working as a researcher in a large chemical company, Mr. Storr has obtained knowledge of a solid oxygen supply system, used in the C-5A Galaxy bombers, by which oxygen is released from a cartridge of sodium chlorate. Storr has learned that oxygen is used as a reliever for persons suffering from heart and respiratory diseases. Up to the present time, instruments using liquid oxygen have been used for this purpose but these have the disadvantage of being bulky, heavy, and relatively dangerous. It has occurred to Storr that the solid oxygen system can readily be modified to make it suitable for medical use. During his spare time, he has designed a small instrument capable of supplying enough oxygen to a person for half an hour. The instrument has the marked advantage of being lighter, smaller, less dangerous, and less costly than any existing instrument for the purpose. The instrument consists of cartridges which can be easily removed and replaced by new cartridges. Thus Storr believes that the solid oxygen system can get wide acceptance as a portable device.

Having secured a patent for his design, Storr has undertaken a feasibility study on his own. First he went to several medical associations and received official medical approval for the product as a reliever in several respiratory diseases, mainly emphysema and asthma. The Tuberculosis and Respiratory Disease Association has supplied Storr with information as to the location of the heaviest sufferers of emphysema and asthma.

Storr has regarded these areas as a basis for evolving his marketing strategy. The highest concentration of possible users is in densely populated urban areas, particularly New York, Philadelphia, Washington, D.C., and Los Angeles. Because of the heterogeneity of the market distribution, a problem has arisen as to the initial scale of operations of the planned company. Clearly three of the major markets for the product are relatively in the same vicinity while the fourth — Los Angeles — will necessitate increased transportation costs. Further, any initial attempt to service the West Coast markets as well as the East will require the establishment of an agency in the Los Angeles area and consequently entail higher overall selling and administration costs. Finally, since the West Coast market comprises 15% of the total market potential while the East Coast represents approximately 60% of the total potential, Storr has decided to supply the East Coast market initially and to enlarge the distribution to cover the West Coast after satisfactory acceptance in the East.

As for determining distribution channels, Storr is somewhat limited by the nature of the product. As with any medical product, it is necessary to gain general medical acceptance and recommendation before attempting direct consumer distribution. Consequently, he intends to make the product initially available only with a doctor's prescription; and after two years, when the public has gained knowledge about, and confidence in, the product, it will then be supplied through drug stores.

The initial favorable response expected from doctors has been conservatively estimated by Storr at 20% and consequently when this figure was applied to the potential market, an estimate of the expected market penetration was obtained. First year sales have been estimated at 10,000 units and are expected to increase rapidly. After five years, the product, according to projections, will eventually reach its maturity stage — a volume of 50,000 units yearly. Thereafter, sales will parallel the market growth at an annual rate of 5% due to population growth, increase in air pollution, and a constant smoking rate.

The design of the product is such that a price had to be determined for replacement cartridges as well as for the total system itself. Since there are no comparable products on the market, Storr determined the full cost of the product based on the volume of his expected sales for the first two years and then applied a 30% profit margin. The resultant prices were as follows:

Initial Total System: $60.00 each
Replacement Cartridges: $3.50 each

These prices will drastically undersell those products being sold which are based on liquid oxygen.

Of course, financing has been an important consideration in determining the feasibility of the venture. Since Storr is not independently wealthy, he has sought external financing. It occurred to him that the Small Business Administration of the federal government was a good source of advice and he therefore contacted them. As a result of his talks with people at this agency, Storr has learned that he is eligible for a major loan to cover the capitalization costs of the proposed company, provided he establishes his factory in one of the six less developed industrial regions in the United States. The loan carries an interest rate which is much lower than that on funds he is able to obtain elsewhere. Further, one of the designated areas for establishment of the factory is the New England States. Proceeding with this information, Storr obtained data on the cost of factory space in places in the Massachusetts area which were within easy reach of New York City and other target market areas. He finally settled on Waterbury, Massachusetts.

Thus Storr has all the necessary information to make the ultimate decision — whether to go ahead or not. He realizes that his present position offers him security during his lifetime although it offers limited prospects. Certainly the venture which he is considering offers the possibility of high profit as well as the satisfaction of managing his own company and being socially successful. On the other hand, there are many risks involved and if the company should fail, a man of his age may find it difficult to get suitable employment immediately.

Choose the appropriate letter (A or B or C or D or E)
for these phrases in accordance with the given directions.

136. Advantages of the solid oxygen system

137. Determination of a price for replacement cartridges

138. The public's knowledge of, and confidence in, the product

139. The underselling of competitive products

140. Obtaining a patent for the design

141. Initial favorable response from doctors

142. The use of the oxygen supply system in the C-5A Galaxy bomber

143. Management of the venture by Storr himself

144. Growth of the market at an annual rate of 5%

145. Difficulty of obtaining suitable employment in Storr's case

146. Official medical approval of the product

147. Eligibility for a major loan

148. Security afforded by his present position

149. The plan to locate the plant in Massachusetts

150. Becoming socially successful

151. The period required by the product to reach its maturity stage

152. The low interest rate of the loan

QUESTIONS ON DATA APPLICATION

Directions: The questions below are to be answered with reference to the same passage (above). For each question, select the correct answer from each of the five choices given.

153. Which of the following characteristics applies (apply) to the solid oxygen supply system?

    I. Easy to carry
    II. Relatively dangerous
    III. Expensive.

    (A) I only
    (B) II only
    (C) I and II only
    (D) I and III only
    (E) I, II, and III

154. In which of the following areas does Mr. Storr wish to enter initially?

    I. The Far West
    II. The Northeast
    III. The Southwest

    (A) I only
    (B) II only
    (C) I and II only
    (D) I and III only
    (E) I, II, and III

155. Which of the following are factors in Storr's arriving at a decision?

    I. His product has official medical approval.
    II. 20% of the doctors will recommend his product.
    III. The market is larger on the East Coast than on the West Coast.

    (A) I only
    (B) II only
    (C) I and II only
    (D) I and III only
    (E) I, II, and III

156. The price of the new product is based on

    I. The full cost
    II. The expected volume of sales
    III. The existing market price

    (A) I only
    (B) II only
    (C) I and II only
    (D) I and III only
    (E) I, II, and III

157. The location of the plant has been determined by

    I. Financial considerations
    II. Production costs
    III. Transportation costs

    (A) I only
    (B) II only
    (C) I and II only
    (D) I and III only
    (E) I, II, and III

158. First-year sales have been forecast at

    (A) 2,000-5,000 units
    (B) 8,000-12,000 units
    (C) 25,000-30,000 units
    (D) 55,000-60,000 units
    (E) 60,000-65,000 units

159. The price arrived at for the initial total system including replacement cartridges is

    (A) $3.50
    (B) $56.50
    (C) $60.00
    (D) $63.50
    (E) $200.00

160. What percentage of the total market does the West Coast represent?

    (A) 2 to 5 percent
    (B) 5 to 9 percent
    (C) 13 to 16 percent
    (D) 25 to 30 percent
    (E) 50 to 60 percent

IF YOU FINISH BEFORE THE TIME IS UP, GO OVER YOUR WORK FOR THIS SECTION ONLY. DO NOT TURN TO ANY OTHER SECTION OF THE TEST. WHEN THE TIME IS UP, GO ON TO THE NEXT SECTION.

SECTION 7A: READING RECALL

Time: 15 Minutes

Directions: Read the following three passages. While
you are reading these passages, bear in mind you will be
asked to recall certain facts and ideas about what you have
read here. After the reading time limit of 15 minutes, you
will not be permitted to turn back to these passages. The
questions based on these passages will be given to you after
the proctor announces that time is up for the reading of
these three passages.

FIRST PASSAGE

The American people were dismayed by the sudden proof that something
had gone wrong with their economic system, that it lacked stability and was
subject to crises of unpredictable magnitude. They had encountered hard
times and temporary depressions before, and such reverses had tended for
over a century to broaden out and to become international misfortunes. But
the depression that began in 1929 proved so severe, so general, and so difficult to arrest, that it caused a "loss of nerve."

Students of economics pointed out that periods of inflation and deflation,
of "boom and bust," had alternated for generations. Any strong stimulus such
as a war might force the economy of the Western world into high gear; when
the fighting ceased, reconstruction and a "backlog" of consumers' orders un-
filled in wartime might for a time keep the machines running at full speed;
but within a decade the market was likely to become satiated and a fall in
demand would then cause a recession. Adjustment and recovery were certain
to come in time, and come the sooner if a new stimulus developed. The threat
of another war, or war itself, that put millions of men in uniform and created
a demand for munitions, was one such stimulus. War provided a limitless
market for expendable goods, the type of goods the machines were best fitted
to supply, and solved unemployment by creating more military and civilian
jobs. Such reasoning as this brought no comfort, however, for it implied a
choice between war and depression, and the cure was worse than the disease.
"Is modern industry a sick giant that can rouse itself only to kill?" one critic
asked. There was no clear answer. But the American people were not willing
to accept such a grim diagnosis and insisted that there must be some method
of coordinating a supply and demand within the framework of a peacetime
economy.

The problem appeared to be as much psychological as economic. In prosperous times business expanded, prices rose, wages increased, and the expectation that the boom would continue indefinitely tempted people to live beyond
their means. They purchased goods on credit, confident that they could meet
the payments later. The increasing prosperity, in part genuine but over-
stimulated by optimism and artificial elements, encouraged farmers and
manufacturers to overproduce until the supply exceeded the capacity of the
market to absorb it. Then when business confidence began to falter, and stock
quotations began to drop, panic set in. Speculators who saw their "paper
profits" vanishing began to unload their securities with a disastrous effect

on prices. Dealers with overloaded shelves slashed their prices to keep their goods moving, and canceled outstanding orders. Manufacturers, seeing orders shrink, reduced output. All down the line the contraction of business left employees without jobs, and lacking wages they could not meet their debts. Once started, this spiral of deflation seemed to have no limit.

It is natural for people to blame others when misfortune strikes, and after 1929 the American people became suddenly critical of their business leaders, who had failed to foresee or avert the swift transition from prosperity to privation. The conviction spread that the heads of great banks and corporations, the promotors and financiers and stockbrokers, had misled the public. Demands raised earlier in American history were revived, demands for "cheap" money with which to pay off debts, demands that the great trusts and monopolies be investigated, demands that the federal government intervene to correct business abuses and aid the destitute. More and more people began to feel that the system of free business enterprise, of unregulated economic competition, so highly praised in the 1920's, must be wrong if it could lead to crises that brought such widespread misery and unemployment.

But President Hoover was firm in his conviction that the American economic system was fundamentally sound and that it would be a mistake for the government to interfere unduly. Government supervision and regulation of business, he felt, would stifle freedom and lead to government control of activities that should be left to private initiative. "You cannot extend the mastery of the government over the daily life of a people," he warned, "without somewhere making it master of people's souls and thoughts." He believed that the government's role should be limited to helping business help itself, and to this end he supported an act (1932) which created the Reconstruction Finance Corporation to aid ailing businesses, as well as hard-pressed states, with government loans. Hoover also inaugurated a public works program which he hoped would effectively relieve unemployment. But beyond such indirect measures as these he did not believe the federal government should go. Meanwhile the burden of providing direct relief for the millions of unemployed and their families was exhausting the resources of state and local governments and private agencies — and still the breadlines formed as jobs and savings went.

SECOND PASSAGE

Medieval Europe abounded in castles. Germany alone had ten thousand and more, most of them now vanished; all that a summer journey in the Rhineland and the south-west now can show are a handful of ruins and a few nineteenth century restorations. Nevertheless, anyone journeying from Spain to the Dvina, from Calabria to Wales, will find castles rearing up again and again to dominate the open landscape. There they still stand, in desolate and uninhabited districts where the only visible forms of life are herdsmen and their flocks, with hawks circling the battlements, far from the traffic and comfortably distant even from the nearest small town: these were the strongholds of the European aristocracy.

The weight of aristocratic dominance was felt in Europe until well after the French Revolution; political and social structure, the Church, the general tenor of thought and feeling were all influenced by it. Over the centuries, consciously or unconsciously, the other classes of this older European society — the clergy, the bourgeoisie and the 'common people' — adopted many of the outward characteristics of the aristocracy, who became their model, their standard, their ideal. Aristocratic values and ambitions were adopted alongside aristocratic manners and fashions of dress. Yet the aristocracy were the object of much contentious criticism and complaint; from the thirteenth century onwards their military value and their political importance were both called in question. Nevertheless, their opponents continued to be their principal imitators. In the eleventh and twelfth centuries, the reforming Papacy and its clerical supporters, although opposed to the excessively aristocratic control of the Church (as is shown by the Investiture Contest) nevertheless themselves first adopted and then strengthened the forms of this control. Noblemen who became bishops or who founded new Orders helped to implant aristocratic principles and forms of government deep within the structure and spiritual life of the Church. Again, in the twelfth and thirteenth centuries the urban bourgeoisie, made prosperous and even rich by trade and industry, were rising to political power as the servants and legal proteges of monarchy. These 'patricians' were critical of the aristocracy and hostile towards it. Yet they also imitated the aristocracy, and tried to gain admittance to the closed circle and to achieve equality of status. Even the unarmed peasantry, who usually had to suffer more from the unrelieved weight of aristocratic dominance, long remained tenaciously loyal to their lords, held to their allegiance by that combination of love and fear, *amor et timor*, which was so characteristic of the medieval relationship between lord and servant, between God and man.

The castles and strongholds of the aristocracy remind us of the reality of their power and superiority. Through the long warring centuries when men went defenceless and insecure, the 'house', the lord's fortified dwelling, promised protection, security and peace to all whom it sheltered. From the ninth to the eleventh centuries, if not later, Europe was in many ways all too open. Attack came from the sea, in the Mediterranean from Saracens and Vikings, the latter usually in their swift, dragon-prowed, easily manoeuvred longboats, manned by some sixteen pairs of oarsmen and with a full complement of perhaps sixty men. There were periods when the British Isles and the French coasts were being raided every year by Vikings and in the heart of the continent marauding Magyar armies met invading bands of Saracens. The name of Pontresina, near St. Moritz in Switzerland, is a memento of the stormy tenth century; it means *pons Saracenorum,* the 'fortified Saracen bridge', the place where plundering expeditions halted on their way up from the Mediterranean.

It was recognized in theory that the Church and the monarchy were the principal powers and that they were bound by the nature of their office to ensure peace and security and to do justice; but at this period they were too weak, too torn by internal conflicts to fulfil their obligations. Thus more and more power passed into the hands of warriors invested by the monarchy and the Church with lands and rights of jurisdiction, who in return undertook to support their overlords and to protect the unarmed peasantry.

Their first concern, however, was self-protection. It is almost impossible for us to realize how primitive the great majority of these early medieval 'castles' really were. Until about 1150 the fortified houses of the Anglo-Norman nobility were simple dwellings surrounded by a mound of earth and a wooden stockade. These were the motte and bailey castles: the motte was the mound and its stockade, the bailey an open court lying below and also stockaded. Both were protected, where possible, by yet another ditch filled with water, the moat. In the middle of the motte there was a wooden tower, the keep or *donjon,* which only became a genuine stronghold at a later date and in places where stone was readily available. The stone castles of the French and German nobility usually had only a single communal room in which all activities took place.

In such straitened surroundings, where warmth, light and comfort were lacking, there was no way of creating an air of privacy. It is easy enough to understand why the life of the landed nobility was often so unrestrained. so filled with harshness, cruelty and brutality, even in later, more 'chivalrous' periods. The barons' daily life was bare and uneventful, punctuated by war, hunting (a rehearsal for war), and feasting. Boys were trained to fight from the age of seven or eight, and their education in arms continued until they were twenty-one, although in some cases they started to fight as early as fifteen. The peasants of the surrounding countryside, bound to their lords by a great variety of ties, produced the sparse fare which was all that the undeveloped agriculture of the early medieval period could sustain. Hunting was a constant necessity, to make up for the lack of butcher's meat, and in England and Germany in the eleventh and twelfth centuries even the kings had to progress from one crown estate to another, from one bishop's palace to the next, to maintain themselves and their retinue.

THIRD PASSAGE

A second major hypothesis would argue that the most important dimension of advanced technological institutions is the social one; that is, the institutions are agencies of highly centralized and intensive social control. Technology conquers nature, as the saying goes. But to do so it must first conquer man. More precisely, it demands a very high degree of control over the training, mobility, and skills of the work force. The absence (or decline) of direct controls or of coercion should not serve to obscure from our view the reality and intensity of the social controls which are employed (such as the internalized belief in equality of opportunity, indebtedness through credit, advertising, selective service channeling, and so on).

Advanced technology has created a vast increase in occupational specialties, many of them requiring many, many years of highly specialized training. It must motivate this training. It has made ever more complex and "rational" the ways in which these occupational specialties are combined in our economic and social life. It must win passivity and obedience to this complex activity. Formerly, technical rationality had been employed only to organize the production of rather simple physical objects, for example, aerial bombs. Now technical rationality is increasingly employed to organize all of the processes necessary to the utilization of physical objects, such as bombing systems, maintenance, intelligence and supply systems. For this reason it seems a mistake to argue that we are in a "post-industrial" age, a concept favored by the *laissez innover* school. On the contrary, the rapid spread of technical rationality into organizational and economic life and, hence, into social life is more aptly described as a second and much more intensive phase of the industrial revolution. One might reasonably suspect that it will create analogous social problems.

Accordingly, a third major hypothesis would argue that there are very profound social antagonisms or contradictions not less sharp or fundamental than those ascribed by Marx to the development of nineteenth-century industrial society. The general form of the contradictions might be described as follows: a society characterized by the employment of advanced technology requires an ever more socially disciplined population, yet retains an ever declining capacity to enforce the required discipline.

One may readily describe four specific forms of the same general contradiction. Occupationally, the work force must be over-trained and under-utilized. Here, again, an analogy to classical industrial practice serves to shorten and simplify the explanation. I have in mind the assembly line. As a device in the organization of the work process the assembly line is valuable mainly in that it gives management a high degree of control over the pace of the work and, more to the point in the present case, it divides the work process into units so simple that the quality of the work performed is readily predictable. That is, since each operation uses only a small fraction of a worker's skill, there is a very great likelihood that the operation will be performed in a minimally acceptable way. Alternately, if each operation taxed the worker's skill there would be frequent errors in the operation, frequent disturbance of the work flow, and a thoroughly unpredictable quality to the end product. The assembly line also introduces standardization in work skills and thus makes for a high degree of interchangeability among the work force.

For analogous reasons the work force in advanced technological systems must be relatively over-trained or, what is the same thing, its skills relatively under-used. My impression is that this is no less true now of sociologists than of welders, of engineers than of assemblers. The contradiction emerges when we recognize that technological progress requires a continuous increase in the skill levels of its work force, skill levels which frequently embody a fairly rich scientific and technical training, while at the same time the advance of technical rationality in work organization means that those skills will be less and less fully used.

Economically, there is a parallel process at work. It is commonly observed that the work force within technologically advanced organizations is asked to work not less hard but more so. This is particularly true for those with advanced training and skills. Brzezinski's conjecture that technical specialists undergo continuous retraining is off the mark only in that it assumes such retraining only for a managing elite. To get people to work harder requires growing incentives. Yet the prosperity which is assumed in a technologically advanced society erodes the value of economic incentives (while of course, the values of craftsmanship are "irrational"). Salary and wage increases and the goods they purchase lose their over riding importance once necessities, creature comforts, and an ample supply of luxuries are assured. As if in confirmation of this point, it has been pointed out that among young people one can already observe a radical weakening in the power of such incentives as money, status, and authority.

IF YOU FINISH BEFORE THE TIME IS UP, GO OVER THESE PASSAGES. DO NOT TURN TO THE QUESTIONS FOR THESE PASSAGES NOR TO ANY OTHER SECTION OF THE TEST. WHEN THE 15 MINUTES ARE UP, GO ON TO SECTION 7B WHICH CONTAINS THE QUESTIONS FOR THESE PASSAGES.

SECTION 7B: READING RECALL

Time: 15 minutes

Directions: Answer the following questions on the basis of what is stated or implied in the passages which you have just read. You are not permitted at any time to turn back to the passages.

QUESTIONS FOR FIRST PASSAGE

161. According to the passage, President Hoover

    (A) urged more and more government regulation
    (B) did little or nothing to aid ailing businesses
    (C) made efforts to relieve unemployment
    (D) had sincere doubts about the soundness of the American economic system
    (E) expressed the belief that we should convert gradually to a socialistic form of government

162. The author indicates that recovery from a recession most likely comes about

    (A) during wartime
    (B) during peacetime
    (C) by decreasing manufacturing
    (D) by lowering wages
    (E) by raising the interest rate

163. Which of the following was *not* a cause of the 1929 Depression?

    (A) too much buying on credit
    (B) rising prices
    (C) overproduction of goods
    (D) lack of economic stability
    (E) political unrest throughout the world

164. When the stock dropped,

    (A) manufacturers immediately increased output
    (B) unemployment decreased
    (C) there was a reduction of business
    (D) dealers increased their prices
    (E) speculators held on to their securities

165. The Reconstruction Finance Corporation

    (A) remodeled old private and government buildings
    (B) served as a price-regulating organization
    (C) helped the unemployed to find jobs during the Depression
    (D) gave government loans to certain businesses
    (E) supported the unemployed by public relief programs

166. Which statement would the author *not* agree to?

    (A) There will continue to be economic crises.
    (B) Hoover and Nixon were beset by the same economic bugbear — a
        spiral of deflation.
    (C) War tends to reduce unemployment.
    (D) War is not the answer to avoiding economic depression.
    (E) The depression of 1929 had psychological roots.

167. As a result of the Depression,

    (A) the value of the free enterprise system was questioned
    (B) more people demanded that the government stay out of business
    (C) people put more trust in business leaders
    (D) a third of the population was unemployed
    (E) the government was forced to increase taxes

168. War is economically useful because

    (A) it implies a choice between war and depression
    (B) it increases unemployment
    (C) the market becomes satiated
    (D) it solves bouts of inflation
    (E) it increases aggregate demand

169. After 1929, the following demands were raised *except*

    (A) abolition of the great financial cartels
    (B) cheap money
    (C) investigation of trusts and monopolies
    (D) intervention of the federal government to correct business abuses
    (E) intervention of the federal government to aid the poor

170. The contraction of business in 1929 led to

    (A) war fever
    (B) increased unemployment
    (C) payment of debts
    (D) demand exceeding supply
    (E) skyrocketing prices

QUESTIONS FOR SECOND PASSAGE

171. Class conflict in the Middle Ages was kept in check by

    (A) the fact that most people belonged to the same class
    (B) tyrannical supressions of rebellions by powerful monarchs
    (C) the religious teachings of the church
    (D) the fact that all other classes admired and attempted to emulate the aristocracy
    (E) the fear that a relatively minor conflict would lead to a general revolution

172. The urban bourgeoisie was hostile to the aristocracy because

    (A) the bourgeoisie was prevented by the aristocracy from seeking an alliance with the kings
    (B) aristocrats often confiscated the wealth of the bourgeoisie
    (C) the bourgeoisie saw the aristocracy as their rivals
    (D) the aristocrats often deliberately antagonized the bourgeoisie
    (E) the bourgeoisie felt that the aristocracy was immoral

173. Castles were originally built

    (A) as status symbols
    (B) as strongholds against invaders
    (C) as simple places to live in
    (D) as luxurious chateaux
    (E) as recreation centers for the townspeople

174. One of the groups that invaded central Europe during the Middle Ages from the ninth century on was the

    (A) Magyars
    (B) Franks
    (C) Angles
    (D) Celts
    (E) Welsh

175. The aristocracy was originally

    (A) the great landowners
    (B) members of the clergy
    (C) the king's warriors
    (D) merchants who became wealthy
    (E) slaves who had rebelled

176. The reform Popes eventually produced an aristocratic church because

    (A) they depended on the aristocracy for money
    (B) they themselves were more interested in money than in religion
    (C) they were defeated by aristocrats
    (D) many aristocrats entered the structure of the church and impressed their values on it
    (E) the aristocrats were far more religious than other segments of the population

177. Hunting served the dual purpose of

   (A) preparing for war and engaging in sport
   (B) preparing for war and getting meat
   (C) learning how to ride and learning how to shoot
   (D) testing horses and men
   (E) getting furs and ridding the land of excess animals

178. The phrase "amor et timor" is used to describe

   (A) the rivalry between bourgeoisie and aristocracy
   (B) the Church's view of man and his relationship to God
   (C) the peasant's loyalty to the aristocracy
   (D) the adaptation of aristocratic manners and dress
   (E) the payment of food in exchange for protection

179. Protection of the peasantry was implemented by

   (A) the King's warriors
   (B) the Magyar mercenaries
   (C) the replacement of wood towers by stone donjons
   (D) the princes of the Church
   (E) the ruling monarchy

180. The effectiveness of the Church and King was diminished by

   (A) ambition of the military
   (B) conflicts and weaknesses within the Church and Royal house
   (C) peasant dissatisfaction
   (D) the inherent flaws of feudalism
   (E) economic instability

QUESTIONS FOR THIRD PASSAGE

181. The term "technical rationality" is used in conjunction with

   (A) a 20th-century euphemism for the industrial revolution
   (B) giving credibility to products of simple technology
   (C) the incorporation of unnecessary skills into economic social living
   (D) effective organization of production processes
   (E) safeguarding against technological over-acceleration

182. The author states that advanced technological institutions exercise control by means of

   (A) assembly-line work process
   (B) advertising, selective service channeling, etc.
   (C) direct and coercive pressures
   (D) salary incentives
   (E) authoritarian managerial staffs

183. The passage indicates that technologically advanced institutions

   (A) fully utilize worker skills
   (B) fare best under a democratic system
   (C) necessarily overtrain workers
   (D) find it unnecessary to enforce discipline
   (E) are operated by individuals motivated by traditional work incentives

184. The value of the assembly line is that it

   I. minimizes the frequency of error
   II. allows for interchangeability among the work force
   III. allows for full utilization of workers' skills

   (A) I and III only
   (B) I and II only
   (C) II and III only
   (D) I, II, and III
   (E) I only

185. Technologies cannot conquer nature unless

   (A) there is unwavering worker allegiance to the goals of the institutions
   (B) there is strict adherence to a *laissez innover* policy
   (C) worker and management are in concurrence
   (D) there is another more intense, industrial revolution
   (E) the institutions have control over the training, mobility and skills of the work force

186. The article states that the work force within the framework of a technologically advanced organization is

   (A) expected to work less hard
   (B) segregated into levels defined by the degree of technical training
   (C) familiarized with every process of production
   (D) expected to work harder
   (E) isolated by the fact of its specialization

187. From the tone of the article, it can be inferred that the author is

   (A) an eloquent spokesman for technological advancement
   (B) in favor of increased employee control of industry
   (C) a social scientist objectively reviewing an industrial trend
   (D) vehemently opposed to the increase of technology
   (E) skeptical of the workings of advanced technological institutions

188. Economic incentives

   (A) are necessary for all but the managerial elite
   (B) are bigger and better in a society made prosperous by technology
   (C) cease to have importance beyond a certain level of luxury
   (D) are impressive only to new members of the work force
   (E) are impressive to all but the radical young

189. According to the article, technological progress requires

        I. increasing skill levels of work force
       II. less utilization of work skills
     III. rich scientific and technical training

    (A) I and II only
    (B) II and III only
    (C) I and III only
    (D) III only
    (E) I, II and III

190. The article states that money, status, and authority

    (A) will always be powerful work incentives
    (B) are not powerful incentives for the young
    (C) are unacceptable to radical workers
    (D) are incentives that are a throwback to 19th-century industrial society
    (E) are incentives evolving out of human nature

IF YOU FINISH BEFORE THE TIME IS UP, GO OVER YOUR WORK FOR THIS SECTION ONLY. DO NOT TURN TO ANY OTHER SECTION OF THE TEST. WHEN THE TIME IS UP, GO ON TO THE NEXT SECTION.

SECTION 8: SENTENCE CORRECTION

Time: 30 minutes

Directions: Each sentence is partly or wholly under-lined. In some cases, what is underlined is correct — in other cases, it is incorrect. The five choices that follow each sentence represent various ways of writing the underlined part. Choice A is the same as the original underlining but Choices B, C, D, and E are different. If, in your judgment, the original sentence is better than any of the changed sentences, select Choice A. If another choice produces the only correct sentence, select that other choice (B or C or D or E).

In making your choice, you should observe the rules of standard written English. Your choice must fulfill the requirements of correct grammar, diction (word choice), sentence structure, and punctuation.

If a choice changes the meaning of the original sentence, do not make that choice.

191. The students requested a meeting with the chancellor since they desired a greater voice in university policy.

    (A) The students requested a meeting with the chancellor
    (B) A meeting with the chancellor was requested by the students
    (C) It occurred to the students to request a meeting with the chancellor
    (D) The chancellor was the one with whom the students requested a meeting
    (E) The students insisted upon a meeting with the chancellor

192. Three American scientists were jointly awarded the Nobel Prize in Medicine for their study of viruses which led to discoveries.

    (A) for their study of viruses which led to discoveries
    (B) for their discoveries concerning viruses
    (C) as a prize for their discoveries about viruses
    (D) the discovery into viruses being the reason
    (E) for their virus discoveries

193. You must convince me of promptness in returning the money before I can agree to lend you $100.

    (A) You must convince me of promptness in returning the money
    (B) The loan of the money must be returned promptly
    (C) You must understand that you will have to assure me of a prompt money return
    (D) You will have to convince me that you will return the money promptly
    (E) You will return the money promptly

194. Because Bob was an outstanding athlete in high school, <u>in addition to a fine scholastic record,</u> he was awarded a scholarship at Harvard.

    (A) in addition to a fine scholastic record,
    (B) also a student of excellence,
    (C) and had amassed an excellent scholastic record,
    (D) his scholastic record was also outstanding,
    (E) as well as a superior student,

195. Although pre-season odds against the Mets had been 100 to 1, <u>the Orioles were trounced by them in the World Series.</u>

    (A) the Orioles were trounced by them in the World Series
    (B) the World Series victors were the Mets who trounced the Orioles
    (C) they won the World Series by trouncing the Orioles
    (D) which is hard to believe since the Orioles were trounced in the World Series
    (E) it was the Mets who trounced the Orioles in the World Series

196. Before you can make a fresh fruit salad, <u>you must buy oranges, bananas, pineapples and peaches are necessary.</u>

    (A) you must buy oranges, bananas, pineapples and peaches are necessary.
    (B) you must buy oranges and bananas and pineapples and peaches.
    (C) you must buy oranges and bananas. And other fruit such as pineapples and peaches.
    (D) you must buy oranges and bananas and other fruit. Such as pineapples and peaches.
    (E) you must buy oranges, bananas, pineapples, and peaches.

197. The physical education department of the school offers instruction <u>to learn how to swim, how to play tennis, and how to defend oneself.</u>

    (A) to learn how to swim, how to play tennis, and how to defend oneself
    (B) in swimming, playing tennis, and protecting oneself
    (C) in regard to how to swim, how to play tennis, and how to protect oneself
    (D) for the purpose of swimming, playing tennis, and protecting oneself
    (E) in swimming, playing tennis, and to protect oneself

198. <u>Joe couldn't wait for his return to his home</u> after being in the army for two years.

    (A) Joe couldn't wait for his return to his home
    (B) There was a strong desire on Joe's part to return home
    (C) Joe was eager to return home
    (D) Joe wanted home badly
    (E) Joe arranged to return home

199. Trash, filth, and muck are clogging the streets of the city and <u>that's not all, the sidewalks are full of garbage.</u>

    (A) that's not all, the sidewalks are full of garbage.
    (B) another thing: garbage is all over the sidewalks
    (C) the garbage cans haven't been emptied for days
    (D) in addition, garbage is lying all over the sidewalks
    (E) what's more, the sidewalks have garbage that is lying all over them

200. Tired and discouraged by the problems of the day, <u>Myra decided to have a good dinner, and then lie down for an hour, and then go dancing.</u>

    (A) Myra decided to have a good dinner, and then lie down for an hour, and then go dancing.
    (B) Myra decided to have a good dinner, lying down for an hour, and then dancing.
    (C) Myra decided to have a good dinner, lie down for an hour, and then dancing.
    (D) Myra decided to have a good dinner, lay down for an hour, and then dance.
    (E) Myra decided to have a good dinner, lie down for an hour, and then go dancing.

201. I am not certain <u>in respect to which courses</u> to take.

    (A) in respect to which courses
    (B) about which courses
    (C) which courses
    (D) as to the choice of which courses
    (E) for which courses I am

202. The people of the besieged village had no doubt <u>that the end was drawing near.</u>

    (A) that the end was drawing near
    (B) about the nearness of the end
    (C) it was clear that the end was near
    (D) concerning the end's being near
    (E) that all would die

203. There isn't a single man among us <u>who is skilled in the art of administering first-aid.</u>

    (A) who is skilled in the art of administering first-aid
    (B) who knows how to administer first-aid
    (C) who knows the administration of first-aid
    (D) who is a first-aid man
    (E) who administers first-aid

204. This is the hole <u>that was squeezed through by the mouse.</u>

    (A) that was squeezed through by the mouse
    (B) that the mouse was seen to squeeze through
    (C) the mouse squeezed through it
    (D) that the mouse squeezed through
    (E) like what the mouse squeezed through

205. <u>She soundly fell asleep</u> after having finished the novel.

    (A) She soundly fell asleep
    (B) She decided to sleep
    (C) She went on to her sleep
    (D) She fell to sleep
    (E) She fell fast asleep

206. <u>Go where he may,</u> he is the life of the party.

    (A) Go where he may,
    (B) Where he may go,
    (C) Wherever he goes,
    (D) Wherever he may happen to go,
    (E) Whatever he does,

207. At first we were willing to support him, <u>afterwards it occurred to us that</u> he ought to provide for himself.

    (A) afterwards it occurred to us that
    (B) that wasn't the thing to do since
    (C) but we came to realize that
    (D) we came to the conclusion, however, that
    (E) then we decided that

208. <u>The statistics were checked and the report was filed.</u>

    (A) The statistics were checked and the report was filed.
    (B) The statistics and the report were checked and filed.
    (C) The statistics were checked and the report filed.
    (D) The statistics and the report were checked and filed respectively.
    (E) Only after the statistics were checked was the report filed.

209. Dick was awarded a medal for bravery <u>on account he risked his life</u> to save the drowning child.

    (A) on account he risked his life
    (B) being that he risked his life
    (C) when he risked his life
    (D) the reason being on account of his risking his life
    (E) since he had risked his life

210. The teacher asked the newly-admitted student <u>which was the country that she came from.</u>

  (A) which was the country that she came from
  (B) from which country she had come from
  (C) the origin of the country she had come from
  (D) which country have you come from?
  (E) which country she was from

211. At the top of the hill <u>to the left of the tall oak</u> is where they live.

  (A) to the left of the tall oak
  (B) where the tall oak is to the left of it
  (C) and the tall oak is to the left
  (D) left of the tall oak
  (E) to the tall oak's left

212. Martin pretended to be asleep <u>whenever she came</u> into the room.

  (A) whenever she came
  (B) at the time she comes
  (C) although she came
  (D) since she came
  (E) by the time she came

213. Once a person starts taking addictive drugs <u>it is most likely he will be led to take more.</u>

  (A) it is most likely he will be led to take more
  (B) he will probably take them over and over again
  (C) it is hard to stop him from taking more
  (D) he is likely to continue taking them
  (E) he will have a tendency to continue taking them

214. We have not yet been informed <u>concerning the one who broke the window.</u>

  (A) concerning the one who broke the window
  (B) about the identity of the individual who is responsible for breaking the window
  (C) of the window-breaker
  (D) as to who broke the window
  (E) who broke the window

215. Having the highest marks in his class, <u>the college offered him a scholarship.</u>

  (A) the college offered him a scholarship
  (B) the college offered a scholarship to him
  (C) he was offered a scholarship by the college
  (D) a scholarship was offered him by the college
  (E) a college scholarship was offered to him

216. <u>The government's failing to keep it's pledges</u> will mean disaster.

    (A) The government's failing to keep it's pledges
    (B) The governments failing to keep it's pledges
    (C) The government's failing to keep its pledges
    (D) The government failing to keep its pledges
    (E) The governments failing to keep their pledges

217. Her father <u>along with her mother and sister insist</u> that she stop smoking.

    (A) along with her mother and sister insist
    (B) along with her mother and sister insists
    (C) along with her mother and sister are insisting
    (D) along with her mother and sister were insisting
    (E) as well as her mother and sister insist

218. Most gardeners like to cultivate <u>these kind of flowers</u> in the early spring.

    (A) these kind of flowers
    (B) these kind of flower
    (C) them kinds of flowers
    (D) those kind of flower
    (E) this kind of flowers

219. The doctor informs us that my aunt <u>has not and never will recover</u> from the fall.

    (A) has not and never will recover
    (B) has not recovered and never will
    (C) has not and never would recover
    (D) has not recovered and never will recover
    (E) had not and never will recover

220. The senator was neither in favor of <u>or opposed to the proposed legislation.</u>

    (A) or opposed to the proposed legislation
    (B) and was not opposed to the proposed legislation
    (C) the proposed legislation or opposed to it
    (D) nor opposed to the proposed legislation
    (E) the proposed legislation or opposed to the proposed legislation

221. <u>Glory as well as gain is to be his reward.</u>

    (A) Glory as well as gain is to be his reward.
    (B) As his reward, glory as well as gain is to be his.
    (C) He will be rewarded by glory as well as gain.
    (D) Glory also gain are to be his reward.
    (E) First glory, then gain, will be his reward.

222. She prefers to write poems which describe the slums and <u>study the habits of the underprivileged.</u>

    (A) study the habits of the underprivileged
    (B) study the underprivileged's habits
    (C) studying the habits of the underprivileged
    (D) to study the habits of the underprivileged
    (E) she prefers to study the habits of the underprivileged

223. <u>By studying during weekends, her grades improved surprisingly.</u>

    (A) By studying during weekends, her grades improved surprisingly.
    (B) By studying during weekends, she improved her grades surprisingly.
    (C) She was surprised to find her grades improved after studying during weekends.
    (D) Her grades, by studying during weekends, improved surprisingly.
    (E) Surprisingly, by studying during weekends, her grades improved.

224. The streets here are <u>as dirty as any other city,</u> according to recent research studies.

    (A) as dirty as any other city
    (B) so dirty as any other city
    (C) dirty like any other city
    (D) as dirty as those of any other city
    (E) as those of any city

225. Betty is buxom, <u>with blue eyes, and has a pleasant manner.</u>

    (A) with blue eyes, and has a pleasant manner
    (B) with eyes of blue, and a pleasant manner
    (C) blue-eyed and pleasant
    (D) blue eyes as well as pleasant
    (E) and has blue eyes as well as a pleasant manner

226. If Jack <u>would have listened to his wife,</u> he would not have bought those worthless stocks.

    (A) would have listened to his wife
    (B) would listen to his wife
    (C) had listened to his wife
    (D) listened to what his wife had said
    (E) would have listened to his wife's advice

227. The bank robber approached the teller quietly, cautiously, <u>and in an unpretentious manner.</u>

    (A) and in an unpretentious manner
    (B) and with no pretense
    (C) and by acting unpretentious
    (D) and by acting unpretentiously
    (E) and unpretentiously

228. The conduct of the judge <u>with the accused</u> seemed very unfair to the jury.

    (A) with the accused
    (B) toward the accused
    (C) as to the man who was accused
    (D) and the accused
    (E) as far as the accused was concerned

229. Every typist in the office <u>except she</u> was out sick at least one day during the past month.

    (A) except she
    (B) except her
    (C) excepting she
    (D) but not her
    (E) outside of her

230. Sam is a professor of theoretical physics, <u>while his brothers are architects</u> with outstanding reputations.

    (A) while his brothers are architects
    (B) also his brothers are architects
    (C) his brothers architects
    (D) as his brothers are architects
    (E) and his brothers are architects

IF YOU FINISH BEFORE THE TIME IS UP, GO OVER YOUR WORK FOR THIS SECTION ONLY. DO NOT TURN TO ANY OTHER SECTION OF THE TEST. WHEN THE TIME IS UP, THE TEST IS OVER.

NOW THAT YOU HAVE COMPLETED PRACTICE TEST 3

1. Turn to the Answer Key on pages 229-230. Do not consider Sections 7 and 8.

2. Count your **correct answers.**

3. Count your **incorrect answers.**

4. Deduct ¼ of the number of incorrect answers from the number of correct answers to get a "**raw score**" of _____.

5. Your "**scaled score**" for this test, according to the Raw Score/Scaled Score Table on page 88, is _____.

ANSWER KEY FOR PRACTICE TEST 3

Section 1: Reading Comprehension

1. A	6. E	11. B	16. C	21. D
2. C	7. E	12. C	17. E	22. E
3. C	8. A	13. A	18. E	23. A
4. B	9. C	14. D	19. A	24. B
5. B	10. B	15. B	20. C	25. D

Section 2: Math Ability

After each answer, there is a hyphenated number (or numbers) in parentheses. This hyphenated number is keyed to Math Refresher (beginning on page 411). The number *before* the hyphen indicates the Math area of the problem:

1 = ARITHMETIC
2 = ALGEBRA
3 = PLANE GEOMETRY
5 = GRAPHS AND CHARTS

The number *after* the hyphen gives you the section (within the Math area) that explains the rule or principle involved in solving the problem.

26. C (2-29)	36. B (1-24)	46. D (2-34)
27. C (1-23, 2-29)	37. D (1-20, 2-20)	47. C (1-27, 2-20)
28. B (1-24)	38. A (2-27)	48. A (1-28)
29. C (2-34)	39. A (3-6)	49. B (2-8, 2-9)
30. C (2-35)	40. B (1-25)	50. B (2-31)
31. D (2-28)	41. A (5-4, 1-25)	51. B (2-3, 2-4)
32. E (1-11, 3-6)	42. E (5-4, 1-25)	52. E (3-6)
33. A (5-4)	43. C (5-4)	53. C (1-25)
34. D (5-4)	44. A (5-4, 2-26)	54. A (2-27)
35. E (2-28)	45. B (1-22)	55. D (2-37)

Section 3: Business Judgment

56. D	61. B	66. C	71. D	76. D
57. A	62. A	67. B	72. E	77. E
58. B	63. E	68. B	73. A	78. B
59. E	64. B	69. E	74. B	79. A
60. B	65. D	70. C	75. C	80. C

ANSWER KEY FOR PRACTICE TEST 3 (continued)

Section 4: Data Sufficiency

81. E	87. E	93. E	99. D	105. C
82. B	88. D	94. C	100. E	106. C
83. C	89. E	95. E	101. C	107. E
84. D	90. C	96. E	102. C	108. D
85. C	91. C	97. D	103. E	109. E
86. D	92. A	98. A	104. B	110. C

Section 5: Grammar and Usage

111. E	116. D	121. D	126. A	131. C
112. C	117. E	122. D	127. D	132. A
113. B	118. A	123. E	128. A	133. B
114. B	119. C	124. D	129. C	134. A
115. B	120. C	125. C	130. B	135. E

Section 6: Business Judgment

136. B	141. D	146. B	151. D	156. C
137. E	142. E	147. B	152. C	157. D
138. D	143. A	148. C	153. A	158. B
139. C	144. D	149. C	154. B	159. D
140. C	145. B	150. A	155. D	160. C

Sections 7A and 7B: Reading Recall

161. C	167. A	173. B	179. A	185. E
162. A	168. E	174. A	180. B	186. D
163. E	169. A	175. C	181. D	187. E
164. C	170. B	176. D	182. B	188. C
165. D	171. D	177. B	183. C	189. E
166. B	172. C	178. C	184. B	190. B

Section 8: Sentence Correction

191. A	199. D	207. C	215. C	223. B
192. B	200. E	208. A	216. C	224. D
193. D	201. B	209. E	217. B	225. C
194. E	202. A	210. E	218. E	226. C
195. C	203. B	211. A	219. D	227. E
196. E	204. D	212. A	220. D	228. B
197. B	205. E	213. D	221. A	229. B
198. C	206. C	214. D	222. D	230. E

EXPLANATORY ANSWERS FOR PRACTICE TEST 3

Section 1: Reading Comprehension

1. **(A)** See paragraph 3: "Third, what is needed nowadays..."

2. **(C)** See paragraph 1: "Without the scientific research of modern psychology..."

3. **(C)** See paragraph 1: "...the primitive stages of propaganda that existed in the time of Pericles."

4. **(B)** See paragraph 1, last two sentences.

5. **(B)** Newton's law of gravitation deals with physics and would be of little use to the propagandist. See paragraph 1: "...modern propaganda is based on scientific analyses of psychology and sociology."

6. **(E)** Throughout the selection, the author expresses favorable attitude toward the propagandist. The very last sentence, for example, states that propaganda "is an object of serious thought, and proceeds along scientific channels."

7. **(E)** The third paragraph states that the Babylonians and Assyrians were Semitic peoples. This refers to their race. Akkadian is a word for their grouping together, Mesopotamian refers to their location, and Sumerians were a different people.

8. **(A)** The very first paragraph tells us that the features of Akkadian civilization were questioned as to whether they were "original or *derivative*... independent creation or a reworking over of material already in existence."

9. **(C)** The final paragraph says that, in Babylonia, Marduk was the national god, while Ashur was the national god in Assyria. Ashur completes the analogy.

10. **(B)** It should be known that Hammurabi was responsible for the penalty stated in his law code of "an eye for an eye, a tooth for a tooth." The other choices would have little to do with the severity of Hammurabi implied in the last paragraph: "In Babylonia, the Hammurabi dynasty... creator and orderer of the universe."

11. **(B)** The very last sentence states that Ashur, national god of Assyria, "possesses the same warlike attributes that are characteristic of his people." Warlike characteristics are not related to any of the other choices in the article.

12. **(C)** Since periodic motion is motion that regularly repeats itself, the motion of a freely falling object is not periodic because it does not repeat, but only occurs once.

13. **(A)** Paragraph 1 states: "... his body will seem thinner in the line of travel. When he lies down with his body in line with the ship's motion... he will now seem shorter from head to toes."

14. **(D)** Paragraph 3 states: "Mass, in a rough sense, is a measure of the amount of matter in an object."

15. **(B)** Paragraph 4 states: "The first method [weighing] is not a very good one, because the results vary with local strength of gravity."

16. **(C)** See the last paragraph (middle): "Mass measured in this way... (to end of paragraph)."

17. **(E)** See paragraph 3: "A lead ball ... greater concentration of matter."

18. **(E)** See paragraph 11: "For it is those labor-intensive services, still so complete

and courteous, that make life pleasant for the British and their visitors." Also see paragraph 12: "There is the smiling young man who pops into your train compartment... or the nurse... or the postman..."

19. **(A)** See paragraph 1: "The fact that we show up poorer in the figures does not really matter."

20. **(C)** See paragraphs 9 and 10: "... British workers really do not want to be more efficient; they prefer a less tidy life... But Ford can and does make cars elsewhere."

21. **(D)** See paragraph 9: "... some psychologists ... would argue that the squabbles and tea breaks are mechanisms to deal with the dreary pressures of the assembly line."

22. **(E)** See paragraph 10: "... Rolls Royce —with feeble management..."

23. **(A)** See paragraph 13: "The answer is to mechanize..." Also see paragraph 15: "... Britain faces the probable necessity of doing things, to maintain contentment, that in fact will make her less contented."

24. **(B)** See paragraph 8: "Henry Ford 2nd has been threatening to cut back his investment in Britain... last year they cost Ford $50 million..."

25. **(D)** See paragraph 7: "... British executives now get lower rewards than French, that automobile workers on the Continent are catching up to, and passing, British wage rates... workers feel their rising expectations are not being met."

EXPLANATORY ANSWERS FOR PRACTICE TEST 3 (continued)

Section 2: Math Ability

26. **(C)** Since s oranges cost v cents we have

$$s \text{ oranges cost } \frac{v}{100} \text{ dollars}$$

and 1 orange costs $\dfrac{s(100)}{v}$ dollars.

Thus, 1 dozen oranges cost $\dfrac{12}{100}\dfrac{v}{s}$ dollars

and w dozen oranges cost $\dfrac{12}{100}\dfrac{wv}{s}$ dollars

27. **(C)** Let x represent the unknown. Then,

$$25\% \left(\frac{1}{9}\right) = 33\frac{1}{3}\%(x)$$

$$\frac{1}{4}\left(\frac{1}{9}\right) = \frac{1}{3}x$$

$$\frac{1}{36} = \frac{1}{3}x$$

$$\frac{1}{12} = x$$

28. **(B)** A 20% discount from $125 leaves $100. Another 10% from $100 leaves $90.

29. **(C)** The sum of his four grades the first term is $(75)(4) = 300$. If his average in the second term is y, then the sum of his 5 grades this term is $5y$. Hence, for 9 courses total,

$$\frac{300 + 5y}{9} = 80$$

$$300 \times 5y = 720$$

$$5y = 420$$

$$y = 84$$

30. **(C)** By the counting principle, the total number of ways the outfits can be chosen is

$$n_1 \times n_2 \times n_3 = 3 \times 4 \times 2 = 24$$

31. **(D)** Let x = the tax on the $225 refrigerator; then form the proportion

$$\frac{150}{14} = \frac{225}{x}$$

Divide both sides by 25, giving

$$\frac{6}{14} = \frac{9}{x}$$

$$6x = 126$$

$$x = 21$$

32. **(E)** Divide length and width by $\frac{1}{2}$.

$$20 \div \frac{1}{2} = 20 \times 2 = 40$$

$$10 \div \frac{1}{2} = 10 \times 2 = 20$$

These numbers represent the number of tiles along length and width. Hence the total number of tiles is $40 \times 20 = 800$.

33. **(A)** Corresponding to 10° on the Centigrade scale is 50° on the Fahrenheit scale.

34. **(D)** Draw the line graph C = F which is the 45° line through the origin. This intersects the given line at the point (−40, −40). Hence, temperature readings are the same on both scales at −40°.

35. **(E)** Let x dollars = price of adult ticket.

⅓ x dollars = price of child's ticket

Then,
$$3x + 3(⅓ x) = \$21.60$$
$$3 x + x = \$21.60$$
$$4 x = \$21.60$$
$$x = \$ 5.40$$

36. **(B)** 10% of $400 is .10 × $400 = $40. After the first discount the coat sells for $400 − $40 = $360. 5% of $360 is .05 × $360 = $18. After the second discount the coat sells for $360 − $18 = $342.

37. **(D)** The containers hold ⅓u and ⅓v respectively. When poured into another container, there is ⅓u + ⅓v in the new container. Hence, the part of the latter container that is full is

$$\frac{⅓u + ⅓v}{w} = \frac{u + v}{3w}$$

38. **(A)** $2^2 \times 5^3$ equals $2 \times 2 \times 5 \times 5 \times 5 = 500$. We can write the following equation.

$$(.001\%)\ 500 = (x\%)(200)$$

$$x = \frac{500}{200}\ (.001) = \frac{5}{2}\ (.001)$$

$$= .0025$$

39. **(A)** Each face of the larger cube has an area of $\frac{600}{6} = 100$ sq. in. Thus the edge of the cube is 10. Each face of the smaller cube has an area of $\frac{150}{6} = 25$ sq. in. Thus the edge of the smaller cube is 5.

Since the ratio of the edges is 10:5 or 2:1, the ratio of the volumes is 8:1. Hence, 8 smaller cubes can be cut from the larger cube.

40. **(B)** 15% of $200 = (.15)(200) = $30.00
(First Discount)

$200 − $30 = $170
(First Net Price)

10% of $170 = (.10)(170) = $17
(Second Discount)

$170 − $17 = $153
(Second Net Price)

41. **(A)** The GNP at start of 1968 was about 675. The GNP at end of third quarter of 1970 was 690. Hence the increase was 15 and the percentage increase is

$$\frac{15}{675} = \frac{1}{45} = 2.2\%\ \text{(approx.)}$$

42. **(E)** Wages at start = 2.90
Wages at end = 3.37
Increase = .47

$$\%\ \text{Increase} = \frac{47}{290} = 17\%\ \text{approx.}$$

43. **(C)** The GNP did increase slowly, as we can see from the flat nature of the graph. Wages did keep pace with the price index, as we see from the percentage increase. The dotted line on the first graph shows a steep rise, indicating a speeding up of the rate of growth of the GNP. Hence, Choice C is *not* true. The graphs indicate D and E to be true.

44. **(A)** Expected increase in 1971 is
$3.40 − 3.35 = .05

Increase in 1969 is
$3.30 − 3.10 = .20

Ratio = $\frac{.05}{.20}$ = 1 : 4 (approx.)

45. **(B)** The percentage mark is

$$\frac{\text{number right}}{\text{number of examples}} \times 100\%.$$ Since the teestee made 45 mistakes, he got 120 − 45 of the problems correct, that is, of course 75.

$$\frac{75}{120} = \frac{5}{8} = 63\% \text{ (approx.)}$$

46. **(D)** The average of the five gains is the sum of the gains divided by 5. Let the unknown fifth gain be G. Then the average gain is

$$\frac{35¢ + 40¢ + 25¢ + 50¢ + G}{5} = 30¢$$

which we are told is the average. Adding and dividing by 5 we find $30¢ + \dfrac{G}{5} = 30¢$. Therefore G = 0¢.

47. **(C)** $y \sqrt{.09} = 6$

$$.3y = 6$$
$$3y = 60$$
$$y = 20$$

48. **(A)** Let x = number of men teachers

4x = number of women teachers

5x = total number of teachers

Hence the number of teachers must be divisible by 5. This is true of all choices except 42.

49. **(B)** Translating the problem statement into an equation,

$$\frac{1}{3} + \frac{1}{4} = \frac{1}{5}x$$

$$\frac{7}{12} = \frac{x}{5}$$

$$12x = 35$$

$$x = \frac{35}{12}$$

50. **(B)** Distance = Rate × Time
If the drives 120 miles at 40 m.p.h., it

takes him $\dfrac{120}{40} = 3$ hours. On his return, the same distance takes him $\dfrac{120}{60} = 2$ hours. He thus travels a total of 240 miles in 5 hours. His average speed is thus

$$\frac{240}{5} = 48 \text{ m.p.h.}$$

51. **(B)** If the product of u and v is positive, they must both be positive or both be negative. In either case the quotient of u and v or $\dfrac{u}{v}$ must also be positive, or

$$\frac{u}{v} > 0.$$

52. **(E)** Let x represent a side of a square. Then the perimeter of the rectangle is 10 x = 140 and x = 14. Thus, area of square is $x^2 = 14^2 = 196$.

53. **(C)** Consider the height and width of the poster to be 10 each. Then its area is 100. If the height is reduced by 30%, it becomes 7, and, if the width is reduced 10%, it becomes 9. Hence, the new area is 63. This new area is

$$\frac{63}{100} = 63\% \text{ of the original}$$

The result will be the same regardless of the dimensions chosen.

54. **(A)** Since fewer men require more hours, the number of hours required is inversely proportional to the number of men painting. Suppose 6 men can paint the fence in x hours; then,

$$\frac{8}{6} = \frac{x}{3}$$

$$6x = 24$$

$$x = 4$$

55. **(D)** If x > y and city C is between city A (x miles) and city B (y miles) then city C's distance from New York is between x miles and y miles. Thus x > z > y.

EXPLANATORY ANSWERS FOR PRACTICE TEST 3 (continued)

Section 3: Business Judgment

56. **(D)** This is a major assumption since Roberts is basing his decision on the continuation of trends·

57. **(A)** The decision to manufacture ovens is being considered within the overall desire to reduce risk.

58. **(B)** Experience in marketing ovens is a major factor since the tube department's lack of experience in marketing could seriously jeopardize the project.

59. **(E)** Capital is not considered a constraint since the Magna Corporation has abundant capital.

60. **(B)** Cheaper labor cost through using the microwave oven would affect demand within the restaurant business, which is an important factor.

61. **(B)** The objective being to reduce risk and increase profit, the decision as to whether to manufacture or to use joint ventures is a major factor.

62. **(A)** The decision as to which product to develop depends on the prestige it will bring to the Magna Corporation.

63. **(E)** The project could be reassigned to other divisions.

64. **(B)** Roberts believes that the high technological skill of the Magna Corporation will give it an advantage in the ability to produce ovens.

65. **(D)** Roberts assumes that contracts with suppliers of raw materials can be arranged.

66. **(C)** This is a minor factor because it affects the demand for ovens within the different restaurant and food-vending businesses, but the major factor is the actual demand for ovens.

67. **(B)** Knowledge of the food industry would affect the ability to market ovens successfully.

68. **(B)** The high demand for ovens is a major factor in the decision as to enter the oven manufacturing business.

69. **(E)** The importance of defense work compatibility is neither specified nor implied.

70. **(C)** This is minor because it affects the total demand for ovens, a major factor.

71. **(D)** Roberts is assuming that the projects contemplated are within his authority and that senior management views will not affect his choice.

72. **(E)** Roberts is considering the corporation as a whole and the objective of greater profit and less risk. Employment is not mentioned.

73. **(A)** Capital is not a constraint, and no mention is made as to the speed of delivery to the consumer.

74. **(B)** Roberts is considering other products for household or general industrial use. Defense contracts would not be included.

75. **(C)** Vending machine use might make the consumer aware of microwave ovens, but such consumer awareness does not apply to the restaurant business.

76. **(D)** The tube department has technological skill but it lacks ample size and oven-marketing experience·

77. **(E)** All of these are assumed.

78. **(B)** The number of eating and drinking establishments declined nearly 20% *on*

a per capita basis. Thus Choice B is the only correct answer.

79. **(A)** The $100,000 restaurants grew from the position of 31.2% of total restaurant sales to 36.1%, a net increase of 4.9% which is less than 6%·

80. **(C)** The passage mentions that the biggest profits are likely to be made for ovens as a whole, through production of ovens for household use. Thus the total profits from the combined vending machine and household markets will be greater than from the restaurant market alone.

EXPLANATORY ANSWERS FOR PRACTICE TEST 3 (continued)
Section 4: Data Sufficiency

81. **(E)** From both statements we can conclude that there is one-half ounce of copper and one-half ounce of gold in the ring. The gold is worth $\frac{1}{2} \times \$35$. We do not, however, know the worth of the copper in the ring.

82. **(B)** The first statement does not provide enough information. Three members of the set, 4, 16 and 36, when squared, are divisible by 8.

    The second statement, however, does provide sufficient information. The only member divisible by a cube is 16. It is divisible by 8.

83. **(C)** According to statement (1), the largest x can be is 50 and according to statement (2) the largest y can be is 30. Thus, the largest $x + y$ can possibly be is 80.

    Since $x + y + \text{Angle } J = 180$,

    we see that Angle J must be at least $100°$ and we can answer the question posed: Yes, the triangle is obtuse.

84. **(D)** We can find the number of boys in camp from statement (1) alone. There are 60 baseball players plus 50 soccer players. However, we have just counted the baseball-and-soccer players twice so we must subtract this number, 15. Thus, the number of boys at camp is $60 + 50 - 15$.

    We can find the number of boys in camp by using statement (2) alone. There are 60 baseball players plus 35 only-soccer players. We have not counted anybody twice. The camp population is $60 + 35$.

85. **(C)** $a + b + c = 180$
    Statements (1) and (2) provide us with the values of a and b. We can substitute and solve for c:

    $$60 + 90 + c = 180$$

    d and c are equal since they are alternate interior angles of parallel lines.

86. **(D)** Distance = Rate × Time. From statement (1) we can set up the following equation:
    Let x equal the time it takes car A to reach the destination. Then

    $$\text{Distance} = 60x = 30(x + \tfrac{1}{4})$$

    We use $\frac{1}{4}$ because 15 minutes is $\frac{1}{4}$ of an hour. This equation can be solved for x and we can then find the distance, $60x$.

    From statement (2) we can set up this equation:

    $$\text{Distance} = 60x = 120(x - \tfrac{1}{8})$$

    This, too, can be solved for x and the distance can be found.

87. **(E)** Both statements do not provide enough information to answer the question.

88. **(D)** Since AB is a straight line,

    $$x + y + z = 180$$

    According to statement (1),

    $$2x + 3y + 2z = 420$$

    Multiply both sides of the first equation by 2:

    $$2x + 2y + 2z = 360$$

    Subtracting this from the second equation, we get

    $$y = 60$$

    According to statement (2),

    $$y = 2x, \quad z = 3x$$

    Substituting this into the original equation, we obtain

    $$x + 2x + 3x = 180$$

    This can be solved for x and we can then obtain y from $y = 2x$.

89. **(E)** From the given information, it is possible to find the number of people in Beth's class but we cannot find out the number of people who got over 80.

90. **(C)** Since one cubic foot of *A* weighs 1.2 grams and there are 1728 cubic inches in a cubic foot, one cubic inch of *A* weighs $\frac{1.2}{1728}$ grams.

By comparing $\frac{1.2}{1728}$ and .003, we can see which gas is heavier.

91. **(C)** The inequality of statement (1) can be simplified:

$$5b + 7 \geqslant 3b + 13$$
$$2b \geqslant 6$$
$$b \geqslant 3$$

The integers satisfying the inequality of statement (2) are −3, −2, −1, 0, 1, 2, 3.

If we use both statements, we see that the answer is $b = 3$.

92. **(A)** Let *T* represent Tom's earnings.

Let *F* represent Fred's earning.
Let *R* represent Robert's earnings.
We are given $T + F + R = \$160$

Statement (1) tells us:
$$3R - 2(T + F) = \$80$$

From the first equation we see that
$$T + F = \$160 - R.$$

Substituting this into the second equation we have
$$3R - 2(\$160 - R) = \$80$$
This equation can be solved for R.

Statement (2) says $T = 2F$. This does not help us solve the problem.

93. **(E)** There is insufficient data to solve the problem. To find BE we would have to know the area of the triangle. This cannot be found from the given information.

94. **(C)** Using both statements, we can solve the problem. Statement (2) informs us that the triangle is right and that Angle *E* is the right angle. Thus, *AD* must be

the hypotenuse. Since the triangle is isosceles, the equal sides must be *AE* and *ED*, both of which are 4 units long. By the Pythagorean Theorem, *AD* is 4 $\sqrt{2}$.

95. **(E)** It is impossible to answer the question posed with the given information because it would be necessary to know how many bags of seeds were needed to cover the backyard.

96. **(E)** In order to find the price of an egg, we need to know the price of a box of eggs and the number of eggs in the box. This information is not given.

97. **(D)** In a rectangle, the diagonals are equal and bisect each other. Thus, $\frac{1}{2} AC = \frac{1}{2} BD$ or $MD = MC$. Since these two sides of triangle DMC are equal, their opposite angles MDC and MCD are equal. From statement 1, angle AMB is 134°. Its opposite vertical angle DMC is also 134°. Letting *x* represent angle DMC and angle MCD, then

$$134 + 2x = 180$$
$$x = 23$$

Therefore, statement 1 is sufficient to answer the question.
In triangle BDC, the sum of the angles is 180°. Since ABCD is a rectangle, angle BCD is 90° and angle DBC is 67° from statement 2. Therefore, letting *x* represent angle BDC,

$$x = 180 - 90 - 67 = 23$$

Thus, statement 2 is sufficient to answer the question.

98. **(A)** First analyze statement 1. Letting *x* represent Sam's present age,

$$x + 14 = 3x + 2$$
$$x = 8$$

Since we do not know Sam's brothers' age, statement 2 does not help solve the problem.

99. **(D)** The equation for the circumference of a circle is $C = 2\pi r$, where r is the radius. If $r = 4$, from statement 1, the circumference is $C = 8\pi$. In statement 2, the area is given as 16π. Since the area of a circle is $A = \pi r^2$,
$$\pi r^2 = 16\pi$$
$$r^2 = 16$$
$$r = 4$$
Again, the circumference is
$$C = 2\pi(4) = 8\pi$$

100. **(E)** These two statements do not pinpoint the height of the tallest boy. For example their heights may be 5 ft. 7 in., 5 ft. 9 in., and 5 ft. 11 in. Or the heights may also be 5 ft. 3 in., 5 ft. 11 in., and 6 ft. 1 in. Thus, there is no exact answer to the question.

101. **(C)** Time equals distance divided by speed. Using the information in both statements we find that the train ride would last 6.36 hours. The train would arrive in Larborn 6.36 hours after midnight.

102. **(C)** The length of a side of a right triangle can be found according to the Pythagorean theorem:
(side 1)^2 + (side 2)^2 = hypotenuse^2.
We know the hypotenuse's length from statement 1. If we let x represent MN and $2x$ represent ML, then x can be found by solving the equation: $x^2 + (2x)^2 = 16^2$.

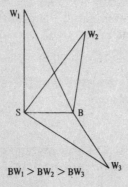

$BW_1 > BW_2 > BW_3$

103. **(E)** Side BW can vary in length depending upon the angle BSW. (See diagram.) Therefore, no single perimeter can be found.

104. **(B)** Since the opposite sides of a square are parallel, alternate interior angles DHG and HGF are equal. Knowing the measure of angle DHG gives us the measure of angle HGF. The measure of angle HIE does not affect the measure of angle HGF.

105. **(C)** According to Statement 1, each cow cost an average of $250. Since Statement 2 tells us that $400 was be average price per cow, the average profit per cow is $150.

106. **(C)** Since a month has 28, 29, 30 or 31 days, then the date in question is either 15, 16, 17 or 18 (Statement 1). According to Statement 2, the date in question is the fifteenth. The only date of the year which satisfies both statements is February 15.

107. **(E)** If only positive values for U and V are considered, then statement 1 provides an answer (no). However, since U and V can also be negative, the answer is not specified. For $U^2 > V$, U can be greater than or less than V.

108. **(D)** Since an inscribed angle of a circle is equal to one-half the measure of the arc it subtends, statement 1 is sufficient to answer the question. Since statement 2 tells us that QS is a diameter, then the angle is inscribed in a semi-circle and is a right angle.

109. **(E)** With the given information we cannot find the length of YZ without knowing the length of the line segment WX.

110. **(C)** If we let 1 equal the total amount earned, then Tim earned .35. If x represents the amount Charles earned, then $1\frac{1}{2}x$ is the amount Alan earned. By solving the equation, $.35 + x + 1\frac{1}{2}x = 1$, we can determine who earned the least amount of money.

EXPLANATORY ANSWERS FOR PRACTICE TEST 3 (continued)

Section 5: Grammar and Usage

111. **(E)** All underlined parts are correct.

112. **(C)** "... pulled out his gun *quickly* ..."
The adverb *quickly*—not the adjective *quick*—should be used to modify the verb *pulled out*.

113. **(B)** "... if you *had waited* for an occasion ..."
In the "if clause" of a past contrary-to-fact condition, one must use the past perfect subjunctive form *had waited*—not the future perfect subjunctive form *would have waited*.

114. **(B)** "... *there* is no necessary connection ..."
We have the expletive use of *there* in this sentence—not the possessive pronoun-adjective *their*.

115. **(B)** "... I knew the winner to be *him* ..."
Since *winner* is the subject of the infinitive *to be, winner* is in the objective case. (The subject of an infinitive is always in the objective case.) The predicate noun or pronoun must be in the same case as the subject. Therefore, the predicate pronoun, in this particular case, must have an objective form *(him)*.

116. **(D)** "... to express *himself*."
The objective form of the reflexive pronoun is *himself*—not *hisself*.

117. **(E)** All underlined parts are correct.

118. **(A)** "I appreciate *your* helping me ..."
The subject of a gerund is in the possessive case. We, therefore, say *your helping*—not *you helping*.

119. **(C)** "... from the wood, *we* can see the blooming lilac ..."
The participle *looking* must modify the subject (which comes right after the comma). It is not the *lilac* that is looking—it is *we* or *one*—that is, a person or persons doing the looking.

120. **(C)** "No sooner had he begun to speak *than* . ."
The correct expression is *no sooner ... than*—not *no sooner ... when*.

121. **(D)** "... raise *their* eyebrows."
The possessive pronoun-adjective is *their*—not *there*.

122. **(D)** "... so that he, *not the lady,* would get the cork."
The *lady* is misplaced in the original sentence. As you see, the correct (or incorrect placement) may make quite a difference in the meaning of the sentence.

123. **(E)** All underlined parts are correct.

124. **(D)** "... but the field supervisor, the sales manager, and *me*."
The preposition *but* is understood before *me*. Since *me* is the object of the preposition *but*, it has an object form *(me)*—not a nominative form *(I)*.

125. **(C)** "... that Williams has an interest *in* and an aptitude for ..."
The preposition *in* must be included after *interest* in order to introduce the object of the preposition *(chemical experimentation)*

126. **(A)** "Manslaughter *occurs when* a person ..."
Avoid using *where* to introduce a definition unless the definition pertains to place or location.

127. **(D)** "The reason ... is *that* they are really insecure."
We say *the reason is that*—not *the reason is because*.

128. **(A)** "*It's* not generally known ..."
We need here the contraction *It's* (meaning *It is*).

129. **(C)** "... is one of the *most poorly* taught subjects ..."
The participle *taught* must be modified by an adverb (*poorly*—the superlative form of which is *most poorly*)—not by an adjective (*poorest*).

130. **(B)** "Developed by the research engineers of Dupont, the new explosive is considered by the government to be ..."
The participle *(Developed)* is not supposed to modify *the government*—it must modify *the new explosive*. That is the reason we have to rearrange the sentence.

131. **(C)** "From *any one* of them ..."
The word *either* refers to one of two. Since we are dealing here with three things (baseball, football, and soccer), we cannot say *either*.

132. **(A)** "After I *had listened* ..."
We must use the past perfect tense *(had listened)* to indicate an action taking place before another past action *(hurried)*.

133. **(B)** "... that the *Mayor's taking* ..."
The possessive form *(Mayor's)* must be used for the noun which modifies the gerund *(taking)*.

134. **(A)** "Having set the bag ..."
The verb *to set* means *to place*. The past participle of *to set* is *having set*. The verb *to sit* means *to rest*. The past participle of *to sit* is *having sat*. This sentence requires the use of the transitive verb *to set* — not the intransitive verb *to sit*.

135. **(E)** All underlined parts are correct.

EXPLANATORY ANSWERS FOR PRACTICE TEST 3 (continued)

Section 6: Business Judgment

136. **(B)** The solid oxygen supply system is a major factor because it would make the venture become profitable.

137. **(E)** The price itself has no relevance with the decision at hand — that is, whether or not to start the venture.

138. **(D)** Storr has to assume that his product will be accepted by the public.

139. **(C)** The lower price is one among several factors rendering the solid oxygen supply system more advantageous than existing systems.

140. **(C)** The patent will give Storr some protection in starting his new business, but it is not a major consideration.

141. **(D)** His pricing policy and profitability expectations are based on this favorable assumption.

142. **(E)** This statement has no relevance with the decision at hand.

143. **(A)** Managing his own business is one of Storr's major ambitions in life.

144. **(D)** On this assumption rest the expectations of growth and profitability in the long run.

145. **(B)** It is a vital risk factor which Storr has to weigh in arriving at his final decision.

146. **(B)** Having the product accepted and recommended by doctors is an essential.

147. **(B)** Storr not being wealthy, the financial issue is of prime importance.

148. **(C)** Though the security of Storr's present situation enters into weighing the risk of the new venture, it is not directly related to his objectives.

149. **(C)** It is a secondary factor related to costs but it is not vital in his decision-making.

150. **(A)** One of Storr's objectives in life is to become socially successful.

151. **(D)** The profitability of the venture rests on an assumption of rapid growth during the first few years.

152. **(C)** The major factor related to financing the venture is the granting of the loan. The interest rate, though important, is secondary in this case.

153. **(A)** The solid oxygen supply system is easy to carry because it is light and small. It is less dangerous and less expensive than the liquid oxygen system.

154. **(B)** Storr plans to enter the East Coast market initially, which includes Washington, D.C. He will cover the West Coast only later on and he does not consider Texas as a potential market.

155. **(D)** The oxygen supply system has received official approval as a reliever for respiratory diseases. The East represents 60% of the total market while the West represents only 15%. Storr estimates a 20% favorable response from doctors but this remains an assumption.

156. **(C)** The price is based on the full cost resulting from the expected sales volume during the first two years. No similar product exists for the moment on the market.

157. **(D)** The plant will be located in a less developed area for financial considerations. New England has been chosen because of its vicinity to the East Coast market. Production cost advantages are not supported by the passage.

158. **(B)** See paragraph 5: "First year sales ... at 10,000 units."

159. **(D)** See paragraph 6: "Initial Total System: $60.00 each ... Replacement Cartridges: $3.50 each."

160. **(C)** See paragraph 3: "Finally, since the West Coast market comprises 15% of the total market potential ..."

EXPLANATORY ANSWERS FOR PRACTICE TEST 3 (continued)

Sections 7A and 7B: Reading Recall

161. **(C)** See paragraph 5, lines 11-12: "Hoover also inaugurated... relieve unemployment."

162. **(A)** See paragraph 2, lines 8-10: "The threat of another war... was one such stimulus."

163. **(E)** Political unrest was the result — not the cause — of the 1929 Depression.

164. **(C)** See paragraph 3, lines 13-14: "All down the line... not meet their debts."

165. **(D)** See paragraph 5, lines 9-11: "...Reconstruction Finance Corporation... with government loans."

166. **(B)** See paragraph 3, last line: "Once started, this spiral of deflation seemed to have no limit." On the other hand, one of President Nixon's major concerns since he took office in 1969 has been how to stop the inflationary spiral from besetting the country.

167. **(A)** See paragraph 4, lines 9-12: "More and more... spread misery and unemployment."

168. **(E)** See paragraph 2: "War provided a limitless market for expendable goods."

169. **(A)** See paragraph 4: All are mentioned except (A).

170. **(B)** See paragraph 3: "...the contraction of business left employees without jobs..."

171. **(D)** The second paragraph states that "the other classes... adopted many of the outward characteristics of the aristocracy."

172. **(C)** The second paragraph implies that the bourgeoisie was "rising to political power" and rivaling the power of the aristocracy.

173. **(B)** The third and fifth paragraphs describe the castles as "strongholds" and "fortified dwellings."

174. **(A)** This information is given in paragraph 3 where it states that "the Magyar armies" harried central Europe.

175. **(C)** The fourth paragraph relates how "power passed into the hands of warriors invested by the monarchy and the Church with lands."

176. **(D)** Paragraph 2 states that "Noblemen who became bishops or who founded new Orders helped to implant aristocratic principles... deep within... the Church."

177. **(B)** The last paragraph states that hunting was a rehearsal for war and it made up "for the lack of butcher's meat."

178. **(C)** See paragraph 2: "Even the unarmed peasantry... long remained tenaciously loyal to their lords, held to their allegiance by that combination of love and fear, *amor et timor*..."

179. **(A)** See paragraph 4: "... warriors... undertook to protect the unarmed peasantry."

180. **(B)** See paragraph 4: "It was recognized in theory that the Church and the monarchy were the principal powers and that they were bound by the nature of their office to ensure peace and security... but... they were too weak, too torn by internal conflicts to fulfil their obligations."

181. **(D)** See paragraph 2: "Formerly, technical rationality had been employed only to organize the production of rather simple physical objects... Now technical rationality is increasingly employed to organize all of the processes necessary to the utilization of physical objects..."

182. **(B)** See paragraph 1: "The absence of direct controls or of coercion should not serve to obscure from our view the ... social controls which are employed (such as ... advertising, selective service channeling, and so on)."

183. **(C)** See paragraph 5: "The force must be relatively over-trained ..."

184. **(B)** See paragraph 4: "The assembly line also introduced standardization in work skills and thus makes for a high degree of interchangeability among the work force ... If each operation taxed the worker's skill there would be frequent errors ..."

185. **(E)** See paragraph 1: "Technology conquers nature ... to do so it must first conquer man ... it demands a very high degree of control over the training, mobility, and skills of the work force."

186. **(D)** See paragraph 6: "... the work force within technologically advanced organizations is asked to work not less hard but more so."

187. **(E)** See paragraph 3: "... there are very profound social antagonisms or contradictions ..." This article is one of skepticism. It frequently points out the contradictions, irrationality and coercive tactics exhibited by advanced technological institutions.

188. **(C)** See paragraph 6: "Salary and wage increases... lose their importance... once an ample supply of luxuries are assured."

189. **(E)** See paragraph 5: "... technological progress requires a continuous increase in the skill levels of its work force, levels which frequently embody a fairly rich scientific and technical training ... those skills will be less and less fully used."

190. **(B)** See paragraph 6: "... among young people one can already observe a radical weakening in the power of such incentives as money, status, and authority."

EXPLANATORY ANSWERS FOR PRACTICE TEST 3 (continued)

Section 8: Sentence Correction

191. **(A)** Choice A is correct. Choice B's passive verb ("was requested") interferes with the flow of the sentence. "It occurred" in Choice C is unnecessary. Choice D is too wordy for what has to be expressed. Choice E changes the meaning of the original sentence — the students did not "insist."

192. **(B)** Choice A is indirect. Choice B is correct. In Choice C, "as a prize" repeats unnecessarily the "Nobel Prize." Choice D is much too awkward. Choice E is incorrect – the scientists did not discover viruses.

193. **(D)** The important thing is not "promptness"; accordingly, Choice A is wrong. Choice B is incorrect because it is not the "loan" that must be returned. In Choice C, "You must understand" is unnecessary. Choice D is correct. Choice E changes the meaning of the original sentence.

194. **(E)** Choice A, as a phrase, hangs without clearly modifying anything else in the sentence. Choice B would be correct if it were preceded and followed by a dash in order to set the choice off from what goes before and after. Choice C is wrong because one does not "amass a scholastic record." Choice D is a complete sentence within a sentence, thus creating a run-on sentence situation. Choice E is correct.

195. **(C)** In Choice A, the use of the passive verb ("were trounced") reduces the effectiveness of expression. Choice B is indirect. Choice C is correct. In Choice D, "which is hard to believe" is unnecessary. Choice E is indirect.

196. **(E)** In Choice A, "are necessary" is not only not necessary, but the expression makes the sentence ungrammatical with the additional complete predicate ("are necessary").

There are too many "ands" in Choice B. Some grammarians call this an "Andy" sentence.
In Choice C, "And other fruit... peaches" is an incomplete sentence – also called a sentence fragment. Choice D also suffers from sentence fragmentation: "Such as pineapples and peaches." Choice E is correct.

197. **(B)** In Choice A, it is unidiomatic to say "instruction to learn." Choice B is correct. Choice C is too wordy. Choice D is not as direct as Choice B. Choice E suffers from lack of parallelism.

198. **(C)** Choice A is awkward and wordy. Choice B is indirect. Choice C is correct. Choice D is unacceptable idiomatically even though the meaning intended is there. Choice E changes the meaning of the original sentence.

199. **(D)** Choice A has incorrect punctuation. A dash (not a comma) is required after "that's not all." In Choice B, the expression "another thing" is too general. Choice C changes the meaning of the original sentence. Choice D is correct. Choice E is too indirectly expressed.

200. **(E)** Choice A suffers from too many "ands" (and-itis). Choices B and C are incorrect because they lack parallel construction. In Choice D, the correct form of the infinitive meaning "to rest" is "(to) lie" – not "(to) lay." Choice E is correct.

201. **(B)** Choice A is awkward. Choice B is correct. Choice C is ungrammatical – "courses" cannot act as a direct object after the copulative construction "am not certain." Choice D is too wordy. Choice E does not make sense.

202. **(A)** Choice A is correct. Choice B is too indirectly stated. Choice C is verbose – since the people "had no doubt," there

is no need to use the expression "it was clear." Choice D is indirect and awkward. Choice E changes the meaning of the original sentence.

203. **(B)** Choice A is too wordy. Choice B is correct. Choice C is indirectly stated. Choices D and E change the meaning of the original sentence.

204. **(D)** Choice A is indirectly stated. Choice B deviates from the original statement. Choice C makes the whole sentence run-on. Choice D is correct. Choice E changes the meaning of the original sentence.

205. **(E)** Choice A is awkward. Choice B has a meaning which differs from that of the original sentence. Choices C and D are unidiomatic. Choice E is correct.

206. **(C)** Choice A is out-of-date. Choice B does not give the meaning intended in the original sentence. Choice C is correct. Choice D is too wordy. Choice E changes the meaning of the original sentence.

207. **(C)** Choices A, B, D, and E are incorrect because each choice begins its own new sentence. Each of these choices, therefore, creates a run-on sentence. Choice C is correct.

208. **(A)** Choice A is correct. Choices B and E change the meaning of the original sentence. Choice C is incorrect grammatically because the verb ellipsis is improper — "the report *was* filed." Choice D is too involved.

209. **(E)** The expression "on account" in Choice A cannot be used as a subordinate conjunction. The expression "being that" in Choice B is always incorrect. Choice C changes the meaning of the original sentence. Choice D is too wordy. Choice E is correct.

210. **(E)** Choice A is too wordy. The double use of the preposition "from" in Choice B is incorrect. Choice C is too wordy. Choice D, as direct discourse, would be correct with the proper punctuation: ...student, "Which country have you come from?" Choice E is correct.

211. **(A)** Choice A is correct. Choice B is awkward. The parenthetical effect of Choice C gives the sentence an ungrammatical structure. The ellipsis of "to the" before the beginning of Choice D, is improper. The possessive use ("oak's") in Choice E results in a bad-sounding sentence.

212. **(A)** Choice A is correct. The present tense in Choice B is incorrect. Choices C, D, and E change the meaning of the original sentence.

213. **(D)** Choices A, B, and E are too wordy. Choice C changes the meaning of the original sentence. Choice D is correct.

214. **(D)** Choice A does not come to the point immediately with the use of the expression "concerning the one." Choice B is too wordy. Choice C is not clear. Choice D is correct. Choice E requires an introductory prepositional compound such as "as to."

215. **(C)** Choices A, B, D, and E are incorrect because of a dangling participle error. In these four choices, the participle "Having" must refer to the subject of the sentence. This subject must follow directly after the participial construction ("Having . . . in his class,"). Accordingly, Choice C is the only correct choice.

216. **(C)** Choice A is incorrect because "its" as a possessive pronoun does not take an apostrophe. Choice B is incorrect because the possessive of "government" ("government's") must be used to modify the gerund "failing." Choice C is correct. Choice D is incorrect for the same reason that Choice B is incorrect. Choice E is incorrect for two reasons: (1) it changes the meaning of the original sentence; (2) even if we change the meaning from singularity to plurality, "governments" must correctly be the possessive form "governments'" to modify the gerund "failing."

217. **(B)** The key to getting the correct answer in this question is knowing this grammatical rule: *When explanatory*

words intervene between the subject and the verb, the number or person of the real subject is not changed. Note that the subject "father" of the original sentence is singular. Accordingly, Choices A, C, D, and E (each of which has a singular subject, "father") are incorrect with a plural verb. Moreover, Choice D changes the present time of the original sentence to past time. Choice B is correct.

218. **(E)** The demonstrative adjective ("this," "that," "these," "those,") must agree in number with the noun ("kind") it modifies. Accordingly, Choices A, B, and D are incorrect. Choice C is incorrect because the personal pronoun "them" may not be used as an adjective. Choice E is correct.

219. **(D)** Choices A, B, C, and E are incorrect because they suffer from incomplete verb comparision. This is a form of improper ellipsis. The corrections would be as follows: Choice A – "has not recovered"; Choice B – "never will recover"; Choice C – (two corrections necessary) "has not recovered" and "never will recover" (the subjunctive "would" should not be used here). Choice E – "has not recovered." Note that in Choice E, the past perfect tense should not be used. Choice D is correct.

220. **(D)** It is important to know that "neither-nor" go together as correlative conjunctions. The pairing of "neither" with "or" is incorrect. Therefore, Choices A, C and E are incorrect. Choice B is awkward. Choice D is correct.

221. **(A)** Choice A is correct. Note that "Glory" is the singular subject which takes the singular verb "is." "Reward" is the predicate nominative after the copulative verb "is." The other four choices are incorrect because they are indirect and awkward.

222. **(D)** Choices A, B, and C are incorrect because they lack parallelism. Note that the infinitive phrase "to write poems" should balance with the infinitive phrase "to study the habits." Choice D, which does have the parallelism required, is correct. Choice E is too wordy.

223. **(B)** This question is concerned with the correct position of the gerund phrase "By studying." Choice A is incorrect because "grades" have been doing the "studying" with such sentence structure. Choices C, D, and E are incorrect for the same reason. Choice B is correct since "she" is obviously the one who is doing the "studying."

224. **(D)** Choice A is incorrect because of the improper omission of the demonstrative pronoun "those." Choices B and C are incorrect for the same reason. Choice D is correct. Choice E is incorrect because we must bring out the comparison with *another* city.

225. **(C)** Parallelism is the important consideration here. Choice C is correct as the only choice that fulfills the requirements of parallel structure.

226. **(C)** Sequence of tenses in contrary-to-fact past situations requires the "had listened" form of the verb. Choice C is therefore correct and all the other choices are incorrect. Moreover, in Choice E, there is no need to use the word "advice" since the rest of the choice implies that advice has been given.

227. **(E)** Choice E is the only correct choice since the other choices lack parallelism. Choice D is incorrect for an additional reason – the predicate adjective "unpretentious" not the adverb "unpretentiously") should be used after the copulative verbal "acting".

228. **(B)** Choice A is incorrect because it is unidiomatic. Choice B is correct. Choices C and E are incorrect because they are too wordy. Choice D improperly omits "conduct of the (accused)."

229. **(B)** The object form of the pronoun must be used for the object of any preposition. Therefore, Choices A and C are incorrect and Choice B is correct. Choice D is incorrect because we need the nominative form of the personal pronoun ("she") as the subject ("but not she"). Choice E is incorrect because it is too informal for the context.

230. **(E)** Choice A is incorrect because "while" pertains to time and should not be substituted loosely for "and." Choice B is incorrect because it does not tie up grammatically with the rest of the sentence. Choice C is incorrect for the same reason. Choice D is incorrect because the subordinate conjunction "as" does not make sense here. Choice E is correct.

Practice Test 4 ⟶

USE THIS SHEET FOR YOUR ANSWERS
PRACTICE TEST 4

Section 1: Reading Recall

1 Ⓐ Ⓑ Ⓒ Ⓓ Ⓔ   7 Ⓐ Ⓑ Ⓒ Ⓓ Ⓔ   13 Ⓐ Ⓑ Ⓒ Ⓓ Ⓔ   19 Ⓐ Ⓑ Ⓒ Ⓓ Ⓔ   25 Ⓐ Ⓑ Ⓒ Ⓓ Ⓔ
2 Ⓐ Ⓑ Ⓒ Ⓓ Ⓔ   8 Ⓐ Ⓑ Ⓒ Ⓓ Ⓔ   14 Ⓐ Ⓑ Ⓒ Ⓓ Ⓔ   20 Ⓐ Ⓑ Ⓒ Ⓓ Ⓔ   26 Ⓐ Ⓑ Ⓒ Ⓓ Ⓔ
3 Ⓐ Ⓑ Ⓒ Ⓓ Ⓔ   9 Ⓐ Ⓑ Ⓒ Ⓓ Ⓔ   15 Ⓐ Ⓑ Ⓒ Ⓓ Ⓔ   21 Ⓐ Ⓑ Ⓒ Ⓓ Ⓔ   27 Ⓐ Ⓑ Ⓒ Ⓓ Ⓔ
4 Ⓐ Ⓑ Ⓒ Ⓓ Ⓔ   10 Ⓐ Ⓑ Ⓒ Ⓓ Ⓔ   16 Ⓐ Ⓑ Ⓒ Ⓓ Ⓔ   22 Ⓐ Ⓑ Ⓒ Ⓓ Ⓔ   28 Ⓐ Ⓑ Ⓒ Ⓓ Ⓔ
5 Ⓐ Ⓑ Ⓒ Ⓓ Ⓔ   11 Ⓐ Ⓑ Ⓒ Ⓓ Ⓔ   17 Ⓐ Ⓑ Ⓒ Ⓓ Ⓔ   23 Ⓐ Ⓑ Ⓒ Ⓓ Ⓔ   29 Ⓐ Ⓑ Ⓒ Ⓓ Ⓔ
6 Ⓐ Ⓑ Ⓒ Ⓓ Ⓔ   12 Ⓐ Ⓑ Ⓒ Ⓓ Ⓔ   18 Ⓐ Ⓑ Ⓒ Ⓓ Ⓔ   24 Ⓐ Ⓑ Ⓒ Ⓓ Ⓔ   30 Ⓐ Ⓑ Ⓒ Ⓓ Ⓔ

Section 2: Math Ability

31 Ⓐ Ⓑ Ⓒ Ⓓ Ⓔ   37 Ⓐ Ⓑ Ⓒ Ⓓ Ⓔ   43 Ⓐ Ⓑ Ⓒ Ⓓ Ⓔ   49 Ⓐ Ⓑ Ⓒ Ⓓ Ⓔ   55 Ⓐ Ⓑ Ⓒ Ⓓ Ⓔ
32 Ⓐ Ⓑ Ⓒ Ⓓ Ⓔ   38 Ⓐ Ⓑ Ⓒ Ⓓ Ⓔ   44 Ⓐ Ⓑ Ⓒ Ⓓ Ⓔ   50 Ⓐ Ⓑ Ⓒ Ⓓ Ⓔ   56 Ⓐ Ⓑ Ⓒ Ⓓ Ⓔ
33 Ⓐ Ⓑ Ⓒ Ⓓ Ⓔ   39 Ⓐ Ⓑ Ⓒ Ⓓ Ⓔ   45 Ⓐ Ⓑ Ⓒ Ⓓ Ⓔ   51 Ⓐ Ⓑ Ⓒ Ⓓ Ⓔ   57 Ⓐ Ⓑ Ⓒ Ⓓ Ⓔ
34 Ⓐ Ⓑ Ⓒ Ⓓ Ⓔ   40 Ⓐ Ⓑ Ⓒ Ⓓ Ⓔ   46 Ⓐ Ⓑ Ⓒ Ⓓ Ⓔ   52 Ⓐ Ⓑ Ⓒ Ⓓ Ⓔ   58 Ⓐ Ⓑ Ⓒ Ⓓ Ⓔ
35 Ⓐ Ⓑ Ⓒ Ⓓ Ⓔ   41 Ⓐ Ⓑ Ⓒ Ⓓ Ⓔ   47 Ⓐ Ⓑ Ⓒ Ⓓ Ⓔ   53 Ⓐ Ⓑ Ⓒ Ⓓ Ⓔ   59 Ⓐ Ⓑ Ⓒ Ⓓ Ⓔ
36 Ⓐ Ⓑ Ⓒ Ⓓ Ⓔ   42 Ⓐ Ⓑ Ⓒ Ⓓ Ⓔ   48 Ⓐ Ⓑ Ⓒ Ⓓ Ⓔ   54 Ⓐ Ⓑ Ⓒ Ⓓ Ⓔ   60 Ⓐ Ⓑ Ⓒ Ⓓ Ⓔ

Section 3: Business Judgment

61 Ⓐ Ⓑ Ⓒ Ⓓ Ⓔ   66 Ⓐ Ⓑ Ⓒ Ⓓ Ⓔ   71 Ⓐ Ⓑ Ⓒ Ⓓ Ⓔ   76 Ⓐ Ⓑ Ⓒ Ⓓ Ⓔ   81 Ⓐ Ⓑ Ⓒ Ⓓ Ⓔ
62 Ⓐ Ⓑ Ⓒ Ⓓ Ⓔ   67 Ⓐ Ⓑ Ⓒ Ⓓ Ⓔ   72 Ⓐ Ⓑ Ⓒ Ⓓ Ⓔ   77 Ⓐ Ⓑ Ⓒ Ⓓ Ⓔ   82 Ⓐ Ⓑ Ⓒ Ⓓ Ⓔ
63 Ⓐ Ⓑ Ⓒ Ⓓ Ⓔ   68 Ⓐ Ⓑ Ⓒ Ⓓ Ⓔ   73 Ⓐ Ⓑ Ⓒ Ⓓ Ⓔ   78 Ⓐ Ⓑ Ⓒ Ⓓ Ⓔ   83 Ⓐ Ⓑ Ⓒ Ⓓ Ⓔ
64 Ⓐ Ⓑ Ⓒ Ⓓ Ⓔ   69 Ⓐ Ⓑ Ⓒ Ⓓ Ⓔ   74 Ⓐ Ⓑ Ⓒ Ⓓ Ⓔ   79 Ⓐ Ⓑ Ⓒ Ⓓ Ⓔ   84 Ⓐ Ⓑ Ⓒ Ⓓ Ⓔ
65 Ⓐ Ⓑ Ⓒ Ⓓ Ⓔ   70 Ⓐ Ⓑ Ⓒ Ⓓ Ⓔ   75 Ⓐ Ⓑ Ⓒ Ⓓ Ⓔ   80 Ⓐ Ⓑ Ⓒ Ⓓ Ⓔ   85 Ⓐ Ⓑ Ⓒ Ⓓ Ⓔ

Section 4: Data Sufficiency

86 Ⓐ Ⓑ Ⓒ Ⓓ Ⓔ   92 Ⓐ Ⓑ Ⓒ Ⓓ Ⓔ   98 Ⓐ Ⓑ Ⓒ Ⓓ Ⓔ   104 Ⓐ Ⓑ Ⓒ Ⓓ Ⓔ   110 Ⓐ Ⓑ Ⓒ Ⓓ Ⓔ
87 Ⓐ Ⓑ Ⓒ Ⓓ Ⓔ   93 Ⓐ Ⓑ Ⓒ Ⓓ Ⓔ   99 Ⓐ Ⓑ Ⓒ Ⓓ Ⓔ   105 Ⓐ Ⓑ Ⓒ Ⓓ Ⓔ   111 Ⓐ Ⓑ Ⓒ Ⓓ Ⓔ
88 Ⓐ Ⓑ Ⓒ Ⓓ Ⓔ   94 Ⓐ Ⓑ Ⓒ Ⓓ Ⓔ   100 Ⓐ Ⓑ Ⓒ Ⓓ Ⓔ   106 Ⓐ Ⓑ Ⓒ Ⓓ Ⓔ   112 Ⓐ Ⓑ Ⓒ Ⓓ Ⓔ
89 Ⓐ Ⓑ Ⓒ Ⓓ Ⓔ   95 Ⓐ Ⓑ Ⓒ Ⓓ Ⓔ   101 Ⓐ Ⓑ Ⓒ Ⓓ Ⓔ   107 Ⓐ Ⓑ Ⓒ Ⓓ Ⓔ   113 Ⓐ Ⓑ Ⓒ Ⓓ Ⓔ
90 Ⓐ Ⓑ Ⓒ Ⓓ Ⓔ   96 Ⓐ Ⓑ Ⓒ Ⓓ Ⓔ   102 Ⓐ Ⓑ Ⓒ Ⓓ Ⓔ   108 Ⓐ Ⓑ Ⓒ Ⓓ Ⓔ   114 Ⓐ Ⓑ Ⓒ Ⓓ Ⓔ
91 Ⓐ Ⓑ Ⓒ Ⓓ Ⓔ   97 Ⓐ Ⓑ Ⓒ Ⓓ Ⓔ   103 Ⓐ Ⓑ Ⓒ Ⓓ Ⓔ   109 Ⓐ Ⓑ Ⓒ Ⓓ Ⓔ   115 Ⓐ Ⓑ Ⓒ Ⓓ Ⓔ

(continued on next page)

Note: At the actual test you will be given an Answer Sheet very much like this sheet in order to record your answers. In doing the following Practice Test, you may prefer to use this Practice Test Answer Sheet. It may, however, be more convenient for you to mark your answer right next to your question after you answer your question.

Section 5: Verbal Ability

116 (A) (B) (C) (D) (E)   121 (A) (B) (C) (D) (E)   126 (A) (B) (C) (D) (E)   131 (A) (B) (C) (D) (E)   136 (A) (B) (C) (D) (E)
117 (A) (B) (C) (D) (E)   122 (A) (B) (C) (D) (E)   127 (A) (B) (C) (D) (E)   132 (A) (B) (C) (D) (E)   137 (A) (B) (C) (D) (E)
118 (A) (B) (C) (D) (E)   123 (A) (B) (C) (D) (E)   128 (A) (B) (C) (D) (E)   133 (A) (B) (C) (D) (E)   138 (A) (B) (C) (D) (E)
119 (A) (B) (C) (D) (E)   124 (A) (B) (C) (D) (E)   129 (A) (B) (C) (D) (E)   134 (A) (B) (C) (D) (E)   139 (A) (B) (C) (D) (E)
120 (A) (B) (C) (D) (E)   125 (A) (B) (C) (D) (E)   130 (A) (B) (C) (D) (E)   135 (A) (B) (C) (D) (E)   140 (A) (B) (C) (D) (E)

Section 6: Business Judgment

141 (A) (B) (C) (D) (E)   146 (A) (B) (C) (D) (E)   151 (A) (B) (C) (D) (E)   156 (A) (B) (C) (D) (E)   161 (A) (B) (C) (D) (E)
142 (A) (B) (C) (D) (E)   147 (A) (B) (C) (D) (E)   152 (A) (B) (C) (D) (E)   157 (A) (B) (C) (D) (E)   162 (A) (B) (C) (D) (E)
143 (A) (B) (C) (D) (E)   148 (A) (B) (C) (D) (E)   153 (A) (B) (C) (D) (E)   158 (A) (B) (C) (D) (E)   163 (A) (B) (C) (D) (E)
144 (A) (B) (C) (D) (E)   149 (A) (B) (C) (D) (E)   154 (A) (B) (C) (D) (E)   159 (A) (B) (C) (D) (E)   164 (A) (B) (C) (D) (E)
145 (A) (B) (C) (D) (E)   150 (A) (B) (C) (D) (E)   155 (A) (B) (C) (D) (E)   160 (A) (B) (C) (D) (E)   165 (A) (B) (C) (D) (E)

Section 7: Grammar and Usage

166 (A) (B) (C) (D) (E)   174 (A) (B) (C) (D) (E)   182 (A) (B) (C) (D) (E)   190 (A) (B) (C) (D) (E)   198 (A) (B) (C) (D) (E)
167 (A) (B) (C) (D) (E)   175 (A) (B) (C) (D) (E)   183 (A) (B) (C) (D) (E)   191 (A) (B) (C) (D) (E)   199 (A) (B) (C) (D) (E)
168 (A) (B) (C) (D) (E)   176 (A) (B) (C) (D) (E)   184 (A) (B) (C) (D) (E)   192 (A) (B) (C) (D) (E)   200 (A) (B) (C) (D) (E)
169 (A) (B) (C) (D) (E)   177 (A) (B) (C) (D) (E)   185 (A) (B) (C) (D) (E)   193 (A) (B) (C) (D) (E)   201 (A) (B) (C) (D) (E)
170 (A) (B) (C) (D) (E)   178 (A) (B) (C) (D) (E)   186 (A) (B) (C) (D) (E)   194 (A) (B) (C) (D) (E)   202 (A) (B) (C) (D) (E)
171 (A) (B) (C) (D) (E)   179 (A) (B) (C) (D) (E)   187 (A) (B) (C) (D) (E)   195 (A) (B) (C) (D) (E)   203 (A) (B) (C) (D) (E)
172 (A) (B) (C) (D) (E)   180 (A) (B) (C) (D) (E)   188 (A) (B) (C) (D) (E)   196 (A) (B) (C) (D) (E)   204 (A) (B) (C) (D) (E)
173 (A) (B) (C) (D) (E)   181 (A) (B) (C) (D) (E)   189 (A) (B) (C) (D) (E)   197 (A) (B) (C) (D) (E)   205 (A) (B) (C) (D) (E)

Section 8: Error Recognition

206 (D) (V) (G) (O)   213 (D) (V) (G) (O)   220 (D) (V) (G) (O)   227 (D) (V) (G) (O)   234 (D) (V) (G) (O)
207 (D) (V) (G) (O)   214 (D) (V) (G) (O)   221 (D) (V) (G) (O)   228 (D) (V) (G) (O)   235 (D) (V) (G) (O)
208 (D) (V) (G) (O)   215 (D) (V) (G) (O)   222 (D) (V) (G) (O)   229 (D) (V) (G) (O)   236 (D) (V) (G) (O)
209 (D) (V) (G) (O)   216 (D) (V) (G) (O)   223 (D) (V) (G) (O)   230 (D) (V) (G) (O)   237 (D) (V) (G) (O)
210 (D) (V) (G) (O)   217 (D) (V) (G) (O)   224 (D) (V) (G) (O)   231 (D) (V) (G) (O)   238 (D) (V) (G) (O)
211 (D) (V) (G) (O)   218 (D) (V) (G) (O)   225 (D) (V) (G) (O)   232 (D) (V) (G) (O)   239 (D) (V) (G) (O)
212 (D) (V) (G) (O)   219 (D) (V) (G) (O)   226 (D) (V) (G) (O)   233 (D) (V) (G) (O)   240 (D) (V) (G) (O)

Practice Test 4

SECTION 1A: READING RECALL

Time: 15 minutes

Directions: Read the following three passages. While you are reading these passages, bear in mind you will be asked to recall certain facts and ideas about what you have read here. After the reading time limit of 15 minutes, you will not be permitted to turn back to these passages. The questions based on these passages will be given to you after the proctor announces that time is up for the reading of these three passages.

FIRST PASSAGE

One of the historical conditions that favors the development of bureaucracy is a money economy. This is not an absolute prerequisite. Bureaucracies based on compensation in kind existed, for example, in Egypt, Rome, and China. Generally, however, a money economy permits the payment of regular salaries, which, in turn, creates the combination of dependence and independence that is most conducive to the faithful performance of bureaucratic duties. Unpaid volunteers are too independent of the organization to submit unfailingly to its discipline. Slaves, on the other hand, are too dependent on their masters to have the incentive to assume responsibilities and carry them out on their own initiative. The economic dependence of the salaried employee on his job and his freedom to advance himself in his career engender the orientation toward work required for disciplined *and* responsible conduct. Consequently, there were few bureaucracies prior to the development of a monetary system and the abolition of slavery.

It has already been mentioned that sheer size encourages the development of bureaucracies, since they are mechanisms for executing large-scale administrative tasks. The large modern nation, business, or union is more likely to be bureaucratized than was its smaller counterpart in the past. More important than size as such, however, is the emergence of special administrative problems. Thus in ancient Egypt the complex job of constructing and regulating waterways throughout the country gave rise to the first known large-scale bureaucracy in history. In other countries, notably those with long frontiers requiring defense, bureaucratic methods were introduced to solve the problem of organizing an effective army and the related one of raising taxes for this purpose. England, without land frontiers, maintained only a small army in earlier centuries, which may in part account for the fact that the trend toward bureaucratization was less pronounced there than in continental nations, which had to support large armies. Weber cites the victory of the Puritans under the leadership of Cromwell over the Cavaliers, who fought more heroically but with less discipline, as an illustration of the superior effectiveness of a bureaucratized army.

The capitalistic system also has furthered the advance of bureaucracy. The rational estimation of economic risks, which is presupposed in capitalism, requires that the regular processes of the competitive market not be interrupted by external forces in unpredictable ways. Arbitrary actions of political tyrants interfere with the rational calculation of gain or loss, and so do banditry, piracy, and social upheavals. The interest of capitalism demands, therefore, not only the overthrow of tyrannical rulers but also the establishment of governments strong enough to maintain order and stability. Note that after the American Revolution such representatives of the capitalists as Alexander Hamilton advocated a strong federal government, while representatives of farmers, in the manner of Jefferson, favored a weak central government.

Capitalism then promotes effective and extensive operations of the government. It also leads to bureaucratization in other spheres. The expansion of business firms and the consequent removal of most employees from activities directly governed by the profit principle make it increasingly necessary to introduce bureaucratic methods of administration for the sake of efficiency. These giant corporations, in turn, compel workers, who no longer can bargain individually with an employer they know personally, to organize into large unions with complex administrative machineries. Strange as it may seem, the free-enterprise system fosters the development of bureaucracy in the government, in private companies, and in unions.

SECOND PASSAGE

The burden of inflation, President Nixon has often said, falls heavily upon the poor, "who are largely defenseless" against price increases on the necessities of life. That view is seldom questioned by politicians, but a growing coterie of economists has lately come to regard it as a misleading oversimplification. Affluent America knows surprisingly little about precisely how inflation affects the poor. What information is available, though, suggests to some experts that inflation — or at least some of the conditions that contribute to it — actually helps many of the poor more than price boosts hurt them.

This heresy has been argued most forcefully by Economists Robinson G. Hollister and John L. Palmer in a study for the University of Wisconsin's Institute for Research on Poverty. They contend that the labor shortages produced by an inflationary boom enable many of the poor to land jobs that otherwise would remain beyond their reach. Using complex mathematical formulas, they support earlier calculations that a reduction in the unemployment rate from 5.4% to 3.5% — experienced by the U.S. between April 1964 and November 1966 — creates 1,042,000 fulltime jobs for poor people who otherwise would be working only part-time or not at all. As for the nonworking poor, Hollister and Palmer found that welfare benefits have generally risen faster than prices. The average monthly check in the program to aid families with dependent children rose 18% during the two years that ended last June. Meanwhile, the consumer price index went up 10%.

Actually, price increases are less painful for the poor than for the middle class and wealthy, the two analysts maintain. They have rejiggered the figures in the Government's consumer price index, which is largely based on middle-class spending patterns, to construct a "poor price index"; it gives more weight to increases in food and rent expenses, less importance to rises in clothing, transportation, medical and education costs. Between 1965 and 1967, the last year for which they calculated the poor price index, it rose 5.1%, compared with a 5.8% increase in the CPI. The Wisconsin researchers conclude that "the poor are not hurt by inflation"—but could be hurt badly by even a "slight" rise in unemployment resulting from a fight against inflation.

This thesis impresses many eminent economists. Says Walter W. Heller, former chairman of the President's Council of Economic Advisers: "I think we have to be very, very careful in suggesting that inflation is the enemy of the poor. It may be their friend in employment terms." Some Government figures buttress the argument. For example, 800,000 of the 5,800,000 U.S. families that were officially defined as poor in 1966 had increased their incomes enough to rise above the poverty line last year. Their gains were achieved even though inflation had meanwhile pushed the poverty line up from $3,317 in annual family income in 1966 to $3,553 in 1968.

THIRD PASSAGE

The relationship between age and income is only casually appreciated by recent theories on the purported redistribution of income. It is known, of course, that the average person's income begins to decline after he is fifty-five years of age, and that it declines sharply after sixty-five. In 1957, 58 per cent of the spending units headed by persons sixty-five years and older earned less than $2,000. The relationship between old age and low income has often been considered a reflection of sociological rather than economic factors — and therefore not to be included in any study of the economy. Actually, the character of the relationship is too integrated to be dissected. However, its significance is mounting with the increase in the number of older persons. The lowest-income groups include a heavy concentration of older persons — in 1957, one-third of all spending units in the $0 – $2,000 class were headed by persons sixty-five years and older; in 1948, it was 28 per cent.

But in economic planning and social policy, it must be remembered that, with the same income, the sixty-five-or-more spending unit will not spend less or need less than the younger spending unit, even though the pressure to save is greater than on the young. The functional ethos of our economy dictates that the comparatively unproductive old-age population should consume in accordance with their output rather than their requirements. Most social scientists have accepted these values; they have assumed that the minimum economic needs of the aged should be lower than those of the younger family. But it is precisely at retirement that personal requirements and the new demands of leisure call for an even larger income if this period is to be something more enjoyable than a wait for death.

The relationship between age and income is seen most clearly in the unionized blue-collar worker. Except for layoffs, which his seniority minimizes, and wage increments for higher productivity, awarded in many industries, his income range is determined by his occupation. But within that income range, the deciding factor is the man's age. After forty-five, the average worker who loses his job has more difficulty in finding a new one. Despite his seniority, the older worker is likely to be downgraded to a lower-paying job when he can no longer maintain the pace set by younger men. This is especially true of unskilled and semiskilled workers.

The early and lower income period of a person's working life, during which he acquires his basic vocational skills, is most pronounced for the skilled, managerial, or professional worker. Then, between the ages of twenty-five and fifty, the average worker receives his peak earnings. Meanwhile, his family expenses rise; there are children to support and basic household durables to obtain. Although his family's income may rise substantially until he is somewhere between thirty-five and forty-five, per capita consumption may drop at the same time. For the growing, working-class family, limited in income by the very nature of the breadwinner's occupation, the economic consequences of this parallel rise in age, income, and obligations are especially pressing. Many in the low-income classes are just as vulnerable to poverty during middle age, when they have a substantially larger income, as in old age. As family obligations finally do begin declining, so does income. Consequently, most members of these classes never have an adequate income.

Thus we see that, for a time, increasing age means increasing income, and therefore a probable boost in income-tenth position. Although there are no extensive data in the matter, it can be confidently asserted that the higher income-tenths have a much greater representation of spending units headed by persons aged thirty-five to fifty-five than do the lower income-tenths. This is demonstrably the case among the richest 5 per cent of the consumer units. The real question is: To what extent does distribution of income-tenths within a certain age group deviate from distribution of income-tenths generally? Although information is not as complete as might be desired, there is more than enough to make contingent generalizations. Detailed data exist on income distribution by tenths and by age for 1935-36 and 1948, and on income-size distribution by age for the postwar years. They disclose sharp income inequalities within every age group (although more moderate in the eighteen-to-twenty-five category) — inequalities that closely parallel the over-all national income pattern. The implication is clear: A spending unit's income-tenth position *within his age category* varies much less, if at all, and is determined primarily by his occupation.

In other words, in America, the legendary land of economic opportunity where any man can work his way to the top, there is only slight income mobility outside the natural age cycle of rising, then falling income. Since most of the sixty-five-and-over age group falls into the low-income brackets and constitutes the largest segment of the $0–$2,000 income class, it is of obvious importance in analyzing future poverty in the United States to examine the growth trends of his group. The sixty-five-and-over population composed 4.0 per cent of the total population in 1900, 5.3 per cent in 1930, 8.4 per cent in 1955, and will reach an estimated 9.6 per cent in 1970 and 10.8 per cent in 2000. Between 1900 and 1975, the total national population is expected to increase 176 per cent, but those from ages forty-five through sixty-four are expected to increase 316 per cent, and those sixty-five and over are expected to increase 572 per cent. Between 1960 and 1975, the population aged eighteen to twenty-five is also expected to grow far more rapidly than the middle-aged population. With the more rapid expansion of these two low-income groups, the young and the old, in the years immediately ahead, an increase in the extent of poverty is probable.

IF YOU FINISH BEFORE THE TIME IS UP, GO OVER THESE PASSAGES. DO NOT TURN TO THE QUESTIONS FOR THESE PASSAGES NOR TO ANY OTHER SECTION OF THE TEST. WHEN THE 15 MINUTES ARE UP, GO ON TO SECTION 1B WHICH CONTAINS THE QUESTIONS FOR THESE PASSAGES.

SECTION 1B: READING RECALL

Time: 15 minutes

Directions: Answer the following questions on the basis of what is stated or implied in the passages which you have just read. You are not permitted at any time to turn back to the passages.

QUESTIONS FOR FIRST PASSAGE

1. The first known large-scale bureaucracy in history occurred in

   (A) England
   (B) China
   (C) Puritan Massachusetts
   (D) Rome
   (E) ancient Egypt

2. Of the following the one that is *least* likely to be bureaucratized is

   (A) a corporation employing 250,000 workers
   (B) a labor union with 10,000 members
   (C) the state government of New York
   (D) the city government of Los Angeles
   (E) a club with 25 members

3. There were few bureaucracies before the development of a monetary system and the abolition of slavery because

   (A) slaves were too independent to submit to discipline
   (B) the payment of salaries is conducive to performance of bureaucratic duties
   (C) organizations were too small to be bureaucratized
   (D) organizations were too large to be bureaucratized
   (E) capitalism leads to bureaucratization in many spheres

4. Capitalists have generally favored a strong Federal government because

   (A) banditry, piracy, and social revolution interfere with attempts to calculate economic risks
   (B) legislators of a weak government are not easily influenced
   (C) such a government holds farmers in check
   (D) they are desirous of an economy whose ups and downs cannot be predicted
   (E) they depend on the president for their existence

5. Expanding business firms use bureaucratic methods because of the need

   (A) to restrict bureau supervisors
   (B) to deal advantageously with unions
   (C) to decentralize the firm
   (D) for efficiency
   (E) for detecting subversion among employees

6. Large corporations are responsible for the development of bureaucracy in labor unions because workers

   (A) lack the incentive to carry out responsibilities on their own initiative
   (B) are too independent of the corporations to submit willingly to discipline
   (C) become estranged from the owners with whom they can no longer bargain individually
   (D) are desirous of improving their skills
   (E) thus feel that they are working in an executive capacity

7. More important than size, a factor which encourages the development of bureaucracy is

   (A) the need for order
   (B) the high level of discipline
   (C) location in an agrarian economy
   (D) the emergence of special administrative problems
   (E) the need for efficiency

8. It can be assumed that Thomas Jefferson

   (A) was strongly in favor of state's rights
   (B) favored strong federal government
   (C) predicted the development of a bureaucratic government
   (D) was more of a patriot than Alexander Hamilton
   (E) recommended strict protection of the competitive market system

9. When workers are removed from the activities governed by the profit principle

   (A) their employer must remain available for individual bargaining
   (B) corporate efficiency increases
   (C) the workers become more involved with their union administration
   (D) it becomes necessary to introduce bureaucratic methods
   (E) bureaucratization can no longer maintain efficiency levels

10. A money economy

   (A) is usually necessary for the development of bureaucracy
   (B) has always been defined as work in exchange for compensation
   (C) existed in ancient Egypt, Rome and China
   (D) requires a worker's disciplined conduct and respect
   (E) prevails in a slave economy

QUESTIONS FOR SECOND PASSAGE

11. Inflation helps the poor because

    (A) money is worth less during an inflationary period
    (B) money is worth more during an inflationary period
    (C) labor shortages created during inflationary periods create more jobs for the poor
    (D) welfare benefits rise more slowly than prices during an inflationary period
    (E) the rich spend more during an inflationary period

12. All of the following would affect the middle class more than the poor *except.*

    (A) an increase in rent
    (B) an increase in education costs
    (C) an increase in clothing expenses
    (D) an increase in travel expenses
    (E) an increase in the cost of air travel

13. Which one of the following would be most aided during an inflationary period?

    (A) a worker with a fixed income
    (B) a landlord
    (C) a school teacher
    (D) a creditor
    (E) a debtor

14. All of the following are measures that would tend to curb inflation *except*

    (A) a decrease in consumer spending
    (B) an increase in interest rates
    (C) an increase in federal spending
    (D) an increase in taxes
    (E) a freeze on wages

15. A circumstance which supports the Hollister-Palmer thesis is

    (A) the increase in the number of families below the poverty line
    (B) the decrease in the number of families below the proverty line
    (C) the rise in the Consumer Price Index
    (D) the drop in federal spending
    (E) none of the above

16. Even the poor who do not land jobs will benefit from inflation because

    (A) taxes will be lower
    (B) the CPI falls more quickly
    (C) welfare benefits will rise faster than prices
    (D) of improvement in the general economic situation
    (E) the inflationary boom will not reach them

17. The "poor price index"

    (A) rises more than the consumer price index
    (B) rises less than the consumer price index
    (C) rises the same amount as the consumer price index
    (D) is an official government statistic
    (E) relates unemployment to the price level

18. President Nixon claims that the burden of inflation

    (A) hits the rich hardest
    (B) hits the rich least of all
    (C) hits the poor hardest
    (D) hits the poor least of all
    (E) hits the middle classes hardest

19. The following assumptions are made in the article:

    I. Both full employment and price stability are desirable.
    II. The non-working poor are on welfare.
    III. There is a trade-off between unemployment and inflation.

    (A) I only
    (B) II only
    (C) III only
    (D) I and II only
    (E) I and II and III

20. Walter W. Heller is

    (A) former chairman of the President's Council of Economic Advisers
    (B) an economist in the Department of Labor
    (C) a member of the cabinet
    (D) creator of the "poor price index"
    (E) creator of the CPI

QUESTIONS FOR THIRD PASSAGE

21. According to the passage, most social scientists erroneously assume that

    (A) personal expenses increase with the age of the spending unit
    (B) the needs of the younger spending unit are greater than those of the aged
    (C) the relationship between old age and low income is an economic and not a sociological problem
    (D) old age population should consume in accordance with their requirements
    (E) leisure living requires increased income

22. It can be inferred that in the 35-55 age category

   (A) income-tenth positions vary greatly
   (B) income-tenth positions vary very little
   (C) earning potential does not resemble the overall national income pattern*
   (D) occupations have little bearing on the income-tenth position
   (E) there is great mobility between income-tenth positions

23. The author believes which of the following?

   I. The aged will continue to increase as a percentage of the total population.
   II. Income inequalities decrease with increasing age.
   III. Managerial and professional workers have greater income mobility than blue collar workers.

   (A) I only
   (B) II only
   (C) III only
   (D) I and II only
   (E) I and III only

24. In the passage the term "functional ethos" means

   (A) national group
   (B) ethnic influence
   (C) prevailing ideology
   (D) biased opinion
   (E) practical ethics

25. The article states that the old age population

   (A) has increased due to longer life expectancy
   (B) exceeds all but the 18-25 age group in growth rate
   (C) is well represented among the higher-income tenths
   (D) is increasing as a percentage of the low-income tenths
   (E) has its greatest numbers among the middle income group

26. According to the author, aside from the natural age cycle, economic opportunity in America is greatly limited by

   I. occupation
   II. income inequality within every age group
   III. class background

   (A) I only
   (B) II only
   (C) III only
   (D) I and III only
   (E) I and II only

27. According to the passage, the older, unionized blue-collar workers are

    (A) assured constant salary until retirement
    (B) given preference over new workers because of seniority
    (C) likely to receive downgraded salary
    (D) more susceptible to lay-off after 40
    (E) encouraged to move to slower-paced but equal-paying jobs

28. The article states that the average worker finds that

    (A) as family obligations begin escalating, income begins to decline
    (B) he reaches economic stability at middle age due to the parallel rise in age, obligations and income
    (C) he earns least while he is acquiring vocational skills
    (D) he reaches peak earning power between the ages of 40-65
    (E) his wage gains coincide with the decline of family needs

29. The article states that within higher income-tenths

    (A) 5% of the spending units are in the 35-55 age group
    (B) the income-tenth increases occur only in the 35-55 age group
    (C) the 35-55 age group have a greater representation than they do with the lower-income tenths
    (D) the retirement age is approximately 10 years younger than that of the general population
    (E) income variables show a higher correlation than those determined by occupation

30. It can be inferred that one could most accurately predict a person's income from

    (A) his age
    (B) his natural age cycle
    (C) his occupation
    (D) his occupation and age
    (E) his seniority position

IF YOU FINISH BEFORE THE TIME IS UP, GO OVER YOUR WORK FOR THIS RECALL PART ONLY. DO NOT TURN BACK TO THE READING PASSAGES NOR TO ANY OTHER SECTION OF THE TEST. WHEN THE 15 MINUTES ARE UP, GO ON TO THE NEXT SECTION.

SECTION 2: MATH ABILITY

Time: 30 minutes

Directions: Each of the problems in this section is followed by five alternatives lettered A through E. Solve each problem and then choose the correct answer. Note that diagrams are not necessarily drawn to scale. Scratchwork may be done on available space on the pages of this section.

31. A man buys a suit which lists for $200 at a 10% discount. He gets an additional 2% discount for paying cash. What does he actually pay for the suit?

   (A) $176
   (B) $170
   (C) $180
   (D) $176.40
   (E) $172.80

32. Harry goes to the post office with $1.00 and spends it all on 5¢ and 2¢ stamps. If he buys some of both, what is the greatest number of 5¢ stamps he could buy?

   (A) 10
   (B) 12
   (C) 14
   (D) 16
   (E) 18

33. A roast beef loses 30% of its weight in cooking. If it weights 12.6 lbs. after cooking, how many pounds did it weigh before cooking?

   (A) 16.4
   (B) 18
   (C) 18.8
   (D) 19.6
   (E) 21

34. In a certain college, all freshmen are required to study French or Spanish or both. If 65% are studying French and 55% are studying Spanish, what percent of the freshmen class is studying both?

   (A) 10%
   (B) 20%
   (C) 40%
   (D) 80%
   (E) 90%

35. A pair of boots cost a teenager $58.80 after he has received a 30% discount. What did the boots cost originally?

    (A) $84.00
    (B) $76.44
    (C) $80.00
    (D) $82.50
    (E) $75.80

36. If $5y = 2y - 6$, what does $y + 5$ equal?

    (A) -3
    (B) 3
    (C) 7
    (D) 5
    (E) -2

37. What is the total cost of borrowing a book from a lending library for n days if the cost for the first 5 days is p cents and the cost for each additional day is q cents?

    (A) $p + q (n - 5)$
    (B) $5p + q (n - 5)$
    (C) $p + qn$
    (D) $p + q(n + 5)$
    (E) $5p + qn$

38. A tourist makes a 540-mile trip during which his car uses from 15 to 18 miles per gallon. If gas varies in price from 32¢ to 40¢ per gallon, what is the difference between the most and least he could spend for gas?

    (A) $2.00
    (B) $2.40
    (C) $3.60
    (D) $4.20
    (E) $4.80

39. A man sold a book for $3.50. His profit was 40% of his cost. What was his profit?

    (A) $1.40
    (B) $1.60
    (C) $1.00
    (D) $1.90
    (E) $2.20

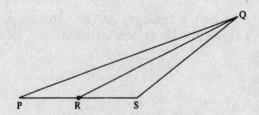

40. In the figure above, $PR = QR$ and $QS = RS$. If Angle RSQ measures 120°, what is the measure of Angle QPR in degrees?

(A) 10°
(B) 20°
(C) 30°
(D) 15°
(E) cannot be determined from given information

41. A mixture is made up of liquids A and B. Liquid A weighs 4 lb. per gallon and liquid B weighs 6.5 lb. per gallon. What is the weight, in pounds, of 2 gallons of the mixture if it is made up of 60% liquid A and 40% liquid B?

(A) 12.4
(B) 5.0
(C) 10.0
(D) 10.5
(E) 21

42. Which of the following fractions is more than one-half?

(A) $\dfrac{9}{20}$

(B) $\dfrac{7}{15}$

(C) $\dfrac{32}{65}$

(D) $\dfrac{73}{147}$

(E) $\dfrac{101}{201}$

43. If there are exactly four times as many women teachers in a school as men teachers, which of the following *cannot* be the number of teachers in the school?

(A) 42
(E) 45
(C) 50
(D) 55
(E) 60

44. A rectangle 20 inches long and 10 inches wide is tiled *completely* with square tiles ½-inch on each side. How many titles are needed?

    (A) 60
    (B) 100
    (C) 200
    (D) 400
    (E) 800

45. Bill can mow 200 square feet of lawn in 12 minutes and Fred can mow 300 square feet in 15 minutes. What is the ratio of Bill's mowing rate to Fred's rate?

    (A) $\dfrac{6}{5}$

    (B) $\dfrac{5}{6}$

    (C) $\dfrac{2}{3}$

    (D) $\dfrac{4}{5}$

    (E) $\dfrac{5}{4}$

46. A boy bicycled up a hill and down the same distance on the other side. He went 5 times as fast going down as up. The whole trip took 9 minutes. How many minutes did it take to go up hill?

    (A) $1\frac{1}{2}$
    (B) 1.8
    (C) 4.5
    (D) 7.2
    (E) $7\frac{1}{2}$

47. Mary can read k pages of a book in 45 minutes. At this rate, how many pages can she read in 2 hours?

    (A) $\dfrac{8k}{3}$

    (B) $\dfrac{3k}{8}$

    (C) $\dfrac{2k}{45}$

    (D) $\dfrac{45}{2k}$

    (E) $15k$

48. A man pays $29.75 for a radio after receiving a 30% discount. What was the list price of the radio?

(A) $38.68
(B) $42.50
(C) $45.00
(D) $48.50
(E) $44.25

Questions 49–51

Income of Persons — U. S. 1961

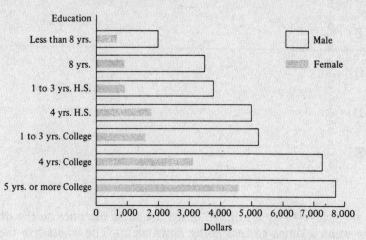

Annual Income According to Years of Education

49. What was the approximate ratio in 1961, of the income of male 4-year college graduates to that of male 4-year high school graduates?

(A) 7 : 5
(B) 2 : 1
(C) 4 : 3
(D) 3 : 2
(E) 7 : 3

50. In 1961, the income of women with 4 years of high school education was approximately what percent of the income of men with 4 years of high school education?

(A) 40%
(B) 20%
(C) 50%
(D) 25%
(E) 60%

51. In 1961, what was the approximate difference in annual income between men with 4 years of college and those with only 8 years of elementary education?

   (A) $2500
   (B) $3000
   (C) $4000
   (D) $5000
   (E) $5500

52. A machine can produce 15 bolts in 12 seconds. At this rate, how many bolts will it produce in 6 minutes?

   (A) 275
   (B) 325
   (C) 350
   (D) 400
   (E) 450

53. A student gets marks of 75 ,82, 86 on three tests. What must be his mark on the next test so that his average for the 4 tests will be 85?

   (A) 97
   (B) 94
   (C) 90
   (D) 88
   (E) 85

Questions 54–57

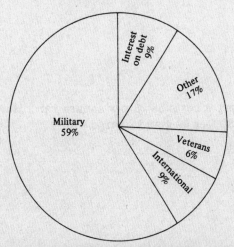

Military 59%

Interest on debt 9%

Other 17%

Veterans 6%

International 9%

1954 National "Budget Dollar" Percent of
U.S. Expenditures on Various Items

54. Approximately how many degrees should there be in the central angle of the sector for military expenditures?

   (A) 220
   (B) 213
   (C) 210
   (D) 208
   (E) 198

55. Approximately what is the ratio of military expenditures to veterans' expenditures?

    (A) 8 : 3
    (B) 9 : 2
    (C) 10 : 1
    (D) 11 : 1
    (E) 6 : 1

56. If the U.S. had total expenditures in 1954 of 120 billion dollars, approximately how many billions did it spend on interest on debt?

    (A) 15.4
    (B) 20
    (C) 9
    (D) 12
    (E) 10.8

57. If 9 billion dollars were spent in 1954 for veterans, what would have been total expenditures for that year in billions?

    (A) 150
    (B) 140
    (C) 160
    (D) 130
    (E) 125

58. A certain carpet costs $8.25 per square yard. How much will a carpet cost if it is 60 feet long and 2 yards wide?

    (A) $640.50
    (B) $1980
    (C) $330
    (D) $660
    (E) $495

59. A shoe store selling shoes from $10 to $20 per pair runs a sale offering one dollar off on each pair of shoes. What can be said about the rate of discount for this sale?

    (A) This is equivalent to a 5% discount
    (B) This is equivalent to a 10% discount
    (C) The discount rate was higher for the more expensive shoes.
    (D) The discount rate was higher for the cheaper shoes.
    (E) The average discount rate was 10%

60. The cost of 5 apples and 6 oranges is 98¢. The total cost of a dozen of each is $2.16. What is the ratio of the cost of an apple to that of an orange?

(A) $\dfrac{6}{5}$

(B) $\dfrac{5}{4}$

(C) $\dfrac{5}{6}$

(D) $\dfrac{4}{5}$

(E) $\dfrac{4}{3}$

IF YOU FINISH BEFORE THE TIME IS UP, GO OVER YOUR WORK FOR THIS SECTION ONLY. DO NOT TURN TO ANY OTHER SECTION OF THE TEST. WHEN THE TIME IS UP, GO ON TO THE NEXT SECTION.

SECTION 3: BUSINESS JUDGMENT

Time: 30 minutes for all Section 3

QUESTIONS ON DATA EVALUATION

Directions: Read the passage. After the passage are Data Evaluation questions (in phrase form) that relate to the passage. Answer each question by choosing the appropriate letter for your answer.

(A) **Major Objective.** The phrase indicates a Major Objective of the business executive in the situation described in the passage.

(B) **Major Factor.** The phrase indicates a Major Factor in the business executive's arriving at a decision. The passage specifically mentions a circumstance or consideration that is fundamental in his coming to the decision.

(C) **Minor Factor.** The phrase indicates a Minor Factor in the business executive's arriving at a decision. The passage specifically states a circumstance or consideration that is secondary in his coming to a decision.

(D) **Major Assumption.** The phrase indicates a Major Assumption in the business executive's arriving at a decision. He is taking for granted certain circumstances or occurrences in his decision-making.

(E) **Unimportant Issue.** The phrase indicates an Unimportant Issue in the business executive's arriving at a decision. The issue is of no importance or of no relevance in his decision-making.

The Supercool Refrigeration Corporation of Chicago has, for several years, been exporting refrigeration units for commercial and domestic use to San Martino, an underdeveloped country in South America whose growth in recent years has been quite rapid. Continuation of present growth trends would indicate a substantially increased demand for both luxury consumer goods and convenient foods. The company's policy is to expand sales in San Martino as quickly as possible, hoping to limit the inroads made by competitors on this lucrative market.

Manufacture of all units is presently performed at the main factory in Chicago. Goods exported to San Martino are taken, at considerable cost, by rail and boat. Breakage and corrosion during the trip are a further, though less important, source of costs. The Chicago factory is of limited size, however, and the growth of export markets taken with the steady increase in demand within the United States has led to an imminent shortage of capacity. If both the home and overseas markets are to be supplied adequately, a new investment in buildings and machinery is called for; the company's presently highly solvent position and high rating on the financial markets mean capital should be readily available for an investment project.

Careful consideration was given to a variety of potential locations for the new works, but eventually the choice narrowed to either expanding the present Chicago works or building a new factory within San Martino. Advice from the sales team was that the entry of competition in the San Martino market could best be restricted by pricing the models as cheaply as possible. The President of the board was in basic agreement with this advice but felt strongly that a continued goal should be the maintenance of the company's reputation for quality merchandise. Only with a reliable "name," he argued, could long-run market penetration be maximized.

The primary sources of cost saving (see Table I) as a result of locating in San Martino were comprised of the elimination of transport costs and the avoidance of a tariff imposed by the government on the import of all consumer goods. This measure was designed to encourage investment within the country.

Cost of Standard Household Unit Sold in San Martino

COST	MANUFACTURED IN CHICAGO	MANUFACTURED IN SAN MARTINO
Materials	$ 50	$ 50
Labor	120	134
Transport	51	4
Damage in Transit (average)	9	2
Basic Cost	230	190
Tariff (20%)	46	0
Wholesale Cost	276	190
Dealer Markup (10%)	28	19
Total Retail Cost	$304	$209

Initially, it was thought that the availability of cheap labor in San Martino would be a major source of savings, but although unskilled labor is available at less than half the American wage, the necessity of importing supervisory and skilled staff from the United States, coupled with the lower productivity of the local workers, more than offset any gain.

The maintenance of quality is important to the company and there was doubt as to the ability of San Martino workers to produce reliable workmanship. Eventually, it was decided that with close supervision and extensive quality control the required standards could be met.

All raw materials used are available in San Martino at close to the United States prices. Cost of construction of buildings would be slightly lower than in Chicago but the higher cost of installing machinery meant that total investment cost would be virtually identical.

A further important issue was a financial matter relating to the instability of the cruzeiro, the unit of currency in San Martino. A devaluation seems likely in the near future and that would increase the basic cost of all imports (before the tariff) and a devaluation of more than 10% would be fatal to any sales drive predicated on the import of goods.

In the light of the foregoing considerations and in view of the impetus that a new overseas base would give to the long-term worldwide sales drive, seen by the President as the logical future of the company, it was decided to build the new factory in San Martino.

Choose the appropriate letter (A or B or C or D or E)
for these phrases in accordance with the given directions.

61. Growth of demand for luxury consumer goods

62. Elimination of damage in transit

63. Avoiding the tariff

64. Growth of convenience food sales

65. Increase in U.S. demand for refrigerators

66. Reducing transportation cost

67. Instability of the cruzeiro

68. Total labor costs in San Martino

69. Rapid expansion of Supercool sales in San Martino

70. Supercool Refrigeration Corporation has been located in Chicago for years

71. Maintaining the company's reputation for good workmanship

72. Total cost of the investment project in either possible location

73. Cost of raw materials in San Martino

74. Expanding sales on a worldwide scale

75. Availability of capital for the project

76. Effect of close supervision and quality control on product quality

77. The limited size of the Chicago factory

QUESTIONS ON DATA APPLICATION

Directions: The questions below are to be answered with reference to the same passage (above). For each question, select the correct answer from each of the five choices given.

78. The dealer mark-up is

      I. the same for goods manufactured in the U.S. and San Martino in dollar terms
     II. lower for goods produced in San Martino in dollar terms
   III. lower for goods produced in San Martino in percentage terms
   IV. the same for goods produced in San Martino and the U.S. in percentage terms

  (A) I only
  (B) I and IV only
  (C) II and IV only
  (D) I and III only
  (E) II and III only

79. The productivity of the U.S. worker is

  (A) expected to be about the same as that of the San Martino worker
  (B) much lower than that of the San Martino worker
  (C) lower than that of the San Martino worker but compensated by close quality control
  (D) rising more rapidly than that of the San Martino worker
  (E) higher than that of the San Martino worker

80. The unskilled wage rates in San Martino are

  (A) high because of an acute labor shortage
  (B) about the same as in the U.S.
  (C) about 20% lower than in the U.S.
  (D) about 50% lower than in the U.S.
  (E) subsidized by the government

81. Pricing as low as possible is desired in order to

  (A) benefit the San Martino consumer
  (B) avoid the tariff totally
  (C) fight inflation in the U.S.
  (D) restrict the entry of competitors in San Martino
  (E) put pressure on workers to increase their productivity

82. The effect of a devaluation of the cruzeiro would be to increase

    (A) the price of a refrigerator made and sold in the U.S.
    (B) the price of a refrigerator made and sold in San Martino
    (C) the price of a refrigerator made in San Martino and sold in the U.S.
    (D) the price of a refrigerator made in the U.S. and sold in San Martino
    (E) transport costs within the U.S.

83. Capital is available for the project because

    (A) bankruptcy would follow if the investment is not made
    (B) the factory in Chicago is to be closed and sold
    (C) of the company's highly solvent position
    (D) of a grant from the San Martino government to encourage investment
    (E) the cost savings due to elimination of transit damage would be so significant

84. Space is short in the Chicago factory because of

    (A) the rapid rise of domestic demand
    (B) the growth of export markets
    (C) a steady rise of domestic demand
    (D) both A and B
    (E) both B and C

85. For a standard household unit sold in San Martino, which manufacturing cost is greater in San Martino than in Chicago?

    (A) Materials cost
    (B) Transport cost
    (C) Basic cost
    (D) Labor cost
    (E) Wholesale cost

IF YOU FINISH BEFORE THE TIME IS UP, GO OVER YOUR WORK FOR THIS SECTION ONLY. DO NOT TURN TO ANY OTHER SECTION OF THE TEST. WHEN THE TIME IS UP, GO ON TO THE NEXT SECTION.

SECTION 4: DATA SUFFICIENCY

Time: 30 minutes

Directions: Each of the questions below is followed by two statements, labeled (1) and (2), in which certain data are given. In these questions you do not actually have to compute an answer, but rather you have to decide whether the data given in the statements are *sufficient* for answering the question. Using the data given in the statements *plus* your knowledge of mathematics and everyday facts (such as the number of days in July), you are to blacken the box on the answer sheet under

(A) if statement (1) ALONE is sufficient but statement (2) alone is not sufficient to answer the question asked.

(B) if statement (2) ALONE is sufficient but statement (1) alone is not sufficient to answer the question asked.

(C) if BOTH statements (1) and (2) TOGETHER are sufficient to answer the question asked, but NEITHER statement ALONE is sufficient.

(D) if EACH statement is sufficient by itself to answer the question asked.

(E) if statements (1) and (2) TOGETHER are NOT sufficient to answer the question asked and additional data specific to the problem are needed.

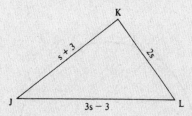

86. What are the lengths of the sides of triangle JKL shown above?

(1) The perimeter is 18.
(2) JK = JL.

87. The cost of butter recently rose 5%. What is the present price?

(1) Butter used to cost 80¢ per pound.
(2) The present price is divisible by 12.

88. In triangle ADE, what is the measure of angle A?

(1) AE = 9 inches
(2) Angle D = 24°

89. How much does Harold weigh?

    (1) If Harold were 5 inches taller, he would weigh 28 pounds more.

    (2) If Harold were 5 inches taller, his weight would increase by 10%.

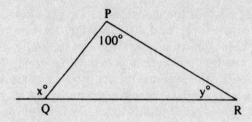

90. In the figure above, what is the value of x?

    (1) PQ = 3 inches

    (2) y = 20°

91. Is the integer k positive or negative?

    (1) k^2 is positive.

    (2) $k + (-k) = 0$

92. How many red marbles are in a box?

    (1) Squaring the number of red marbles would have the same effect as tripling it.

    (2) There are ten marbles in the box.

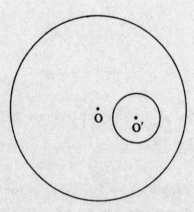

93. What is the distance between the centers of the two circles shown above?

    (1) The area of the large circle is 25π.

    (2) The area of the small circle is π.

94. p and q are integers. Furthermore, $3 \leq p \leq 7$.
What is p? ($\leq$ means equal to or less than; $<$ means less than)

(1) $1 < q < 5$
(2) $p \leq q$

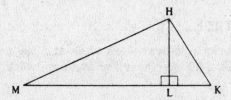

95. In the diagram above, what is the length of ML?

(1) LK = 2 feet.
(2) HK = 3 feet, HM = 6 feet

96. On line segment AB, C lies between A and B.
Furthermore, D lies between C and B. What is the length of CD?

(1) AB = 19 inches. AC = DB
(2) DB = 5 inches.

97. A group of cows and chickens walk about in a farm yard. Altogether, there are 18 animals. How many cows are there?

(1) More than half the animals are chickens.
(2) The total number of legs is 44.

98. Is quadrilateral EFGH a parallelogram?

(1) EF + FG = 10 inches.
(2) FG + GH = 10 inches.

99. x, y, and z are the measures of the three angles of a triangle. Which is the smallest?

(1) $z = 62°$
(2) $x < y$

100. What is the depth of the water in a fish tank?

(1) The water in the tank weighs 124 pounds.
(2) The tank has a capacity of 200 pounds of water and a volume of 3 cubic feet.

101. A certain school has an auditorium with 25 rows. Each row has from 30 to 35 seats. If the auditorium is filled up, what percent of the school can it hold?

(1) The school has 2000 students and 70 teachers.
(2) The rows average 32 seats each.

102. Eight pounds of corn meal are needed to feed 32 pigs for one day. How many pounds of meal are consumed by the pigs of Mr. Hardwick's farm each day?

    (1) There are 109 pigs on the farm.
    (2) In one week 190¾ pounds of meal is consumed.

103. George worked 42 hours this week. How much did he earn?

    (1) George works a 35-hour work week at $3.00 per hour.
    (2) George gets $4.00 per hour for overtime work.

104. Is the average of 60 numbers less than 20?

    (1) One-fifth of the numbers are exactly 10.
    (2) One-half of the numbers are less than 30.

105. What is the volume of a given cube?

    (1) The area of each face is 4.
    (2) The length of the diagonal of one face is $2\sqrt{2}$.

106. In triangle TRE, is there a right angle?

    (1) Angle R is greater than twice angle E.
    (2) Angle T is 70°.

107. Alice can sell her lemonade at 5¢ or 10¢ per glass. At which price would she make more money?

    (1) Alice would sell 15 glasses per hour at 10¢ per glass.
    (2) Alice would sell 3 times as much lemonade at 5¢ per glass as she would at 10¢ per glass.

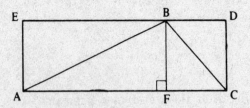

108. In the figure above, what is the length of BC?

    (1) AF is 6 inches.
    (2) AB is 8 inches, AC is 9 inches.

109. Five girls stand in a row. What is the weight of the third girl?

    (1) The third girl is 75% of the average weight.
    (2) Their total weight is 600 pounds.

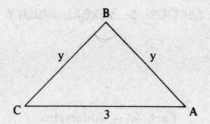

110. In the triangle above, what is the measure of angle B?

    (1) The perimeter of the triangle is less than 10 and greater than 5
    (2) Angle A is less than 60°

111. Is y less than $\dfrac{15}{16}$?

    (1) $y + 2 = \dfrac{25}{16}$

    (2) $y < \dfrac{11}{16}$

112. Is Harry younger than John?

    (1) John is two years younger than Jim
    (2) Jim is two years younger than Harry.

113. City X has two libraries. Does the total number of books in both libraries exceed 18,000?

    (1) One library has twice as many books as the other library.
    (2) One library has 9000 books.

114. Is $\dfrac{2}{5}x$ greater than $\dfrac{3}{5}y$?

    (1) x is greater than y
    (2) $x + y = 1$

115. What is the value of x and y?

    (1) The point (x, y) lies in the first quadrant.
    (2) $x = y$

IF YOU FINISH BEFORE THE TIME IS UP, GO OVER YOUR WORK FOR THIS SECTION ONLY. DO NOT TURN TO ANY OTHER SECTION OF THE TEST. WHEN THE TIME IS UP, GO ON TO THE NEXT SECTION.

SECTION 5: VERBAL ABILITY

Time: 30 minutes

Part A — Antonyms

Directions: In each question, you will find a capitalized word which is followed by five choices. Select from these choices that word whose meaning is *opposite* to the meaning of the capitalized word.

116. TRAVAIL

    (A) excitement
    (B) exaggeration
    (C) solicitude
    (D) trouble
    (E) relaxation

117. CUDGEL

    (A) unravel
    (B) caress
    (C) agitate
    (D) prefer
    (E) silence

118. FACTITIOUS

    (A) untruthful
    (B) spontaneous
    (C) peaceful
    (D) superstitious
    (E) magnified

119. INVETERATE

    (A) beginning
    (B) uninvited
    (C) illiterate
    (D) literate
    (E) cumulative

120. PRODIGAL

    (A) corruptible
    (B) lackadaisical
    (C) religious
    (D) provident
    (E) egocentric

121. ESCHEW

    (A) welcome
    (B) swallow whole
    (C) borrow
    (D) save
    (E) reset

122. ERUDITE

    (A) polite
    (B) flimsy
    (C) prolific
    (D) humble
    (E) ignorant

123. DIVISIVE

    (A) multiplying
    (B) derisive
    (C) farseeing
    (D) acceptable
    (E) unifying

Part B — Analogies

Directions: In each question, you will first see two capitalized words. Try to establish a relationship between these two words. Then select from the five lettered word-pairs that word pair which bears a relationship which is the same as that of the two capitalized words.

124. LABEL : CLASSIFICATION ::

    (A) joke : amusement
    (B) organization : disorder
    (C) river : swimming
    (D) land : safety
    (E) beauty : perfection

125. SHACKLED : UNFETTER ::

    (A) land: sea
    (B) omen : sign
    (C) give : take
    (D) hurt : comfort
    (E) chain : link

126. CHAIR : BENCH ::

    (A) street : sidewalk
    (B) ruler : yardstick
    (C) wood : steel
    (D) pig : elephant
    (E) glass : cup

127. SMOKE : POLLUTION ::

    (A) water : river
    (B) war : death
    (C) vaccination : immunity
    (D) degeneration : decay
    (E) iron : strength

128. HYPOTHESIS : EXPERIMENTATION ::

    (A) prediction : conclusion
    (B) film : camera
    (C) science : achievement
    (D) reality : fantasy
    (E) opinion : debate

129. OXYGEN : RESPIRATION ::

    (A) improvement : care
    (B) camera : photography
    (C) sunlight : photosynthesis
    (D) hydrogen : digestion
    (E) drama : acting

130. REQUEST : REFUSAL ::

    (A) eating : obesity
    (B) deny : affirmation
    (C) try : failure
    (D) swim : sinking
    (E) struggle : victory

131. CONFIDENCE : DECEPTION ::

    (A) hostility : kindliness
    (B) walking : running
    (C) dissent : commotion
    (D) blanket : heat
    (E) giant : pygmy

Part C — Sentence Completions

Directions: In each of the following sentences, one or two words are missing. From the five choices, select that choice which fits in best with the rest of the sentence.

132. Lacking _____, he enjoyed everything from the best to the worst in food.

    (A) censure
    (B) discrimination
    (C) consideration
    (D) plausibility
    (E) competition

133. The _____ in the Bible are both entertaining and instructive.

    (A) syllables
    (B) abatements
    (C) milestones
    (D) parables
    (E) utilities

134. After remaining _____ for some time the object began to move _____ upward.

    (A) stationary .... imperceptibly
    (B) illuminated .... variously
    (C) invisible .... partially
    (D) secondary .... rapidly
    (E) fragile .... undulatingly

135. The orchestra was _____ by the addition of several violins and cellos.

    (A) rescinded
    (B) resounded
    (C) omitted
    (D) conceived
    (E) augmented

136. Because of the poor _____, the singers' voices could barely be heard.

    (A) matrix
    (B) acoustics
    (C) implementation
    (D) reduction
    (E) attenuation

137. Because the lawyer's _____ was considered so good, his _____ were always respected.

    (A) clientele .... whims
    (B) knowledge .... antiquities
    (C) judgment .... decisions
    (D) intuition .... reservations
    (E) diplomacy .... institutions

138. _____ may conceivably be a virtue, if it is not _____.

    (A) frugality .... invalidated
    (B) ambition .... traditional
    (C) rivalry .... skeptical
    (D) nobility .... inevitable
    (E) inconsistency .... habitual

139. The _____ of perpetual motion has been abandoned and _____ many times, but it is now regarded as impossible.

    (A) argument .... implemented
    (B) theory .... resurrected
    (C) revision .... ignored
    (D) method .... revamped
    (E) calculation .... rejected

140. There was danger of another _____ with workers because of the difficulty of providing sufficient police protection during the _____ downtown noon hour.

    (A) clash .... teeming
    (B) emergency .... migrant
    (C) reduction .... varying
    (D) misconception .... designated
    (E) disclosure .... unspecified

IF YOU FINISH BEFORE THE TIME IS UP, GO OVER YOUR WORK FOR THIS SECTION ONLY. DO NOT TURN TO ANY OTHER SECTION OF THE TEST. WHEN THE TIME IS UP, GO ON TO THE NEXT SECTION.

SECTION 6: BUSINESS JUDGMENT

Time: 30 minutes for all of Section 6

QUESTIONS ON DATA EVALUATION

Directions: Read the passage. After the passage are Data Evaluation questions (in phrase form) that relate to the passage. Answer each question by choosing the appropriate letter for your answer.

(A) **Major Objective.** The phrase indicates a Major Objective of the business executive in the situation described in the passage.

(B) **Major Factor.** The phrase indicates a Major Factor in the business executive's arriving at a decision. The passage specifically mentions a circumstance or consideration that is fundamental in his coming to the decision.

(C) **Minor Factor.** The phrase indicates a Minor Factor in the business executive's arriving at a decision. The passage specifically states a circumstance or consideration that is secondary in his coming to a decision.

(D) **Major Assumption.** The phrase indicates a Major Assumption in the business executive's arriving at a decision. He is taking for granted certain circumstances or occurrences in his decision-making.

(E) **Unimportant Issue.** The phrase indicates an Unimportant Issue in the business executive's arriving at a decision. The issue is of no importance or of no relevance in his decision-making.

The research department of the Progressive Floor Treatments Company has developed a high quality polymer resin which will allow the firm to produce an excellent water-based floor polish at less than two-thirds of the present cost. All raw materials are low cost and readily available. The new process is also unusually simple, which is important since labor accounts for about three-quarters of production costs. Changing over to the new process will halve the labor required, and all workers can be unskilled, whereas previously 25% of production workers were skilled men. Furthermore, the polymer resin can be sold directly to industrial users, providing funds to finance other ventures. Patent rights have been applied for, and no problems are expected in that area.

The company has, until now, concentrated all its efforts on the bulk market for polish, supplying commercial users such as factories, offices, and public buildings. The management has resisted the temptation to enter the household market, in view of the high level of competition and the far greater size of companies engaged in that market. Given that the research department is confident that the cost advantage resulting from the innovation will continue for at least two years before being wiped out by advances of a similar magnitude by prospective competitors, the company now feels compelled to investigate the retail market.

The investigation was undertaken by way of several small-scale test markets over a wide geographical area, and by calling in specialist research companies. The test markets indicated that consumers showed virtually no response to price reductions, suggesting that heavy advertising expenditures would be the effective method of breaking into the market. However, advertising proved effective only where the salesmen were successful in obtaining a good distribution of the product among prospective outlets. Here the company faced the problem that the performance of its industrial salesmen was inadequate, as compared to that of the task force of retail salesmen brought in to assist in the operation. In order to secure prime space in the retail outlets, attention to point of sale merchandising and consideration of introductory offers both proved to be valuable, whilst experimentation with packaging produced no consumer response. Additionally, the test marketing produced no reaction from the prospective competitors, and research indicated that they were most unlikely to retaliate by price cutting, since their losses would be considerable.

The Progressive Floor Treatments Company's current situation was also taken into account by the marketing manager. From his own point of view, the retail market offered "safety in numbers." In the industrial operation, increasing numbers of customers had been handing over their cleaning problems to contractors, with the result that Progressive's hundred largest customers recently accounted for 91% of the company's turnover, compared with 82% five years previously, and 73% ten years previously. According to the marketing manager's estimates, the retail market could double Progressive's turnover, within the two year period, by which time a share of the retail market would be secured. However, he was seriously concerned by the company's total lack of experience in the retail field, though this was counterbalanced, to an extent, by considerable expertise with the product itself.

Consultations within the company provided further information. The company accountant was alarmed at the capital costs of the venture, but he considered that it should reverse the trend of declining profitability, caused by the concentration of customers. The problem here was that the large cleaning contractors had succeeded in negotiating special contracts on large quantities. Furthermore, a dramatic increase in numbers of customers would ease his cash flow problems, which were becoming acute because of the large size and small number of customers. However, he was adamant that the retail venture must generate rapid returns on capital invested, as the cost of borrowing the necessary short-term funds could prove disastrous. He and the marketing manager did agree on one point: the innovation represented a windfall gain which was unlikely to be repeated and, hence, should be exploited to the maximum extent possible.

To this appraisal were added the estimates produced by specialists from outside the firm. The economy, as a whole, was expected to continue to be sluggish, and at the less general level, estimates for new building starts were low. However, a high proportion of new flooring was expected to be of the plastic variety, with the result that the total market for water-based polish was expected to increase marginally.

Choose the appropriate letter (A or B or C or D or E) *for these phrases in accordance with the given directions.*

141. The doubling of the company's turnover within two years

142. The price of the new retail product

143. The performance of the industrial salesmen in the retail market

144. Unlikelihood of competitors' retaliating by price cutting

145. "Safety in numbers" offered by the retail market

146. Effectiveness of point of sale merchandising

147. Easing the cash flow problem

148. The cost advantage resulting from the innovation continuing for two years

149. Sales of the polymer resin to industrial customers

150. Exploiting the patent to the maximum extent possible

151. Good distribution of the new retail product

152. The cost of raw materials

153. Heavy advertising expenditure

154. Reversing the trend of declining profitability

155. The expectation of patent rights

156. The company's lack of experience in the retail market

157. The rapid return on capital invested

QUESTIONS ON DATA APPLICATION

Directions: The questions below are to be answered with reference to the same passage (above). For each question, select the correct answer from each of the five choices given.

158. For which of the following reasons is the company considering entering the retail market?

    I. Profits are falling in the current situation.
    II. It expects rapid growth if it does so.
    III. The cost advantage resulting from the innovation will cover the heavy advertising expenditures.

  (A) I only
  (B) II only
  (C) III only
  (D) I and III only
  (E) I and II and III

159. Why does the accountant favor the retail project?

    I. It eases the cash flow problem.
    II. It should increase profits.
    III. It will eliminate special contracts.

  (A) I only
  (B) II only
  (C) III only
  (D) I and II only
  (E) I and II and III

160. Which of the following is true of the company's industrial salesmen?

  (A) They are inadequate.
  (B) They perform poorly in the retail market.
  (C) They perform adequately in the industrial market and poorly in the retail market.
  (D) They are too busy with the industrial market to take on the retail selling job, at which they are in any case inadequate.
  (E) They perform adequately in both markets.

161. Which of the following is true of the company's present situation?

    I. Profits have been declining.
    II. Turnover has been declining.
    III. The number of customers has been declining.

  (A) I only
  (B) I and II only
  (C) I and III only
  (D) I and II and III
  (E) III only

162. What will the company be selling and to which outlets, regardless of the decision concerning entering the retail market?

     I. Floor polish to industrial and commercial outlets
     II. Floor polish to retail outlets
     III. Polymer resin to industrial users

(A) I only
(B) I and II only
(C) I and II and III
(D) I and III only
(E) None of the above are applicable

163. Why does the marketing manager favor the project?

     I. Because the company has experience with the product
     II. Because the project will double turnover
     III. Because the project will reduce risk
     IV. Because it will improve the company's cash flow

(A) I and II and III and IV
(B) I and II and III only
(C) II and III only
(D) I and III only
(E) II only

164. In which of the following ways does the company view the growth of the market for water based polish?

     I. It is necessary for the success of the project.
     II. It depends on both the quantity of new buildings and the proportions of new floor area on which plastic based flooring material is used.
     III. It is a contributory factor, but not of great importance.
     IV. It depends on the quantity of new buildings.

(A) I only
(B) I and II only
(C) II only
(D) II and III only
(E) I and IV only

165. Because more and more customers had been delegating their cleaning problems to contractors, the firm's 100 largest customers accounted for an increase of what percent of its turnover compared with its turnover a decade ago?

(A) 91%
(B) 82%
(C) 73%
(D) 9%
(E) 18%

IF YOU FINISH BEFORE THE TIME IS UP, GO OVER YOUR WORK FOR THIS SECTION ONLY. DO NOT TURN TO ANY OTHER SECTION OF THE TEST. WHEN THE TIME IS UP, GO ON TO THE NEXT SECTION.

SECTION 7: GRAMMAR AND USAGE

Time: 30 minutes

Directions: In each question, you will find a sentence with four words (or phrases) underlined. In some sentences one of the underlined words (or phrases) is incorrect in the light of the rules of standard written English for grammar, correct usage, and choice of words. No sentence has more than one error. You are to assume that the rest of the sentence (whatever is not underlined) is correct. If you find an error, choose the letter (A *or* B *or* C *or* D) of that underlined word (or phrase) which is incorrect. If you find no error, fill in answer space E.

166. When one leaves his car to be repaired, he assumes that the mechanic
             A   B   C

will repair the car good. No error.
             D   E

167. Bob could easily have gotten a higher score on his college entrance
                 A   B

test if he would have read more in his school career. No error.
           C   D   E

168. Any modern novelist would be thrilled to have his stories compared
      A   B   C

with Dickens. No error.
      D   E

169. When my Uncle Pancho's plane arrives at the airport in San Diego,
           A   B   C

I shall already have left San Diego for Mexico City. No error.
         D   E

170. Many people in the United States don't scarcely know about the
                       A   B

terrible hardships that the Vietnamese are experiencing in their
                          C

war - ravaged country. No error.
       D   E

171. Cesar Chavez, president of the United Farm Workers Union,
called for a Congressional investigation of certain California lettuce
     ‾‾‾‾‾
       A
growers whom, he said, were giving bribes to a rival union. No error.
        ‾‾‾‾‾   ‾‾‾‾‾‾‾‾‾‾‾   ‾‾‾‾‾‾‾‾‾‾ ‾‾‾‾‾‾‾‾
          B   C   D   E

172. The automobile industry is experimenting with a new type of a motor
                           ‾‾‾‾‾‾‾‾‾‾‾‾‾‾   ‾‾‾‾‾‾‾‾‾‾‾‾
                                 A   B
that will consume less gasoline and cause much less pollution. No
                    ‾‾‾‾   ‾‾‾‾‾   ‾‾
                      C   D
error.
‾‾‾‾‾
  E

173. The girl who won the beauty contest is nowhere near as beautiful
             ‾‾‾‾‾‾‾   ‾‾‾‾‾‾‾‾‾‾‾
                A   B
as my mother was when she was a bride. No error.
           ‾‾‾‾ ‾‾‾   ‾‾‾‾‾‾‾‾
             C   D   E

174. Sitting opposite my sister and me in the subway were them same
             ‾‾‾‾‾‾‾‾   ‾‾   ‾‾‾‾
                A   B   C
men who walked alongside us and tried to pinch us on Fifth Avenue.
               ‾‾‾‾‾‾‾‾‾
                   D
No error.
‾‾‾‾‾‾‾‾
   E

175. Even if Detroit could provide nonpolluting cars by the original dead-
     ‾‾‾‾‾‾‾   ‾‾‾‾‾‾‾‾‾‾‾
        A   B
line to meet prescribed Federal standards for clean air, the effect in
             ‾‾‾‾‾‾‾‾‾‾
                 C
big cities would be slight because only new cars would be properly
                                     ‾‾‾‾
                                       D
equipped. No error.
          ‾‾‾‾‾‾‾‾
             E

176. Of the two-cars that the Smiths have, the Plymouth is,
                                      ‾‾‾‾
                                        A
without any question, the cheapest to run. No error.
‾‾‾‾‾‾‾‾‾‾‾‾‾‾‾‾‾‾‾   ‾‾‾‾‾‾‾‾ ‾‾‾‾‾‾ ‾‾‾‾‾‾‾‾
        B   C   D   E

177. Since one of their members was a prisoner of war in Vietnam, the
     _____A
     family felt badly when they heard over the radio that the peace talks
     _____B_____C
     were to be discontinued. No error.
     _____D_____E

178. Man cannot live by bread alone, or can he live without bread.
     ____A_____B_____C_____D
     No error.
     ____E

179. Have you read in the *Columbia Spectator* that Jeff's leg was broken
     _____A_____B_____C
     while playing football? No error.
     _____D_____E

180. Having swam two-thirds of the distance across the English Channel,
     _____A_____B_____C
     Dixon could not give up now. No error.
     _____D_____E

181. George Foreman did like he said when he forecast that he would
     _____A_____B
     knock out Joe Frazier to win the world's heavyweight championship.
     ____C_____D
     No error.
     ____E

182. In the discussion, one speaker held that, since we live in a
     _____A
     money-oriented society, the average individual cares little about
     ____B_____C
     solving anyone's else problems. No error.
     _____D_____E

183. Due to the meat boycott, the butchers were doing about half of the
     ___A_____B_____C
     business that they were doing previous to the boycott. No error.
     _____D_____E

184. We requested the superintendent of the building to clean up the
$\overline{}$
A
storage room in the basement so that the children had enough space
$\overline{}$ $\overline{}$ $\overline{}$
B   C   D
for their bicycles. No error.
$\overline{}$
E

185. Lidocaine's usefulness as a local anesthetic was discovered by two
$\overline{}$ $\overline{}$
A   B
Swedish chemists who repeatedly tested the drug's effects on their
$\overline{}$ $\overline{}$
C   D
bodies. No error.
$\overline{}$
E

186. Namath played a real fine game in spite of the fact that the Jets
$\overline{}$ $\overline{}$
A   B
lost by a touchdown which the opposing team scored in the last
$\overline{}$ $\overline{}$
C   D
minute of play. No error.
$\overline{}$
E

187. You may not realize it but the weather in Barbados during Christmas
$\overline{}$ $\overline{}$ $\overline{}$
A   B   C
is like New York in June. No error.
$\overline{}$ $\overline{}$
D   E

188. Stores were jammed with last-minute Christmas shoppers, but the
$\overline{}$ $\overline{}$
A   B
festive spirit was slightly disrupted by homemade bombs that
$\overline{}$
C
exploded at two department stores. No error.
$\overline{}$ $\overline{}$
D   E

189. The teacher did not encourage the student any even though the boy
$\overline{}$
A
began to weep when he was told that his poor marks would
$\overline{}$ $\overline{}$
B   C
likely hold up his graduation. No error.
$\overline{}$ $\overline{}$
D   E

190. Nixon has stated that he has always had a great interest and ad-
$\overline{}$ $\overline{}$ $\overline{}$
A   B   C
miration for the work of the British economist Keynes. No error.
$\overline{}$ $\overline{}$
D   E

191. <u>According to</u> the most recent estimates, Greater Miami
         A

     <u>has more than</u> 450,000 <u>Spanish-speaking</u> residents, of <u>who</u>
         B   C   D

     about 400,000 are Cubans. <u>No error.</u>
                                 E

192. Sharon planned to pay <u>around</u> a hundred dollars <u>for</u> a new spring
                           A   B

     coat but when she saw a gorgeous coat <u>which sold</u> for two hun-
                                             C

     dred dollars, she decided <u>to buy</u> it. <u>No error.</u>
                              D   E

193. Had Lincoln <u>have been</u> alive during World War II, he
                   A

     <u>would have regarded</u> the racial <u>situation in</u> the armed
             B   C

     forces as a <u>throwback</u> to pre-Civil War days. <u>No error.</u>
                   D   E

194. Members of the staff <u>of the District Attorney</u> made more than
                                  A

     $100,000 from a <u>get-rich-quick</u> scheme in which investors <u>were bilked</u>
                       B   C

     of about $1-million. <u>No error.</u>
              D   E

195. The reason <u>that</u> Roberto Clemente, the great baseball star, was on
                A

     the plane that <u>crashed</u> was <u>because</u> he was <u>on his way</u> to help the
                   B   C   D

     victims of the earthquake. <u>No error.</u>
                            E

196. Although Hank was the captain of our high school track team, and

     <u>was hailed</u> as the fastest man on the team, I have <u>no doubt about</u>
         A   B

     <u>my being able</u> to run faster than <u>him</u> today. <u>No error.</u>
        C   D   E

197. <u>These kind</u> of people who have little education, who have no desire
        ^A

for cultural pursuits, and whose sole purpose <u>is acquiring</u> wealth,
                                    ^B

are not the <u>type</u> I wish <u>to associate with</u>. <u>No error</u>.
         ^C   ^D   ^E

198. <u>Whether</u> the sales campaign <u>succeeds</u> <u>will probably not be known</u> for
        ^A   ^B   ^C

at least a year, but it is clear now that the stakes <u>are</u> high. <u>No error</u>.
                                        ^D   ^E

199. Neither Sam Atkins <u>nor</u> Henry Miller, sales representatives for the
                   ^A

company, presented <u>their</u> summaries of sales <u>before</u> the deadline
                   ^B   ^C

<u>for doing so</u>. <u>No error</u>.
   ^D   ^E

200. A recent poll <u>has indicated</u> that Harold, who is a Senior at South
               ^A

Palmetto High School, is considered <u>brighter</u> than <u>any student</u> in the
                              ^B   ^C

<u>senior class</u> at that school. <u>No error</u>.
    ^D   ^E

201. The question <u>arises</u> <u>as to who</u> <u>should go out</u> this morning in this
              ^A   ^B   ^C

below-zero weather to clean the snow from the garage entrance, you

or <u>me</u>. <u>No error</u>.
   ^D   ^E

202. Since I <u>loved</u> her very much when she was alive, I prize my
           ^A

<u>mother's-in-law</u> picture and I <u>wouldn't</u> sell it for <u>all the money</u> in
        ^B   ^C   ^D

the world. <u>No error</u>.
         ^E

203. <u>Had I have been</u> in my <u>brother's</u> position, I•would have <u>hung up</u>
       ^A   ^B   ^C

the phone <u>in the middle</u> of the conversation. <u>No error</u>.
         ^D   ^E

204. Lie detectors measure physiological changes in respiration, perspira-
     ——   ———————   —————————————
      A   B   C
tion, blood pressure, and muscular grip. No error.
      ——————————   ————————
           D   E

205. The company is planning a series of lectures for their executives
                                 ——————   ————
                                   A   B
so that they may be aware of how to deal with racial problems that
——————
  C
may occur from time to time. No error.
        —————————————————— ————————
               D   E

IF YOU FINISH BEFORE THE TIME IS UP, GO OVER YOUR WORK FOR
THIS SECTION ONLY. DO NOT TURN TO ANY OTHER SECTION OF THE
TEST. WHEN THE TIME IS UP, GO ON TO THE NEXT SECTION.

SECTION 8: ERROR RECOGNITION

Time: 30 minutes

Directions: Among the sentences in this group are some which cannot be accepted in formal, written English for one or another of the following reasons:

Poor Diction: The use of a word which is improper either because its meaning does not fit the sentence or because it is not acceptable in formal writing.

Examples

The audience was strongly *effected* by the senator's speech.

The dean made an *illusion* to the Boer War in his talk.

Verbosity: Repetitious elements adding nothing to the meaning of the sentence and not justified by any need for special emphasis.

Examples

At that time there was *then* no right of petition.

In the last decade television production has advanced *forward* with great strides.

Faulty Grammar: Word forms and expressions which do not conform to the grammatical and structural usages required by formal written English (errors in case, number, parallelism, and the like).

Examples

Everyone in the delegation had *their* reasons for opposing the measure.

The commission decided to reimburse the property owners, to readjust the rates, and that they would extend the services in the near future.

No sentence has more than one kind of error. Some sentences have no errors. Read each sentence carefully; then on your answer sheet blacken the box under:

D If the sentence contains an error in diction;
V If the sentence is verbose;
G If the sentence contains faulty grammar;
O If the sentence contains none of these errors.

206. In a violent outburst, the superpatriot angrily tore up the peace placard which was being carried by one of the demonstrators.

207. He was sheathing with anger when he read the newspaper article about his dealing with gangsters.

208. The men were tired, and they had worked hard, and the day was hot.

209. A series of debates between major candidates were scheduled for the Labor Day weekend.

210. The editorial extolled the weaknesses of the Mayor's slum-rebuilding program.

211. After being wheeled into the infirmary, the nurse at the desk asked me several questions.

212. Che Guevara was a guerrilla leader who recruited Bolivians into a rebel army to battle against the authorities.

213. When the little girl saw the face in her bedroom window, she screamed piercingly.

214. The American people, dismayed by the sudden proof that something had gone wrong with their economic system, that it lacked stability and was subject to crises of unpredictable magnitude.

215. An old miser who picked up yellow pieces of gold had something of the simple ardor of a child who picks out yellow flowers.

216. The millennium will have arrived when parents give appropriate responsibilities to we teenagers.

217. The customers demanded that the crooked merchants be persecuted to the fullest extent of the law.

218. Unless there can be some assurance of increased pay, factory morale, all ready low, will collapse completely.

219. Entering our bedroom shortly after midnight, a terrific explosion was heard by my wife and me.

220. Mynette, who was born in France, is now a neutralized citizen of the United States.

> No sentence has more than one kind of error. Some senten-
> ces have no errors. Read each sentence carefully; then on
> your answer sheet blacken the box under:
>
> **D** If the sentence contains an error in diction;
> **V** If the sentence is verbose;
> **G** If the sentence contains faulty grammar;
> **O** If the sentence contains none of these errors.

221. Morphine and other narcotic drugs are valuable medically; if misused, however, it can cause irreparable damage.

222. In Latin America, the new governments fell under the control of wealthy and aristocratic landowners, almost invariably of European blood.

223. On any given weekend – especially holiday weekends – the number of highway deaths is predictable.

224. The Congressman made an angry, impassive attack on the proposed tax increase.

225. We did the job as good as we could; however, it did not turn out to be satisfactory.

226. Nuclear scientists should be particularly skilled in investigative research.

227. If I would have had more time, I would have written a much more interesting and a far more thorough report.

228. A UN investigation has revealed that prisoners of war were coerced by force to enter the narrow caves where they were compelled to live like animals.

229. Though Seaver pitched real well, the Reds scored four runs in the ninth inning as a result of two Met errors.

230. The landlord effected a change in personnel by first dismissing his superintendent and then replacing two porters who were screwy.

231. Each of the hotel's 500 rooms were equipped with high quality air-conditioning and color television.

232. At the end of the performance, the audience applauded vigorously with enthusiasm.

233. The professor was not only an accomplished violinist but also an excellent portrait artist, having studied it in his spare time.

234. By 1763, when the French and Indian War ended, the American colonies had grown to be a strong and thriving part of the British Empire.

No sentence has more than one kind of error. Some sentences have no errors. Read each sentence carefully; then on your answer sheet blacken the box under:

D If the sentence contains an error in diction;
V If the sentence is verbose;
G If the sentence contains faulty grammar;
O If the sentence contains none of these errors.

235. Hitler, though allowing his subleaders to be identified with certain political organizations, appeared to endorse all.

236. At the Christmas party, the boss was so vociferous and noisy that we decided to leave before the food was served.

237. More leisure, as well as an abundance of goods, are attainable through automation.

238. His arithmetic is poor largely because he is weak in fractions and decimations.

239. Because Henry IV acted to depose the Pope, Gregory, in turn, excommunicated Henry and cut him off from communion with the church.

240. It is therefore possible to question the wisdom of applying civil disobedience in respect to a particular act or law; it is possible to advise delay and caution.

IF YOU FINISH BEFORE THE TIME IS UP, GO OVER YOUR WORK FOR THIS SECTION ONLY. DO NOT TURN TO ANY OTHER SECTION OF THE TEST. WHEN THE TIME IS UP, THE TEST IS OVER

NOW THAT YOU HAVE COMPLETED PRACTICE TEST 4

1. Turn to the Answer Key on pages 303-304. Do not consider Sections 7 and 8.

2. Count your **correct answers.**

3. Count your **incorrect answers.**

4. Deduct ¼ of the number of incorrect answers from the number of correct answers to get a **"raw score"** of _____.

5. Your **"scaled score"** for this test, according to the Raw Score/Scaled Score Table on page 88, is _____.

ANSWER KEY FOR PRACTICE TEST 4

Section 1: Reading Recall

1. E	7. D	13. E	19. E	25. D
2. E	8. A	14. C	20. A	26. D
3. B	9. D	15. B	21. B	27. C
4. A	10. A	16. C	22. A	28. C
5. D	11. C	17. B	23. E	29. C
6. C	12. A	18. C	24. C	30. C

Section 2: Math Ability

After each answer, there is a hyphenated number (or numbers) in parentheses. This hyphenated number is keyed to Math Refresher (beginning on page 411). The number *before* the hyphen indicates the Math area of the problem:

$$1 = \text{ARITHMETIC}$$
$$2 = \text{ALGEBRA}$$
$$3 = \text{PLANE GEOMETRY}$$
$$5 = \text{GRAPHS AND CHARTS}$$

The number *after* the hyphen gives you the section (within the Math area) that explains the rule or principle involved in solving the problem.

31. D (1-24, 1-25)	41. C (1-25)	51. C (5-5)
32. E (2-22)	42. E (1-20)	52. E (2-30)
33. B (1-25)	43. A (1-28)	53. A (2-34)
34. B (1-21)	44. E (3-6)	54. B (5-3, 1-25)
35. A (1-24, 2-22)	45. B (2-26)	55. C (5-3, 2-26)
36. B (2-22, 2-12)	46. E (2-31)	56. E (5-3, 1-25)
37. A (2-11)	47. A (2-28)	57. A (5-3, 1-25)
38. E (1-20)	48. B (1-24)	58. C (3-6, 1-17)
39. C (1-25)	49. A (5-5, 2-26)	59. D (1-25)
40. D (3-1, 3-4)	50. A (5-5, 1-22)	60. B (2-26, 2-25)

Section 3: Business Judgment

61. D	66. A	71. A	76. C	81. D
62. C	67. B	72. E	77. C	82. D
63. A	68. C	73. E	78. C	83. C
64. D	69. A	74. A	79. E	84. E
65. C	70. E	75. E	80. D	85. D

ANSWER KEY FOR PRACTICAL TEST 4 (continued)

Section 4: Data Sufficiency

86. D	92. A	98. E	104. E	110. E
87. A	93. E	99. C	105. D	111. D
88. E	94. E	100. E	106. E	112. C
89. C	95. C	101. C	107. B	113. E
90. B	96. C	102. D	108. C	114. E
91. E	97. B	103. C	109. C	115. E

Section 5: Verbal Ability

116. E	121. A	126. B	131. A	136. B
117. B	122. E	127. B	132. B	137. C
118. B	123. E	128. E	133. D	138. E
119. A	124. A	129. C	134. A	139. B
120. D	125. D	130. C	135. E	140. A

Section 6: Business Judgment

141. A	146. C	151. B	156. B	161. C
142. E	147. A	152. C	157. B	162. D
143. E	148. D	153. B	158. E	163. B
144. D	149. C	154. A	159. D	164. D
145. A	150. A	155. D	160. D	165. E

Section 7: Grammar and Usage

166. D	174. C	182. D	190. C	198. E
167. C	175. E	183. A	191. D	199. B
168. D	176. C	184. D	192. A	200. C
169. E	177. B	185. E	193. A	201. D
170. A	178. C	186. A	194. E	202. B
171. B	179. D	187. D	195. C	203. A
172. B	180. A	188. E	196. D	204. E
173. B	181. A	189. A	197. A	205. B

Section 8: Error Recognition

206. V	213. V	220. D	227. G	234. O
207. D	214. G	221. G	228. V	235. O
208. G	215. O	222. O	229. G	236. V
209. G	216. G	223. O	230. D	237. G
210. D	217. D	224. D	231. G	238. D
211. G	218. D	225. G	232. V	239. V
212. O	219. G	226. V	233. G	240. O

EXPLANATORY ANSWERS FOR PRACTICE TEST 4

Sections 1A and 1B: Reading Recall

1. **(E)** See paragraph 2: "Thus in ancient Egypt ... first-known large scaled bureaucracy in history."

2. **(E)** See paragraph 2: "It has already been mentioned that sheer size encourages the development of bureaucracies..." The smallest group is thus likely to be bureaucratized."

3. **(B)** See paragraph 1: "... a money economy permits the payment ..."

4. **(A)** See paragraph 3: "Arbitrary actions ..."

5. **(D)** See paragraph 4: "The expansion of business firms ..."

6. **(C)** See paragraph 4: "These giant corporations, in turn, compel workers ..."

7. **(D)** See paragraph 2: "More important than size as such, however, is the emergence of special administrative problems."

8. **(A)** See paragraph 3: "... Jefferson, favored a weak central government."

9. **(D)** See paragraph 4: "... removal of most employees from activities directly governed by the profit principle make it increasingly necessary to introduce bureaucratic methods of administration for the sake of efficiency."

10. **(A)** See paragraph 1: "One of the historical conditions that favors the development of bureaucracy is a money economy."

11. **(C)** The second paragraph, discussing the Hollister-Palmer thesis, states: "...labor shortages ... enable many of the poor to land jobs ..."

12. **(A)** The third paragraph discusses the Poor Price Index, which puts a greater emphasis upon commodities, such as rent and food, for which the poor pay a greater percentage of their money.

13. **(E)** A debtor would gain because he must pay a fixed sum of money. The money he pays to the creditor during an inflationary period is worth less in purchasing power as compared to the money he borrowed.

14. **(C)** An increase in federal spending is one of the major causes of inflation according to the Keynesian philosophy.

15. **(B)** A decrease in the number of families below the poverty line would indicate that some of the poor are gaining money. Hollister and Palmer contend that inflation may aid the poor.

16. **(C)** See paragraph 2: "As for the non-working poor ... welfare benefits have generally risen faster than prices."

17. **(B)** See paragraph 3: "Between 1965 and·1967 ... the poor price index ... rose 5.1% compared with a 5.8% increase in the CPI."

18. **(C)** See paragraph 1: "The burden of inflation, President Nixon has often said, falls heavily upon the poor ..."

19. **(E)** I and III are the themes of the article. Although a trade-off is assumed to be inevitable, the poor, it is claimed, fare better in employment terms with inflation than with price stability. For II, see paragraph 2, which talks about the "non-working poor" and the "program to aid families with dependent children."

20. **(A)** See paragraph 4: "Walter Heller, former chairman of the President's Council of Economic Advisers ..."

21. **(B)** See paragraph 2: "Most social scientists ... have assumed that the min-

imum economic needs of the aged should be lower than those of the younger family."

22. **(A)** See paragraph 5: "(The data) disclose sharp income inequalities within every age group..."

23. **(E)** For I, see paragraph 6: "Those sixty-five and over are expected to increase 572 per cent." For III, see paragraph 4: "For the growing working-class family, limited in income by the very nature of the breadwinner's occupation..."

24. **(C)** See paragraph 2: The sentence after the "functional ethos" sentence refers to "these values."

25. **(D)** See paragraph 6: "With the more rapid expansion of these two low-income groups, the young and the old..."

26. **(D)** For I, see paragraph 5: "A spending unit's income tenth position *within his*

age category varies much less, if at all, and is determined primarily by his occupation." For III, see paragraph 4: "For the growing working-class family, limited in income by the very nature of the breadwinner's occupation..."

27. **(C)** See paragraph 3: "Despite his seniority, the older worker is likely to be downgraded to a lower-paying job..."

28. **(C)** See paragraph 4: "The early and lower income period of a person's working life, during which he acquires his basic vocational skills..."

29. **(C)** See paragraph 5: "...the higher-income tenths have a much greater representation of spending headed by persons aged thirty-five to fifty-five than do the lower income tenths."

30. **(C)** See paragraph 5: "A spending unit's income tenth position is... determined primarily by his occupation."

EXPLANATORY ANSWERS FOR PRACTICE TEST 4 (continued)

Section 2: Math Ability

31. **(D)** If \$200 is the list price, then the first net price is $200 - .10(200) = 180$. The final net price is

$$180 - .02 (180) = \$176.40.$$

32. **(E)** Let $x =$ no. of 5¢ stamps
    $y =$ no. of 2¢ stamps

Thus,

$$5x + 2y = 100$$
$$5x = 100 - 2y$$
$$x = \frac{100 - 2y}{5}$$

Since x must be a whole number, the numerator of the fraction must be divisible by 5 and this is only possible when y is a multiple of 5. The greatest value of x occurs when y is the least multiple of 5.

Hence,

$$y = 5 \text{ and } x = \frac{100 - 2\ (5)}{5} = \frac{90}{5} = 18.$$

33. **(B)** Let $x =$ no. of lbs. before cooking; then,

$$x - .30x = 12.6$$

Multiply by 10, giving

$$10x - 3x = 126$$
$$7x = 126$$
$$x = 18$$

34. **(B)** Out of every 100 Freshmen, 65 are studying French and 55 are studying Spanish. Let x be the number of Freshmen studying both subjects in a group of 100. Then $(65 - x)$ study French only and $(55 - x)$ study Spanish only; so that

$$(65 - x) + (55 - x) + x = 100$$
$$120 - x = 100$$
$$x = 20$$

35. **(A)** Let $x =$ the original cost
    $.30x =$ the amount of discount

Then

$$x - .30x = \$58.80$$
$$.70x = \$58.80$$
$$x = \$84.00$$

36. **(B)** $5y = 2y - 6$
    $$3y = -6$$
    $$y = -2$$
    $$y + 5 = -2 + 5 = 3$$

37. **(A)** The cost for the first 5 days is p cents. This leaves $(n - 5)$ days at q cents per day.

Hence, total cost $= p + q(n - 5)$

38. **(E)** If he uses 15 miles per gallon, he will use $\frac{540}{15} = 36$ gallons. If he uses 18 miles per gallon, he will use $\frac{540}{18} = 30$ gallons. The most he could spend would be

$$36 \times .40 = \$14.40$$

The least he could spend would be

$$30 \times .32 = \$9.60$$

The difference is

$$\$14.40 - \$9.60 = \$4.80.$$

39. **(C)** Let x = the cost

    $.4x$ = the profit

    $x + .4x = 3.50$; multiply by 10

    $10x + 4x = 35$

    $14x = 35$

    $x = \$2.50$

    profit = $\$3.50 - \$2.50$

    $= \$1.00$

40. **(D)** Let m Angle $QPR = x°$

    Then m Angle $PQR = x°$ (base Angles of isosceles $\triangle$)

    Angle $QRS = 2x$ (exterior Angle of $\triangle PQR$)

    Angle $RQS = 2x$ (base Angles of isosceles $\triangle$)

    Then, in $\triangle QRS$

    $2x + 2x + 120 = 180°$

    $4x = 60$

    $x = 15°$

41. **(C)** Two gallons of the mixture contains $.60 \times 2 = 1.2$ gallons of liquid A and

    $.40 \times 2 = .8$ gallon of liquid B

    Liquid A weighs $1.2 \times 4 = 4.8$ lb.

    Liquid B weighs $.8 \times 6.5 = 5.2$ lb.

    Total weight $= 4.8 + 5.2 = 10.0$ lb.

42. **(E)** For a fraction to have a value more than $\frac{1}{2}$, its numerator must be more than half its denominator. This is only true for

    $$\frac{101}{201}$$

43. **(A)** Let x = *no.* of men teachers

    then $4x$ = *no.* of women teachers

    $5x$ = total *no.* of teachers

    Since x is an integer, $5x$ must be divisible by 5. Hence, 42 *cannot* be the number of teachers. All other choices are multiples of 5.

44. **(E)** If the rectangle is 20 inches long, we can place $20 \div \frac{1}{2} = 40$ tiles along the length.

    If it is 10 inches wide, we can place $10 \div \frac{1}{2} = 20$ tiles along the width.

    Hence, $40 \times 20 = 800$ tiles are needed.

45. **(B)** Bill's rate $= \dfrac{200}{12}$ *sq.ft./*min.

    Fred's rate $= \dfrac{300}{15} = 20$ *sq.ft./*min.

    Ratio $= \dfrac{\frac{200}{12}}{20} = \dfrac{10}{12} = \dfrac{5}{6}$

46. **(E)** Let x = no. of minutes to go down the hill. Then $5x$ = no. of minutes to go up the hill.

    $5x + x = 9$

    $6x = 9$

    $x = 1\frac{1}{2}$

    $5x = 5 \times 1\frac{1}{2} = 7\frac{1}{2}$ minutes

47. **(A)** 45 minutes $= \dfrac{45}{60} = \dfrac{3}{4}$

    Let x = no. of pages in 2 hours

    then $\dfrac{k}{\frac{3}{4}} = \dfrac{x}{2}$

    $x = \dfrac{8k}{3}$

48. **(B)** Let x = list price.

    Then $x - .3x = 29.75$

    Now multiply both sides by 10.

    $10x - 3x = 297.5$

    $7x = 297.5$

    $x = \$42.50$

49. **(A)** Male 4 yr. college graduates earned about $7200.

   Male 4 yr. high school graduates earned about $4900.

   $$\text{Ratio} = \frac{7000}{5000} \approx 7 : 5$$

50. **(A)** Females earned about $1700
   Males earned about $4900

   $$\frac{1700}{4900} \approx \frac{2}{5} = 40\%$$

51. **(C)** Men with 4 years of college earned about $7200.

   Men with 8 years of elementary education earned $3500.

   Difference is about $4200.

52. **(E)** Let x no. of bolts in 6 minutes.

   Then, $$\frac{15}{12} = \frac{x}{60 \times 6}$$

   $$12x = 15 \times 360$$

   $$x = 450$$

53. **(A)** Let $m =$ his mark on the 4th test.

   Then, $$\frac{75 + 82 + 86 + m}{4} = 85$$

   $$243 + m = 340$$

   $$m = 97$$

54. **(B)** 59% of 360 = .59 (360)

   $$= 213° \text{ approx.}$$

55. **(C)** $$\frac{\text{Military}}{\text{Veterans}} = \frac{59}{6} = 10 : 1 \text{ approx.}$$

56. **(E)** Interest on debt = 9% of 120

   $$= .09 \ (120)$$

   $$= 10.8$$

57. **(A)** Let $y =$ total expenditures.

   Then $.06y = 9$

   $$6y = 900$$

   $$y = 150$$

58. **(C)** Area $$= \frac{60}{3} \times 2$$

   $$= 20 \times 2 = 40 \text{ sq. yd.}$$

   $40 \times 8.25 = \$330$

59. **(D)** A $1 discount on a $10 pair of shoes is the same as $\frac{1}{10} = 10\%$ discount. A $1 discount on a $20 pair of shoes is the same as $\frac{1}{20} = 5\%$ discount. Hence, the discount rate is higher for the cheaper shoes (D).

60. **(B)** Let $x =$ cost of apple
   $y =$ cost of orange

   $$5x + 6y = 98$$

   $$12x + 12y = 216$$

   Now, multiply first equation by (−2) to get

   $$-10x - 12y = -196$$

   Now, add the above to the second equation:

   $$\begin{array}{r} 12x + 12y = 216 \\ -10x - 12y = -196 \\ \hline 2x = 20 \end{array}$$

   $$x = 10$$

   Substitute $x = 10$ in first equation

   $$50 + 6y = 98$$

   $$6y = 48$$

   $$y = 8$$

   $$\frac{x}{y} = \frac{10}{8} = \frac{5}{4}$$

EXPLANATORY ANSWERS FOR PRACTICE TEST 4 (continued)

Section 3: Business Judgment

61. **(D)** The growth of demand for luxury goods is a projection of trends and therefore an assumption.

62. **(C)** The saving due to the elimination of damage is a plus but is not basic to the decision.

63. **(A)** The avoidance of the tariff is one of the keys to location in San Martino. It is, therefore, a major objective.

64. **(D)** Again, this is an assumption resting on the continuation of present trends.

65. **(C)** The growth of U.S. demand contributes to the initial shortage of factory space but does not play a major part in the final decision.

66. **(A)** The dramatic reduction in transportation is a major source of saving and the final decision revolves about this major objective.

67. **(B)** The instability of the cruzeiro could lead to a devaluation which would wreck the sales effort if based on importing the goods. If is, therefore, a major factor.

68. **(C)** Initially, cheap labor looks important but the total cost proves, in the end, to have only a minor impact.

69. **(A)** This is a major short-term goal.

70. **(E)** The length of time that Supercool has been in Chicago is irrelevant to the present decision.

71. **(A)** As stated by the President, this is a major objective.

97. **(E)** Total costs are roughly the same in each location. This issue is not important.

73. **(E)** Raw materials cost the same in each place — not important at all.

74. **(A)** This is a major long-term company goal.

75. **(E)** Capital is freely available for the project in either location — an unimportant issue.

76. **(C)** The use of close supervision can offset the low skill level of local of local workers — a minor factor.

77. **(C)** The limited size of the Chicago plant is a contributory factor to the required expansion, but is not an important part of the final decision.

78. **(C)** The dealer markup is a constant 10% for goods produced in the U.S. or San Martino, but the higher basic cost of goods delivered in San Martino from abroad and the effect of the tariff lead to a higher wholesale cost and dollar value of the dealer markup.

79. **(E)** The productivity of U.S. workers must be higher than that of San Martino workers since it offsets much lower wage rates. Nothing is actually stated about the rates at which productivity is increasing.

80. **(D)** The wage rates are stated to be over 50% lower than in the U.S.

81. **(D)** The sales force advised that the most effective way of restricting the entry of competition would be by pricing the product as low as possible.

82. **(D)** The effect of a devaluation of the cruzeiro would be to increase the prices of all goods brought into San Martino — in this case, refrigerators made in the U.S.

83. **(C)** The availability of capital to start the project is contingent only on the company's present solvency.

84. **(E)** Space is said to be short because of "the growth of export markets taken with the steady increase of home demand."

85. **(D)** It can be seen from the table that Labor costs in Chicago are $120 whereas Labor costs in San Martino are $134. It can also be seen that Labor costs are the only type of costs which are greater in San Martino than in Chicago.

EXPLANATORY ANSWERS FOR PRACTICE TEST 4 (continued)

Section 4: Data Sufficiency

86. **(D)** According to statement (1)

$$(s + 3) + (2s) + (3s - 3) = 18$$

From this equation we can find the value of s and, thus, the lengths of the three sides.
According to statement (2),

$$s + 3 = 3s - 3$$

Again, we can solve this equation for s and obtain the lengths of the sides.

87. **(A)** To find the present price of butter, use the data provided in statement (1). The present price equals 80¢ + 5% of 80¢.
The second statement does not help solve the problem.

88. **(E)** Both statements together do not provide enough information to determine the measure of Angle A.

89. **(C)** By using the information from both statements we can deduce that 28 pounds is 10% of Harold's present weight. Thus, since 10% equals 1/10,

$$\frac{1}{10} x = 28 \text{ pounds}$$
$$x = 280 \text{ pounds}$$

90. **(B)** An exterior angle of a triangle is equal to the sum of the two remote interior angles.
Statement (2) provides us with the value of y so we can find the value of x:
$$x° = 100° + y° =$$
$$100° + 20° = 120°$$

91. **(E)** Both statements are true for both positive and negative numbers so they do not help us determine what k is.

92. **(A)** Statement (1) tells us that there are 3 red marbles in the box. If squaring a number has the same effect as tripling it, then that number must be 3.
Statement (2) adds no useful information.

93. **(E)** The area of a circle of radius r is πr^2. Statement (1) tells us that the large circle is of radius 5 and statement (2) tells us that the small circle is of radius 1. This information, however, is insufficient to solve the problem.

94. **(E)** From the given information we can conclude that p belongs to the set $\{3, 4, 5, 6\}$.
Statement (1) tells us that q belongs to the set $\{2, 3, 4\}$.
Statement (2), therefore, asserts that p is either 3 or 4, but we still do not know exactly which one.

95. **(C)** If we use both statements (1) and (2), we have the lengths of segments LK, HK, and HM. By using the Pythagorean Theorem in triangle HLK, we can calculate the length of segment HL. By using the Pythagorean Theorem in triangle MHL, we can find the length of ML, since we know the lengths of HL and HM.

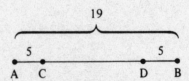

96. **(C)** From the given information we can see that
AC + CD + DB = 19 inches
and
AC = DB = 5 inches
See the diagram above. It is evident that we can now find the length of CD.

97. **(B)** Let C be the number of cows. Then $18 - C$ is the number of chickens. Each cow has four legs and each chicken has two legs. According to statement (2), we can write this equation:

$$4C + 2(18 - C) = 44$$

This can be solved for C.

98. **(E)** The information contained in both statements is not enough to answer the question. The quadrilateral could still be a parallelogram or not. See diagram.

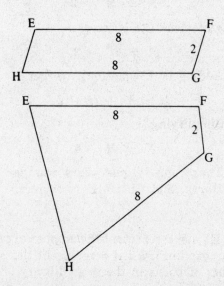

99. **(C)** Both pieces of data are needed to see that x is the smallest. We know that $z = 62°$. Both x and y cannot be greater than 62° since this would mean that the sum of the angles of the triangle was more than 180°. x must be less than z as well as being less than y.

100. **(E)** From the information given in the two statements it is not possible to find out the volume of the water in the tank. We cannot find out the depth unless we know the area of the bottom of the tank.

101. **(C)** From statement (1) we can conclude that there are 2070 people in the school. From the second statement we see that there are 25×32 or 800 seats in the auditorium. From these two facts we can calculate the percent of the school's population which will fit into the auditorium.

102. **(D)** Using statement (1) we can find the amount of meal consumed each day by setting up the following proportion:

$$\frac{8}{32} = \frac{x}{109}$$

This can be solved for x.
Using statement (2) we can solve the problem by dividing $190\frac{3}{4}$ pounds by 7, the number of days in a week.

103. **(C)** By using both statements (1) and (2) we can calculate George's earnings for the week. He worked for 35 hours at $3.00 per hour and for 7 overtime hours at $4.00 per hour. His earnings were $35 \times \$3 + 7 \times \$4$.

104. **(E)** Both statements together do not provide enough information to answer the question. For instance, suppose, consistent with the two statements, that the numbers were: 20 "zeros," 10 "tens," and 30 "ones." The average of these is less than 20.

On the other hand, suppose that the numbers were 10 "tens" and 50 "twenty-nines." This average is more than 20.

105. **(D)** From the first statement we can conclude that the length of each side is 2. The volume can be found by cubing 2.

From the second statement we can also find that the length of each side is 2 by using the Pythagorean Theorem. Thus, we can solve the problem by using the second statement alone also.

106. **(E)** Using the data given in both statements, we still cannot be sure whether or not the triangle is a right one. The angles could be 70°, 20°, 90° or they could also be something like 70°, 21°, 89°.

107. **(B)** According to statement (2), for every one glass of lemonade Alice sells at 10¢, she could sell three glasses at 5¢. Thus, she would make 15¢ for every 10¢ of business at the higher price. We can see it would be better to sell at the lower price.

The first statement provides no useful information.

108. **(C)** The first statement provides us with the length of AF and the second statement provides us with the length of AB. By applying the Pythagorean Theorem to triangle ABF, we can find the length of BF. The length of AC, provided in statement (2), minus the length of AF gives us the length of FC. By applying the Pythagorean Theorem to triangle BFC, knowing the lengths of FC and BF, we can find the length of BC.

109. **(C)** We can find the average weight by dividing 5 into the total weight, 600 pounds, which is provided by statement (2). The weight of the third girl can be found by taking 75% of this average, as indicated by statement (1).

110. **(E)** The two inequalities given by the two statements do not provide enough information to answer the question.

111. **(D)** Statement (1) enables us to solve for y exactly. Thus from Statement (1) we can determine whether y is less than $\frac{15}{16}$. Statement (2) tells us that y is less than $\frac{11}{16}$. Thus y must certainly be less than $\frac{15}{16}$. Thus Choice D is correct.

112. **(C)** Here we should substitute algebraic variables for Harry's age, John's age, and Jim's age. Let H represent Harry's age, N represent John's age, and M represent Jim's age. In algebraic notation, Statement (1) becomes

$$N = M - 2$$

Statement (2) becomes

$$M = H - 2$$

Adding both equations, we get

$$N + M = M + H - 2 - 2$$

Simplifying,

$$N = H - 4$$

Thus John is *four* years younger than Harry, and Choice C is correct.

113. **(E)** Let x represent the number of books in one library. Let y represent the number of books in the other library.

Statement (1) can be interpreted as

$$x = 2y \ or \ y = 2x$$

Statement (2) can be interpreted as

$$x = 9000 \ or \ y = 9000$$

If $x = 2y$ and $x = 9000$, then $y = 4500$ and so, $x + y = 13,500$. However, if $y = 2x$ and $x = 9000$, then $y = 18,000$ and $x + y = 27,000$. So we see that in one case we have the total number of books less than 18,000 (that is, 13,500) and in the other case we have that the total number of books is greater than 18,000 (that is, 27,000). Therefore we need additional data to solve the problem.

114. **(E)** Note that if $x = \dfrac{3}{5}$ and $y = \dfrac{2}{5}$,

Statement (1) *and* Statement (2) are satisfied. With these values for x and y,

$$\dfrac{2}{5}x = \dfrac{2}{5} \times \dfrac{3}{5} = \dfrac{6}{25} \text{ and } \dfrac{3}{5}y =$$

$$\dfrac{3}{5} \times \dfrac{2}{5} = \dfrac{6}{25} \text{ so } \dfrac{2}{5}x = \dfrac{3}{5}y. \text{ How-}$$

ever, if $x = \dfrac{3}{4}$ and $y = \dfrac{1}{4}$, Statements

(1) and (2) are also both satisfied. With these new values for x and y,

$$\dfrac{2}{5}x = \dfrac{2}{5} \times \dfrac{3}{4} = \dfrac{6}{20} \text{ and } \dfrac{3}{5}y =$$

$$\dfrac{3}{5} \times \dfrac{1}{4} = \dfrac{3}{20} \text{ so, } \dfrac{2}{5}x > \dfrac{3}{5}y$$

Therefore, we need more information to determine exactly the answer to our question.

115. **(E)**

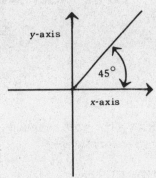

All points on the line which is 45° above the X-axis (see figure above) lie in the first quadrant and also have the x-coordinate equal to the y-coordinate. But the values of x and y (even though they may be equal) may be between 0 and infinity. Thus, additional information is needed to determine their exact values.

EXPLANATORY ANSWERS FOR PRACTICE TEST 4 (continued)

Section 5: Verbal Ability

PART A — ANTONYMS

116. **(E)** TRAVAIL: toil; anguish.
Antonym: *relaxation.*

117. **(B)** CUDGEL: beat.
Antonym: *caress.*

118. **(B)** FACTITIOUS: artificial; affected; not spontaneous.
Antonym: *spontaneous.*

119. **(A)** INVETERATE: habitual; confirmed; deep-rooted.
Antonym: *beginning.*

120. **(D)** PRODIGAL: lavish; extravagant; wasteful.
Antonym: *provident.*

121. **(A)** ESCHEW: shun; avoid.
Antonym: *welcome.*

122. **(E)** ERUDITE: learned; scholarly.
Antonym: *ignorant.*

123. **(E)** DIVISIVE: causing division; creating dissension.
Antonym: *unifying.*

PART B — ANALOGIES

124. **(A)** Just as a label is created by man for the purpose of classification, a joke is created by man for the purpose of amusement. Choice C suggests that the purpose of a river is to swim, but one must remember that a river serves many other purposes and was not created by man.

125. **(D)** A person who is shackled or confined and not free to move, will find relief and freedom when he is unfettered. Similarly, a person who is hurt will find relief when he is comforted in some way.

126. **(B)** A chair and a bench are both used for the purpose of sitting; their difference lies in the greater size of the bench. Similarly, a ruler and yardstick are both used for the purpose of measuring, though the yardstick is larger than the ruler. In Choice D, certainly an elephant is larger than a pig, though the relationship of purpose does not function here.

127. **(B)** Just as smoke is a major cause of pollution, war is a major cause of death. Both express, however, great harm caused by man. In Choice C, a vaccination causes immunity, but this is beneficial and so does not apply to this analogy.

128. **(E)** A hypothesis, or educated guess, is quite necessary before carrying out experimentation so that one may know exactly what he is to look for. In the same way, an opinion is needed to debate so that one may know what he is to argue for and against. Indeed, film is needed for a camera to function (B), but film is not created in the mind as are both hypotheses and opinions.

129. **(C)** Just as respiration in animals depends upon oxygen from the atmosphere, to provide the organism with energy, plants depend upon sunlight to carry out photosynthesis which provides them with energy. In Choice B, a camera is needed for photography, but the relationship is not a biological one as are the other two.

130. **(C)** When one requests, he expects an acceptance — to get a refusal to the request is completely negative. Simimilarly, when one tries, he expects success — if the result is failure, then this too is negative. The relationship expresses a negative response to an action.

131. **(A)** Just one person's deception reduces confidence in another person, so kindliness reduces hostility.

PART C — SENTENCE COMPLETIONS

132. **(B)** Discrimination is the *ability* to *distinguish* between good, bad, and indifferent.

133. **(D)** Parables are *stories* or *fables* that illustrate a moral or ethical point while relating a simple incident.

134. **(A)** Choices B and C would fit the first blank but neither would make sense in the second blank.

135. **(E)** The orchestra was *enlarged*, or *increased*, by the extra instruments.

136. **(B)** Acoustics refers to the *sound-carrying capacities* of a hall or room.

137. **(C)** Choices B, D, and E might be used in the first blank, but none of them would suit the second blank.

138. **(E)** Although every other choice here might fit the first blank, no combination except Choice E makes sense in both blanks.

139. **(B)** The point is that the *idea* of devising a perpetual motion machine was abandoned and *brought to life* again many times, before being finally dismissed as impossible.

140. **(A)** There was danger of another *battle* or *fight* during the *extremely crowded* downtown noon hour.

EXPLANATORY ANSWER FOR PRACTICE TEST 4 (continued)

Section 6: Business Judgment

141. **(A)** This is a major objective in the decision process, since the management of the company must expect their prestige and remuneration to be at least in part a function of company size.

142. **(E)** It is stated that consumers showed virtually no response to price reductions. Price consequently does not enter the decision process at all, on the information provided.

143. **(E)** Even for the test market, a task force had to be brought in. The industrial sales force is fully occupied. The company has simply learned that it should leave the salesmen where they are, and recruit new men with retail experience.

144. **(D)** This is an assumption, which is of considerable importance, since the other firms in the market are said to be far larger. They could use their greater resources in a price-cutting war to keep out the new entrant. It does *not* follow from the fact that price proved to be an unimportant variable for the newcomer, that consumers will not react to price cutting by the market leaders.

145. **(A)** The marketing manager clearly considers that the current situation is too risky, and considers risk reduction a goal.

146. **(C)** Merchandising is stated to be valuable, but a minor factor relative to advertising and securing wide distribution, without which sales were inadequate.

147. **(A)** To the accountant, this is a major objective.

148. **(D)** This is a major assumption, since rapid technical progress among the prospective competitors could deprive the firm of the high profits required to finance their advertising campaign, which is necessary to break into the market.

149. **(C)** This is a minor factor, as it contributes to funding the operation, though only to a limited extent. The accountant still requires rapid returns on the capital invested in the retail project, because of the costs of borrowing.

150. **(A)** The accountant and marketing manager appear to regard this as a goal in its own right. It is offered as a further reason for entering the retail market.

151. **(B)** This is a major factor since, without distribution, the sales effort failed in the test markets. Therefore, it is reasonable to assume that if good distribution cannot be achieved, the objectives will not be attained.

152. **(C)** The raw materials are said to be cheap. The matter may be regarded as a minor factor since it is clear that only a small part of production costs depends upon raw material prices.

153. **(B)** This is a major factor since adequate sales appear to depend jointly on effective distribution and heavy advertising.

154. **(A)** This should be self-evident. Firms with no profits cease to exist — at least, in a private enterprise system.

155. **(D)** This is clearly a major assumption. Without a patent, the company cannot proceed, for it will have a cost advantage over the larger firms for a very limited period. They would simply duplicate the new product.

156. **(B)** The marketing manager considers this a real danger, despite offsetting factors. The company's lack of experience in the retail market could possibly prevent the attainment of major objectives.

157. **(B)** This is a major factor, because the company could fail if it cannot recover its capital outlays in a short period.

158. **(E)** All of these reasons are mentioned.

159. **(D)** He mentions I and II specifically.

160. **(D)** A task force had to be brought in for the test market, and performed better than the industrial salesmen.

161. **(C)** No statement was made about turnover, but both I and III are explicitly mentioned.

162. **(D)** II depends on the decision, while III is implied to be profitable regardless of the decision and I forms the current basis of the business.

163. **(B)** All these appear to be favorable points to the marketing manager. IV is brought up only by the accountant.

164. **(D)** The whole discussion is in terms of the firm's ability to break into the market, with the mention of market growth added only later. Hence III is true rather than I. Also II is a more complete statement than IV.

165. **(E)** The firm's 100 largest customers accounted for 91% of the turnover as compared with 73% ten years ago. 91% — 73% = 18%. Therefore the percent increase was 18%.

EXPLANATORY ANSWERS FOR PRACTICE TEST 4 (continued)

Section 7: Grammar and Usage

166. **(D)** "...will repair the car *well*."
The adverb (*well*) — not the adjective (*good*) — is used to modify the verb (*will repair*).

167. **(C)** "...if he *had read* more..."
The "if" clause of a contrary-to-fact past tense requires the verb *had read* — not *would have read*.

168. **(D)** "...to have his stories *compared with those of Dickens*."
We have an improper ellipsis in the original sentence. The additional words (*those of*) are necessary to complete the meaning of the sentence.

169. **(E)** All underlined parts are correct.

170. **(A)** "Many people in the United States *scarcely know*..."
Omit the word *don't*. The word *scarcely* is sufficiently negative to express the meaning intended.

171. **(B)** "...*who*, he said, were giving bribes..."
The subject of the dependent clause must have a nominative case form (*who*) — not an objective case form (*whom*).

172. **(B)** "...with a new *type of* motor..."
Do not use the article *a* or *an* after *kind of, type of, sort of,* etc.

173. **(B)** "...is not *nearly* as beautiful..."
Do not use the expression *nowhere near* for *not nearly*.

174. **(C)** "...were *those* same men..."
The demonstrative pronoun-adjective form (*those*) — not the personal pronoun form (*them*) — must be used to modify the noun *men*.

175. **(E)** All underlined parts are correct.

176. **(C)** "...the *cheaper* to run."
Since we are here comparing two things, we must use the comparative degree — not the superlative degree (*cheapest*).

177. **(B)** "...the family felt *bad*..."
In this sentence, an adjective (*bad*) — not an adverb (*badly*) — is used after a "sense" verb (*felt*).

178. **(C)** "...*nor* can he live without bread."
The coordinate conjunction *nor* is used when the alternative statement is negative.

179. **(D)** "...Jeff's leg was broken while *he was playing* football?"
We have a dangling elliptical clause in the original sentence. We must make clear that *Jeff was playing football*. Otherwise, the sentence may be understood to mean that *Jeff's leg was playing football*.

180. **(A)** "*Having swum* two-thirds of the distance..."
The past participle of *swim* is *having swum*.

181. **(A)** "George Foreman did *as* he said..."
The conjunction (*as*) should be used to introduce the dependent clause (*as he said*) — not the preposition (*like*).

182. **(D)** "...about solving *anyone else's* problems." Say *anyone else's, somebody else's,* etc. Do *not* say *anyone's else, somebody's else.*

183. **(A)** "*Because of* the meat boycott..."
Do not begin a sentence with the words *due to. Due* is an adjective. As an adjective, is must have a noun to modify.

184. **(D)** "...so that the children *would have* enough space..."
In a clause expressing purpose, the subjunctive form of the verb (*would have*) — not the indicative form (*had*) should be used.

185. **(E)** All underlined parts are correct.

186. **(A)** "Namath played a *really* fine game..."
An adverb (*really*) — not an adjective (*real*) — is used to modify the adjective *fine*.

187. **(D)** "... is like *that of* New York in June." We have an improper ellipsis here. We must include the words *that of*, meaning *the weather of*.

188. **(E)** All underlined parts are correct.

189. **(A)** "The teacher did not encourage the student *in any way* even though..."
We cannot properly use the indefinite pronoun *any* to modify the verb (*did not encourage*). The adverbial phrase *in any way* should be used for this purpose.

190. **(C)** "...a great interest *in* and admiration for the work of..."
We are not permitted to omit the preposition *in* since it is necessary to introduce the object of the preposition (*work*).

191. **(D)** "...of *whom* about..."
The object of the preposition must take the objective form (*whom*) — not the nominative form (*who*).

192. **(A)** "Sharon planned to pay *about*..."
About means *approximately;* *around* means *on all sides.*

193. **(A)** "Had Lincoln *been* alive..."
In a past contrary to fact situation, the "if clause" verb should take the form *had been* — not *had have been.*

194. **(E)** All underlined parts are correct.

195. **(C)** "...was *that* he was on his way..."

196. **(D)** "...no doubt about my being able to run faster than *he* today." The nominative case (*he* — not *him*) must be used after the conjunction *than* when the pronoun is the subject of an eliptical clause ("than he can run today").

197. **(A)** *"These kinds* of people..."
A plural pronoun-adjective (*These* — not *this*) must be used to modify a plural noun (*kinds*).

198. **(E)** All underlined parts are correct.

199. **(B)** "...presented *his* summaries of sales...
Singular antecedents (*Atkins* and *Miller*) which are joined by *or* or *nor* are referred to by singular pronouns (*his*, in this case — not *their*).

200. **(C)** "...brighter than *any other* student...
As the original sentence stands, Harold is brighter than himself. In a comparative construction, we must be sure that, if A and B are compared, A is not included as part of B.

201. **(D)** "...you or *I.*"
A pronoun which is an appositive of a subject must, like the subject, be in the nominative case. The word *who* is the subject of the clause "who should go out..." The subject of a clause or a sentence is in the nominative case. The pronouns which act as appositives to the subject must, accordingly, have nominative case forms (*you and I* — not *you and me*).

202. **(B)** "I prize my *mother-in-law's* picture..." When you form the possessive of a compound word, you must add the *apostrophe* and *s* only to the last word in the compound.

203. **(A)** "Had I *been* in my brother's position..."

204. **(E)** All underlined parts are correct.

205. **(B)** "The company is planning a series of lectures for *its* executives..."
A singular pronoun-adjective (*its* — not *their*) must be used to refer to a collective noun (*company*) when the members of the collective noun are considered as a unit.

EXPLANATORY ANSWERS FOR PRACTICE TEST 4 (continued)

Section 8: Error Recognition

206. **(V)** "In a violent outburst, the superpatriot tore up the peace placard..." Since the superpatriot was in a *violent outburst*, there is no need to add the word *angrily*.

207. **(D)** "He was *seething* with anger when he read the newspaper article about his dealings with gangsters." *Sheathing* means protecting by means of a covering. *Seething* means boiling.

208. **(G)** "The men were tired because they had worked hard on a hot day." Avoid the "and-and" construction. The thought is better expressed by a complex sentence in which the more (or most) important idea is the main clause: *"The men were tired..."*

209. **(G)** "A series of debates...*was* scheduled..." *Series* is a collective noun with a feeling of singularity. As a singular subject, it takes a singular verb (*was scheduled*).

210. **(D)** "The editorial *exposed* the weaknesses of the Mayor's slum-rebuilding plan." To *extol* means to praise. *To expose* means to lay open to criticism.

211. **(G)** "...into the infirmary, *I* was asked several questions by the nurse at the desk." It is *I* who was being wheeled – not the *nurse*. The participial construction should modify the subject. In the original sentence, the subject is *nurse*.

212. **(O)** The sentence contains no errors.

213. **(V)** "When the little girl... she screamed." The word *scream* means to utter a long, loud, *piercing* cry.

214. **(G)** "The American people *were dismayed...*" The original sentence is fragmentary (incomplete) since it lacks a verb.

215. **(O)** The sentence contains no errors.

216. **(G)** "...to *us* teenagers." The pronoun-adjective modifying the object of the preposition must be objective in form. *Teenagers* is the object of the preposition *to*. The pronoun-adjective modifying teenagers must, therefore, be the object form (*us* – not *we*).

217. **(D)** "The customers demanded that the crooked merchants be *prosecuted* to the fullest extent of the law." *Persecute* means to harass with cruel or oppressive treatment. *Prosecute* means to carry on a legal proceeding against someone.

218. **(D)** "...factory morale, *already* low..." *All ready* means everybody (is) ready. The adverb *already* modifying the adjective *low* is correct here.

219. **(G)** "Entering our bedroom shortly after midnight, *my wife and I* heard a terrific explosion." The present participle (*Entering*) must refer to the subject of the sentence (*my wife and I*).

220. **(D)** "Mynette, who was born in France, is now a *naturalized* citizen of the United States." *To neutralize* is to render ineffective. To *naturalize* is to confer the rights and privileges of citizenship upon an alien.

221. **(G)** "...*they* can cause irreparable damage." We have a plural subject: *Morphine* and *drugs*. Accordingly, the pronoun which occurs later in the sentence must be plural (*they*) since a pronoun must agree with its antecedent in number.

222. **(O)** The sentence contains no errors.

223. **(O)** The sentence contains no errors.

224. **(D)** "The Congressman made an angry, *impassioned* attack on the proposed tax increase."
Impassive means not feeling emotion. *Impassioned* means filled with emotion.

225. **(G)** "We did the job as *well* as we could..."
The adverb *well* must be used to modify the verb *did*. The adjective *good* is incorrect for such modification.

226. **(V)** "Nuclear scientists should be especially skilled in *research*."
Eliminate *investigative* since the word *research* implies investigation.

227. **(G)** "If I *had had* more time..."
In a contrary to fact condition in the past, the "if clause" must have a past perfect subjunctive form (*had had*).

228. **(V)** "A UN investigation has revealed that prisoners of war were coerced to enter..." *Coerce* means to compel *by force*.

229. **(G)** "Though Seaver pitched *really* well ..."
The adverb *well* must be modified by another adverb such as *really* – not by an adjective such as *real*.

230. **(D)** "...who were *irrational* (or *crazy*)."
The word *screwy* is slang for *irrational* or *crazy*.

231. **(G)** "Each of the hotel's 500 rooms *was* equipped..."
The singular subject (*Each*) requires a singular verb (*was equipped* – not *were equipped*).

232. **(V)** "At the end... the audience applauded *vigorously*."
An audience that applauds *vigorously* certainly has *enthusiasm*

233. **(G)** "The professor... portrait artist, having studied *art* in his spare time."
The professor did not study *artist* – he studied *art*.

234. **(O)** The sentence contains no errors.

235. **(O)** The sentence contains no errors.

236. **(V)** "At the Christmas party, the boss was so *vociferous* that..."
Since the word *vociferous* implies noisiness, there is no need to include *noisy* in the original sentence.

237. **(G)** "More leisure...*is* attainable..."
Since the subject (*leisure*) is singular, the verb must be singular (*is attainable*).

238. **(D)** "His arithmetic is poor because he is weak in fractions and *decimals*."
Decimation means destruction of one out of every ten. *Decem* in Latin means ten. A *decimal* pertains to the number ten.

239. **(V)** "Because Henry IV... *excommunicated* Henry."
Excommunicate means to cut off from communion with the church.

240. **(O)** The sentence contains no errors.

Practice Test 5 ⟶

USE THIS SHEET FOR YOUR ANSWERS
PRACTICE TEST 5

Section 1: Reading Comprehension

1 Ⓐ Ⓑ Ⓒ Ⓓ Ⓔ   6 Ⓐ Ⓑ Ⓒ Ⓓ Ⓔ   11 Ⓐ Ⓑ Ⓒ Ⓓ Ⓔ   16 Ⓐ Ⓑ Ⓒ Ⓓ Ⓔ   21 Ⓐ Ⓑ Ⓒ Ⓓ Ⓔ
2 Ⓐ Ⓑ Ⓒ Ⓓ Ⓔ   7 Ⓐ Ⓑ Ⓒ Ⓓ Ⓔ   12 Ⓐ Ⓑ Ⓒ Ⓓ Ⓔ   17 Ⓐ Ⓑ Ⓒ Ⓓ Ⓔ   22 Ⓐ Ⓑ Ⓒ Ⓓ Ⓔ
3 Ⓐ Ⓑ Ⓒ Ⓓ Ⓔ   8 Ⓐ Ⓑ Ⓒ Ⓓ Ⓔ   13 Ⓐ Ⓑ Ⓒ Ⓓ Ⓔ   18 Ⓐ Ⓑ Ⓒ Ⓓ Ⓔ   23 Ⓐ Ⓑ Ⓒ Ⓓ Ⓔ
4 Ⓐ Ⓑ Ⓒ Ⓓ Ⓔ   9 Ⓐ Ⓑ Ⓒ Ⓓ Ⓔ   14 Ⓐ Ⓑ Ⓒ Ⓓ Ⓔ   19 Ⓐ Ⓑ Ⓒ Ⓓ Ⓔ   24 Ⓐ Ⓑ Ⓒ Ⓓ Ⓔ
5 Ⓐ Ⓑ Ⓒ Ⓓ Ⓔ   10 Ⓐ Ⓑ Ⓒ Ⓓ Ⓔ   15 Ⓐ Ⓑ Ⓒ Ⓓ Ⓔ   20 Ⓐ Ⓑ Ⓒ Ⓓ Ⓔ   25 Ⓐ Ⓑ Ⓒ Ⓓ Ⓔ

Section 2: Math Ability

26 Ⓐ Ⓑ Ⓒ Ⓓ Ⓔ   32 Ⓐ Ⓑ Ⓒ Ⓓ Ⓔ   38 Ⓐ Ⓑ Ⓒ Ⓓ Ⓔ   44 Ⓐ Ⓑ Ⓒ Ⓓ Ⓔ   50 Ⓐ Ⓑ Ⓒ Ⓓ Ⓔ
27 Ⓐ Ⓑ Ⓒ Ⓓ Ⓔ   33 Ⓐ Ⓑ Ⓒ Ⓓ Ⓔ   39 Ⓐ Ⓑ Ⓒ Ⓓ Ⓔ   45 Ⓐ Ⓑ Ⓒ Ⓓ Ⓔ   51 Ⓐ Ⓑ Ⓒ Ⓓ Ⓔ
28 Ⓐ Ⓑ Ⓒ Ⓓ Ⓔ   34 Ⓐ Ⓑ Ⓒ Ⓓ Ⓔ   40 Ⓐ Ⓑ Ⓒ Ⓓ Ⓔ   46 Ⓐ Ⓑ Ⓒ Ⓓ Ⓔ   52 Ⓐ Ⓑ Ⓒ Ⓓ Ⓔ
29 Ⓐ Ⓑ Ⓒ Ⓓ Ⓔ   35 Ⓐ Ⓑ Ⓒ Ⓓ Ⓔ   41 Ⓐ Ⓑ Ⓒ Ⓓ Ⓔ   47 Ⓐ Ⓑ Ⓒ Ⓓ Ⓔ   53 Ⓐ Ⓑ Ⓒ Ⓓ Ⓔ
30 Ⓐ Ⓑ Ⓒ Ⓓ Ⓔ   36 Ⓐ Ⓑ Ⓒ Ⓓ Ⓔ   42 Ⓐ Ⓑ Ⓒ Ⓓ Ⓔ   48 Ⓐ Ⓑ Ⓒ Ⓓ Ⓔ   54 Ⓐ Ⓑ Ⓒ Ⓓ Ⓔ
31 Ⓐ Ⓑ Ⓒ Ⓓ Ⓔ   37 Ⓐ Ⓑ Ⓒ Ⓓ Ⓔ   43 Ⓐ Ⓑ Ⓒ Ⓓ Ⓔ   49 Ⓐ Ⓑ Ⓒ Ⓓ Ⓔ   55 Ⓐ Ⓑ Ⓒ Ⓓ Ⓔ

Section 3: Business Judgment

56 Ⓐ Ⓑ Ⓒ Ⓓ Ⓔ   61 Ⓐ Ⓑ Ⓒ Ⓓ Ⓔ   66 Ⓐ Ⓑ Ⓒ Ⓓ Ⓔ   71 Ⓐ Ⓑ Ⓒ Ⓓ Ⓔ   76 Ⓐ Ⓑ Ⓒ Ⓓ Ⓔ
57 Ⓐ Ⓑ Ⓒ Ⓓ Ⓔ   62 Ⓐ Ⓑ Ⓒ Ⓓ Ⓔ   67 Ⓐ Ⓑ Ⓒ Ⓓ Ⓔ   72 Ⓐ Ⓑ Ⓒ Ⓓ Ⓔ   77 Ⓐ Ⓑ Ⓒ Ⓓ Ⓔ
58 Ⓐ Ⓑ Ⓒ Ⓓ Ⓔ   63 Ⓐ Ⓑ Ⓒ Ⓓ Ⓔ   68 Ⓐ Ⓑ Ⓒ Ⓓ Ⓔ   73 Ⓐ Ⓑ Ⓒ Ⓓ Ⓔ   78 Ⓐ Ⓑ Ⓒ Ⓓ Ⓔ
59 Ⓐ Ⓑ Ⓒ Ⓓ Ⓔ   64 Ⓐ Ⓑ Ⓒ Ⓓ Ⓔ   69 Ⓐ Ⓑ Ⓒ Ⓓ Ⓔ   74 Ⓐ Ⓑ Ⓒ Ⓓ Ⓔ   79 Ⓐ Ⓑ Ⓒ Ⓓ Ⓔ
60 Ⓐ Ⓑ Ⓒ Ⓓ Ⓔ   65 Ⓐ Ⓑ Ⓒ Ⓓ Ⓔ   70 Ⓐ Ⓑ Ⓒ Ⓓ Ⓔ   75 Ⓐ Ⓑ Ⓒ Ⓓ Ⓔ   80 Ⓐ Ⓑ Ⓒ Ⓓ Ⓔ

Section 4: Data Sufficiency

81 Ⓐ Ⓑ Ⓒ Ⓓ Ⓔ   87 Ⓐ Ⓑ Ⓒ Ⓓ Ⓔ   93 Ⓐ Ⓑ Ⓒ Ⓓ Ⓔ   99 Ⓐ Ⓑ Ⓒ Ⓓ Ⓔ   105 Ⓐ Ⓑ Ⓒ Ⓓ Ⓔ
82 Ⓐ Ⓑ Ⓒ Ⓓ Ⓔ   88 Ⓐ Ⓑ Ⓒ Ⓓ Ⓔ   94 Ⓐ Ⓑ Ⓒ Ⓓ Ⓔ   100 Ⓐ Ⓑ Ⓒ Ⓓ Ⓔ   106 Ⓐ Ⓑ Ⓒ Ⓓ Ⓔ
83 Ⓐ Ⓑ Ⓒ Ⓓ Ⓔ   89 Ⓐ Ⓑ Ⓒ Ⓓ Ⓔ   95 Ⓐ Ⓑ Ⓒ Ⓓ Ⓔ   101 Ⓐ Ⓑ Ⓒ Ⓓ Ⓔ   107 Ⓐ Ⓑ Ⓒ Ⓓ Ⓔ
84 Ⓐ Ⓑ Ⓒ Ⓓ Ⓔ   90 Ⓐ Ⓑ Ⓒ Ⓓ Ⓔ   96 Ⓐ Ⓑ Ⓒ Ⓓ Ⓔ   102 Ⓐ Ⓑ Ⓒ Ⓓ Ⓔ   108 Ⓐ Ⓑ Ⓒ Ⓓ Ⓔ
85 Ⓐ Ⓑ Ⓒ Ⓓ Ⓔ   91 Ⓐ Ⓑ Ⓒ Ⓓ Ⓔ   97 Ⓐ Ⓑ Ⓒ Ⓓ Ⓔ   103 Ⓐ Ⓑ Ⓒ Ⓓ Ⓔ   109 Ⓐ Ⓑ Ⓒ Ⓓ Ⓔ
86 Ⓐ Ⓑ Ⓒ Ⓓ Ⓔ   92 Ⓐ Ⓑ Ⓒ Ⓓ Ⓔ   98 Ⓐ Ⓑ Ⓒ Ⓓ Ⓔ   104 Ⓐ Ⓑ Ⓒ Ⓓ Ⓔ   110 Ⓐ Ⓑ Ⓒ Ⓓ Ⓔ

(continued on next page)

Section 5: Grammar and Usage

111 Ⓐ Ⓑ Ⓒ Ⓓ Ⓔ	116 Ⓐ Ⓑ Ⓒ Ⓓ Ⓔ	121 Ⓐ Ⓑ Ⓒ Ⓓ Ⓔ	126 Ⓐ Ⓑ Ⓒ Ⓓ Ⓔ	131 Ⓐ Ⓑ Ⓒ Ⓓ Ⓔ
112 Ⓐ Ⓑ Ⓒ Ⓓ Ⓔ	117 Ⓐ Ⓑ Ⓒ Ⓓ Ⓔ	122 Ⓐ Ⓑ Ⓒ Ⓓ Ⓔ	127 Ⓐ Ⓑ Ⓒ Ⓓ Ⓔ	132 Ⓐ Ⓑ Ⓒ Ⓓ Ⓔ
113 Ⓐ Ⓑ Ⓒ Ⓓ Ⓔ	118 Ⓐ Ⓑ Ⓒ Ⓓ Ⓔ	123 Ⓐ Ⓑ Ⓒ Ⓓ Ⓔ	128 Ⓐ Ⓑ Ⓒ Ⓓ Ⓔ	133 Ⓐ Ⓑ Ⓒ Ⓓ Ⓔ
114 Ⓐ Ⓑ Ⓒ Ⓓ Ⓔ	119 Ⓐ Ⓑ Ⓒ Ⓓ Ⓔ	124 Ⓐ Ⓑ Ⓒ Ⓓ Ⓔ	129 Ⓐ Ⓑ Ⓒ Ⓓ Ⓔ	134 Ⓐ Ⓑ Ⓒ Ⓓ Ⓔ
115 Ⓐ Ⓑ Ⓒ Ⓓ Ⓔ	120 Ⓐ Ⓑ Ⓒ Ⓓ Ⓔ	125 Ⓐ Ⓑ Ⓒ Ⓓ Ⓔ	130 Ⓐ Ⓑ Ⓒ Ⓓ Ⓔ	135 Ⓐ Ⓑ Ⓒ Ⓓ Ⓔ

Section 6: Business Judgment

136 Ⓐ Ⓑ Ⓒ Ⓓ Ⓔ	141 Ⓐ Ⓑ Ⓒ Ⓓ Ⓔ	146 Ⓐ Ⓑ Ⓒ Ⓓ Ⓔ	151 Ⓐ Ⓑ Ⓒ Ⓓ Ⓔ	156 Ⓐ Ⓑ Ⓒ Ⓓ Ⓔ
137 Ⓐ Ⓑ Ⓒ Ⓓ Ⓔ	142 Ⓐ Ⓑ Ⓒ Ⓓ Ⓔ	147 Ⓐ Ⓑ Ⓒ Ⓓ Ⓔ	152 Ⓐ Ⓑ Ⓒ Ⓓ Ⓔ	157 Ⓐ Ⓑ Ⓒ Ⓓ Ⓔ
138 Ⓐ Ⓑ Ⓒ Ⓓ Ⓔ	143 Ⓐ Ⓑ Ⓒ Ⓓ Ⓔ	148 Ⓐ Ⓑ Ⓒ Ⓓ Ⓔ	153 Ⓐ Ⓑ Ⓒ Ⓓ Ⓔ	158 Ⓐ Ⓑ Ⓒ Ⓓ Ⓔ
139 Ⓐ Ⓑ Ⓒ Ⓓ Ⓔ	144 Ⓐ Ⓑ Ⓒ Ⓓ Ⓔ	149 Ⓐ Ⓑ Ⓒ Ⓓ Ⓔ	154 Ⓐ Ⓑ Ⓒ Ⓓ Ⓔ	159 Ⓐ Ⓑ Ⓒ Ⓓ Ⓔ
140 Ⓐ Ⓑ Ⓒ Ⓓ Ⓔ	145 Ⓐ Ⓑ Ⓒ Ⓓ Ⓔ	150 Ⓐ Ⓑ Ⓒ Ⓓ Ⓔ	155 Ⓐ Ⓑ Ⓒ Ⓓ Ⓔ	160 Ⓐ Ⓑ Ⓒ Ⓓ Ⓔ

Section 7: Analysis of Explanations

161 Ⓐ Ⓑ Ⓒ Ⓓ Ⓔ	169 Ⓐ Ⓑ Ⓒ Ⓓ Ⓔ	177 Ⓐ Ⓑ Ⓒ Ⓓ Ⓔ	185 Ⓐ Ⓑ Ⓒ Ⓓ Ⓔ	193 Ⓐ Ⓑ Ⓒ Ⓓ Ⓔ
162 Ⓐ Ⓑ Ⓒ Ⓓ Ⓔ	170 Ⓐ Ⓑ Ⓒ Ⓓ Ⓔ	178 Ⓐ Ⓑ Ⓒ Ⓓ Ⓔ	186 Ⓐ Ⓑ Ⓒ Ⓓ Ⓔ	194 Ⓐ Ⓑ Ⓒ Ⓓ Ⓔ
163 Ⓐ Ⓑ Ⓒ Ⓓ Ⓔ	171 Ⓐ Ⓑ Ⓒ Ⓓ Ⓔ	179 Ⓐ Ⓑ Ⓒ Ⓓ Ⓔ	187 Ⓐ Ⓑ Ⓒ Ⓓ Ⓔ	195 Ⓐ Ⓑ Ⓒ Ⓓ Ⓔ
164 Ⓐ Ⓑ Ⓒ Ⓓ Ⓔ	172 Ⓐ Ⓑ Ⓒ Ⓓ Ⓔ	180 Ⓐ Ⓑ Ⓒ Ⓓ Ⓔ	188 Ⓐ Ⓑ Ⓒ Ⓓ Ⓔ	196 Ⓐ Ⓑ Ⓒ Ⓓ Ⓔ
165 Ⓐ Ⓑ Ⓒ Ⓓ Ⓔ	173 Ⓐ Ⓑ Ⓒ Ⓓ Ⓔ	181 Ⓐ Ⓑ Ⓒ Ⓓ Ⓔ	189 Ⓐ Ⓑ Ⓒ Ⓓ Ⓔ	197 Ⓐ Ⓑ Ⓒ Ⓓ Ⓔ
166 Ⓐ Ⓑ Ⓒ Ⓓ Ⓔ	174 Ⓐ Ⓑ Ⓒ Ⓓ Ⓔ	182 Ⓐ Ⓑ Ⓒ Ⓓ Ⓔ	190 Ⓐ Ⓑ Ⓒ Ⓓ Ⓔ	198 Ⓐ Ⓑ Ⓒ Ⓓ Ⓔ
167 Ⓐ Ⓑ Ⓒ Ⓓ Ⓔ	175 Ⓐ Ⓑ Ⓒ Ⓓ Ⓔ	183 Ⓐ Ⓑ Ⓒ Ⓓ Ⓔ	191 Ⓐ Ⓑ Ⓒ Ⓓ Ⓔ	199 Ⓐ Ⓑ Ⓒ Ⓓ Ⓔ
168 Ⓐ Ⓑ Ⓒ Ⓓ Ⓔ	176 Ⓐ Ⓑ Ⓒ Ⓓ Ⓔ	184 Ⓐ Ⓑ Ⓒ Ⓓ Ⓔ	192 Ⓐ Ⓑ Ⓒ Ⓓ Ⓔ	200 Ⓐ Ⓑ Ⓒ Ⓓ Ⓔ

Section 8: Sentence Correction

201 Ⓐ Ⓑ Ⓒ Ⓓ Ⓔ	209 Ⓐ Ⓑ Ⓒ Ⓓ Ⓔ	217 Ⓐ Ⓑ Ⓒ Ⓓ Ⓔ	225 Ⓐ Ⓑ Ⓒ Ⓓ Ⓔ	233 Ⓐ Ⓑ Ⓒ Ⓓ Ⓔ
202 Ⓐ Ⓑ Ⓒ Ⓓ Ⓔ	210 Ⓐ Ⓑ Ⓒ Ⓓ Ⓔ	218 Ⓐ Ⓑ Ⓒ Ⓓ Ⓔ	226 Ⓐ Ⓑ Ⓒ Ⓓ Ⓔ	234 Ⓐ Ⓑ Ⓒ Ⓓ Ⓔ
203 Ⓐ Ⓑ Ⓒ Ⓓ Ⓔ	211 Ⓐ Ⓑ Ⓒ Ⓓ Ⓔ	219 Ⓐ Ⓑ Ⓒ Ⓓ Ⓔ	227 Ⓐ Ⓑ Ⓒ Ⓓ Ⓔ	235 Ⓐ Ⓑ Ⓒ Ⓓ Ⓔ
204 Ⓐ Ⓑ Ⓒ Ⓓ Ⓔ	212 Ⓐ Ⓑ Ⓒ Ⓓ Ⓔ	220 Ⓐ Ⓑ Ⓒ Ⓓ Ⓔ	228 Ⓐ Ⓑ Ⓒ Ⓓ Ⓔ	236 Ⓐ Ⓑ Ⓒ Ⓓ Ⓔ
205 Ⓐ Ⓑ Ⓒ Ⓓ Ⓔ	213 Ⓐ Ⓑ Ⓒ Ⓓ Ⓔ	221 Ⓐ Ⓑ Ⓒ Ⓓ Ⓔ	229 Ⓐ Ⓑ Ⓒ Ⓓ Ⓔ	237 Ⓐ Ⓑ Ⓒ Ⓓ Ⓔ
206 Ⓐ Ⓑ Ⓒ Ⓓ Ⓔ	214 Ⓐ Ⓑ Ⓒ Ⓓ Ⓔ	222 Ⓐ Ⓑ Ⓒ Ⓓ Ⓔ	230 Ⓐ Ⓑ Ⓒ Ⓓ Ⓔ	238 Ⓐ Ⓑ Ⓒ Ⓓ Ⓔ
207 Ⓐ Ⓑ Ⓒ Ⓓ Ⓔ	215 Ⓐ Ⓑ Ⓒ Ⓓ Ⓔ	223 Ⓐ Ⓑ Ⓒ Ⓓ Ⓔ	231 Ⓐ Ⓑ Ⓒ Ⓓ Ⓔ	239 Ⓐ Ⓑ Ⓒ Ⓓ Ⓔ
208 Ⓐ Ⓑ Ⓒ Ⓓ Ⓔ	216 Ⓐ Ⓑ Ⓒ Ⓓ Ⓔ	224 Ⓐ Ⓑ Ⓒ Ⓓ Ⓔ	232 Ⓐ Ⓑ Ⓒ Ⓓ Ⓔ	240 Ⓐ Ⓑ Ⓒ Ⓓ Ⓔ

Practice Test 5

SECTION 1: READING COMPREHENSION

Time: 30 minutes

Directions: Each of the reading passages in this section is followed by questions based on its content. After reading the passage, choose the best answer to each question. The questions are to be answered on the basis of what is stated or implied in the passage.

From my Old-Norse textbook back in Iceland I had become familiar with battle poetry rooted in sea-robber experience and the warlike spirit of petty Scandinavian kings, the so-called Scaldic poetry. Most of it is composed by Icelandic Scalds (poets or bards) either itinerant or engaged as house poets of kings and pirates.

This is a poetry of grim beauty composed by happy warriors in the most intricate of metres. It is considered by encyclopaedists to contain some of the most beautiful verses inspired by fighting in any age and any nation. Modern battle descriptions, including death-rolls (anemic impersonal body counts; Hill No. this or that), make pale reading to Icelanders compared to the Scaldic accounts of the famous battles of yore in which a great hero is dying a formidable death in almost every verse and battle is praised as the acme of human existence, war as the consummate glory of man.

This poetry is very particular about light and color in a battle; and about the right hour of day to fight one. The hour before daybreak is all right because it lends to the crimson of liquid blood a nice admixture of an azure sky and the silvery grey of a fading moon. Most good battles take place at dawn when you may behold the blue of your naked steel reddened by your worthy enemy's blood in perfect juxtaposition with the golden radiance of the rising sun. You delight in the frolics of blue colliding edges, accompanied by that seething din which this poetry holds to be characteristic of lethal wounds. Spears are singing and skulls crack with a thundering sound. The "flower of the wound" is one of the beautiful names given to a sword.

A battle is the "divine service," or mass, of swords; it also is the fun of swords; a happy bout of carnage; a kill spree. In all the poems the names of places where famous battles were fought are given; so are the names of chieftains and prominent heroes. A single poem might record a few dozen battles; one mentions fifty. Battles and heroes may or may not have their origin in reality. But you are left in the dark why all these battles were fought. The question seems never to have arisen. For all you know they might have been fought for fun, maybe not for fun of those who were actually slain, but for the many others who were supposed to hear the story and learn the poem. It is significant that a Scaldic poem never misses one elaborate passage of big joy, that is the joy of the hungry raven and the eagle and the swift-moving wolves amidst the fresh-reeking carrion of the battlefield. At times you might think the only idea of all the wars was to produce plenty of "warm prey" for empty-stomached scavengers.

In the Norse war-poetry you will note that a battle story never stands as a substitute, symbol or *exemplum* for anything outside itself; it never tries to put over on you any moral or give you tips about how to change the world for the better or save it. Evidently these poets were living in a perfect world.

To them war is the real thing; moreover, it is the thing of which it is always real fun to hear the news, the game of games, the Super-Olympics of which other Olympics are a substitute or a symbol.

The situation has not changed much since Scaldic times; anything to do with war still makes good copy. As our ancestors, we have the feeling that war is always with us, a *casus belli* is always round the corner. There are always plenty of facile "becauses." You open a war with someone because you think he is weaker than you or because he is your equal or you fear that he is stronger than you — all equally natural and legitimate arguments in favor of declaring war: let us go ahead and kill them! If you are afraid of being killed yourself, you are a scoundrel and a coward.

In our Western cultures male adulthood means being ripe for a kill spree. This is called conscription age. Nice people say war is all right as long as only young men are sent off to die honorably on the battlefield, but think it is immoral to kill girls, old men and kids, Why?

In this case, as so often in ethnology, we do not have the rationale. Some enlightening stories about this thing may be read in fairy tales, mythology and poetry, even in the Bible: Saul killed one thousand. David killed ten thousand. Prophets and scientists, students of this syndrome, have several explanations about why only young men should be shot, but not girls etc., but each one of their conclusions is disputed by the next bunch of experts.

Looking at the matter from the outside, for instance from the Moon, which might be as good a place for wisdom as any (or Iceland, for that matter), war looks like the fulfillment of a pact between two partners of mutually executing each other's young men. In recent years there have been symptoms, even forebodings, of a conceivable reverse in the situation. If wonderful young men with the future in their lustering eyes should take over one of these days as they threaten to do, let us pray they are not going to march us old devils off to die honorably in some faraway hell of which you don't even know the name, still less the number of the hill on the top of which you are going to be killed.

1. The writer of this passage

    (A) wrote war poetry
    (B) is a young man in his early thirties
    (C) is a Biblical scholar
    (D) is a Latin professor
    (E) spent his youth in a Northern country

2. Which paragraph has the most figurative language?

   (A) second
   (B) third
   (C) fourth
   (D) seventh
   (E) ninth

3. The author

   (A) is unsure about whether war is a good thing
   (B) doesn't indicate a definite point of view in regard to war
   (C) strongly favors war
   (D) strongly opposes war
   (E) believes that wars should be fought by the old

4. The tone of the last paragraph is

   (A) semiserious
   (B) sympathetic
   (C) angry
   (D) matter-of-fact
   (E) devil-may-care

5. Scaldic poetry

   (A) sought to improve society
   (B) stressed the importance of peace
   (C) explained why battles were fought
   (D) spoke about death lists and battle hills
   (E) may be considered today beautiful poetry

6. It is the belief of the writer that

   (A) only cowards refuse to fight
   (B) war is the only real thing
   (C) people love to read about war happenings
   (D) war is necessary
   (E) the Bible is inaccurate

Once upon a time, up to about 50 years ago, all *hatters* (hat makers) were thought to be mad. Therefore, a person behaving strangely was said to be "mad as a hatter." You certainly recall the Mad Hatter from Lewis Carroll's *Alice's Adventures in Wonderland*.

More than any other group, hatters were subject to *mercurialism*—poisoning caused by intake of the liquid metal, *mercury*. Mercurialism can cause brain damage. Symptoms of such damage are shaking of the body, odd behavior, garbled speech, blurred vision, and loss of muscular co-ordination. These symptoms were considered the signs of "hatters' madness."

Hatters used mercury and mercury compounds (chemical combinations of mercury and other elements) to process fur and felt for hats. In the hot stuffy rooms where hatters toiled, mercury easily vaporized. As a result, the hatters inhaled quantities of mercury each day. They also "ate" the metal, which rubbed off their unwashed hands onto food the hatters consumed. Over a number of years, this day-to-day intake of mercury tended to damage the kidneys, intestines, and, eventually, the brains of hatters.

Scientists now believe that damage to the brain is caused by a class of *organic* (containing carbon) mercury compounds known as the *methylmercury group*.

Mercury is no longer used in the hat industry. And industries that continue to use the liquid metal observe very strict safety precautions. Thus, it would seem that mercury poisoning and hatters' "madness" are things of the past.

But are they?

Various mercury compounds are widely used to kill many of the world's more than 40,000 different species of *fungi*. And, as a result of this use, mercury is reportedly showing up in our food, air, and water.

Fungi form a large class of plants whose members range from slime molds to mushrooms. A common feature of fungi is a lack of chlorophyll, the green coloring matter of most plants. Because of this lack of chlorophyll, fungi are unable to "process" their own food. Some species obtain nutrients from dead plant and animal matter. But many others are *parasitic* — they steal nutrients from other living organisms.

Some fungi, such as yeasts, penicillin, and mushrooms, are beneficial to man. But many fungi are pests. These species, which live on dead matter, speed the decay of books, clothes, stored food, furniture, and other useful things.

The parasitic species are even more dangerous. They can destroy vital food crops such as wheat, oats, corn, rice, and potatoes. More than a hundred years ago, Ireland's entire potato crop rotted in the fields as the result of an attack by a parasitic fungus.

Similar famines would be frequent events if effective *fungicides* (fungi killers) weren't used to protect growing food plants. And mercury compounds are very effective fungicides.

Farmers and foresters around the world use various mercury compounds to shield their delicate seedlings from fungus attacks. In particular, methylmercury compounds are widely used because they can kill many different kinds of fungi.

Wherever mercury compounds are used in agriculture, government agencies, such as our own Food and Drug Administration (FDA), set strict rules on when, where, and how these substances should be applied. The strict rules are intended to keep mercury out of the food we eat and the water we drink. But, in spite of these precautions, reports from Sweden claim that mercury may pollute the food we eat.

For a long time, Swedish farmers, like U.S. farmers, have treated seeds with mercury compounds to protect them and the plants growing out of them from fungi attacks.

By successfully curbing the spread of destructive fungi, the use of mercury compounds greatly increased the outputs of fields and forests in the U.S. and Sweden.

But about 15 years ago, a few Swedish scientists sounded an alarm. They warned that by splashing fields and forests with mercury compounds and by dumping mercury wastes from factories into streams and lakes, the Swedish people were risking widespread mercury poisoning.

The scientists became concerned when they discovered that many birds and other wild animals were dying of mercury poisoning. How did the birds become poisoned? They ate mercury-treated seeds. How did the other animals become poisoned? They ate poisoned birds or their eggs.

This prompted several questions: If wild birds were eating mercury-treated seeds, might not domestic fowl also pick up such seeds blown in on the wind or dropped by passing birds?

In the beginning, few people heeded the scientists' warnings. Then news of mercury poisoning tragedies in Japan shocked the Swedish government and people into action.

Between 1953 and 1960, 110 people in Japan's Minimata Bay area died mysteriously. Investigations revealed that the people had eaten fish containing quantities of methylmercury. Where did the mercury compound come from? It was dumped into the bay by a plastics manufacturing plant.

The Japanese government closed that plant and started strictly regulating the use and disposal of mercury compounds. But this didn't prevent another tragedy. In 1965, 26 people at Niigata, Japan, were struck by mercury poisoning. Five died. All the victims had eaten fish containing mercury. And again the culprit was a plastics plant.

7. This reading passage attributes the strange behavior of hat makers to

   (A) a character created by Lewis Carroll
   (B) the eating of mercury in hat shops
   (C) the hatter's neglect to wash before eating
   (D) a parasitic fungus
   (E) eating poisoned fish

8. It is *not* true that

   (A) mercury may pollute food
   (B) food supplies are protected with fungicides
   (C) fish may contain mercury
   (D) fungi may be good for mankind
   (E) fungi make their own food

9. A form of fungi is

   (A) chlorophyll
   (B) a toadstool
   (C) a book
   (D) a potato
   (E) mercury

10. The passage states that mercury is no longer used in the hat industry. Why then are there still mercury poisonings?

   (A) The FDA has been ineffective.
   (B) Mercury is effective as a fungicide.
   (C) There is a high mercury content in plastic.
   (D) Many are unable to recognize the metal.
   (E) Many products containing mercury are imported from Japan.

11. When the public was first informed of the mercury poisoning tragedies, the general reaction was one of

   (A) indifference
   (B) disbelief
   (C) anger
   (D) desire for inmediate action
   (E) request for factual proof

12. The true origin of the poisoning of the birds could best be traced back to

   (A) the fungi destroying crops
   (B) other poisoned birds
   (C) the wind carrying mercury-treated seeds
   (D) the farmer trying to protect his seedlings
   (E) the research done by scientists

It began midsummer 1944 as a dream in the mind of Adolf Hitler. By late autumn, Wehrmacht planners had transformed the dream into battle orders. Hitler proposed to regain the offensive by deploying Germany's last reserves to smash through a lightly held sector of the Belgian front. His panzers would entrap as many as 30 U.S. and British divisions, capture the strategic supply port of Antwerp, and perhaps end the war in the West with a negotiated peace. Hitler thought of it as another Dunkirk and code-named it *"Wacht am Rhein* [Watch on the Rhine]." Allied archives would later refer to "the Battle of the Ardennes." To men who were there, it was "the breakthrough" or "the Battle of the Bulge."

Several officers under Field Marshal Gerd von Rundstedt, Commander in Chief in the West, protested that Hitler had set an impossible timetable by ordering a two-day rush to the Meuse, 50 miles distant. *"Das ist unwiderruflich* [This is irrevocable]," said General Alfred Jodl, Chief of Operations at supreme headquarters, slamming his fist on a conference table. One officer suggested that Hitler was trying for a *grosser Schlag,* a grand slam. Why not, he proposed to Jodl, settle instead for a more attainable *kleiner Schlag,* or little slam, by advancing only as far as Liege? Jodl was unmoved.

Hitler promised 300,000 troops for the attack and strong Luftwaffe support. Manteuffel recalls that during one seven-hour meeting, Hitler asked Reichsmarschall Hermann Göring how many planes he could provide. "Three thousand," Goring said instantly. "You know Goring," Hitler said, to Manteuffel. "I think we shall have 2,000." The actual count was about 900.

Hitler had a strong reason for not accepting the opinions of his generals.

The generals had been wrong about both Czechoslovakia and Poland. None of the generals believed that such blitz campaigns were possible. Even in France, the German military predicted that the campaign would last much more than six weeks. Hitler was proved right, and ever afterward he followed his own judgment. Naturally, France was the last time he was right.

Had Hitler been persuaded to call off his attack, Europe might have followed a different course. According to Manteuffel, Stalin knew all about *Wacht am Rhein* through a security leak in German headquarters. He said nothing to his allies. Instead, he waited until the German offensive was spent, then sent the Red Army dashing across Eastern Europe a month after the Ardennes battle began. Stalin was apparently aware that the last 200,000 members of the German army's strategic reserve were among the men committed to the Ardennes. Had those reserves been available for the Eastern Front, they might have stopped or delayed the Russians. U.S. soldiers, as a result, might have met Russian troops at the Oder instead of on the Elbe, 125 miles farther west. The British would have reached the German rocket base at Peenemünde before the Russians captured its secrets. U.S. and British columns would have been first into Berlin. Moreover, the Russians would have lost the psychological advantage they have exploited throughout Eastern Europe by billing themselves as the true conquerors of the Third Reich.

13. According to the German generals, why was the Hitler plan doomed for failure?

    (A) It did not provide for protection of the eastern front.
    (B) It provided for the German army to move too far too fast.
    (C) It did not provide adequate defense for Berlin.
    (D) It put the last remaining German troops on the defensive.
    (E) It sought a confrontation with British and American troops.

14. Approximately how many planes supported the German troops?

    (A) 900
    (B) 2000
    (C) 3000
    (D) 9000
    (E) 300,000

15. Hitler ignored the advice of his generals because

    (A) they had been proved wrong in the past
    (B) they had little experience with the war in the west
    (C) the Allied troops were overextended
    (D) he was a madman
    (E) he was envious of their previous successes

16. All the following are probable reasons for Stalin's not telling the Allies about *Wacht am Rhein* except:

    (A) He found out about the plan only after the Ardennes battle began.
    (B) He wanted to make it easier for the Russian troops to break through the Eastern Front.
    (C) He wanted the Russians to get the rocket secrets of Peenemünde.
    (D) He wanted Russia to be known as "The liberator of Eastern Europe."
    (E) He wanted the Russians to get to Berlin first.

17. According to the author, Hitler ordered the Western offensive because

    (A) of his desire to capture Russia
    (B) of his desire to gain a negotiated peace in the West
    (C) he expected to win a military victory in the West
    (D) he wanted to conquer Belgium
    (E) he hoped to get Russia on his side by such an offensive

18. What was the result of the German offensive?

    (A) The Germans defeated the Allies at Antwerp and controlled the West.
    (B) After initial losses, the Allies prevented the Germans from extending the "Bulge" and then broke through into Germany.
    (C) The Russians were ambushed by a secret patrol on the Eastern Front.
    (D) Hitler proved to his generals that he was right all along.
    (E) The British, but not the Americans, asked for a negotiated peace.

What is it that people today fail to understand about what is happening to them? What is happening is that they are using up their planet at a fearsome rate and may soon pass the point where their total habitat can sustain human life. Man's world is slipping away from him. His habits, his thoughts, his actions run counter to the essentials of his existence. He has created national governments for the purpose of giving him maximum protection, but he has no way of protecting himself against the governments. In the act of contending with one another, the governments have become instruments of race suicide and world holocaust.

Whatever man's successes in intermediate organization, he has failed to create an organization of the whole. His finest energies have gone into interim projects. The need to apply his intelligence to the operation of human society itself has yet to lay a claim on his awareness or his reason. After at least 200,000 years of evolution, man's instincts and tropisms are still strongly tribal.

Most of what man does is irrelevant to his main problems; his ingenuity has been applied to everything except the need to make his planet safe for human habitation. He has cut into his natural environment with large slashes. His sources of food are being sealed over by the tar and cement of his cities and highways. Next to destructive force, he produces nothing in greater volume than his garbage. He has made his sky an open sewer and his rivers and lakes a poisonous brew. He has pumped his foul wastes into the seas and has stared balefully at billions of floating dead fish.

Instead of fortifying his plants against insects with rich loam and compost, he has attacked them indiscriminately with chemicals, violating the chain of life and killing off the birds that are far more essential to his own spirit than many of his commodities. By going against nature, he has warred against beauty of line, movement, and sound. He has been mucking up his own planet, but has the arrogance to go searching for life elsewhere in the universe.

What has been happening to people that they don't understand is that they have made a geographical entity out of their world without a philosophy for ennobling it, a plan for conserving it, or an organization for sustaining it. Men crave to do good, to act reasonably and think decently. But goodness and decency and wisdom must have a world purpose in our time if life and thought are to have any meaning at all.

19. The author would be opposed to

    (A) a stronger United Nations
    (B) moon flights sponsored by the government
    (C) pollution control
    (D) conservation of natural resources
    (E) organic farming

20. The basic contrast in this selection is that of man's

    (A) efforts and their results
    (B) arrogance and his humility
    (C) past and present
    (D) accomplishments on land and in the sea
    (E) seeking peace and waging war

21. The following concept is stressed in the selection:

    (A) "The survival of the fittest."
    (B) "Good guys never win pennants."
    (C) "To the victor belong the spoils."
    (D) "Man cannot live on bread alone."
    (E) "Where there's a will there's a way."

22. The word "holocaust" (first paragraph, last line) means

    (A) holiness
    (B) cooperation
    (C) expansion
    (D) destruction
    (E) empty victory

23. The tone of the article is one of

    (A) concealed humor
    (B) hopeless resignation
    (C) stoic calm
    (D) unbridled anger
    (E) alarming concern

24. The author in speaking of "interim projects" (paragraph 2) implies that

    (A) "There is a tide in the affairs of men."
    (B) "Mankind cannot see the forest for the trees."
    (C) "A rose by any other name would smell as sweet."
    (D) "Conscience is but a word that cowards use."
    (E) "The paths of glory lead but to the grave."

25. To which of the following would the author *not* be favorably disposed?

    I. Having additional research trips to the moon.
    II. Building an airport in the Everglades (Florida).
    III. Barring factories from the shores of the Hudson River (New York).

    (A) I and II only
    (B) II and III only
    (C) I and III only
    (D) II and III only
    (E) I, II, and III

IF YOU FINISH BEFORE THE TIME IS UP, GO OVER YOUR WORK FOR THIS SECTION ONLY. DO NOT TURN TO ANY OTHER SECTION OF THE TEST. WHEN THE TIME IS UP, GO ON TO THE NEXT SECTION.

SECTION 2: MATH ABILITY

Time: 30 minutes

Directions: Each of the problems in this section is followed by five alternatives lettered A through E. Solve each problem and then choose the correct answer. Note that diagrams are not necessarily drawn to scale. Scratchwork may be done on available space on the pages of this section.

Questions 26–29 refer to the following pictorial graph:

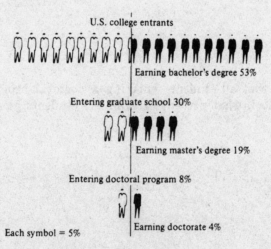

How Many Get Degrees

U.S. college entrants

Earning bachelor's degree 53%

Entering graduate school 30%

Earning master's degree 19%

Entering doctoral program 8%

Each symbol = 5%

Earning doctorate 4%

This breakdown shows what happens to every 100 persons who enter college.

26. What percent of those people who enter a doctoral program succeed in earning a doctorate?

(A) 4%
(B) 8%
(C) 25%
(D) 50%
(E) 100%

27. If 200,000 people enter U.S. colleges how many of these are expected to earn a master's degree?

   (A) 34,000
   (B) 27,000
   (C) 78,000
   (D) 52,000
   (E) 38,000

28. A graduate school has an enrollment of 1500. How many students can be expected to earn their master's degree?

   (A) 860
   (B) 490
   (C) 1030
   (D) 950
   (E) 780

29. Assuming that all students entering a doctoral program came from a grad school, what percent of graduate students go on to a doctoral program?

   (A) 16%
   (B) 30%
   (C) $26\frac{2}{3}$%
   (D) $41\frac{1}{4}$%
   (E) 8%

30. A rectangular plot of land 100 feet × 200 feet is divided into as many square 900 square feet sections as possible for vegetable gardens. How many square feet of land are left unused?

   (A) 5550
   (B) 10,880
   (C) 2090
   (D) 6700
   (E) 3800

Questions 31–32

Distance It Takes Car to Stop at Given Speeds

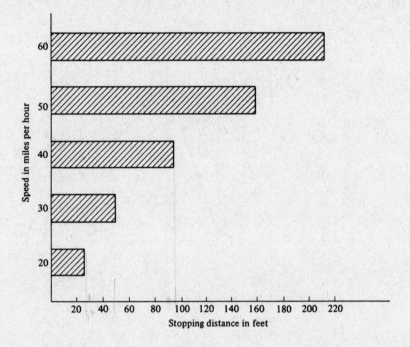

31. From the bar graph above, what is the approximate ratio of the stopping distance at 40 m.p.h. to that at 20 m.p.h.?

(A) 2:1
(B) 3:1
(C) 4:1
(D) 3:2
(E) 5:3

32. What is the approximate ratio of the stopping distance at 60 m.p.h. to that at 30 m.p.h.?

(A) 4:1
(B) 3:1
(C) 2:1
(D) 3:2
(E) 5:2

---

33. If a boy can mow a lawn in t minutes, what part can he do in 15 minutes, if he works at a uniform rate?

(A) $t - 15$
(B) $15 - t$
(C) $\dfrac{15}{t}$
(D) $\dfrac{t}{15}$
(E) $15\,t$

34. A radio costing $60 is sold for $80. What is the percent profit on the selling price?

(A) 33⅓%   (D) 60%
(B) 25%   (E) 80%
(C) 20%

35.

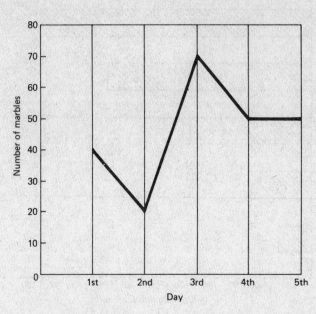

John bought a certain number of marbles every day for 5 days. The number he bought each day is given on the graph above. What is the average number of marbles John bought each day?

(A) 230   (D) 45
(B) 46   (E) 70
(C) 50

36. ⅔ of the members of a committee are women; ¼ of the male members of the committee are married. If there are 9 bachelors in the committee, how many members are there altogether?

(A) 28
(B) 32
(C) 30
(D) 36
(E) 38

37. A storekeeper has merchandise valued at $2,340. After cutting prices, his merchandise costs 82% of its original value. How much does the merchandise now cost?

(A) $1876.00
(B) $1900.00
(C) $1918.80
(D) $1954.60
(E) $2000.00

Questions 38–39 refer to the tables below.

DEATH FROM HEROIN IN NYC

ALL AGES

1950-1954	465
1955-1959	611
1960-1964	1,299
1965-1969	2,935

TEENAGERS

	15 and Under	All Teens
1960	0	15
1964	0	38
1967	0	79
1969	20	224

38. Teenagers under 15 years of age accounted for what percentage of the total teenage heroin deaths in 1969?

(A) 20%
(B) 9%
(C) 8%
(D) 22%
(E) 10%

39. Between the period 1955-59 and the period 1960-64, the number of heroin deaths recorded in New York increased by

(A) 688
(B) 1636
(C) 146
(D) 2324
(E) 23

40. If a sheet of cardboard has an area of 186 square inches, and two pieces of size 6 inches by 3 inches are cut out, what is the area of the remaining cardboard?

(A) 168
(B) 150
(C) 132
(D) 123
(E) 114

COMPOSITION OF CONCRETE BY WEIGHT

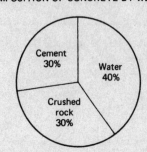

41. The graph above shows the composition of concrete. If one ton of concrete is mixed, how many pounds of cement are needed

(A) 300   (D) 600
(B) 400   (E) 700
(C) 500

42. If a man buys several articles for n cents per dozen and sells them for $\frac{n}{9}$ cents per article, what is his profit, in cents, on each article?

(A) $\frac{n}{36}$ (D) $\frac{4n}{3}$

(B) $\frac{n}{12}$ (E) $\frac{n}{18}$

(C) $\frac{3n}{4}$

Questions 43–44

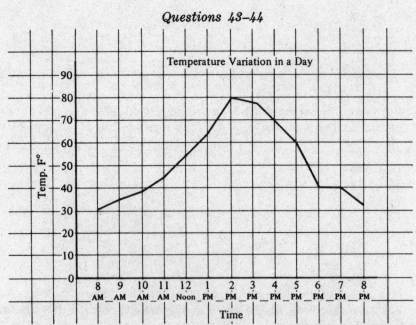

43. What is the approximate percentage increase in temperature from 8 A.M. to noon?

(A) 50%   (D) $83\frac{1}{3}\%$
(B) 60%   (E) $87\frac{1}{2}\%$
(C) $72\frac{1}{2}\%$

44. During what hour did the temperature increase the greatest amount?

    (A) 9 to 10 A.M.
    (B) 10 to 11 A.M.
    (C) 11 A.M. to 12 noon
    (D) 12 noon to 1 P.M.
    (E) 1 P.M. to 2 P.M.

45. A company has a net profit of $10,000 per month. If it reinvests $2,000 of this every month, what percentage of its profits does it reinvest?

    (A) 10%
    (B) 15%
    (C) 20%
    (D) 25%
    (E) 30%

46. Subtract 3 from the number n. Multiply the result by 3. Add 3 and then divide this result by 3. What is the final result?

    (A) n
    (B) $n - 1$
    (C) $n + 1$
    (D) $n - 2$
    (E) $n + 2$

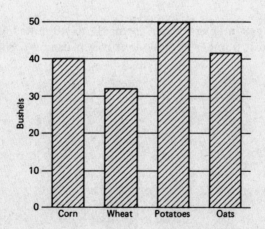

47. The preceding graph indicates the harvest of certain crops on a small farm. How many bushels of oats were harvested?

    (A) 20
    (B) 32
    (C) 40
    (D) 42
    (E) 50

48. Which of the following must be odd?

> I. The product of two even numbers.
> II. The product of two odd numbers.
> III. The sum of an odd and an even number.

(A) none
(B) I only
(C) II and III only
(D) I and III only
(E) I, II, and III

49. There are 5 males and 6 females who volunteered to serve on a committee. If the committee consists of one male and one female, how many different committees are possible?

(A) 24
(B) 26
(C) 28
(D) 30
(E) 32

50. An auto's gas mileage runs from 12 to 18 miles per gallon. What is the greatest number of gallons it might use on a 360-mile trip?

(A) 20
(B) 22
(C) 25
(D) 28
(E) 30

51. If $p = \frac{3}{5} q$, and q is a positive integer, which of the following could be a value of p?

(A) 13
(B) 16
(C) 22
(D) 25
(E) 18

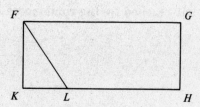

52. In the figure above, FGHK is a rectangle of area 80. If KL = ¼ KH, what is the area of triangle FKL?

    (A) 8
    (B) 10
    (C) 12
    (D) 14
    (E) 15

Questions 53–54

New York Stock Exchange
WEEK ENDED APRIL 10, 1971

New York Times Weekly Combined Averages

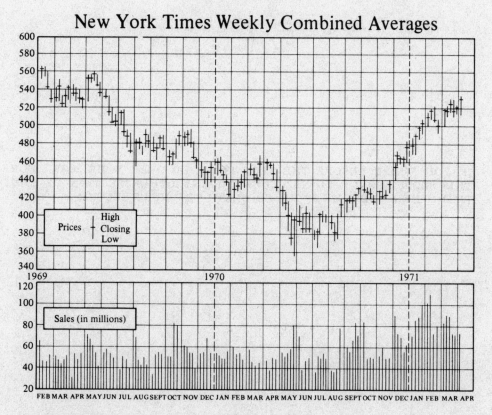

53. The lowest amount reached by the combined averages in the period indicated by the graph was about

    (A) 420
    (B) 400
    (C) 340
    (D) 380
    (E) 355

54. The highest amount reached by the combined averages was about

(A) 540
(B) 580
(C) 565
(D) 535
(E) 600

55. The indicator on a can of milk shows it is $\frac{1}{4}$ full. When t more gallons are poured in, the indicator rests at the $\frac{5}{8}$ mark. What is the total capacity of the can? (in gallons)

(A) $8t$

(B) $3t$

(C) $\dfrac{3t}{8}$

(D) $\dfrac{8t}{3}$

(E) $\dfrac{4t}{3}$

IF YOU FINISH BEFORE THE TIME IS UP, GO OVER YOUR WORK FOR THIS SECTION ONLY. DO NOT TURN TO ANY OTHER SECTION OF THE TEST. WHEN THE TIME IS UP, GO ON TO THE NEXT SECTION.

SECTION 3: BUSINESS JUDGMENT

Time: 30 minutes for all of Section 3

QUESTIONS ON DATA EVALUATION

Directions: Read the passage. After the passage are Data Evaluation questions (in phrase form) that relate to the passage. Answer each question by choosing the appropriate letter for your answer.

(A) **Major Objective.** The phrase indicates a Major Objective of the business executive in the situation described in the passage.

(B) **Major Factor.** The phrase indicates a Major Factor in the business executive's arriving at a decision. The passage specifically mentions a circumstance or consideration that is fundamental in his coming to the decision.

(C) **Minor Factor.** The phrase indicates a Minor Factor in the business executive's arriving at a decision. The passage specifically states a circumstance or consideration that is secondary in his coming to a decision.

(D) **Major Assumption.** The phrase indicates a Major Assumption in the business executive's arriving at a decision. He is taking for granted certain circumstances or occurrences in his decision-making.

(E) **Unimportant Issue.** The phrase indicates an Unimportant Issue in the business executive's arriving at a decision. The issue is of no importance or of no relevance in his decision-making.

The chemical industry has undergone some profound technological changes in the last few years. In particular, the change of techniques and the greater degree of mechanization has enabled tasks which formerly required two or three workers to be easily accomplished by a single man. The Sigma Chemical Company has not been slow in recognizing and implementing the new processes, and its stock of equipment and machinery is among the most modern in the industry. Nor is capital short in quantity; the value of total plant and machinery per worker is $105,000 compared to $110,000 for the industry leader and $93,500 for the industry-wide average.

Despite the modern equipment employed and the ability of a capable and aggressive sales force to sell the entire product either to industry or directly to consumers, the company's profit record is dismal and the value of shares on the stock exchange considerably depressed. The J.C. McClelland Organization, a firm of management consultants, was retained and given the task of identifying the causes of the present low-profit levels and suggesting ameliorative action. The President of the Sigma Company emphasized, with the full concurrence of the Board, that no plan or proposal should, in any way, threaten the harmonious relationships at present existing between management and union; the company's strike record was the best in the industry and it was regarded as of paramount importance that this be maintained.

As anticipated by the Company, the McClelland report pointed to low labor productivity as the basic problem and indicated two underlying causes. First, because of the long-term nature of the previous contract, work practices were predicated on the older industrial methods of production now made obsolete by the new techniques. This meant too many men were being employed on each task and this was a cause of the low productivity. A second lesser cause was that the loyalty and long service of the work force had led to a situation in which a disproportionate percentage were between the ages of 55 and 65. These workers, so the consultants had found, were slow in reaching peak efficiency when working with new processes.

After reviewing the report, the Board of Directors met and agreed that major steps should be taken to increase the profitability of the enterprise by way of increasing the labor productivity. Such steps, however, should not impair management-worker relations and should also serve as a model enhancing the company's stature as a responsible employer and supplier.

It was clear from the outset of the Board's discussion that the plan would have to be comprehensive, paying much attention to detail. The plan would also require extensive, possibly delicate, negotiation with the union. Indeed, the success of the effort depended on the responsible and capable union officials that Sigma was fortunate to be dealing with. Sigma's personnel department would also be required to work strenuously and ably throughout the negotiations, but it was felt that the vigorous and imaginative officers would be equal to the task. Without the known cooperation between these two groups the plan would be jeopardized.

The basis of the scheme lay in the payment of substantial lump-sum separation payments to older workers who wished to retire within the two years following the initiation of the scheme. This payment, it was thought, would hasten the planned retirement of older workers and so reduce both the size of the work force and the proportion of older workers in it. Each retiree would receive two weeks' pay for each year of service with the company.

The rest of the plan was directed at the improvement of productivity among the remaining workers. This was to be achieved by a system of productivity reward. On the basis of small sections of the total factory, each worker's weekly pay would be increased by 40% of the increase of output per worker over a specified level. The system crucially depended on the divisibility of the factory into appropriately small units where the effort made by each worker would have a perceptible impact on output. This was necessary to maximize incentive effects. The bonus scheme should not only increase the output of existing workers, but also have the effect of attracting able, more skilled workers, enabling the recruiting officers to be more selective. Conceivably these workers might be drawn from competitors, further improving the company's relative profitability. Moreover, the new arrangements would give the company greater flexibility to implement new techniques and product lines.

The union's concern related to the remuneration of retiring and remaining workers and to the physical safety of those who were staying. The payment of bonuses related to increase in output could lead to accident by the encouragement of hasty and reckless behavior. It was agreed, therefore, that part of the planned package would be a tightening of safety procedures (already in excess of federal requirements) and a special safety training program.

The initial cost of the whole plan would be substantial and its implementation depended on the ability of the company to raise the required funds. The depressed share prices led to the rejection of a new issue as a means of raising funds and resort would have to be made to the loan market. Outside factors could lead to problems but the company Treasurer was certain that the money could be borrowed.

A final consideration was that the rapidly rising remuneration of factory workers would lead to discontent among the clerical and supervisory staff. These people were not in the union nor able to be covered by the type of agreement applied to the factory workers. However, the three-year contract recently signed by this group meant immediate action was out of the question, and the company's improved profit position would enable compensatory remunerations to be made in the future.

Choose the appropriate letter (A or B or C or D or E)
for these phrases in accordance with the given directions.

56. The more rapid retirement of workers in response to separation pay

57. Maximization of profit

58. Low productivity of the work force under the present system

59. New safety regulations and training

60. Possible difficulties in the loan market

61. Government safety regulations

62. Increased productivity of workers under the new incentive scheme

63. Maintenance of harmonious relations between management and union

64. Responsible and capable union officials

65. Luring workers away from rival concerns

66. The ability to expand the plant and introduce new products

67. Ability to gather the finance to implement the scheme

68. Attitude of clerical and supervisory staff

69. Ability of the sales force to sell increased product

70. Attraction of young, skilled workers by higher rewards

71. Improvement of company image

72. Inability of older workers to work efficiently with new techniques

QUESTIONS ON DATA APPLICATION

Directions: The questions below are to be answered with reference to the same passage (above). For each question, select the correct answer from each of the five choices given.

73. Consultants found that the low productivity was due to

    (A) overmanning
    (B) too little capital per worker
    (C) outmoded capabilities of the work force
    (D) both A and B
    (E) both A and C

74. In the matter of buying the latest equipment, the company was

    (A) a leader in the industry
    (B) behind the rest of the industry
    (C) average
    (D) below average
    (E) well above average

75. The existing overmanning was due to

    (A) poor union-management relations
    (B) incorrect choice of productive techniques
    (C) a contract related to outdated techniques
    (D) older workers requiring assistance
    (E) federal safety regulations

76. The divisibility of the plant into small units was important

    (A) so workers could be trained in a small range of tasks
    (B) to maximize the incentive effort
    (C) to tighten safety regulations
    (D) to negotiate separately with a small group of workers at a time
    (E) to implement a shift work system

77. Each retiring worker would receive

    (A) one year's salary
    (B) two months' salary
    (C) one week's salary for each year's service
    (D) two weeks' salary for each year's service
    (E) six months' salary

78. Safety was thought to be a concern under the new scheme because

    (A) workers would be less experienced
    (B) the new technology was unsafe
    (C) young workers had a bad accident record
    (D) workers might hurry unsafely to get greater bonuses
    (E) of a reduction in the number of safety officers

79. Issuing new shares as a means of finance was ruled out because

    (A) share capital must be linked to new building
    (B) new shares had recently been issued
    (C) federal laws prohibited a new issue
    (D) share prices were depressed
    (E) management could not be freed for the new issue

80. If the Sigma Chemical Company employs 1000 workers, the value of the total plant and machinery is

    (A) over $100,000,000
    (B) greater than the value for 1000 workers of the industry leader
    (C) less than the industry-wide average for 1000 workers
    (D) less than $105,000
    (E) the same as the industry-wide average per 1000 workers

IF YOU FINISH BEFORE THE TIME IS UP, GO OVER YOUR WORK FOR THIS SECTION ONLY. DO NOT TURN TO ANY OTHER SECTION OF THE TEST. WHEN THE TIME IS UP, GO ON TO THE NEXT SECTION.

SECTION 4: DATA SUFFICIENCY

Time: 30 minutes

Directions: Each of the questions below is followed by two statements, labeled (1) and (2), in which certain data are given. In these questions you do not actually have to compute an answer, but rather you have to decide whether the data given in the statements are *sufficient* for answering the question. Using the data given in the statements *plus* your knowledge of mathematics and everyday facts (such as the number of days in July), you are to blacken the box on the answer sheet under

(A) if statement (1) ALONE is sufficient but statement (2) alone is not sufficient to answer the question asked.

(B) if statement (2) ALONE is sufficient but statement (1) alone is not sufficient to answer the question asked.

(C) if BOTH statements (1) and (2) TOGETHER are sufficient to answer the question asked, but NEITHER statement ALONE is sufficient.

(D) if EACH statement is sufficient by itself to answer the question asked.

(E) if statements (1) and (2) TOGETHER are NOT sufficient to answer the question asked and additional data specific to the problem are needed.

81. W is one of the following numbers: 8, 10, 13, 17, 22. Which number is W?

    (1) W is a prime number.
    (2) $\frac{1}{2}$W > 6.

82. Can Phil buy the radio with $30?

    (1) The radio now costs $\frac{5}{6}$ of its former price.
    (2) After cutting the price of the radio the store's profit has decreased by $\frac{1}{2}$.

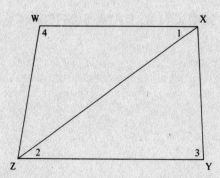

83. Is XY parallel to WZ?

    (1) Angle 1 = Angle 2
    (2) WZ > XY

84. If $a > c$, is $b > d$? ($a, b, c, d \neq 0$)
    (1) $ab = cd$.
    (2) $c = 2d$.

85. On the xy plane, A is located at (2,3) and B is located at (3,1). What is the perimeter of ABC?

    (1) C is 2 units away from B.
    (2) Angle ABC = 90°.

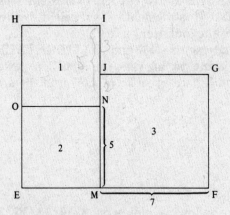

86. If Figure 1 is congruent to Figure 2, what is the length of IJ?

    (1) Area 3 = (GF)²
    (2) $\sqrt{\text{Area 1}}$ = EO

87. A circulation manager of a high school newspaper must deliver papers to students and teachers. Will an order of 3200 papers be sufficient?

    (1) There are 15 times as many students as teachers in the school.
    (2) There are 30 students in each class.

88. What does WXY equal?

    (1) W = X + Y
    (2) WXYZ = 6Z

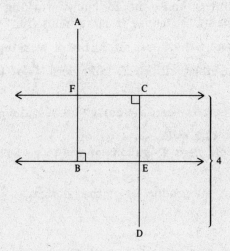

89. What is the length of FB?

    (1) ED = 2
    (2) AF = 2

90. An encyclopedia consists of 24 books. What is the weight of the twelfth book?

    (1) The first 12 books weigh 22 pounds.
    (2) The last 12 books weigh 25 pounds.

91. What is the volume of the cube?

    (1) The diagonal of a face measures $3\sqrt{2}$.
    (2) The sum of the edges is 36.

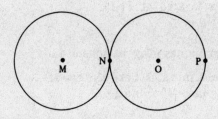

92. Is Circle M congruent to circle O?

    (1) $NP = MO$
    (2) $MN = 3$

93. Which number is greatest, *C*, *D*, or *E*?

    (1) $2D > 2E > 2C$

    (2) $C + 2 = D \geqslant E$

94. If Jeff can paint a house in 15 hours working alone, how long will it take to paint the house if Mike helps him?

    (1) Mike can paint the house in 20 hours working alone.

    (2) Working together with Jeff, Mike does $\dfrac{3}{7}$ of the total work.

95. Or the average how far can the car go on 20 gallons of gas?

    (1) It averages 12.2 miles on 1 gallon.

    (2) The car would need 45 gallons of gas to go 549 miles.

96. Which is greater, the product *ef* or the quotient, $\dfrac{e}{f}$.

    (1) $0 < ef < 1$

    (2) $0 < f < e < 1$

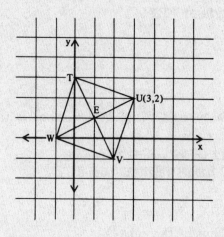

97. What is the length of a side of square *TUVW*?

    (1) A line perpendicular to *WV* from *E* measures $\dfrac{\sqrt{10}}{2}$.

    (2) Point *E* is located at (1,1).

98. How long must James stay in school daily?

    (1) There are 4 minutes between classes.

    (2) Each class lasts 40 minutes.

99. There are 4000 students in a school, all of whom take a course in English and/or Math. How many students take both subjects?

    (1) 640 students take only English.

    (2) 525 students take only Math.

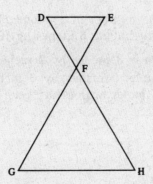

100. What is the length of *DF*?

    (1) *DE* is parallel to *GH*.
    (2) *FG* = 2*EF*

101. How many apples are needed to make 2 gallons of apple juice?

    (1) 3 apples are needed to make 1 pint of apple juice.
    (2) 17 oranges are needed to make 2 gallons of orange juice.

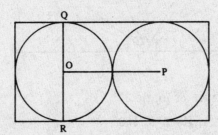

102. Two congruent circles *O* and *P* are inscribed in the above rectangle. What is the area of the rectangle?

    (1) *OP* = 4
    (2) *QR* = 4

103. A building and 3 sides of fencing enclose a rectangular 100-square-yard lot. How many feet of total fencing are needed for the 3 sides?

    (1) The building is 75 feet long.
    (2) 4 yards of fencing are needed on one of the sides.

104. If the river is flowing downstream at a rate of 3 miles per hour, how long will it take Harold to row 10 miles upstream?

    (1) He starts upstream at 10 A.M.
    (2) He rows at a rate of 5 miles per hour.

105. What is the maximum number of photographs that can be placed on photographic paper measuring 8 inches by 10 inches?

   (1) Each photograph is 3 inches by 2 inches.
   (2) Only 2 photographs 5 inches by 6 inches fit on the last piece of photographic paper which has been printed.

106. Is M an integer?

   (1) $2M$ is an integer.
   (2) $M + 2$ is an integer.

107. How much fuel will a 120 horsepower engine consume in $2\frac{1}{2}$ hours?

   (1) Fuel costs 20 cents a pound.
   (2) The engine utilizes $\frac{2}{3}$ pound of fuel per horsepower per hour.

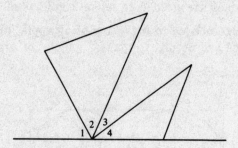

108. What is the measure of angle 3?

   (1) Angle 1 + Angle 2 = 103°
   (2) Angle 1 + Angle 4 = 92°.

109. Which detergent costs less per ounce — super-economy size or family size?

   (1) Super-economy size contains $\frac{1}{4}$ pound more than family size.
   (2) Super-economy size costs 77¢ whereas family size costs 20¢ less.

110. If she types at her average pace, can the secretary finish the 1750-word report in 20 minutes?

   (1) She types 6000 words per hour.
   (2) In 10 minutes she can type 1000 words.

IF YOU FINISH BEFORE THE TIME IS UP, GO OVER YOUR WORK FOR THIS SECTION ONLY. DO NOT TURN TO ANY OTHER SECTION OF THE TEST. WHEN THE TIME IS UP, GO ON TO THE NEXT SECTION.

SECTION 5: GRAMMAR AND USAGE

Time: 30 minutes

Directions: In each question, you will find a sentence with four words (or phrases) underlined. In some sentences one of the underlined words (or phrases) is incorrect in the light of the rules of standard written English for grammar, correct usage, and choice of words. No sentence has more than one error. You are to assume that the rest of the sentence (whatever is not underlined) is correct. If you find an error, choose the letter (A *or* B *or* C *or* D) of that underlined word (or phrase) which is incorrect. If you find no error, fill in answer space E.

111. <u>Besides</u> <u>being</u> an outstanding student, he is <u>also</u> a leader in school
 A   B   C

 government and a <u>trophy-winner</u> in school sports. <u>No error.</u>
                    D   E

112. If any signer of the Constitution <u>was</u> to return to life <u>for a day,</u> his
                                        A   B

 <u>opinion</u> of our amendments <u>would be</u> interesting. <u>No error.</u>
  C   D   E

113. The dean <u>of the college,</u> together <u>with</u> some other faculty members,
              A   B

 <u>are</u> planning a conference for the purpose of <u>laying</u> down certain
  C   D

 regulations. <u>No error.</u>
               E

114. If one lives in Florida <u>one day</u> and in Iceland <u>the next,</u> he is <u>certain</u> <u>to</u>
     A   B   C   D

 feel the change in temperature. <u>No error.</u>
                                  E

115. <u>Now</u> that the stress of examinations and interviews <u>are</u> over, we can
     A   B

 all <u>relax</u> for awhile. <u>No error.</u>
 C   D   E

116. The industrial trend is in the direction of more machines and less
                     A   B   C   D

     people. No error.
           E

117. The American standard of living is still higher than most of the
                                A   B   C

     other countries of the world. No error.
             D   E

118. At last, late in the afternoon, a long line of flags and colored umbrellas
        A   B

     were seen moving toward the gate of the palace. No error.
        C   D   E

119. Due to the failure of the air-cooling system, many in the audience
        A

     had left the meeting before the principal speaker arrived. No error.
         B   C   D   E

120. Psychologists and psychiatrists will tell us that it is of utmost impor-
                                  A

     tance that a disturbed child receive professional attention as soon as
              B   C   D

     possible. No error.
           E

121. After waiting in line for three hours, much to our disgust, the tickets
           A   B   C

     had been sold out when we reached the window. No error.
         D   E

122. That angry outburst of Father's last night was so annoying that it
                      A

     resulted in our guests packing up and leaving this morning. No error.
             B   C   D   E

123. Sharp advances last week in the wholesale price of beef is a strong
        A   B

     indication of higher meat costs to come, but so far retail prices con-
                         C

     tinue favorable. No error.
           D   E

124. An acquaintance with the memoirs of Elizabeth Barrett Browning

and Robert Browning <u>enable</u> us to appreciate the <u>depth of influence</u>
      A   B

that two people of talent can have <u>on</u> <u>each other</u>. <u>No error</u>.
            C D   E

125. The supervisor <u>was advised</u> to give the assignment to <u>whomever</u>
       A   B

<u>he believed</u> had a strong sense of responsibility, and the courage <u>of</u> his
 C   D

conviction. <u>No error</u>.
     E

126. If he <u>would have lain</u> quietly as instructed by the doctor, he <u>might not</u>
   A B   C

<u>have had</u> a second heart attack. <u>No error</u>.
 D   E

127. The founder and, <u>for many years</u>, the <u>guiding spirit</u> of the "Kenyon
       A   B

Review" is John Crowe Ransom, <u>who</u> you must know <u>as</u> an out-
              C   D

standing American critic. <u>No error</u>.
        E

128. <u>Though</u> you may not <u>agree with</u> the philosophy of Malcolm X, you
 A   B

must admit that he <u>had</u> tremendous influence <u>over</u> a great many
        C   D

followers. <u>No error</u>.
    E

129. There is no objection to <u>him</u> joining the party <u>provided</u> he is willing
          A   B

to <u>fit in</u> with the plans of the group and is <u>ready</u> and able to do his
  C   D

share of the work. <u>No error</u>.
      E

130. Ceremonies were opened by a drum and bugle corps of Chinese chil-
     ‾‾‾‾‾‾‾‾‾   ‾‾‾‾‾‾‾‾‾‾
         A   B

dren parading up Mott Street in colorful uniforms. No error.
             ‾‾   ‾‾‾‾‾‾‾‾‾‾‾‾‾‾‾‾‾   ‾‾‾‾‾‾‾‾
               C   D   E

131. The reason most Americans don't pay much attention to rising African
               ‾‾‾‾‾‾‾‾‾‾‾‾‾‾   ‾‾‾‾   ‾‾‾‾‾‾
                    A   B   C

nationalism is because they really do not know modern Africa.
             ‾‾‾‾‾‾‾
                D

No error.
‾‾‾‾‾‾‾‾
   E

132. The farmer felt badly about his prize cow's being eliminated from
                   ‾‾‾‾‾   ‾‾‾‾‾ ‾‾‾‾‾‾‾‾‾‾‾‾‾‾‾
                     A   B   C

competition. No error.
‾‾‾‾‾‾‾‾‾‾‾   ‾‾‾‾‾‾‾‾
     D   E

133. The Federal Aviation Administration ordered an emergency inspec-
                                         ‾‾‾‾‾‾‾
                                            A

tion of several Pan American planes on account of a Pan American
    ‾‾   ‾‾‾‾‾‾‾‾‾‾‾‾‾
     B   C

Boeing 707 had crashed on Bali, in Indonesia. No error.
          ‾‾‾‾‾‾‾‾‾‾   ‾‾‾‾‾‾‾‾
              D   E

134. A gang of armed thieves, directed by a young woman, has raided the
           ‾‾‾‾‾‾‾‾‾‾‾‾‾   ‾‾‾‾‾‾‾‾‾‾
                 A   B

mansion of a gold-mining millonaire near Dublin late last night.
             ‾‾‾‾‾‾‾‾‾‾‾   ‾‾‾‾‾‾‾‾‾‾‾
                  C   D

No error.
‾‾‾‾‾‾‾‾
   E

135. I had a male chauvinist pig dream that the women of the world rose up
     ‾   ‾‾‾‾‾‾‾‾‾‾‾‾‾‾‾   ‾‾‾‾‾‾‾
       A   B   C

and denounced the women's liberation movement. No error.
                  ‾‾‾‾‾‾‾‾‾‾‾‾‾‾‾‾‾‾‾‾‾‾‾‾‾‾‾   ‾‾‾‾‾‾‾‾
                            D   E

IF YOU FINISH BEFORE THE TIME IS UP, GO OVER YOUR WORK FOR THIS
SECTION ONLY. DO NOT TURN TO ANY OTHER SECTION OF THE TEST.
WHEN THE TIME IS UP, GO ON TO THE NEXT SECTION.

SECTION 6: BUSINESS JUDGMENT

Time: 30 minutes for all of Section 6

QUESTIONS ON DATA EVALUATION

Directions: Read the passage. After the passage are Data Evaluation questions (in phrase form) that relate to the passage. Answer each question by choosing the appropriate letter for your answer.

(A) **Major Objective.** The phrase indicates a Major Objective of the business executive in the situation described in the passage.

(B) **Major Factor.** The phrase indicates a Major Factor in the business executive's arriving at a decision. The passage specifically mentions a circumstance or consideration that is fundamental in his coming to the decision.

(C) **Minor Factor.** The phrase indicates a Minor Factor in the business executive's arriving at a decision. The passage specifically states a circumstance or consideration that is secondary in his coming to a decision.

(D) **Major Assumption.** The phrase indicates a Major Assumption in the business executive's arriving at a decision. He is taking for granted certain circumstances or occurrences in his decision-making.

(E) **Unimportant Issue.** The phrase indicates an Unimportant Issue in the business executive's arriving at a decision. The issue is of no importance or of no relevance in his decision-making.

When founded 75 years ago by the present owner's grandfather, the Whitworth Machine Tool Company had enjoyed the advantages of an excellent location. The factory had been built on the outskirts of Brookdale, a growing city, near a newly completed railway line, which provided cheap transportation of raw materials and the finished product. The rapid industrial growth of the region had been based on a rich coalfield. The cheap coal had led both to cheap electric power and the establishment of several steelworks. These enterprises provided the raw materials for Whitworth and the many other engineering firms in the area. This agglomeration constituted a reliable market for Whitworth's product, and continued immigration led to an abundance of skilled labor.

These favorable circumstances continued for half a century, but the last twenty-five years had seen a persistent erosion of the profitability of the Company. When Charles Whitworth assumed control of the Company on the death of his father, it was apparent that drastic remedial action was necessary. Charles had spent very little prior time with the Company, partly because he preferred the Coast, where he lived, to the inland industrial area where the Company was located. His thorough study of the Company's situation led to a series of reports, which, viewed collectively, adequately diagnosed the problem. The basis of the trouble lay in the exhaustion of the coalfields and the closure of the mines, which had once employed over 30,000 men. The four major steelworks had followed, relocating close to raw material supplies. One by one, the other engineering firms had left, draining the pool of skilled labor, so that the Whitworth Company now faced wage rates 25% above the national average. The loss of local markets and materials, however, was of little importance owing to the development of cheap road travel; transportation was now a minor element in total costs.

The Whitworth factory, once suburban, had been swallowed up by the expanding city, and now lay in a high rental area, devoted almost entirely to service trades and retail establishments, which required central locations and were able to withstand high rents. For the Whitworth Company these developments meant only an inflated site rent and growing city property taxes, which together now accounted for an alarming 22% of costs.

Furthermore, the years of decline had seen a bitter struggle between management and powerful local unions. The outcome of a recent series of strikes was the ruin of the Company's reputation for reliability.

Wages were now the largest single item of costs, followed by electric power, which had risen in price since the exhaustion of local coal. Power now accounted for 27% of costs and was likely to rise even higher·

Charles Whitworth briefly considered the possibility of an overhaul and re-equipment of the present premises. This he deemed unwise in the extreme since the city had long threatened compulsory acquisition of the premises as part of an urban renewal program. In such an event, the city would finance relocation and provide a new site, but it seemed more likely that the procrastination would continue. This and other factors inflicted a high level of uncertainty on the enterprise which dogged long-range planning and damaged morale. Charles considered it vital that this uncertainty be lessened.

Consequently, he investigated alternative locations, two of which seemed promising. The less drastic was a move to Palmer, a township on the outskirts of the city, meaning an escape from high rents and city taxation. The twin problems of high labor cost and poor union-management relations would not, however, be solved. Further, Charles loathed the suburbs and would like to see a clean break ending the firm's lengthy association with the city and its environs.

The other alternative was Newport, a coastal town within a rapidly developing area. Charles wanted to continue living in this pleasant environment near the sea. An important problem with this alternative was the possibility that his management would resign rather than move, a serious problem in the light of his own inexperience. No objections were voiced against his initial proposal; and, consequently encouraged, he planned ahead on the basis of continued acquiescence. He thought that, as long as management did not resign *en masse*, he would be able to replace those individuals who did. His other reservation concerning the move was that, since the Company was unknown in the new area, credit availability would initially he difficult.

Beyond this, the Newport location seemed excellent. Labor was available at much lower rates than near Brookdale, and a State-financed retraining scheme ensured a liberal supply of appropriate skills, conserving the firm's own training resources. Power was cheaper and transportation would be no problem if a nearby interstate link-up was completed shortly, as Charles expected. Because of the greater distance, moving costs would be higher, but would be largely offset by a State relocation grant and federal tax credits. These two factors would help ensure a smooth transition, but the following data were also helpful in opting for the Newport site.

Estimated Running Costs

	Brookdale	Palmer	Newport
Income of skilled worker per year ($)	19000	18500	16500
State payroll tax per worker ($)	200	200	300
City property tax (% of assessed value)	5	—	—
Rental per sq.ft. per year ($)	40	20	25
Electricity rates per k.w./hr ($)	10	8	5

Choose the appropriate letter (A or B or C or D or E) *for these phrases in accordance with the given directions.*

136. Improved labor relations

137. Willingness of management to move away

138. Proximity of the company to its markets

139. The availability of skilled labor

140. Completion of the interstate highway connection at Newport

141. The cost of electric power

142. The cost of transporting raw materials

143. Meeting the owner's desire to live in a pleasant coastal area

144. The rental costs of factory premises

145. The advantages of a city center location

146. Reducing the current high level of uncertainty

147. The price of soft water

148. The city's continued procrastination on the issue of demolition and relocation of the Brookdale factory

149. The State retraining scheme for labor at the coastal location

150. Moving into an area where the company is not known

151. The lack of a rail link at the coastal location

152. The expectation of continued low wages in Newport

QUESTIONS ON DATA APPLICATION

Directions: The questions below are to be answered with reference to the same passage (above). For each question, select the correct answer from each of the five choices given.

153. Which of the following describes the reasons why the steelworks moved?

      I. Development of coastal cities
     II. Relocation of engineering companies
   III. Exhaustion of coalfield
   IV. Need to locate near raw materials
     V. A State relocation grant

  (A) I and V only
  (B) I and III only
  (C) III and V only
  (D) III and IV only
  (E) I, II, III, IV, and V

154. What proportion of costs is accounted for by transport costs?

  (A) More than 30%
  (B) 27%
  (C) A maximum of 24%
  (D) Definitely less than 20%
  (E) Exactly one-quarter

155. For which of the following reasons *had* the original location been so good?

      I. Good transportation
     II. Abundant skilled labor
   III. Cheap electric power
   IV. A good local market for the product
     V. Local availability of raw materials

  (A) I and IV only
  (B) II and V only
  (C) I, III and V only
  (D) I, II, IV and V only
  (E) I, II, III, IV, and V

156. If 30 square feet of floor space and 200 k.w. hours of electricity are required per worker, per year, then total per worker rent and electricity costs per year are

    I. $450 less in Newport than in Palmer
    II. $450 more in Newport than in Palmer
    III. $600 less in Newport than in Palmer
    IV. $1450 less in Newport than in Brookdale
    V. $1000 less in Palmer than in Brookdale

(A) I only
(B) II and V only
(C) III and IV only
(D) IV and V only
(E) I, IV, and V only

157. Which of the following could be said of the present labor situation at Brookdale?

(A) Skilled labor is still plentiful.
(B) The State retraining program is a source of skilled labor.
(C) The labor union is weak.
(D) The labor union is strong.
(E) Strikes are very rare.

158. Which of the following factors is a major contributor to total costs?

(A) Transportation costs
(B) Electric power prices
(C) The price of steel
(D) The cost of health insurance for employees
(E) Mortgage payments

159. Which of the following is true of the present owner?

(A) He is an expert in industrial location.
(B) He was the cause of the falling profits.
(C) He is a skilled engineer.
(D) He has little management expertise.
(E) He is sorry to break ties with Brookdale.

160. Which of the following is true of the comparison of the three sites in the table?

(A) Newport is best on all counts.
(B) Brookdale is worst on all counts.
(C) Palmer is as good as, or better than, Brookdale on all counts.
(D) Newport is better than, or as good as, Palmer on all counts.
(E) Newport is better than Palmer on the majority of considerations.

IF YOU FINISH BEFORE THE TIME IS UP, GO OVER YOUR WORK FOR THIS SECTION ONLY. DO NOT TURN TO ANY OTHER SECTION OF THE TEST. WHEN THE TIME IS UP, GO ON TO THE NEXT SECTION.

SECTION 7: ANALYSIS OF EXPLANATIONS

Time: 30 minutes

Directions: In the following, a factual situation and a result are presented. After the result is presented, a set of statements is given. For each of the statements given, you are to choose

- (A) if the statement contradicts or is not consistent with the factual situation, or with the result, or with both the factual situation and the result.

- (B) if (A) is not true and if the statement possibly explains the result.

- (C) if (A) and (B) are not true and if the statement can be deduced from the factual situation, or from the result, or from both the factual situation and the result.

- (D) if (A), (B), and (C) are not true and if the statement supports or weakens an explanation of the result.

- (E) if (A), (B), (C), and (D) are not true and if the statement is not relevant to an explanation of the result.

Consider and eliminate each of the choices in the order (A), (B), (C), (D), and (E). The very first choice that cannot be eliminated is the correct answer.

Set 1

Situation:

The law firm of Colson, Borg, and Temple, had been attempting for some time to fill a vacancy caused by the sudden and unexpected death of Max Jasmine, a former partner. After much deliberation, the three senior partners concluded that they required a skillful lawyer who was articulate, handsome, and between the ages of thirty and forty years old. They proceeded to interview two candidates whom they felt met the necessary prerequisites. However, prior to the final selection of a new partner, George Jasmine, the twenty-four-year-old son of the deceased, arrived at the law firm and presented Colson, Borg, and Temple with a newly acquired diploma from Harvard Law School, and a completed job application for his father's vacated position.

Result:

George Jasmine was made a partner of Colson, Borg, and Temple.

370 / Graduate Management Admission Test

161. The firm was not absolutely rigid in its requirements for a new partner.

162. The three senior partners felt a tremendous loyalty to Max Jasmine, and desired to repay him posthumously for his services.

163. Max Jasmine died of old age.

164. George Jasmine was particularly inarticulate, and possessed numerous scars on his face.

165. George Jasmine graduated first in his class from law school, and demonstrated expertise in numerous legal fields.

166. The older Jasmine's body was never recovered from a plane crash.

167. Both candidates for the partnership were found to have forged their law school transcripts.

168. Max Jasmine, prior to his death, had become invaluable as a tax specialist.

169. One of the two candidates was dismissed because he was forty-two years old.

170. The job left behind by Max Jasmine was not hastily filled.

Set 2

Situation:

Corbet Browning had been operating a steel foundry in Southern Pennsylvania for over thirty years. Although Browning, for a good portion of that period, had enjoyed much prosperity in his business, in recent times his economic situation fell into a marked decline. Dismayed by current developments, Browning hired a highly touted cost-analyst, Bently Gordon, to study his predicament. After much deliberation, Gordon concluded that upwardly spiraling labor and material costs, combined with a decrease in job contracts, were to blame for the foundry's diminishing profits. He recommended that Browning aggressively solicit new contracts, as well as cut his staff by 50% to ten employees — the minimum required to run a foundry his size. Acting upon his advice, Browning found that all went well until the spring of 1977, when a Board of Inquiry cited his foundry for violation of the newly-drafted Pollution Control Act of Pennsylvania.

Result:

In June of 1977, Browning decided to sell his business to the United States Steel Corporation.

171. Prior to the institution of Gordon's recommendations, eighteen people were employed in Browning's foundry.

> (A) if the statement contradicts or is not consistent
>   with the factual situation, or with the result,
>   or with both the factual situation and the result.
> (B) if (A) is not true and if the statement possibly
>   explains the result.
> (C) if (A) and (B) are not true and if the state-
>   ment can be deduced from the factual situation,
>   or from the result, or from both the factual sit-
>   uation and the result.
> (D) if (A), (B), and (C) are not true and if the
>   statement supports or weakens an explanation
>   of the result
> (E) if (A), (B), (C), and (D) are not true and if
>   the statement is not relevant to an explanation
>   of the result.

172. Those foundries found to be in violation of the Pollution Control Act were given five years to make the necessary corrections.

173. In recent years the foundry had accepted a number of contracts that involved working with copper, in addition to steel.

174. U.S. Steel made Browning a fair and equitable offer towards the purchase of his foundry.

175. The Pollution Control Board demanded that Browning make alterations in his plant that, if performed, would be so costly as to wipe out any profit made by the foundry in the next two years.

176. After making the study, Gordon felt that little could be done with regard to curbing the rising costs of materials.

177. The Pollution Control Act was the first law of its kind in the United States.

178. Browning acknowledged that, after thirty years of running an unsuccessful business, it was time to get out.

179. Without the aid of Gordon, Browning was likely to hire more people than was absolutely necessary.

180. Browning decided that a man of his age should not subject himself to the physical and emotional strain of running a business, but rather, should retire gracefully.

Set 3

Situation:

Carswell Morse, a long time star of the stage and screen, was facing stiff competition from the newly discovered talent, Morgan Betz, for the leading role in Franco Bordelli's newest motion-picture extravaganza. Although a close friend of Bordelli, as well as an excellent actor, Morse feared that the financial backers of the film were anxious to introduce a new personality as the star. Desperate for the part, Morse changed his name and hired a plastic surgeon to alter his facial characteristics.

Result:

The "new" Carswell Morse was offered the leading role in Bordelli's new film.

181. After the operation, Morse was universally acknowledged to be the most handsome actor of the day.

182. Following the operation, the surgeon was arrested for practicing medicine without a license.

183. This was Bordelli's first major motion picture.

184. Morgan Betz abandoned his acting ambitions in order to pursue a career in law, prior to the hiring of Morse.

185. In the movie business, those who finance the film have a greater say in the selection of actors than does the director.

186. Bordelli's wife, Tamara, was also offered a role in the film.

187. Morse feared that Bordelli would hire the lesser qualified Betz just to spite him.

188. Once recognized nationally, Morse's appearance after surgery was foreign to even his most devoted fans.

189. The acting business is not run on the seniority system.

190. The "new" Carswell Morse retained his expertise as a thespian, while presenting a fresh visage to the public.

Set 4

Situation:

Joseph Marshall, a highly respected executive of the Bone-Dry Anti-Perspirant Company, was in serious disagreement with his colleagues over the chemical contents of the company's product. One of Marshall's acquaintances, a Bone-Dry researcher, financed independently by Marshall,

(A) if the statement contradicts or is not consistent with the factual situation, or with the result, or with both the factual situation and the result.
(B) if (A) is not true and if the statement possibly explains the result.
(C) if (A) and (B) are not true and if the statement can be deduced from the factual situation, or from the result, or from both the factual situation and the result.
(D) if (A), (B), and (C) are not true and if the statement supports or weakens an explanation of the result.
(E) if (A), (B), (C), and (D) are not true and if the statement is not relevant to an explanation of the result.

had invented a new chemical, Methyl Phenyl Hydro Chlorate (MPHC), which Marshall wanted to incorporate into "Bone-Dry." Marshall's peers rejected his suggestion, so he decided to form a new company called No-Fear Deodorants. The product was a non-aerosol pump spray which used MPHC. Marshall embarked on a nation-wide campaign to advertise his new deodorant as an alternative to products which used harmful chemicals that could destroy the ozone layer of the atmosphere. Furthermore, he hired Elmore Jones, the well known Phoenix professional basketball super-star to do the TV commercials. After the first year, sales were going very well except for the Southwestern region of the country which was only breaking even.

Result:

In June 1980, two years after going into business, No-Fear Deodorants went bankrupt.

191. In August 1979, aerosol sprays were banned in the United States.

192. MPHC was found to be carcinogenic in November 1979.

193. Elmore Jones retired from professional basketball in September 1972.

194. Marshall did not have absolute authority over the chemical contents of "Bone-Dry."

195. No-Fear was found to be in minor violation of the U.S. labor laws.

196. No-Fear was heavily in debt when Marshall took over the company.

197. In June 1979, a new non-aerosol product called "Un-Deodorant," priced half as much as "No-Fear," appeared on the market.

198. The researcher who invented MPHC retained his original position at the Bone-Dry Anti-Perspirant Company.

199. Marshall had little experience in the anti-perspirant business.

200. A boycott against "No-Fear" was organized in May 1980 since it was found that Marshall had contributed considerable money to the Weathermen Radical Left movement.

IF YOU FINISH BEFORE THE TIME IS UP, GO OVER YOUR WORK FOR THIS SECTION ONLY. DO NOT TURN TO ANY OTHER SECTION OF THE TEST. WHEN THE TIME IS UP, GO ON TO THE NEXT SECTION.

SECTION 8: SENTENCE CORRECTION

Time: 30 minutes

Directions: Each sentence is partly or wholly underlined. In some cases, what is underlined is correct — in other cases, it is incorrect. The five choices that follow each sentence represent various ways of writing the underlined part. Choice A is the same as the original underlining but Choices B, C, D, and E are different. If, in your judgment, the original sentence is better than any of the changed sentences, select Choice A. If another choice produces the only correct sentence, select that other choice (B or C or D or E).

In making your choice, you should observe the **rules of** standard written English. Your choice must fulfill the requirements of correct grammar, diction (word choice), sentence structure, and punctuation.

If a choice changes the meaning of the original sentence, do not make that choice.

201. Such of his novels as was humorous were successful.

   (A) Such of his novels as was humorous were successful.
   (B) Such of his novels as were humorous were successful.
   (C) His novels such as were humorous were successful.
   (D) His novels were successful and humorous.
   (E) Novels such as his humorous ones were successful.

202. Being that the plane was grounded, we stayed over till the next morning so that we could get the first flight out.

   (A) Being that the plane was grounded, we stayed over
   (B) In view of the fact that the plane was grounded, we stayed over
   (C) Since the plane was grounded, we stayed over
   (D) Because the plane was grounded, we stood over
   (E) On account of the plane being grounded, we stayed over

203. He never has and he never will keep his word.

   (A) He never has and he never will
   (B) He has never yet and never will
   (C) He has not ever and he will not
   (D) He never has or will
   (E) He never has kept and he never will

204. The teacher <u>felt badly because she had scolded the bright child</u> who was restless for want of something to do.

   (A) felt badly because she had scolded the bright child
   (B) felt badly why she had scolded the bright child
   (C) felt bad because she had scolded the bright child
   (D) felt bad by scolding the bright child
   (E) had felt badly because she scolded the bright child

205. This book <u>does not describe the struggle of the Blacks to win their voting rights that I bought.</u>

   (A) does not describe the struggle of the Blacks to win their voting rights that I bought
   (B) does not describe the Black struggle to win their voting rights that I bought
   (C) does not, although I bought it, describe the struggle of the Blacks to win their voting rights
   (D) which I bought does not describe the struggle to win for Blacks their voting rights
   (E) that I bought does not describe the struggle of the Blacks to win their voting rights

206. <u>Barbara cannot help but think</u> that she will win a college scholarship.

   (A) Barbara cannot help but think
   (B) Barbara cannot help but to think
   (C) Barbara cannot help not to think
   (D) Barbara can help but think
   (E) Barbara cannot but help thinking

207. In spite of <u>Tom wanting to study,</u> his sister made him wash the dishes.

   (A) Tom wanting to study
   (B) the fact that Tom wanted to study
   (C) Tom's need to study
   (D) Tom's wanting to study
   (E) Tom studying

208. The old sea captain <u>told my wife and me</u> many interesting yarns about his many voyages.

   (A) my wife and me
   (B) me and my wife
   (C) my wife and I
   (D) I and my wife
   (E) my wife along with me

209. A great many students from several universities <u>are planning to, if
the weather is favorable, attend next Saturday's mass rally in Wash-
ington</u>.

    (A) are planning to, if the weather is favorable, attend next Satur-
day's mass rally in Washington

    (B) are planning, if the weather is favorable, to attend next Satur-
day's mass rally in Washington

    (C) are planning to attend, if the weather is favorable, next Satur-
day's mass rally in Washington

    (D) are planning to attend next Saturday's mass rally in Wash-
ington, if the weather is favorable

    (E) are, if the weather is favorable, planning to attend next Satur-
day's mass rally in Washington

210. Jane's body movements are <u>like those of a dancer</u>.

    (A) like those of a dancer

    (B) the same as a dancer

    (C) like a dancer

    (D) a dancer's

    (E) like those of a dancer's

211. This is one restaurant I won't patronize because <u>I was served a fried
egg by the waitress that was rotten</u>.

    (A) I was served a fried egg by the waitress that was rotten

    (B) I was served by the waitress a fried egg that was rotten

    (C) a fried egg was served to me by the waitress that was rotten

    (D) the waitress served me a fried egg that was rotten

    (E) a rotten fried egg was served to me by the waitress

212. Watching the familiar story unfold on the screen, he was glad <u>that
he read the book with such painstaking attention to detail</u>.

    (A) that he read the book with such painstaking attention to detail.

    (B) that he had read the book with such painstaking attention to
detail.

    (C) that he read the book with such attention to particulars.

    (D) that he read the book with such intense effort.

    (E) that he paid so much attention to the plot of the book.

213. If anyone requested tea instead of coffee, <u>it was a simple matter to
serve it to them</u> from the large percolator at the rear of the table.

    (A) it was a simple matter to serve it to them

    (B) it was easy to serve them

    (C) it was a simple matter to serve them

    (D) it was a simple matter to serve it to him

    (E) he could serve himself

214. He bought <u>some bread, butter, cheese and decided</u> not to eat them until the evening.

    (A) some bread, butter, cheese and decided
    (B) some bread, butter, cheese and then decided
    (C) a little bread, butter, cheese and decided
    (D) some bread, butter, cheese, deciding
    (E) some bread, butter, and cheese and decided

215. The things the children liked best were <u>swimming in the river and to watch the horses being groomed by the trainer.</u>

    (A) swimming in the river and to watch the horses being groomed by the trainer.
    (B) swimming in the river and to watch the trainer grooming the horses.
    (C) that they liked to swim in the river and watch the horses being groomed by the trainer.
    (D) swimming in the river and watching the horses being groomed by the trainer.
    (E) to swimming the river and watching the horses being groomed by the trainer.

216. A reward was offered <u>to whoever would return the dog to its owner.</u>

    (A) to whoever would return the dog to its owner.
    (B) to whomever would return the dog to its owner.
    (C) to whosoever would return the dog to its owner.
    (D) to whomsoever would return the dog to its owner.
    (E) to whichever person would return the dog to its owner.

217. <u>Irregardless of the outcome of the battle,</u> neither side will be able to claim a decisive victory.

    (A) Irregardless of the outcome of the battle,
    (B) Irregardless of how the battle ends,
    (C) Regardless of the outcome of the battle,
    (D) Despite the outcome of the battle,
    (E) Irregardless of the battle,

218. One of the finest examples of early Greek sculpture <u>are to be found in the British Museum</u> in London.

    (A) are to be found in the British Museum
    (B) were to be found in the British Museum
    (C) are found in the British Museum
    (D) is to be found in the British Museum
    (E) are in the British Museum

219. We were surprised at him canceling the order without giving any previous indication of his intentions.

   (A) We were surprised at him canceling the order without giving any previous indication of his intentions.

   (B) We were surprised that he canceled the order and didn't tell anyone.

   (C) His canceling the order surprised us all.

   (D) We were surprised at his canceling the order without giving any previous indication of his intentions.

   (E) We were surprised at him canceling the order and not letting anyone know about it.

220. When going for an interview, a high school graduate should be prepared to answer the questions that will be asked of him without hesitation.

   (A) a high school graduate should be prepared to answer the questions that will be asked of him without hesitation.

   (B) a high school graduate should without hesitation be prepared to answer the questions that will be asked of him.

   (C) a high school graduate should be prepared without hesitation to answer the questions that will be asked of him.

   (D) a high school graduate should be prepared to answer without hesitation the questions that will be asked of him.

   (E) a high school graduate should be prepared to answer the questions without hesitation that will be asked of him.

221. This test was as hard, if not harder than, the one I took last week.

   (A) This test was as hard,

   (B) This test was so hard,

   (C) This test was as hard as,

   (D) This test was so hard as,

   (E) This was a test as hard,

222. We took a plane from JFK Airport which carried few passengers.

   (A) We took a plane from JFK Airport which carried few passengers.

   (B) The plane that was taken by us from JFK Airport carries few passengers.

   (C) The plane we took carried few passengers.

   (D) We took a plane which carried few passengers from JFK Airport.

   (E) The plane which we took from JFK Airport carried few passengers.

223. I wanted to and would have gone to the play if I had the money.

   (A) I wanted to and would have gone

   (B) Having wanted to, I would have gone

   (C) I wanted to go and would have gone

   (D) Although I wanted to go and would have gone

   (E) I wanted and would have gone

224. Either I'll go to the store today or tomorrow morning.

   (A) Either I'll go to the store today or tomorrow morning.
   (B) Either I'll go to the store today or I'll go tomorrow morning.
   (C) I'll go to the store today, or if not today, then tomorrow morning.
   (D) I'll go to the store either today or tomorrow morning.
   (E) I'll go either today or tomorrow morning to the store.

225. For a while he had a job after school, which caused his grades to suffer.

   (A) which caused his grades to suffer
   (B) and for this reason his grades were suffering
   (C) and this caused his grades to suffer
   (D) so his grades suffered as a result of this
   (E) this was the reason his grades suffered

226. When a student learns a foreign language, he must not only learn to speak and write it, but understand the culture of those who speak it.

   (A) but understand the culture of those who speak it.
   (B) and he must understand the culture of those who speak it.
   (C) he must understand the culture of those who speak it.
   (D) but must also understand the culture of those who speak it.
   (E) but in addition he must also understand the culture of those who speak it.

227. The paintings of Dali, like many artists, have been both applauded as great masterpieces and dismissed as rubbish.

   (A) like many artists
   (B) like most other artists
   (C) like the paintings of many artists
   (D) like many other paintings
   (E) like those of many other artists

228. Because the sick man laid in bed for several months, he developed pneumonia.

   (A) Because the sick man laid in bed
   (B) Because the sick man had laid in bed
   (C) Because the sick man had lain in bed
   (D) Because the sick man is laying in bed
   (E) Because the sick man lies in bed

229. The pollution bills recently passed by the House are different than those that were vetoed earlier

   (A) different than those
   (B) different from those
   (C) different to those
   (D) different from the earlier ones
   (E) different to the ones

230. <u>Neither you nor I are going to agree</u> with the speaker; sometimes, however, it is a good idea to listen to someone whom one may disagree with.

    (A) Neither you nor I are going to agree
    (B) Neither of us are going to agree
    (C) Neither you nor me is going to agree
    (D) Neither you nor I am going to agree
    (E) Neither I nor you am going to agree

231. <u>After having completed his experiments on cancer,</u> the scientist tried to determine if his findings could be used to help prevent this dreaded disease.

    (A) After having completed his experiments on cancer
    (B) As soon as he completed his experiments on cancer
    (C) Having completed his experiments on cancer
    (D) After the experiments of the scientist on cancer were completed
    (E) When his experiments on cancer are completed

232. The principal, as well as the students and faculty, <u>is trying to affect</u> constructive changes in the school curriculum.

    (A) is trying to affect
    (B) try to affect
    (C) are trying to effect
    (D) is trying to effect
    (E) does try to encourage

233. Because of the recent General Motors strike, <u>less men will be hired in the coming year.</u>

    (A) less men will be hired in the coming year
    (B) not as many men will be hired in the coming year as before
    (C) in the coming year less men will be hired
    (D) few men will be hired in the coming year
    (E) fewer men will be hired in the coming year

234. <u>If the director would have changed</u> some of the dialogue in the script, the scene would have worked better.

    (A) If the director would have changed
    (B) If changes had been made in
    (C) If the director had changed
    (D) Had there been changes made in
    (E) If there would have been changes in

235. <u>Neither Bill nor Jack had their money with them.</u>

    (A) Neither Bill nor Jack had their money with them.
    (B) Neither of the boys had their money with them.
    (C) Neither Bill or Jack had his money with him.
    (D) Neither boy had his money with him.
    (E) Neither Bill nor Jack had his money with him.

236. He is not only chairman of the Ways and Means Committee, but also of the Finance Committee.

(A) He is not only chairman of the Ways and Means Committee, but also of the Finance Committee.

(B) He is the chairman not only of the Ways and Means Committee, but also of the Finance Committee.

(C) He is the chairman of the Ways and Means Committee and the chairman of the Finance Committee.

(D) Not only is he the chairman of the Ways and Means Committee, but also of the Finance Committee.

(E) Both the Finance Committee and the Ways and Means Committee are committees in which he is the chairman.

237. First the student did research in the library, and then his English composition was written.

(A) and then his English composition was written

(B) and then the English composition was written by the student

(C) and following this he then wrote his English composition

(D) and then he wrote his English composition

(E) then he wrote his English composition

238. Two candidates for the U.S. Senate, Buckley and him, made speeches to the group.

(A) Two candidates for the U.S. Senate, Buckley and him, made speeches to the group.

(B) Two candidates for the U.S. Senate, Buckley and he, made speeches to the group.

(C) Buckley and him, two candidates for the U.S. Senate, made speeches to the group.

(D) Speeches to the group were made by Buckley and he, two candidates for the U.S. Senate.

(E) Buckley and he made speeches to the group.

239. A student of American history for many years, Stephen Douglas and his economic policies were thoroughly familiar to him.

(A) A student of American history for many years

(B) After having been a student of American history for many years

(C) He was a student of American history for many years

(D) Being that he was student of American history for many years

(E) Since he was a student of American history for many years

240. Does anyone know <u>to who this book belongs</u>?

    (A) to who this book belongs
    (B) to whom this book belongs to
    (C) to whom this book belongs
    (D) who this book belongs to
    (E) to whom this belongs

IF YOU FINISH BEFORE THE TIME IS UP, GO OVER YOUR WORK FOR THIS
SECTION ONLY. DO NOT TURN TO ANY OTHER SECTION OF THE TEST.
WHEN THE TIME IS UP, THE TEST IS OVER

**NOW THAT YOU HAVE
COMPLETED PRACTICE TEST 5**

1. Turn to the Answer Key on pages
384-385. Do not consider Sections
7 and 8.

2. Count your **correct answers.**

3. Count your **incorrect answers.**

4. Deduct ¼ of the number of incorrect
answers from the number of correct
answers to get a **"raw score"** of
_____.

5. Your **"scaled score"** for this test, according to the Raw Score/Scaled
Score Table on page 88, is _____.

ANSWER KEY FOR PRACTICE TEST 5

Section 1: Reading Comprehension

1. E	6. C	11. A	16. A	21. D
2. B	7. C	12. D	17. B	22. D
3. D	8. E	13. B	18. B	23. E
4. A	9. B	14. A	19. B	24. B
5. E	10. B	15. A	20. A	25. A

Section 2: Math Ability

After each answer, there is a hyphenated number (or numbers) in parentheses. This hyphenated number is keyed to Math Refresher (beginning on page 411). The number *before* the hyphen indicates the Math area of the problem:

$$1 = \text{ARITHMETIC}$$
$$2 = \text{ALGEBRA}$$
$$3 = \text{PLANE GEOMETRY}$$
$$5 = \text{GRAPHS AND CHARTS}$$

The number *after* the hyphen gives you the section (within the Math area) that explains the rule or principle involved in solving the problem.

26. D (5-1)	37. C (1-25)	48. C (1-28)
27. E (1-24)	38. B (1-22, 5-2)	49. D (2-35)
28. D (2-28)	39. A (5-2)	50. E 1-20)
29. C (1-28)	40. B (3-6)	51. E (1-5, 1-28)
30. E (3-7)	41. D (5-3, 1-25)	52. B (3-6)
31. C (5-5, 2-26)	42. A (2-7)	53. E (5-4, 5-5)
32. A (5-5, 2-26)	43. D (5-4, 1-22)	54. C (5-4, 5-5)
33. C (2-37)	44. E (5-4)	55. D (2-22)
34. B (1-25)	45. C (1-22)	
35. B (5-4, 2-34)	46. D (2-10)	
36. D (2-20)	47. D (5-5)	

Section 3: Business Judgment

56. D	61. E	66. C	71. A	76. B
57. A	62. D	67. B	72. C	77. D
58. B	63. A	68. E	73. E	78. D
59. C	64. B	69. E	74. E	79. D
60. C	65. C	70. D	75. C	80. A

ANSWER KEY FOR PRACTICE TEST 5 (continued)

Section 4: Data Sufficiency

81. E	87. E	93. A	99. C	105. A
82. E	88. B	94. D	100. E	106. B
83. C	89. A	95. D	101. A	107. B
84. A	90. E	96. B	102. D	108. E
85. C	91. D	97. D	103. D	109. E
86. C	92. A	98. E	104. B	110. D

Section 5: Grammar and Usage

111. E	116. D	121. C	126. A	131. D
112. A	117. C	122. B	127. C	132. A
113. C	118. C	123. B	128. E	133. C
114. E	119. A	124. A	129. A	134. B
115. B	120. E	125. B	130. D	135. E

Section 6: Business Judgment

136. B	141. B	146. A	151. E	156. E
137. B	142. C	147. E	152. D	157. D
138. C	143. A	148. D	153. D	158. B
139. B	144. B	149. C	154. C	159. D
140. D	145. E	150. C	155. E	160. C

Section 7: Analysis of Explanations

161. C	169. A	177. E	185. C	193. E
162. B	170. C	178. A	186. E	194. C
163. A	171. A	179. C	187. A	195. D
164. D	172. D	180. B	188. D	196. A
165. B	173. E	181. B	189. C	197. B
166. E	174. B	182. E	190. B	198. E
167. B	175. B	183. A	191. D	199. A
168. E	176. C	184. D	192. B	200. B

Section 8: Sentence Correction

201. B	209. D	217. C	225. C	233. E
202. C	210. A	218. D	226. D	234. C
203. E	211. D	219. D	227. E	235. E
204. C	212. B	220. D	228. C	236. B
205. E	213. D	221. C	229. B	237. D
206. A	214. E	222. E	230. D	238. B
207. D	215. D	223. C	231. C	239. E
208. A	216. A	224. D	232. D	240. C

EXPLANATORY ANSWERS FOR PRACTICE TEST 5

Section 1: Reading Comprehension

1. **(E)** See the first paragraph: "From my own Norse textbook back in Iceland ..."

2. **(B)** Read the third paragraph aloud. Note the figurative expressions such as "the crimson of liquid blood," "the blue of your naked steel," "seething din," – and finally, "spears are singing and skulls crack with a thundering sound."

3. **(D)** Throughout the passage the author implies that war is stupid and cruel.

4. **(A)** Although the author does not literally mean the things he says about "mutually executing each other's young men," and marching "us old devils off to die honorably," he really seeks to bring out the inhumaneness of war.

5. **(E)** See paragraph 2: "It is considered ... to contain some of the most beautiful verses."

6. **(C)** See paragraph 7: "The situation has not changed ... still makes good copy."

7. **(C)** The third paragraph states that the metal rubbed off onto their unwashed hands and onto their food.

8. **(E)** Paragraph 8 states that fungi are unable to make their own food.

9. **(B)** A toadstool is a poisonous mushroom. All mushrooms belong to the fungus family. Fungi lack chlorophyll so Choice A is wrong. Fungi can destroy books and potatoes among other things, so Choices C and D are wrong. Mercury (Choice E) is a metallic element.

10. **(B)** Stated in paragraph 7: "Various mercury compounds are widely used to kill many of the world's more than 40,000 different species of fungi." Prior

to this, it was stated that mercury poisoning still menaces us, and the fact that mercury combats fungi is a logical reason.

11. **(A)** Stated in the third from the last paragraph: "In the beginning, few people heeded the scientists' warnings." Only after more tragedies, were people motivated to act.

12. **(D)** See paragraphs 14-17: Originally the farmers would shield their delicate seedlings from fungus attacks by using mercury compounds. It was only after his realizing that fungi were destroying his crops that he applied the mercury; the seeds would then be carried by the wind and eaten by other birds.

13. **(B)** The second paragraph tells about the protest of the German officers against the Hitler plan.

14. **(A)** The third paragraph states: "The actual count (of planes) was about 900."

15. **(A)** The fourth paragraph deals entirely with the miscalculations of the German generals as compared with Hitler's previous correct military judgment.

16. **(A)** The fifth paragraph states that Stalin was aware of the plan through a security leak and did not tell the allies because of the reasons outlined in choices B, C, and D.

17. **(B)** The first paragraph states: "His panzers ... with a negotiated peace."

18. **(B)** A result of the Battle of the Bulge was that after initial losses the Allies finally broke through into Germany. The failure of Hitler's plan is hinted at throughout the passage.

19. **(B)** In the last sentence of the fourth paragraph, the author states that man

"has the arrogance to go searching for life elsewhere in the universe." The reference is obviously to the billions of dollars and tremendous effort devoted to getting a few moon rocks.

20. **(A)** The entire selection deals with the fact that man's efforts have not resulted in a better way of life. An example of this idea is stated in the last sentence of the third paragraph: "He has pumped his foul wastes into the seas and has stared balefully at billions of floating dead fish."

21. **(D)** In the fourth paragraph, the author states that man is "killing off the birds that are far more essential to his own spirit than many of his commodities. By going against nature, he has warred against beauty of line, movement, and sound." Hence, the author feels that there is something far more important than material things to bring about happiness.

22. **(D)** The word "holocaust" comes from the Greek: "holos" = whole and "kaustos" = burnt. A holocaust is wholesale destruction and loss of life, especially by fire.

23. **(E)** In the first paragraph the author's alarming concern is revealed by the statement that men are "using up their planet at a fearsome rate and may soon pass the point where their total habitat can sustain human life. Man's world is slipping away from him." Such alarming concern is reiterated throughout the passage.

24. **(B)** Man is not looking far enough ahead. His projects are interim (temporary) ones. He is not considering his heirs. Will he have any?

25. **(A)** The author is obviously opposed to the "I" and "II" types of projects. For his opposition to "I" see paragraph 3: "Most of what man does ... to make his planet safe for human habitation." His opposition to "II" and his favoring of "III" are expressed clearly throughout paragraph 4.

EXPLANATORY ANSWERS FOR PRACTICE TEST 5 (continued)

Section 2: Math Ability

26. **(D)** The graph shows that 8% of those who enter college eventually enter a doctoral program and 4% of those who enter college earn a doctorate. Thus,

$$\frac{4\%}{8\%} = 50\%$$ of those entering a doctoral program earn a doctorate.

27. **(E)** The graph shows that 19% of college entrants earn a master's degree.

$$19\% \text{ of } 200,000 =$$
$$(.19)(200,000) =$$
$$38,000$$

28. **(D)** We can set up the following proportion:

$$\frac{19}{30} = \frac{x}{1500}$$

Where $x = 1500 \left(\frac{19}{30}\right)$

$$= (50)(19) = 950$$

29. **(C)** 30% of college entrants go to graduate school and 8% of college entrants go on to a doctoral program. The percent of grad students who go on to a doctoral program is

$$\frac{8\%}{30\%} = \frac{4}{15}$$
$$= 26\tfrac{2}{3}\%$$

30. **(E)** Let $s =$ the length of one side of the small squares. Then $s^2 = 900$ so $s = \sqrt{900}$ $= 30$ feet. The number of these 30-foot by 30-foot squares that can fit along the 100-foot side is 3 and the number that can fit along the 200-foot side is 6.

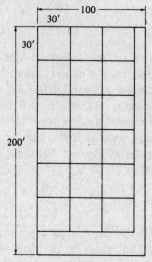

There are 18 squares, each of area 900 square feet. The total area of the squares is $18 \times 900 = 16,200$ square feet. The total area of the plot is $100 \times 200 = 20,000$ square feet. The area which is unused is $20,000 - 16,200 = 3,800$ square feet.

31. **(C)** At 40 m.p.h. stopping distance is 95 feet.

At 20 m.p.h., stopping distance is 25 feet.

Ratio $= \dfrac{95}{25} = \dfrac{19}{5} = 4{:}1$ approximately

32. **(A)** At 60 m.p.h., stopping distance is 212 feet.

At 30 m.p.h., stopping distance is 50 feet.

Ratio $= \dfrac{212}{50} = 4{:}1$ (approx.)

33. **(C)** He mows $\dfrac{1}{t}$ of the lawn per minute.

Hence, in 15 minutes, he can do $\dfrac{15}{t}$ of the lawn.

34. **(B)** Selling price = $80

    Cost = $60

    Profit = 80 − 60 = $20

    % Profit on
    Selling Price = $\frac{20}{80} = \frac{1}{4} = 25\%$

35. **(B)** On the first day John bought 40 marbles, the second day 20 marbles, 70 marbles the third day, and 50 marbles on each of the next two days. To find the average, add up the number of marbles bought and divide by the number of days. John bought a total of 230 marbles in 5 days. 230 ÷ 5 = 46.

36. **(D)** Let m = no. of males on the committee

    $\frac{3}{4}m$ = no. of bachelors

    Thus,

    $$\frac{3}{4}m = 9$$
    $$n = 12$$

    Let x = no. of members of the committee. Then,

    $$\frac{1}{3}x = 12$$
    $$x = 36$$

37. **(C)** 82% = .82. To find 82% of $2340, you must multiply $2340 by .82.

    $$\begin{array}{r} \$2340 \\ \times\ .82 \\ \hline 4680 \\ 18720 \\ \hline \$1918.80 \end{array}$$

38. **(B)** The under-15 group accounted for 20 of the 224 deaths. This is

    $$\frac{20}{224} \times 100\% \text{ or very close to } 9\%$$

39. **(A)** The deaths in the first period were 611; in the second, 1299.
    The rise was 1299 − 611 or 688.

40. **(B)** Each of the pieces removed has an area of 6 × 3 or 18 square inches. Cutting out two such pieces removes 2 × 18 or 36 square inches from the original 186. This leaves 186 − 36 or 150 square inches left.

41. **(D)** One ton equals 2000 pounds. The graph shows that concrete is 30% cement. 30% of 2000 is 2000 × .30 = 600.

42. **(A)** If he buys one dozen for n cents, then his cost per article is $\frac{n}{12}$. His selling price per article is $\frac{n}{9}$.

    His profit is selling price minus cost, or

    $$\frac{n}{9} - \frac{n}{12} = \frac{4n - 3n}{36} = \frac{n}{36} \text{ cents per article}$$

43. **(D)** Increase is 55 − 30 = 25° F.
    Hence,

    $$\frac{25}{30} = \frac{5}{6} = 83\frac{1}{3}\%$$

44. **(E)** The greatest increases occur when the line rises most steeply. This appears to be from 1 to 2 P.M.

45. **(C)** The percentage of its profit that the company reinvests is equal to

    $$\frac{\text{Amount Invested}}{\text{Total Profit}} \times 100\% \text{ which equals}$$

    $$\frac{\$\ 2,000}{\$10,000} \times 100\% \text{ or } 20\%.$$

46. **(D)** The result is $\frac{3(n-3)+3}{3}$ which can be simplified as follows:

    $$\frac{3(n-3)+3}{3} = \frac{3n - 9 + 3}{3}$$

    $$= \frac{3n - 6}{3}$$

    $$= n - 2$$

47. **(D)** Look only at the bar marked oats. The top of the bar is above the horizontal line marked 40 bushels, but below the 50 bushel line. The answer must be between 40 and 50 bushels. 42 bushels is the correct choice.

48. **(C)** The product of two even numbers is even. The product of two odd numbers is odd. The sum of an odd and even number is odd.
Hence, II and III only.

49. **(D)** Suppose that one male is picked. Then any of six females could be picked to complete the committee. The number of different committees must then be equal to six times the number of males. Since there are 5 male volunteers, there are 30 possible committees.

50. **(E)** The auto will use the greatest number of gallons if it runs only 12 miles per gallon.

In this case, it will use

$$\frac{360}{12} = 30 \text{ gallons}$$

51. **(E)** Since all choices for values of p are integers, q must be a multiple of 5, and hence p must be a multiple of 3. Therefore, the only possible value of p is 18.

52. **(B)** Since $KL = \frac{1}{4} KH$, the triangle FKL has the same altitude as the rectangle but its base is $\frac{1}{4}$ that of the rectangle. Hence, the area of the rectangle is

$$A = bh = 80$$

The area of the triangle is

$$
\begin{aligned}
A &= \tfrac{1}{2} \left(\tfrac{1}{4}b\right)(h) \\
&= \tfrac{1}{8} bh \\
&= \tfrac{1}{8} (80) \\
&= 10
\end{aligned}
$$

53. **(E)** The low reading for the final week of May 1970 appears to be about 355.

54. **(C)** From the upper graph, the high reading for the second week in Feb. 1969 was about 565.

55. **(D)** Let x = capacity of tank in gallons. Then

$$\tfrac{1}{4}x + t = \tfrac{5}{8}x$$

Multiplying through by 8,

$$
\begin{aligned}
2x + 8t &= 5x \\
8t &= 3x \\
t &= \tfrac{3}{8}x
\end{aligned}
$$

EXPLANATORY ANSWERS FOR PRACTICE TEST 5 (continued)

Section 3: Business Judgment

56. **(D)** The hypothesis is untested and, though it seems a logical development, it might not be realized. Older workers, for example, might be prepared to forego separation benefits in order to get larger present pay packets.

57. **(A)** The basic goal of the firm is to make greater profits.

58. **(B)** It is the reason that a scheme is required in the first place.

59. **(C)** The safety regulations are secondary to the basic plan, and fit in with management philosophy of maintaining good relations with labor.

60. **(C)** Any difficulties can be troublesome but not insuperable.

61. **(E)** Safety regulation is already in excess of government requirements.

62. **(D)** The response of workers to the new scheme is still uncertain.

63. **(A)** The company is very much concerned about its labor relations and seeks, under any scheme, to maintain good relations.

64. **(B)** Without this, the scheme is admittedly unworkable.

65. **(C)** This is a side issue to the main concern of raising the poor work-force productivity.

66. **(C)** Expanding the plant and product line is not central to the success of the scheme.

67. **(B)** Without capital, the scheme cannot be implemented at all.

68. **(E)** In the decision at hand, the clerical and supervisory staff have no say, and they cannot disrupt the agreement because of their own contract.

69. **(E)** The sales force is not discussed in the passage.

70. **(D)** It is not known whether the new scheme will attract new workers.

71. **(A)** The company image is important to the company.

72. **(C)** This is contributory to the overall low productivity, but is not a major cause of the low productivity.

73. **(E)** The consultants found that the low productivity was attributable to both overmanning and the inability of the older workers to work efficiently with the latest production techniques.

74. **(E)** The first paragraph states that the company was among the most modern in terms of capital stock.

75. **(C)** The overmanning was due to a contract which was based on older production techniques which had required more men for a task than the number of men now required.

76. **(B)** The divisibility of the plant was required so that the extra work effort of each man might lead to a significant increase in output. The greater output, in turn, resulted in higher wages – maximizing the incentive effort.

77. **(D)** This is clearly stated in the text.

78. **(D)** Although some of the other choices might be true, no mention is made of them in the text.

79. **(D)** The poor profit performance has led to a low share valuation on the Stock Exchange. New issues would not raise much of the needed finance.

80. **(A)** Since the value of total plant and machinery per worker is $105,000, for 1000 workers it is $105,000,000, a figure which is over $100,000,000. Thus Choice A is correct. Choice B is incorrect because the total plant and machinery per worker is $105,000 as compared to $110,000 for the industry leader. Choice C is incorrect because the industry-wide average is $93,500 per worker which is less than $105,000 per worker. Choice D is incorrect for the reason that Choice A is correct. Choice E is incorrect for the same reasoning that Choice C is incorrect.

EXPLANATORY ANSWERS FOR PRACTICE TEST 5 (continued)

Section 4: Data Sufficiency

81. **(E)** Statement 1 tells us that W is either 13 or 17. Statement 2 does not tell us which one of those two numbers is W since half of each is $6\frac{1}{2}$ and $8\frac{1}{2}$ respectively.

82. **(E)** Without knowing the original price of the radio it is not possible to answer the question.

83. **(C)** Statement 1 tells us that WX is parallel to ZY, since the alternate interior angles are equal. If XY is also parallel to WZ, then WXYZ is a parallelogram and opposite sides of a parallelogram are equal. But, according to statement 2, WZ is not equal to XY. Therefore, XY cannot be parallel to WZ.

84. **(A)** Since ab and cd are equal in statement 1, if a is greater than c, then d must be greater than b, not less than. Statement 2 is totally unrelated to the size of b and is therefore insufficient to answer the question.

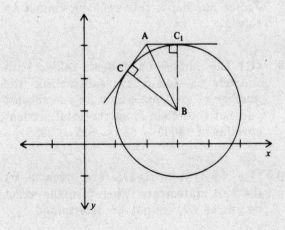

85. **(C)** From statement 1, C lies on the locus of points 2 units away from B which is a circle of radius 2 with B as the center. From statement 2, angle ABC = 90° or a right angle. The two tangents drawn from A to the locus circle are equal and form a right angle with the radius drawn to the point of tangency. Therefore, $BC = BC_1 = 2$. The distance AB can be found by the formula $d = \sqrt{(x_2 - x_1) + (y_2 - y_1)^2}$ where x and are the coordinates of points A and B. Finally, the distance AC can be found by the Pythagorean theorm $AB^2 = AC^2 + BC^2$, and since $AC = AC_1$, the perimeter of triangles ACB and AC_1B are equal and one answer can be found.

86. **(C)** According to statement 1, Figure 3 is a square. According to statement 2, Figure 2 is a square. By congruency, then, Figure 1 is also a square. With the lengths of the sides given in the diagram, we can derive that IM is 10 and JM is 7. Therefore IJ is the difference, 3.

87. **(E)** The total number of students and teachers must be determined in order to answer the question. Since the total number of classes in the school is not given, the answer cannot be determined.

88. **(B)** Since W, X, and Y are all independent variables, statement 1 is insufficient to answer the question. In statement 2, we can divide both sides of the equation by Z. This tells us that the product WXY is 6.

89. **(A)** The right angles in the diagram tell us that $FCEB$ is a rectangle. Thus $CE = FB$. From statement 1, $CE = 4 - 2 = 2$. Therefore, $FB = 2$. In statement 2,, the length of AF tells nothing about the length of FB.

90. **(E)** Since the weight of each book is not constant, the weight of one book cannot be found with the given information.

91. **(D)** Each face of a cube is a square. The height, length, and width of a cube are equal. By the Pythagorean theorem, where s represents the length of an edge,

$$2s^2 = (3 \sqrt{2})^2$$

$$s = 3$$

Thus the volume is $s^3 = 3^3 = 27$. This shows that statement 1 is sufficient. From statement 2, the 12 edges of the cube total 36. The length of one edge is 3. The volume is then 27.

92. **(A)** From statement 1, $NP = MO$ or $MN + NO = NO + OP$. This says that $OP = MN$, or that the radii are congruent. Statement 2 alone is insufficient.

93. **(A)** Dividing each member of the inequality in statement 1 by 2, we find that D is greater than either E or C. According to statement 2, C is less than D, but E may be equal to D. Therefore, statement 2 is inconclusive.

94. **(D)** From statement 1, we can set up the following equation where x is the number of hours needed, $\frac{1}{15}$ is the part of the job Jeff can do in one hour, and $\frac{1}{20}$ is the part of the job Mike can do in one hour.

$$x \left(\frac{1}{15} + \frac{1}{20} \right) = 1 \text{ job}$$

Solving for x gives the answer. Thus, $x = 8\frac{4}{7}$ hours. From statement 2, using only Mike's rate,

$$x \left(\frac{1}{15} \right) = \frac{4}{7} \text{ job}$$

Solving for x, $\quad x = 8\frac{4}{7}$ hours.

95. **(D)** For statement 1, multiply 12.2 by 20 to find how far the car can go with 20 gallons of gas. For statement 2 set up a proportion and solve for x:

$$\frac{45}{54a} = \frac{20}{x}$$

$$x = 244 \text{ miles.}$$

96. **(B)** From statement 2 we find that both e and f are between 0 and 1. Therefore they are both fractions. When a larger fraction is divided by a smaller fraction the quotient will be a number larger than either of them. For example $\dfrac{\frac{1}{2}}{\frac{1}{3}}$ $= \frac{3}{2}$. When two proper fractions are multiplied the product is smaller than either of the factors. For example $\frac{1}{2} \cdot \frac{1}{3} = \frac{1}{6}$. Therefore the quotient is greater than the product.

97. **(D)** For statement 1, the point where the two diagonals of a square meet is the center of the square. A line from E to WV, perpendicular to WV, is one-half the length of a side of the square. Therefore the length of a side is $\sqrt{10}$. Use the distance formula in conjunction with statement 2. Half the distance of the diagonal as measured by EU is $\sqrt{5}$. The diagonal is $2\sqrt{5}$ units long. Use the Pythagorean theorem for a length of a side. $2x^2 = (2\sqrt{5})^2$. The length of a side x is $\sqrt{10}$.

98. **(E)** Without knowing how many classes James has daily, this problem cannot be solved.

99. **(C)** The number of students taking both subjects is found by subtracting the number of students who take one subject and not the other from the total student enrollment. $4000 - 640 - 525 = 2835$.

100. **(E)** No definite figures are given us by the two statements. Therefore the exact length of DF cannot be determined.

101. **(A)** There are 16 pints in 2 gallons. From statement 1, if 3 apples are needed to make 1 pint of apple juice then 48 apples are needed to make 16 pints of apple juice. Statement 2 is not relevant since it is quite possible that different numbers of apples and oranges are needed to make a quantity of apple or orange juice.

102. **(D)** The height of the rectangle is equal to the diameter of the circles. The base is equal to twice the diameter. *OP* is the length of one diameter since it is the combination of two equal radii of the congruent circles. Therefore the dimensions of the rectangle are 4 and 8, and the area is 32. From statement 2 we are also given the length of a diameter. We can use the same method to solve the problem.

103. **(D)** From statement 1 we learn that the building is 75 feet, or 25 yards long. Since there are 100 square yards of area enclosed, two of the sides of fencing must have a length of 100 divided by 25, or 4 yards (12 feet). The other side, facing the building, must have a length equal to the length of the building (75 feet) since opposite sides of a rectangle are equal. Therefore 99 feet of fencing is needed altogether. From statement 2 we find out directly that one of the sides alongside the building is 4 yards long. Then we can solve as above.

104. **(B)** Without knowing when the voyage ended, statement 1 is useless. However from statement 2 we can find the solution. Harold is rowing upstream at 5 miles per hour, but the current is pushing him back at a rate of 3 miles per hour. Therefore he is actually moving upstream at a rate of 2 miles per hour. He will need 5 hours to row the 10 miles upstream.

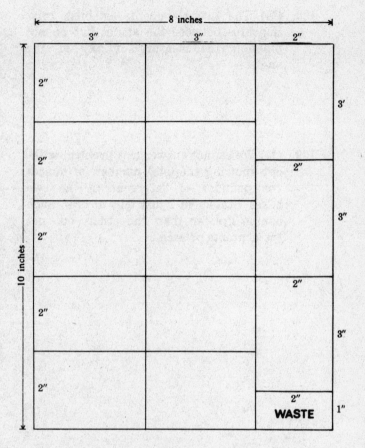

105. **(A)** 13 photographs can be printed on the paper. (See the above solution diagram.) Some of the photographic paper will be waste.

106. **(B)** Statement 1 is insufficient because twice any integer or twice any integer plus $\frac{1}{2}$ will yield an integer. ($2 \times 2 = 4$; $2 \times 2\frac{1}{2} = 5$). However when one adds an integer to an integer, an integer is always the result. ($2 + 2 \times 4$). Therefore statement 2 is sufficient to answer the question.

107. **(B)** Statement 1 reveals nothing relating to the problem since the question does not ask for cost. However using statement 2 we can find the answer. The engine will use 80 pounds of fuel per hour. In $2\frac{1}{2}$ hours it will use 200 pounds of fuel.

108. **(E)** The two statements establish relationships between the angles but do not pinpoint the measure of any of the angles.

109. **(E)** We cannot answer this problem without knowing the total number of ounces (or pounds) of detergent in the two boxes. Statement 1 just tells us how much one is greater than the other, but not the contents of each.

110. **(D)** From (1) we know that 6000 words are typed in 60 minutes. Set up a proportion:

$$\frac{60}{6000} = \frac{20}{x}$$

x is the number of words typed in 20 minutes.

Solve for x.

$$x = 2000.$$

Therefore she can finish the 1750-word report in the given time. Set up a similar proportion to solve the problem from the information in statement 2.

EXPLANATORY ANSWERS FOR PRACTICE TEST 5 (continued)

Section 5: Grammar and Usage

111. **(E)** All underlined parts are correct.

112. **(A)** "If any signer of the Constitution *were* to return to life . . ."
The verb in the "if clause" of a present contrary-to-fact conditional statement must have a past subjunctive form *(were)*.

113. **(C)** "The dean of the college . . . *is* planning . . ."
The subject of the sentence *(dean)* is singular. Therefore, the verb must be singular *(is planning)*.

114. **(E)** All underlined parts are correct.

115. **(B)** "Now that the stress . . . *is* over . . ."
The subject of the subordinate clause is singular *(stress)*. Accordingly, the verb of the clause must be singular *(is* – not *are)*. Incidentally, *examinations* and *interviews* are not subjects – they are objects of the preposition *of*.

116. **(D)** ". . . of more machines and *fewer* people."
We use *fewer* for persons and things that may be counted. We use *less* for bulk or mass.

117. **(C)** ". . . than *that of most* of the other countries of the world."
We must have parallellism so that the word *standard* in the main clause of the sentence acts as an antecedent for the pronoun *that* in the subordinate clause. As the original sentence reads, the American standard of living is still higher than the countries themselves.

118. **(C)** ". . . a long line of flags . . . *was* seen . . ."
The subject of the sentence is singular *(line)*. Therefore, the verb must be singular *(was seen)*.

119. **(A)** "*Because of* the failure . . ."
Never start a sentence with *Due to*.

120. **(E)** All underlined parts are correct.

121. **(C)** "After waiting in line for three hours, the tickets had, *much to our disgust*, been sold out when we reached the window."
Avoid squinting constructions – that is, modifiers that are so placed that the reader cannot tell whether they are modifying the words immediately preceding the construction, or the words immediately following the construction.

122. **(B)** ". . . resulted in our *guests'* packing up . . ."
A noun or pronoun immediately preceding a gerund is in the possessive case. Note that the noun *guests* followed by an apostrophe is possessive.

123. **(B)** "Sharp advances . . . *are* . . ."
Since the subject of the sentence is plural *(advances)*, the verb must be plural *(are)*.

124. **(A)** "An acquaintance with the memoirs . . . *enables* us . . ."
Since the subject of the sentence is singular *(acquaintance)*, the verb must be singular *(enables)*.

125. **(B)** ". . . to *whoever* . . . had a strong sense . . ."
The subject of the subordinate clause is *whoever* and it takes a nominative form *(whoever* – not *whomever)* since it is a subject. Incidentally, the expression *he believed* is parenthetical so that it has no grammatical relationship with the rest of the sentence.

126. **(A)** "If he *had lain* . . ."
The verb in the "if clause" of a past contrary-to-fact conditional statement must take the *had lain* form – not the *would have lain* form.

127. **(C)** ". . . John Crowe Ransom, *whom* you must know as an outstanding American critic."
The direct object of the subordinate clause—or of any clause or sentence—must be in the objective case and, accordingly, must take the objective form *(whom*—not *who).*

128. **(E)** All underlined parts are correct.

129. **(A)** "There is no objection to *his* joining . . .
We have here a pronoun that is acting as the subject of the gerund *joining.* As a subject of the gerund, the pronoun must be in the possessive case *(his).*

130. **(D)** ". . . of Chinese children parading *in colorful uniforms* up Mott Street."
In the original sentence, *in colorful uniforms* was a misplaced modifier.

131. **(D)** "The reason . . . is *that* . . ."
We must say *the reason is that*—not *the reason is because.*

132. **(A)** "The farmer felt *bad* about . . ."
After the copulative verb *(felt),* the word referring to the subject is a predicate adjective *(bad)*—not an adverb *(badly).*

133. **(C)** ". . . *because* a Pan American Boeing 707 had crashed . . . "
The word group *on account of* has the function of a preposition. We need a subordinate conjunction *(because)* here in order to introduce the clause.

134. **(B)** " . . . *raided* the mansion . . . "
The past tense *(raided)* — not the present perfect tense *(has raided)* — is necessary because the sentence has a specific past time reference *(last night).*

135. **(E)** All underlined parts are correct.

EXPLANATORY ANSWER FOR PRACTICE TEST 5 (continued)

Section 6: Business Judgment

136. **(B)** This is a major factor, since poor labor relations are said to have lost the company its reputation for reliability. This clearly affects profitability, which is an objective.

137. **(B)** This is a major factor. Charles Whitworth knows he is too inexperienced to run the firm, and he needs to be assured that at least some of the management will remain with the Company during and after the move.

138. **(C)** The passage says that the loss of local markets was of little importance owing to improvements in transportation.

139. **(B)** This is clearly a major factor since labor costs are said to be the largest single element in costs.

140. **(D)** This is a major assumption. Charles Whitworth seems not to question the completion of the road.

141. **(B)** Electric power accounts for 27% of production costs.

142. **(C)** This is a minor factor. Since transportation has improved, it is a matter of little importance.

143. **(A)** Living near the coast is an objective to the decision maker.

144. **(B)** A major factor, since rent is said to be a large part of costs at present.

145. **(E)** There is no intimation that a city center location has any advantages for the Whitworth Company. It is an unimportant issue.

146. **(A)** Risk reduction is an objective. Charles "considered it vital that this uncertainty be lessened."

147. **(E)** There is nowhere any mention of the price of soft water. It therefore does not appear to be a factor in the decision, and is an unimportant issue.

148. **(D)** This is a major assumption. Charles Whitworth rejects the possibility of city action before making his decision.

149. **(C)** This is a minor factor. The major factor is the availability of cheap labor. Having the labor trained by the State is an extra bonus, but not a major issue.

150. **(C)** This is a minor factor. The only concern here is that credit may be less easily obtainable, but there is no intimation that the firm has problems in this area.

151. **(E)** This is an unimportant issue, and is not mentioned.

152. **(D)** This is a major assumption. If Newport wages rise markedly, then the advantage of Newport in this respect would be negated.

153. **(D)** Coal is an input in the manufacture of steel. The exhaustion of the coal has brought about the need to relocate near some other raw material source.

154. **(C)** Wages are stated to be the largest single item of costs, and therefore must be at least as great and probably slightly more than the 27% accounted for by electric power. The two together add up to 54% at minimum. Rent and city taxes take up a further 22%, leaving a maximum residual of (100—76)% or 24%.

155. **(E)** All five of these factors are mentioned as former advantages of the company's original site in Brookdale.

156. **(E)** From the information in the passage we can establish the following data:

	Brookdale	Palmer	Newport
Rent cost for 30 sq. ft.	$1200	$ 600	$ 750
Cost of 200 k.w. hours	2000	1600	1000
Total Cost	$3200	$2200	$1750

From the above we can see that the cost in Newport is $450 less than in Palmer (I). The cost in Palmer is $1000 less than in Brookdale (V), and the cost in Newport is $1450 less than in Brookdale (IV). The other two options are not true.

157. **(D)** From the text, we know that skilled labor is no longer plentiful, labor unions are strong and strikes are not rare. There is no mention of a retraining program at Brookdale.

158. **(B)** Transportation costs are, we are told, not important — nor is the price of steel. Charles Whitworth is, however, concerned about the price of power. No mention is made of mortgage payments nor the cost of employee health insurance, and we assume, therefore, they are not important.

159. **(D)** We know that the present owner, Charles Whitworth, is new to the firm, and has little management experience. Far from being reluctant to break ties with Brookdale, he is eager to do so, and since he is newly involved in the firm, he cannot be blamed for the prior poor profit record. No mention is made of skill in either engineering or industrial location.

160. **(C)** Newport is not the best on all counts, as payroll tax is highest in Newport. For the same reason, Brookdale is not the worst in all respects. Palmer, however, is better than Brookdale on every consideration, except in the matter of payroll tax. The latter is the same for both locations. Choice C is therefore true. Newport is better than Palmer in two respects, and worse in two, with one tied. Therefore, Choices D and E are false.

EXPLANATORY ANSWER FOR PRACTICE TEST 5 (continued)

Section 7: Analysis of Explanations

161. **(C)** This statement is implied in the fact situation. Recall that the firm decided to hire someone between thirty and forty years of age. Nevertheless, the twenty-four-year-old George Jasmine was given the job. The correct answer is thus Choice C.

162. **(B)** Here we are presented with a possible explanation of the result. Conceivably, George was offered the position because of his father's influence on the senior partners. The correct answer is Choice B.

163. **(A)** The correct answer is Choice A, as the statement contradicts the fact situation. Max Jasmine's death was "sudden and unexpected," and thus he could not have died of old age.

164. **(D)** From this statement it is evident that George Jasmine possessed none of the qualities desired by the senior partners. The statement thus strengthens the contention that he was given the job because the partners were loyal to Max. The correct answer must be Choice D.

165. **(B)** Here the correct answer is clearly Choice B, since the fact that George possessed excellent credentials is a possible explanation for his being made partner.

166. **(E)** This statement is clearly irrelevant to the fact situation and to the result. We are not concerned with how Max died, nor with what became of the body. The correct answer is Choice E.

167. **(B)** This statement provides an adequate explanation of the result as it is conceivable that George was hired because the other two candidates were eliminated from the competition. The correct answer is therefore Choice B.

168. **(E)** We are not concerned with any aspects of Max Jasmine's career with the law firm. What is of importance is only that he died, thus leaving a position empty. The statement is irrelevant and the correct answer is Choice E.

169. **(A)** We are presented here with a statement that contradicts the fact situation. Recall that the partners interviewed two candidates whom they felt met the requirements. One of these requirements was to be between thirty and forty. Thus, it is impossible that one of the candidates was forty-two, and the correct answer is Choice A.

170. **(C)** This statement is implied in the fact situation. The partners had attempted to fill the position "for some time," and selected candidates only "after much deliberation." The job was thus not hastily filled, and the correct answer is Choice C.

171. **(A)** This statement clearly contradicts the fact situation. Browning cut his staff by 50% to ten employees. This leaves us with an original workforce of twenty, not eighteen. The correct answer is therefore Choice A.

172. **(D)** This statement weakens the contention that Browning decided to sell his business because of pressure exerted by the Pollution Control Board. He is given five years to comply with the new law, yet he sells his business within three months of the law's enactment. The correct answer is thus Choice D.

173. **(E)** The fact that the foundry also worked with copper has absolutely no bearing on the problem posed in the fact situation, nor on the result. It is irrelevant, and the correct answer is thus Choice E.

174. **(B)** This statement provides a possible explanation of the result. Despite the problems that the foundry faced, U.S. Steel was willing to purchase it at a fair price. Conceivably, this is what influenced Browning to sell. The correct answer is thus Choice B.

175. **(B)** The answer to this question is Choice B as the statement provides a possible explanation of the result. The demand for costly alterations, made by the Pollution Control Board may have influenced Browning to sell his business.

176. **(C)** Recall that Gordon attributed the problem to rising labor and material costs, as well as to lack of contracts. Yet his recommendations concerned only labor and contracts, not materials. The statement is implied in the passage, and the answer is Choice C.

177. **(E)** What is relevant is only how the Pollution Control Act affects Browning. We are not concerned with the uniqueness of the act. This statement is irrelevant and the correct answer is Choice E.

178. **(A)** This statement clearly contradicts the fact situation. Recall that most of Browning's years with the foundry were profitable. Only a few of the years were unsuccessful. The correct answer is therefore Choice A.

179. **(C)** Recall that Browning was employing twenty people, or ten more than was determined necessary by Bently Gordon. This statement is thus implied in the fact situation, and the correct answer is Choice C.

180. **(B)** In this statement we are presented with a possible explanation of the result. Browning had been operating the foundry for thirty years, and in recent years he was confronted with a number of problems. Quite conceivably, he decided that he had worked hard and was now entitled to retire. The correct answer is therefore Choice B.

181. **(B)** This statement presents a possible explanation of the result. It is quite conceivable that Morse was offered the job because of his good looks.

182. **(E)** This statement is irrelevant to the fact situation. We are concerned with the doctor only with regard to his operating on Morse. The doctor's personal problems are of little consequence here.

183. **(A)** The answer to this question is clearly Choice A. Recall that Bordelli was undertaking his "newest motion picture extravaganza." This contradicts the notion that it was his first major motion picture.

184. **(D)** This statement weakens the contention that Morse was offered the role because of his operation. Recall that he was competing with Betz. Now that Betz is out of the running, Morse might have been hired even if he had never undergone surgery.

185. **(C)** This statement is implied in the fact situation which states that Morse feared that the financial backers would choose to hire Betz, even though Bordelli might have favored Morse.

186. **(E)** This statement is totally foreign to the fact situation. The acting career of Bordelli's wife is irrelevant. The correct answer is thus clearly E.

187. **(A)** This statement clearly contradicts the fact situation. Recall that Morse was a "close friend" of Bordelli. Bordelli would therefore do nothing to "spite him."

188. **(D)** This statement supports the contention that Morse was offered the role because of his operation. Recall that the financial backers wished to introduce someone new.

189. **(C)** This statement is implied by the fact situation. Morse has been in the acting business a long time, while Betz is a relative newcomer. Nevertheless, both in-

dividuals are competing on equal ground for the same position.

190. **(B)** This statement presents a possible explanation of the result. Morse's acting abilities have not suffered as a result of surgery, and he is able to give the backers exactly what they want — a new face. The correct answer is thus B.

191. **(D)** Since "No-Fear" is a non-aerosol spray, the banning of aerosols should have increased sales. This statement weakens an adequate explanation for the company's failing.

192. **(B)** The finding of MPHC, one of "No Fear's" ingredients, to be carcinogenic could definitely have forced "No-Fear" off the market. This is an adequate explanation for the company's failure.

193. **(E)** The product still did well in its first years of existence, six years after Jones's retirement. So, apparently Jones was still well-known in 1978, the inaugural year. The date of his retirement is irrelevant.

194. **(C)** This is implied in the situation since it is stated that Marshall's colleagues disagreed with him and that he formed a new company.

195. **(D)** This would strengthen the explanation that the company was mismanaged overall. Minor violations would not in and of themselves force a company to go bankrupt.

196. **(A)** This is clearly contradicted by the situation since it stated that No-Fear Deodorants was a new company and, therefore, could not have had any accumulated debts.

197. **(B)** The price difference is enough to have led to the result. This could have caused "No-Fear" to go out of business.

198. **(E)** The fact that the researcher kept his job is irrelevant. All that was important was his invention of MPHC, which belonged to Marshall.

199. **(A)** The passage clearly states that Marshall was a respected executive at "Bone-Dry". He had to have adequate experience in the anti-perspirant field, so the statement contradicts the facts.

200. **(B)** A boycott is a sufficient explanation for the company's bankruptcy.

EXPLANATORY ANSWERS FOR PRACTICE TEST 5 (continued)

Section 8: Sentence Correction

201. **(B)** Choice A is incorrect because the plural verb ("were") is necessary. The reason for the plural verb is that the subject "as" acts as a relative pronoun whose antecedent is the plural noun "novels." Choice B is correct. Choice C is awkward. Choice D changes the meaning of the original sentence – so does Choice E.

202. **(C)** Choice A is incorrect – never start a sentence with "being that." Choice B is too wordy. Choice C is correct. Choice D is incorrect because we "stayed" – not "stood." Choice E is incorrect because "on account of" may never be used as a subordinate conjunction.

203. **(E)** Avoid improper ellipsis. Choices A, B, C, and D are incorrect for this reason. Choice E is correct. The word "kept" must be included since the second part of the sentence uses another form of the verb ("keep").

204. **(C)** Choice A is incorrect because the copulative verb "felt" takes a predicate adjective ("bad") — not an adverb ("badly"). Choice B is incorrect for the same reason. Moreover, we don't say "felt bad why." Choice C is correct. Choice D is incorrect because the verbal phrase "by scolding" is awkward in this context. Choice E is incorrect because of the use of "badly" and because the past perfect form of the verb ("had felt") is wrong in this time sequence.

205. **(E)** Choices A, B, and C are incorrect because the part of the sentence that deals with the buying of the book is in the wrong position. Choice D is incorrect because the meaning of the original sentence has been changed. According to this choice, others besides Blacks have been struggling. Choice E is correct.

206. **(A)** Choice A is correct. The other choices are unidiomatic.

207. **(D)** Choice A is incorrect because the possessive form of the noun ("Tom's") must be used to modify the gerund ("wanting"). Choice B is too wordy. Choice C changes the meaning of the original sentence. Choice D is correct. Choice E is incorrect for the same reason that Choice A is incorrect. Also, Choice E changes the meaning of the original sentence.

208. **(A)** Choice A is correct. Choice B is incorrect because "wife" should precede "me." Choice C is incorrect because the object form "me" (not the nominative form "I") should be used as the indirect object. Choice D is incorrect for the reasons given above for Choices B and C. Choice E is too roundabout.

209. **(D)** Choices A, B, C, and E are incorrect because of the misplacement of the subordinate clause ("if the weather is favorable"). Choice D is correct.

210. **(A)** Choices B and C are incorrect because of improper ellipsis. The words "those of" are necessary in these choices. Choice D is incorrect because the "body movements" are not "a dancer's." The possessive use of "dancer's" is incorrect in Choice E.

211. **(D)** The clause "that was rotten" is misplaced in Choices A, B, and C. Choice D is correct. Choice E is incorrect because the passive use of the verb is not as effective as the active use, in this context.

212. **(B)** Choice A uses wrong tense sequence. Since the reading of the book took place before the watching of the picture, the reading should be expressed in the past perfect tense, which shows action prior to the simple past tense. Choice B corrects the error with the use of the past perfect tense, "had read," instead of the past tense, "read." Choices C, D, and E do not correct the mistake, and Choice E in addition changes the meaning.

213. **(D)** Choices A is wrong because the word "them," being plural, cannot properly take the singular antecedent, "anyone." Choices B and C do not correct this error. Choice D corrects it by substituting "him" for "them." Choice E, while correcting the error, changes the meaning of the sentence.

214. **(E)** Choice A contains a "false series," meaning that the word "and" connects the three words in the series – bread, butter, cheese – with a wholly different clause, instead of with a similar fourth word. The series, therefore, needs its own "and" to complete it. Only Choice E furnishes this additional "and."

215. **(D)** Choice A violates the principle of parallel structure. If the first thing the children liked was "swimming" (a gerund), then the second thing they liked should be, not "to watch" (an infinitive), but "watching" (the gerund). Choice B does not improve the sentence. Choice C repeats the beginning of the sentence with the repetitious words "that they liked." Choice D is correct. Choice E simply reverses the gerund and the infinitive without correcting the error.

216. **(A)** Choice A is correct. Choice B wrongly substitutes the objective case "whomever" for the nominative "whoever," the subject of the verb "would return." Choice C uses the the form "whosoever," which while correct, is legalistic and not needed here. Choice D again uses the objective case. Choice E is awkward.

217. **(C)** There is no such word as "irregardless." Therefore Choices A, B, and E cannot be right. "Despite" in Choice D does not give the same meaning as "regardless." Choice C is the correct one.

218. **(D)** Choice A wrongly uses the plural verb "are to be found" after the subject of the sentence, "One." (The plural word "examples" is not the subject of the prepositional phrase "of the finest examples.") Choice B simply uses the same plural verb in the past tense instead of the present. Choice C does not correct

the error. Choice D does, by using the singular verb "is." Choice E is incorrect because of the use of the plural verb "are."

219. **(D)** Choice A fails to use the possessive case of the pronoun that governs a gerund. Choice B changes the meaning of the sentence. Choice C corrects the error but omits a necessary part of the meaning. Choice D is correct. Choice E retains the error of Choice A and, in addition, distorts the meaning of the sentence.

220. **(D)** Choices A, B, C, and E should place the adverbial phrase "without hesitation" after the infinitive it modifies, "to answer." Since the meaning is to "answer without hesitation," the phrase "without hesitation" should be placed right after the infinitive "to answer." This is done in Choice D.

221. **(C)** Choices A, B, and E suffer from incomplete comparison. The conjunction (a second "as") is required to complete the comparison: "This test was as hard... *as* the one I took last week." Choice D is incorrect because the conjunction "so" should be used in a negative construction: "This test was *not* so hard..." Choice C is correct because it completes the comparison.

222. **(E)** Choice A is incorrect because the plane and *not* JFK Airport carried few passengers. Choice B is incorrect because there is a lack of agreement in the verb tenses. Also the active voice should be used. See correct Choice E. Choice C does not include a reference to JFK Airport which is necessary to the meaning of the original sentence. Choice D is ambiguous. E is correct.

223. **(C)** Choice A is incorrect because the word "go" is needed after the word "to" (otherwise the sentence means "I wanted to gone"). Choice B also requires the word "go" after "to". Choice C is correct. In Choice D, the word "although" changes the original sentence to a fragment. Choice E requires the word "to go" after "wanted."

224. **(D)** Choices A and B are incorrect because "Either" should be placed before "today." Choice C is too wordy. Choice D is correct. Choice E is awkward.

225. **(C)** Choice A is incorrect because "which" should be used to refer to a noun or pronoun and *not* a clause, as it is used here. In Choice B, there is a lack of agreement in the verb tenses. Choice C is correct. Choice D is awkward. Choice E is a complete sentence, making the original a run-on sentence.

226. **(D)** Choice A is incorrect because the expression "not only" must be accompanied by "but also." B is also incorrect for this reason. C is a complete sentence, making the original a run-on sentence. Choice D is correct. In Choice E, the words "in addition to" are unnecessary.

227. **(E)** Choices A and B are incorrect because there is improper ellipsis of "like those." Choice C is too wordy. Choice D changes the meaning of the original sentence. Choice E is correct.

228. **(C)** Choice A is incorrect because "laid" is the past tense of the verb "to lay," and the verb required is "to lie." Choice B is incorrect because "had laid" is the past perfect tense of the verb "to lay." Choice C is correct. Choice D is incorrect because it is in the present tense and it also is a form of the verb "to lay." Choice E is in the present tense – it should be in the past perfect tense.

229. **(B)** In making a comparison, the word "different" is followed by the word "from" rather than by the word "than." For this reason, Choices A, C, and E are incorrect. Choice D uses the word "from" correctly but the choice includes the unnecessary repetition of "earlier." Choice B is, of course, correct.

230. **(D)** Choices A and E are incorrect because in a "neither-nor" construction, the verb agrees with the noun or pronoun that follows "nor." Choice B is incorrect because "neither" must be followed by a singular verb. Choice C is incorrect because the nominative form of the pronoun ("Neither you nor <u>I</u>") should be used, since "I" is a subject in the sentence. Choice D is correct.

231. **(C)** Choice A is incorrect because the verb should be the past perfect form ("had completed") to indicate an action that took place prior to "tried." Choice B changes the meaning of the original sentence. Choice C is correct. Choice D is awkward. Choice E changes the tense of the original sentence.

232. **(D)** Choice A uses the word "affect" incorrectly. It means "to influence" and in the original sentence it is incorrectly used to mean "to bring about." Choice B also uses the word "affect" incorrectly and in addition the verb needed is "is trying" as it refers to the principal *only*. Choice C is incorrect because the singular verb is required. Choice D is correct. Choice E is not correct because it changes the meaning of the original sentence.

233. **(E)** Choice A is incorrect because the word "fewer" should be used instead of "less" because "less" denotes amount or degree and "fewer" denotes number. Choice B is not correct because "as before" is superfluous. Choice C is incorrect for the same reason as Choice A (above). Choice D changes the meaning of the original sentence. Choice E is correct.

234. **(C)** Choice A is incorrect because in this past contrary to fact situation, the verb of the "if" clause should be expressed in the past perfect tense ("had changed"). Choice B does not include a reference to the director, which is necessary to the meaning of the original sentence. Choice C is correct. Choice D is incorrect because it does not include a reference to the director, which, as indicated previously, is necessary to the meaning of the original sentence. Choice E omits a reference to the director and also uses "would have been" incorrectly.

235. **(E)** Choices A and B are incorrect because when two singular antecedents are joined by "nor," they should be referred to by a singular pronoun. Also, Choice B does not include the names of the boys, which were included in the original sentence. Choice C uses the word "or" incorrectly, rather than "nor." Choice D does not include the names of the boys and so it changes the meaning of the original sentence. Choice E is correct.

236. **(B)** Choice A is incorrect because the words "not only . . . but also" should be placed immediately before the parallel terms, which are "of the Ways and Means Committee" and "of the Finance Committee." Choice B is correct. Choice C is too wordy. Choice D is incorrect because it does not place the words "not only . . . but also" directly before the parallel terms. Choice E is awkward.

237. **(D)** Choices A and B are incorrect because they both contain an unnecessary shift from active to passive voice, resulting in awkwardness. Choice C is too wordy. Choice D is correct. Choice E is a complete sentence making the original a run-on sentence.

238. **(B)** Choice A is incorrect because "Buckley" and "him" are in apposition with "candidates," the subject of the sentence. Since the subject is nominative, the appositive must also be nominative; hence "he" should be used instead of "him." Choice B is correct. Choice C uses "him" incorrectly for "he." The use of the passive voice ("were made") makes Choice D unnecessarily indirect. Choice E omits "two candidates for the U.S. Senate" which is necessary to the meaning of the sentence.

239. **(E)** Choices A and B are incorrect because they are both misplaced as modifiers — it is not clear who is the student. Choice C is a complete sentence making the original sentence a run-on sentence. Choice D is incorrect because "being that" is poor English. Choice E is correct.

240. **(C)** Choice A is not correct because the word "who" is incorrectly used; as the object of the preposition, the word "whom" is used. In Choice B, the second "to" is redundant. Choice C is correct. Choice D uses the word "who" instead of "whom." Choice E does not include a reference to the book, which is in the original sentence.

Part Two

GMAT Math Refresher

The pages immediately following will help you to review for every type of Math question which appears on the actual test. These are the areas covered in this study section:

ARITHMETIC
ALGEBRA
PLANE GEOMETRY
GRAPHS & CHARTS

Every single Math question which you encountered in the preceding 5 GMAT Practice Tests has been keyed to the Math Review Section which follows.

GMAT MATH REFRESHER

Arithmetic

(including Fractions, Decimals, Percentage, Exponents and Roots, Whole Numbers)

FRACTIONS

1–1   A fraction indicates a division, or a part of a number. Since fractions are numbers, they can be added, subtracted, multiplied, and divided. The numerator of a fraction tells how many parts we have. The denominator tells the total number of parts there are. Thus, in $3/4$, the numerator is 3, the denominator is 4, and the fraction means 3 divided by 4, or 3 parts out of 4.

> Since a fraction is a division, and division by zero is undefined, the denominator of a fraction cannot be zero. If the numerator is zero (and the denominator is not zero), then the fraction equals zero.

When working with fractions, an important rule to remember is:

> The value of a fraction is unchanged when the numerator and denominator are multiplied by the same quantity.

For example:

$$\frac{5}{9} = \frac{5 \times 3}{9 \times 3} = \frac{15}{27}$$

$$\frac{4}{8} = \frac{4 \times \frac{1}{4}}{8 \times \frac{1}{4}} = \frac{1}{2}$$

A number like $5\frac{1}{3}$ is called a mixed number. It means $5 + \frac{1}{3}$.

1–2   <u>To write a fraction as a mixed number:</u>

1) If the denominator is larger than the numerator, leave the fraction as it is.
2) If the denominator is smaller than the numerator, divide the numerator by the denominator. The whole number of the mixed number is the quotient. The numerator in the mixed number is the remainder, and the denominator is the same as in the original fraction.

For example: Write $19/7$ as a mixed number.
$19 \div 7 = 2$, remainder 5. The mixed number is $2\frac{5}{7}$.

1–3   <u>To write a mixed number as a fraction:</u>

1) The numerator is the whole number times the denominator, plus the old numerator.
2) The denominator is the old denominator.

For example: Express $5\frac{1}{3}$ as a fraction.

$$\text{numerator: } 5 \times 3 + 1 = 16$$
$$\text{denominator: } 3 \qquad \text{Therefore, } 5\frac{1}{3} = \frac{16}{3}$$

1–4   <u>To reduce a fraction to lowest terms:</u>

1) Divide both numerator and denominator by whole numbers which divide into both (numerator and denominator) evenly.
2) If there are no whole numbers which divide both numerator and denominator evenly, the fraction is in lowest terms.

For example: Reduce $\frac{30}{12}$ to lowest terms.

$$\frac{30}{12} = \frac{10}{4} \quad \text{(dividing numerator and denominator by 3)}$$

$$\frac{10}{4} = \frac{5}{2} \quad \text{(dividing numerator and denominator by 2)}$$

Now $\frac{5}{2}$ is in lowest terms.

Or, we could have divided the numerator and denominator by 6 right away to get $\frac{5}{2}$.

1–5   <u>To multiply fractions:</u>

1) Multiply the numerators to get the numerator of the product.
2) Multiply the denominators to get the denominator of the product.

For example: $\dfrac{3}{5} \times \dfrac{2}{7} = \dfrac{6}{35}$

Another example: Multiply $\dfrac{2}{9}$ by 4.

To do this, we represent 4 as $\dfrac{4}{1}$. Then $\dfrac{2}{9} \times 4 = \dfrac{2}{9} \times \dfrac{4}{1} = \dfrac{8}{9}$.

<u>To multiply fractions by cancellation:</u>

A short cut in multiplying is to reduce to lowest terms while multiplying. This is called cancelling.

For example: Multiply $\dfrac{3}{14} \times \dfrac{49}{6}$.

The 3 in the numerator and the 6 in the denominator can both be divided by 3.

We are left with $\dfrac{1}{14} \times \dfrac{49}{2}$. Now the 49 and the 14 can both be divided by 7.

This leaves $\frac{1}{2} \times \frac{7}{2}$. Therefore $\frac{3}{14} \times \frac{49}{6} = \frac{1}{2} \times \frac{7}{2} = \frac{7}{4}$. Cancelling can take place only between numerators and denominators. Two numbers in the numerator cannot be cancelled with each other. Two numbers in the denominator cannot be cancelled with each other.

> The word "of" is sometimes used in problems instead of "times". For example: $\frac{1}{3}$ of $\frac{3}{10}$ means $\frac{1}{3} \times \frac{3}{10}$ or $\frac{1}{10}$.

1–6 The reciprocal of a fraction:

The reciprocal of a fraction is a fraction with numerator and denominator interchanged.

For example: The reciprocal of $\frac{2}{3}$ is $\frac{3}{2}$. Since $7 = \frac{7}{1}$, the reciprocal of 7 is $\frac{1}{7}$.

To divide fractions:

To divide one fraction by another, multiply the first fraction by the reciprocal of the divisor.

For example: Divide $\frac{2}{3}$ by $\frac{1}{4}$. $\frac{2}{3} \div \frac{1}{4} = \frac{2}{3} \times \frac{4}{1} = \frac{8}{3}$.

Or, divide $\frac{5}{7}$ by 7. $\frac{5}{7} \div \frac{7}{1} = \frac{5}{7} \times \frac{1}{7} = \frac{5}{49}$.

1–7 To change a fraction to an equal fraction with a different denominator:

First, decide what denominator you want. Then, find the new numerator. To do this, multiply the original fraction by the new denominator.

For example: Write $\frac{4}{5}$ as a fraction with 15 as denominator.

$$\frac{4}{5} = \frac{\left(\frac{4}{5} \times 15\right)}{15} = \frac{12}{15}$$

since $\frac{4}{5} \times 15 = 12$.

Another example: How many twelfths are there in $\frac{4}{5}$?

We must write $\frac{4}{5}$ as a fraction with 12 as the denominator. The numerator is $\frac{4}{5} \times 12$ or $\frac{48}{5} = 9^3/_5$. There are $9^3/_5$ twelfths in $\frac{4}{5}$.

1–8 To add fractions:

1) If the denominators are the same, simply add the numerators, and leave the denominator alone.

For example: $\frac{2}{5} + \frac{1}{5} = \frac{3}{5}$.

2) If the denominators are different, we must find a common denominator. One common denominator is the product of the different denominators. Then express both fractions with the common denominator as the denominator. Then just add the numerators.

For example: Add $\frac{3}{5} + \frac{1}{7}$.

The common denominator is 5×7 or 35.

$$\frac{3}{5} = \frac{\left(\frac{3}{5} \times 35\right)}{35} = \frac{21}{35}. \quad \frac{1}{7} = \frac{\left(\frac{1}{7} \times 35\right)}{35} = \frac{5}{35}. \quad \frac{21}{35} + \frac{5}{35} = \frac{26}{35}.$$

Therefore $\frac{3}{5} + \frac{1}{7} = \frac{26}{35}$.

The least common denominator:

You do not have to use the product of the denominators as the common denominator. Sometimes there is a smaller common denominator. The least common denominator is the smallest number that can be divided by both denominators evenly.

For example: Add $\frac{2}{7} + \frac{1}{14}$.

The least common denominator is 14. $\quad \frac{2}{7} = \frac{\left(\frac{2}{7} \times 14\right)}{14} = \frac{4}{14}.$

Therefore, $\frac{2}{7} + \frac{1}{14} = \frac{4}{14} + \frac{1}{14} = \frac{5}{14}.$

Another example is: If Mary bought $\frac{5}{3}$ yd. of blue cloth, $\frac{2}{9}$ yd. of green cloth, and $\frac{8}{3}$ yd. of yellow cloth, how many yards did she buy in all?
We must add $\frac{5}{3} + \frac{2}{9} + \frac{8}{3}$. First, $\frac{5}{3} + \frac{8}{3} = \frac{13}{3}$. Then add $\frac{13}{3} + \frac{2}{9}$. The least common

denominator is 9. $\quad \frac{13}{3} = \frac{\left(\frac{13}{3} \times 9\right)}{9} = \frac{39}{9}. \quad \frac{39}{9} + \frac{2}{9} = \frac{41}{9}.$
Therefore $\frac{5}{3} + \frac{2}{9} + \frac{8}{3} = \frac{41}{9}$. Mary bought $\frac{41}{9}$ or $4\frac{5}{9}$ yds. of cloth.

1–9 ### To subtract fractions:

1) If the denominators are the same, subtract numerators and keep the denominators the same.

For example: $\frac{5}{7} - \frac{3}{7} = \frac{2}{7}.$

2) If the denominators are different, express both fractions with a common denominator, and then subtract numerators.

For example: Find $\frac{2}{3} - \frac{1}{6}.$

The least common denominator is 6. $\frac{2}{3} = \frac{\left(\frac{2}{3} \times 6\right)}{6} = \frac{4}{6}$. Then, $\frac{2}{3} - \frac{1}{6} = \frac{4}{6} - \frac{1}{6} = \frac{3}{6} = \frac{1}{2}$.

Another example: One-third less than 5 is?

We must find $5 - \frac{1}{3}$. The common denominator is 3, since 5 means $\frac{5}{1}$.

$\frac{\frac{5}{1} \times 3}{3} = \frac{15}{3}$. Then, $5 - \frac{1}{3} = \frac{15}{3} - \frac{1}{3} = \frac{14}{3} = 4\frac{2}{3}$.

1-10   Complex fractions:

A complex fraction is a fraction whose numerator or denominator is itself a fraction.

For example: $\frac{2/3}{5/7}$ is a complex fraction. A complex fraction may be simplified by division. Thus, $\frac{2/3}{5/7} = \frac{2}{3} \div \frac{5}{7} = \frac{2}{3} \times \frac{7}{5} = \frac{14}{15}$.

1-11   To add, subtract, multiply or divide mixed numbers, or mixed numbers and fractions:

First change all mixed numbers to fractions, and then use the rules for operating with fractions.

For example: Multiply $3\frac{1}{3} \times \frac{1}{10}$.

$3\frac{1}{3} = \frac{10}{3}$, so $3\frac{1}{3} \times \frac{1}{10} = \frac{10}{3} \times \frac{1}{10} = \frac{1}{3}$.

> In doing problems with fractions on a multiple-choice test, remember that you must obtain the answer in the right form. For example, if the choices given are mixed numbers, then you must convert your answer to a mixed number; if the choices are in lowest terms, you must reduce your answer to lowest terms.

DECIMALS

1-12   A decimal fraction is a fraction whose denominator is a power of 10 — that is, the denominator is 10, 100, 1000, etc.

For example: $\frac{313}{1000}$ is a decimal fraction. It can also be written .313; the first digit after the decimal point stands for tenths, the second digit stands for hundredths, and the third stands for thousandths, etc. Thus, $.313 = \frac{3}{10} + \frac{1}{100} +$ $\frac{3}{1000}$ or $\frac{313}{1000}$. Also .007 means $\frac{7}{1000}$ or $\frac{0}{10} + \frac{0}{100} + \frac{7}{1000}$. A number of the form 17.36 means $17 + .36$ or $17^{36}/_{100}$.

> **Adding zeros on the *right* side of a decimal fraction does not change the value of the decimal fraction.**

Thus, $.3 = .30$, since the first decimal means $\frac{3}{10}$ and the second means $\frac{30}{100}$.

1–13   To multiply a decimal by a power of 10:

Move the decimal point to the right, one place for each zero in the power of 10.

For example: What is 100×32.812?
Since 100 has two zeros, we must move the decimal point two places to the right: $100 \times 32.812 = 3281.2$.

Another example: Find 1000×37.68.
We can write $37.68 = 37.680$, and now we can move the decimal point three places to the right. $1000 \times 37.680 = 37680$.

To divide a decimal by a power of 10:

We must move the decimal place to the left, one place for each zero in the power of 10.

For example: What is $17.23 \div 100$?
Moving the decimal point two places to the left, we get $17.23 \div 100 = .1723$.

Another example: What is $11.4 \div 10000$?
Before we move the decimal point four places to the left, we write $11.4 = 0011.4$; now $0011.4 \div 10{,}000 = .00114$.

1–14   To convert a decimal to a fraction:

1) The numerator of the fraction is found by multiplying the decimal by the power of 10 required to make the decimal a whole number.
2) The denominator of the fraction is the power of 10 you multiplied by.

For example: Change .812 to a fraction.
We must multiply .812 by 1000 to make it a whole number. Therefore $.812 = \frac{(.812 \times 1000)}{1000}$ or $\frac{812}{1000}$. This could be reduced if required.

1–15   <u>To add decimal numbers:</u>

1) Align the numbers so that the tenths are written under tenths, the hundredths are written under hundredths, etc.
2) The decimal point goes right under the decimal point in the numbers being added. Then, add as you add whole numbers.

For example: Add 10.9, 15.73, and 22.001.
Write the sum like this:

$$
\begin{array}{r}
10.9 \\
15.73 \\
\underline{22.001} \\
48.631
\end{array}
$$

1–16   <u>To subtract decimal numbers:</u>

1) If one number has more decimal places than the other, add zeros at the right end so that there are the same number of decimal places in the two numbers.
2) Align the numbers, tenths under tenths, etc. Put the decimal point **under** the decimal point in the numbers being subtracted. Subtract as with whole numbers.

For example: What is $17.19 - 8.4$?
First write 8.4 as 8.40 and then subtract:

$$
\begin{array}{r}
17.19 \\
- \ 8.40 \\
\hline
8.79
\end{array}.
$$

Another example: If one store sells a shirt for $10 and another sells it for $3.35 less, how much does it cost in the cheaper store?
We must subtract $3.35 from $10, so write $10 as $10.00 and then subtract:

$$
\begin{array}{r}
\$10.00 \\
- \ 3.35 \\
\hline
\$\ 6.65
\end{array}
$$

1–17   <u>To multiply two decimal numbers:</u>

1) Just multiply the numbers as if they were whole numbers.
2) The number of decimal places in the answer is the sum of the number of decimal places in the factors.

For example: What is 3.1×2.7?
There will be two decimal places in the answer:

$$
\begin{array}{r}
3.1 \\
\times 2.7 \\
\hline
217 \\
\underline{62} \\
8.37
\end{array}
$$

Another example: Multiply .75 by 3.2.
There will be three decimal places in the answer:

$$
\begin{array}{r}
.75 \\
\times 3.2 \\
\hline
150 \\
225 \\
\hline
2.400
\end{array}
$$

1-18   To divide decimal fractions:

1) Multiply the divisor by the power of 10 required to make it a whole number.
2) Multiply the number being divided by the same power of 10.
3) The decimal point in the quotient is right above the decimal point in the number being divided.
4) Add zeros at the end of the number being divided to express the remainder as a decimal.

For example: What is $51 \div 1.2$?
To make 1.2 a whole number, we multiply by 10. We must multiply 51 by 10 also. We now divide $510 \div 12$. We add one zero after the decimal point.

$$
\begin{array}{r}
42.5 \\
12\overline{)510.0} \\
48 \\
\hline
30 \\
24 \\
\hline
60
\end{array}
$$

Therefore, $51 \div 1.2 = 42.5$.

Note: Sometimes the remainder cannot be expressed as a decimal no matter how many zeros are added after the number being divided. In this case, the remainder is usually expressed as a fraction.

1-19   To convert a fraction to a decimal:

1) Write the numerator with a decimal point and zeros after it.
2) Divide the numerator by the denominator.

For example: Write $\frac{2}{125}$ as a decimal.
We write 2 as 2.000 and then divide:

$$
\begin{array}{r}
.016 \\
125\overline{)2.000} \\
1\,25 \\
\hline
750 \\
750
\end{array}
$$

Therefore $\frac{2}{125} = .016$

> Problems with decimals will not usually involve messy arithmetic. The important point is to keep track of where the decimal point belongs.

1-20   To do problems with fractions and decimals, it is usually best to convert the decimals to fractions.

For example: If a boy ran .3 miles one day and $\frac{1}{3}$ mile the next, how many miles did he run in all?

To do this, express .3 as $\frac{3}{10}$ and then add: $\frac{1}{3} + \frac{3}{10} = \frac{19}{30}$.

PERCENTAGE

1–21   Percent is another method of describing parts of a whole; other ways of doing so are fractions and decimals. In a fraction, the denominator can be any number, and it is sometimes hard to compare fractions such as $\frac{1}{286}$ and $\frac{3}{597}$. Percents are like fractions whose denominator is always 100; thus, percents describe parts of a hundred or the number of hundredths.

Suppose a student does 80 problems correctly out of 100 problems in an exam. There are several ways to describe the part of the whole exam he has done correctly: $\frac{80}{100}$ (fraction) or .80 (decimal) or simply 80 hundredths. The word "hundredths" is replaced by the symbol "%" when we use percents. The part of the exam the student has correct is 80%, read "80 percent". Note that $1 = \frac{100}{100} = 100\%$. 100% of a number equals the entire number.

1–22   Since percents, fractions, and decimals are equivalent in describing parts of a whole, it is possible to convert a percent into a decimal and a fraction, and a decimal or fraction into a percent. It is convenient to do so because in doing calculations involving percents, it is not so easy to work with percents directly. Normally, one changes percents to either fractions or decimals since they are easier to work with.

1) To change decimals into percents, the rule is to multiply the decimal by 100 (move the decimal point 2 places to the right) and then add the sign "%" at the end.

For example: Change .365 into a percent.
Multiply .365 by 100, .365 × 100 = 36.5
Therefore, .365 = 36.5%

2) To change a fraction into a percent, there are two methods:
   a) Change the fraction into an equal fraction whose denominator is 100. Then the percent is the numerator with the sign "%" at the end.

   For example: Change $\frac{4}{25}$ into a percent.
   Change $\frac{4}{25}$ into an equal fraction with 100 as the denominator.

   $$\frac{4}{25} = \frac{16}{100}$$

   Therefore, $\frac{4}{25} = 16\%$

   b) First change the fraction into a decimal by dividing the denominator into the numerator. Then change the decimal into a percent.

For example: Change $^4/_{25}$ into a percent.
First change $^4/_{25}$ into a decimal.

$$\frac{4}{25} = 4 \div 25 = .16$$

Then change .16 into a percent.

$$.16 \times 100 = 16 \qquad .16 = 16\%$$

Therefore, $^4/_{25} = .16 = 16\%$.

3) To change a percent into a decimal, remove the percent sign and divide the number by 100.
For example: Change 25% into a decimal.
Remove the percent sign in 25% to get 25. Then divide 25 by 100.
$25 \div 100 = .25$
Therefore, $25\% = .25$

4) To change a percent into a fraction, remove the percent sign and form a fraction using the remaining number as the numerator and 100 as the denominator. Reduce the fraction if necessary.

For example: Change 25% into a fraction.
Remove the percent sign in 25% to get 25. Then form the fraction with 25 as the numerator and 100 as the denominator, or the fraction $^{25}/_{100}$. $^{25}/_{100}$ reduces to $^1/_4$. Therefore, $25\% = ^1/_4$.

1–23   The following table is a list of common percents and their equivalent fractions and decimals.

Percent	Fraction	Decimal
100%	1	1.0
50%	$^1/_2$	.5
25%	$^1/_4$	.25
75%	$^3/_4$	.75
80%	$^4/_5$	.8
60%	$^3/_5$	.6
40%	$^2/_5$	.4
20%	$^1/_5$	.2
10%	$^1/_{10}$	.1
5%	$^1/_{20}$	.05
$12^1/_2\%$	$^1/_8$	.125
$87^1/_2\%$	$^7/_8$	.875
$33^1/_3\%$	$^1/_3$	.333 . . .*
$66^2/_3\%$	$^2/_3$	.666 . . .*
$16^2/_3\%$	$^1/_6$	.1666 . . .*

*Note: These are called repeating decimals and will never "come out even." When these occur, use fractions instead of decimals to solve problems.

1–24   The two most common types of percent problems are interest problems and discount problems. To solve these problems, first change the rate (if the rate is given, it is usually given in percent) from a percent to either a decimal or a fraction, and then substitute into the formulas.

A. For simple interest problems, the formula used to solve the problems is

$$\text{Interest} = \text{Rate} \times \text{Principal} \times \text{Time}$$

For example: Mr Jones has $1400 in the bank. If the interest rate is 5%, how much money does he have in the bank after 1 year?

The total amount he has in the bank after 1 year is the money he had originally plus the interest.

$$\text{Principal} = \$1400$$
$$\text{Rate} = 5\%$$
$$\text{Time} = 1 \text{ year}$$

First, change 5% to a decimal.

$$5\% = 5 \div 100 = .05$$

Write down the formula for interest.

$$\text{Interest} = \text{Rate} \times \text{Principal} \times \text{Time}$$
$$= .05 \times \$1400 \times 1$$
$$= \$70$$

The amount of money he has after 1 year is $1400 + $70 = $1470.

B. For the discount problems, the formula is

$$\text{Amount of Discount} = \text{Rate of Discount} \times \text{Original Price}$$

For example: The original price of a painting is $40. If the discount price is $36, find the rate of discount.

The amount of discount is the original price minus the discount price.
Amount of Discount = $40 − $36 = $4
Original Price = $40
Write down the formula for discount problems.
Amount of discount = Rate of Discount × Original Price
$$\$4 = \text{Rate of Discount} \times \$40$$
Rate of Discount = $4 ÷ $40 = .1
Since the rate is normally expressed in percent, change .1 to a percent.
$$.1 \times 100 = 10$$
$$.1 = 10\%$$
Therefore, the rate of discount is 10%.

1–25   In general, problems involving percent fall into 3 categories. Consider the following statement:

$$15 \text{ is } 50\% \text{ of } 30$$

Whenever any two of the numbers given above are known, the third one can be found. The 3 types of problems involving percent are then to find one of the 3 numbers. The possible problems relating to the statement above are:

1) What is 50% of 30?

To find the answer, change 50% to either a fraction or a decimal, and then multiply by 30..

$$50\% = \frac{1}{2} = .5$$
$$\frac{1}{2} \times 30 = 15 \qquad .5 \times 30 = 15$$

Both give the same answer.

2) 15 is what percent of 30?

To find the answer, either divide 15 by 30 to give a decimal or form the fraction with 15 as the numerator and 30 as the denominator. Then change either to a percent.

$$15 \div 30 = .5 \qquad \qquad \frac{15}{30} = \frac{1}{2}$$
$$.5 = 50\% \qquad \qquad \frac{1}{2} = 50\%$$

3) 15 is 50% of what number?

To find the answer, first change 50% to either a fraction or decimal, and then divide 15 by that number.
$$50\% = \frac{1}{2} = .5$$
$$15 \div \frac{1}{2} = 15 \times 2 = 30 \qquad 15 \div .5 = 30$$

To do a problem involving percent, it is really a question of figuring out which of the 3 types of percent problems it is. Once you know the correct type, you just follow the rules to find the answer.

For example: John weighs 165 pounds. If Jack weighs 10% less than John, how much does Jack weigh?

To find out Jack's weight, we must first find out how much is Jack lighter than John in pounds. Since we know that John weighs 165 pounds and Jack weighs 10% less than that, we are involved with a type 1 problem.

What is 10% of 165?

$$10\% = .1$$

Multiply .1 by 165, $.1 \times 165 = 16.5$
So, Jack weighs 16.5 pounds less than John.

$$165 - 16.5 = 148.5$$

Jack weighs 148.5 pounds.

EXPONENTS AND ROOTS

1–26   An exponent tells how many times a number is to be used as a factor. For example, in the expression 4^3, the exponent 3 means that we are to multiply $4 \times 4 \times 4$. The expression 5^4 means $5 \times 5 \times 5 \times 5$. If the exponent is zero, the value of the expression is always 1. Thus, $3^0 = 10^0 = 1$. If the exponent is 1, the value of the expression is the number whose exponent is 1. Thus, $3^1 = 3$, and $7^1 = 7$.

Problems with exponents can be done by remembering that exponents just count factors. For example: Evaluate $3^4 \times 3^3$. Since 3^4 means use 3 as a factor four times, and 3^3 means use 3 as a factor three times, and since we then multiply the results, we are using 3 as a factor $3 + 4$ or 7 times. Therefore $3^4 \times 3^3 = 3^7$. Similarly, $4^5 \div 4^2 = 4^3$, because we are dividing out two of the five factors of 4, leaving three factors of 4, or 4^3.

A negative exponent indicates the reciprocal of a positive exponent. Thus, $5^{-2} = \dfrac{1}{5^2}$.

1–27   The square of a number is the number multiplied by itself. For example, $4^2 = 4 \times 4 = 16$. The square root of a given number is a number whose square is the original number. Thus, the square root of 16, written $\sqrt{16}$ is 4 since $4 \times 4 = 16$. (The $\sqrt{}$ symbol always means a positive number.)

> The key relationship in simplifying square roots is: The square root of a product is the product of the square roots.

To simplify a square root, try to find a factor of the number under the square root sign that is a perfect square (4, 9, 16, 25, etc.). If such a factor can be found, then we can simplify.

For example: $\sqrt{32} = \sqrt{16 \times 2} = \sqrt{16} \times \sqrt{2} = 4\sqrt{2}$; this cannot be simplified further.

Similarly the sum $\sqrt{3} + \sqrt{2}$ cannot be simplified. We can add expressions with square roots only if the numbers inside the square root sign are the same.

For example: Add $\sqrt{50} + \sqrt{2}$. First, $\sqrt{50} = \sqrt{25 \times 2} = \sqrt{25} \times \sqrt{2} = 5\sqrt{2}$. Then, $\sqrt{50} + \sqrt{2} = 5\sqrt{2} + \sqrt{2} = 6\sqrt{2}$.

Similarly, the cube of a number is the number multiplied by itself 3 times. For example, since $8 = (2)(2)(2)$, 8 is the cube of 2. A cube root of a given number is a number whose cube is the given number. Thus, 2 is a cube root of 8, written $\sqrt[3]{8} = 2$.

WHOLE NUMBERS

1–28   The whole numbers are 0, 1, 2, 3, 4, and so on. The whole numbers have some special definitions and properties. In this section, the word "number" refers only to whole numbers.

1) A number is *divisible* by another number if the second number divides into the first number without any remainder. For example: 10 is divisible by 5.

2) A number that is divisible by 2 is called an *even* number. Examples of even numbers are 0, 2, 4, 6, and 8.

3) A number that is not even is an *odd* number. Examples of odd numbers are 1, 3, 5, 7, and 9.

4) *Consecutive* means following in the natural order. For example: 15, 16, 17, and 18 are consecutive whole numbers. 2, 4, and 6 are consecutive even numbers. 11, 13, and 15 are consecutive odd numbers.

> **Note:**
> (a) Consecutive numbers differ by 1, consecutive even numbers differ by 2, and consecutive odd numbers differ by 2.
> (b) In the whole numbers, the even numbers and odd numbers alternate. In other words, an even number is followed by an odd number and an odd number is followed by an even number.

5) A number is a *multiple* of another number if it is divisible by the second number. For example: 10 is a multiple of 5, and 10 is a multiple of 2.

6) A number is a *factor* of another number if the second number is divisible by the first number. For example: 2 is a factor of 10, 5 is a factor of 10, and 1 and 10 are also factors of 10.

> **Note:** Any number is always a multiple of itself and 1. 1 and the number itself are always factors of that number.

7) A *composite* number is any number that has more than 2 factors. Examples of composite numbers are 10 and 12. 10 has 4 factors (1, 2, 5, and 10) and 12 has 6 factors (1, 2, 3, 4, 6, and 12).

8) A *prime* number is any number that has exactly 2 different factors, itself and 1. The first 10 prime numbers are 2, 3, 5, 7, 11, 13, 17, 19, 23, and 29.

> **Note:**
> (a) 2 is the only even prime number. Every other even number has at least 3 factors: 1, 2, and itself.
> (b) 1 is neither a prime number nor a composite number since it has only one factor: 1.

9) If a factor of a number is a prime number, it is a *prime factor*. For example: Of the factors of 10, the prime factors are 2 and 5.

10) To factor is to express the number as the product of its factors, excluding 1 and itself. For example: To factor 10, write 10 as (2)(5) In this case the factors 2 and 5 are prime factors; so 10 is factored into prime factors.

To factor a number into prime factors:

First factor out the smallest prime factor and then factor out the next smallest prime factor and so on. Continue to factor out the prime factors until it is not possible to factor any further (until all the factors are prime factors).

For example: Factor 200 into prime factors.

First factor the 2's out of 200.

$$200 = (2)(100)$$
$$= (2)(2)(50)$$
$$= (2)(2)(2)(25)$$

The next smallest factor is 5.

$$200 = (2)(2)(2)(5)(5)$$

Since all the factors are prime numbers, 200 cannot be factored any further.

1–29   To find out whether or not a number is prime:

See whether the number has any factor other than itself and 1; if it does not have any, then it is a prime. To find the factors of a number, the following divisibility tests will be helpful:

Division tips:

1) A number is divisible by 2 if its last digit is even.

   For example: 342 is divisible by 2 since the last digit, 2, is even. 356,771 is not divisible by 2 since its last digit, 1, is odd.

2) A number is divisible by 3 if the sum of its digits is divisible by 3.

   For example: 528 is divisible by 3 since $5 + 2 + 8 = 15$ which is divisible by 3.   721 is not divisible by 3 since $7 + 2 + 1 = 10$ which is not divisible by 3.

3) A number is divisible by 4 if the number formed by the last two digits is divisible by 4.

   For example: 987,528 is divisible by 4 since the number formed by the last 2 digits, 28, is divisible by 4.   926 is not divisible by 4 since 26 is not divisible by 4.

4) A number is divisible by 5 if its last digit is either 0 or 5.

   For example: 340 is divisible by 5 since the last digit is 0.   344 is not divisible by 5 since the last digit is 4.

5) A number is divisible by 6 if it is divisible by both 2 and 3.

   For example: 546 is divisible by 6 since it is divisible by 2 (its last digit is even) and by 3 ($5 + 4 + 6 = 15$ which is divisible by 3).   521 is not divisible by 6 since it is not divisible by 2.

6) A number is divisible by 8 if the number formed by the last 3 digits of the number is divisible by 8.

For example: 5064 is divisible by 8 since 64 is divisible by 8.   5121 is not divisible by 8 since 121 is not divisible by 8.

7) A number is divisible by 9 if the sum of its digits is divisible by 9.

For example: 1782 is divisible by 9 since $1 + 7 + 8 + 2 = 18$ which is divisible by 9.   782 is not divisible by 9 since $7 + 8 + 2 = 17$ which is not divisible by 9.

Algebra

*(including Signed Numbers, Algebraic Expressions,
Factoring, Equations, Ratio and Proportion, Rate and Work,
Averages, Combinations, Inequalities)*

SIGNED NUMBERS

2–1   When a larger positive number is subtracted from a smaller positive number, the result is a negative number. For example, $5 - 10 = -5$, read "minus 5." A signed number is a number with a plus or minus sign associated with it. In dealing with signed numbers, if the sign is omitted, it is understood to be plus. Thus $+10 = 10$.

2–2   To add two signed numbers:

1) If the numbers have the same sign, add them as if they were unsigned numbers, and then use the sign they both had. For example, $(+3) + (+4) = +7$. Or, $(-2) + (-4) = -6$.
2) If the numbers have a different sign, subtract them as if they were unsigned numbers. If you subtract a smaller number from a larger one, the result is positive. For example, $(-2) + (+5) = 5 - 2 = +3$. If you subtract a larger number from a smaller one, the result is negative. For example, $(+3) + (-6) = 3 - 6 = -3$.

Another example: Find $(+1) + (-2) + (+3) + (-4) + (+5)$.
We add all the numbers with the same sign. $(+1) + (+3) + (+5) = +9$. $(-2) + (-4) = -6$. We now have to add $(+9) + (-6) = 9 - 6 = +3$.

To subtract two signed numbers:

Just change the sign of the number being subtracted and then add.

For example: $(-3) - (+6) = (-3) + (-6) = -9$.
Or, $(-5) - (-3) = (-5) + (+3) = 3 - 5 = -2$.

2–3   To multiply two signed numbers:

1) The sign of the answer is given by the following rule: If the numbers have the same sign, the product is positive. If the numbers have different signs, the product is negative.
2) Then just multiply the numbers as if they were unsigned.

For example: Since $3 \times 5 = 15$, we have $(+3) \times (+5) = +15$, $(+3) \times (-5) = -15$, $(-3) \times (+5) = -15$, and $(-3) \times (-5) = +15$.

2–4   To divide two signed numbers:

1) Find the sign of the quotient just as in the rule for multiplication.
2) Then just divide the numbers as if they were unsigned numbers.

For example: $(+25) \div (-5) = -5$, but $(-25) \div (-5) = +5$.

The rules for division of signed numbers stipulate that a fraction is positive if its numerator and denominator have the same sign, and a fraction is negative if its numerator and denominator have different signs.

Thus, $\dfrac{-1}{+2} = \dfrac{+1}{-2} = -\dfrac{1}{2}$, but $\dfrac{-1}{-2} = +\dfrac{1}{2}$.

2–5 <u>To multiply or divide strings of numbers:</u>

1) Multiply and divide as if the numbers were unsigned.
2) The sign of the result is positive if there is an even number of minus signs. The sign is negative if there is an odd number of minus signs.

For example: What is $(-2)^5$?

Since the exponent is odd, there is an odd number of minus signs in the product, and the sign of $(-2)^5$ is $-$. Since $2^5 = 32$, $(-2)^5 = -32$.

ALGEBRAIC EXPRESSIONS

2–6   If we want to express arithmetical rules, or geometrical facts, or everyday formulas in general terms, we use algebra. In algebraic expressions we use letters to represent numbers. (Algebraic expressions can contain both letters and numbers.) To indicate that the area of a rectangle is its base multiplied by its height, we write $A = bh$. The "A" stands for the area, the "b" stands for the length of the base, and the "h" stands for the height. When two letters are written together without a symbol between them (or with a dot between them), they are to be multiplied. Thus $2x$ means 2 times x, and $7b^2$ means 7 times b squared or 7 times b times b. If we wanted to express the fact that, in general, the order in which numbers are added does not matter, we could write $x + y = y + x$.

Since algebraic expressions represent numbers, we can add, subtract, multiply, and divide them.

2–7   <u>To add and subtract algebraic expressions:</u>

The addition and subtraction of algebraic expressions is possible only if the letters in the expressions are the same, and have the same exponents. (Expressions like these are called "like terms," and adding and subtracting them is called "combining like terms.") Thus $2x + x = 3x$, and $y^2 - 3y^2 = -2y^2$, but $3x + 2y^2$ cannot be simplified. Note: in an expression like $2y^3$, the 2 is called a coefficient and combining like terms involves adding coefficients.

The important rule to remember in adding and subtracting algebraic expressions is the rule for removing parentheses: If the sign before the parentheses is +, just remove the parentheses. If the sign before the parentheses is −, change the sign of every expression inside the parentheses and then remove the parentheses.

For example: Simplify $x - (-x + 1)$.
Remove the parentheses in $x - (-x + 1)$. We change the $-x$ to $+x$, and the $+1$ to -1, and then write $x - (-x + 1) = x + x - 1 = 2x - 1$.

Another example: Simplify $(x + 2y) - (x - 3y)$.
We remove the first parentheses, but before we can remove the second parentheses we must change signs: x becomes $-x$, and $-3y$ becomes $+3y$. Now, $(x + 2y) - (x - 3y) = x + 2y - x + 3y = +5y$.

2-8   To add algebraic expressions which are fractions:

Proceed just as in adding regular fractions. The product of the different denominators is a common denominator.

For example: Add $\dfrac{2}{x} + \dfrac{3}{y}$.

The common denominator is xy. $\dfrac{2}{x} = \dfrac{2y}{xy}$, and $\dfrac{3}{y} = \dfrac{3x}{xy}$.

Therefore, $\dfrac{2}{x} + \dfrac{3}{y} = \dfrac{2y}{xy} + \dfrac{3x}{xy} = \dfrac{2y + 3x}{xy}$

2-9   To multiply simple algebraic expressions:

Do the numerical and letter multiplication separately, and then multiply the results.

For example: Multiply 2x by $3x^2$.
First, $2 \times 3 = 6$, and then $x^2 \cdot x = x^3$. Altogether $(2x)(3x^2) = 6x^3$.

> The key in multiplying algebraic expressions is the distributive law. In general, it says $a(b + c) = ab + ac$. Also $a(b - c) = ab - ac$.

For example: Multiply $(x + 2)(x + 3)$.
First, $(x + 2)(x + 3) = (x + 2)x + (x + 2)3$ by the distributive law. Using the distributive law again, $(x + 2)x = x^2 + 2x$, and $(x + 2)3 = 3x + 6$. Altogether, $(x + 2)(x + 3) = x^2 + 2x + 3x + 6 = x^2 + 5x + 6$.

Another example: Multiply $(2y + 1)(y - 5)$.
We use the distributive law to get

$$
\begin{aligned}
(2y + 1)(y - 5) &= (2y + 1)y - (2y + 1)5 \\
&= 2y^2 + y - (10y + 5) \\
&= 2y^2 + y - 10y - 5 \\
&= 2y^2 - 9y - 5
\end{aligned}
$$

2-10   To divide simple algebraic expressions:

Divide the numerical and letter part of the expressions separately. Thus, $15x^2y^2 \div 5xy = (15 \div 5)(x^2 \div x)(y^2 \div y) = 3xy$. Dividing is like reducing a fraction. We simply divide numerator and denominator by the factors they have in common.

For example: Divide $21a^2b^3$ by $14a^2b^5$.

We form the fraction $\dfrac{21a^2b^3}{14a^2b^5}$. Since the numerator and denominator both contain the factors 7, a^2, and b^3, we can divide numerator and denominator by these factors. We are left with 3 in the numerator, and 2 and b^2 (from $b^5 \div b^3 = b^2$) in the denominator. Therefore, $21a^2b^3 \div 14a^2b^5 = \dfrac{3}{2b^2}$.

To do other division problems, we can use the distributive law. For division, the distributive law is $\dfrac{a+b}{c} = \dfrac{a}{c} + \dfrac{b}{c}$ and $\dfrac{a-b}{c} = \dfrac{a}{c} - \dfrac{b}{c}$.

For example: Divide $72y^3 + 16y^2$ by $8y$.

First, we use the distributive law, so that $\dfrac{72y^3 + 16y^2}{8y} = \dfrac{72y^3}{8y} + \dfrac{16y^2}{8y}$. Now $72y^3 \div 8y = 9y^2$, and $16y^2 \div 8y = 2y$. Therefore, $(72y^3 + 16y^2) \div 8y = 9y^2 + 2y$.

There are other division problems, such as $(x^2 + 7x + 12) \div (x + 3)$ which require the ability to factor more complicated algebraic expressions. If we can factor the expressions involved, then we can use the procedures outlined above. (See the next section on factoring.) If we cannot factor the expressions, then the division process is similar to division of whole numbers, and this is generally not tested.

In problems involving the simplification of algebraic expressions, you must be careful to get the answer in the form given in the choices after the problem.

2–11   Some problems involve converting words into algebraic expressions. In this case, the important thing is to let some letter stand for the words "a number". The choices after the problem will tell you which letter.

For example: How would one represent 12 more than four times a certain number?
Say we let n stand for that certain number. Then four times the number is $4n$, and 12 more than that is $4n + 12$.

Another example: Represent the amount by which 22 exceeds 7 times a number.
Let the number be n. Then 7 times the number is $7n$; 22 exceeds $7n$ by the amount $22 - 7n$.

2–12   Since the letters in an algebraic expression stand for numbers, and since we add, subtract, multiply, or divide them to get the algebraic expression, the algebraic expression itself stands for a number. When we are told what value each of the letters in the expression has, we can evaluate the expression.

In evaluating algebraic expressions, place the value you are substituting for a letter in parentheses. (This is important when a letter has a negative value.)

For example: What is the value of the expression $a^2 - b^3$ when $a = -2$, and $b = -1$? $a^2 - b^3 = (-2)^2 - (-1)^3 = 4 - (-1) = 5$.

If you can, simplify the algebraic expression before you evaluate it.

For example: Evaluate $\dfrac{32a^6b^2}{8a^4b^3}$ if $a = 4$, and $b = -2$.

First we divide:

$$\frac{32a^6b^2}{8a^4b^3} = \frac{4a^2}{b}. \text{ Then } \frac{4a^2}{b} = \frac{4(+4)^2}{-2} = -32.$$

2-13   Sometimes problems about evaluations are presented differently. Addition and multiplication are two examples of operations: We take two numbers and "operate" on them to get a third number. Many different operations could be defined (we could operate on one, two, or more numbers). These operations are defined by an algebraic expression. To invent an operation *, we might say $a * b = ab + a + b$. Then, to find $3 * 4$, we evaluate $ab + a + b$ with $a = 3$ and $b = 4$. Thus, $3 * 4 = 3 \cdot 4 + 3 + 4 = 19$.

An operation is undefined if the denominator of an algebraic expression defining it is zero.

For example: Say $a \& b = \dfrac{a^2 - b^2}{ab}$. Find $x \& x$. When is $x \& x$ undefined?

Since $a \& b = \dfrac{a^2 - b^2}{ab}$, $\quad x \& x = \dfrac{x^2 - x^2}{x^2} = \dfrac{0}{x^2} = 0$, if x is not 0. If $x = 0$, then $x \& x$ is undefined because the denominator would be zero.

FACTORING

2-14   The factors of an expression are two or more expressions whose product is equal to the first expression.

For example: The factors of $x^2 + xy$ are x and $x + y$ since their product $x(x + y)$ is equal to $x^2 + xy$.

To factor any expression is to write the expression as the product of its factors. There are 3 special types of factoring.

2-15   A. A factor that divides into each term of the expression is called a common factor.

For example: For the expression $x^2 + xy$, x divides into each term of the expression. So x is a common factor.

To factor an expression with a common factor:

1) Find the largest common factor of all the terms in the expression. This is one of the factors of the expression.
2) Divide the expression by the largest common factor. The quotient is the other factor.
3) Write the answer as the product of the two factors.

For example: Factor $4x^2 + 2x$.
Step 1: 2x is a factor of both $4x^2$ and 2x, and it is the largest common factor.
Step 2: Divide the expression by the largest common factor.

$$(4x^2 + 2x) \div 2x = 2x + 1$$

Step 3: Write the answer as the product of the factors.
Therefore, $4x^2 + 2x = 2x(2x + 1)$

2–16   **B.** If an expression has two terms and the expression consists of one perfect square minus another perfect square, the expression is a difference of two squares. For example: $x^2 - y^2$ is a difference of two squares and so is $4m^2n^2 - 4$. The second case is a difference of two squares since $4m^2n^2$ is a perfect square ($4m^2n^2 = (2mn)^2$) and 4 is a perfect square ($4 = 2^2$).

To factor a difference of two squares:

1) Take the square root of each of the perfect squares.
2) One of the factors is the sum of the square roots. The other factor is the difference of the square roots (the first minus the second).
3) Write the answer as the product of the two factors.

For example: Factor $4m^2n^2 - 4$.
Step 1: Take the square root of each perfect square.
$$\sqrt{4m^2n^2} = 2mn \qquad \sqrt{4} = 2$$

Step 2: One factor is the sum of the square roots, 2mn + 2. The other factor is the difference of the square roots, 2mn − 2.

Step 3: Write the answer as the product of the factors. Therefore, $4m^2n^2 - 4 = (2mn + 2)(2mn - 2)$

2–17   **C.** The third type is the factoring of trinomials into binomials. A trinomial is an expression with 3 unlike terms such as $x^2 + 2x + 1$, and mn + n + 1; and a binomial is an expression with 2 unlike terms such as x + 2 and m + n^2.

For example: $x^2 + 3x + 2 = (x + 2)(x + 1)$ is an example of a trinomial, $x^2 + 3x + 2$, being factored into factors, x + 2 and x + 1, which are binomials.

Not all trinomials can be factored into binomials. Examples of such trinomials are mn + n + 1 and $x^2 + 3x + 1$. It is not easy to determine whether a trinomial can be factored or not without actually attempting to factor the expression.

Even with trinomials which can be factored, there is no definite method of finding the factors directly. The method used here requires trial and error.

<u>To factor a trinomial of the form $x^2 + bx + c$ where b and c are numbers:</u>

1) First write down the first term of each factor, which is x. (x)(x)
2) To find the second term of each factor, find two numbers whose product is equal to c and whose sum is equal to b. (This requires trial and error.)
3) Write the answer as the product of the two factors.

For example: Factor $y^2 - 5y + 6$.

<u>Step 1</u>: Write down the first term of each factor which is y.

$$(y \quad)(y \quad)$$

<u>Step 2</u>: To find the other term of each factor, find two numbers whose product is 6 and whose sum is -5. The following pairs of numbers have 6 as their product:

$$\begin{array}{ll} 1, 6 & 2, 3 \\ -1, -6 & -2, -3 \end{array}$$

Of these, the only pair of numbers whose sum is -5 is -2 and -3. So, -2 and -3 are the second terms of the factors. Thus, the factors are $y - 2$ and $y - 3$.

<u>Step 3</u>: Write the answer as the product of the factors.

$$y^2 - 5y + 6 = (y - 2)(y - 3)$$

2-18   <u>To factor a trinomial of the form $ax^2 + bx + c$ where a, b, and c are numbers:</u>

1) Find all possible pairs of binomials in which the product of the first terms is equal to ax^2 and the product of the second terms is equal to c.
2) Of these pairs, find the pair of binomials whose product is equal to the trinomial by multiplying each pair.

For example: Factor $2x^2 - 7x - 4$.

<u>Step 1</u>: Find all possible pairs of binomials in which the product of the first terms is equal to $2x^2$ and the product of the second terms is equal to -4. $2x - 2$ and $x + 2$ is a possible pair since the product of the first terms, 2x and x, is $2x^2$ and the product of the second terms, -2 and 2, is -4.

All possible pairs are:

$2x - 2$ and $x + 2$	$2x + 2$ and $x - 2$
$2x - 1$ and $x + 4$	$2x + 4$ and $x - 1$
$2x + 1$ and $x - 4$	$2x - 4$ and $x + 1$

<u>Step 2</u>: Multiply these pairs of binomials to find the pair whose product is $2x^2 - 7x - 4$. The only correct pair is $2x + 1$ and $x - 4$. Therefore, $2x^2 - 7x - 4 = (2x + 1)(x - 4)$.

Note: In a multiple-choice test, it is sometimes easier to multiply in each choice given to find the answer rather than trying to find the factors.

2-19   To factor an expression completely is to factor the expression into expressions which cannot be factored any further.

To factor an expression completely:

1) Look for any common factor. If there is any common factor, factor it out.
2) Factor the resulting expressions until they can not be factored any further.

For example: Factor completely $10y^2 - 40$.
Step 1: Factor out the common factor 10.

$$10y^2 - 40 = 10(y^2 - 4)$$

Step 2: $y^2 - 4$ is a difference of two squares and can still be factored into $(y + 2)(y - 2)$. Therefore, $10y^2 - 40 = 10(y + 2)(y - 2)$.

Another example: Factor completely $x^2 - 5x + 4$.
There is no common factor. So factor completely simply means factor the expression. $x^2 - 5x + 4$ is factored $(x - 1)(x - 4)$. Therefore, factored completely, $x^2 - 5x + 4 = (x - 1)(x - 4)$.

EQUATIONS

2-20   An equation is a statement that two expressions are equal. The reason for learning to solve equations is that knowing how to solve equations makes solving problems easier. Some examples of equations are $10 + 5 = 15$, $4x - 5 = 10$, formulas such as $A = l \times w$ (area = length × width), and proportions.

In the equation $4x - 5 = 10$, the equal sign indicates that the expression to the right of it is to have the same value as the expression to the left of it ($4x - 5$ is to have the same value as 10). There are 4 properties of equations which later will be used to solve equations with unknowns:

1) If the same expression is added to both expressions of an equation, the resulting expressions are still equal.

For example: $10 + 5 = 15$
Add 6 to the left expression $10 + 5$ to get $10 + 5 + 6$ and add 6 to the right expression 15 to get $15 + 6$. The two resulting expressions $10 + 5 + 6$ and $15 + 6$ have equal values.

$$10 + 5 + 6 = 15 + 6$$

This, of course, can be checked by adding the numbers to get $21 = 21$.

2) If the same expression is subtracted from both expressions of an equation, the resulting expressions are still equal.

For example: $10x + 5x = 15x$
Subtract 5x from the expression $10x + 5x$ to get $10x + 5x - 5x$ and subtract 5x from the expression 15x to get $15x - 5x$. The resulting expressions have the same value.

$$10x + 5x - 5x = 15x - 5x$$

Combining the terms shows that the two expressions are equal.

$$10x = 10x$$

3) If both expressions of an equation are multiplied by the same expression, the resulting expressions are equal.

For example: $5x^2 + 2 = 10$
Multiply the expression $5x^2 + 2$ by 6 to get $6(5x^2 + 2)$ or $30x^2 + 12$, and multiply the expression 10 by 6 to get 60. The resulting expressions have the same value.

$$30x^2 + 12 = 60$$

4) If both expressions of an equation are divided by the same nonzero expression, the resulting expressions are still equal.

For example: $7y = 14$
Divide the expression $7y$ by 7 to get $\frac{7y}{7}$ or y, and divide the expression 14 by 7 to get $\frac{14}{7}$ or 2. The resulting equation is equivalent to the original equation.

$$y = 2 \text{ is equivalent to } 7y = 14$$

2-21   In algebra, the expressions consist of both constants such as 0, 15, or any other number, and variables which are represented by letters. The variables in an equation stand for unknowns. Solving an equation which has unknowns means finding values for the unknowns which, when substituted into the equation, will make the two expressions in the equation equal.

For example: Consider the equation $2x = 10$.
To solve the equation is to find a value or values for x which will make the equation true. In this case only when $x = 5$ does the equation hold.

$$2x = 10$$

When 5 is substituted for x,

$$2(5) = 10$$
$$10 = 10 \text{ which is obviously true.}$$

With any other value such as $x = 6$, the equation does not hold. When 6 is substituted into the equation,

$$2(6) = 10$$
$$12 = 10 \text{ which is not true.}$$

2-22   The simplest kind of equation to solve is an equation with only one unknown and in which the exponent of the unknown is no larger than 1. Such an equation is called a linear equation with one unknown. Examples of this kind of equation are $5x = 20$, $10y - 6 = 4$, $x + 1 = 0$, and $2x + 2 = 3x$.

To solve a linear equation with one unknown:

1) Use properties 1 and 2 (see Section 2-20) to put all terms involving the unknown on one side of the equation and all constant terms on the other side.

2) Combine the like terms, if necessary.
3) Use properties 3 or 4 (see Section 2-20) to isolate the unknown—that is, to have only the unknown on one side of the equation. (Make the coefficient of the variable 1.) When the unknown is isolated, the equation is solved because the value of the unknown is on the other side of the equation.

For example: Solve the equation $3x = 15$.
Step 1 is already completed since the only term involving the unknown is on one side of the equation and the constant term is on the other side.
Step 2 is already completed also.
Step 3: To isolate x in the equation $3x = 15$, apply property 4 (see Section 2-20). Divide both expressions of the equation by 3. The resulting expressions $\frac{3x}{3}$ and $\frac{15}{3}$ are equal.

$$\frac{3x}{3} = \frac{15}{3}$$

$$x = 5$$

Therefore the value for x is 5.

> After solving an equation, the answer should be checked to make sure that it is correct. To check the answer, substitute the value found for the unknown into the original equation and then simplify to see if the expressions are equal.

To check the above example, substitute 5 for x in the equation.

$$3x = 15$$
$$3(5) = 15$$
$$15 = 15$$

Thus, the answer is correct.

Another example: Solve the equation $10x + 17 = 3x - 4$.
Step 1: Put all terms involving x on one side and the constant terms on the other.
Subtract 17 from both sides of the equation.

$$10x + 17 - 17 = 3x - 4 - 17$$
$$10x = 3x - 21$$

Subtract 3x from both sides of the equation.

$$10x - 3x = 3x - 21 - 3x$$
$$7x = -21$$

Step 2 has already been done.
Step 3: Isolate the unknown.

Divide both sides by 7.

$$\frac{7x}{7} = \frac{-21}{7}$$
$$x = -3$$

To check that -3 is the correct value for x, substitute -3 into the equation.

$$10x + 17 = 3x - 4$$
$$10(-3) + 17 = 3(-3) - 4$$
$$-30 + 17 = -9 - 4$$
$$-13 = -13$$

Therefore, the answer checks out.

> Note: Sometimes an equation such as $x^3 + 3x = x^3 + 6$ may not look like a linear equation since there are x^3 terms in it. However, if the equation is simplified by subtracting x^3 from both sides, the resulting equation is $3x = 6$ which is a linear equation and can be solved.

2-23   A quadratic equation is an equation in which the unknown's highest power is 2. Examples of quadratic equations with one unknown are $3x^2 + 8x + 5 = 0$, $x^2 = 3x + 4$, and $y^2 + 2y = 4y - 1$.

A method for solving quadratic equations is factoring. This method is based on a principle for multiplying numbers.

> If the product of two factors is zero, then at least one of the factors is zero.

For example: $(x + 3)(x - 1) = 0$

Since the product of the two factors is zero, then either $x + 3 = 0$ or $x - 1 = 0$.

To solve quadratic equations by factoring:

1) Use properties 1 and 2 (see Section 2-20) to put all terms on one side of the equation, while the other side is 0.
2) Combine the like terms, if necessary.
3) Factor the expression.
4) Since the product of the factors is 0, the equation will hold if at least one of the factors is equal to zero. So set the factors equal to 0.
5) Solve the resulting equations.

For example: Solve the equation $x^2 - 25 = 0$.

<u>Steps 1 and 2</u> have already been taken.

<u>Step 3</u>: Factor the expression $x^2 - 25$.

$x^2 - 25$ is factored into $(x + 5)(x - 5)$. So,

$$(x + 5)(x - 5) = 0$$

<u>Step 4</u>: Set each factor equal to 0.

$$x + 5 = 0 \quad \text{or} \quad x - 5 = 0$$

<u>Step 5</u>: Solve the resulting equation.

$$x + 5 = 0$$
$$x = -5$$
$$x - 5 = 0$$
$$x = 5$$

The answer is either $x = -5$ or $x = 5$.

To check whether the answer is correct, substitute $x = -5$ and then $x = 5$ into the original equation.

First, $x = -5$,

$$x^2 - 25 = 0$$
$$(-5)^2 - 25 = 0$$
$$25 - 25 = 0$$
$$0 = 0$$

Then, $x = 5$,

$$x^2 - 25 = 0$$
$$5^2 - 25 = 0$$
$$25 - 25 = 0$$
$$0 = 0$$

Therefore, the answer is correct.

Another example: Solve the equation $y^2 = 5y - 4$.

<u>Step 1</u>: Put all terms on one side of the equation. Subtract 5y from both sides and add 4 to both sides.

$$y^2 - 5y + 4 = 5y - 4 - 5y + 4$$
$$y^2 - 5y + 4 = 0$$

<u>Step 2</u> has already been taken.

<u>Step 3</u>: Factor the expression $y^2 - 5y + 4$.

$y^2 - 5y + 4$ is factored into $(y - 1)(y - 4)$.

So,

$$(y - 1)(y - 4) = 0$$

<u>Step 4</u>: Set each factor equal to 0.

$$y - 4 = 0 \quad \text{or} \quad y - 1 = 0$$

<u>Step 5</u>: Solve the resulting equations.

$$y - 4 = 0 \qquad y - 1 = 0$$
$$y = 4 \qquad y = 1$$

Therefore, the answer is either $y = 4$ or $y = 1$. To check the answer, substitute first $y = 4$ into the original equation and then $y = 1$.

First, $y = 4$,

$$y^2 = 5y - 4$$
$$4^2 = 5(4) - 4$$
$$16 = 20 - 4$$
$$16 = 16$$

Then, $y = 1$,

$$y^2 = 5y - 4$$
$$1^2 = 5(1) - 4$$
$$1 = 5 - 4$$
$$1 = 1$$

Therefore, the answer is correct.

2–24 Solving equations with more than one unknown:

An equation may have more than one unknown. In this case, there is generally no specific solution for the unknowns; each unknown can have almost any value depending on the values of the other unknowns. Examples of equations with more than one unknown are $x + 2y = 56$, $m + n + p = 0$, and $3x + 7y + z = 2$. In problems which have equations with more than one unknown, you are usually asked to solve for one unknown in terms of the others.

The method used in solving for one unknown in terms of the others in a linear equation is basically the same as the method used in solving a linear equation with only one unknown.

For example: Solve the equation $2x + 3y = 6$ for x.
Step 1: Use properties 1 and 2 (see Section 2-20) to put all terms involving x on one side of the equation and all the other terms on the other side.
Subtract 3y from both sides of the equation, then combine terms:

$$2x + 3y - 3y = 6 - 3y$$
$$2x = 6 - 3y$$

Step 2: Use property 4 (see Section 2-20) to isolate x.
Divide both sides by 2.

$$\frac{2x}{2} = \frac{6 - 3y}{2}$$

$$x = \frac{6 - 3y}{2}$$

Once x is alone on one side of the equation and does not appear on the other side, the problem is really finished. x is equal to the expression on the other side which is in terms of y and constants.

2–25 Sometimes, we must use the solution of one equation to solve another.

For example: If $xy + \frac{y}{x} = 10$, and $x + 3 = 5$, find y.

First, we solve $x + 3 = 5$, to get $x = 2$.

We then substitute 2 for x in the equation $xy + \frac{y}{x} = 10$ to get $2y + \frac{y}{2} = 10$.

Combining like terms, we get $\frac{5}{2}y = 10$. Now we multiply both sides of the equation by 2 to get $5y = 20$. Dividing both sides by 5, we get $y = 4$.

RATIO AND PROPORTION

2–26 A ratio is a comparison between two numbers or between two measurements with the same units. For example, $2 : 3$ and 2 feet : 3 feet are both ratios. However, 1 yard : 3 gallons is not a ratio, because yards and gallons are not the same units. $2 : 3$ is read "the ratio of 2 to 3".

A ratio can be considered a fraction. The ratio $2 : 3$ could be written as the fraction $\frac{2}{3}$. Since, when we consider ratios, we are interested only in the relative size of the two numbers or quantities, ratios can be reduced just like fractions. For example, $6:9$ is equal to $2:3$ because $\frac{6}{9} = \frac{2}{3}$. Other operations are performed just as they are with fractions. For example, what ratio is twice the ratio $3:4$? $3:4$ is $\frac{3}{4}$. Twice $\frac{3}{4}$, or $2 \times \frac{3}{4}$, equals $\frac{3}{2}$. Therefore the ratio $3:2$ is twice the ratio $3:4$.

2-27   If two quantities are related by a formula, a change in one quantity might cause the other quantity to change. We could be required to find the change in one quantity given the change in the other. To do this:
1) Pick a letter to stand for the original value of the quantity whose change we are given.
2) Find the ratio of the following —   New value : Original value.

For example: The area of a circle is πr^2, where π is a constant and r is the radius of the circle. What happens to the area if the radius is doubled?
Let x equal the original radius. Then πx^2 is the original value of the area. The new radius is double the original, or 2x. The new area is $\pi(2x)^2$ or $4\pi x^2$. The ratio of New area : Original area is $4\pi x^2 : \pi x^2$ or $4:1$. Doubling the radius multiplies the area by 4.

Another example: Light intensity is found by the formula $\frac{I}{d^2}$, where I is a constant, and d is the distance from the light. If the distance from the light is tripled, what happens to the intensity?
Let the original distance be x. Then the original intensity was $\frac{I}{x^2}$. The new distance is 3x and the new intensity is $\frac{I}{(3x)^2}$, or $\frac{I}{9x^2}$. The ratio of New intensity : Original intensity is $\frac{I}{9x^2} : \frac{I}{x^2}$ or $\frac{1}{9} : 1$. The intensity was multiplied by $\frac{1}{9}$ when the distance tripled. In these problems, the formulas are well known, or they will be given.

2-28   A proportion is simply a statement that two ratios are equal. An example of a proportion is $4:5 = 8:10$, which is read "4 is to 5 as 8 is to 10". Since ratios are fractions, problems with proportions generally involve equations with fractions. These can be solved by clearing the equation of fractions.

For example: What number is to 12 as 3 is to 4?

We are asked to solve the proportion $x:12 = 3:4$. This can be written $\frac{x}{12} = \frac{3}{4}$.

We multiply both sides of the equation by 12, and we get $x = 12 \times \frac{3}{4}$, or $x = 9$.

> In general, proportions can be solved by using the rule: "The product of the extremes equals the product of the means." In the proportion $a:b = c:d$, the extremes are the outside terms, a and d. The means are the inside terms, b and c. The rule says that $ad = bc$. By dividing both sides of $ad = bc$ by two of the terms of the proportion, we can get various proportions equivalent to $a:b = c:d$.

For example: If x is to y as m is to n, then x is to m as _____?
We are given that x : y = m : n. Using "the product of the means equals the product of the extremes" rule, we get xn = my. Dividing both sides of this equation by mn, we get $\frac{x}{m} = \frac{y}{n}$. Therefore, x is to m as y is to n.

Another example: If 3 pounds of apples cost 57¢, how much do 10 pounds of apples cost?

We set up the proportion $\frac{3 \text{ lbs.}}{10 \text{ lbs.}} = \frac{57¢}{x¢}$. The units cancel out. Using the product of the extremes equals the product of the means, we get 3x = 570, or x = 190. 10 pounds cost 190¢ or $1.90.

2–29 To solve scale problems, express the given information as a proportion.

For example: If 1 inch on a map represents 10 miles, then 2 inches represent 20 miles, etc. This can be expressed in a proportion,

$$\frac{1 \text{ inch}}{2 \text{ inches}} = \frac{10 \text{ miles}}{20 \text{ miles}}$$

In a problem, one of the terms in the proportion may be unknown.

For example: If one inch on a map represents 30 blocks, how many inches would be needed to represent 135 blocks?
We set up the proportion

$$\frac{1 \text{ inch}}{x \text{ inches}} = \frac{30 \text{ blocks}}{135 \text{ blocks}}$$

The units cancel, and we must solve the proportion $\frac{1}{x} = \frac{30}{135}$. The product of the means equals the product of the extremes, so

$$30x = 135$$
$$x = 4\tfrac{1}{2}$$

Therefore $4\tfrac{1}{2}$ inches are required to represent 135 blocks.

2–30 To convert from one unit of measurement to another, we use proportions.

(This makes sense only if the different units are measuring the same thing.)

For example: How many inches are there in 100 centimeters if there are 2.5 centimeters in 1 inch?
We set up the proportion

$$\frac{1 \text{ inch}}{x \text{ inches}} = \frac{2.5 \text{ centimeters}}{100 \text{ centimeters}}$$

The units cancel and we have

$$\frac{1}{x} = \frac{2.5}{100}$$

or 2.5x = 100.   x = 40. Therefore there are 40 inches in 100 centimeters.

RATE AND WORK

2–31   To do problems dealing with distance:

1) Use this formula: Distance = Rate × Time.
2) If parts of the trip are at different rates (speeds), then to find the total distance, or the total time, you must separate the parts of the trip.

For example: If a boy flew from New York to Chicago, a distance of 1600 miles at the rate of 400 miles an hour, and then took a train home at the rate of 80 miles an hour, how long did the whole trip take?
We must use the formula Distance = Rate × Time, or Time = Distance ÷ Rate. First, Time going = 1600 ÷ 400 = 4 hours. Then, Time returning = 1600 ÷ 80 = 20 hours. The total trip took 20 + 4 or 24 hours.

If a wind or river current is helping a traveler, then his total speed is the normal speed (in windless conditions or still water) plus the speed of the wind or current. If the wind or current is hindering the traveler, then his speed is his normal speed minus the speed of the wind or river current.

For example: A man can row 2 miles an hour in still water. If he rows with the current helping him along, he can go 20 miles in 5 hours. How fast is the current? Let s be the speed of the current. Then (s + 2) is his speed when the current is aiding him.

Distance = Rate × Time, so 20 = (s + 2)5, or 20 = 5s + 10, and s = 2 miles per hour.

2–32   To do work problems:

Write an equation to tell how much of the work is done in one hour. Usually the unknown will be how long it takes two men working together to do a job, or how long it takes one man working alone to do the job.

The key is: If it takes x hours to do a job, $\frac{1}{x}$ of the job is done each hour.

For example: Bill can do a job alone in 5 hours. Bob can do it alone in 4 hours. If they work together, how long will it take?

Let x be the time it takes them to do the job together. Then $\frac{1}{x}$ is the part of the job they do in one hour. But Bill does $\frac{1}{5}$ of the work in one hour, and Bob can do $\frac{1}{4}$ of the work in one hour. Therefore, $\frac{1}{x} = \frac{1}{4} + \frac{1}{5}$. Multiplying by 20x, we get $20 = 5x + 4x = 9x$. $x = \frac{20}{9}$ or $2\frac{2}{9}$ hours.

Another example: Jim and John can do a job together in 5 hours. It takes Jim twice as long to do the job alone as it takes John to do the job alone. How long will it take Jim to do the job alone?

Let x be the time it takes John to do the job alone. Then it takes 2x hours for Jim to do the job alone. In one hour, they do $\frac{1}{5}$ of the work. John does $\frac{1}{x}$ of the work and Jim does $\frac{1}{2x}$ of the work. Therefore, $\frac{1}{5} = \frac{1}{x} + \frac{1}{2x}$. Multiplying by 10x, we get $2x = 10 + 5 = 15$. $x = 7\frac{1}{2}$. Since it takes 2x hours for Jim to do the job alone, it would take him 15 hours to complete the entire job.

Measurement Table

2-33 The following table can be used to solve simple measurement problems:

Length	1 foot = 12 inches
	1 yard = 3 feet
	1 mile = 5280 feet
Time	1 minute = 60 seconds
	1 hour = 60 minutes
Volume	1 quart = 2 pints
	1 gallon = 4 quarts
Weight	1 pound = 16 ounces
	1 ton = 2000 pounds

Consider this problem: How many ounces are there in 4 pounds 3 ounces? 1 pound = 16 ounces, so 4 pounds = 4 × 16 = 64 ounces. Therefore 4 pounds 3 ounces = 64 + 3 = 67 ounces.

AVERAGES

2-34 The average of a number of values is the sum of all the values divided by the number of values. The formula for finding the average of a list of values is

$$\text{Average} = \frac{\text{Total sum of the values}}{\text{Number of values}}$$

For example: Find the average of the following numbers: 10, 5, 110, 130, and 65.
To find the average of the numbers, first find the total sum.
Total sum = 10 + 5 + 110 + 130 + 65
= 320
Since there are five numbers, divide the total sum by 5.

$$\text{Average} = \frac{\text{Total sum of the values}}{\text{Number of values}} = \frac{320}{5} = 64$$

To solve problems involving averages:

All you have to remember is the formula for the average, and know how to apply the formula.

For example: The sum of a list of numbers is 486 and the average for the numbers is 40.5. How many numbers are there in the list?
The problem asks for how many numbers there are in the list. So, let n be the number of numbers in the list. Write the formula for the average.

$$\text{Average} = \frac{\text{Total sum of the values}}{\text{Number of values}}$$

From the problem, the total sum is 486 and the average is 40.5. Substitute the values into the formula.

$$40.5 = \frac{486}{n}$$

Solve the equation by multiplying both sides of the equation by n.

$$40.5 \, n = 486$$

Divide both sides by 40.5.

$$n = 486 \div 40.5$$
$$n = 12$$

There are 12 numbers in the list.

COMBINATIONS

2-35   Suppose that a job has 2 different parts. There are m different ways of doing the first part and there are n different ways of doing the second part. The problem is to find the number of ways of doing the entire job. For each way of doing the first part of the job, there are n ways of doing the second part. Since there are m ways of doing the first part, the total number of ways of doing the entire job is m × n. The formula that can be used is

Number of ways = m × n

For any problem which involves 2 actions or 2 objects, each with a number of choices, and asks for the number of combinations, the formula can be used. For example: A man wants a sandwich and a drink for lunch. If a restaurant has 4 choices of sandwiches and 3 choices of drinks, how many different ways can he order his lunch?
Since there are 4 choices of sandwiches and 3 choices of drinks, using the formula

Number of ways = 4(3)
= 12

Therefore, the man can order his lunch 12 different ways.

2-36   Suppose there are two groups, each with a certain number of members. It is known that some members of one group also belong to the other group. The problem is to find how many members there are in the 2 groups altogether. To find the numbers of members altogether, use the following formula:

Total number of members = Number of members in group I
+ Number of members in group II
− Number of members common to both groups

For example: In one class, 18 students received A s for English and 10 students received A's in math. If 5 students received A's in both English and math, how many students received at least one A?
In this case, let the students who received A's in English be in group I and let those who received A's in math be in group II.

Using the formula:
Number of students who received at least one A
$$= \text{Number in group I} + \text{Number in group II} - \text{Number in both}$$
$$= 18 + 10 - 5 = 23$$
Therefore, there are 23 students who received at least one A.

> In combination problems such as those on the preceding page, the problems do not always ask for the total number. They may ask for any of the four numbers in the formula while other three are given. In any case, to solve the problems, use the formula.

INEQUALITIES

2–37 An inequality is a statement that one expression is greater than or less than another expression. Thus, $3 > 1$ is an inequality which says 3 is greater than 1. $3 < 5$ is an inequality which says 3 is less than 5. Also, if a number n is positive, we can write $n > 0$, and if n is negative, we can write $n < 0$.

> The statement $a > b$ and $b < a$ mean the same thing. The symbol $>$ or $<$ always points to the lesser expression. The statement $x \neq y$ means x does not equal y (x may be greater than y or less than y). Note that $\geq$ means "greater than or equal to" and $\leq$ means "less than or equal to."

2–38 To do problems involving inequalities, use the following rules:

1) Inequalities can be added in this way: If $a > b$, and $c > d$, then $a + c > b + d$. Also if $a > b$ and $c = d$, then $a + c > b + d$. The rules for $a < b$ follow similarly.

2) Inequalities can be multiplied in this way: If $a > b$, and if $c > 0$, then $ac > bc$. If $a > b$ and $c < 0$ then $ac < bc$. That is, multiplying by a negative number reverses the inequality

For example: For what values of x is $3x > x + 2$ a true statement?
Just as in working with equations, we must get x alone on one side of the inequality, $3x > x + 2$. We can add $-x$ to both sides of the inequality. $3x + (-x) > x + 2 + (-x)$, or $2x > 2$. Now we multiply both sides by $\frac{1}{2}$ to get $x > 1$. Therefore $3x > x + 2$ is true whenever $x > 1$.

Another example: If $a > b$, then when is the inequality $ax^2 > bx^2$ true? If $x = 0$, then both sides are zero, and ax^2 is not greater than bx^2. But, if x is not equal to zero, then $x^2 > 0$, since any number multiplied by itself cannot be negative. Since $a > b$, and $x^2 > 0$, we can multiply by x^2 to get $ax^2 > bx^2$. Therefore, $ax^2 > bx^2$ is true unless $x = 0$.

2-39   Some problems with inequalities give certain statements as true, and then ask which of several inequalities (or other statements) could not be true. To do these problems, you must be able to show that the reverse of one of the choices is always true.

For example: If $x + 2P = y$, and P is positive, which of the following statements could not be true?

(a) $x > y$ (b) $x + P > -y$ (c) $y = P$ (d) $y + x > 1$ (e) $y > x + 1$.

Since P is positive, 2P is positive or $2P > 0$. Multiplying this by -1, we get that $-2P < 0$ (reversing the inequality). Now we add $x + 2P = y$ and $-2P < 0$, to get $x + 2P + (-2P) < y + 0$, or $x < y$. Since $x < y$ is always true, $x > y$ can never be true. The correct choice is (a).

2-40   To compare fractions:

1) Change the given fractions to fractions with the same denominator (you can use one of the original denominators).
2) The greater fraction is the one with the greater numerator.

For example: Which fraction is greater, $\frac{1}{4}$ or $\frac{7}{27}$?

We can change $\frac{1}{4}$ to $\dfrac{\frac{1}{4} \times 27}{27} = \dfrac{6^{3}/_{4}}{27}$. Since $7 > 6^{3}/_{4}$, $\frac{7}{27} > \frac{1}{4}$.

> If a fraction has a positive numerator and denominator, then if the numerator increases the fraction increases; if the denominator increases, the fraction decreases.

Plane Geometry

(including Angles, Lines, Polygons, Triangles, Circles)

ANGLES

3–1   1) An angle is formed by 2 lines meeting at a point. The point at which the lines meet is called the vertex of the angle, and the lines are called the sides of the angle. The symbol "∠" is used to indicate an angle.

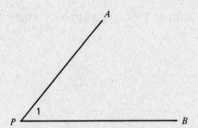

An angle can be named 3 different ways:
(a) According to its vertex point (∠P)
(b) According to the names of the endpoints of the lines forming the angle — the vertex is the middle term (∠APB, ∠BPA).
(c) According to the number indicated inside an angle (∠1).
2) When two lines meet, they form 4 angles. Each pair of opposite angles are called vertical angles.

For example:

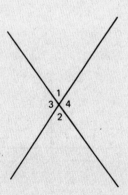

∠3 and ∠4 are vertical angles; ∠1 and ∠2 are vertical angles.

3) Vertical angles are equal.
In the example, ∠3 = ∠4 and ∠1 = ∠2.
4) A straight angle is one whose sides lie on the same straight line.

For example:

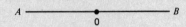

∠ AOB is a straight angle.

A straight angle measures 180°.

5) Two angles whose sum is 180° are supplementary angles.

For example:

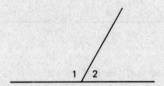

∠ 1 and ∠ 2 are supplementary angles.
6) Two angles supplementary to the same angle are equal.
7) A right angle is half of a straight angle. The symbol "⌐" indicates a right angle.

For example:

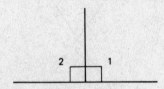

∠ 1 and ∠ 2 are right angles.

A right angle measures 90°.

8) Two angles whose sum is 90° are complementary angles.

For example:

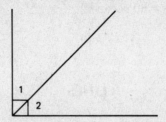

∠1 and ∠2 are complementary angles.

9) Two angles complementary to the same angle are equal.

10) Adjacent angles are two angles with the same vertex and a common side (one angle is not inside the other).

For example:

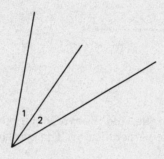

∠1 and ∠2 are adjacent angles.

11) An angle bisector of an angle is a line that cuts the original angle in half (bisect means to divide into 2 equal parts).

For example:

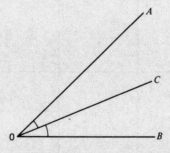

∠AOC = ∠COB, so OC is an angle bisector of ∠AOB.

Angle Measures

$1° = 60'$ (that is, 1 degree = 60 minutes)
$1' = 60''$ (that is, 1 minute = 60 seconds)

LINES

3–2 1) In a plane, two lines are parallel if they never meet.
2) Two lines are perpendicular if they meet at right angles.

For example:

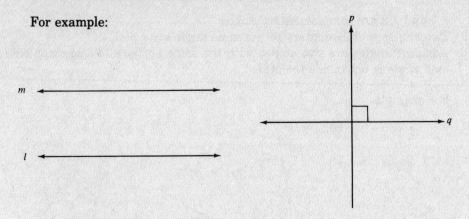

Lines l and m are parallel and the symbol for parallel is "‖". (Line l ‖ line m)
Line p and line q are perpendicular. The symbol for perpendicular is "⊥".
(Line p ⊥ line q)

3) Two points determine a line. This can also be expressed as: Only one line can pass through any two points.
4) Two different lines can meet at no more than one point.
5) If two lines in a plane are perpendicular to the same line, they are parallel.

For example:

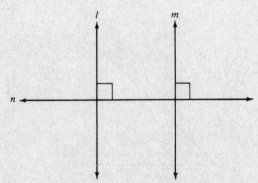

Line l and line m are perpendicular to line n. So, line l and line m are parallel.

6) If two lines are parallel to the same line, they are parallel.

For example:

Line l and line m are parallel to line n. So, line l and line m are parallel.

7) If a line is perpendicular to one of two parallel lines, it is perpendicular to the other.

For example:

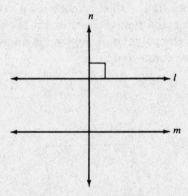

Line l and line m are parallel. Since line n is perpendicular to line l, it is also perpendicular to line m.

8) A line that cuts through two lines is a transversal line. (The transversal usually cuts parallel lines.)

9) If two lines are parallel, and are cut by a transversal line,
   a) the alternate interior angles are equal
   b) the corresponding angles are equal
   c) consecutive interior angles are supplementary.

For example: Line l and line m are parallel. Line n is a transversal line.

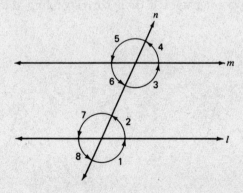

∠2 and ∠6 are alternate interior angles and so are ∠3 and ∠7. So, ∠2 = ∠6, and ∠3 = ∠7.   ∠1 and ∠3 are a pair of corresponding angles and so are ∠2 and ∠4, ∠6 and ∠8, and ∠5 and ∠7. So, ∠1 = ∠3; ∠2 = ∠4, ∠6 = ∠8, and ∠5 = ∠7.   ∠2 and ∠3 are a pair of consecutive angles and so are ∠6 and ∠7. So, ∠2 is supplementary to ∠3, and ∠6 is supplementary to ∠7.

10) If two lines are cut by a transversal and if either a) the alternate interior angles are equal or b) the corresponding angles are equal or c) the consecutive angles are supplementary, then the two lines are parallel.

POLYGONS

3–3   1) A polygon is a plane figure that consists of a set of points and a set of line segments joining the points. Each point is called a vertex, and each segment is a side of the polygon. A polygon is named by giving its vertices in the order they are connected.

For example:

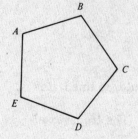 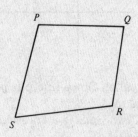 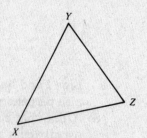

The polygons in the figure are ABCDE, PQRS, and XYZ. If a line were drawn from A to C, the line segment AC would be a diagonal of the polygon ABCDE, since it connects two non-adjacent vertices.

2) A regular polygon is a polygon in which all the sides are equal and all the angles are equal.

3) Two polygons are congruent if their corresponding sides and angles are equal.

For example:

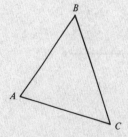 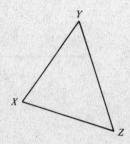

Polygons ABC and XYZ are congruent, since AB = XY, AC = XZ, ∠A = ∠X, ∠B = ∠Y, etc.

4) Two polygons are similar if their angles are equal and their corresponding sides are in proportion.
5) A triangle is a polygon with 3 sides.
6) A quadrilateral is a polygon with 4 sides.
7) A pentagon is a polygon with 5 sides.
8) A hexagon is a polygon with 6 sides.

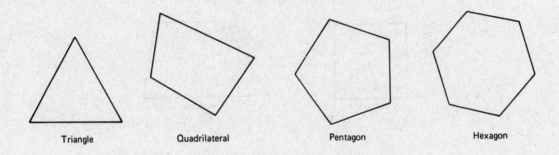

| Triangle | Quadrilateral | Pentagon | Hexagon |

9) A parallelogram is a quadrilateral with the 2 pairs of opposite sides parallel. The pairs of opposite sides are equal, and the pairs of opposite angles are also equal.

For example:

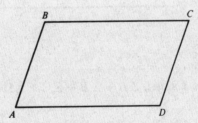

AB∥CD, AB = CD, ∠A = ∠C, etc.

10) A rhombus is a parallelogram with all sides equal.
11) A rectangle is a parallelogram with 4 right angles.
12) A square is a rectangle with 4 equal sides.
13) A trapezoid is a quadrilateral with 1 pair of parallel sides. The two parallel sides are called bases; the other sides are called legs. The median of a trapezoid is the line segment connecting the midpoints of the legs.

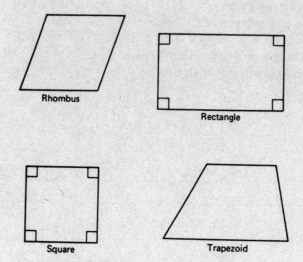

14) The sum of the interior angles of a polygon with n sides is 180°(n − 2).

For example:

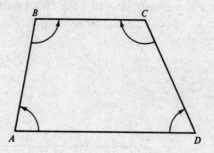

Since the figure has 4 sides, ∠A + ∠B + ∠C + ∠D = 180°(4 − 2) or 360°.

TRIANGLES

3–4   1) An equilateral triangle is one with three equal sides.
2) An isosceles triangle is one with two equal sides.
3) A right triangle is one with a right angle.
4) The sum of the interior angles of a triangle is 180°.
5) Each angle of an equilateral triangle measures 60°.
6) Two triangles are similar if the corresponding angles are equal.

For example:

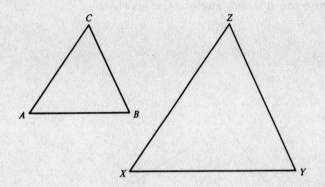

$\angle$ A = $\angle$ X, $\angle$ B = $\angle$ Y, and $\angle$ C = $\angle$ Z. So, triangle ABC is similar to triangle XYZ.

7) If 2 triangles are similar, then the corresponding sides are proportional. In the above figure,

$$\frac{AB}{XY} = \frac{BC}{YZ} = \frac{AC}{XZ}.$$

8) In any triangle, the sides opposite equal angles are equal.

For example: In triangle ABC, $\angle$ A = $\angle$ C. So, AB = BC.

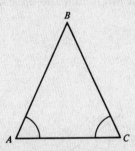

9) In any triangle, the angles opposite equal sides are equal.
10) The sum of any 2 sides of a triangle is greater than the third side.

For example:

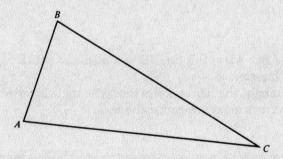

AB + BC is greater than AC.   AC + BC is greater than AB.   AB + AC is greater than BC.

11) In any triangle, the side opposite the largest angle is the longest and the side opposite the smallest angle is the shortest.

For example:

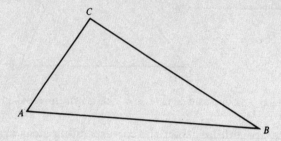

In triangle ABC, ∠C is the largest angle. So, AB is the longest side. ∠B is the smallest angle. So, AC is the shortest side.

12) A median of a triangle is a line segment joining the vertex and the midpoint of the opposite side.

13) An angle bisector of a triangle is a line segment bisecting an angle and joining the vertex of that angle and the opposite side.

For example:

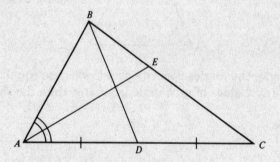

In triangle ABC, AD = DC. So, BD is a median. ∠BAE = ∠CAE. So, AE is an angle bisector.

14) In a right triangle, the side opposite the right angle is called the hypotenuse and the other two sides are called the legs.

> **Pythagorean Theorem: In a right triangle, the sum of the squares of the two legs is equal to the square of the hypotenuse.**

For example: In right triangle ABC, $AC^2 + BC^2 = AB^2$

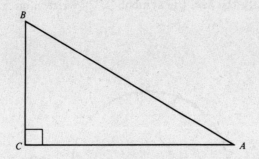

CIRCLES

3-5 1) When there is only one circle with a given center, the circle is named by its center.

2) A radius of a circle is a line segment from the center to a point on the circle. (The plural of radius is radii.) All the radii of the same circle are equal.

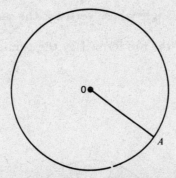

This circle is called circle O. OA is a radius of circle O.

3) A chord of a circle is a line segment whose endpoints are on the circle. A diameter is a chord which passes through the center. If a line passes through the center of a circle and is perpendicular to a chord, then it bisects the chord.

For example:

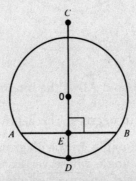

AB is a chord of circle O. Since CD passes through O and is perpendicular to AB, AE = BE.

4) An arc of a circle is any part of the circle. An arc of a circle is named by its endpoints; to identify the arc, the symbol "⌢" is written on top.

For example:

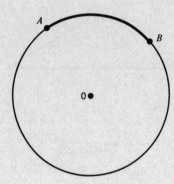

The indicated arc is $\overset{\frown}{AB}$. There are actually 2 arcs (the circumference of the circle has been divided into two parts). The smaller arc is usually meant by the symbol "⌢".

5) A central angle is an angle whose vertex is the center of the circle.

An intercepted arc is the arc formed by the points where the sides of the angle meet the circle.

For example:

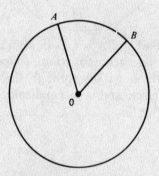

∠AOB is a central angle, and $\overset{\frown}{AB}$ is the intercepted arc for central angle ∠AOB.

6) An arc can be measured in degrees. The degree measure of an arc is the same as that of its central angle. In the diagram above, $\overset{\frown}{AB}$ = ∠AOB.

7) An inscribed angle is an angle whose vertex is on the circle and whose sides are chords of the circle. An inscribed angle is one half of the central angle of its intercepted arc.

For example:

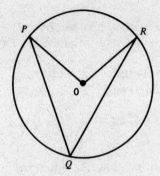

∠PQR is an inscribed angle, and therefore ∠PQR = ½∠POR. Specifically, an angle inscribed in a semi-circle (half of a circle) is a right angle.

8) Concentric circles are circles with the same center.

9) A tangent to a circle is a line that touches the circle at only one point. From a point outside the circle, 2 tangents can be drawn to the circle. These tangents are equal. Also, the radius to the point where the tangent meets the circle is perpendicular to the tangent.

For example:

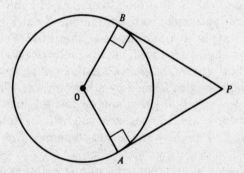

PA = PB, OA ⊥ PA, and OB ⊥ PB.

FORMULAS

3–6

Triangle: Area = $\frac{1}{2}$bh (b = base, h = height)
                Perimeter = a + b + c (a, b, and c are the 3 sides)

Rectangle: Area = lw (l = length, w = width)
                Perimeter = 2(l + w)

Square: Area = s^2 (s = side of square)
            Perimeter = 4s

Parallelogram: Area = bh (b = base, h = height)
                      Perimeter = sum of 4 sides

Trapezoid: Area = $\frac{1}{2}$(a + b)h   (a and b are the two bases, h = height)
                Median = $\frac{1}{2}$(a + b)

Circle: d = 2r   (d = diameter, r = radius)
            Circumference = $2\pi r = \pi d$
            Area = πr^2

3–7

GEOMETRY TIPS

There is no general method for attacking geometry problems. If the problem requires that you make some statement about a figure, think about the theorems which apply to a statement of that kind. For example, if you want to show that two angles are equal, list the methods for showing that two angles are equal: vertical angles, angles of similar triangles, angles opposite equal sides in a triangle, angles formed by a bisector, etc. Then examine the given information to see which of these approaches might work. Examine the diagram carefully for clues. (Sometimes you will be told that the diagram is drawn to scale.) You might want to add some new line segments to the given diagram.

In doing problems which require a numerical answer, try breaking up the problem into parts. If you cannot find the answer directly, try to find the length of other line segments, or the measure of other angles, which might lead to the unknown quantity you are looking for. To find the area of a figure, divide the figure up into parts whose area you can find (triangles, rectangles, etc.) and then add these to find the total area.

Graphs and Charts

HELPFUL HINTS

5–1

Here are some things to remember when doing problems based on graphs or charts:

1. Understand what you are being asked to do before you begin figuring.
2. Check the dates and types of information required. Be sure that you are looking in the proper columns, and on the proper lines, for the information you need.
3. Check the units required. Be sure that your answer is in thousands, millions, or whatever the question calls for.
4. In computing averages, be sure that you add the figures you need and no others, and that you divide by the correct number of years or other units.
5. Be careful in computing problems asking for percentages.
   (a) Remember that to convert a decimal into a percent you must multiply it by 100. For example 0.04 is 4%.
   (b) Be sure that you can distinguish between such quantities as 1% (1 percent) and .01% (one-hundredth of 1 percent), whether in numerals or in words.
   (c) Remember that if quantity X is greater than quantity Y, and the question asks what percent quantity X is of quantity Y, the answer must be greater than 100 percent.

5–2

TABLE CHART TYPE

CONSUMPTION OF FUELS FOR PRODUCTION OF ELECTRIC ENERGY
(1959 – 64)

	1959	1960	1961	1962	1963	1964
Bituminous and lignite coal (thousands of short tons)	165,794	173,882	179,612	190,941	200,193	223,162
Anthracite coal (thousands of short tons)	2,629	2,751	2,509	2,297	2,139	2,239
Fuel oil (thousands of barrels)	88,263	85,340	85,736	85,768	93,314	101,162
Gas (millions of cubic feet)	1,628,509	1,724,762	1,825,117	1,955,974	2,144,473	2,321,889

1. In which year did the greatest number of kinds of fuel show an increase in consumption over that of the preceding year?

   (A) 1960
   (B) 1961
   (C) 1962
   (D) 1963
   (E) 1964

   The table shows some increases and some decreases from one year to the next. What is requested here is the year in which there were more increases than in other years—not the amount of increased use, simply the number of increases. You are allowed to use the blank columns and margins in the test booklet for scratch paper. You can jot down the numbers 1960, 1961, and so on, in a column, and beside each date set down a plus for each increase you find. Three kinds of fuel (all but fuel oil) showed an increase in 1960. You will find three increases in 1961, 1962, and 1963, also. There were *four* increases in 1964, however, and E is the answer to the question.

2. For the period shown, the approximate average amount of gas consumed annually for the production of electric energy was, in millions of cubic feet,

(A) 1,933   (D) 1,933,500
(B) 11,597   (E) 1,932,833,000
(C) 1,890,045

To find the average amount of gas consumed annually, find the row on the table marked "Gas." Add the amount of gas consumed each year and divide by the number of years (6). The exact figure by this method is 1,933,454. Since you have been asked for an *approximate* average, you could have skipped the last three digits in each number and considered them zeros. This would give a total of 11,597,000, or an annual average of something over 1,932,000. You do not need to divide into the last three zeros of the approximate total to get the approximate average.

It is a good practice to check the question to see whether the units asked for in the question are the same units you have found in your answer. If they are not, make the necessary changes. In this question, you are asked the amount in millions of cubic feet and your answer is in the same units. Therefore, you have finished the problem. Look at your choices. D is closest to the amount you have computed and should be selected as your answer.

3. In 1962, approximately what percentage of the total amount of coal used in production of electrical energy was anthracite coal?

(A) 1%   (D) 4%
(B) 2%   (E) 5%
(C) 3%

Before you do any figuring, think how you would solve this problem. First, you must find the total amount of coal consumed in 1962, and then you will have to find what percent of that whole amount was anthracite coal. The percent of anthracite coal will be the amount of anthracite coal divided by the total amount of coal consumed and multiplied by 100. Now you are ready to do the problem. Look at the table and note that there are two rows giving amounts of coal used. Look under 1962 and add the amounts for these two rows for that year (190,941 + 2,297 = 193,238 thousands of short tons). The amount of anthracite coal used was 2,297 thousands short tons. The percentage of the total amount of coal that was anthracite would be 2,297 divided by 193,238 or 0.011. Since the question asks for percent and your computation has given you a decimal, you must multiply the decimal by 100 (0.011 × 100 = 1.1 percent). The closest answer in the choices given is A. (In this question, as in question 2, you could have computed an approximate answer by working with round numbers. Dropping the last three zeros, you could have divided 2 by 193; and you could have seen that the percentage is just over 1 percent and not nearly 2 percent.)

4. In which year did the gas consumed in producing electric energy show the greatest increase in cubic feet over that of the preceding year?

(A) 1960
(B) 1961
(C) 1962
(D) 1963
(E) 1964

The last row of the table will give the numbers needed to answer a question of gas consumption. When you have to make several computations, you can often save time by using shortcuts.

Try rounding the figures by disregarding the last three digits. The 1960 increase was about 96 thousand (1,724 − 1,628 = 96). In succeeding years it was 101 thousand, 130 thousand, 189 thousand, and 177 thousand. The greatest increase over the preceding year occurred in 1963, and the answer is D.

5. The total amount of coal consumed in the production of electrical energy in 1964 was approximately what percent of that consumed in 1959?

(A) 57%
(B) 75%
(C) 134%
(D) 150%
(E) 168%

The total amount of coal is computed by adding the amounts in the first two rows of the table for each of the 2 years involved in the question. Rounding the figures to the nearest hundred, you will get 223,200 + 2,200 or 225,400 thousands of short tons for 1964. The 1959 total, rounded in the same way, is 168,400. Since you have been asked what percent the 1964 total was of that consumed in 1959, you would divide 225,400 by 168,400. (Since the 1964 total is larger than the 1959 total, you know that your answer must be over 100 percent. You can eliminate choices A and B before you compute.) The number 225,400 divided by 168,400 equals approximately 1.34. Remember that the question asks for *percent*. Therefore multiply 1.34 by 100. Your product is 134%, which is choice C.

5–3

PIE CHART TYPE

LUMBER PRODUCTION, BY KIND OF WOOD, UNITED STATES, 1962

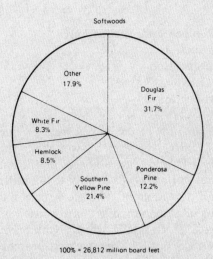

100% = 26,812 million board feet

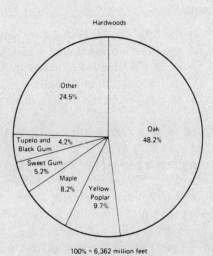

100% = 6,362 million feet

The next 3 questions are based on this chart:

1. Of the two kinds of pine (ponderosa and southern yellow) shown in 1962, yellow pine constituted, to the nearest whole percent,

   (A) 21%   (D) 65%
   (B) 35%   (E) 80%
   (C) 60%

To compare these figures, which are in the same "pie chart," you do not need to calculate the number of board feet. Instead you add the two percentages (21.4 + 12.2 = 33.6), and calculate what percentage of that total is represented by yellow pine. Of the choices given, the answer is closest to D.

2. In 1962 yellow poplar and sweet gum production was, in millions of board feet,

   (A) 947.9   (D) 94,794
   (B) 1,170.6   (E) 947,938,000
   (C) 3,994.9

Look at the pie charts. Yellow poplar and sweet gum lumbers are on the hardwoods chart. To compute the production of yellow poplar and sweet gum, add their percentages as found on the chart (9.7% + 5.2% = 14.9%). The total production of hardwoods is 6,362 million board feet; yellow poplar and sweet gum make up 14.9% of this total. Multiply the total by the percentage ($6,362 \times 14.9\% = 6,362 \times 0.149 = 947.9$ millions of board feet). Choice A is 947.9 and the answer.

Notice some of the wrong choices: D will be chosen if you forget that 14.9% is 0.149 and you multiply by 14.9. E will be chosen if you forget that the chart is already expressed in millions of board feet and you multiply the correct answer by 1 million. B and C might be chosen if you use total production of softwoods instead of hardwoods. C is 14.9% of the softwoods. B is the total amount of softwoods divided by approximately 14.9.

3. In 1962 the amount of ponderosa pine lumber produced was most nearly equal to

   (A) the total of maple and tupelo and black gum production
   (B) one-fourth the amount of oak production
   (C) twice the amount of sweet gum production
   (D) the production of all hardwoods shown as "other"
   (E) 10 percent of the total lumber production

Look at the charts and compute the amount of ponderosa pine produced ($26,812 \times 12.2\%$ or $26,812 \times 0.122 = 3,271.064$). Now each answer choice must be considered and all but one rejected. A, B, C, and D are all based on the hardwoods chart. Notice that the total amount of hardwoods is only 6,362 million board feet. Ponderosa pine is almost half that amount. Therefore, only hardwoods that equal almost 50 percent of the total amount of all hardwoods would be in equal supply with ponderosa pine. A, B, C, and D are out. Oak production, 48 percent of the total, at first looks good, but B is "one-fourth the amount of oak production," so B is eliminated. Only E is left. Let us see whether it is the answer. The total lumber production is the total amount of hardwoods plus the total amount of softwoods (26,812 million board feet + 6,362 million board feet), or 33,174 million board feet. Ten percent of this amount (0.10 × 33,174) is 3,317.4. This is very nearly the same amount that you figured for ponderosa pine. E is the best choice as an answer.

LINE GRAPH TYPE

5–4 In working on this type of graph, you are permitted to use the edge of a sheet of paper, or your pencil, as a straightedge to help you in making estimates. For example, in the graph shown below, you might want to estimate the amount of income from dairy products in 1950. You would want to know how much of the distance between the lines marked 3000 and 4000 is below the point where the dotted line marked "DAIRY PRODUCTS" crosses the date line marked "1950." Laying your pencil across that point, parallel to the 4000 line, would help you to see that it is about three-fourths of the way up from 3000—in other words, the income from dairy products is about 3,750 millions of dollars for 1950.

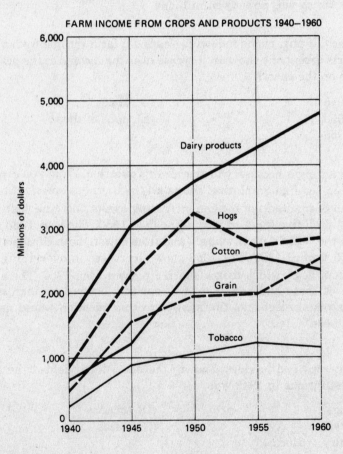

FARM INCOME FROM CROPS AND PRODUCTS 1940–1960

1. The total farm income from crops and products in 1960 was, in millions of dollars, approximately

(A) 4,700
(B) 13,500
(C) 14,500

(D) 4,700,000
(E) 13,500,000

To compute the total income from a chart like this, it is necessary to estimate the income from each item shown on the chart for the year mentioned and add all the estimates. The chart shows figures in millions of dollars, and since the question asks for the same, it will not be necessary to add any zeros to the figure you obtain. Use the blank space in the test booklet for figuring. Be sure you are looking at the correct year. Estimate the amount where each of the product lines meets the 1960 line at the extreme right of the chart. Tobacco seems to be about 1200, grain is easily estimated to be 2500, cotton a little lower—perhaps 2400, hogs about 2800, and dairy products about 4700. Adding these estimates gives a total of 13,600. Among the answer choices you have 13,500 and 14,500. It is most unlikely that you have underestimated by as much as 800, so you can discard 14,500 as a possible answer and mark 13,500, or B. The wrong alternative E, which adds three zeros to this, might be chosen if you had not noticed that the required answer is in millions of dollars and doesn't need more zeros. Alternatives A and D might be selected if you thought that the top line in the chart represented the total of all the amounts. Since dairy products brought in the greatest amount of income, 4,700 million dollars in 1960, that error would give you answer A, and D would be the choice if you made an additional error of adding three zeros to the estimate, which was already in millions.

2. In which, if any, of the following years did farm income from all crops and products except one show an increase over the income of the preceding year shown on the chart?

(A) 1945   (D) 1960
(B) 1950   (E) none of these
(C) 1955

No estimating is necessary to answer this question. What you are looking for is a date on the line graph that shows all the lines but one *slanting up* to it— that is, all of the items of income *increasing* except one. The year 1945 shows increases in all five kinds of income; so does 1950. The year 1960 shows a decrease in the income from tobacco and from cotton, both lines slanting down from 1955 toward 1960. But 1955 shows increases in everything except the income from hogs, which took a sharp dip down from 1950. The answer is C, therefore. If there had *not* been any year that showed an increase in every type of income except one, the answer to this question would have been E, "none of these."

3. Of the crops and products shown, the one which yielded the next to the smallest income in 1940 was

(A) hogs   (D) tobacco
(B) grain   (E) cotton
(C) dairy products

Again, no estimating is necessary for this fairly easy question. All you need to find is the line that is the second from the bottom where they meet the 1940 dateline. Since the lines are not labeled at the point where they begin, you must trace this line upward until you find where it is labeled "GRAIN."

4. Farm income in 1960 from the sale of hogs showed a percentage decrease from the 1950 income of approximately

(A) 88%   (D) 25%
(B) 66%   (E) 12%
(C) 33%

First estimate the 1950 income from the sale of hogs, where the line crosses the 1950 line. It appears to be about 3250 on the chart. It is not necessary to work with the figure $3,250,000,000 (as $3,250 million would look written out). The figures read from the chart can be handled so as to give results in percentages. The 1960 income is about 2800, where the line meets the right-hand edge of the graph. The *decrease from the 1950 income,* in terms of per-centage, is found by calculating what percentage of the 1950 income is the amount by which it dropped. The drop between 1950 and 1960 is about 450 (3250 − 2800). Dividing this by 3250 gives a quotient of 0.138 or 13.8 percent. Different persons will, no doubt, make different estimates in reading figures from a graph but the final computations from estimates that are made from the proper place in the graph will be closer to the correct answer than to any of the other answer choices given. In this question, the *approximate* percent-age is required, and the best answer is E.

5–5

BAR GRAPH TYPE

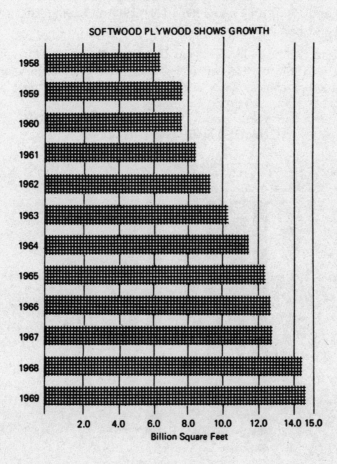

SOFTWOOD PLYWOOD SHOWS GROWTH

Billion Square Feet

1. What was the ratio of soft plywood produced in 1958 as compared with 1967?

(A) 1:1
(B) 2:3
(C) 1:2

(D) 3:4
(E) 1:3

To answer this question, you will have to measure the bars accurately. In 1958, 6.4 billion square feet of plywood were produced. In 1967, 12.8 billion square feet were produced. The ratio of 6.4:12.8 is the same as 1:2. The correct answer is C.

2. For the years 1958 through 1963, excluding 1962, how many billion square feet of plywood were produced altogether?

(A) 23.2
(B) 29.7
(C) 34.1

(D) 40.7
(E) 50.5

All you have to do is to measure the bar for each year — of course, don't include the 1962 bar — and estimate the length of each bar. Then you add the five lengths. 1958 = 6.4; 1959 = 7.8; 1960 = 7.9; 1961 = 8.4; 1963 = 10.2. The total is 40.7. The correct answer is D.

3. Between which consecutive odd years and between which consecutive even years was the plywood production jump greatest?

(A) 1965 and 1967; 1958 and 1960
(B) 1963 and 1965; 1964 and 1966
(C) 1959 and 1961; 1960 and 1962

(D) 1961 and 1963; 1960 and 1962
(E) 1963 and 1965; 1962 and 1964

The jump from 1963 to 1965 was from 10.3 to 12.4 = 2.1 billion square feet. The jump from 1962 to 1964 was from 9.2 to 11.4 = 2.2 billion square feet. None of the other choices show such broad jumps. The correct answer is, therefore, E.

5–6

CUMULATIVE GRAPH TYPE

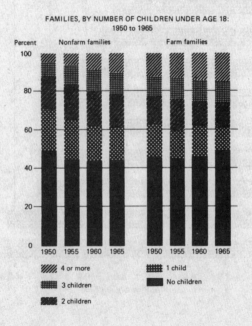

FAMILIES, BY NUMBER OF CHILDREN UNDER AGE 18:
1950 to 1965

1. The combined years in which there were fewest Nonfarm families with 3 children were

   (A) 1950 and 1955   (D) 1950 and 1960
   (B) 1955 and 1960   (E) 1955 and 1965
   (C) 1960 and 1965

The best way to answer a Cumulative Graph question is to use your ruler— or, if a ruler is not available, some straight edge on which you can measure off. Eye inspection is also an aid in answering Cumulative Graph questions. In this particular question, eye inspection will indicate that 1950 is the year when there were fewest Nonfarm "3-children" families. This 1950 cross-hatching measures $1/8$ of an inch. The 1955 crosshatching measures $3/16$ of an inch. Together, the $1/8 + 3/16 = 5/16$ inches, which is the smallest of the pair choices given. The correct answer, therefore, is A. Incidentally, in Cumulative Graph questions, do not be misled by the upper positions of partial quantities. The top positions have nothing to do with the size or amount of a specific division.

2. Which statement is *not* true?

   (A) In 1960, there were more "2-child" Nonfarm families than "2-child" Farm families.
   (B) There were more "4-children or more" families (Farm and Nonfarm) in 1965 than in any other year indicated.
   (C) From 1950-1960, there was a general decrease in the "No children" category for Nonfarm families.
   (D) A comparison of the year showing the smallest number of "4-children or more" Farm families with the year showing the greatest number of "4-children or more" Nonfarm families reveals that the "4-children or more" Farm families outnumbered the "4-children or more" Nonfarm families.
   (E) From 1955-1965, there was a general decrease in the "No-children" category for Farm families.

Eye inspection will show that the number of "No children" Nonfarm families generally decreased from 1950 to 1960, but the number of "No children" Farm families generally increased from 1955 to 1965. The correct answer is, therefore, E.

3. The combined 1965 "No-children" and "4-children or more" Nonfarm families made up approximately what percent of all 1965 Nonfarm families?

   (A) 45%   (D) 66%
   (B) 52%   (E) 73%
   (C) 59%

The "No-children" black bar goes up to 42%. The "4-children or more" diagonal-line bar extends from about 90% to 100%. $42 + 10 = 52$. Therefore, B is the correct answer.

Part Three

Data Sufficiency Study and Practice

Tips for Solving Data Sufficiency Problems

The Data Sufficiency section of the GMAT contains questions that test your reasoning ability. Many candidates have trouble solving these problems because they are unaccustomed to the unusual nature of these problems. Working with Data Sufficiency problems (beginning on page 477) will get you used to the reasoning necessary to attack such problems successfully.

Data Sufficiency problems are different from other Math problems in that they do not ask you to choose one of five answers as the solution to a specific mathematical question. Rather, you are required to determine whether the data provided in reference to a given question is sufficient for answering the question. The general format of the Data Sufficiency question is a question followed by two statements labeled (1) and (2). Often there will be an accompanying diagram. For example:

What is the area of the rectangle shown above?

(1) AB is twice as long as BC.
(2) AD is 5 meters long.

Directions: Each of the questions below is followed by two statements, labeled (1) and (2), in which certain data are given. In these questions you do not actually have to compute an answer, but rather you have to decide whether the data given in the statements are *sufficient* for answering the question. Using the data given in the statements *plus* your knowledge of mathematics and everyday facts (such as the number of days in July), you are to blacken the box on the answer sheet under

(A) if statement (1) ALONE is sufficient but statement (2) alone is not sufficient to answer the question asked,

(B) if statement (2) ALONE is sufficient but statement (1) alone is not sufficient to answer the question asked,

(C) if BOTH statements (1) and (2) TOGETHER are sufficient to answer the question asked, but NEITHER statement ALONE is sufficient.

(D) if EACH statement is sufficient by itself to answer
the question asked,

(E) if statements (1) and (2) TOGETHER are NOT
sufficient to answer the question asked and additional data specific to the problem are needed.

You need not memorize these choices — the meaning of each letter
will be given to you on the actual test. It is important that you fully understand the meaning of each choice.

The first step in solving a Data Sufficiency problem is to look at the
question asked without the two statements. You will not be able to answer the question because you will need more data. Now examine statement
(1) only. See whether you now have enough data to answer the question.
Remember, or note down, whether statement (1) *alone* was enough to
solve the problem. Now look at statement (2) alone and see whether it
provides enough data to enable you to answer the question.

Often, you will have to use both statements to answer the question;
and, sometimes, both statements will not provide enough information.

The answer to the sample question given is C. *Both* statements
are needed to answer the question. The first statement alone certainly
does not provide enough information to enable you to find the area of
the rectangle. The second statement alone does not either. But if we use
both pieces of information, we can find the area and thus solve the
problem: AD is 5 meters long, BC must also be 5 meters long, and so,
AB is 10 meters long. Thus, the area of the rectangle is 50 square meters.

There are several things that should be kept in mind when doing Data
Sufficiency problems.

I. It is unnecessary to obtain exact numerical answers for each
question asked. It is only necessary to recognize that you can
obtain such an answer from certain data. For instance, consider
the problem:

What is the sum of a certain list of 15 numbers?

(1) The first number is 1, the second number is 2,
and so on, until the last number is 15.

(2) The average of the numbers is 8.

The answer to this question is "D" since statement (1) alone provides
sufficient data (it tells us all the entries on the list) and statement (2)
alone provides enough data since, to get the sum, we can multiply the average, 8, by 15.

The point is, we do *not* have to actually sum up 1, 2,. . . 15 or even
multiply 8 by 15. This would be wasting valuable time.

When doing Data Sufficiency problems do not waste time by pushing
through unnecessary calculations.

Of course, any calculations which are needed to determine the usefulness of certain data must be done.

II. If you find that statement (1) alone is sufficient to answer the question do not blindly put down A and go on to the next problem. Look at statement (2) alone also. If (2) also is sufficient, the answer is "D".

III. It is assumed that you have, and can use, certain basic knowledge. For example, if a problem mentions the month of May, it is assumed you know there are 31 days in May. You are expected to use such data even though it is not in a labeled statement.

THE FIVE DIFFERENT DATA SUFFICIENCY QUESTIONS

I. WHERE CHOICE A is the ANSWER

Example: How much change does Mary receive from a $5 bill?
(1) Mary buys a total of 6 oranges at 15¢ each.
(2) Mary receives more than $3 in change.

Look at (1). If Mary buys a total of 6 oranges at 15¢ each, it is easy to figure out how much money Mary spends (6×15¢). There is no need to multiply out however. Since she gives a $5 bill, we can certainly determine how much change she will receive ($5.00 - \$.15 \times 6$). Again no need to compute. Therefore we can certainly answer the question by using statement (1). Statement (2) does not tell us anything definite so it can not be used to answer the question. Thus Choice A is correct.

II. WHERE CHOICE B is the ANSWER

Example: How many people are there at the party?
(1) The party has between 20 and 30 people.
(2) The number of the people at the party is a prime number between 24 and 30. (A prime number cannot be divided by another number evenly.)

Certainly statement (1) alone cannot answer the question. Now look at statement (2): The only prime number between 24 and 30 is *29* since 29 can be divided evenly only by itself. Thus statement (2) can be used to answer the question. Therefore Choice B is correct.

III. WHERE CHOICE C is the ANSWER

Example: Is $x + y$ positive?
(1) $x^3 = 20y$
(2) $y^3 = -129$

Look at statement (1): This does not tell us anything about $x + y$. Now look at statement (2). This tells us that y is negative (since y^3 is negative). Unfortunately, this does not answer our question. However, if y is negative (from statement (2), then according to statement (1), x must be negative. The reason for this is that x^3 is now negative. There fore, by using statements (1) and (2) we have shown that both x and y are negative. Therefore, $x + y$ must be negative and this answers our question. Thus, Choice C is correct.

IV. WHERE CHOICE D is the ANSWER

Example: Which is greater, 37 or y^2?
(1) $y > \sqrt{38}$
(2) $y = 7$

Look at statement (1): $y > \sqrt{38}$. This implies that $y^2 > \sqrt{38} \times \sqrt{38}$.

$$\sqrt{38} \times \sqrt{38} = 38$$

So statement (1) implies that $y^2 > 38$. Thus y^2 is surely greater than 37 and we have answered the question. Now look at statement (2): If $y = 7$, then $y^2 = 49$ and certainly $y^2 = 49 > 37$. Thus statement (2) answers our question. Since both statements (1) and (2) answer our question by themselves, Choice D is correct.

V. WHERE CHOICE E is the ANSWER

Example: What is the perimeter of triangle ABC?
(1) Triangle ABC is a right triangle.
(2) The area of triangle ABC = 30.

Statement (1) alone certainly does not answer our question because the fact that a triangle is a right triangle (contains a right angle) does not tell us anything about the perimeter of the triangle. Statement (2) tells us that the area is 30. Statement (2) alone will not tell us what the perimeter of the triangle is. Now suppose we looked at statements (1) and (2) together. Call the sides of the triangle x, y, and z where z is the hypotenuse (longest side opposite the 90° angle). The area of the right triangle is ½ the product of the shorter sides (½ base × height) so the area of the triangle is

$$\tfrac{1}{2}xy = 30$$

The perimeter of the right triangle is however

$$x + y + z$$

Therefore just because we know what the value of ½xy is, we cannot determine the value of $x + y + z$. Accordingly, Choice E is correct. We, therefore, need additional information to answer our question.

At this point, you are urged to use the foregoing "Tips for Solving Data Sufficiency Problems" in the solution of such problems. Following are "Practice Problems in Data Sufficiency." These questions are much like the Data Sufficiency problems that you will encounter on the actual GMAT.

55 PRACTICE PROBLEMS IN DATA SUFFICIENCY*

Directions: Each of the questions below is followed by two statements, labeled (1) and (2), in which certain data are given. In these questions you do not actually have to compute an answer, but rather you have to decide whether the data given in the statements are *sufficient* for answering the question. Using the data given in the statements *plus* your knowledge of mathematics and everyday facts (such as the number of days in July), you are to blacken the box on the answer sheet under

- (A) if statement (1) ALONE is sufficient but statement (2) alone is not sufficient to answer the question asked,

- (B) if statement (2) ALONE is sufficient but statement (1) alone is not sufficient to answer the question asked,

- (C) if BOTH statements (1) and (2) TOGETHER are sufficient to answer the question asked, but NEITHER statement ALONE is sufficient.

- (D) if EACH statement is sufficient by itself to answer the question asked,

- (E) if statements (1) and (2) TOGETHER are NOT sufficient to answer the question asked and additional data specific to the problem are needed.

1. In a given parallelogram, what is the measure of Angle *b*?

   (1) Angle *d* = 80°.
   (2) The sum of Angles *a*, *c*, and *d* is 280°.

2. If we assume a constant reading rate, can Joel finish the book in 6 hours?

   (1) Joel reads 54 pages an hour.
   (2) In 2 hours, he reads half the book.

3. How many hits must a batter get to raise his batting average to .300?

   (1) He has batted 56 times.
   (2) He has 14 hits now.

*Solutions for these problems begin on page 487.

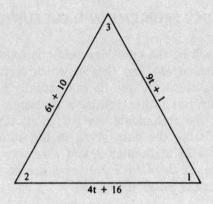

4. What is the perimeter of the triangle?

   (1) Angle 1 = Angle 2 = Angle 3
   (2) Angle 2 = 60°.

5. How long will it take Howie to finish the job alone?

   (1) Howie and Donald together finish the job in 6 hours.
   (2) Donald would need 10 hours to complete the job alone.

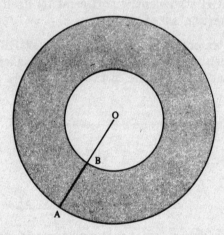

6. What is the ratio of the shaded area to the unshaded area of the concentric circles?

   (1) $OA = 3OB$
   (2) $AB = 2OB$

7. How far is Birenburg from Ferenci?

   (1) Ferenci is 37 miles from Pebbly Corners.
   (2) Birenburg is 56 miles from Pebbly Corners.

8. Is C an odd number?

   (1) The reciprocal of C is greater than .1 and less than .12.
   (2) $2C$ is an even number.

9. In triangle *MNO*, does Angle *MNO* equal Angle *MON*?

   (1) $ON = MN$
   (2) Angle $OMN = 73°$

10. Is the average age of the men less than 32?

    (1) One-third of the men are younger than 25.
    (2) One-half of the men are between 25 and 30 years old.

11. What is the length of the square's diagonal?

    (1) The perimeter of the square is $16\sqrt{2}$.
    (2) The area of the square is 32.

12. If deebis, dlowds, and flestrungs are units of measurement, is a deebi greater than a dlowd?

    (1) 5 deebis = 1 dlowd.
    (2) 1 dlowd = 7 flestrungs.

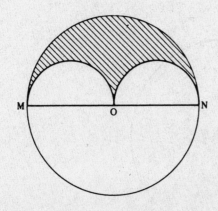 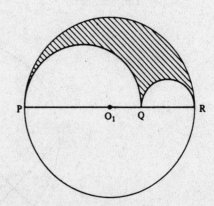

13. If both circles O and O_1 have radii of 6, what is the ratio of the shaded area of semicircle O to the shaded area of semicircle O_1?

    (1) $MO = ON$
    (2) $PQ = 2\ QR$

14. How many minutes does the clock lose a day?

    (1) The clock reads 6:00 when it is really 5:48.
    (2) The clock is 40 seconds fast each hour.

15. Is angle *l* greater than angle *m* in triangle *LMN*?

    (1) $55 \leq m \leq 70$
    (2) $55 \leq n \leq 70$

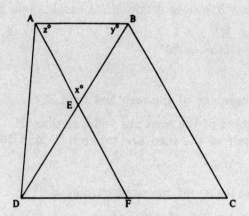

16. In trapezoid *ABCD*, what is the length of *AB*?

    (1) $x = y = z$
    (2) $EB = 6$

17. Does $L = M$?

    (1) $\dfrac{M}{L} = 1$.

    (2) $LM = M^2$.

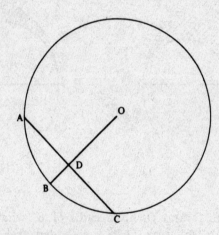

18. What is the diameter of the circle?

    (1) $AC = 16$
    (2) $DB = 6$

19. What is the area of square *EFGH*?

    (1) $EG = 13$
    (2) $FH = 13$

20. If a hockey team gains 2 points for a win, 1 point for a tie, and no points for a loss, how many points does the team now have?

    (1) The team has won 13 more games than it has tied.
    (2) The team has played 52 games.

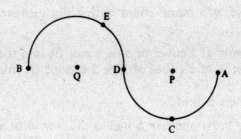

21. *Q* and *P* are the centers of the arcs. What is the length of *ACDEB*?

    (1) $QE = 6\frac{1}{2}$
    (2) $QP = DA$

22. How many pints of oil are contained in the can?

    (1) $\frac{1}{2}$ pint of oil fills up $\frac{1}{5}$ of the can.
    (2) 5 pints of oil are needed to fill 2 cans.

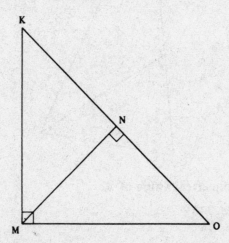

23. What is the length of *KO*?

    (1) $MN = 5\sqrt{2}$
    (2) $KM = MO = 10$

24. How much did George weigh before his diet?

    (1) He lost 8 pounds.
    (2) He now weighs $\frac{23}{24}$ of his former weight.

25. How much time will a computer need to solve 150 problems?

    (1) The computer needs 50 seconds to solve the first problem.
    (2) A man needs 6 hours to solve the 150 problems.

26. Which element weighs the most, Argon, Sodium, or Sulfur?

    (1) 2 atoms of Sulfur weigh more than one atom of Argon or one atom of Sodium.
    (2) 2 atoms of Sodium weigh less than one atom of Argon or one atom of Sulfur.

27. The contents of how many cubes with sides measuring 2 can fit into a container?

   (1) The contents of 3 cubes of side 4 can fit into the container.
   (2) The contents of 8 cubes of side 3 cannot fit into the container.

28. What is Wayne's height?

   (1) If Wayne grew another 5 inches, he would be as tall as Marty.
   (2) If Marty were 8 inches shorter, he would be as tall as Wayne was last year.

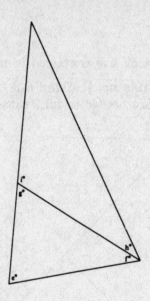

29. What is the numerical value of e?

   (1) $h + g = 115$
   (2) $i - f = 75$

30. How many yards of cloth must Mrs. Roth buy to make 3 identical dresses?

   (1) She needs 3 yards of cloth to make one such dress.
   (2) Usually she averages 4 yards of cloth per dress.

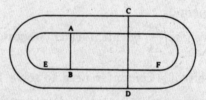

31. If the straight portion of the track EF is 100 yards long, how much longer is a lap for a runner on the outer track than for a runner on the inner track?
   (The curved portions of the track are semicircles.)

   (1) $CD = 20$ yards
   (2) $AB = 10$ yards

32. How many words are listed in the 1280 page dictionary?

    (1) Page 387 lists 50 words.
    (2) There are 2000 words listed under "A."

33. If there were 52,000 people living in Woodridge in 1968, what was the percentage increase in population from 1967 to 1968?

    (1) Since 1960 the average percentage population increase was 5.3%
    (2) In 1967 there were 48,000 people living in Woodridge.

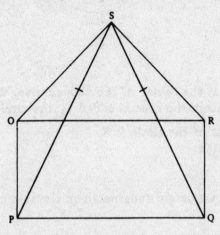

PS = SQ

34. In the above figure, $ORQP$ is a rectangle, angle OSR is a right angle, and triangle PQS is isosceles. What is the measure of angle PSQ?

    (1) Angle $SPQ = 70°$
    (2) Angle $QSR = 25°$

35. What was the average temperature during August?

    (1) The high temperature for August 6 was 98°F.
    (2) The low temperature for August 10 was 63°F.

36. If A and B are numbers, which weighs more, A feathers or B stones?

    (1) $A = 700 B$
    (2) 2 pounds $= A$ feathers $= B$ stones

37. What grade must Perry receive on his next exam so that his total average for the term will be 90?

    (1) The next test will be the sixth of the term.
    (2) His average is now 88.

38. Judy walked from Monticello to Liberty, a walking distance of 10 miles. If she left Monticello at 9 A.M., what was her average walking speed in miles per hour?

    (1) Judy walked into Liberty at 20 minutes past noon.
    (2) Judy arrived in Liberty after walking $3\frac{1}{2}$ hours.

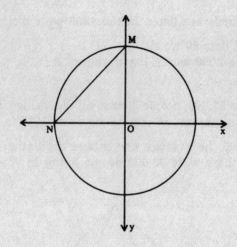

39. The origin is at the center of the above circle. Will the point located at (3,2) be within the area bounded by the circle?

    (1) The radius of the circle is 3.
    (2) $MN = 3\sqrt{2}$

40. Can Truck A pass safely underneath an elevated highway 12 feet above the ground?

    (1) Truck B can pass safely underneath the highway.
    (2) Truck B is taller than Truck A.

41. Is the base of isosceles triangle -1 greater than the base of isosceles triangle 2?

    (1) The vertex of triangle 1 measures 32°.
    (2) The vertex of triangle 2 measures 54°.

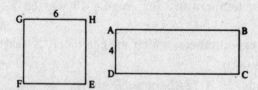

42. By how much do the perimeters of the above square and rectangle differ?

    (1) Their areas are equal.
    (2) $GF + BC = AB + 1$

43. Are the 2 circles congruent?

    (1) Chord AB on the first circle is twice the length of chord XY on the second circle.
    (2) Their areas are equal.

44. If Karen has 95¢ in nickels, dimes, and quarters, how many dimes has she?

    (1) She has twice as many dimes as quarters.

    (2) Quarters account for $\dfrac{10}{19}$ and nickels account for $\dfrac{1}{19}$ of the value of her change.

45. What day of the week is it?

    (1) Today is March 25.
    (2) February 25 was a Monday.

46. Is the triangle scalene, isosceles, or equilateral?

    (1) The sides of the triangle are in the ratio of 3:4:5.
    (2) The angles of the triangle are unequal.

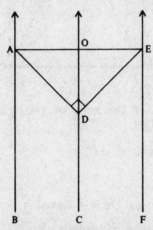

(The vertical lines are parallel.)

47. *AB* is parallel to *EF* and Angle *ADE* is a right angle. What is the measure of angle *BAD*?

    (1) Angle *FED* = 45°
    (2) *AE* is perpendicular to *EF*

48. What is the length of the diagonal of the rectangular solid?

    (1) The height of the solid is 3 inches.
    (2) The rectangular base measures 6 inches by 8 inches.

49. Are there more than 200 pictures in the 67-page book?

    (1) There is at least 1 picture on each page.
    (2) There are no more than 3 pictures on any given page.

50. How many sides does the regular polygon have?

    (1) Each interior angle measures 120°.
    (2) The sum of the interior angles is 720°.

51. What is the length of the bed?

    (1) The sum of 2 different yardsticks measures the length exactly.

    (2) If stretched out fully, a man 6 feet 6 inches tall would not fit into the bed.

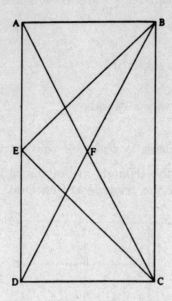

52. In rectangle *ABCD*, if the area of triangle *ACE* is 4, what is the area of triangle *BDE*?

    (1) *E* is the midpoint of *AD*.

    (2) *BC* = 8

53. How many pencils does Dennis have?

    (1) He bought 2 boxes of pencils.

    (2) He lent 2 pencils to George.

54. If $D = 7$, *E* is how many units greater than *F*?

    (1) $E = D + F$

    (2) $\dfrac{E}{D} = F - 5$

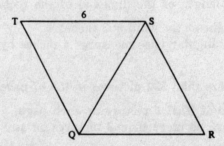

55. In rhombus *QRST* what is, the length of *QS*?

    (1) Angle *QTS* = 60°

    (2) *RS* = *TS*

SOLUTIONS FOR DATA SUFFICIENCY PROBLEMS

1. **(D)** Since opposite angles of a parallelogram are equal, statement 1 is sufficient. Statement 2 is sufficient since the sum of the angles of a parallelogram is 360° and, knowing the total measure of 3 angles, we can find the measure of the fourth.

2. **(B)** Statement 1 would be sufficient if we knew the length of the book. Statement 2 is sufficient since, knowing that half of the book will be read in 2 hours and that the reading rate is constant, we find that it will take Joel 4 hours to complete the book.

3. **(C)** Using both statements, we can set up the following equation: x = the number of hits the batter must get.

$$\frac{14 + x \text{ hits}}{56 + x \text{ at bat}} = .300$$

$$x = 4$$

4. **(A)** Knowing that Angle 1 = Angle 2 = Angle 3 tells us that the triangle is equilateral. We can thus set any 2 sides of the triangle equal to each other and solve for t. Adding the lengths of the sides will give the perimeter. Statement 2 alone is insufficient to draw any conclusions.

5. **(C)** Using statement 1 we can set up the following equation: H = the amount of time Howie needs to finish the job alone. $\frac{1}{H}$ is the part of the job he completes in 1 hour.
D = the amount of time Donald needs to finish the job alone. $\frac{1}{D}$ is the part of the job Donald completes in 1 hour. According to statement 2, $D = 10$.

$$\frac{1}{H} + \frac{1}{10} = \frac{1}{6}$$

$$H = 15$$

6. **(D)** The area of the shaded area is the area of the circle with radius OA minus the area of the circle with radius OB. Since $A = \pi r^2$, the ratio is

$$\frac{\text{shaded area}}{\text{unshaded area}} =$$

$$\frac{\pi(OA)^2 - \pi(OB)^2}{\pi(OB)^2} = \frac{(OA)^2 - (OB)^2}{(OB)^2}$$

Substituting from statement 1, the ratio is

$$\frac{9(OB)^2 - (OB)^2}{(OB)^2} = \frac{8}{1}$$

Substituting from statement 2,

$$OA = OB + AB = 30B$$

which is the same as statement 1.

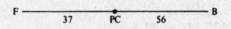

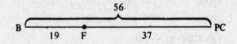

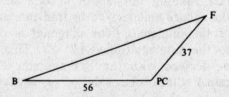

7. **(E)** Birenburg can be anywhere between 19 and 93 miles from Ferenci.

8. **(A)** The only number whose reciprocal is less than .12 and greater than .1 is 9. (Its reciprocal is .11.) Twice any number is even, therefore Statement 2 is inconclusive.

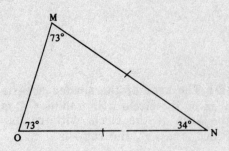

9. **(C)** Sketch a diagram and use the information in both statements to answer the question. Remember: Base angles of an isosceles triangle are equal. The answer is no.

10. **(E)** The given information is insufficient. Let us show this by two counter-examples:

GROUP A
TOTAL = 6 men
3 men = 27 years old
2 men = 22 years old
1 man = 40 years old
Avg. age = 27.5

GROUP B
TOTAL = 6 men
3 men = 26 years old
2 men = 23 years old
1 man = 80 years old
Avg. age = 34.0

11. **(D)** Finding the length of one side of the square enables you to find the length of the diagonal. (The diagonal is equal to the side multiplied by $\sqrt{2}$. This can be derived with the Pythagorean Theorem.) Since one side of a square is equal to $\frac{1}{4}$ of the perimeter, the side can be found using statement 1. Since the area of a square is equal to a side squared, the length of the side can also be found from statement 2.

12. **(A)** Statement 1 tells us that a deebi is equal to $\frac{1}{5}$ of a dlowd, and is therefore smaller. Statement 2 alone does not tell us anything about a deebi.

13. **(C)** The area of circle O is 36 since $MO = ON = 6$ from statement 1. The area of the shaded portion is the area of the semicircle (18π) minus the area of the two smaller semicircles, each having radius 3. Thus,

$$18\pi = \left[\ \frac{3^2\pi}{2} + \frac{3^2\pi}{2}\ \right] = 18\pi - 9\pi = 9\pi$$

From statement 2, in circle O, the radii of the two inner semicircles are 4 and 2. Using the same formula shown above, we find the area of the shaded portion to be 8π. The ratio is 9:8.

14. **(B)** Statement 1 is inconclusive. Although we know that by 6, the clock was 12 minutes slow, we do not know when the true time and the clock time were the same. Therefore we cannot project this difference over a full day. However statement 2 tells us how much time is lost per hour. Multiplying 40 seconds per hour by 24 hours will give you the amount of time lost per day.

15. **(E)** Assuming the minimum values for m and n, l will be 70°. Assuming the maximum values for m and n, l will be 40°. We cannot tell if l is greater than m from this information.

16. **(C)** Knowing that angles x, y, and z are equal tells us that ABE is equilateral and all its sides are equal If side EB is 6, then side AB will also be 6.

17. **(A)** In statement 1, multiply both sides of the equation by L to find that $M = L$. Note that the only way L could be 0 would be if $M = 0$, since $\frac{M}{L} = 1$. Thus if $L = 0$, $M = 0$ and $M = L$. Statement 2 is not sufficient *alone* to answer the question of whether $L = M$. The reason for this is that the equation of Statement 2

$$LM = M^2$$

holds if $M = 0$ and L is *any* value. Thus Statement 1 *alone* is sufficient but Statement 2 alone is not sufficient. Therefore, Choice A is correct.

18. **(E)** The diameter is indeterminable since there can be many different circles with these lengths for *AC* and *DB*.

19. **(D)** If we letter the square in a clockwise direction, *EG* and *FH* are diagonals. By using the Pythagorean theorem, the length of a side of a square can be immediately determined from the length of the diagonal. Squaring the length of a side gives the area.

20. **(E)** Since we do not know how many games the team has lost, we cannot determine the exact number of wins and ties. Consequently the total points of the team cannot be found.

21. **(C)** Knowing statement 2 enables us to determine that the radii of the semicircles are equal. (Subtract *DP* from each side of the equation $QD + DP = DP + PA$) Knowing the length of the radius from statement 1 enables us to find the circumference of the arcs.

22. **(D)** Set up proportions:

$$\frac{\frac{1}{2}\text{ pint}}{\frac{1}{5}\text{ can}} = \frac{x}{1\text{ can}} \qquad x = 2\tfrac{1}{2}\text{ pints}$$

$$\frac{5\text{ pints}}{2\text{ cans}} = \frac{x}{1\text{ can}} \qquad x = 2\tfrac{1}{2}\text{ pints}$$

23. **(B)** Knowing the length of the altitude to the hypotenuse of a right triangle cannot alone tell us the length of the sides. However knowing the length of two sides of a right triangle enables us to find the length of the third side.

24. **(C)** 8 pounds represents $\frac{1}{24}$ of George's former weight. Multiplying 8 by 24 gives us the former weight or 192.

25. **(E)** Statement 1 is insufficient since the rate for solving each problem is not necessarily a constant. Statement 2 is insufficient since we do not have a comparison of the computer's and the man's rate of solving problems.

26. **(E)** From the given information, it cannot be determined which element is heaviest.

27. **(E)** From statement 1 we can determine that 192 cubic units of volume can be contained in the container. From statement 2 we can determine that 8 cubes of 27 cubic units each cannot fit into the container. Therefore the container cannot hold 216 cubic units. Since the contents of anywhere between 24 to 27 cubes of side 2 can fit into the container, we cannot determine the exact number of cubes which will fit into the container.

28. **(E)** We cannot determine Wayne's present height without knowing either Marty's height or Wayne's height last year.

29. **(B)** The measure of an exterior angle of a triangle *i* is equal to the sum of the two opposite interior angles *f* and *e*. Substituting $f + e$ for *i* in statement 2, we get $f + e - f = 75$, or $e = 75$.

30. **(A)** Since the question says that the three dresses are identical, then all we must know is the amount of cloth needed for one such dress and then multiply by 3. Statement 1 provides this information. In this case statement 2 does not apply.

31. **(C)** Both the runner on the outer and the inner track would run equal lengths on the two straightaway portions of the track. However they do run different lengths along the curved portions of the track. (The two outer and inner semicircles constitute one full circle each.) Therefore all we must find is the diameter of each circle to find the lengths of the curved portions of the track. Circumference $= \pi d$. The diameter of the outer track is 20 yards and the diameter of the inner track is 10 yards. The curved portion of the outer track is 20π. The curved portion of the inner track is 10π. The runner on the outer track will have to run 10π yards longer than a runner on the inner track.

32. **(E)** Since the number of each page varies and since there is a different number of words under each letter we cannot determine the total number of words in the dictionary from the given information.

33. **(B)** Statement 1 tells only the average percentage population increase and does not tell us the increase from 1967 to 1968. However from the information given in the question (52,000 people) and from statement 2 we can determine the percentage population increase between those two years.

34. **(D)** Angle, SPQ, a base angle of isosceles triangle PQS, measures $70°$, according to statement 1. Therefore the other base angle also measures $70°$ and angle PSQ, the vertex angle, measures $40°$, the difference between $180°$ and the two base angles. Now we examine statement 2. $PS = SQ$ because they are equal sides of an isosceles triangle. Since $ORQP$ is a rectangle, opposite sides OP and RQ are equal, and all its angles are right angles. Since the base angles of the isosceles triangle are equal, their complementary angles, OPS and SQR are equal. Using the side-angle-side theorem, we have proved triangle SRQ and SOP congruent and all corresponding parts are equal. Since (according to statement 2) angle $QSR = 25°$, angle OSP also equals $25°$. Since OSR is a right angle, angle PSQ equals $90° - 2(25°) = 40°$.

35. **(E)** The given information relates only to isolated days and does not give any total information dealing with the question.

36. **(B)** Although A may be a greater number than B, the question asks for weight, not numbers. Statement 2 provides the answer for the question, that their weights are equal.

37. **(C)** From both statements we determine that Perry has earned 5×8 or **440** total points on his tests. For his new average to be 90, his total points must be 540. (When 540 is divided by 6 tests, the average is 90.) Therefore he must earn 100 on his next exam to gain a 90 average.

38. **(D)** From statement 1 and the facts given in the question, we can determine that Judy walked for $3\frac{1}{3}$ hours. (Statement 2 gives us this information immediately.) Since the walking rate is equal to the total distance walked divided by the time needed to walk that distance, we find that the walking speed equals 3 miles per hour.

39. **(D)** From statement 1, for a point to be within the area bounded by the circle, the distance between that point and the origin must be less than 3. By the distance formula,

$$d = \sqrt{(3-0)^2 + (2-0)^2} = \sqrt{13}$$

This is greater than 3 and therefore the point is not within the circle. Statement 2 tells us that MN, the hypotenuse of the right triangle formed by M, N, and the origin, is $3\sqrt{2}$ units long. Since the radii of the circle, OM and ON, are equal, we can determine the length of the radius using the Pythagorean theorem:

$$2x^2 = 3\sqrt{2} = 18$$
$$x = 3$$

Now we can proceed as in statement 1 to answer the question.

40. **(C)** Truck B, a taller truck, can safely pass under the highway. Therefore Truck A, a shorter truck, can also safely pass under the highway.

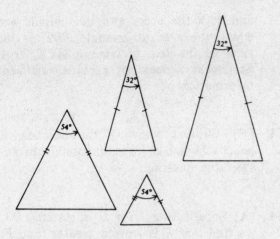

41. **(E)** The base of either triangle can be larger than the other as shown by the solution diagram.

42. **(D)** Since one side of the square is 6, its perimeter is four times that, or 24. Its area is $6 \times 6 = 36$. The rectangle's area is also 36 from statement 1. The height of the rectangle is 4. Since the area of a rectangle is given by the formula: Area $=$ Base $\times$ Height, the base must be 9. Its perimeter is 30. The difference in the perimeters is 6. In statement 2, $GF = 6$ (one side of the square) and $BC = 4$ (opposite sides of a rectangle area equal). Substituting these figures in the equation, we get $AB + 1 = 10$ $AB = 9$. We proceed as above to find the respective perimeters and the difference between them.

43. **(B)** Statement 1 tells virtually nothing because we do not know the location of the given chords. However from statement 2 we know that the circles are congruent because circles with equal areas are congruent.

44. **(B)** Statement 1 is inconclusive. However from statement 2 we can determine that dimes account for $\frac{8}{19}$ of the value of the change. $\frac{8}{19}$ of 95¢ is 40¢. Karen has 4 dimes.

45. **(E)** If February 25 is a Monday, March 25 will be a Monday in a non-leap year and a Tuesday in a leap year. If we knew whether it was a leap year or not, we could answer the question.

46. **(D)** From statement 1 we know that all the sides are unequal, therefore making the triangle scalene. Since the angles of the triangle are unequal from statement 2, the sides are unequal, making the triangle scalene.

47. **(A)** Since angle $FED = 45°$, alternate interior angle ODE also equals 45°. Since angle ADE is 90°, then complementary angle ADO equal 45°. Alternate interior angle BAD also equals 45°. Statement 2 is not needed to answer the question.

48. **(C)** The diagonal of the rectangular solid is the hypotenuse of the right triangle formed by the height at an edge of the solid and the diagonal of the base. The height is 3 inches. The diagonal of the base is found with the Pythagorean theorem. $6^2 + 8^2 = $ (hypotenuse)^2. The hypotenuse equals $\sqrt{84}$. Using the Pythagorean theorem again we will find the length of the diagonal. $3^2(\sqrt{84})^2 = $ (diagonal)^2.
The diagonal equals $\sqrt{93}$.

49. **(E)** Since there are between 1 and 3 pictures on each page, there can be between 67 and 201 pictures in the book. However we do not definitely know whether there are more than 200 pictures in the book.

50. **(D)** The following formula gives the measures of each angle in a regular polygon:

$$A = \frac{(n\text{-}2)\ 180°}{n}$$

where A is the measure of each angle and n is the number of sides in the polygon. For statement 1, substitute 120° for A in the formula.

$$120° = \frac{(n-2)\ 180°}{n}$$

$$120n = 180n - 360$$

$$60n = 360$$

$$n = 6$$

For statement 2, transform the equation into the following form by multiplying both sides by n:

$$An = (n-2)\ 180°$$

Substitute 720° for An since the measure of the angle multiplied by the number of sides gives the total sum of the interior angles.

$$720° = (n-2)\ 180°$$

$$4 = n - 2$$

$$n = 6$$

51. **(A)** A yardstick measures 1 yard. The sum of 2 yardsticks is 2 yards. From statement 2 all we know is that the bed is less than 6 feet 6 inches long, but we do not know the exact length.

52. **(A)** From statement 1, $AE = ED$. Thus the two triangles ACE and BDE have equal bases. The sides of the rectangle ($AB = DC$) represent the equal heights of the two triangles. Since $A = \frac{1}{2}$ bh, and both the bases and the heights are equal, the area of triangle BDE is the same as the area of triangle ACE, or 4. Statement 2 does not provide sufficient information.

53. **(E)** Without knowing the number of pencils in a box, it is impossible to answer the question.

54. **(A)** Substituting 7 for D in statement 1, we find that E is 7 units greater than F. However in statement 2 the difference between E and F is not a constant. For example $E = 42$ and $F = 11$ solves the equation. E is 31 units greater than F in this case. In another example E may be 28 and F would then be 9. The difference between them is then 19. Therefore statement 2 is inconclusive.

55. **(A)** In a rhombus, all sides are equal. Therefore $TS = TQ$ and the base angles opposite them in triangle TQS are equal. Since angle QTS is 60° from statement 1, the two equal base angles are also 60°. The triangle is therefore equilateral and all its sides are equal. QS also equals 6. Statement 2 does not tell us anything we did not know before since all sides of a rhombus are equal.

Part Four

Tips for Answering
Business Judgment Questions

TIPS FOR ANSWERING BUSINESS JUDGMENT*
QUESTIONS

About the Business Judgment Passage

In the Business Judgment section, you are given a passage of about 1000 to 1500 words in length. Each passage describes a practical business situation in which a person or persons have to make a decisión related to that situation. The passage focuses on the problems encountered in making a decision, while presenting facts and conditions relevant to the situation. In the course of reading the passage, you will find suggestions as to how to achieve the goal. You will also see that the decision maker is influenced by many factors, some important and some not so important. You will find that the decision maker has several many important objectives or goals. The decision maker also makes many serious assumptions which may possibly lead him to making the wrong decision.

About the Business Judgment Questions

After reading the passage, you will encounter two sets of questions — the Data Evaluation type and the Data Application type. About two-thirds of the questions are of the first type, Data Evaluation. Each question of the Data Evaluation type is presented as a *single phrase*. The phrase describes either (1) and *objective* of the decision maker, or (2) a *factor* which influences the decision maker's decision, or (3) an *assumption* of the decision maker or (4) an *issue* that is unimportant to the decision.

You are to choose (A) if the phrase represents a

MAJOR OBJECTIVE — That is, a *goal* of the decision maker. A major objective is something that the decision maker desires. Note that the decision maker may want to achieve many goals. Thus, he may have many major objectives.

You are to choose (B) if the phrase represents a

MAJOR FACTOR — That is, a primary factor which influences the decision maker in his decision. A major factor is usually a consideration that is explicitly mentioned in the pasage. And usually, the decision maker has no real control over these factors.

You are to choose (C) if the phrase represents a

MINOR FACTOR — That is, a factor which secondarily or indirectly influences the decision maker with his decision. A minor factor is either a *subset* of a *major factor* or a factor which is relatively unimportant as compared to a major factor.

*Business Judgment is also called Practical Judgment.

You are to choose (D) if the phrase represents a

MAJOR ASSUMPTION — That is, an assumption that the decision maker makes in arriving at the decision. It is something that the decision maker takes for granted or assumes to be true. Note that it is an *important* assumption. Indeed, if the decision maker makes too many of these MAJOR ASSUMPTIONS, it may lead him to making a wrong or unwise decision.

You are to choose (E) if the phrase represents an

UNIMPORTANT ISSUE — That is, an issue which has no relevance to the decision at hand, or is unimportant in the decision maker's arriving at a decision. In other words, this issue has no importance or relevance to the decision-making process.

The Data Evaluation Question-Type

We will now present a sample passage which contains the Data Evaluation type questions. Read the passage. Then for each of the five phrases that follow, choose.

(A) if the phrase is MAJOR OBJECTIVE

(B) if the phrase is a MAJOR FACTOR

(C) if the phrase is a MINOR FACTOR

(D) if the phrase is a MAJOR ASSUMPTION

(E) if the phrase is an UNIMPORTANT ISSUE

After you have answered the five questions, read the explanatory answers that follow. IMPORTANT NOTE: The passage that follows is much shorter than the passages that you will get on you GMAT. The short passage is used here to introduce you to the DATA EVALUATION question-type.

Read the following passage in an analytical manner. You are advised to underline important words or phrases as you read the passage. When you start answering the questions, quick reference to the underlinings should aid you in answering the questions. It is usually wise to involve yourself with the passage as if *you* were the decision maker and had the responsibility of the decision maker's actions. Remember, however, to treat his considerations *objectively* and *critically*.

A Business Judgment Situation

Bob Martin had always been fascinated with the idea of operating his own candy store or soda fountain. After his physician told him to move from New York to a warmer area, he decided to open a candy store. Being financially independent, he could put as much money into the venture as he wished, without worrying about profit or loss. He preferred a large store, but would settle for a medium-size or even a small one. He believed the people to be friendlier in the Southwest than in other regions, and so investigated sites in that area. He found four possible choices:

    a. a medium-sized store in Barstow, in the middle of the hot Mojave Desert;

    b. a large store in Flagstaff, where, because of the high elevation even summer nights could grow nippy;

    c. a small but artistically decorated and expensive store in warm Albuquerque;

    d. a large store in sun-baked Phoenix.

He opened up his store in Phoenix.

DATA EVALUATION QUESTIONS

1. Reaping of a huge profit from the store
2. Climate in the area where the store is located
3. Having an owner-operated business
4. Friendliness of people in Phoenix
5. Elevation of Flagstaff

ANSWERS

1. (E) Since Bob is "financially independent," he can choose his site "without worrying about profit or loss." Thus, this is an UNIMPORTANT ISSUE.

2. (B) Bob needs warm weather. He must, therefore, weigh the possible locations with regard to their climate. Since this variable directly affects the decision, it is a MAJOR FACTOR.

3. (A) Since Bob Martin was fascinated with the idea of operating a soda fountain, it would appear that an owner-operated business was a MAJOR OBJECTIVE of the decision maker.

4. (D) *Believing* this item to be true was the basis for Bob's proceeding to arrive at a decision. It is thus a MAJOR ASSUMPTION.

5. (C) Since climate at each site is a Major Factor, and since the elevation of Flagstaff contributes to the climate at that site, this item is a MINOR FACTOR.

The Data Application Question Type

The second set of questions appearing in the Business Judgment section is the Data Application type. Data Application questions comprise about one-third the total number of questions in the Business Judgment section. The Data Application question-types are straightforward multiple-choice questions which relate to information discussed in the passage. Occasionally, the Data Application questions may refer to material presented in a chart or table in the passage. Following is a sample Data Application question which is related to the previous passage:

It could be reasonably concluded from the business situation described that Bob Martin

    (A) had most of his money tied up in investments

    (B) chose to open his store in Phoenix because Phoenix was a major city.

    (C) did not care to decorate his store artistically

    (D) was considering stores only with sea-level elevation

    (E) lived on the East Coast of the United States before opening up his store in Phoenix.

ANSWER

Choice E is the correct answer. The passage states that "his physician told him to move from New York to a warmer area." Thus, it is reasonable to assume that Bob Martin lived in New York (which is on the East Coast of the United States) before he opened up his store. Choice A is incorrect because we have no way of determining whether this is true or not. Choice B is incorrect because there is no mention in the passage of whether Bob Martin was interested in Phoenix because it was a major city. Choice C is incorrect. Although Bob Martin did not choose the artistically decorated store in Albuquerque, it does not follow that he did not care to decorate his store in Phoenix artistically. Choice D is incorrect because Bob Martin was also considering a store in Flagstaff which, according to the passage, had *high* elevation.

More Suggestions for Answering Business Judgment Questions

1. If the decision outcome is contrary to what is presented in the beginning and/or middle of the passage, it is very probable that many of the factors, objectives, and assumptions, will be found toward the end of the passage, or in a table or chart at the end of the passage. If you have little time to read the entire passage, it would be wise to concentrate on the last part of the passage.

2. There are usually 50 questions in the Business Judgment section. Since all the questions on the GMAT have equal weight, the Business Judgment section is a very important one in determining your overall GMAT score.

3. Make sure that you thoroughly understand what the Data Evaluation choices refer to. That is, make sure you know and feel comfortable with what is meant by

(A) MAJOR OBJECTIVE   (C) MINOR FACTOR

(B) MAJOR FACTOR   (D) MAJOR ASSUMPTION

(E) UNIMPORTANT ISSUE

You should *memorize*: Choice A refers to MAJOR objective. Choice B refers to MAJOR FACTOR, etc.

4. In answering the Data Application questions, be on the lookout for specific and relevant information appearing in the passage. Sometimes a chart or list is included in the passage. In making any calculations, be sure that you include all of the required calculational steps. Do not spend too much time on a computational type question if you see that it is very difficult for you to answer or comprehend it.

5. In the Data Evaluation questions, watch for "first-word keys." For example: *Cost of equipment.* Cost is a first-word key. Note that *cost* must refer to a FACTOR, an ASSUMPTION, or an UNIMPORTANT ISSUE. *Cost could not* refer to an OBJECTIVE. Another example: *Maintaining proper environment. Maintaining* is a first-word key. *Maintaining* must refer to an OBJECTIVE, an ASSUMPTION, or an UNIMPORTANT ISSUE. *Maintaining could not* refer to a FACTOR.

Finally, we offer two more important suggestions to "whip you" into good shape for the important Business Judgment section of the GMAT.

1. When you answer the Business Judgment questions in each of the five Practice Tests in this book, study carefully the explanatory answers for those questions which you answered incorrectly. In this way, you will strengthen your technique of answering Business Judgment questions that may cause you difficulty on the actual test.

2. Compose your own Business Judgment situation — then make up your own Data Evaluation and Data Application questions — and compose your own explanatory answers for each question you make up. This valuable exercise will give you a great feel for what to look for in answering Business Judgment questions.

Part Five

GMAT Grammar and Usage Refresher

The following pages will prove very helpful since you will find in these pages a brief but to-the-point review for every type of Grammar and Usage question which appears on the actual GMAT.

This "Refresher" includes the following essential areas of Grammar and Usage:

The Parts of Speech	**Tense**
Clauses and Phrases	**Verbals**
The Sentence and Its Parts	**Mood and Voice**
Verbs	**Adjective Modifiers**
Nouns and Pronouns	**Adverbial Modifiers**
Subject-Verb Relationship	**Connectives**

Correct Usage: Choosing the Right Word

GRAMMAR AND USAGE REFRESHER*

CHAPTER 1
The Parts of Speech

1a Noun

A **noun** is a word that names a **person, place, thing** or **idea.**

Persons	Places	Things	Ideas
nurse	forest	banana	love
Henry	Miami	shoe	democracy
uncle	house	television	hunger
Chicano	airport	notebook	cooperation

A noun that is made up of more than one word is called a **compound noun.**

Persons	Places	Things	Ideas
Martin Luther King	high school	telephone book	energy crisis
cab driver	Puerto Rico	car key	arms race
movie star	dining room	park bench	light year
federal judge	Middle East	pork chop	market value

1b Pronoun

A **pronoun** is a word used **in place of a noun.**

> Buy a newspaper and bring **it** home.
>   (The pronoun "it" stands for the noun "newspaper.")

> Marlene went to the party but **she** didn't stay long.
>   (The "pronoun "she" stands for the noun "Marlene.")

A **pronoun** may be used **in place of a noun or a group of nouns.**

> Pedro wanted to see the polar bears, camels, and tropical birds, **which** were at the zoo.
>   (The pronoun "which" stands for the nouns "polar bears, camels, and tropical birds.")

> When Mark, Steven, Teresa, and Barbara became eighteen, **they** registered to vote.
>   (The pronoun "they" stands for the nouns "Mark, Steven, Teresa and Barbara.")

The **noun that the pronoun replaces** is called the **antecedent** of the pronoun.

> The **plates** broke when **they** fell.
>   (The noun "plates" is the antecedent of the pronoun "they.")

*An index to this entire Grammar Refresher section begins on page 571.

Avoid confusion by repeating the noun instead of using a pronoun if more than one noun might be considered to be the antecedent.

> The lamp hit the table when **the lamp** was knocked over.
> (**Not:** The lamp hit the table when **it** was knocked over.)

1c   Verb

A **verb** is a word or group of words that **expresses action or being**.

> The plane **crashed** in Chicago. (action)

> Soccer **is** a popular sport. (being)

1d   Adjective

An **adjective** is a word that **modifies a noun or pronoun**.

Note: In grammar, to modify a noun means to describe, talk about, explain, limit, specify, or change the character of a noun.

> Susan brought us **red** flowers.
> (The adjective "red" describes the noun "flowers.")

> Everyone at the party looked **beautiful.**
> (The adjective "beautiful" describes the pronoun "everyone.")

> **Several** people watched the parade.
> (The adjective "several" does not actually describe the noun "people"; it limits or talks about how many "people" watched the parade.)

> Those shoes are her **favorite** ones.
> (The adjective "favorite" defines or specifies which "ones.")

> They have **two** children.
> (The adjective "two" limits or specifies how many "children.")

1e   Adverb

An **adverb** is a word that **modifies** the meaning of **a verb, an adjective, or another adverb**.

> The librarian spoke **softly.**
> (The adverb "softly" describes or explains how the librarian "spoke.")

> Jackie Onassis is **extremely** rich.
> (The adverb "extremely" talks about or specifies how "rich" Jackie Onassis is.)

> The job is **very** nearly completed.
> (The adverb "very" limits or specifies how "nearly" the job is completed.)

1f Preposition

A **preposition** is a word that **connects a noun or pronoun to another word** in the sentence.

> The mayor campaigned **throughout** the city.
>   (The preposition "throughout" connects the noun "city" to the verb "campaigned.")

A **preposition connects** a noun or pronoun to another word in the sentence **to show a relationship**.

> The wife **of** the oil executive was kidnapped.
>
> A friend **of** mine is a good lawyer.
>
> The strainer **for** the sink is broken.
>
> The floor **under** the sink is wet.
>
> David wants to work **in** the city.
>
> The accident occurred **about** eight o'clock.

1g Conjunction

A **conjunction** is a word that **joins words, phrases, or clauses.**

> Alan's father **and** mother are divorced. (two words joined)
>
> Is your favorite song at the end **or** in the middle of the record? (two phrases joined)
>
> You may swim in the pool **but** don't stay long. (two clauses joined)

(See Chapter 12 for a discussion of how prepositions and conjunctions act as connectives.)

1h Interjection

An **interjection** is a word (or group of words) that **expresses surprise, anger, pleasure, or some other emotion.**

> **Aha!** I've caught you.
>
> **Oh no!** What have you done now?

An **interjection** has **no grammatical relation** to another word.

> **Ouch!** I've hurt myself.

1i   A word may belong to more than one part of speech, depending on its meaning.

Example 1

Everyone **but** Sam was invited to the wedding. (preposition)

The Orioles won the pennant **but** the Angels came close to winning. (conjunction)

Harry has **but** ten dollars left in his bank account. (adverb)

Example 2

He lives **up** the street. (preposition)

It's time to get **up.** (adverb)

The sun is **up.** (adjective)

Every life has its **ups** and downs. (noun)

I'll **up** you five dollars. (verb)

Note: Just for fun—what is the part of speech of the word "behind" in this sentence?

Attempting to save Annie, the fireman ran for the door, dragging her **behind.**

Our answer is an adverb, meaning "at the rear." If your answer was a noun—Oh my! The noun means a certain part of the human body. We won't tell you which part.

CHAPTER 2
Clauses and Phrases

2a   Clauses

A **clause** is a **group of words** within a sentence.

From his room, **he could see the park.** (one clause)

The children loved the man   who sold ice cream. (two clauses)

A **clause contains a subject and a verb.**

subject   verb
↓   ↓
Before the race, **the jockeys inspected their horses.** (one clause)

subject   verb   subject   verb
↓   ↓   ↓   ↓
When the   rain   stopped,   the air   was   cooler. (two clauses)

2b   There are two types of clauses: main and subordinate.*

main clause
During the riot, several people got hurt.

subordinate clause   main clause
When she won the lottery, Mrs. Ya-ching shouted with joy.

A **main clause** makes sense by itself.

We got the day off.

A **main clause** expresses a complete thought.

The fire was put out.
   (**Not:** When the fire was put out.)

It rained this morning.
   (**Not:** Because it rained this morning.)

A **subordinate clause** does not make sense by itself.

While the washing machine was broken, we couldn't wash anything.
   (The subordinate clause does not make sense without the rest of the
   sentence.)

Because a subordinate clause does not make sense by itself, a subordinate clause cannot stand as a complete sentence.

While the washing machine was broken. . . .

---

*A main clause may be called an independent clause. A subordinate clause may be called a dependent clause.

A subordinate clause depends on a particular word in a main clause to make the subordinate clause mean something.

main clause   subordinate clause

Jack abandoned the car **which had two flat tires.**
(The subordinate clause depends on the noun "car" in the main clause to describe the car.)

main clause   subordinate clause

The job was offered to Ann **because she was best qualified.**
(The subordinate clause depends on the verb "was offered" in the main clause to explain **why** the job was offered.)

main clause   subordinate clause

My new neighbor is the one **who is waving.**
(The subordinate clause depends on the pronoun "one" in the main clause to tell **who** is waving.)

A subordinate clause may be used in a sentence as an **adjective,** an **adverb** or a **noun.**

Woody Allen's new film is the funniest movie **that he has made yet.**
(The subordinate clause acts like an adjective because it modifies —talks about—the noun "movie.")

The child giggled **while he was asleep.**
(The subordinate clause functions like an adverb because it modifies the verb "giggled.")

Please tell me **what this is all about.**
(The subordinate clause acts like a noun because it is the object of the action verb "tell.")

2c Phrases

A phrase is a group of words within a sentence.

Thurmon Munson died **in a plane crash.** (one phrase)

Let's sit **under that apple tree.** (one phrase)

At the top   of the hill   there were some cows grazing. (two phrases)

The phrase itself does not contain a subject or a verb.

subject   verb
↓   ↓
Many streets **in the city** need repairs.

A phrase does not make sense by itself.

Ellen has a collection **of beautiful earrings.**
(The phrase "of beautiful earrings" does not make sense by itself; therefore, the phrase cannot stand alone as a complete sentence.)

A phrase may begin with a preposition, a participle, a gerund, or an infinitive.

preposition
↓
Put the milk **into** the refrigerator. (prepositional phrase)

participle
↓
There are several people **waiting** in line. (participial phrase)

gerund
↓
Running ten miles a day is hard work. (gerund phrase)

infinitive
↓
To sing well take a lot of practice. (infinitive phrase)

A **phrase** may be used as a **noun,** an **adjective** an **adverb.**

A doctor's job is **to heal people.**
(The infinitive phrase acts like a noun because it names the doctor's job.)

Raising his hands, the pope blessed the crowd.
(The participial phrase acts like an adjective because it describes the pope.)

Most stores close **at five o'clock.**
(The prepositional phrase acts like an adverb because it tells when most stores close.)

CHAPTER 3
The Sentence and Its Parts

3a A **sentence** is a **group of words** that has a **subject** and a **verb.**

subject   verb
↓   ↓
The **concert began** at midnight.

subject   verb
↓   ↓
During the storm, the **electricity was knocked out.**

3b A sentence may be **declarative, interrogative,** or **exclamatory.**

A declarative sentence **states or asserts.**

Inflation is a serious problem.

An **interrogative** sentence **asks a question.**

How long must we suffer?

An **exclamatory** sentence **expresses emotion***

What a fool he is!

A sentence expresses a **complete thought.**

The price of gold has gone up.

Bus service will resume on Friday morning.

Note: Because a sentence expresses a complete thought, a sentence makes sense by itself.

Peter likes to tend his vegetable garden. (complete thought)

Peter likes. (incomplete thought—not a sentence)

The gasoline shortage created serious problems. (complete thought)

The gasoline shortage. (incomplete thought—not a sentence).

3c **The four types of sentences according to structure are the following:**

(1) **Simple**	Everyone likes music.
(2) **Compound**	The Simons put their house up for sale on Friday, and it was sold by Monday.

*An "exclamatory sentence" is sometimes called an "imperative sentence."

(3) **Complex**   If you want good Szechuan cooking, you should

go to the Hot Wok Restaurant.

(4) **Compound-Complex**   Bob met Sally, who was in town for a few

days, and they went to a museum.

3d   Simple sentence

A **simple sentence** is made up of **one main clause** only.

I love you.

A simple sentence may be of any length.

The old man sitting on the park bench is the father of a dozen men and women besides being the grandfather of nearly forty children.

Note: A simple sentence **does not have a subordinate clause** in it.

3e   Compound sentence

A **compound sentence** has **two or more main clauses**.

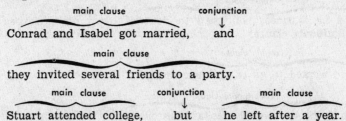

Conrad and Isabel got married,   and

they invited several friends to a party.

Stuart attended college,   but   he left after a year.

Each main clause in a compound sentence may stand by itself as a simple sentence—as long as the conjunction is left out.

conjunction
↓

Carlos will arrive by plane tonight,   and   Maria will go to the airport to meet him. (compound sentence)

Carlos will arrive by plane tonight. (simple sentence)

Maria will go to the airport to meet him. (simple sentence)

Note: A compound sentence does not have any subordinate clauses.

3f   Complex sentence

A complex sentence contains only one main clause and one or more subordinate clauses.

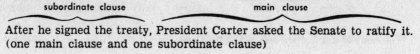

After he signed the treaty, President Carter asked the Senate to ratify it. (one main clause and one subordinate clause)

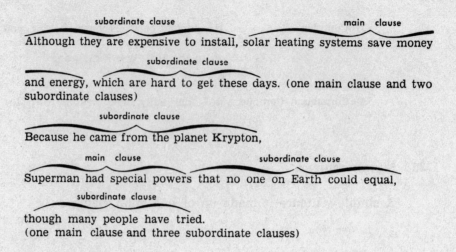

subordinate clause / main clause

Although they are expensive to install, solar heating systems save money

subordinate clause

and energy, which are hard to get these days. (one main clause and two subordinate clauses)

subordinate clause

Because he came from the planet Krypton,

main clause / subordinate clause

Superman had special powers that no one on Earth could equal,

subordinate clause

though many people have tried.
(one main clause and three subordinate clauses)

3g Compound-complex sentence

A compound-complex sentence is made up of **two or more main clauses and one or more subordinate clauses.**

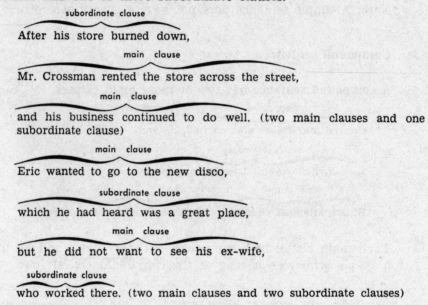

subordinate clause

After his store burned down,

main clause

Mr. Crossman rented the store across the street,

main clause

and his business continued to do well. (two main clauses and one subordinate clause)

main clause

Eric wanted to go to the new disco,

subordinate clause

which he had heard was a great place,

main clause

but he did not want to see his ex-wife,

subordinate clause

who worked there. (two main clauses and two subordinate clauses)

Note: For helpful guidance as to which sentence type to use, turn to "Vary Your Sentence Patterns," page 191.

3h The parts of a sentence

The basic parts of a sentence are a **subject,** a **verb,** and a **complement.***

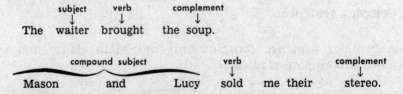

subject / verb / complement

The waiter brought the soup.

compound subject / verb / complement

Mason and Lucy sold me their stereo.

*The complement is discussed on pages 519-521.

3i Subject

A subject of a sentence is the word (or group of words) that **tells who or what is being talked about.**

> **Ann Landers** gives advice to millions of Americans.
>> (Because Ann Landers is being talked about, "Ann Landers" is the subject of the sentence.)

> High **taxes** caused many businesses to close.
>> (Because we are told that high taxes caused businesses to close, the noun "taxes" is the subject of the sentence.)

> **Whoever goes to bed last** should shut off the lights.
>> (Because we are told that whoever goes to bed last should do something, the noun clause "whoever goes to bed last" is the subject of the sentence.)

> **Brushing one's teeth and getting checkups regularly** are two important parts of good dental care.
>> (Because brushing one's teeth and getting checkups are discussed, the two gerund phrases are the **compound subject** of the sentence.)

3j A subject may be a **noun, pronoun, verbal, phrase,** or **clause.**

(1) A subject is usually a **noun.**

> Our **wedding** will be held outdoors.

> The **White House** is the home of the president.

> The **police** arrested the anti-nuclear energy demonstrators.

(2) A subject may be a **pronoun.**

> **He** always gets his way. (personal pronoun used as the subject)

> **Hers** is the tan raincoat. (possessive pronoun used as the subject)

> **What** did you do? (interrogative pronoun used as the subject)

> **That** is my car. (demonstrative pronoun used as the subject)

> **Everyone** was happy. (indefinite pronoun used as the subject)

(3) A subject may be a **verbal.***

> **To begin** is the hardest part of the job. (infinitive used as the subject)

> **Jogging** is good exercise. (gerund used as a subject)

Note: A participle may not be used as a subject.

---

*See Chapter 8.

(4) A subject may be a phrase.

Smoking cigarettes is unhealthy. (gerund phrase used as a subject)

To obey the law is everyone's duty. (infinitive phrase used as a subject)

(5) A subject may be a subordinate clause.

Whatever you decide is all right.

That Danny had cancer saddened his friends.

What will happen is going to surprise you.

Who will star in the movie will be announced.

3k Verb

A verb is a word or group of words that **usually tells what the subject does.**

Annie **skated** down the street.

Your baby **has dropped** his toy.

President Nixon **resigned.**

The telephone **is ringing.**

Two or more verbs may have one subject.

They **defeated** the Cubs but **lost** to the Pirates.

Dick **works** during the day and **goes** to school at night.

A verb may express a state or condition.

Lynn **appears** puzzled. (Or: Lynn **appears to be puzzled.**)

The stew **tastes** delicious.

Jason and Martha **are** good friends.

3l The three kinds of verbs are **transitive, intransitive,** and **linking.**

3m A transitive verb tells what its subject does to someone or to something.

The cat **caught** the mouse.

Phil **washed** the dishes.

Carol's mother **slapped** the boy.

3n   An intransitive verb tells what its subject does. The action of the intransitive verb does not affect someone or something else.

The old man **slept** in his chair.

The audience **applauded**.

All of the job applicants **waited** patiently.

Note: Many verbs may be transitive or intransitive.

He **will return** the book tomorrow. (transitive)

The manager **will return** in an hour. (intransitive)

Whether a verb is transitive or intransitive depends on how it is used in the sentence.

Chuck **opened** the package.
(The verb is transitive because the action was carried out on something.)

The door **opened** slowly.
(The verb is intransitive because the action by the subject "door" did not affect anything else.)

3o   A linking verb links the subject with a noun or a pronoun or an adjective.

"Jaws" was a terrifying **film**. (noun)

It's **I**.* (pronoun)

The child in this old photograph is **I**. (pronoun)

The girl who loves Peter is **she**. (pronoun)

The Beatles were **popular** in the 1960's. (adjective)

A linking verb may link the subject with an infinitive, a gerund, or a noun clause.

Stephanie's greatest pleasure is **to sing**. (infinitive)

Herb's mistake was **lying**. (gerund)

David's new job seemed **what he had hoped for**. (noun clause)

Linking verbs are to be, to appear, to grow, to seem, to remain, to become, and verbs that involve the senses, such as to look, to smell, to feel, to sound, and to taste.

Karen and Valerie **are** sisters.

Ben **is** strong.

---

*In spoken English, it is acceptable to say "It's me" or "It's us." It is not acceptable, however, to say "It's him," "It's her," or "It's them."

Eric **appears** healthy.

The situation at the prison **remains** tense.

Gertrude **feels** better.

Jim **sounds** angry.

A verb that appears to be a sense-linking verb may not actually be a sense-linking verb.

The milk **smells** sour. (linking verb)

The dog **smells**, the fire hydrant. (transitive verb)

Tony **looked** sad. (linking verb)

Rosie **looked** through the window. (intransitive verb)

Note: The use of a particular verb determines whether that verb is sense-linking **or** transitive **or** intransitive.

3p

Transitive verb	Intransitive verb	Linking verb
1. Expresses action	1. Expresses action	1. Does not express action
2. Is followed by a direct object which receives the action	2. Is not followed by a direct object	2. May be followed by a noun or an adjective

Transitive verb:

```
subject    trans.     direct
           verb       object
  ↓   |     ↓          ↓
Keith     shot    a    deer.
```

Intransitive verb:

```
subject          intrans.
                   verb
  ↓                 ↓
Jimmy            grinned.
```

Linking verb:

```
           link.      predicate
subject    verb        noun
  ↓         ↓           ↓
Juanita    is     a    nurse

           link.      predicate
subject    verb      adjective
  ↓         ↓           ↓
Lenny     looks       sick.
```

CHAPTER 4
Verbs

4a **Five characteristics of every verb are number, person, tense, mood, and voice.**

4b **Number shows whether the subject of the verb is singular or plural.**

>Maggie **drives** well. (singular)
>
>Adam and Peter **drive** dangerously. (plural)
>
>Joan's grandmother **is** in Atlanta. (singular)
>
>Arthur's parents **are** from Texas. (plural)

A verb must always agree in number with its subject.

subject   verb

Emily   lives alone. (subject and verb both singular)

subject   subject   verb

Dennis   and   Chuck   live   together. (subject and verb both plural)

4c **Person tells whether the subject of the verb is speaking, being spoken to, or being spoken about.**

>I **am** the person in charge. (first person)
>
>You **are** my best friend. (second person)
>
>Bill **is** not here. (third person)
>
>I **swim** at the YMCA. (first person)
>
>You **come** with me. (second person)
>
>Rosa **speaks** Spanish and French. (third person)

All three persons may be singular or plural in number.

	Singular	Plural
First person	I run	we run
Second person	you run	you run
Third person	he runs	
	she runs	they run
	it runs	

Note: The same verb form frequently is used for different persons and different numbers.

> I **love** ice cream. (first person singular)
> We **love** ice cream. (first person plural)
> They **love** ice cream. (third person plural)

4d Tense shows when the action of the verb takes places—whether in the present, the past, or the future.

> A plane **is passing** over our house right now. (present)
>
> Our guests **are** here. (present)
>
> Two U.S. astronauts **walked** on the moon in 1969. (past)
>
> The workmen **were** here yesterday. (past)
>
> We'll **pay** you tomorrow. (future)
>
> Many people **will be** at the party tomorrow. (future)

4e Mood indicates how a sentence is used—whether it is a statement or a question, a command or a request, a wish or a condition.

> Dinner **is** ready. (statement)
>
> Does Elizabeth **work** in New Jersey? (question)
>
> **Go** away! (command)
>
> Please **pass** me the bread. (request)
>
> If it **doesn't** rain, we can go. (condition)

The three kinds of moods are indicative, imperative, and subjunctive.

The indicative mood is used to express a statement or a question.

> Two firemen **were** injured in the blaze. (statement)
>
> **Are** you going out tonight? (question)

The imperative mood expresses a command or a request.

> **Turn** off that radio! (command)
>
> **May** I have a menu? (request—not question)

Note: The imperative mood is frequently indicated by leaving out the pronoun "you."

> (You) **Stop** that!

The subjunctive mood may be used to show that a wish rather than a fact is being expressed.

I wish I **were** ten years younger.

4f **Voice indicates whether the subject acts or is acted upon.**

The dog **barked** at the stranger.

The baby **was kissed** several times.

A verb in the active voice shows that the subject is doing something.

The thieves **wounded** the bank teller. (active voice)

The curtains **blocked** out view. (active voice)

A verb in the passive voice shows that something is being done to the subject.

The garbage **was picked up** this morning. (passive voice)

Tyrone's car **is being washed.** (passive voice)

4g **Complement**

A complement may be one or more words that come after either a transitive or a linking verb.

            complement
                ↓
Fire destroyed the **building**. (transitive verb)

        complement
            ↓
The cat seemed **startled**. (linking verb)

          complement   complement
              ↓   ↓
Tony bought his **wife** a silver **necklace**. (transitive verb)

          complement
              ↓
Adam will be **president** someday. (linking verb)

A complement completes the meaning of the verb.

The junta took **control of the government.**

A baseball broke the **window.**

4h **The four ways that a complement may be used in a sentence are 1) as a direct object of the verb, 2) as an indirect object of the verb, 3) as a predicate noun,* and 4) as a predicate adjective.**

Sally waters her **garden** every day. (direct object, receiving the action of the verb)

*A predicate noun is also called a predicate nominative.

Vincent gave his **brother** a basketball. (indirect object, telling to whom the action of the verb was directed)

Note: The noun "basketball" is the direct object of the transitive verb "gave"; therefore, "basketball" is also a complement.

Arthur Fiedler was the **conductor** of the Boston Pops. (predicate noun, renaming the subject after the linking verb)

Alaska is **huge**. (predicate adjective, describing the subject after the linking verb)

4i A complement used as a direct object of the verb may be a noun, a pronoun, or a subordinate clause.

Uncle Nate plants **vegetables** each spring. (noun used as direct object)

You should see **her** now. (pronoun used as direct object)

Tell me **what you know about life insurance**. (subordinate clause used as direct object)

4j A complement used as an indirect object of the verb may also be a noun, a pronoun, or a subordinate clause.

The nurse sent the **patient** a bill. (noun used as indirect object)

Will you do **me** a favor? (pronoun used as indirect object)

Give **whoever calls today** this information. (subordinate clause used as indirect object)

Note: From the three examples above, you can see that **an indirect object must always be accompanied by a direct object.**

The three sentences above—which have indirect objects—may be expressed in a different way.

The nurse sent a bill **to the patient**.

Will you do a favor **for me**?

Give this information to **whoever calls today**.

In these three sentences, the prepositional phrases serve the purpose of indirect objects.

4k A complement that acts as a predicate noun may be a noun, a pronoun, a verbal, a phrase, or a clause.

> Juan's uncle is a **bus driver.** (noun)
>
> It is **she.** (pronoun)
>
> Fred's favorite sport is **sailing.** (gerund)
>
> President Sadat's desire is **to make peace.** (infinitive phrase)
>
> Fixing cars is **what Tom does best.** (noun clause)

4l A complement that acts like a predicate adjective may be an adjective or an adjective phrase.

> Laverne and Shirley are **funny.** (adjective)
>
> The lecture was **about alcoholism.** (adjective phrase)

Note: Both predicate nouns and predicate adjectives may be called predicate complements.

CHAPTER 5
Nouns and Pronouns

5a   Nouns

The five types of nouns are **1) proper, 2) common, 3) collective, 4) concrete,** and **5) abstract.***

5b   A proper noun names a particular person, place, or thing.

> Cesar Chavez, San Clemente, Statue of Liberty
> (Proper nouns always begin with a capital letter.)

5c   A common noun names a general sort of person, place, or thing.

> waitress, store, table

5d   A collective noun names a group of individuals.

> congregation, class, political party

> (A collective noun is singular in form, but it refers to many people.)

5e   A concrete noun names any material object that is inanimate.

> apple, hat, ball, box, desk, book, shirt

5f   An abstract noun names a quality, state, or idea.

> truth, motion, beauty

5g   Pronouns

The six kinds of pronouns are **1) personal, 2) relative, 3) interrogative, 4) indefinite, 5) demonstrative,** and **6) reflexive.**

5h   A personal pronoun stands for the speaker, the person spoken to, or the person or thing spoken about.

> **I** am going out.
>   (The first person "I" is speaking.)

> **You** should see the traffic jam downtown.
>   (The second person "you" is being spoken to.)

> **She** wants to become a lawyer.
>   (The third person "she" is being spoken about.)

---

*A noun may be of more than one type. For example, "table" is both a common noun and a concrete noun.

The **personal pronouns** are the following:

I, you, he, she, it, we, they, me, us, him, her, them

The **possessive** forms of the personal pronouns are the following:

my, mine, yours, his, hers, its, our, ours, their, theirs

A pronoun should be in the same person as the noun or pronoun it refers to.

The tree was damaged when lightning struck **it**. (noun and pronoun in third person)

Everyone knows that **he** should dress well to make a good impression. (both pronouns in third person)
(Not: **Everyone** knows that **you** should. . .)

5i The **relative pronouns** are the following:

who (whom), which, what, that

A relative pronoun may begin a subordinate clause.

The child, **who** was alone, looked unhappy.

A relative pronoun connects the main clause to the subordinate clause.

The problem was in the gas line, **which** was rusty.
(The relative pronoun "which" joins the main clause to the subordinate clause it begins.)

A relative pronoun stands for a noun in the main clause.

Sharon gave me the money **that** I needed.
(The relative pronoun "that" stands for the noun "money" in the main clause.)

When to use the relative pronoun "whom"

"Whom" is the objective case form of "who." We use "whom" as a direct object, an indirect object, or an object of the preposition.

The men **whom** you see are waiting for work.
(The relative pronoun "whom" is the direct object of the verb "see.")

Hansen is the person to **whom** Wilmot gave the bribe money.
(The relative pronoun "whom" is the indirect object of the verb "gave.")

The typewriter was stolen by the messenger about **whom** the office manager had been suspicious.
(The relative pronoun "whom" is the object of the preposition "about.")

5j An interrogative pronoun asks a question.

> **Who** wants to start first?
>
> **What** did Richard do then?
>
> **Which** should I take?
>
> **Whose** is this jacket?
>
> **Whom** do you want to speak to?

5k An indefinite pronoun refers to a number of persons, places, or things in a general way.

> **None** of the dishes was broken.
>
> Mark finds **everything** about boats interesting.
>
> I'll bring you **another**.
>
> **Some** of my friends buy lottery tickets.

Other commonly used indefinite pronouns are the following:

> any, both, few, many, most, one, other, several, such

5l A demonstrative pronoun points out a specific person or thing.

> **This** is not my handwriting.
>
> May I have two of **those**?
>
> **That** is my brother.
>
> **These** are my best friends.

Note: Interrogative, indefinite, and demonstrative pronouns may be used as adjectives.

> **Which** dessert do you want? (interrogative adjective)
>
> **Every** time I try to skate I fall down. (indefinite adjective)
>
> **That** dress costs too much. (demonstrative adjective)

5m A reflexive pronoun refers back to the noun it stands for.

> I hurt **myself** while jogging.
>
> Amy considers **herself** an adult.

A reflexive pronoun may be the **direct object of a verb,** the **indirect object of a verb,** the **object of a preposition,** or a **predicate noun.**

> Kim pushed **himself** and finished the race. (direct object)
>
> Ray brought **himself** a new watch. (indirect object)
>
> Buffie likes to be by **herself.** (object of a preposition)
>
> Mr. Thompson is just not **himself** lately. (predicate nominative)

Note: Do not use "hisself" for "himself," or "theirselves' for "themselves."

5n Three characteristics shared by all nouns and pronouns are gender, number, and case.

5o Gender indicates the sex of the person or thing named—whether masculine, feminine, or neuter.

> **Adam** wants some ice cream, but **he** is on a diet.
> ("Adam" and the pronoun "he" are both masculine in gender.)
>
> **Alice** said **she** was ready.
> ("Alice" and the pronoun "she" are both feminine in gender.)
>
> The **movie** was good, but **it** was too long.
> ("Movie" and the pronoun "it" are neither masculine nor feminine; therefore, they are both neuter in gender.)

A pronoun should be in the same gender as the noun it refers to.

5p Number indicates whether one or more than one person or thing is named.

> Here is a **letter** for you.
> (The one letter is singular in number.)
>
> Many **cars** were involved in the accident.
> (Many "cars" are plural in number.)

Note: A collective noun is singular in form, but usually plural in meaning.

> The **audience** was upset by the delay.
> ("Audience" in singular in number, although many people are in the audience.)

A pronoun should be in the same number as the noun it refers to.

> The **dishes** are not clean, so don't use **them.**
> ("Dishes" and the pronoun "them" are both plural in number.)
>
> **Hockey** is a lot of fun, but **it** is rough.
> ("Hockey" and the pronoun "it" are both singular in number.)

A pronoun that refers to a collective noun that is considered as a unit should be singular in number.

The home team won **its** final game of the season.

A pronoun that refers to a collective noun that is considered as a group of individuals should be plural.

The visiting team felt **they** deserved to win.

A pronoun that refers to an indefinite pronoun antecedent must be singular.

Almost anyone can earn a good living if **he** or **she** works hard.

A pronoun must be singular if it refers to singular antecedents joined by "or" or "nor."

Neither Earle nor Jeff could find **his** coat.

5q   Case shows how a noun or pronoun is used in a sentence.

They stayed out all night.
   ("They" is the subject.)

Natalie knew **him.**
   ("Him" is the object of the transitive verb.)

Craig thinks this hat is **his.**
   ("His" is a pronoun that shows ownership.)

The three cases are nominative, objective, and possessive.

5r   The nominative case names the subject of a verb or the predicate noun of a linking verb.

Susan and **I** will call you tonight. (subjects)

My best friends are **Katherine** and **you.** (predicate nouns)

A noun in the nominative case usually is placed before a verb.

Mr. Garcia opened a dry cleaning business.

Ida answered the telephone.

Personal pronouns in the nominative case have the following forms:

I, you, he, she, it, we, they

The subject of a subordinate clause must be in the nominative case even if the clause itself acts as a direct object or an object of a preposition.

Show me **who** is waiting to see me. (subordinate clause as direct object)

Discuss this form with **whoever** applies for the job. (subordinate clause as object of a preposition)

5s **The objective case indicates that nouns and pronouns act as direct objects, indirect objects, or objects of prepositions.**

The storm forced **them** to stay home. (direct object)

Victor enjoyed meeting **her.** (direct object)

Sally called **us, Mary** and **me, into her office.** (direct objects)

The cab driver gave **me** good directions. (indirect object)

Our supervisor showed **him** and **me** some contracts. (indirect objects)

Annette had trouble teaching **them** how to type. (indirect object)

Several of **us** want more food. (object of the preposition)

Between **you** and **me, I** don't like our boss. (objects of the preposition)

Note: Each noun or pronoun in a compound object must be in the objective case.

A noun is in the objective case if it is placed after a transitive verb or after a preposition.

He saw **Greta Garbo.**

Ernie went into the **store.**

Personal pronouns in the objective case have the following forms:

me, you, him, her, it, us, them

5t Only two personal pronouns "we" ("us") and "you"—may also be used as **adjective pronouns.**

We women have responded to the challenge of the 1980's.

They are discriminating against **us** women.

You boys should play more quietly.

Note: The adjective pronoun "we" is in the nominative case when it modifies a subject. The adjective pronoun "us" is in the objective case when it modifies an object of a verb or an object of a preposition.

We Democrats support President Carter's bid for re-election. (nominative case when modifying subject)

Mom sent **us** children to bed. (objective case when modifying direct object of verb)

Won't you give **us** boys a chance to earn some money? (objective **case** when modifying indirect object of verb)

Many Orientals were on the plane with **us** Americans. (objective **case** when modifying object of a preposition)

5u   **The objective case is used by nouns and pronouns that are the subject of an infinitive.**

Paul's father wants **him** to help paint the house.

Should Fred ask **her** to join the club?

A noun or pronoun following the infinitive **to be** must, like its subject, be in the objective case.

Pat didn't expect my friend to be **him.**

Note: If the infinitive **to be** has no subject, the noun or pronoun that comes after the infinitive is in the nominative case.

My twin brother is often thought to be **I.** (nominative case)

5v   **The possessive case indicates ownership.**

Martha's home is in Ohio.

This book is **mine.**

Possession is generally shown by using an apostrophe:

Bumbry's error   men's room

child's toy   ship's crew

Ownership may be shown by an "of" phrase.

The handle **of the door** is broken.

The "of" phrase is used in formal English to show possession by inanimate things or to avoid awkward constructions.

The passage **of the bill** now in Congress will mean lower taxes.
    Not: The bill's passage. . . .)

The sister **of my uncle's wife** is eighty years old.
    (Not: My uncle's wife's sister. . . .)

Personal and relative pronouns have distinct forms to show the possessive case.

The following are personal pronouns (possessive form):

my, mine, your, yours, his, her, hers, our, ours, their, theirs, its*

That dress is **hers.**

Ours is the house on the left.

"Whose" is a relative pronoun (possessive form.)*

No one knows **whose** it is.

The possessive forms **my, your, his, our, their,*** and **whose** are called adjective pronouns because they modify nouns.

Your shirt has a button missing.

My family is very large.

Their apartment costs a lot of money.

The woman **whose** typewriter I borrowed, gave it to me.

The possessive case is used by nouns and pronouns that come before a gerund.

Buba's shouting attracted a large crowd. (noun)

My being sick caused me to miss an important lecture. (pronoun)

The possessive case of a compound noun is indicated by adding **'s** to the **last word of the compound noun.**

A movie **star's** life is glamorous.

The **Governor of California's** speech attacked the president.

Pope John Paul II's visit to the United States pleased millions.

Note: The plural of a compound noun is formed by adding to the principal noun.

chief of police (singular)   chief of police's (singular possessive)
chiefs of police (plural)   chiefs of police's (plural possessive)

---

*"Its" is the possessive form of the personal pronoun "it." "It's" is a contraction of "it is."
"Whose" is the possessive form of the relative pronoun "who"; "who's" is a contraction of "who is."
"Their" is the possessive form of the relative pronoun "they"; "they're" is a contraction of "they are."

5w An **appositive** is a **noun or pronoun** usually placed next to another noun or pronoun to rename it.

> Two guys, **Nestar and his cousin,** were already there. (identifies the subject)

> Clarinda's dog **Sonya** eats only hamburgers. (renames the subject)

Note: An appositive must always be in the same case as the noun it renames.

> We, **my brother and I,** are going hunting together. (both subject and appositive in nominative case)

> Uncle Joe gave us, **Stuart and me,** tickets to the World Series. (both object and appositive in case)

5x **Direct address** and **nominative absolute** constructions are **always in the nominative case.**

Direct address consists of a noun (or pronoun) which names a particular person when someone else addresses that person.

> **Willy,** please come here immediately.

A nominative absolute consists of a noun plus a participle.

> **The money having been spent,** the boys decided to go home.

CHAPTER 6
Subject-Verb Relationship

6a **A verb must agree with its subject in number and in person.**

> Dr. Shu has office hours from 8 until 4.
> (The third person singular form of "to have" agrees with the subject "Dr. Shu.")

> Robin I **play** squash every Tuesday.
> (The first person plural form of "to play" agrees with the compound subject "Robin and I.")

6b **Collective nouns are followed by singular or plural verbs according to the sense of the sentence.**

> The jury **has** asked for more time.
> (The third person singular is used because the jury is considered to be a unified body.)

> The jury **are** unable to agree.
> (The third person plural is used because the jury is considered to be a group of twelve persons.)

To summarize, a **collective noun** is **singular** when it refers to a group as a single unit.

> A minority in Congress **is** delaying passage of the bill.

A **collective noun** is **plural** when it refers to the individual members of the group.

> A minority of Congressmen **want** to defeat the bill.

6c **Some indefinite pronouns are always singular in meaning.**

> **Each** of the candidates **wants** an opportunity to discuss his beliefs.

> **Anyone** is allowed to use the public beach.

> **Any one** of us **is** willing to help.

Some indefinite pronouns are always plural in meaning.

> **Many** of the drawings **were** beautiful.

> **A few** of the windows **were** broken.

> **Several** of Joe's friends **are** sorry that he left.

6d A verb should be **singular** if its subject has "every" or "many a" just before it.

> **Many a woman feels** entitled to more in life than just housework.

> **Every man, woman, and child wants** to be happy.

Some **indefinite pronouns** may be **singular or plural,** depending on the meaning of the sentence.

Some of the books **have** been lost.

Some of the work **was** completed.

All of the ice cream **is** gone.

All of the men **have** left.

Most of the talk **was** about football.

Most of the people **were** dissatisfied.

6e **When singular subjects are joined by "or" or "nor," the subject is considered** to be singular.

Neither the mother **nor** her daughter **was** ever seen again.

One or the **other** of us **has** to buy the tickets.

6f **When one singular and one plural subject are joined by "or" or "nor," the subject closer to the verb determines the number of the verb.**

Neither the plumber nor the painters **have** finished.

Either the branch offices or the main office **closes** at 4.

6g **When the subjects joined by "or" or "nor" are of different persons, the subject nearer the verb determines the person.**

She or you **are** responsible.

You or she **is** responsible.

To avoid such awkward sentences, place a verb next to each subject.

Either she **is** responsible or you **are.**

Either you **are** responsible or she **is.**

6h **Even if the verb comes before the subject, the verb agrees with the true subject in number and person.**

Are the cat and the dog fighting? (The cat and the dog are. . . .)

Coming at us from the left **was** an ambulance. (An ambulance was. . . .)

There **are** two things you can do.* (Two things are. . . .)

There **is** only one bottle left.* (Only one bottle is. . . .)

---

*In this sentence, *there* is an expletive. An expletive is a word that gets a sentence started, but it is not a subject. Another expletive is *it*.

6i **Interrogative pronouns and the adverbs "where," "here," and "there" do not affect the number or person of the verb when they introduce a sentence.**

subject
↓
What is the **name** of your friend?

subject
↓
What **are** the **addresses** of some good restaurants?

subject
↓
Who **is** the **man** standing over there?

subject
↓
Who **are** those **people?**

subject
↓
Here **comes** my **friend.**

subject
↓
Here **come** my **parents.**

6j **When a predicate noun (following a linking verb) differs in number from the subject, the verb must agree with the subject.**

Our biggest problem **is** angry customers.

More gas guzzlers **aren't** what this country needs.

6k **Parenthetical phrases** or other modifiers that come between the subject and verb **do not change the number or person of the true subject**—which the verb agrees with.

The amount shown, plus interest, **is** due on Friday.

The president, together with his advisers, **is** at Camp David.

CHAPTER 7
Tense

7a **Tense specifies the moment of an action or condition.**

We **are walking** to the park. (present moment)

We **will walk** to the park tomorrow. (future moment)

We **walked** to the park yesterday. (past moment)

I **have worked** here for three years. (action begun in the past and continued into the present)

I **had worked** in Chicago for four years before I left. (past action completed **before** another past action)

I **will have worked** here six months next Friday. (past action to be completed sometime in the future)

7b **The six tenses are present, past, future, present perfect, past perfect, and future perfect.**

7c **The present tense** shows that an action is **happening in the present** or that a condition exists now.

I **live** here. (action)

He **is** busy now. (condition)

The **present tense** forms of **to work, to have,** and **to be** follow:

to work	to have	to be
I work	I have	I am
you work	you have	you are
he ⎫ she ⎬ works it ⎭	he ⎫ she ⎬ has it ⎭	he ⎫ she ⎬ is it ⎭
we work	we have	we are
you work	you have	you are
they work	they have	they are

The present tense may indicate **habitual action** or **habitual condition,** or **a general truth.**

Judy **leaves** her office every day at 5 o'clock. (habitual action)

Dana **is** allergic to chocolate. (habitual condition)

Two and two **are** four. (general truth)

The present tense may express **future time with the help of an adverb.**

adverb
↓
Gary flies to Washington **tomorrow**.

adverb
↓
We are going to see a movie **tonight**.

7d The **present perfect tense** shows that an action which **began in the past** is **still going on in the present.**

Betsy and I **have been** in New York for two years. (and are still in New York)

The Johnson family **has owned** a plumbing supply company for sixty years. (and still owns it)

The **present perfect tense** may show that an action **begun in the past was just completed at the present time.**

Our men have worked on your car until now.

Charlayne has just walked in.

The **present perfect tense** is formed with **have or has and a past participle.**

I **have eaten** too much.

Nina **has** always **loved** music.

7e The **past tense** shows that an action **occurred some time in the past** but has **not continued into the present.**

Laura's doctor **advised** her to lose weight.

The plane **landed** on time.

Susan **was living** in Philadelphia then. (progressive form)

We **went** along for the ride.

If the verb in the main clause is in the past tense, the verb in the subordinate clause must also be in the past tense.

The surgeon told his patient that an operation **was** necessary.
(**Not:** The surgeon told his patient that an operation **will be** necessary.)

Lenny said that he **would meet** Frank at 7:30.
(**Not:** Lenny said that he **will meet** Frank at 7:30.)

The past tense (first, second, and third person — singular and plural) is often formed by adding "ed" to the infinitive (without "to.")

Jim **helped** us many times.

We **called** you last night.

7f The **past perfect tense** indicates that an **action was completed before another action began.**

> I remembered the answer after **I had handed** in my exam.
>
> Kenny **had bought** the tickets before he met Ruth.
>
> Margaret **had worked** very hard, so she took a vacation.

Note: The **past tense** shows that an event happened at any time in the past, but the **past perfect tense** indicates that an event happened before another event in the past.

> Paula **had finished** dressing before I woke up.
>   (Not: Paula **finished** dressing before I woke up.)
>
> Jake **had** already **left** by the time I arrived.)
>   (Not: Jake already **left** by the time I arrived.)

The past perfect tense is formed with "had" and a past participle.

> Peter **had said** he would call before twelve.

7g The **future tense** indicates that an **action is going to take place sometime in the future.**

> All of us **will pay** more for heat this winter.
>
> The weatherman says it **will rain** tomorrow.
>
> **Will** you **join** us for lunch, Eric?
>
> **I'll go** away this weekend.

The future tense is formed with "will" and the infinitive (without "to").

> Don **will take** you to the airport.

7h The **future perfect tense** is used to express a **future action that will be completed before another future action.**

> By the time we get home,* my parents **will have gone** to bed.
>
> We'll start eating after you **(will) have washed** your hands.
> Helena **will have finished** her work when we meet her at the office.

The future perfect tense is formed with "will have" and a past participle.

> Patty **will have quit** her job by Christmas.

---

*See page 535 (top), which discusses how a present tense may express future time.

7i **All six tenses may be expressed in a progressive form by adding a present participle of a verb to the appropriate form of "to be."**

The Cosmos **are winning.** (present progressive)

The Cosmos **were winning.** (past progressive)

The Cosmos **have been winning.** (present perfect progressive)

The Cosmos **had been winning.** (past perfect progressive)

The Cosmos **will be winning.** (future progressive)

The Cosmos **will have been winning.** (future perfect progressive)

7j **Principal parts of irregular verbs**

We call a verb like "eat" an irregular verb. Any verb that changes internally to form the past participle is an iregular verb.

Present Tense	Past Tense	Past Participle	Present Participle
eat	ate	eaten	eating
begin	began	begun	beginning
blow	blew	blown	blowing
break	broke	broken	breaking
burst	burst	burst	bursting
catch	caught	caught	catching
choose	chose	chosen	choosing
come	came	come	coming
do	did	done	doing
drink	drank	drunk	drinking
drive	drove	driven	driving
fall	fell	fallen	falling
find	found	found	finding
fly	flew	flown	flying
freeze	froze	frozen	freezing
give	gave	given	giving
go	went	gone	going
grow	grew	grown	growing
know	knew	known	knowing
lay (place)	laid	laid	laying
lie (rest)	lay	lain	lying
ring	rang	rung	ringing
raise	raised	raised	raising
rise	rose	risen	rising
run	ran	run	running
set	set	set	setting
sit	sat	sat	sitting
speak	spoke	spoken	speaking
steal	stole	stolen	stealing
swim	swam	swum	swimming
take	took	taken	taking
throw	threw	thrown	throwing
wear	wore	worn	wearing
write	wrote	written	writing

CHAPTER 8

Verbals

8a A verbal is a word formed from a verb.

> **Skiing** can be dangerous.
>
> We could hear our neighbors **arguing**.
>
> Bonnie and Clyde worked hard **to succeed**.

8b The three kinds of verbals are gerunds, participles, and in-finitives.

8c A gerund acts like a noun.

> **Smoking** is not allowed in many stores.
>
> **Traveling** by train can be fun.
>
> Mark's favorite sport is **boating**.

A gerund ends in "ing."

> Nureyev's **dancing** is terrific.
>
> **Flying** is the fastest way to get there.

A phrase that begins with a gerund is called a gerund phrase.

> **Paying bills** on time is a good habit.
>
> **Leaving my friends** made me sad.

8d A participle acts like an adjective.

> The police stopped the **speeding** car.
>
> The **tired** children were sent to bed.

A present participle ends in "ing."

> A priest comforted the **dying** woman.
>
> **Running**, the girl caught up with her friends.

Note: A present participle looks like a gerund because they both end in "ing." A present participle, however, is used as an adjective, not as a noun.

A past participle usually ends in "d," "ed," "t," "n," or "en."

Used clothing is cheaper than new clothes.

Woody left **written** instructions for his assistant.

A phrase that begins with a participle is called a participial phrase.

Getting off the elevator, I met a friend.

Questioned by the police, several witnesses described the robbery.

8e   An infinitive is used as a noun or an adjective or an adverb.

Franz loves **to dance.** (noun)

Our candidate has the ability **to win.** (adjective)

Lisa practices every day **to improve.** (adverb)

An infinitive usually begins with "to," but not always.

Sally wants **to know** if you need a ride.

Help me **wash** my car. (Or: Help me **to wash** my car.)

A phrase introduced by an infinitive is called an infinitive phrase.

His only desire was **to save money.** (infinitive phrase used as a noun)

There must be a way **to solve this problem.** (infinitive phrase used as an adjective)

The doctor is too busy **to see you now.** (infinitive phrase used as an adverb)

8f   Gerunds may be present or perfect.

Good **cooking** is her specialty. (present)

Your **having arrived** on time saved me. (perfect)

A gerund in the present form refers to an action happening at the same time as the action of the main verb.

Swimming is fun.

Running a mile tired him out.

Taking driving lessons will help you drive better.

A gerund in the perfect form refers to an action that was completed before the time of the main verb.

He believes his recovery is a result of his **having prayed.**

Our **having read** the book made the movie boring.

8g Participles may be present, past, or perfect.

The woman **sitting** on the couch is my mother. (present)

Warned by his doctor, Jack began to exercise. (past)

Having been recognized, Elton John was mobbed by his fans. (perfect)

A present participle refers to **action happening at the same time as the action of the main verb.**

present
↓
Smiling broadly, the president **answers** questions from the audience.

past
↓
Smiling broadly, the president **answered** questions from the audience.

present
↓
Holding up his hands, the teacher **is asking** for silence.

past
↓
Holding up his hands, the teacher **asked** for silence.

A past participle sometimes refers to action happening at the same time as the action of the main verb.

Irritated by his sister, Raphael yelled at her.

Dressed up, Tom looks like a new man.

A past participle sometimes refers to action that happened before the action of the main verb.

Burned by the sun, Mary is suffering.

Awakened by the noise, we looked outside.

The perfect participle always refers to action occurring before the action of the main verb.

Having finished work, we can leave.

Having seen that movie, we went somewhere else.

Having left home in a hurry, Michael forgot his raincoat.

8h Infinitives may be present or perfect.

Albert likes **to read** all day. (present)

Tina was supposed **to have brought** the money. (perfect)

The present infinitive shows an action occurring at the same time as the action of the main verb.

I **am trying to finish** this puzzle. (both present)

Jerry **looked** around **to see** who was there. (both past)

Dana **will call to ask** you for some advice. (both future)

The present infinitive may indicate action or a state of being at some future time.

I hope **to see** you again.

I expect **to be** there in an hour.

He intended **to write** to us.

An infinitive is never used in a subordinate clause which begins with "that."

I expect everyone to remain seated.

I expect that everyone will remain seated.
    (**Not:** I expect that everyone to remain seated.)

The perfect infinitive expresses action occurring before that of the main verb.

I am sorry not **to have met** you before.

He claims **to have seen** a flying saucer.

Avoid using the perfect infinitive after main verbs in the past or past perfect tense.

I had expected **to receive** my mail today.
    (**Not:** I had expected **to have received.** . . .)

They hoped **to join** us for dinner.
    (**Not:** They hoped **to have joined** us. . . .)

Mike would have liked to ask Alice for a date, but he was too shy.
    (**Not:** Mike would have like **to have asked** Alice. . . .)

CHAPTER 9

Mood and Voice

9a   Mood

The **three moods** that a verb may express are **indicative, imperative,** and   **subjunctive.**

9b   The indicative mood indicates that the action or state is something believed to be true.

> I **am** the greatest.
>
> She **sings** beautifully.

The **indicative** mood is **used in asking a question.**

> **Are** you Mr. Feldman?
>
> **Does** Tom **want** to watch "Saturday Night Live"?

9c   The imperative mood expresses a command or a request or a suggestion.

> **Answer** the telephone. (command)
>
> **Give** me a napkin, please. (request)
>
> **Try** turning the handle the other way. (suggestion)

The imperative mood is not only more emphatic than the indicative mood—it is more quickly and easily understood.

> **Give** me that letter. (imperative)
>
> I would appreciate it if you would give me that letter. (indicative)

9d   The subjunctive mood is often used to express a wish or a condition that is not real—that is, contrary to fact.

> I wish the weather **were** nicer.
>
> If this paint **were** dry, we could sit on the bench.
>
> Debbie suggested that Carol **stay** at her apartment.
>
> Carl asked that Stan **agree** to pay for the damage.

The subjunctive mood is also used to express purpose or intention.

> Connie said that she **would visit** her mother at Easter.
> (**Not:** Connie said that she **will visit** her mother at Easter.)
>
> We made box lunches so that we **would have** food for the trip.
> (**Not:** We made box lunches so that we **had** food for the trip.)

The subjunctive mood is mainly indicated by **two forms of the verb "to be."** The forms are **"be"** and **"were."**

Be good.

If I **were** president, I'd nationalize the oil industry.

The present subjunctive uses "be" for all three persons, both singular and plural.

I be, you be, he be, we be, they be

I have one wish—that I **be** president some day.

Mrs. Diggs insists that you **be** given a bonus.

I asked that the child not **be** punished.

The judge ordered that the tenants **be** allowed to stay.

The more common form of the subjunctive is the past subjunctive form "were" for all three persons, both singular and plural.

If $\left\{ \begin{matrix} I \\ you \\ he \\ we \\ they \end{matrix} \right\}$ were here, everything would be all right.

The subjunctive mood for verbs other than "to be" is formed by using the present tense first person singular form for all persons.

Mary suggested that Ronald **keep** an extra pair of eyeglasses.

The umpire insisted that the manager **leave** the field.

9e   Choosing between the subjunctive and indicative mood.

One should show how he sees a situation: **contrary to fact or within the realm of possibility.** He does this by choosing either the subjunctive mood or the indicative mood.

If his statement **be** true, this is a case of fraud. (subjunctive)
    (One indicates that he thinks it is highly improbable that the statement is true.)

If his statement **is** true, this may be a case of fraud. (indicative)
    (The writer indicates that it is quite possible that the statement may be true.)

If he **were** at the meeting, he would. . . .) (subjunctive)
    (The speaker tells the listener that the man is not at the meeting.)

If he **was** at the meeting, he would have been able to speak to the point. (indicative)
    (Perhaps the man **was** at the meeting; one doesn't know.)

Had the first payment been made in April, the second would be due in September. (subjunctive)

(The speaker indicates that the payment was **not** made in April.)

If the first payment **was** made in April, the second will be due in September. (indicative)

(Perhaps it was made; perhaps not—the speaker doesn't know.)

Do not use "would have" instead of "had" in "if" clauses to express the past perfect tense of the subjunctive.

If he **had worked** harder, he would have a better job.

(**Not:** If he **would have worked** harder. . . .)

9f   Voice

A verb is either in the active voice or in the passive voice.

9g   A verb in the active voice indicates that the subject performs an action.

Maggie **reads** every night before going to sleep.

The fire **burned** the entire house.

A verb in the active voice stresses the subject or actor rather than the action.

9h   A verb in the passive voice indicates that something is being done to the subject.

The children **were given** lunches to take to school.

The television **was turned** off by my dad.

A verb in the passive voice stresses the action rather than the actor.

9i   All transitive verbs—verbs whose action affects something or someone—can be used in the passive voice.

Johnny Bench **caught** the ball. (active)

The ball **was caught** by Johnny Bench. (passive)

9j **To form the passive,** the object of the transitive verb in the active voice is moved ahead of the verb, thus becoming the subject. A form of "to be" is added to the main verb. The subject of the active sentence is either left out or expressed in a prepositional phrase.

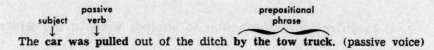

The **tow truck pulled** the **car** out of the ditch. (active voice)

The **car was pulled** out of the ditch **by the tow truck.** (passive voice)

9k **If the active sentence has an indirect object as well as a direct object, either the indirect object or the direct object may be the subject of the passive sentence.**

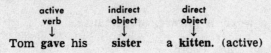

Tom gave his   sister   a kitten. (active)

A **kitten was given** by Tom to his sister. (passive)

Tom's **sister was given** a kitten by Tom. (passive)

9l The **passive voice is appropriate** to express an action **when the actor is unknown.**

The door had been locked before we arrived.

Note: In general, avoid the passive voice for clearer, more forceful sentences.

CHAPTER 10
Modifiers – Adjectives, Adjective Phrases and Clauses

10a   Modifiers

A modifier adds information to another word in the sentence.

> **Blue** flowers were growing in the field.
> (The adjective "blue" adds color to the noun "flowers.")

> Vera paints **beautifully.**
> (The adverb "beautifully" tells how Vera paints.)

10b   Modifiers may be a word, a phrase, or a clause.

> Billy put on a **clean** shirt. (word)

> The wristband **of her watch** was broken. (phrase)

> Andy liked the painting **that was done by his friend.** (clause)

There are **various types** of modifiers.

> Jill brought us **fresh** fruit. (adjective as modifier)

> Bob's friends greeted him **warmly.** (adverb as modifier)

> Rudy enjoyed the ride **from Birmingham to Atlanta.** (adjective phrase as modifier)

> The rent will increase **after this month.** (adverb phrase as modifier)

> Louise holds two jobs **because she supports her sons in college.** (subordinate clause as adverbial modifier)

> The houses **where American presidents were born** are museums. (subordinate clause as adjectival modifier)

10c   Adjectives modify nouns

The six kinds of adjectives are the following:

Limiting: Many children are bused to school.

Numerical: Four days have passed since I saw her.

Descriptive: Striped wallpaper hung in the hall.

Proper: American and **Russian** flags lined the parade route.

Pronoun: My book has a torn cover.

Article: A letter has arrived.

10d   Articles

The **articles "a" and "an"** (indefinite articles) indicate that the **noun they modify is an example of a general type.**

> **A** dove symbolizes peace. (any dove)
>
> **A** doctor saves lives. (any doctor)
>
> **An** ambulance brings people to hospitals (any ambulance)

Note: Do not use the articles "a' or "an" after "kind of," "type of," or "sort of."

> A mango is **a kind of fruit.**
>   (Not: ...a kind of a fruit)
>
> The Citation is **a new type of car.**
>   (Not: ...a new type of a car.)
>
> That sound gives me **a sort of weird feeling.**
>   (Not: ...a sort of a weird feeling.)

The article "the" (definite article) **indicates that the noun it modifies is a particular noun.**

> **The** winner received ten thousand dollars. (specific person)
>
> **The** lamp over there is sold. (specific thing)

10e   Single adjectives and compound adjectives

A single adjective usually comes immediately before the word it modifies.

> Help me carry this **heavy** package.

A compound adjective consists of **two or more words serving as a single adjective.**

> The drought made the earth **bone dry.**
>
> My dictionary is **up to date.**

When a **compound adjective** comes **before a noun, the words are joined by a hyphen.**

> Woody Allen was my **next-door** neighbor.
>
> A **large-scale** map is hanging on the wall.

When the modifying words follow a noun, they are not hyphenated, unless they are normally hyphenated compounds.

> This book is **well written.**
>
> My new watch is **self-winding.** (normally hyphenated)

When two or more adjectives come before a noun but do not act jointly, they are not hyphenated.

Jim was wearing a white silk shirt.

I've had a long, hard day.

Note: If the word "and" can be inserted between two adjectives that come before a noun without destroying the meaning of the sentence, put a comma in between the two adjectives; otherwise, do not.

Miss Cameron is a kind, generous person. (kind **and** generous)

Show us your new suit.

(**Not:** ...your, new suit.)

10f   Two or more adjectives may follow the word they modify to make the sentence read more smoothly.

The children, **tired and hungry,** were difficult to control.

10g   Most adjectives may show greater or lesser degrees of their characteristic quality.

Today was **cold.** (characteristic quality)

Tomorrow will be **colder** than today. (greater)

The day after will be the **coldest.** (still greater)

Yesterday was **less cold** than today. (lesser)

The day before was the **least cold** this week. (lesser still)

Some adjectives do not show comparison.

Jennifer is **pregnant.**
   (She cannot be **more** or **less** pregnant.)

This salad dressing is **perfect.**
   (**Not:** ...is **more** or **less** perfect.)

10h   The three degrees of comparison are positive, comparative, and superlative.

Tania is **happy.** (positive degree)

Lenny is **happier** than Frank. (comparative degree)

Wayne is the **happiest** of all. (superlative degree)

The positive degree simply names the quality expressed by an adjective.

I like **spicy** food.

The **comparative degree** indicates that the quality described by an adjective exists in one person to a **greater or lesser degree** than in another person or thing.

> Susan looks **older** than Liz. (greater)
>
> Marlo was **more excited** than her brother. (greater)
>
> This street is **less clean** than the one where I live. (lesser)

The greater form of the comparative degree is formed by adding "er" to the positive degree or by inserting "more" before the positive form.

> rich + er = **richer**
>
> rich + more = **more rich**

The lesser form of the comparative degree is formed by inserting "less" before the positive form.

> rich + less = **less rich**

Note: Use the comparative degree when comparing only two things.

The **superlative degree** indicates that the quality described by an adjective exists in the **greatest or least degree** in one person or thing.

> Rufus is the **friendliest** dog I know. (greatest)
>
> Florence seems the **least nervous** of us all. (least)

Note: Use the superlative degree when comparing more than two things.

10i **Some adjectives do not follow the regular methods of forming their comparative and superlative degrees.**

Positive degree	Comparative degree	Superlative degree
good	better	best
bad	worse	worst
little	less, lesser	least

(A dictionary will provide the irregular comparisons of such adjectives.)

Most adjectives of three syllables or more are compared by the use of "more" and "most," rather than by the endings "er" and "est."

> Tim is **more capable** of managing a business than Jon.
>
> Alma is the **most wonderful** girl I know.

10j   Avoid double comparisons which are formed by adding both "more" or "most" and "er" or "est."

> Alan is the **brightest** little boy.
>   (Not: ...the **most brightest**. . . .)

> Eric is a **better** eater than his brother.
>   (Not: ...a **more better** eater. . . .)

10k   **When two things are compared, both things should be clearly accounted for.**

> **These clothes** look cleaner than **those (clothes).**

> **George** looks older than **he** used to.

An ellipsis is the leaving out of one or more words that are grammatically important but that are understood by the reader.

> Harvey plays soccer better than **I** (do).

> **While** (he was) waiting for the pitch, Al Bumbry clenched the bat tightly.

Incomplete subordinate clauses that cause confusion, similar to the confusion caused by **dangling modifiers,** may be corrected by supplying the missing words.

> Margaret's dress was torn while **she was** climbing over the fence.
>   (**Not:** Margaret's dress was torn while climbing over the fence.)

Use the word "other' or "else" to separate the thing being compared from the rest of the group of which the word is a part.

> **This car** gets better mileage than all the **other** cars.

> **Mary Beth** is more beautiful than anyone **else** around.

10l   **Infinitives, infinitive phrases, participles, and participial phrases may act as adjectives.**

> Mr. Garcia is the man **to know** if you want a bank loan. (infinitive as adjective)

> This is a day **to remember always.** (infinitive phrase as adjective)

> **Screaming,** Nancy woke up from her nightmare. (present participle as adjective)

> **Covering his face,** the defendant walked past the reporters. (participial phrase as adjective)

10m   **Infinitive and participial phrases that begin a sentence must be able to refer, both logically and grammatically, to the subject of the main clause.**

> **To qualify for the job, you** need a high school diploma.
>   (**Not:** To qualify for the job, a high school diploma is needed. A "high school diploma" cannot apply for the job.)

> **Rushing to finish, Tina** made some errors.
>   (**Not:** Rushing to finish, some errors were made by Tina. "Errors" cannot rush to finish.)

10n   **Infinitive and participial phrases are called dangling modifiers if they cannot logically and grammatically attach to the subject of the main clause.**

> **To apply for a credit card,** an application form must be filled out. (infinitive phrase as dangling modifier)

> **Being an only child,** my parents spoiled me. (participial phrase as dangling modifier)

Sentences with dangling modifiers may be corrected either by supplying the subject that the phrase can sensibly modify or by changing the phrase to an introductory adverbial clause.

> To apply for a credit card, **one** must fill out an application. (Or: **When one applies for a credit card,** an application form must be filled out.)

> Being an only child, **I** was spoiled by my parents. (Or. **Because I am an only child,** I was spoiled by my parents.)

10o   **A prepositional phrase may act as an adjective**

> The violent storm damaged the roof **of our house.**

> Her leaving **without saying a word** irritated me.
>   (also considered a gerund phrase)

10p   **A subordinate clause may act as an adjective**

> Thanks for the present **that you gave me.**

> The woman **who can help you** is not at her desk.

> This ring, **which belonged to my grandmother,** is valuable.

> The building **where they used to live** is being torn down.

> There is never a time **when Ed isn't busy.**

Subordinate clauses that act as adjectives may state essential information or nonessential information.

> The train **that you need to take** is leaving from Track 12. (information essential to describe which train)

> Peter loves his car, **which he hasn't finished paying for.** (information this is nonessential to describe which car)

10q Restrictive and nonrestrictive clauses

Restrictive clauses, which contain essential information, are not set apart by commas.

> The secondhand radio **that I bought for five dollars** works beautifully. (restrictive clause)

Nonrestrictive clauses, which contain secondary information that is not essential to the sentence, are set off by commas.

> My friend Dina, **whom I've known for years,** wants me to visit her. (nonrestrictive clause)

10r "Whose" is the possessive form for the relative pronouns "who," "which," and "that."

> The boy **whose** father died had to get a job.

> The dog **whose** leg was broken runs well now.

> Mr. Temple, **whose** wife is a ballerina, teaches French.

> The book **whose** cover is damaged is half price.

10s A word, phrase, or clause should be placed as close as possible to the word it modifies.

> Give me a glass of **cold** beer.
>   (**Not:** Give me a cold glass. . . .)

> We need someone **with experience** to cook breakfast.
>   (**Not:** We need someone to cook breakfast with experience.)

> Grant wore a felt hat **that was obviously too small on his head.**
>   (**Not:** Grant wore a felt hat on his head that was obviously too small.)

10t **A misplaced modifier is a word, phrase, or clause that is misplaced in the sentence so that it modifies the wrong word.**

Wrong: Mrs. Kent was injured while preparing her husband's dinner in a horrible manner.

Right: Mrs. Kent was injured in a horrible manner while preparing her husband's dinner.

Wrong: The old farmer went to the barn to milk the cow with a cane.

Right: The old farmer with the cane went to the barn to milk the cow.

Wrong: The flames were extinguished before any damage was done by the Fire Department.

Right: The flames were extinguished by the Fire Department before any damage was done.

10u **Squinting modifiers** are modifiers that are misplaced so that the reader cannot tell if the word, phrase, or clause modifies the words immediately before the modifier or immediately after.

Wrong: Henry said **today** he would wash his car.

Right: **Today** Henry said he would wash his car. (**Or:** Henry said he would wash his car **today**.)

Wrong: The dentist told him **frequently** to use dental floss.

Right: The dentist **frequently** told him to use dental floss. (**Or:** The dentist told him to use dental floss **frequently**.)

CHAPTER 11

Modifiers (continued) – Adverbs, Adverbial Phrases and Clauses

11a Adverbs modify verbs, adjectives, and adverbs.

> Don runs **slowly**. (modifies verb)
>
> Emily is an **extremely** gifted pianist. (modifies adjective)
>
> Eric Heiden skates **incredibly** well. (modifies adverb)

11b The five kinds of adverbs are classified by the questions they answer.

How? Adverbs of manner.

> She sings **well**. He speaks **clearly**.

Where? Adverbs of place or direction.

> Take me **home**. She was just **here**. He went **out**.

When? Adverbs of time.

> Bring it **immediately**. I'll see you **tomorrow**.

How much? Adverbs of degree or measure.

> That's **enough**. A little **more**, please.

Why? Adverbs of cause, reason, or purpose.

> He left **because** he was afraid.
>
> I have ten dollars, **so** we can go out.

11c The following words can be either adjectives or adverbs, depending on their use.

above	fast	only
better	first	slow
cheap	hard	well
deep	long	
early	much	

> The sign said to drive **slow**. (adverb)
>
> **Slow** drivers can be dangerous. (adjective)
>
> Mark Spitz can swim **better** than I can. (adverb)
>
> Lucy feels **better** now. (adjective)

11d Distinguish carefully **when an adverb should follow a linking verb** and **when a predicate adjective should be used** to follow the linking verb.

> Sharon looks **bad**. (predicate adjective meaning that Sharon doesn't look healthy)
>
> Miguel looks **badly**. (adverb meaning that Miguel is doing a poor job looking for something)
>
> Carmen smells **sweet**. (predicate adjective meaning that Carmen has a sweet scent)
>
> Roses smell **sweetly**. (adverb **incorrectly** meaning that roses sniff the air sweetly!)

11e While speaking, one may incorrectly drop the "ly" ending from common adverbs.

> I'm **real** glad you called.
>   (**Correct**: I'm **really** glad you called.)
>
> He **sure** is lucky.
>   (**Correct**: He **surely** is lucky.)

Do not drop the "ly" ending unless a shorter form is correct.

> I bought it **cheaply**. (Or: I bought it **cheap**.)
>
> Come **quickly**! (Or: Come **quick**!)

The adverbs "hardly," "scarcely," "only," and "barely" should not be used with a negative verb construction

> Ernie has hardly any free time.
>   (**Not**: Ernie **hasn't** hardly any free time.)
>
> Rose and I have scarcely worked this week.
>   (**Not**: Rose and I **haven't** scarcely worked this week.)

11f **An adverb may show greater or lesser degrees** of its characteristic quality

> Peter arrived **early**.
>
> Adam came **earlier** than Peter.
>
> Amy came **earliest** of all.

The positive degree simply names the quality expressed by an adverb.

> Stephanie runs **quickly**.

The **comparative degree** indicates that the quality described by an adverb exists for one person or thing to **a greater or lesser degree** than for another person or thing.

> New air conditioners run **more efficiently** than old ones.

> Nat draws **less well** than Monica.

The **comparative degree** of adverbs is formed by inserting **"more" or "less" before the positive degree form,** unless there is an irregular form for the comparative degree.

> Charles works **more diligently** than Mark.

> Barbara gets angry **less often** than Steven.

> This stereo sounds **better** than mine. (irregular form)

The **superlative degree** indicates the quality described by the adverb exists in the **greatest or least degree** for one person or thing.

> Ben works **most carefully** when someone is watching.

> Elaine explained the problem the **most clearly.**

> His was the **least carefully** written report.

The **superlative degree** of adverbs is formed by inserting **"most" or "least" before the positive degree form.**

> Who was voted **"most likely"** to suceed"?

> Tracy Austin played **least skillfully** during the first set.

When two persons or things are being compared, the comparison should be clear.

> I love chocolate more than **Umberto** does.
> > **(Not:** I love chocolate more than Umberto. Such an incomplete comparison might be interpreted to mean that I love chocolate more than I love Umberto.)

11g An infinitive or an infinitive phrase may be used as an adverb.

> Robert was willing **to go.** (infinitive used as adverb)

> I am writing **to explain my behavior last night.** (infinitive phrase used as adverb)

11h A prepositional phrase may be used as an adverb.

> We left **for the weekend.**

> The old man sat **on the park bench.**

> The coach supported his team **in every way.**

11i A subordinate clause may be used as an adverb.

> Mrs. Maurillo forgot her umbrella **when she left.**

> **Because they cooperated with him,** the president thanked several members of Congress.

11j An adverb or an adverbial phrase should be placed as close as possible to the word it modifies.

> Joanne worked **without complaining** while her husband went to school.
> (**Not:** Joanne worked while her husband went to school **without complaining.**)

Note how an adverbial misplacement may change the meaning of a sentence.

> The room can be painted **only** by me.
> (not by anyone else)

> The room can **only** be painted by me.
> (not wallpapered)

> **Only** the room can be painted by me.
> (not the outside of the house)

11k An adverbial clause may be placed either at the beginning of a sentence or, in its natural order, after the main clause.

> **After you have read this letter,** you will understand my reasons.

> You will understand my reasons **after you have read this letter.**

Note: An adverbial clause is followed by a comma when it is used to introduce a sentence.

11l Adverbial phrases and clauses should be placed so that only one meaning is possible.

> **After the movie** we all agreed to go for some ice cream. (Or: We all agreed to go for some ice cream **after the movie.**)
> (**Not:** We all agreed **after the movie** to go for some ice cream.)

> Ask Kay to call me **when she gets in.** (Or: **When she gets in,** ask Kay to call me).
> (**Not:** Ask Kay **when she gets in** to call me.)

CHAPTER 12

Connectives

12a   A connective joins one part of a sentence to another part.

Phillip **and** Dennis are giving a concert tonight.
(The connective "and" joins the two parts of the compound subject.)

Did you go out **or** did you stay home last night?
(The connective "or'" joins the two independent clauses.)

The banks are closed **because** today is a holiday.
(The connective "because" joins the main clause to the subordinate clause.)

The investigation **of** the robbery has been completed.
(The connective "of" joins the noun "robbery" to the noun "investigation.")

12b   A connective may be a preposition, a conjunction, an adverb, or a pronoun.

Josie left her scarf **on** the bus. (preposition)

Mr. Fernandez campaigned for the presidency **but** he lost. (conjunction)

Kevin looked back **because** someone was shouting. (conjunction)

Ernie left his home an hour ago; **therefore**, he should be here any minute. (adverb)

The letter **that** was mailed this morning should arrive tomorrow. (pronoun)

12c   Prepositions as connectives

A preposition may be **a word or a compound.** A compound consists of two or more words that function as one word.

Come **over** here. (word)

Women live longer than men **according to** statistics. (compound)

12d   A preposition joins a noun or pronoun to the rest of the sentence.

One   *prep.*↓ **of**   the **windows** is broken. (noun)

Josh is worried *prep.*↓ **about** his **health.** (noun)

These bags have nothing *prep.*↓ **in** **them.** (pronoun)

Choosing the correct preposition is often based on **idiomatic usage** — that is, the way English is used, whether or not it contradicts strict grammatical rules.

12e Some commonly used prepositional idioms are the following:

absolve	from	[blame]
abstain	from	[drinking]
accede	to	[a request]
accommodate	to	[a situation]
accompanied	by	[a lady (a person)]
accompanied	with	[applause (a thing)]
account	for	[one's actions]
account	to	[one's superior]
acquit	of	[a crime]
adapted	to	[his requirements]
adapted	from	[a novel]
adept	in	[selling a product]
adequate	to	[the demand]
adequate	for	[her needs]
agree	to	[a proposal (an idea)]
agree	with	[the teacher (a person)]
amenable	to	[an offer]
angry	with	[my cousin (a person)]
angry	at	[a remark (a thing)]
annoyed	by	[the noise (a thing)]
annoyed	with	[the child (a person)]
appreciative	of	[their efforts]
averse	to	[hard work (an idea)]
basis	for	[agreement]
capable	of	[getting high marks]
concur	with	[the mayor (a person)]
concur	in	[the decision (an idea)]
confer	with	[someone (a person)]
confer	about	[something (a thing)]
conform	to	[the rules]
correspond	to	[what I said (a thing)]
correspond	with	[his lawyer (a person)]
differs	from	[her sister (a person)]
differs	with	[what was done (a thing)]

disappointed	in	[you (**a person**)]
disappointed	with	[the result (**a thing**)]
enter	into	[an agreement]
enter	upon	[a career]
excepted	from	[further responsibility]
exempt	from	[taxes]
expect	from	[your investment (**a thing**)]
expect	of	[his assistant (**a person**)]
familiar	to	[me (**a person**)]
familiar	with	[the proceedings (**a thing**)]
free	of	[his wife (**a person**)]
free	from	[her nagging (**a thing**)]
identical	with	[something else]
ignorant	of	[his rights]
incompatible	with	[fellow workers]
independent	of	[his relative]
infer	from	[a statement]
involved	in	[a project (**a thing**)]
involved	with	[a friend (**a person**)]
liable	to	[damages (**a thing**)]
necessity	for	[food (**a thing**)]
necessity	of	[avoiding trouble (**doing something**)]
proficient	in	[a skill]
profit	by	[knowledge]
responsible	to	[the owner (**a person**)]
responsible	for	[paying a debt (**a thing**)]
talk	to	[the group (**one person talks**)]
talk	with	[my friends (**all talk**)]
variance	with	[another]
wait	at	[the church (**a place**)]
wait	for	[your uncle (**a person**)]
worthy	of	[consideration]

12f Prepositions should not be used needlessly.

Where is your brother?
(**Not:** Where is your brother **at**?)

Where are you going?
(**Not:** Where are you going **to**?)

Pete started on another project.
(**Not:** Pete started **in** on another project.)

We agreed to divide the housework.
(**Not:** We agreed to divide **up** the housework.)

Prepositions are sometimes left out by mistake.

Irene talked to me **about** her new job and **about** why she left her old one.
(**Not:** Irene talked to me about her new job and why. . . .)

Dr. Rosen was puzzled **by** and concerned **about** Ellen's nightmares.
(**Not:** Dr. Rosen was puzzled and concerned about. . . .)

Note: Two different prepositions are needed for this last sentence.

12g Conjunctions as connectives

A conjunction is a word that joins words, phrases, clauses, or sentences.

Nixon **and** Agnew ended their political careers by resigning (words joined)

The mouse ran out of the kitchen **and** into the living room. (phrases joined)

Casino gambling in Atlantic City has helped some **but** it has hurt others. (clauses joined)

Sally has the ability to do the job; **however,** she has too many personal problems. (sentences joined)

12h Conjunctions are coordinate, correlative, or subordinate.

A **coordinate conjunction** and a **correlative conjunction** connect grammatical elements of equal rank. A **subordinate conjunction** connects grammatical elements of unequal rank.

12i Coordinate conjunctions include the following words in order to connect two equal elements.

and, but, or, nor, so, yet

On our vacation we will go to Boston **or** to Cape Cod. (two phrases)

My two favorite colors are blue **and** green. (two words)

I told Stanley that I couldn't leave my house, **so** he should come over tonight. (two subordinate clauses)

Phil was eager to try the new restaurant, **but** he moved away before trying it. (two independent clauses)

12j Correlative conjunctions include the following **word pairs** in order to connect two equal elements.

> either . . . or, neither . . . nor, not only . . . but also,
> both . . . and, if . . . then, since . . . therefore

> Take **either** the dark meat **or** the light meat. (two words)

> **Not only** has Rick quit school, **but** he has **also** left town. (two independent clauses)

> **Both** the Baltimore Orioles **and** the Pittsburgh Pirates won the pennant in 1979. (two words)

> I have seen her **neither** in the movies **nor** on television. (two phrases)

Note: The correlative conjunctions "neither... nor" should never be written "neither... or.")

Each member of the pair of correlative conjunctions must be followed by the same grammatical construction.

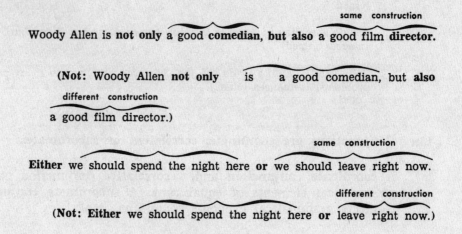

Woody Allen is **not only** a good **comedian, but also** a good film **director.** [same construction]

(**Not:** Woody Allen **not only** is a good comedian, but **also** [different construction] a good film director.)

Either we should spend the night here or we should leave right now. [same construction]

(**Not:** Either we should spend the night here or leave right now.) [different construction]

12k Conjunctive adverbs

A **conjunctive adverb** may be considered a **type of coordinate conjunction.**

Conjunctive adverbs include the following words which **serve to connect two equal elements.**

> therefore, however, consequently, accordingly,
>
> furthermore, besides moreover, nevertheless, still

Although the clause introduced by a conjunctive adverb is grammatically independent, it is logically dependent on the preceding clause for complete meaning.

> A storm knocked down our electric wires; **therefore,** we had to eat by candlelight.

> A bad traffic accident ahead of us caused us to be delayed; **nevertheless,** we made the party on time.

> You have not paid your rent for six months; **accordingly,** I am going to see a lawyer.

Independent clauses joined by a conjunctive adverb should be separated by a semicolon (;) or a period.

> Frank and Marty delayed their vacation one week; **consequently,** I was able to join them.

> The judge awarded custody of the child to its mother. **Moreover,** the judge set strict guidelines for visiting privileges.

Certain phrases may act as conjunctive adverbs.

> Eunice wanted to buy a fur coat; **on the other hand,** she was trying to save money for a car.

> We saw many interesting towns and cities on our tour. **In addition,** we met several nice people.

12l Join only the **same parts of speech** with coordinate conjunctions or with correlative conjunctions. **Faulty parallelism will result if different parts of speech are combined.**

> Correct: Jim's day consisted of waking up early, working all day, **and** going back to bed. (three gerund phrases)

> Faulty: Jim's day consisted of waking up early, working all day, **and** then to go back to bed. (two gerund phrases combined with an infinitive phrase)

> Correct: The president's plan was a disappointment **not only** to the leaders of big business, **but also** to the leaders of organized labor. (two prepositional phrases)

> Faulty: The president's plan was a disappointment **not only** to the leaders of big business, but also the leaders of organized labor. (one prepositional phrase and one noun)

12m Connecting elements of unequal rank

A less important idea should be put into a subordinate clause; the more important idea should be expressed in the main or independent clause.

main idea   subordinate idea

Bill is going to work for his father, although he was offered other jobs.

12n **Subordination may be introduced by a subordinate conjunction, by a relative pronoun, or by a relative adverb.**

Eva will want to go straight to bed **after** she comes back from her exercise class. (subordinate conjunction)

I bought the sneakers **that** you wanted. (relative pronoun)

We saw the house **where** they filmed "Gone with the Wind." (relative adverb)

A subordinate conjunction introduces an adverbial clause.

My mother can knit a sweater **while** she watches television. (adverbial clause tells **when**)

Tell me what he looks like **so that** I'll recognize him. (adverbial clause tells **why**)

12o **Some relative pronouns introduce adjective clauses.**

Everyone wants a job **that** he likes.

The woman **who** walked across the United States has written a book about her experience.

Bobby gave Connie a new tennis racket, **which** she needed.

Other relative pronouns introduce noun clauses.

Tell me **what** you did.

This book has **whatever** you want to know about scuba diving.

Invite **whomever** you like.

12p **A relative adverb introduces an adjective clause.**

Do you remember the night **when** we locked ourselves out of the house?

Chris will be at the place **where** we met him last time.

CHAPTER 13
Correct Usage: Choosing the Right Word

"The difference between the right word and the almost-right word is the difference between lightning and the lightning bug (firefly)."

— Mark Twain

13 **A, an.** The indefinite article *a* is used before a consonant sound; the indefinite article *an* is used before a vowel sound. Say *a plan, an idea.*

Accept, except. *Accept* means *to receive; except* when used as a verb means *to leave out.* (We *accepted* the gift. Pedro's name was *excepted* from the honor roll.) The word *except* is used most often as a preposition. *Everyone went except me.*

Affect, effect. *Affect* is a verb which means to *influence.* (Winning the sweepstakes will *affect* his attitude.) *Effect,* as a noun, means *an influence.* (Smoking has an *effect* on one's health.) *Effect,* as a verb means to *bring about.* (The teacher's praise *effected* a change in the student.)

Affected, as an adjective, has the meaning of *false.* (She had an *affected* way of speaking.)

Aggravate, irritate. *Aggravate* means to make worse. (Drinking iced water will *aggravate* your cold.) *Irritate* means to *annoy* or *exasperate.* (Mary's continuous chattering *irritated* me.)

Ain't. Do not use this expression.

Already, all ready. *Already* means *before* or *by a certain time.* (Mike said that he had *already* done the job.) *All ready* means *completely ready.* (When the buzzer sounded, the horses were *all ready* to start running.)

All right, alright. The only correct spelling is *all right.*

Altogether, all together. *Altogether* means *entirely, wholly.* (Jane is *altogether* too conceited to get along with people.) *All together* means *as a group.* (After the explosion, the boss was relieved to find his workers *all together* in front of the building.)

Among, between. *Among* is used with more than two persons or things. (The manager distributed the gifts *among* all of the employees.) *Between* is used only with two persons or things. (The steak was divided *between* the two children.)

Amount, number. *Amount* is used to refer to things in bulk. (The war costs a great *amount* of money.) *Number* is used to refer to things that can be counted. (A large *number* of pupils attend this school.)

And etc. This is incorrect. The abbreviation *etc.* stands for the Latin *et cetera.* The *et* means *and;* the *cetera* means *other things.* It is wrong to say *and etc.* because the idea of *and* is already included in the *etc.*

Anyways, anywheres, everywheres, somewheres. These expressions are not correct. Omit the final *s* after each.

As, like. *As*, used as a conjunction, is followed by a verb. (Please do it *as* I told you to.) *Like* may not be used as a conjunction. If it is used as a preposition, it is not followed by a verb. (This ice cream looks *like* custard.)

Awful. See **Terrific, terrible.**

Being that. *Being that* is incorrect for *since* or *because*. (*Since* you are tired, you ought to rest.)

Beside, besides. *Beside* means *alongside of; besides* means *in addition to.* (Nixon sat *beside* Autry at the baseball game.) (There is nobody *besides* her husband who understands Ann.)

Between. See **Among.**

Bring, take. Consider the speaker as a starting point. *Bring* is used for something carried in the direction of the speaker. (When you return from lunch, please *bring* me a ham sandwich.) *Take* is used for something carried away from the speaker. (If you are going downtown, please *take* this letter to the post office.)

Bunch. *Bunch* means cluster. Do not use *bunch* for group or crowd. (This is a large *bunch* of grapes.) (A *crowd* of people were at the scene of the accident.)

But that, but what. Do not use these expressions in place of *that* in structures like the following: I do not question *that* (not *but that*) you are richer than I am.

Can't hardly. Don't use this double negative. Say *can hardly.*

Continual, continuous. *Continual* means happening at intervals. (Salesmen are *continually* walking into this office.) *Continuous* means going on without interruption. (Without a moment of dry weather, it rained *continuously* for forty days and forty nights.)

Could of. Do not use for *could have.*

Data. Although *data* is the plural of *datum*, idiom permits the use of this word as a singular. Some authorities still insist on *Data are gathered* rather than *Data is gathered* or *these data* rather than *this data.* Most persons in computer programming now say *Data is gathered* or *this data.*

Deal. Do not use this term for *arrangement* or *transaction.* (He has an *excellent arrangement* (not *deal*) *with the manager.*)

Different from, different than. *Different from* is correct. *Different than* is incorrect. (His method of doing this is *different from* mine.)

Discover, invent. *Discover* means to see or learn something that has not been previously known. (They say the Vikings, not Columbus, *discovered* America.) *Invent* means to create for the first time. (William S. Burroughs *invented* the adding machine.)

Disinterested, uninterested. *Disinterested* means without bias. (An umpire must be *disinterested* to judge fairly in a baseball game.) *Uninter-*

ested means not caring about a situation. (I am totally *uninterested* in your plan.)

Doesn't, don't. *Doesn't* means *does not;* *don't* means *do not.* Do not say *He don't* (*do not*) when you mean *He doesn't* (*does not*).

Due to. At the beginning of a sentence, *due to* is always incorrect. Use, instead, *on account of, because of,* or a similar expression. (*On account of* bad weather, the contest was postponed.) As a predicate adjective construction, *due to* is correct. His weakness was *due to* his hunger.

Each other, one another. *Each other* is used for two persons. (The executive and his secretary antagonize *each other.*) *One another* is used for more than two persons. (The members of the large family love *one another.*)

Effect. See **Affect.**

Enthuse. Do not use this word. Say *enthusiastic.* (The art critic was *enthusiastic* about the painting.)

Equally as good. This expression is incorrect. Say, instead, *just as good.* (This car is *just as good* as that.)

Farther, further. *Farther* is used for a distance that is measurable. (The farmer's house is about 100 yards *farther* down the road.) *Further* is used to express the extension of an idea. (A *further* explanation may be necessary.)

Fewer, less. *Fewer* applies to what may be counted. (Greenwich Village has *fewer* conservatives than liberals.) *Less* refers to degree or amount. (*Less* rain fell this month than the month before.)

Flout, flaunt. *Flout* means to mock or insult. (The king *flouted* the wise man when the latter offered advice.) *Flaunt* means to make a pretentious display of. (The upstart *flaunted* his diamond ring.)

Further. See **Farther.**

Get. *Get* means *to obtain* or *receive.* Get should not be used in the sense of *to excite, to interest,* or *to understand.* Say: His guitar playing *fascinates* (not *gets*) me. Say: When you talk about lifestyles, I just don't *understand* (not *get*) *you.*

Good, well. Do not use the adjective *good* in place of the adverb *well* in structures like the following: John works *well* (not *good*) in the kitchen. Jim Palmer pitched *well* (not *good*) in last night's game.

Graduate. One *graduates from,* or *is graduated from,* a school. One does *not graduate a school.* (The student *graduated* [or was graduated] from high school.)

Had of. Avoid this for *had.* Say: My father always said that he wished he *had* (not *had of*) gone to college.

Hanged, hung. When a person is *executed,* he is *hanged.* When anything is *suspended* in space, it is *hung.*

Hardly. See **Can't hardly.**

Healthful, healthy. *Healthful* applies to *conditions that promote health.* *Healthy* applies to *a state of health.* Say: Stevenson found the climate of Saranac Lake very *healthful.* Say: Mary is a very *healthy* girl.

If, whether. Use *whether* — not *if* — in structures that follow verbs like *ask, doubt, know, learn, say.* Say: Hank Aaron didn't know *whether* (not *if*) he was going to break Babe Ruth's homerun record.

Imply, infer. The speaker *implies* when he suggests or hints at. (The owner of the store *implied* that the patron stole a box of toothpicks.) The listener *infers* when he draws a conclusion from facts or evidence. (From what you say, I *infer* that I am about to be discharged.)

In, into. *In* is used to express a location, without the involvement of motion. (The sugar is *in* the cupboard.) *Into* is used to express motion from one place to another. (The housekeeper put the sugar *into* the cupboard.)

In regards to. This is incorrect. Say *in regard to* or *with regard to.*

Invent. See **Discover.**

Irregardless. Do not use *irregardless.* It is incorrect for *regardless.* (You will not be able to go out tonight regardless of the fact that you have done all of your homework.)

Its, it's. *Its* is the possessive of *it; it's* is the contraction for *it is.*

Kind of, sort of. Do not use these expressions as adverbs. Say: Ali was *quite* (not *kind of* or *sort of*) witty in his post-fight interview.

Kind of a, sort of a. Omit the *a.* Say: What *kind of* (not *kind of a* or *sort of a*) game is lacrosse?

Lay, lie. See "Principal Parts of Irregular Verbs" — page 537.

Learn, teach. *Learn* means *gaining knowledge. Teach* means *imparting knowledge.* Say: He *taught* (not *learned*) his brother how to swim.

Leave, let. The word *leave* means *to depart.* (I *leave* today for San Francisco.) The word *let* means to allow. (*Let* me take your place.)

Less, fewer. See **Fewer, less.**

Liable, likely. *Liable* means exposed to something unpleasant. (If you speed, you are *liable* to get a summons.) *Likely* means probable, with reference to either a pleasant or unpleasant happening. (It is *likely* to snow tomorrow.)

Locate. Do not use *locate* to mean *settle* or *move to.* Say: We will *move to* (not *locate in*) Florida next year.

Might of, must of. Omit the *of.*

Myself, himself, yourself. These pronouns are to be used as intensives. (The Chairman *himself* will open the meeting.) Do not use these pronouns when *me, him,* or *you* will serve. Say: We shall be happy if Joe and *you* (not *yourself*) join us for lunch at the Plaza.

Nice. See **Terrific, terrible.**

Number, amount. See **Amount, number.**

Of, have. Do not use *of* for *have* in structures like *could have.*

Off of. Omit the *of.* Say: The book fell *off* (not *off of*) the shelf.

Pour, spill. When one *pours,* he does it deliberately. (He carefully *poured* the wine into her glass.) When one *spills,* he does it accidentally. (I carelessly *spilled* some wine on her dress.)

Practical, practicable. *Practical* means *fitted for actual work. Practicable* means *feasible* or *possible.* Say: My business partner is a *practical man.* Say: The boss did not consider the plan *practicable* for this coming year.

Principal, principle. *Principal* applies to a *chief* or the *chief part* of something. *Principle* applies to a *basic law.* Say: Mr. Jones is the *principal* of the school. Professor White was the *principal* speaker. Honesty is a good *principle* to follow.

Raise, rise. See "Principal Parts of Irregular Verbs" — page 537.

Reason is because. Do not use the expression *reason is because* — it is always incorrect. Say the *reason is that.* (The *reason* Jack failed the course *is that* he didn't study.)

Regardless. See **Irregardless.**

Respectfully, respectively. *Respectfully* means *with respect* as in the complimentary close of a letter, *respectfully yours. Respectively* means that each item will be considered *in the order given.* Say: This paper is *respectfully* submitted. Say: The hero, the heroine, and the villain will be played by Albert, Joan, and Harry *respectively.*

Rise, raise. See "Principal Parts of Irregular Verbs" — page 537.

Said. Avoid the legalistic use of *said* like *said letter, said plan, said program* except in legal writing.

Should of. Do not use for *should have.*

Sit, set. See "Principal Parts of Irregular Verbs" — page 537.

Some. Do not use *some* when you mean *somewhat.* Say: I'm confused *somewhat* (not *some*).

Spill, pour. See **Pour, spill.**

Suspicion. Do not use *suspicion* as a verb when you mean *suspect.*

Take, bring. See **Bring, take.**

Teach, learn. See **Learn, teach.**

Terrific, terrible. Avoid "lazy words." Many people don't want to take the trouble to use the exact word. They will use words like *terrific, swell, great, beautiful,* etc. to describe anything and everything that is favorable. And they will use words like *terrible, awful, lousy, miserable,* etc. for whatever is unfavorable. Use the exact word. Say: We had a *delicious* (not *terrific*) meal. Say: We had a *boring* (not *terrible*) weekend.

This kind, these kind. *This kind* is correct — as is *that kind, these kinds,* and *those kinds.* (My little brother likes *this kind* of pears.) *These kind* and *those kind* are incorrect.

Try and. Do not say *try and*. Say *try to*. (*Try to* visit me while I am in Florida.)

Uninterested. See **Disinterested.**

Wait for, wait on. *Wait for* means *to await; wait on* means *to serve*. Say: I am waiting *for* (not *on*) Carter to call me on the telephone.

Way, ways. Do not use *ways* for *way*. Say: It is a long *way* (not *ways*) to Japan.

Where. Do not use *where* in place of *that* in expressions like the following: I see in the newspaper *that* (not *where*) a nuclear reactor may be built a mile away from our house.

Would of. Do not use for *would have*.

GRAMMAR AND USAGE INDEX

*This Index does not include items listed in Chapter 13 (Correct Usage: Choosing the Right Word). Since these Correct Usage items are in alphabetical order, it will be easy for you to locate any Correct Usage explanation whatsoever.